Exploring British Politics

Visit The Politics Chamber at **www.pearsoned.co.uk/politicschamber** to access a wealth of valuable politics resources, including:

- Guides to studying politics
- Information on the political process
- Short essays on careers in politics

From the Politics Chamber, click through to the Companion Website for *Exploring British Politics*, or visit the website directly at **www.pearsoned.co.uk/garnett**. Here you will find:

- Regular updates on a range of political topics
- Discussion questions
- Extensive links to relevant sites on the web

PEARSON
Education

We work with leading authors to develop the strongest educational materials in politics, bringing cutting-edge thinking and best learning practice to a global market.

Under a range of well-known imprints, including Longman, we craft high quality print and electronic publications which help readers to understand and apply their content, whether studying or at work.

To find out more about the complete range of our publishing, please visit us on the World Wide Web at: www.pearsoned.co.uk

Exploring British Politics

Mark Garnett and Philip Lynch

PEARSON
Longman

Harlow, England • London • New York • Boston • San Francisco • Toronto • Sydney • Singapore • Hong Kong
Tokyo • Seoul • Taipei • New Delhi • Cape Town • Madrid • Mexico City • Amsterdam • Munich • Paris • Milan

Pearson Education Limited
Edinburgh Gate
Harlow
Essex CM20 2JE
England

and Associated Companies throughout the world

Visit us on the World Wide Web at:
www.pearsoned.co.uk

First published 2007

ISBN-13: 978-0-582-89431-0
ISBN-10: 0-582-89431-X

British Library Cataloguing-in-Publication Data
A catalogue record for this book is available from the British Library

Library of Congress Cataloging-in-Publication Data

Garnett, Mark, 1963–
    Exploring British politics / Mark Garnett and Philip Lynch.
        p. cm.
    Includes bibliographical references and index.
    ISBN-13: 978-0-582-89431-0 (alk. paper)
    ISBN-10: 0-582-89431-X (alk. paper)
        1. Public administration – Great Britain. 2. Great Britain – Politics and government. I. Lynch, Philip, 1967–II. Title.

JN318.G37 2007
320.441–dc22   2006046473

10 9 8 7 6 5 4 3 2 1
11 10 09 08 07

Typeset in Sabon 10/12½ by 3

Printed by Ashford Colour Press Ltd., Gosport

The publisher's policy is to use paper manufactured from sustainable forests.

For our textbook children,
Amelia and Alec

Brief contents

Part 4 Political parties

Part 5 Participation

Part 6 Conclusions

Contents

Supporting resources
Visit **www.pearsoned.co.uk/politicschamber** to find valuable politics resources

Politics Chamber
- Guides to studying politics
- Information on the political process
- Short essays on careers in politics

Companion Website
Visit **www.pearsoned.co.uk/garnett** for:
- Regular updates on a range of political topics
- Discussion questions
- Extensive links to relevant sites on the web

For more information please contact your local Pearson Education sales representative or visit **www.pearsoned.co.uk/politicschamber**

Guided tour

Chapter 18

Referendums and pressure groups

Learning outcomes

After reading this chapter, you will:

* Be able to outline the major forms of non-electoral participation in the UK.
* Appreciate the chequered history of referendums in UK politics.
* Understand the complex relationship between pressure groups and liberal democracy.

Introduction

The French philosopher Jean-Jacques Rousseau (1712–78) once jeered that the English people are only 'free' during elections. He meant that these were the only occasions when members of the public could behave like true citizens, and take a meaningful part in making the laws by which they were governed. Even at election time, during the eighteenth century this citizenship was a privilege enjoyed by a few rather than a right extended to the many. Women were not allowed to vote, and most men were ruled out by the wide range of qualifications applied in different constituencies.

Despite the different context of today, Rousseau's remark is a convenient summary of a major dilemma for all representative democracies. Elections give citizens a regular opportunity to dismiss unsatisfactory representatives. But normally that judgement can only be delivered at the end of a term of office, by which time many unpopular or damaging decisions could have been made. In the UK, instead

of submitting themselves to the electorate as soon as they lose public confidence, governments usually hang on in the hope that their prospects will improve. There are, though, ways in which citizens can register their feelings between elections. In this chapter we will look at referendums, pressure groups and other forms of participation in the UK, in order to assess whether or not they overcome Rousseau's challenge.

Referendums

Referendum a mechanism allowing voters to choose between different courses of action in a particular policy area.

Referendums are ballots in which citizens are asked to give their views on specific policies. As such, they can be seen as a return to the kind of direct democracy which was practised in Athens and elsewhere in the ancient world, and which inspired Rousseau (see Chapter 1).

Case study: 18.1

Referendums in the UK

1973. The 'Border poll' in Northern Ireland

Voters in Northern Ireland were asked if they wanted to remain within the UK. There was an overwhelming 'yes' vote, but this proved very little since opponents of the Union organised an effective boycott. Critics claimed that the referendum was nothing more than a way of confirming what everyone knew already – that the majority in Northern Ireland was Protestant and favoured the link with the rest of Britain. In their eyes the real problem was the status of the Catholic minority.

1975. Continued UK membership of the European Economic Community

The first UK-wide referendum was held on 5 June 1975, over Britain's membership of what was then the European Economic Community (EEC). The Labour Prime Minister, Harold Wilson, resorted to the vote because his party was seriously divided. A 'yes' vote, he hoped, would give him the authority to override the objections of colleagues who wanted the UK to withdraw. On a high turnout (nearly two-thirds) the 'yes' campaign secured what could be presented as a conclusive result. Almost every region of the UK voted in favour of membership. In England, there was a 69 per cent 'yes' vote. But critics could argue that the poll had been held too late. On a question of such importance, voters should have been asked whether they wanted to join in the first place. By 1975 the 'no' camp was fighting an uphill battle, asking people to overturn a decision which had already been taken. Furthermore, the 'yes' campaign was much better funded.

Learning Objectives list the topics covered and what you should understand by the end of the chapter

Case studies bring key issues to the fore with real life examples of politics in action

Key terms introduce and define important words and concepts throughout the text

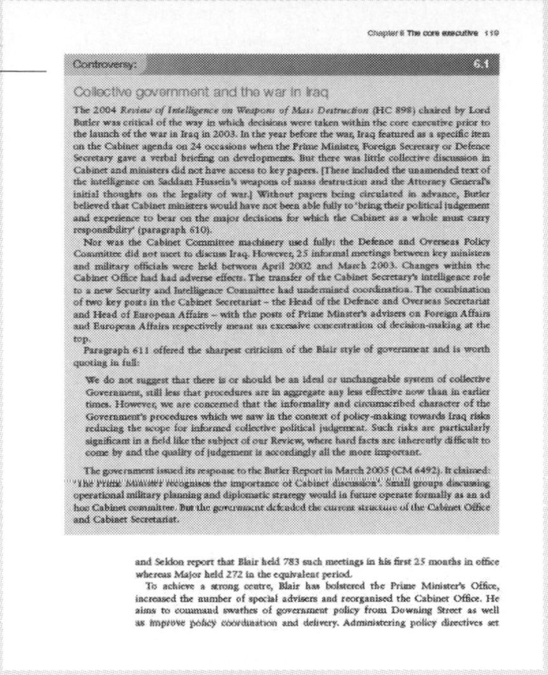

Controversy: 6.1

Collective government and the war in Iraq

The 2004 *Review of Intelligence on Weapons of Mass Destruction* (HC 898) chaired by Lord Butler was critical of the way in which decisions were taken within the core executive prior to the launch of the war in Iraq in 2003. In the year before the war, Iraq featured as a specific item on the Cabinet agenda on 24 occasions when the Prime Minister, Foreign Secretary or Defence Secretary gave a verbal briefing on developments. But there was little collective discussion in Cabinet and ministers did not have access to key papers. (The handful the unamended text of the intelligence on Saddam Hussein's weapons of mass destruction and the Attorney General's initial thoughts on the legality of war.) Without papers being circulated in advance, Butler believed that Cabinet ministers would have not been able fully to 'bring their political judgement and experience to bear on the major decisions for which the Cabinet as a whole must carry responsibility' (paragraph 610).

Nor was the Cabinet Committee machinery used fully: the Defence and Overseas Policy Committee did not meet to discuss Iraq. However, 25 informal meetings between key ministers and military officials were held between April 2002 and March 2003. Changes within the Cabinet Office had had adverse effects. The transfer of the Cabinet Secretary's intelligence role to a new Security and Intelligence Committee had weakened coordination. The combination of two key posts in the Cabinet Secretariat – the Head of the Defence and Overseas Secretariat and Head of European Affairs – with the posts of Prime Minister's advisers on Foreign Affairs and European Affairs respectively meant an excessive concentration of decision-making at the top.

Paragraph 611 offered the sharpest criticism of the Blair style of government and is worth quoting in full:

> We do not suggest that there is or should be an ideal or unchangeable system of collective Government, still less that procedures are in aggregate any less effective now than in earlier times. However, we are concerned that the informality and circumscribed character of the Government's procedures which we saw in the context of policy-making towards Iraq risks reducing the scope for informed collective political judgement. Such risks are particularly significant in a field like the subject of our Review, where hard facts are inherently difficult to come by and the quality of judgement is accordingly all the more important.

The government issued its response to the Butler Report in March 2005 (CM 6492). It claimed: 'The Prime Minister recognises the importance of Cabinet discussion'. Small groups discussing operational military planning and diplomatic strategy would in future operate formally as an ad hoc Cabinet committee. But the government defended the current structure of the Cabinet Office and Cabinet Secretariat.

and Seldon report that Blair held 783 such meetings in his first 25 months in office whereas Major held 272 in the equivalent period.

To achieve a strong centre, Blair has bolstered the Prime Minister's Office, increased the number of special advisers and reorganised the Cabinet Office. He aims to command swathes of government policy from Downing Street as well as improve policy coordination and delivery. Administering policy directives set

---

Each chapter contains Controversy boxes that discuss issues that have been and continue to be sources of debate

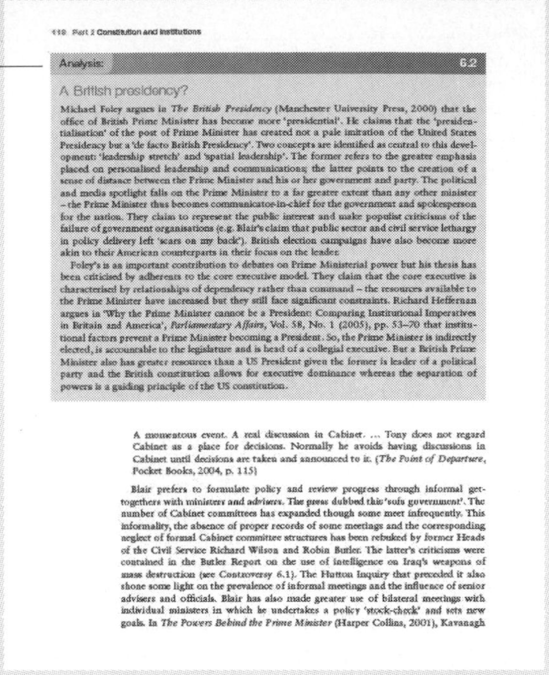

Analysis: 6.2

A British presidency?

Michael Foley argues in *The British Presidency* (Manchester University Press, 2000) that the office of British Prime Minister has become more 'presidential'. He claims that the 'presidentialisation' of the post of Prime Minister has created not a pale imitation of the United States Presidency but a 'de facto British Presidency'. Two concepts are identified as central to this development: 'leadership stretch' and 'spatial leadership'. The former refers to the greater emphasis placed on personalised leadership and communication; the latter points to the creation of a sense of distance between the Prime Minister and his or her government and party. The political and media spotlight falls on the Prime Minister to a far greater extent than any other minister – the Prime Minister thus becomes communicator-in-chief for the government and spokesperson for the nation. They claim to represent the public interest and make populist criticisms of the failure of government organisations (e.g. Blair's claim that public sector and civil service lethargy in policy delivery left 'scars on my back'). British election campaigns have also become more akin to their American counterparts in their focus on the leader.

Foley's is an important contribution to debates on Prime Ministerial power but his thesis has been criticised by adherents to the core executive model. They claim that the core executive is characterised by relationships of dependency rather than command – the resources available to the Prime Minister have increased but they still face significant constraints. Richard Heffernan argues in 'Why the Prime Minister cannot be a President: Comparing Institutional Imperatives in Britain and America', *Parliamentary Affairs*, Vol. 58, No. 1 (2005), pp. 53–70 that institutional factors prevent a Prime Minister becoming a President. So, the Prime Minister is indirectly elected, is accountable to the legislature and is head of a collegial executive. But a British Prime Minister also has greater resources than a US President given the former is leader of a political party and the British constitution allows for executive dominance whereas the separation of powers is a guiding principle of the US constitution.

A momentous event. A real discussion in Cabinet. ... Tony does not regard Cabinet as a place for decisions. Normally he avoids having discussions in Cabinet until decisions are taken and announced to it. (*The Point of Departure*, Pocket Books, 2004, p. 115)

Blair prefers to formulate policy and review progress through informal get-togethers with ministers and advisers. The press dubbed this 'sofa government'. The number of Cabinet committees has expanded though some meet infrequently. This informality, the absence of proper records of some meetings and the corresponding neglect of formal Cabinet committee structures has been rebuked by former Heads of the Civil Service Richard Wilson and Robin Butler. The latter's criticisms were contained in the Butler Report on the use of intelligence on Iraq's weapons of mass destruction (see Controversy 6.1). The Hutton Inquiry that preceded it also shone some light on the prevalence of informal meetings and the influence of senior advisers and officials. Blair has also made greater use of bilateral meetings with individual ministers in which he undertakes a policy 'stock-check' and sets new goals. In *The Powers Behind the Prime Minister* (Harper Collins, 2001), Kavanagh

---

Analysis boxes take a closer look at a particular event or issue for a deeper understanding

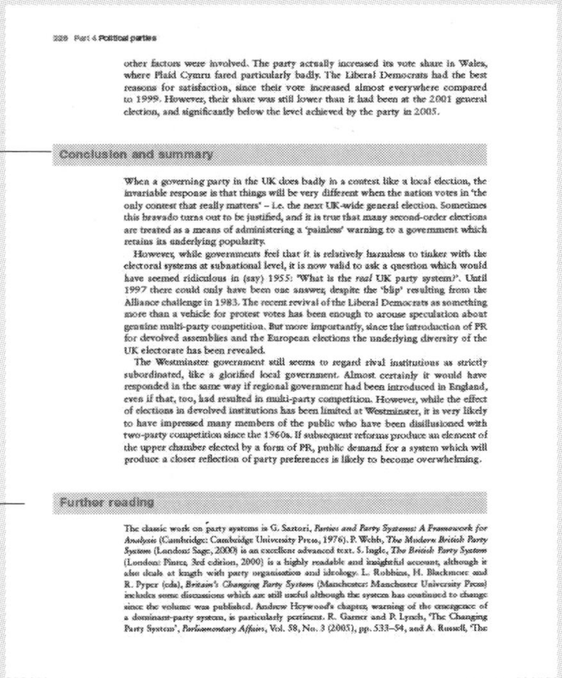

---

other factors were involved. The party actually increased its vote share in Wales, where Plaid Cymru fared particularly badly. The Liberal Democrats had the best reasons for satisfaction, since their vote increased almost everywhere compared to 1999. However, their share was still lower than it had been at the 2001 general election, and significantly below the level achieved by the party in 2005.

Conclusion and summary

When a governing party in the UK does badly in a contest like a local election, the invariable response is that things will be very different when the nation votes in 'the only contest that really matters' – i.e. the next UK-wide general election. Sometimes this bravado turns out to be justified, and it is true that many second-order elections are treated as a means of administering a 'painless' warning to a government which retains its underlying popularity.

However, while government feel that it is relatively harmless to tinker with the electoral systems at subnational level, it is now valid to ask a question which would have seemed ridiculous in (say) 1955: 'What is the *real* UK party system?'. Until 1997 there could only have been one answer, despite the 'blip' resulting from the Alliance challenge in 1983. The recent revival of the Liberal Democrats as something more than a vehicle for protest votes has been enough to arouse speculation about genuine multi-party competition. But more importantly, since the introduction of PR for devolved assemblies and the European elections the underlying diversity of the UK electorate has been revealed.

The Westminster government still seems to regard rival institutions as strictly subordinated, like a glorified local government. Almost certainly it would have responded in the same way if regional government had been introduced in England, even if that, too, had resulted in multi-party competition. However, while the effect of elections in devolved institutions has been limited at Westminster, it is very likely to have impressed many members of the public who have been disillusioned with two-party competition since the 1960s. If subsequent reforms produce an element of the upper chamber elected by a form of PR, public demand for a system which will produce a closer reflection of party preferences is likely to become overwhelming.

Further reading

The classic work on party systems is G. Sartori, *Parties and Party Systems: A Framework for Analysis* (Cambridge: Cambridge University Press, 1976). P. Webb, *The Modern British Party System* (London: Sage, 2000) is an excellent advanced text. S. Ingle, *The British Party System* (London: Pinter, 3rd edition, 2000) is a highly readable and insightful account, although it also deals at length with party organisation and ideology. L. Robbins, H. Blackmore and R. Pyper (eds), *Britain's Changing Party System* (Manchester: Manchester University Press) includes some discussions which are still useful although the system has continued to change since the volume was published. Andrew Heywood's chapters warning of the emergence of a dominant-party system, is particularly pertinent. R. Garner and P. Lynch, 'The Changing Party System', *Parliamentary Affairs*, Vol. 58, No. 3 (2005), pp. 533–54, and A. Russell, 'The

---

Conclusion and summaries bring together the key issues dealt with in the chapter succinctly and clearly to aid understanding.

Every chapter is supported by a Further Reading section to help you find more information and continue your study

Party System: Deep Freeze or Gentle Thawing?', *Parliamentary Affairs*, Vol. 58, No. 2 (2005), pp. 351–65 take account of more recent developments.

Much of the literature on general elections includes assessments of the state of the party system. Particularly useful in this respect are P. Norris and C. Wlezein (eds), *Britain Votes 2005* (Oxford: Oxford University Press, 2005) and A. Geddes and J. Tonge (eds), *Britain Decides: The 2005 General Election* (London: Palgrave, 2005). The significance of electoral systems is assessed in P. Dunleavy, 'Facing up to Multi-Party Politics', in *Parliamentary Affairs*, Vol. 58, No. 3 (2005), pp. 503–32 and P. Dunleavy and H. Margetts, 'The Impact of UK Electoral Systems', in P. Norris and C. Wlezein (eds) *Britain Votes 2005* (Oxford: Oxford University Press, 2005), pp. 198–213.

Useful overviews of the various party systems within the UK include a selection of articles that have appeared in *Politics Review*. On the 2005 general election, see D. Denver, 'Four-Party Competition in Scotland', *Politics Review*, Vol. 15, No. 2 (2005), pp. 19–21; J. Bradbury, 'Labour Power under Pressure in Wales', *Politics Review*, Vol. 15, No. 2 (2005), pp. 16–18, and J. Tonge, 'DUP and Sinn Fein Triumph in Northern Ireland', *Politics Review*, Vol. 15, No. 2 (2005), pp. 10–13. On elections to the devolved assemblies, see D. Denver, '2003 Scottish Parliament elections: Messages for Unpopular Parties', *Politics Review*, Vol. 13, No. 2, (2003), pp. 28–31 and J. Bradbury, '2003 Welsh Assembly elections: Labour reclaims Power', *Politics Review*, Vol. 13, No. 2, (2003), pp. 22–6.

Websites

The official websites of British political parties contain details on their election results and policies. Richard Kimber's politics 'gateway' www.psr.keele.ac.uk/parties.htm provides links. The websites of the main parties in the UK are:

Conservative Party www.conservative-party.org.uk

Labour Party www.labour.org.uk

Liberal Democrats www.libdems.org.uk

Plaid Cymru www.plaid-cymru.wales.com

Scottish National Party www.snp.org.uk

British National Party www.bnp.net

Greens www.greenparty.org.uk

Respect www.respectcoalition.org

United Kingdom Independence Party www.independenceuk.org

Democratic Unionist Party www.dup.org.uk

Ulster Unionist Party www.uup.org/

Sinn Fein www.sinnfein.ie

Social Democratic and Labour Party www.sdlp.ie

Websites provide a wealth of valuable resources for further study and interest

Guide to features

Case studies

Controversy boxes

Figures

Tables

Timelines

Preface

At the time of writing (June 2006), teachers of UK politics are confronted by an apparent paradox. As an academic subject, politics is more popular than ever, and there is an increasing demand for courses covering the UK. At the same time, though, the political process seems to be trapped in a spiral of decline. For more than a decade, the public and private activities of politicians have brought the profession into disrepute. The recent decline in voter turnout has provoked a great deal of soul-searching, but there have been few constructive measures which might reverse the trend.

The situation poses difficult problems for anyone writing a textbook on UK politics. However, we believe that the new opportunities are more striking. For one thing, the long years of Conservative rule after 1979 made it difficult to avoid undue bias. Even her warmest admirers freely admit that Margaret Thatcher was a divisive prime minister. Amongst the general public, she polarised opinion to the extent that those who refrained from criticism stood accused of being too sympathetic. Under John Major (1990–97), the Conservatives were equally controversial, even if the reasons for critical comment ('sleaze', and divisions over Europe) were different.

The experience of Labour government since 1997 allows academic commentators to overcome many of these difficulties. First, some of the trends which could be identified under the Conservatives have taken on a more 'permanent' aspect. Perhaps the most noteworthy development has been a shift from 'government' to 'governance', with many traditional state functions now being performed by agencies of various kinds. This leads to obvious questions about democratic accountability, which can now be discussed as a crucial general theme in UK politics, rather than an opportunity to praise or blame the Conservatives. Also, while the argument for devolution was in a state of suspended animation between 1979 and 1997 due to Conservative opposition, all three main parties have now accepted Labour's constitutional settlement in this respect. So this important area of speculation before 1997 has been conclusively settled, at least for the foreseeable future.

Another advantage of writing a textbook at this time is that the previous dissatisfaction with the main political parties has now been registered in indisputable statistics, rather than opinion polls. Even in 1992, when the Conservatives received a record number of votes, it was possible to detect an increase in pressure group activity. But the voting habit was hard to break, even in people who had begun to channel most of their political energies outside the long established parties. For many people the period from 1997 to 2001 marked a 'tipping point'. In some cases, this might have been because negative reasons for voting no longer applied – i.e.

some Conservatives might have abstained because Tony Blair was not perceived to be a serious threat. Equally, though, many voters might have lost their positive reasons for voting. Whatever the reasons – and polling evidence on this subject can never be conclusive – after 2001, no objective observer could deny that the main parties were no longer inspiring a sufficient proportion of UK citizens to cast a vote.

There is obvious scope for a textbook which focuses on the key themes of (i) the shift from government to governance and (ii) the character of British democracy, rather than simply bolting institutional change and apathy onto an existing argument. Teachers of UK politics also require a textbook which is *comprehensive*, *concise* and *coherent*. These needs have dictated the composition of the present volume. In particular, unlike other authors, we have decided not to include a substantial separate section on 'issues'. Debate on subjects like the economy and the public services is vulnerable to regular change, in relation to underlying assumptions as well as details. We judge that it is more important to provide students and teachers with a sound understanding of the context in which specific policies are developed, which involves a discussion of such factors as the media and pressure groups, as well as the core institutions and actors in the UK polity. While it is impossible to understand contemporary UK politics without a good grounding in historical developments since 1945, a textbook which attempted a detailed discussion of the period would also be of unusable bulk. In the present volume, we have provided a sketch of the most relevant events in the post-war period, and provided students with a comprehensive guide to further reading. We hope that readers who used our *AS UK Government and Politics* (Deddington: Philip Allan, 2nd edition, 2005) will appreciate a similar accessible style and benefit from the greater scope and in-depth analysis we provide in this book.

We are very grateful to the five referees who read earlier versions of these chapters for their thorough and helpful comments:

Jacqui Briggs, University of Lincoln
Dan Hough, University of Sussex
Alistair Jones, De Montfort University
Joanna McKay, Nottingham Trent University
Liz Sperling, Liverpool John Moores University

Philip Lynch would also like to thank Stephen Hopkins and Richard Whitaker for their comments on draft chapters. Thanks are due to the staff of Pearson Education for their advice and assistance, particularly Morten Fuglevand, Andrew Peart and Peter Hooper.

On a personal note, each of the authors was preparing to become a father for the first time when we started this project; at its finish, we are proud fathers of lively toddlers. Special thanks are due to our partners, Dili and Mandy for their support and patience and to our children Amelia and Alec, to whom this book is dedicated.

Acknowledgements

We are grateful to the following for permission to reproduce copyright material:

Table 2.2 from *Twentieth Century British Political Facts*, Palgrave/Macmillan (Butler, D. and Butler, G. 2000); Table 6.1 and 18.1 from *AS UK Government and Politics*, 2nd ed, Philip Allan Updates (Garnett, M. and Lynch, P. 2005); Figure 10.1 and 11.1 reproduced by permission of Ordnance Survey on behalf of HMSO. © Crown copyright 2006. all rights reserved. Ordnance Survey Licence number 100030901; Table 11.7 from Devolution and Britishness in Economic and Social Research Council, *Devolution Briefing* no 35 table 3. ESRC Programme on Devolution and Constitutional Change, (School of Social and Political Studies, University of Edinburgh. Curtice, J. 2005); Table 16.5 from *Changed voting changed politics: lessons of Britain's experience of PR since 1997*, p34. final report. (The Constitution Unit, School of Public Policy, UCL 2004)

Photographs:

p7, © Jon Bower/Alamy. p15, © eye35.com/Alamy p24, © Setboun Michel/Sygma/Corbis. p31, Courtesy of The Advertising Archives. p49, © AP/EMPICS. p57, © Colin Jones/Topfoto. p70, ©PA/EMPICS. p.72, © Matthew Polak/Sygma/Corbis. p.89, © Tim Graham/Getty Images. p.99, © John Stillwell/PA/jd/EMPICS. p.117, © Ken Lennox/Mirrorpix. p.120, © Graeme Robertson/Getty Images. p.123, © PA/Topfoto. p.142, © PA/Topfoto. p.147, © PA/Topfoto. p.152, © ArenaPAL/Topfoto. p.168, © Getty Images. p170, © Peter MacDiarmid/Reuters/Corbis. p.199, © Richard Austin/Rex Features. p206, © David Fisher/Rex Features. p. 221, © David Davies/PA/EMPICS. p.230, © Mirrorpix. p.247, © James Fraser/Rex Features. p.257, © Mirrorpix. p 262, © Belfast News Letter/Mirrorpix. p.284, © AFP/Getty Images. p.290, © Harry Prosser/Mirrorpix. p.314, Reproduced with permission of Punch ltd. p.317, © D. Gaywood/Rex Features. p.336, © Getty Images. p.340, © AFP/Getty Images. p. 371, © Ray Tang/Rex Features. p.374, © Topfoto. p.392, © Reuters/Corbis. p.403, Courtesy of The Electoral Commission. p.437, © Mirrorpix. p.443, © Rex Features. p.460, © Dan Chung/Reuters/Corbis. p.466, © Alisdair Macdonald/ Rex Features. p.478, © AP/EMPICS. p.483, © Nicholas Bailey/Rex Features.

Part 1
Context

Chapter 1

Understanding British politics

Learning outcomes

After reading this chapter, you will:

- Appreciate that the subject-matter of politics is open to competing interpretations.
- Understand that there are various approaches to the study of British politics.
- Become familiar with the concept of 'liberal democracy'.
- Understand the issues involved in a shift from 'government' to 'governance' in the UK.

Introduction

Teachers of British politics today are faced with an interesting dilemma. On the one hand, the subject is increasingly popular among students. At the same time, though, there is undoubtedly a strong feeling of public dissatisfaction with the political process itself. The profession of politics is not highly regarded and voter turnout was a matter of concern even before the 2001 general election when less than 60 per cent of the electorate registered a preference. This was the worst turnout since 1928 when the UK adopted universal suffrage for people over 21. The situation improved in 2005, but only slightly.

Despite occasional dissenting voices, until the mid-1960s it was common to present the British political system as a success story: the product of gradual progress over several centuries towards a democratic society in which all citizens could feel represented and involved in the political process. Nowadays it is much easier to find deep-rooted faults. In this book, we have reflected common criticisms of the UK political system. But the main purpose is to enable students to approach British politics in an analytical spirit. By the end of the book, they should have learned something about their own ideas, as well as reaching a deeper understanding of the subject.

This introductory chapter outlines some of the perspectives from which British politics can be analysed and introduces the key themes of the book. The main text is divided into five parts:

- *Context*: exploring the historical, economic and social background to contemporary British politics.
- *Constitution and institutions*: covering the uncodified British constitution, its parliament, the legal system, the office of Prime Minister.
- *Multi-level governance*: explaining recent developments relating to the changing state, local government, devolution within the UK and the European Union (EU).
- *Political parties*: discussing party systems, ideology and the structure of the main parties.
- *Participation*: assessing electoral systems, voting behaviour, referendums and pressure groups.

UK politics, representative democracy and the 'Westminster Model'

Executive: the branch of government responsible for putting laws into operation. In the UK, the executive consists of the Prime Minister, other members of the Cabinet and junior ministers.

Legislature: the part of government which makes laws. In the UK, the Westminster parliament is the legislative body, and is dominated by the elected House of Commons.

Judiciary: the branch of government which decides disputes about the law, punishing individuals who have been convicted of illegal acts by the courts, and decides whether agents of the state have properly applied laws passed by the legislature.

Broadly speaking, there are two ways in which a country's politics can be understood. The most familiar approach is to focus on specific institutions, practices and people: for example, parliament, elections and party leaders. The advantage of this view of politics, exemplified in the UK by the 'Westminster Model', is that the subject-matter is clearly delineated. It takes politics to be a specialised activity, undertaken by experts.

The Westminster Model reflects the long-standing UK tradition of strong centralised government, run by strictly-disciplined political parties. On the Westminster Model the government (the **executive**) is dominant, backed by a majority in the House of Commons (the main element of the **legislature**) and by a professional civil service. In the UK the executive and legislature are 'fused', that is, the effective head of the executive, the Prime Minister, derives his or her power from control of the legislature. There is no codified constitution, and institutions like the **judiciary** and local government can be reshaped according to the wishes of the government, so long as parliament agrees. This system is highly unusual. In most democratic countries, the executive, legislature and judiciary are kept separate in accordance with a codified constitution (see Chapter 5).

The Westminster Model approach to UK politics was followed by most political scientists until the 1970s. It encouraged students to focus on such questions as the role of the Prime Minister, the influence of parliament, and ministerial responsibility. Outside academia, advocates of the Westminster Model claimed that it provided government which combined the virtues of strength and flexibility. In a two-party system (see Chapter 14), the majority party would be able to implement its policy programme because parliamentary discipline would ensure the loyalty of its elected representatives. The parliamentary opposition would point out its real (or perceived) failings, in the hope of replacing it at a subsequent election. On any working day, virtually all of the key actors in UK politics could be found either in the parliament at Westminster, or in the surrounding area of Whitehall.

However, there is an inherent tension between this view of UK politics and the long-accepted notion that Britain is a 'representative democracy'. In such systems, when politicians take decisions they are acting on behalf of the people who elected them. Since 1928 the UK electorate has included all adults (with a few exceptions such as criminals serving prison sentences). In a representative democracy, MPs must submit themselves for re-election at periodic intervals. Parliament has the power to change the existing arrangement, under which a new election cannot be delayed more than five years after the previous one. But it would be most unlikely to do so, except at a time of grave national emergency (thus, for example, there was no general election between 1935 and 1945). The most likely changes to British democratic institutions and practices will either widen the franchise further (by reducing the voting age to 16), make participation easier (e.g. by introducing new voting methods or changing polling day from the traditional Thursday to a weekend), or bring the outcome closer to voter preferences (by introducing some form of proportional representation) (see Chapter 16).

Voters and voting behaviour are thus clearly part of the subject matter of politics. And people can vote (or abstain from voting) for a wide variety of reasons, from hard-headed assessments of political programmes to half-remembered parental influences or even an irrational passion for a particular candidate. Thus, in order to understand even the formal political process in any representative democracy like the UK, it seems sensible to look beyond specific institutions, and to examine developments within society as a whole. Yet participation in politics by the general public is not restricted to voting. Between elections people can try to influence decisions by writing to their MPs, signing petitions or joining demonstrations. They might even take their objections to government policy to the length of breaking the law. All of these activities ought to be included in an account of the politics of a representative democracy (see Chapter 18).

The decline of the Westminster Model

Long before the advent of universal electoral suffrage in the UK, members of the political class developed a theory which promised to reconcile the Westminster Model with representative institutions. On this view, members of parliament were elected because voters decided that they could trust them to exercise judgement on their behalf. At the next election they would be assessed on their records. This made them *representatives* in a strict sense, rather than *delegates* who would be subjected to constant instruction by their constituents between elections.

Whatever the merits of the theory of representation when it was first expounded, since the eighteenth century it has been undermined by the emergence of tightly-disciplined political parties. Instead of being judged on their individual records, candidates tend to win or lose depending on the popularity of their parties at the national level. But even this departure from the old idea of representation could be squared with the Westminster Model. It could be argued that a party which won an overall majority of MPs in the House of Commons had secured a 'mandate' from the voters – that is, the winning party's policy programme had been approved by the electorate as a whole. Even if they had no insight into the individual character of their constituency representative, voters had expressed a preference for his or her party; and thanks to the disciplinary procedures exercised at Westminster through the 'whipping' system, MPs could be expected to act in accordance with the popular mandate.

At least in part, the present dissatisfaction with politics in the UK can be attributed to this stubborn attachment to the Westminster Model. There is a tendency for any group of 'specialists' to become isolated from the rest of the public. In some professions this need not be a disaster. But MPs are particularly vulnerable to the charge that they are 'out of touch' with developments in society as a whole. It is not that politicians have no interest in winning public respect; indeed, most of them have a pathological desire to be loved. They also seem keener than ever to find out what the public is thinking between elections, fussing over opinion polls and focus groups. However, when they receive this information they tend to filter it through the mind-set of the 'Westminster Village' – a network of media people and policy advisers, all of whom tend to view politics in the same way and to reinforce each other's responses to political developments.

By seeking out any evidence of party disunity in the hope of filling up its political coverage with dramatic stories, the media has undoubtedly helped to create the context in which MPs are ordered to stay loyal and 'on message' at all times (see Chapter 4). But the disciplinary impulse has always been present to some extent. In particular, parties which either hold office or believe that they will soon form a government have a tendency to vote *en bloc* against any measure which threatens to diminish the power of the executive. Thus, for example, Labour came to power in 1997 promising to 'modernise' key elements of the constitution, notably the House of Lords. An obvious move in this strategy would have been to introduce elections to the upper house. Yet this would have increased its authority, making it a potential rival to the Commons. Tony Blair emphasised this point and although MPs were theoretically allowed a free vote on the future of the Lords, the Labour whips privately intervened in support of the prime minister's preference for a wholly appointed chamber. The vote ended in fiasco with the Commons rejecting all of the options for reform.

Despite the problems over Lords reform, the first two terms of Labour government after 1997 produced important constitutional reforms which weakened the Westminster Model. Devolution to Scotland, Wales and Northern Ireland has undermined old ideas about London's dominance (see Chapter 11) as has UK membership of the European Union (see Chapter 12). There have also been moves to introduce a more independent judiciary, particularly through the Human Rights Act 1998 (see Chapter 8). The UK government has often been reluctant to loosen its grip; for example, Labour tried unsuccessfully to dictate the choice of the First Secretary in the devolved Welsh administration.

Beyond the Westminster Model

It can thus be argued that the Westminster Model is not just inaccurate as a description of politics in a representative democracy like the UK. It also has a more

To understand contemporary British politics, we must look beyond Westminster (© Jon Bower/Almay)

practical impact, helping to explain that while people are apparently still interested in political *issues*, they are increasingly disillusioned with the political *process*.

The approach in this book reflects the continuing relevance of the Westminster Model. However, we move beyond this narrow focus and adopt an approach to politics which gives equal prominence to public participation. The difficulty with a broader definition is placing a limit on the subject-matter of politics. Which social phenomena should count as 'political'? In this book we confine ourselves to the most obvious factors. Social changes, such as the decline of class voting, the improved status of women, and questions of culture and ethnicity clearly have a significant bearing on the political landscape. But changing economic factors are also important. For example, up to 1979 UK governments made it a priority to protect domestic manufacturing industry, which had originally propelled the country to worldwide power. Since the election of the first Thatcher government in 1979, manufacturing industry has been allowed to decline. The service sector, particularly the financial concerns based in the City of London, has been given priority.

One important political by-product of this trend has been the dramatic decline of the balance of payments (the difference between the value of UK imports and exports) as a factor in electoral fortunes. Labour lost the 1970 general election at least in part because the balance of payments dipped into a small deficit just before the poll. The small (and temporary) 'trade gap' of May 1970 would nowadays be regarded as a triumph; in 1992 the deficit on trade in goods was a record £46.3 billion, yet the Conservative government was re-elected. The shift from manufacturing to services has had additional consequences. Manufacturing was more suited to the development of life-long political allegiances, and was associated with a relatively inflexible class structure. Now that most people work in the service sector, class boundaries are regarded as more fluid and people on the whole are far less reliable in their voting behaviour (see Chapter 17).

When Britain's world status was higher, students of politics could relegate consideration to the outside world to short discussions of foreign policy. This option is no longer available. In a 'globalised' economy – accompanied by daily talk of worldwide terrorist networks – an insular understanding of UK politics is obviously inadequate. British politicians are affected on a day-to-day basis by the decisions of other actors on the world stage; and agreement on one subject does not preclude tensions elsewhere. In 2002, as Blair was discussing an invasion of Iraq with US President George W. Bush, the EU was locked in a battle over the protection of the American steel industry against European imports. Blair himself was hopeful that one day he could persuade the British people to join the European single currency (the euro), which was widely regarded as a potential rival to the mighty US dollar. These diverse and sometimes contradictory considerations were not secondary distractions from the business of politics; they formed an integral part of the context in which political decisions were taken in the UK, and even those voters who were unaware of this wider stage would feel their effects.

Liberal democracy

In studying UK politics, then, we are addressing much more than a set of institutions in London, and the people who operate within them. Social, economic and global factors are all relevant to a proper understanding of the subject. They are discussed in more detail in Chapters 2 and 3. But the study of politics involves more than the identification of relevant subject-matter and the accumulation of evidence. Some scholars have argued that politics can and should be studied 'scientifically' – that is, with the kind of objectivity which is associated with the natural sciences. However, such hopes are misplaced. There is some scope for objective study in politics; for example, statistics based on electoral data can be analysed in a way which leaves little room for reasonable doubt. But the question of 'objectivity' is highly problematic even before we start to assemble the raw data. Why do we decide that some statistics are more important than others? And while certain figures presented in graphs might give rise to conclusions which no reasonable observer can dispute, invariably we find ourselves trying to explain the findings in a wider context, which brings in factors like ideologies, which are not susceptible to 'scientific' evaluation (see Chapter 15).

No student of British politics today can approach the subject without feeling the influence of liberal democratic ideas. The phrase 'liberal democracy' is liable to create some confusion, particularly since the third largest party in the UK is called the Liberal Democrats. But there is no better shorthand term for the broad framework of ideas within which UK politics has been conducted for many decades. Indeed, it can be argued that a strong element of liberal democracy in the UK predates the relatively recent introduction of universal adult suffrage. That is because liberal democracy is not about a specific electoral system, as the phrase might suggest. Rather, the precepts of liberal democracy assert that elections should be free from intimidation or other forms of corruption, and the outcome broadly representative of public opinion. Thus, for example, the result of the 2000 US presidential election was not disputed because the winning candidate, George W. Bush, happened to win fewer votes than his rival Al Gore. That was accepted as a by-product of the electoral system under which the contest took place. The system itself was open to criticism, but few people seriously suggested that the contest between Bush and Gore should be re-run using a different method to compile the results. Rather, the argument concerned the way in which the decisive state of Florida had conducted the election, with allegations that some voters were prevented from reaching the polls and serious questions about the way in which the votes had been counted. This would have been a clear breach of liberal democratic principles.

The idea that political controversies should be settled by 'free and fair' procedures rather than by the use of force is the key principle of liberal democracy. This does not mean that the resort to force is outside the domain of politics. Ultimately, the authority of the liberal democratic state rests on the recognition by its citizens that it can legitimately resort to force in certain circumstances. However, in liberal democracies it is assumed that force will be exercised within a framework of laws and accepted procedures. This principle is summed up in the phrase 'the rule of law'. This means that all citizens should be treated equally; and if they are accused of a crime they should be given a fair and open trial. In the UK this principle dates back to mediaeval times; hence the fierce controversy over the treatment of suspected terrorists in the wake of the attacks on the US of 11 September 2001 (see Chapter 8).

State: a political association that has a monopoly of force within a territory.

In liberal democracies, the **state** is supposed to exist for the benefit of its citizens rather than vice-versa. As rational, autonomous individuals, they should be protected as they conduct their daily business, so long as they do not break the laws. This sphere of private activity, and the associated voluntary organisations (like charities, clubs, trade unions and political parties themselves) is often covered by the umbrella term of **civil society**. Unless people are allowed to associate freely for their own purposes, it is asserted, the political institutions of **liberal democracy** will be meaningless.

Civil society: the sphere of voluntary activity, where associations can be formed independently of the state.

Liberal democracy: a state governed in accordance with long-established liberal principles, such as the right to participate in free and fair elections, freedom of expression, and the impartial administration of justice.

Pluralism

In theory, at least, liberal democracies accept the notion that reasonable people will reach different conclusions about political issues. In their daily lives, they will also have a wide range of interests which often conflict; and they should be free to express their views in association with others who feel the same. Politics, on this view, is about the peaceful adjustment of such interests. The ideal outcome of political debate will be a compromise which satisfies all sides. But if this is impossible, at least all the parties to the dispute should be left satisfied that nothing has prevented them from winning a fair hearing.

Pluralism: the belief that the existence of different peoples and opinions within a society is healthy.

These ideas are associated with another key liberal democratic principle – that of **pluralism**. This underpins the principle of free speech, which can be exercised within the scope of the law even by people who express unpopular views. Originally, pluralist thinkers like the French philosopher Voltaire (1694–1778) and John Stuart Mill (1806–73) in Britain argued that pluralism was the best guarantee of intellectual progress; if unpopular ideas are suppressed, the public is likely to miss out on beneficial ideas. Thus pluralists argue that the dissemination of ideas should be as free as possible. In particular, there must be minimal state interference in the activities of the media. During the Cold War in which liberal democracies were ranged against 'totalitarian' Communist regimes, western propagandists tended to argue that whether or not society actively benefited from free speech, at least it was permitted in their countries – unlike the Soviet Union and its allies, where the state controlled the flow of information to the public.

More generally, pluralist ideas can be contrasted with the elitist position (see below). While elitists want to keep the impact of public opinion on decision-making down to a minimum, pluralists argue that it should be maximised. For pluralists, the existence of political 'specialists' is problematic in itself. It may be the case that such people are more knowledgeable on political matters, and win the respect of the public through their ability to express their ideas. The key point for pluralists is that they should always be open to challenge, and that in debate they should have no other advantage than the respect they have earned from their previous record. For pluralists, the unthinking assumption that 'the government always knows best' is the death-knell of a free society.

The limits of liberal democracy

While liberal democratic ideas have been widely accepted for many years in Western Europe and North America, they have received an additional impetus since the late 1980s with the virtual disappearance of old-style Communist regimes like the Soviet Union. Other countries which remain formally Communist, like China, seem gradually to be moving towards liberal democratic practices in some respects, even if free and open elections are still absent. It has been argued, most famously by the US writer Francis Fukuyama, that the worldwide triumph of liberal democracy is inevitable. Among other reasons, it is claimed that liberal democracies are associated with free economies, which are far more efficient than totalitarian states. Thus liberal democracy is not just morally superior to any alternative; it also works better. These arguments lend support to the view that liberal democracies are justified in interfering in the internal affairs of so-called 'failing' (or 'rogue') states, like Iraq. On

| Analysis: | 1.1 |

Elitism

Elitists argue that politics is a specialised activity, and that the most important decisions should be left to people with the relevant qualifications. In its purest form, elitism is anti-democratic; according to some elitists, allowing the general public to influence important decisions is a recipe for disaster. Thus, while pluralists think that things are going well when political leaders are representative of society, elitists take this as a sign that things have gone wrong. On the elitist view, leaders should be better than the people they govern.

However, some elitists accept democracy, on the grounds that the parties who compete for votes are themselves elites. 'Democratic elitists' argue that politicians who rise to the top of their parties are likely to have acquired the skills necessary for good government. On this view, free competition between organised parties is unlikely to be damaging to a state, since the rulers at any time will still constitute an elite, even if they have been chosen by voters who have a limited knowledge of politics.

this view, even the imposition of liberal democracy by armed force will improve the lives of people who currently lack its benefits.

However, even those who accept the superiority of liberal democratic ideas can continue to question the extent to which they are actually reflected in the institutions and practices of a particular state at a specific time. In the case of the UK, we have already referred to concerns about the impact of the Westminster Model, the party system and the media. A more general question is how readily liberal democracy can accommodate significant inequalities of wealth. Pluralists might accept that key business interests have a special right to be heard by governments, since their fortunes can affect a nation's general prosperity. But when questions seem to be settled by the size of a bank balance rather than the weight of an argument, many liberal democratic assumptions begin to ring hollow. In the UK this difficulty has been recognised by new restrictions on party funding through the Political Parties, Elections and Referendums Act 2000. Unlike the US, the UK also has strict guidelines on the nature and extent of party-political coverage on radio and television. However, during the 1990s concerns were raised that money could win privileged access to decision-makers, regardless of the conduct of elections (see Chapter 14).

A second question is the appropriate response of liberal democracies to new terrorist threats. In the UK this problem had been debated long before 11 September 2001, because of the campaign of violence by Irish terrorists which began in the early 1970s. Among other things, this had already prompted the erection of iron gates at the entrance to Downing Street (in 1989, when Margaret Thatcher was prime minister). However justified for security reasons, this was still a regrettable symbol of an enforced distance between politicians and the people. It even prevented demonstrations of spontaneous enthusiasm, so that when Blair approached Number 10 after Labour's landslide victory in May 1997 the television footage of rejoicing citizens in Downing Street was actually a stage-managed display from selected party supporters.

The new terrorist threat, understandably, has led to an extension of tight security to many other public buildings. MPs are still accessible to the public in other ways. But when they take decisions which affect the civil rights even of a small minority of people – or vote to take the country into war – it is legitimate to ask whether they are truly accountable to their real employers, who elect them and pay their salaries. In a rapidly changing context, this remains one of the key principles of liberal democracy. The weakness of accountability was a serious flaw in the old Westminster Model. If, as the evidence suggests, true accountability has been weakening in recent years there is a danger that decision-makers could lose sight of the necessary balance between liberty and security, thus fulfilling a major aim of the enemies of Western liberal democracy.

The other concern arising from the Iraq war was that liberal democracy was becoming too vulnerable to the influence of money. The role of the US was particularly vulnerable to this charge. Critics suspected that the ideal of a 'liberated' Iraq was merely introduced as a smokescreen for the real motive, which was to gain control of the country's extensive oil reserves. The fact that the US President George W. Bush was heavily financed by oil companies – and had previously been Governor of the oil-dominated state of Texas – did nothing to allay these fears. Bush had also resisted attempts to tackle the problem of global pollution, allegedly for the same reason. No-one believed that Tony Blair had committed UK forces to the assault

Controversy: 1.1

Economics and liberal democracy

During the 1970s and 1980s, a key element of the case for a free market economy was the notion that it had a mutually supportive relationship with liberal democracy. On this view, excessive state intervention was a threat to political as well as economic freedom. Supporters of the free market used the example of the Soviet Union – where the ruling party controlled the media, the economy, and the political process – to argue that freedom was indivisible. They also borrowed an older argument, that countries which traded freely with each other were most unlikely to resort to force to settle their disagreements. Thus the free market was the best guarantee of international peace as well as domestic prosperity.

Conservative electoral success between 1979 and 1997 – and the Labour acceptance of most key Conservative arguments – suggested that the free marketers had won the debate. The circumstances in which the Soviet Union collapsed pointed to the same conclusion. Under Mikhail Gorbachev, economic reforms had been introduced in advance of democratic institutions. The result was a growing demand for political freedom, which could not be contained within the old Soviet system. However, subsequent events suggest a more complex relationship between the economy and politics. Although Russia is no longer Communist, its blood-soaked intervention in Chechnya is a distinct echo of the old days. Meanwhile, social inequalities have widened to an extent which is unthinkable even in Western democracies. A tiny handful of people have become wildly rich through a flawed privatisation process; and something like a 'mafia' threatens to fill the vacuum left by the all-powerful Communist Party. Although he has been elected, president Putin exercises an iron grip over the electronic media.

The Russian example suggests that a liberal economy can co-exist with a political culture in which democracy is either absent or meaningless. The same lesson can be derived from Far Eastern states, like Malaya. In the 1990s, while Western intellectuals were hailing the inevitable triumph of liberal democracy, such states were experiencing dramatic rates of economic growth while heavily curtailing personal liberty.

Recent experience suggests that while a (relatively) free economy may help to underpin political freedoms, it is by no means a guarantee that citizens will enjoy real influence over their leaders. In fact, the ideal business context is one in which investors are insured against political upheaval, so that they can plan ahead. It is not necessary for a government to keep a majority of its citizens happy in order to enjoy prolonged tenure of office. So long as the government serves the interests of the most influential sections of society, along with most of the media and the armed forces, it can expect to stay in power. In a consumerist society like the UK (or the US), democratic practices can be allowed in the reasonable expectation that they will never produce unprofitable outcomes.

on Iraq because he was under the direct influence of the oil industry. But since his position was clearly influenced by the US determination to depose the regime of Saddam Hussein, critics argued that it amounted to the same thing. There had been instances when the Blair government was accused of granting privileged access to business-people who had contributed to its election coffers. Similar allegations had beset the previous Conservative government.

Although opinions will always be divided about the Iraq war, it seems reasonable to suggest that the course of events lent support to the ideas of democratic elitists (see Analysis 1.1), rather than their pluralist opponents. In the UK, the most spectacular evidence was the sudden swing of public opinion once the government had decided to embark on the war, even though the quality of the arguments had not significantly changed (indeed, the fact that the Iraqi regime did not instantly use weapons of mass destruction, despite the overwhelming force deployed against it, reinforced the views of those who doubted the formal justification for war). On the view of democratic elitists, ordinary people are actually relieved when 'experts' take decisions out of their hands. However, we also argued above that there is likely to be a connection between an elitist view of politics and a decline in electoral turnout. This implies that democratic elitists are mistaken in their view of human nature, and that many people want to live in a society which truly reflects pluralist ideas. On present trends, the ironic outcome may be that the people most likely to participate in elections are the ones who would be happy to leave decisions to others, while those who are eager to make a meaningful contribution stay at home. In such circumstances, active citizens are more likely to participate in politics through pressure groups (see Chapter 18). These have a valuable place in a liberal democracy, but it is doubtful whether the system would survive if large numbers of people regarded them, rather than political parties, as the only realistic vehicle to effect change.

The changing state

The emergence of a more demanding (and fickle) electorate is one important explanatory factor behind recent changes in the UK state. It was commonly argued during the mid-1970s that the British state had become 'overloaded' with functions, reducing government effectiveness and stretching democratic accountability beyond reasonable limits. For example, ministers were supposed to be accountable to parliament for the performance of nationalised industries, whose detailed operations they were most unlikely to understand. More controversially, it could also be argued that detailed supervision of the economy – particularly through direct government intervention designed to control inflation – had proved counterproductive in practice (see Chapter 2).

The Conservative Party won the 1979 general election under a leader who was determined to reverse Britain's relative decline in global status, and Margaret Thatcher believed that a radical change in the role of the state was a crucial part of this process. In theory, Thatcher was a staunch supporter of the Westminster Model: she had a deep respect for the idea of parliamentary sovereignty, for example. Yet the effect of her reforms was to undermine traditional understandings of British government and politics.

The most spectacular change during the 1980s was the government's programme of privatisation, under which the state sold off its holdings in several major industries (see Chapter 9). In many cases – particularly where the privatised firms still enjoyed a dominant market position – direct political control was replaced by a regime of appointed regulators. In addition, many of the more traditional functions of the central state were 'hived off' to semi-autonomous agencies and a distinction was drawn between 'policy' and 'operational matters' (see Chapter 9). Ministers could still be held responsible for the first, but not for day-to-day operations. The prisons, for example, had been regarded as the direct responsibility of the Home Secretary. Once the Prison Service had been given agency status, embarrassing escapes could be blamed on the chief executive and subordinate officials – even if the escapes took place against a background of prison overcrowding and low staff morale, caused by government policy.

Before 1979, the Conservatives promised to abolish many of the semi-official bodies known as 'quangos' (quasi-autonomous non-governmental organisations), which were not directly accountable to the public despite the fact that they distributed billions of pounds of government revenue. However, the emergence of a 'regulatory state' under Thatcher actually meant that the number and cost of quangos increased. Before it came into office in 1997 Labour was also committed to a cull of quangos, but in practice its efforts were equally ineffectual. In 2005 it was estimated that there were more than 500 of such bodies, including such obscure organisations as the British Potato Council and the Milk Development Council. Opposition parties focused on the continued existence of quangos and promised reform; but judging by the experience of the past quarter-century, it seems that governments of all parties will find them too useful to reduce their numbers and their spending-power.

The relationship between local authorities and central government also underwent a considerable change in this period. Thatcher and her allies believed that the services offered by local government, such as council housing, created a large body of dependent 'clients' who were likely to vote for the party which offered the most generous provision, regardless of efficiency. The government also objected to the tendency of Labour-controlled councils to spend ratepayers' money on political campaigns, often on behalf of minority groups. The effect of successive measures imposed by central government was to force local councils to base their services on value for money, and radically to reduce their scope for independent political initiative. As a result, by the end of the twentieth century most councils were more like businesses than political entities.

In 1990 Conservative policy towards local government rebounded against Thatcher, when the new community charge (or poll tax) caused widespread resentment. However, this controversy ended by increasing the scope of central government interference, because the Treasury was forced to provide more generous subsidies in order to cushion the impact of the new tax (and its successor, the council tax). While Labour has been less antagonistic towards local authorities since it returned to office in 1997, councils have adjusted to their new role rather than readopting their old one. In particular, there is no sign that councils will recover their former prominence in housing provision. Rather, even a Labour government has preferred to work through unelected housing associations. Other building projects are now conducted in partnership with private companies.

Government: decision-making through formal institutions and rules.

Governance: decision-making by multiple actors in networks.

From 'government' to 'governance'

A positive way of interpreting these developments is to say that the UK has moved from the old Westminster Model of **government** to a new style of **'governance'** (see

Chapter 9). Even in the Thatcher years, the central state gave orders and expected obedience. However, some governmental decisions actually made it more difficult to ensure compliance – for example, ministers no longer exercised direct control over nationalised industries, and although at first ministers continued to treat agencies as subordinates, eventually they were always likely to maximise their sphere of independent action.

It would be going too far to say that the Thatcher years saw a general relaxation of central control – if anything, the experience of local authorities suggested that Westminster was increasing its power. However, from a wider perspective many developments of the 1979–97 period can be seen as complementary to some important New Labour reforms. In particular, the introduction of devolved institutions in Scotland, Wales and Northern Ireland has encouraged political scientists to talk about a shift from 'government' to 'governance'. Instead of handing down decisions from London, ministers now have to think in terms of negotiation and bargaining. Not only do they have to take into account the more powerful subnational bodies, but they also deal on a regular basis with supranational organis-ations like the European Union (EU) and the United Nations (UN). From this perspective, another notable move from government to governance was Labour's immediate decision to give control over interest-rates to a committee of the Bank of England. Previously this key economic lever had been under the control of the Chancellor of the Exchequer.

However one assesses the real significance of recent changes, it is unhelpful to study UK politics in the traditional fashion, focusing on the Westminster Model and the dominance of central government. However, it is too easy to talk of a completed transition from government to governance in the UK. Three obvious problems remain. First, the notion of 'governance' suggests that central dictation has given way across the board to a process of bargaining with a variety of institutions. But even after the establishment of devolved institutions, central government has tried

The Scottish Parliament: the new face of the multi-level UK polity (© eye35.com/Almay)

to interfere with important business, like the choice of First Minister in Wales. Other legislation passed since 1997, for example the Human Rights Act 1998 (see Chapter 8) and the Freedom of Information Act 2000, have obvious potential to reduce the power of central government over British citizens. But both measures have caused some disquiet in government circles, and their full implications are yet to be felt.

Second, in specific areas – notably in matters of national security, but also in their attempts to reform public services – Westminster politicians have actually become more determined to push through their ideas, even in the face of concerted opposition. Far from 'rolling back' the frontiers of the state, the central government has tried to compensate for its loss of influence in certain areas by extending it in others (i.e. greater interference in matters which were previously governed by personal choice, such as hunting with dogs, and smoking in public places). Third, the transition to governance has been accompanied by a definite reduction in the extent to which ministers can be held responsible for decisions of a political nature. For example, in 2005 Blair openly criticised the operations of the Child Support Agency, which had been set up as a result of a political decision, without any fear that a member of his government would have to resign as a result of institutional failures.

Thus, while it is certainly possible to detect a shift from government to governance, it is worth questioning whether this is more apparent than real, and to ask whether the trend is beneficial in a liberal democracy. The key to such a system is that the people who make important decisions should be held accountable by members of the general public. With its falling electoral turnouts, the UK is hardly unique in facing a 'crisis of accountability' at the time of writing (June 2006); but students should be aware that future changes in the UK state might make this problem worse rather than better.

Conclusion and summary

The UK is usually counted among the world's most successful representative democracies. Although it has not been free from violent outbreaks, since the seventeenth century it has avoided the kind of revolutionary upheavals which have affected so much of the European mainland. It has a strong tradition of free and fair elections, and upholds other key liberal democratic principles such as the right to free speech.

However, in the circumstances of the early twenty-first century it would be a mistake to embark on the study of UK politics in a spirit of complacency. We have identified several potent threats to pluralism and liberal democracy, if those terms are to retain any of their original meaning. The most obvious danger is the impact of global terrorism. But this new threat has materialised at a time when an increasingly diverse and demanding electorate already had good reasons for unease. It is impossible to deny that rich business interests enjoy privileged access to decision-makers, and serious doubts have been cast on the integrity of all UK governments since 1979. In addition, ever-tighter party discipline at Westminster forces ambitious MPs to support certain policies in public, regardless of strong personal reservations. It seems increasingly difficult to hold ministers to account for their actions through the traditional mechanisms of parliamentary debate. The result has been to reinforce an accountability gap which, in any case, is widening under the influence of global developments.

All of these factors help to explain the recent decline in electoral turnout in the UK, and a growing feeling of disillusionment with the political process. This is the most worrying development of all, since the concept of representative democracy obviously depends on a high level of participation. The best antidote to apathy is information, and there are signs that many of the problems facing the political process in the UK are inadequately understood. Thus a critical study of UK politics is more important today than at any time since the institution of universal suffrage.

Further reading

W.H. Greenleaf, *The British Political Tradition* (London: Methuen, 3 volumes, 1983 and 1987) is a magisterial account which identifies different traditions in the study of British politics. L. Tivey, *Interpretations of British Politics* (London: Harvester Wheatsheaf, 1988) is a shorter study of interpretations of British politics. A. Gamble, 'Theories of British Politics', *Political Studies*, Vol. 38, No. 3 (1990), pp. 404–20, M. Bevir and R. Rhodes, 'Studying British Government: Reconstructing the Research Agenda', *British Journal of Politics and International Relations*, Vol. 1, No. 2 (1999), pp. 215–39 and J. Dearlove, 'The Political Science of British Politics', *Parliamentary Affairs*, Vol. 35 (1982), pp. 436–55 are good overviews of developments in the study of British politics.

W. Bagehot, *The English Constitution* (Oxford: Oxford Paperbacks, 2001, original 1867) and A.V. Dicey, *Introduction to the Study of the Law and the Constitution* (Indianapolis: Liberty Fund, 1982, original 1885) are classic texts. A.H. Birch, *Representative and Responsible Government* (George Allen & Unwin, 1964) sets out some of the key attributes of the Westminster Model. D. Marsh, J. Buller, C. Hay, J. Johnstone, P. Kerr, S. McAnulla and M. Watson, *Postwar British Politics in Perspective* (Oxford: Polity Press, 1999) challenges the orthodox Westminster Model perspective. R. Rhodes, *Understanding Governance: Policy Networks, Governance, Reflexivity and Accountability* (Buckingham: Open University Press, 1997) is a collection of Rhodes's influential work on the move from government to governance.

Websites

Two 'gateways' providing links to a series of useful websites on politics in the UK are highly recommended: the Political Studies Association www.psa.ac.uk and Richard Kimber's Political Science Resources site www.psr.keele.ac.uk.

Chapter 2

UK government in context

Learning outcomes

After reading this chapter, you will:
- Have an understanding of the main political developments in Britain since 1945, judging the relative impact of changes and continuity.
- Be able to identify the most important developments in the UK's economic and foreign policy since 1945.
- Appreciate the leading themes from the past which are relevant to an understanding of contemporary politics.

Introduction

Despite the far-reaching changes in British politics since the mid-1970s, it is impossible to understand contemporary developments without some knowledge of previous events. Even the most radical British politician still has to work through long-established institutions, which have developed distinctive practices and attitudes over the years. Also, memories of the past have been crucial factors in shaping the most important political projects of recent years. Thatcherism was a conscious reaction against the trend of previous post-war policies. For their part the 'New' Labour modernisers, headed by Tony Blair, were determined to make their party electable again after defeats stretching back to 1979.

Conventionally, textbooks on British politics take 1945 as their historical starting point. This is more debatable today since Britain is so different from the country that emerged, bruised though unbeaten, from the Second World War. However, the economic and social reforms of the 1945–51 Labour government established a general policy framework which was accepted by most politicians until the mid-1970s, and even today its legacy is crucially important. For this reason the present chapter will use the traditional timeframe, in order to explain the elements of change and continuity in British politics.

The post-war 'consensus'

The 1945 general election resulted in a landslide victory for the Labour Party, led by Clement Attlee. The result was seen as a judgement on the record of inter-war governments, most of which had been dominated by the Conservatives. There had been two Labour governments between 1918 and 1939, but in neither case did the party enjoy an overall majority in the Commons and between them the stints in office lasted little more than three years. With a majority of almost 150 after the 1945 election, and backed by a widespread feeling that previous governments had failed the country, Labour finally had the chance to put its ideals into practice.

Nationalisation: the transfer of private assets into public ownership, often as public corporations.

The Attlee government is associated above all with **nationalisation** and the welfare state. Under the first policy, several key industries were brought under public ownership: coal (1946), electricity (1947), gas, railways and canals (1948) and iron and steel (1949). The Bank of England was also nationalised, in 1946. Many critics and supporters regarded these measures as the first steps towards the implementation of a fully-fledged socialist programme. However, although the scale of Labour's programme was a radical break from the past, nationalisation itself was not new. The BBC and the London Passenger Transport Board had been set up as public corporations between the wars, and the distribution (rather than generation) of electricity was entrusted to a government board in 1926. Also, coal and the railways had been struggling badly in private hands; despite this, the previous owners were generously compensated when they were taken over by the state. Generally speaking, the nationalised concerns were seen either as natural monopolies, utilities whose survival was essential to the country, or both. Iron and steel was by far the most controversial measure, and it was returned to private hands by the Churchill government in 1953.

The Attlee government also pursued an ambitious programme of social reform. It introduced Family Allowances (1945), compulsory National Insurance (1946), and the National Health Service (NHS, 1946). These policies represented a concentrated attack on the economic insecurity which had afflicted many workers between the wars. Britons were now offered assistance when in need at all stages of life – literally from 'the cradle to the grave', since family allowances were payable for every child after the first one, and the National Insurance Act provided state subsidies for funerals. These measures followed the 1942 Beveridge Report into social policy, which had been accepted (with different degrees of enthusiasm) by all three main parties. As with nationalisation, although they represented a comprehensive and ambitious package in combination, the individual policies built on previous reforms, notably those of the Liberal government of H.H. Asquith (1908–16). Significantly, Labour did not abolish private education or healthcare, thus ensuring that the

Table 2.1 British governments, 1945–2005

Period	Party	Overall majority	Share of the vote (%)
1945–50	Labour	146	47.8
1950–1	Labour	5	46.1
1951–5	Conservative	17	48.0
1955–9	Conservative	58	49.7
1959–63	Conservative	100	49.4
1963–4	Labour	4	44.1
1966–70	Labour	96	48.7
1970–4	Conservative	30	46.5
1974	Labour	−33	38.0
1974–9	Labour	3	40.2
1979–83	Conservative	43	44.9
1983–7	Conservative	144	42.5
1987–92	Conservative	102	43.4
1992–7	Conservative	21	41.9
1997–2001	Labour	179	43.2
2001–2005	Labour	167	42.0
2005–	Labour	67	35.2

Note: The Labour government formed after the February 1974 general election relied on support from minority parties.

rich still had access to superior services in these fields. The wartime coalition had passed another important piece of social legislation, the Education Act (1944) which proposed the raising of the school leaving age to 16 (though this change was delayed for nearly 30 years). It also reorganised secondary schools into a tripartite system (grammar, modern and technical schools) whose pupils were selected by examination at 11.

Apart from the Beveridge Report, the other key wartime development in domestic policy was the 1944 White Paper on Unemployment. This document, inspired by the great liberal economist John Maynard Keynes (1883–1946), committed postwar governments to policies which promised to ensure a 'high and stable level of employment'. This was always going to be a priority for a post-war government of any colour, so long as a majority of voters had vivid memories of the 1930s, tainted by economic depression and an official unemployment rate which had rarely dipped below two million. But the White Paper added an official imprint to a political necessity. Keynes's followers assumed that it would be possible to manage the economy in such a way that unemployment could be kept under control without

Analysis: **2.1**

Consensus

In UK politics, the term 'consensus' has been used to indicate a broad agreement between the major parties on the main elements of policy, even if the parties continue to disagree about the precise way in which such policies should be implemented. It is usually accepted that such a consensus was in operation between 1945 and the mid-1970s; according to some commentators, a similar situation has arisen since Tony Blair became Labour's leader in 1994.

Keynesianism: an economic doctrine based on the work of Keynes which advocates that government should intervene in the economy to manage demand.

causing excessive inflation. The key economic lever of **Keynesianism** was 'demand management'; taxes and interest rates could be manipulated to increase or reduce demand depending on whether the economy was stagnant or overheated. In this way, unemployment and inflation could be kept relatively constant, avoiding the 'boom and bust' which was associated with pre-war capitalism. Confidence in the Keynesian economists was increased by the knowledge that civil service expertise had helped Britain in its fight against the Nazis. This mood was summed up by the Labour MP (and subsequent Cabinet minister Douglas Jay) who wrote in 1947 that 'the gentleman in Whitehall really does know better what is good for people than the people know themselves'.

The 'gentleman in Whitehall' would have been kept busy enough in normal times by Labour's industrial and social policies. But the Attlee government was faced with the additional task of restoring an economy which had been ravaged by the war effort. Wartime rationing was retained (and even extended in 1946 to bread) in order to reduce domestic consumption. The level of imports had to be controlled while British industry devoted the bulk of its energies to recovering export markets which had been lost during the war. In particular, Britain had to finance a yawning trade gap with America. Soon after the end of the war Keynes himself negotiated a loan from the Americans, but the terms of repayment were harsh. The government was desperate to avoid devaluing sterling against the dollar, since this would involve a loss of prestige at home and abroad. In September 1949 speculation against the pound made devaluation unavoidable, and the value of Britain's currency was reduced by almost a third, from $4.03 to $2.80. Already the government had started relaxing its restrictions on domestic consumption, conscious that the public was becoming impatient with enforced material sacrifices. But it was too late. Labour's majority almost disappeared in the 1950 general election, largely because of continued economic 'austerity'.

The global context

Even at the end of the twentieth century, many Britons had not absorbed the real lessons of the two world wars which made the period from 1914 to 1945 the bloodiest in human history. The country had fought throughout the two conflicts, and on both occasions emerged on the winning side. It was hardly surprising that many members of the public found it hard to accept that Britain had actually been one of the chief losers.

Realities were obscured by the fact that Britain was allowed to punch above its new weight. It was made a permanent member of the United Nations Security Council, along with the United States of America (USA), the Union of Soviet Socialist Republics (USSR, also known as the Soviet Union), China and France. It helped to found the North Atlantic Treaty Organisation (NATO) in 1949. In 1952 it successfully tested an atomic bomb, the new badge of 'great power' status; only America and the USSR had preceded it in joining the nuclear club. Optimists like Churchill could argue that Britain was uniquely placed to influence world affairs, since its geographical situation made it a part of Europe, its monarch was head of the far-flung Commonwealth, and ties of language and culture were assumed to give it a 'special relationship' with the United States (see Analysis 2.2).

Analysis: 2.2

The 'special relationship'

Since the Second World War, it has generally been assumed by the British political establishment, the media and the public that the country enjoys a unique place in the affections of the American people, reflected in an unshakable diplomatic and military alliance.

However, there have always been dissenters from this positive view. During the 1970s there were divisions over America's intervention in the Vietnam War, and in the following decade there was fierce resistance to the siting of American-controlled cruise missiles in Britain. Since the terrorist actions of September 2001, and the subsequent 'war on terror', the nature of the 'special relationship' has become more controversial than ever.

There are at least three ways of interpreting the history of UK–US relations:

1. There is indeed a 'special relationship'. Although Britain is not America's equal in economic might, and spends far less on defence, its armed forces are highly skilled and (relatively) well equipped. Above all, the Americans know that the British are their most reliable allies. This was proved during the course of the Cold War, and the legacy continues in a new age of terrorism. The Americans will listen to British advice, because they have an identical interest in ensuring a peaceful, democratic world.

2. There is indeed a 'special relationship', but it is a friendship between thieves. Throughout the Cold War Britain was no more than a willing stooge for the US. Both countries had an interest in the economic exploitation of the Third World and in resisting popular liberation movements. Once the British Empire was wound down America began to exploit Britain itself, using it as a glorified 'aircraft carrier' during the 1980s, when the installation of cruise missiles on British soil actually made an attack from the Soviet Union more likely. However, now that the Cold War is over Britain has once again become a valued partner in crime, seeking economic self-interest in places like Iraq.

3. Britain does have a natural affinity for America, based on culture and language. However, the relationship on both sides has been dictated by necessity rather than sentiment. During the Cold War British dependence on America brought many unfortunate results, but the alternative scenario would have been worse. Now that the Cold War is over, the British can afford to be more selective in their support for their ally, and to take a more sober look at the reality of the relationship over the years. To base one's foreign policy on unthinking support for America in all things is a (potentially disastrous) mistake; the record shows that the Americans certainly have not extended the same compliment to Britain since 1940.

The first attitude is characteristic of the Conservative Party, but has been followed by Tony Blair since 1997; the second is fairly common within 'Old Labour', but is more typical of Marxists who may or may not support Labour. The third would probably be endorsed by a majority of academic observers, and may be growing more popular in Britain since the war on Iraq in 2003.

However, in the post-war period none of these links was a source of unmixed satisfaction to the British. As we have seen, the Americans provided a loan but on hard-headed terms – very much in keeping with its attitude between 1939 and December 1941 when, contrary to the notion of a 'special relationship' between the two countries, it entered the Second World War because of a Japanese attack rather than its love for the British. In 1948 Britain benefited under the more generous Marshall Plan, designed by the Americans to promote economic reconstruction in Europe as a whole. NATO seemed an essential bulwark against the military power of the USSR, which blockaded West Berlin in 1948 having previously inspired a Communist coup in Czechoslovakia. But American friendship continued to come at a price. Britain was expected to maintain a large peace-time army: even three years after the end of war in Europe its strength was still one million, and a system of compulsory peace-time national service was introduced. Britain contributed to the US-inspired Korean War of 1950–53, involving expenditure which forced the Attlee government to impose charges on false teeth and spectacles previously supplied free by the NHS. This move provoked the resignation from the government of Aneurin Bevan (1897–1960), the founder of the NHS.

In this crucial respect, the post-war 'consensus' was shaped not by socialism (see Chapter 15), but by the anti-socialist Americans. The Attlee government was a committed participant in the Cold War against the USSR, but it was very much a junior partner. The message conveyed by America's economic dealings with Britain was echoed in the passage by the US Congress of the MacMahon Act (1946) which prevented any cooperation on nuclear technology with other countries. Britain was not excepted from its terms until 1958, despite the fact that it had shared its knowledge freely with America during the war.

Perhaps the most important reason for American ambivalence about Britain was its Empire. After all, the US was at one time a British colony and celebrates its victorious War of Independence on 4 July every year (although casual observers of the British media would not be able to guess the identity of the country which had fought against the American liberators). If Churchill had remained Prime Minister there could have been a serious divergence on this subject after the war, because he had a strong romantic attachment to the British Empire. But Labour was far more willing to speed up the dismantling of the Empire, particularly in countries where there were unmistakable symptoms of resistance. Thus India and Pakistan were granted independence in 1947, followed by Burma and Ceylon (later Sri Lanka) in 1948. In the same year, British troops left Palestine, which the country had administered under an international mandate since 1922.

The Empire was gradually being transformed into a loose association of self-governing states known as the Commonwealth (see Case study 2.1). But it still left Britain with obligations and perceived interests which made it difficult to contemplate a serious move towards close cooperation with other European states. For the same reason, the US constantly urged Britain to seek its destiny in Europe. But in 1950 the Labour government rejected an invitation from France to join the European Coal and Steel Community, the first step towards the later European Economic Community (EEC) and the European Union (EU). However, Britain did join the intergovernmental Council of Europe and signed its Convention on Human Rights in 1950. The experience of total war had convinced all the main parties that they should get involved in any European initiative that seemed likely to help avoid a future conflict, but only if there was no question of a loss of sovereignty (see Chapter 12). This was a rather ironic attitude, since the force of events had already required Britain to surrender much of its capacity for independent action to the Americans.

The Commonwealth

The (British) Commonwealth today includes 53 states which were formerly incorporated within the British Empire, but now enjoy self-government. Representing around 1.8 billion citizens (almost a third of the global population), in theory it could be a potent force in global politics. Until the 1970s, senior British politicians spoke fondly of the country's historic ties with its former colonies. However, UK membership of the EEC helped to loosen the bond, and positive sentiments were also undermined by public unease at the extent of immigration from certain Commonwealth countries. Margaret Thatcher resented the tendency of Commonwealth leaders to attack UK policy on issues like sanctions against the racist regime in South Africa, and with some justification, since the moral lectures were often delivered by dictators. The Commonwealth has caused less embarrassment to Thatcher's successors, but this is partly because interest among the media and the public has declined. Memories of the Empire are fading and the interests of Commonwealth states are now far too diverse for it to be an effective organisation.

For Britons, the lowering of the union flag was a poignant symbol of the end of Empire (© Setboun Michel/Sygma/Corbis)

Interlude: Conservative government 1951–59

In hindsight, the 1950s looks like a period of relative calm in British politics. The Conservatives won three consecutive general elections (1951, 1955 and 1959) under three different leaders (Churchill 1951–55, Sir Anthony Eden 1955–57, and Harold Macmillan 1957–63). Domestically, there was little policy change of significance. As we have seen, the new government left most of the nationalised utilities in state hands. There was some disquiet among Conservative MPs about the likely cost and

Case study: 2.2

The political implications of 'consensus'

Whatever the precise nature of the post-war political framework, it certainly increased the responsibilities facing British governments:

- *Keynesian demand management*: government is held responsible if inflation or unemployment rise too steeply.
- *Nationalisation*: government is held accountable for poor performance of state-run industries. Ministers have a direct role in pay talks, and can be blamed for strikes.
- *Social services*: spending on welfare has to be maintained at a high (and preferably rising) level.

Once governments had taken on these responsibilities it was very difficult to back away from them, whatever the beliefs of the party in power. There were implications for international politics, too. The Attlee government set the post-war precedent of acting as if Britain retained 'great power' status, even though its capacity for independent action was much reduced. Subsequent governments had to keep up this act, for fear of alienating large sections of the media and electorate.

implications of the welfare state, but the Guillebaud Report (1956) into the NHS indicated that it would be sustainable. General elections were decided on issues of general competence, and on the ability of the parties to deliver the increased and painless prosperity which, for the first time in history, most voters were now learning to expect as a key government responsibility.

The main developments were in Britain's relationship with the outside world. The Suez misadventure of 1956 proved that the UK was now subservient to the US (see Case study 2.3). It destroyed the premiership of Anthony Eden, but not his government. The fact that the Conservative Party was able to recover quickly enough to win the 1959 general election underlines the new predominance of domestic issues in British politics.

The other key development in international affairs was Britain's refusal to join the emerging EEC. It sent only a junior representative to the talks which led up to the signature of the Treaty of Rome (1957) and at first was disinclined to take the new initiative seriously. However, towards the end of the decade the government had second thoughts. It was impressed by rising living standards in the EEC countries, and concluded that future prosperity would be best secured by membership of an alternative trading bloc. In November 1959 it helped to establish the European Free Trade Association (EFTA), with Austria, Denmark, Norway, Portugal, Sweden and Switzerland. For Eurosceptics the brief career of this organisation was a lost opportunity for Britain, because it lacked the political dimension which made them suspicious of the EEC. However, it soon became clear that its members lacked the collective industrial and economic muscle of the rival organisation.

Case study: 2.3

Suez

In July 1956 the Egyptian President, General Nasser, nationalised the Suez Canal Company, in which the British and French governments were major shareholders. This was in retaliation for the refusal of Britain and America to finance the construction of a new dam on the River Nile. The new British Prime Minister Sir Anthony Eden was outraged by Nasser's decision, and a secret plan was hatched to seize the canal. Israel was to attack Egypt, and Britain and France would send troops under the pretence of restoring order. Although the operation began smoothly, with the capture of Port Said by the British in early November 1956, the action was condemned by the United Nations. The US President Eisenhower was incensed – not least because the Soviet Union took advantage of the crisis to suppress a revolt in its client state of Hungary – and the Americans encouraged speculation against sterling on the international exchanges. With their currency on the verge of collapse, the British backed down. Eden resigned early the next year.

Suez divided opinion in the UK itself. Within the Conservative Party some MPs remained convinced that Britain would have secured its objectives had it pressed on. But to have done so would have risked conflict with the Soviet Union, which had replaced the Western powers as Nasser's ally as a result of the row over the dam. The real reason for the unhappiness of the Conservative 'Suez Group' was that the incident had exposed Britain's reduced status in the world. Even after the humiliating climb-down, the reality of Suez was obscured by the revelation that Eden's judgement had been affected by a chronic illness. Eden's successor Harold Macmillan dealt with the situation so skilfully that Suez had little effect on Conservative fortunes in the next general election (1959).

The age of corporatism, 1959–70

In July 1957 Harold Macmillan coined one of the best-known of post-war political phrases, when he told a party rally that 'most of our people have never had it so good'. Two years later his government fought an election with the slogan 'Life's better with the Conservatives. Don't let Labour ruin it'. Macmillan's speech is usually taken as a sign of complacency, but in fact he was warning that prosperity was far from secure. One major problem was that Britain was still not producing enough consumer goods to satisfy domestic demand, so that when governments tried to stimulate economic activity the result was a significant increase in the country's import bill. In turn, this put pressure on sterling; so governments had to act to curb demand as soon as trouble seemed to be brewing. The result was a policy pattern which became known as 'stop–go', with the government pressing the economic accelerator (usually before elections, to make voters feel more prosperous) then slamming on the brakes (normally very soon after the election).

One obstacle to 'sustainable' economic growth was Britain's poor industrial relations. Disruptive strike action made Britain an unreliable trade partner for overseas customers, and also weakened the ability of domestic firms to compete with foreign producers in the home market. The solution was to bring harmony to the workplace by devising corporatist, or more precisely neo-corporatist, institutions which would allow constructive talks between both sides of industry (see Analysis

Corporatism and neo-corporatism

The corporatist approach to economic management rests on the view that the interests of employers and workers can be reconciled if their chief representatives meet regularly to discuss current problems under the benign guidance of the government. It is an *elitist* theory, assuming that the leaders of trade unions and employers' organisations can influence the behaviour of their ordinary members. Its reputation has been tarnished by the fact that it was first practiced in a systematic way by the fascist dictator Mussolini in inter-war Italy (see Chapter 1).

The term neo-corporatism is used to designate a more democratic version of the process. But even this is criticised by pluralists, mainly on the grounds that the arrangement provides inadequate representation for consumer interests.

2.3). The elected government would mediate between unions and employers as an honest broker, just as it hoped to do on the international stage whenever the US and the Soviet Union fell out.

Despite mixed results, this approach lasted until Margaret Thatcher came to power in 1979. One predictable effect was yet another addition to the political implications of 'consensus' (see Case study 2.2). Now almost any strike or wage settlement was seen as a government responsibility. In response, politicians were tempted into further intervention, thinking, for example, of ways to punish firms which gave their workers pay rises which threatened to increase inflation.

Macmillan was also impressed by the apparent success of French governments, which took an active role in economic planning. This process promised to reduce even further the uncertainty of life in a capitalist society. If the government knew about the intentions of individual firms, it could try to manage the economy in order to help fulfil plans for overall economic growth in future. The Labour government of Harold Wilson (1964–70) built on Macmillan's strategy, producing in 1965 a national economic plan. However, this was derailed by further international speculation against the pound. There was a serious sterling crisis in 1966, and the currency was devalued again (from $2.80 to $2.40) in 1967. As before, the attempt to stave off devaluation was based on cuts in government expenditure: a dramatic economic 'stop', when the national plan had been all about 'go'.

In August 1961 the Macmillan government finally applied to join the EEC. Key factors in the policy change included pressure from US President John F. Kennedy, the prosperity of EEC and hopes that Britain might have real influence over the EEC's development from within. But French President Charles de Gaulle vetoed the application in 1963, citing Britain's subservience to the US. In 1967 Wilson made a fresh bid for membership of the EEC but again de Gaulle vetoed it, noting both Britain's continued closeness to the US and her weak economy. There was plenty of evidence to support de Gaulle's claim about Britain being a client state of the US. Britain might have its own nuclear bomb, but this deterrent depended on US missile technology. In the dramatic 1962 crisis caused by the delivery of Soviet nuclear weapons to Cuba, Britain was barely consulted by its ally. The coolness in the 'special relationship' persisted even though Britain was rapidly divesting itself of its Empire. During the 1960s independence was granted to numerous countries, including Uganda (1962), Kenya (1963), and Singapore (1965). Macmillan had spoken of a 'wind of change' blowing through Africa, and the prospect of majority (black) rule in the British colony of Southern Rhodesia provoked a unilateral declaration of independence by its white-dominated government. Britain lacked the power to resolve this situation, either by economic sanctions or by force, until civil war forced the illegal government to back down in 1980 (after which Rhodesia won legal independence as Zimbabwe, with the British acting as mediators).

The end of consensus, 1970–79

The Labour government of 1964–70 was a major disappointment to its original supporters. But after the devaluation of sterling the economic outlook improved, and at least Wilson had managed to keep Britain out of America's war in Vietnam. It was a major surprise when he was defeated by Edward Heath's Conservatives in the 1970 general election. Heath was a sign that a 'wind of change' had blown through his party; he was a grammar-school boy from relatively humble origins, and in 1965 had become the first Conservative leader to be elected by his parliamentary colleagues. He also had no illusions about the 'special relationship' and accepted Britain's reduced role in the world.

Heath's 1970 election programme was based on the argument that Wilson had mismanaged the economy. His own hopes of an economic resurgence arose from his confidence that he could persuade the French to allow Britain to join the EEC. He was helped in this task by the fact that he was known as a genuine enthusiast for European cooperation, but more importantly by de Gaulle's resignation from the French Presidency in 1969. Britain's became a member on 1 January 1973 and the decision was confirmed by the first ever national referendum, held in 1975 (see Chapter 12).

Heath hoped that membership of the EEC would cement Britain's post-war economic strategy. UK firms would be forced to compete for markets on equal terms with efficient European counterparts. Among other things, this would give them a clear incentive to work harmoniously with their employees, as the corporate approach indicated. But the economic message was ignored by both sides of industry. Far from embracing the new challenges and opportunities at home, British capitalists preferred to seek easier profits by investing abroad. Meanwhile, workers continued to demand higher wages unrelated to productivity. Heath's attempt to reform the unions, following a half-hearted effort by Wilson in the late 1960s, further increased the militant mood. Industrial action by the National Union of Mineworkers (NUM) forced him to call a general election in February 1974, and the Conservatives were narrowly beaten.

In opposition, the Labour Party had developed radical policies as a response to what many regarded as Wilson's 'betrayal' of socialism. Wilson himself seemed shaken when his party won in February 1974; he had expected (and probably half-hoped) to lose. The main problem he inherited was price inflation, which had been rising for some time but was given an additional spur by the increased cost of oil (see case study 2.4). Having disappointed his supporters in the 1960s, Wilson knew

Government 'overload'

In the mid-1970s commentators identified a systematic crisis in British government. The various responsibilities we discussed above might have been manageable in good times. But they were interconnected; and trouble in one quarter could easily have a knock-on effect elsewhere. In particular, satisfactory government performance hinged on economic growth, which would promote feelings of prosperity, fund better public services, etc.

To make matters worse, governments had invested so heavily in the successful operation of their strategies that in times of trouble they felt compelled to intervene still further. Thus Wilson and Heath both responded to rising inflation by trying to control prices and incomes by law. In the short-term these measures were reasonably successful, but after a while both sides of industry lost patience with them. In trying to do too much, it seemed to many commentators that the British state was unable to perform any of its functions satisfactorily. Although warnings about 'overload' came from a variety of sources, in the circumstances of the mid-1970s their effect was to lend support to the 'New Right' critique of the post-war consensus as a whole.

in advance that his record could be no better this time round. His situation might have improved slightly if he had secured a comfortable parliamentary position. But when he called a new election, in October 1974, Labour won only 18 more seats. Wilson kept a low profile throughout this second premiership, which ended with his surprise resignation in April 1976. In a clear symptom of underlying malaise in British politics, conspiracy theorists quickly assumed that Wilson's departure could not have been voluntary. Some thought that he was hiding a secret which left him open to blackmail by a foreign power. In fact, he had decided to step down some time earlier.

In September 1976, at the Labour Party conference, Wilson's successor James Callaghan effectively announced the end of the post-war consensus when he argued that the British had been 'living on borrowed time'. Instead of facing up to its underlying problems, the country had run up crippling debts in an attempt to maintain living standards. He continued: 'We used to think that you could spend your way out of a recession and increase employment by cutting taxes and boosting government spending. I tell you in all candour that that option no longer exists'.

Callaghan's speech indicated that the government would no longer be guided by Keynesian ideas. It could no longer make the fight against unemployment its top priority. Now the main target would be inflation. Callaghan hoped that his remarks would impress international financiers, who were speculating against sterling once again. The government had already applied for emergency relief from the International Monetary Fund (IMF), an organisation established in 1944 to foster economic stability. Callaghan and his Chancellor Denis Healey knew that the price of assistance from the IMF would be savage cuts in public expenditure. The government was struggling to survive in parliament, where its slender overall majority was further depleted by by-election defeats. In 1977 it made a pact with the Liberals, which shored up its position for a while. But unemployment was rising, and although Callaghan persuaded union leaders to restrain their pay demands

Case study: 2.4

The fuel crisis, 1973–74

If one international event helped to destroy the post-war British 'consensus', it was the Yom Kippur war which broke out between Israel and Arab forces in October 1973. After their decisive defeat, Arab states punished Western nations for having supplied Israel with its superior weaponry. Their own weapon was an economic asset – oil. Restrictions on supply caused a more than four-fold increase in the cost of oil. All Western nations were badly affected, but although Heath had tried to adopt a neutral stance towards the conflict in the Middle East Britain suffered more than most because its economic position was already weak. British-based oil companies snubbed the Prime Minister when he asked them for special help.

In the short term there were power cuts and limits on the British working week. The crisis strengthened the bargaining position of the miners, triggering Heath's departure from office. But the most lasting legacy was a considerable boost to domestic inflation, which had been rising anyway because of a general increase in other commodity prices on the world market. As the effect of the oil price filtered through the economy, in August 1975 Britain's annual inflation rate reached a record 27 per cent.

they were unable to control their rank-and-file members. In the winter of 1978–79, quickly dubbed 'the winter of discontent', there were numerous strikes, notably in the public services. Britain was beginning to look ungovernable. Callaghan hung on, in the hope that he could call an election in circumstances which would allow Labour to win a workable parliamentary majority. But he ran out of time, losing a vote of confidence in the House of Commons on 28 March 1979.

Thatcherism, 1979–97

In hindsight, Conservatives like to claim that the country was ready for a radical change of direction in the spring of 1979. The old consensus politics had palpably failed, and voters eagerly grasped the Thatcherite alternative. This account is understandable, given the affection that Thatcher still commands within her party. But it is a myth. First, the party concealed its true intentions from the electorate. In 1978 it had attacked the government's record with a poster portraying a lengthy dole queue with the slogan, 'Labour isn't working'. Yet Conservative policies were bound to cause a significant rise in unemployment, at least in the short term (see Table 2.2). Second, the Conservative share of the vote in 1979 showed a distinct lack of public enthusiasm. Heath did better in 1970: Thatcher's level of electoral support never matched the 46.5 per cent he secured in that year.

From one perspective, Thatcherism can be seen as an attempt to solve the problem of government 'overload' (see Analysis 2.4). The strategy involved four core elements:

- *Monetarism*: bearing down on inflation by controlling the money supply, rather than trying directly to control wages and prices (see Analysis 2.5).

Table 2.2 Unemployment, 1947–93

Year	Maximum figure (month)
1947	1 900 000 (February)
1950	404 000 (January)
1960	461 000 (January)
1970	628 000 (January)
1978	1 608 000 (August)
1980	2 244 000 (December)
1982	3 097 000 (December)
1983	3 225 000 (January)
1984	3 284 000 (September)
1985	3 346 000 (September)
1986	3 408 000 (January)
1987	3 297 000 (January)
1988	2 722 000 (January)
1989	2 074 000 (January)
1990	1 850 000 (December)
1991	2 552 000 (December)
1992	2 983 000 (December)
1993	3 062 000 (January)

Note: During the Thatcher years there were numerous changes to the way in which unemployment statistics were compiled, almost invariably resulting in a reduction of the official figure. It is therefore more than likely that the maximum tally (in January 1986) was an under-estimate, and possible that the number of people out of work in January 1993 exceeded the previous record.

Source: D. Butler and G. Butler, *Twentieth Century British Political Facts*, 2000, reproduced with permission of Palgrave Macmillan

Conservative propaganda highlights Labour's economic record, 1978 (Saatchi and Saatchi advertising poster) (© Advertising archives)

Analysis:	2.5

Monetarism

Monetarism is an economic theory based on the notion that the rate of inflation depends on the supply of money. Monetarists argue that if the amount of money in circulation remains broadly stable, prices and incomes have to follow a similar trend unless businesses want to go bankrupt and workers to price themselves out of jobs. Direct attempts to control prices and incomes by law, as practised by successive Labour and Conservative governments, were thus either irrelevant or (more likely) damaging to the economy.

The monetarist theory lay at the centre of Thatcherism, since economic mismanagement was held to be the underlying cause of Britain's post-war woes. Its importance to the Thatcher government is reflected in the tendency of critics to denounce *all* Conservative policy as a product of 'monetarist' thinking. The Thatcher governments certainly brought inflation under control. However, critics claim that monetarism had little or nothing to do with this achievement. In practice monetarism is far more complicated than the basic theory suggests. It proved very difficult to define 'money', let alone to control the quantity in circulation at any given time (or the speed of its circulation). The Thatcher governments regularly set targets for the money supply, but most commentators agree that they were usually missed. Instead, high unemployment sharply reduced the amount of demand in the economy. This could have been predicted under the supposedly discredited Keynesian approach – except that Keynes himself would have deplored the waste of human resources.

- *Privatisation*: selling off state-owned industries rather than subsidising their losses (or indeed trying to run them profitably).
- *Trade union reform*: gradually restricting trade union rights in a series of measures (7 important Acts between 1979 and 1990), while refusing to become involved in the settlement of disputes.
- *Hiving off*: entrusting many functions of central government to semi-autonomous agencies, thus blurring the conventional lines of departmental responsibility.

The overall purpose was to ensure that although government would do much less, when it acted it would be much more effective, thus restoring its authority. The implementation of the strategy required a quality which Thatcher possessed in abundance – determination. Even when the official unemployment figures exceeded three million (in September 1982) she refused to back down. But the other essential ingredient was luck. The possession of North Sea oil cushioned the government from the full effects of the severe economic recession of 1979–81. More importantly, the Conservatives benefited from a feeling of national revival after the Falklands War of April–June 1982. The conflict with Argentina had at least in part been triggered by the government's own policy of naval spending cuts, which encouraged the regime of General Galtieri to think that the islands could be taken without any retaliation from Britain. As it turned out, there could have been no better opportunity for Thatcher to show that her tough rhetoric on foreign affairs was matched by an appetite for action. In her second term she showed equal determination in refusing to settle a year-long miners' strike (1984–85), but here too she was lucky because the NUM President Arthur Scargill had for many years been portrayed as a dangerous extremist in the press and made several disastrous tactical errors during the dispute.

Of course, Thatcherism was about much more than government retreat from the 'overloaded' responsibilities of the 1970s. In fact, this was one reason why Thatcher stirred up such strong antagonism. After 1976 Labour itself talked in monetarist terms, but only to appease the financial markets. While it was obvious that the Callaghan government hated the necessity of focusing on inflation and cutting government expenditure, Thatcher gave the impression of relishing this task. She believed that excessive taxation had been holding back an entrepreneurial spirit among the British people, and was happy to apply much of the revenue from North Sea oil and the privatisation of state-run industries to reduce the burden on the well-to-do. The government's first budget (1979) set the tone, reducing income tax from 33 to 30 per cent and almost doubling Value Added Tax (VAT) which was levied on everyone regardless of income. At the same time, the top rate of income tax on earned income was slashed from 83 to 60 per cent (in 1988 this was cut further, to 40 per cent).

Ultimately it was Thatcher's crusading zeal that precipitated her downfall. The community charge, popularly known as the 'poll tax', was brought in to replace the existing system of local government taxation (based on the rateable value of properties) after her third election win in 1987. Always impatient with any symptoms of opposition, the government had already legislated to 'cap' the rates of high-spending authorities (1984) and in 1985 abolished the Greater London Council (GLC). The poll tax had initially been rejected by ministers as an alternative to the rates. But by 1987 the government tended to assume that any of its policies would eventually be accepted, however strong the initial outcry. With the poll tax, it miscalculated badly. At the end of March 1990, a demonstration in London turned into a riot. In October 1990 the Conservatives lost the Eastbourne seat to the Liberal Democrats, even though the vacancy had arisen because of the IRA's assassination of Thatcher's personal friend Ian Gow and a sympathetic vote for the government might have been expected in normal circumstances. Michael Heseltine, a known opponent of the poll tax who had resigned from the cabinet in January 1986 after disagreeing with the Prime Minister over policy and the conduct of cabinet meetings, challenged for the party leadership in the following month. Heseltine also took a positive view of the UK's engagement with Europe, whereas Thatcher took no trouble to conceal her growing hostility, creating more unease within the party. Thatcher won the first ballot of Conservative MPs, but by an insufficient margin to prevent a second contest. Recognising, very reluctantly, that she would probably lose this further ballot, she resigned.

Although Thatcher's successor John Major was far less confrontational and quickly replaced the poll tax with the council tax (based, in part, on the value of a property), his election was not the signal for a change of direction. Privatisation continued, reaching into areas where even Thatcher would have hesitated (notably the railways). Although the Conservatives won the 1992 general election against expectations, within a few months they had plunged into an economic crisis from which they had not recovered a decade later. 'Black Wednesday' (16 September 1992) actually improved Britain's economic prospects. But the political damage arose not just because it left the government looking helpless. The crisis also brought to a head divisions within the Conservative Party over Europe.

Controversy: 2.1

Thatcherism: for and against

Characteristic arguments of supporters and opponents of the changes of the Thatcher years

For	Against
Monetarism might have proved difficult to implement, but it revolutionised the economic climate in Britain, proving that the government would never take the soft inflationary option.	Monetarism proved unworkable, as expected, and caused years of unnecessary suffering. Even well-run businesses went bankrupt as a result of high interest rates.
Thatcher tamed the trade unions.	It was important to curb the power of trade unions, but Thatcher swung the balance too far in favour of employers.
Thatcher attacked local government because many councils were irresponsible and some were corrupt.	In attacking local government Thatcher showed her contempt for opposition and her preference for centralised power.
Privatisation was a runaway success, producing a 'shareholding democracy' and proving that the state cannot run major enterprises.	Privatisation was a barefaced swindle, in which public assets were sold well below their real market value. Most of the companies have been poorly run since they were sold off. Many small shareholders realised a quick profit, leaving important utilities in the hands of giant institutional investors.
Thatcher stood up for British interests in Europe, and increased the country's standing in the world.	Thatcher proved to Britain's European partners that the country would never be a cooperative partner and damaged Britain's reputation abroad because she was too subservient to the US.

Thatcherism abroad, 1979–97

Prior to her election as Prime Minister, Thatcher had appeared to be a lukewarm pro-European. She had campaigned for a 'yes' vote in the 1975 referendum, although her contribution was small compared to that of her predecessor Edward Heath. But at the Dublin Summit in 1979 she bluntly demanded a rebate from Britain's budgetary contribution. Although a satisfactory compromise was eventually negotiated, it was obvious that under Thatcher Britain would be an 'awkward partner' in Europe (see Chapter 12).

Thatcher agreed to the Single European Act (1986) which pointed towards the introduction of a European single currency and reduced the scope of Britain's right to veto decisions in the Council of Ministers. But her true opinion was revealed in her Bruges speech of September 1988. She attacked the idea of an interfering European 'superstate', referring to her success in reducing the scope of government activity at home. Her opposition to membership of the European Exchange Rate Mechanism (ERM) cost her the services of her Chancellor Nigel Lawson, who thought that the ERM would provide a more reliable guarantee of financial discipline than monetarist theory, which he had tacitly abandoned. Nevertheless,

Lawson's successor John Major persuaded her at a moment of extreme political weakness (October 1990) to commit Britain to the ERM after all. The mechanism fixed the value of the pound in relation to other European currencies, though some commentators warned that sterling was too high at the time of joining.

In the following month Thatcher's continued antagonism towards European integration triggered another resignation, that of her long serving (or suffering) colleague Geoffrey Howe (Chancellor 1979–83, Foreign Secretary 1983–9 Lord President of the Council 1989–90). Howe's resignation speech crystallised opposition to Thatcher within her own party, thus proving that the House of Commons can still have a significant effect on events, and providing the context for Heseltine's leadership challenge.

The fact that after the 1990 leadership election Thatcher was succeeded by Major, who had cajoled her into signing up to the ERM, suggested a more cooperative stance towards the EC. But Major's hope of keeping Britain at 'the very heart of Europe' turned sour after Black Wednesday. Ministers felt that their European partners had not been very active in resisting the speculation against sterling which led to Britain's enforced decision to leave the ERM.

By this time Major had already agreed to further European integration at the Maastricht Summit of December 1991, albeit with opt-outs for Britain on the proposed single currency and social policy. He now had the task of winning parliamentary approval for the Maastricht Treaty, against a background of growing Conservative discontent (fuelled by Thatcher, now in the House of Lords). In July 1993 Conservative Eurosceptics voted tactically with Labour on a motion deploring the Maastricht opt-out on social policy, resulting in a government defeat by 8 votes. Although the government won a vote of confidence on the following day, its slender parliamentary majority (down to 17, on paper, by July 1993) gave the Eurosceptics power well out of proportion to their numbers. In November 1994, seven Tory MPs had the party whip withdrawn as a result of their repeated disobedience. Another Eurosceptic refused to accept the whip in protest. Less than a year later the 'whipless wonders' were asked to return to the fold, so desperate was the government's plight.

Ironically, Major's Conservatives had received in 1992 more votes than any previous British political party. The Thatcherite project of restoring government authority was being undermined by the first-past-the-post electoral system, which had left the government with an inadequate parliamentary majority. Major was urged to improve his position by taking a more Eurosceptic stance, but this would not have been credible given his earlier pronouncements. Instead, in June 1995 he took the unprecedented step of resigning as party leader (though not as Prime Minister), challenging his critics to put up a candidate. Although he survived the ensuing election (against the former Secretary of State for Wales, John Redwood), his authority was only damaged further. In 1996 he became more antagonistic towards Europe, as a result of the ban on imports of British beef in the wake of the BSE outbreak. But by this time his European colleagues were confident that he would lose the next election, which could not be more than a year away. During the 1997 election campaign Major was unable to take a convincing line on Europe, trapped between his powerful pro-European Chancellor Kenneth Clarke and the majority of his parliamentary colleagues who were by this time predominantly 'sceptical'.

Critics on both sides of the argument make much of Major's inability to heal divisions over Europe. But it must be remembered that he had inherited a poisonous situation from Thatcher, in whose downfall Europe had played a crucial part. Unluckily for Major, he lacked Thatcher's compensation of warm relations with the US. Although Britain was an active partner during the first Gulf War (1991), Major could not hope to form with George Bush senior (1989–93) the kind of bond which had quickly developed between his predecessor and Ronald Reagan (1981–89). Thatcher and Reagan agreed on economic policy and the proper role of the state. They also shared a deep hostility to the USSR. In opposition Thatcher had been dubbed the 'iron lady' by the Soviet media for her uncompromising rhetoric, and as Prime Minister she gladly allowed America to install nuclear missiles on British territory. By the time that Major became Prime Minister, the Communist bloc had collapsed and Germany had been reunified (October 1990). The reality of the 'special relationship' was suddenly exposed, when President Bush made no attempt to hide his view that in the new circumstances Germany was as good (or as useful) a friend as Britain.

Even when Thatcher was Prime Minister the limitations on the 'special relationship' were apparent. During the Falklands War the Reagan administration was bitterly divided, with some key officials preferring to maintain good relations with Argentina. Astonishingly, in October 1983 Reagan's troops invaded the Commonwealth island of Grenada without proper consultation – a Suez in reverse, with a very different outcome reflecting America's ability to override any objections from a third party. Even loyal Thatcherites like Norman Tebbit were dismayed in April 1986 when US planes took off from British bases in a futile raid on Libya (other European countries had refused to let the planes fly over their territory). In other circumstances, under a Prime Minister who enjoyed less support from the media, these incidents would have caused grave and lasting embarrassment.

Blair and New Labour

Already damaged by Europe, the Major government finally sank under allegations of ministerial misdeeds (whether financial or sexual). A new election was delayed for as long as possible, but the reckoning finally came on 1 May 1997. Labour supporters, starved of success for so long, hailed a new dawn under a charismatic leader who won an overwhelming parliamentary majority (even if his party's share of the vote was considerably less than it had been in 1950, when it received a majority of only five seats).

After his victory, Blair promised that his party would 'govern as New Labour', sticking to its (limited) campaign pledges. This was actually a signal that the government would adhere to the general approach followed by the Conservatives, even though Blair had promised to give a new priority to 'welfare' issues like health and education.

We have seen that during the 1970s it became clear to most observers that the British state had over-reached itself, taking on responsibilities which it could not fulfil. This situation was transformed during the Thatcher–Major years, mainly because these Conservative governments were successful in disengaging themselves from (most) industrial disputes. Under Blair, the record has been mixed. From the point of view of making life easier for ministers, there have been three steps forward and three back:

1. The most obvious change has been devolution to Scotland, Wales and Northern Ireland. With important governmental functions transferred to the constituent nations of the UK, ministers based in London have fewer factors to take into account (despite the wide variety of conditions within England itself). By contrast, despite the arguments of Eurosceptics and New Labour's adherence to the social chapter of the Maastricht Treaty, membership of the EU has not seriously reduced the remit of the UK government and parliament since 1997 (see Chapter 12).

2. The government gave the Bank of England operational independence. This decision, which was not mentioned in Labour's 1997 manifesto, deprived Chancellors of the Exchequer of a key economic instrument (the control of interest rates) which arguably had provided more headaches than benefits during the Thatcher years. The Bank can now be blamed if inflation gets out of control; but it is also likely to carry the can if Britain suffers an economic recession, or if the value of the pound fluctuates too wildly.

3. Ministers can now rely on far more support from special advisers (or 'spin-doctors'). This gives them an important second line of defence against adverse publicity. Sometimes the advisers can themselves become a problem, but the advantages of a skilful public relations team are obvious (for example, bad news can be disguised in a way which was never contemplated in the 1970s).

However, the role of government has been made more complicated by three developments:

1. State spending on certain public services (notably education and health) has been greatly expanded. Although New Labour has not made a significant change in the institutional framework established by the Conservatives, the level of public expectation has risen, and in spite of their concerted efforts ministers have arguably made themselves more vulnerable to criticisms relating to the performance of the public services than ever before.

2. The Thatcher governments claimed that they reduced the level of interference in the economy, but passed new laws on trade unions, local government and criminal justice with far more regularity than any of their predecessors. Similarly, New Labour has shown a much greater willingness than previous governments to interfere with personal habits and pastimes. Hunting, smoking, the treatment of children and even eating habits are now under parliamentary scrutiny as never before, leading to accusations of a 'nanny state'. The Blair governments' response to the terrorist threat has been highly reminiscent of the Thatcherite authoritarianism, which Labour denounced when it was in opposition.

3. The incorporation into British law of the European Convention on Human Rights (by means of the Human Rights Act 1998 (HRA)) has increased the burdens on British ministers. Even before 1998, governmental decisions were being challenged more frequently in the British courts (see Chapter 8). Now legislation must be checked before passage to ensure that it complies with the terms of the HRA, and if the courts rule that it fails this test there is an expectation that it will have to be revised.

Overall, however, it would be reasonable to conclude that the British state is in no imminent danger of 'overloading' as it was in the 1970s. There is, for example, little prospect that fully-fledged corporatism will be revived, that trade unions, employers and government representatives will be meeting in the near future to discuss the prospects of individual industries.

Conclusion and summary

The role of the prime minister

During the course of our survey, there has been a tendency for the names of individual Prime Ministers to appear with increasing frequency. This is no accident. Although his government introduced many radical measures, Attlee acted as something like a low-profile 'chairman of the board' in Cabinet. Blair, by contrast, dominates the public image of his government (although behind the scenes Gordon Brown has a comparable influence). The impact of the electronic media is important here (see Chapter 4), making the Prime Minister seem more 'presidential'. In this respect, at least, Blair is following Thatcher's example. During the 1980s, for example, Thatcher's official spokesman, Bernard Ingham, often announced that the Prime Minister would be taking a special interest in a subject when the relevant departmental minister seemed to be struggling. This practice has continued under Blair (though in both cases the announcements were rarely followed by any concrete evidence of prime ministerial action).

We saw that the House of Commons can still have a crucial influence over events, in cases like the resignation speech of Geoffrey Howe and the Maastricht debates. However, these episodes are much more the exception than the rule, and Blair is rarely in the Commons except for his weekly visit for Prime Minister's Question Time. The television studio is far more important than Westminster. While the Commons has been declining for many decades, the eclipse of the Cabinet is strictly a post-war phenomenon. Nowadays Prime Ministers tend to transact business directly with their relevant colleagues (and with their unelected special advisers) rather than asking the Cabinet to give a collective opinion.

The role of democracy

An implicit theme of the survey up to the mid-1970s was the tendency of governments to use Keynesian techniques of demand management to manipulate the British economy so that elections coincided with times of maximum prosperity. Naturally this practice would not have appealed to Keynes himself. Even so, no-one can deny that it had serious consequences for the economy, leading in particular to the process of 'stop–go'.

In this respect, at least, the end of the Keynesian consensus could have been a welcome development. But ingrained habits die very hard, and politicians have continued to try to generate a 'feel-good factor' at election time. Difficult decisions can still be put off, and populist measures brought forward, depending on the electoral timetable. The Blair government is no different from its immediate predecessors in this respect. Whoever was originally to blame for this development – and whether or not it is an inevitable feature of liberal democracy – it has certainly contributed to a deepening cynicism among politicians and voters alike.

The international scene

Throughout this chapter we have encountered strong evidence to suggest that the so-called 'special relationship' with America is a product of wishful thinking. It would be far more accurate to say that since 1945 the relationship has been generally warm, with occasional 'hot-spots' like the period 1981–89 when the political leaders of Britain and America admired each other personally and agreed on ideological questions.

But over time an illusion can take on some of the trappings of reality. In particular, the expectation that Britain should be the most trusted partner of the United States has become ingrained among most media commentators and voters. Blair took this facet of post-war policy further than any of his predecessors. For most of her premiership Thatcher dealt with Presidents who represented the Republican Party, which has traditionally been linked with the Tories. Furthermore, cooperation with America could always be justified by the Cold War alliance against the USSR. Neither of these factors can explain Blair's relationship with George W. Bush. An alliance against terror after the events of 11 September 2001 was fully in line with post-war British policy, but it was always questionable that this cause would be helped by a war on Iraq. Bush supported many policies which were anathema to New Labour, on subjects such as welfare, capital punishment and abortion. But this did not prevent Blair from treating him with even more respect than he gave to Bush's predecessor, the Democrat Bill Clinton. Indeed, Blair's anxiety to befriend Bush seemed to reflect his desire at all times to take the course which was most likely to annoy traditional Labour supporters at home.

Iraq exposed the old divisions between Britain and its major European partners, reminding observers of the reasons why de Gaulle vetoed British membership of the EEC back in the 1960s. Nevertheless, Blair sought to echo John Major's desire to be 'at the very heart of Europe'. He persisted with this rhetoric even though he recognised his inability to take Britain into the single currency, despite his personal popularity and a crushing majority in the Commons.

Perhaps the best way of understanding Blair's attitude to foreign policy is to see it as an attempt to cling to one aspect of the post-war consensus (excepting the brief interlude under the Europhile Heath) at a time when it was increasingly difficult to do so. Thus Blair tried to say both 'yes' and 'no' to Europe when a definitive answer was pressing; and he risked his premiership by saying an unequivocal 'yes' to America when it might have been safer for him to give a qualified response. For a Prime Minister who is engrossed with the idea of leaving a constructive legacy at home and abroad, foreign policy has proved to be a very unfortunate distraction. However, institutional developments suggest that British Prime Ministers will continue to dabble in this field, rather than taking a sustained interest in domestic affairs where decisive interventions are far more difficult. Foreign affairs give Prime Ministers the chance to imagine that they are truly 'speaking for Britain'. In the domestic sphere, by contrast, the change from 'government' to 'governance' is all too apparent.

Further reading

For an excellent survey from the end of the Second World War to the fall of Thatcher, see A. Sked and C. Cook, *Post-War Britain: A Political History* (London: Penguin, 4th edition, 1993). A concise overview is provided by D. Kavanagh and P. Morris, *Consensus Politics: From Attlee to Major* (Oxford: Blackwell, 2nd edn, 1994). For contrasting viewpoints on Britain's economic performance, see A. Gamble, *Britain in Decline: Economic Policy, Political Strategy and the British State* (London: Macmillan, 4th edition, 1994), W. Hutton, *The State We're In* (London: Vintage, 1996) and G. Bernstein, *The Myth of Decline: The Rise of Britain since 1945* (London: Pimlico, 2004). On the debate about the post-war 'consensus', see D. Kavanagh and P. Morris, *Consensus Politics: from Attlee to Major* (Oxford: Blackwell, 1994) and H. Jones and M. Kandiah (eds), *The Myth of Consensus. New Views on British History, 1945–64* (London: Macmillan, 1996). Useful statistical information can be found in D. Butler and G. Butler, *Twentieth Century British Political Facts 1900–2000* (Palgrave, 2000), and the same authors' *British Political Facts since 1979* (Palgrave, 2005).

While there are many good books covering post-war developments as a whole, some studies of specific periods are well worth reading. P. Hennessy, *Never Again* (London: Jonathan Cape, 1992) gives a detailed and highly-readable account of the Attlee governments. For an important article on the crucial years of the post-war period see A. King, 'Overload: Problems of Governing in the 1970s', *Political Studies*, Vol. 33 (1975), pp. 284–96. On the Thatcher years, see I. Gilmour, *Dancing with Dogma: Britain under Thatcherism* (London: Simon & Schuster, 1992) for a highly critical account; on the other side of the debate is S.R. Letwin, *The Anatomy of Thatcherism* (London: Fontana, 1992). On Blair's first government see A. Seldon (ed.), *The Blair Effect* (London: Little, Brown, 2001) and on the second, A. Seldon and D. Kavanagh (eds), *The Blair Effect, 2001–5* (Cambridge: Cambridge University Press, 2005).

On the history of Britain's relations with the wider world, see A. Gamble, *Beyond Europe and America: The Future of British Politics* (London: Palgrave, 2003); S. George, *An Awkward Partner: Britain in the European Community* (Oxford: Oxford University Press, 3rd edition, 1998); D. Reynolds, *Britannia Overruled* (Harlow: Longman, 1991) and D. Sanders, *Losing an Empire, Finding a Role* (London: Macmillan, 1990).

Changes in the role of the British Prime Minister since 1945 are traced in P. Hennessy, *The Prime Minister. The Office and its Holders since 1945* (London: Penguin, 2001) and M. Foley, *The Rise of the British Presidency* (Manchester: Manchester University Press, 1993). See also Simon James, *British Cabinet Government* (London: Routledge, 2nd edition, 1998).

Websites

The National Archives and Public Record Office at Kew maintain documents from central government departments. A small selection of their material is available online at www.hmc.gov.uk/nra and www.pro.gov.uk. A useful 'gateway' providing links to primary documents on British history is http://library.byu.edu/~rdh/eurodocs/uk.html. The Thatcher Foundation www.margaretthatcher.org/ has an extensive collection of material available online.

Chapter 3

Economy and society

Learning outcomes

After reading this chapter, you will:

- Understand some of the key social and economic features of contemporary Britain.
- Be able to assess the main causes of division and cohesion in British society.
- Appreciate the relevance of social and economic factors to an understanding of British politics.

Introduction

No political system can be understood in any depth without at least a basic awareness of the social and economic context in the relevant territory. This is particularly true in liberal democracies, whose politicians are expected at least to take note of public demands, and whose institutions can lose credibility unless they are adapted to accommodate social and economic change. In turn, governments affect social and economic life, for example, by making some practices illegal, by subsidising industries or changing the tax and benefit systems.

British society has been transformed since the Second World War ended in 1945, and although some trends are now reasonably stable, predictions about the future are extremely hazardous. In an increasingly complex and ever-changing social context, it is vital for governments to base their decisions on reliable statistics. Business ventures, academics and news organisations also conduct research into social and economic trends. With so much publicly available information to choose from, in this chapter we will focus on the data with the greatest political relevance.

Britain: a divided nation?

It would be a mistake to exaggerate the extent to which Britain is divided. Most developed nations are subject to similar internal tensions, and some are much less successful in containing potential friction. However, the most important socio-economic features of contemporary Britain can most usefully be introduced by exploring these divisions.

National and regional divisions

The United Kingdom consists of four territories: England, Scotland, Wales (collectively known as Great Britain) and Northern Ireland. England has the largest population by far (see Table 3.1); its greater size, economic strength and military muscle have always been reflected in its relations with its UK partners. Wales was the first of the smaller countries to come under English rule, having been conquered in the Middle Ages. After centuries of sporadic conflict Scotland united with England under the terms of the 1707 Act of Union, although it retained many of its distinctive institutions in, for example, the legal and religious spheres. Ireland followed suit in 1801. In 1922, after a bloody civil war, the island of Ireland was partitioned with six northern counties staying within the United Kingdom of Great Britain and Northern Ireland.

Political tensions between the component parts of the UK are discussed in the context of devolution in Chapter 11. It is important to stress that although commentators usually focus on differences between the four nations, they have significant internal contrasts of their own in terms of culture, religion and economic prosperity. For example, Scotland contains both the rural Highlands and the central belt dominated by the large cities of Glasgow and Edinburgh. The Welsh language is in common use in the north west of that country, but the eastern area adjacent to the English border is heavily Anglicised. Northern Ireland is itself a product of religious and cultural conflict, which has continued with varying degrees of intensity since 1922.

The demand for devolution to Scotland and Wales led to referendums in both countries in 1979. In Wales the proposition was defeated, while in Scotland the

Table 3.1 Population of UK, 2001

United Kingdom (total)	59 533 700	100%
England	49 855 700	83.7%
Scotland	5 057 400	8.5%
Wales	2 938 000	4.9%
Northern Ireland	1 702 600	2.9%

Source: 2001 census, Office for National Statistics, www.ons.gov.uk

majority in favour was insufficient to meet the requirements of the relevant legislation. However, during the 1980s nationalist feeling remained strong and it was widely felt that the Conservative governments at Westminster gave priority to England's economic interests. While many parts of Wales and Scotland suffered economic decline in those years, some regions in England itself were hit just as badly. The north east, in particular, saw the decimation of its coal industry after the bitter strike of 1984–85. In the UK as a whole, two million manufacturing jobs disappeared between 1979 and 1987 (see Case study 3.1).

Regional inequalities within England are summed up by the often-used expression 'the north–south divide'. Yet this is an inexact, short-hand phrase for a complex phenomenon. Economic decline left parts of the north almost unaffected, while some areas in the south were far from prosperous. London included affluent boroughs like Kensington and Chelsea, as well as areas of serious deprivation like Lambeth and Tower Hamlets. It was no accident that in 1981, when England was affected by a spate of inner-city rioting, some of the worst incidents occurred in the south, in places like Brixton in south London and the St Paul's district of Bristol. During the economic recession at the end of the 1980s many of those southern areas which had escaped the previous downturn were badly affected, and many new homeowners found that their properties were worth less than the value of the mortgage (a phenomenon known as 'negative equity'). The remaining property 'hot-spots' presented politicians with the pitfalls of prosperity, because public servants like teachers and nurses found it increasingly difficult to buy houses there.

These examples underline the danger of drawing general conclusions even about individual cities in the UK, let alone the much larger and more diverse countries or regions. The localised contrasts have remained and even deepened despite the fact that economic fortunes tend to reinforce themselves: a booming area can be expected to attract new businesses hoping for a share in the prosperity, while firms which depend on thriving markets will be tempted to change their location if other big employers move away. In part, these trends have been softened by deliberate government action. Even during the free-market Thatcher years, generous subsidies were offered in order to attract new businesses into the depressed areas. Evidence of geographical inequality was regarded as politically tolerable, but only to a certain level.

The country versus the cities

Until fairly recently it has been easy to overlook another tension which cuts across regions of the UK. But in the early stages of the Industrial Revolution the rural/urban split was a key domestic political issue. The parliamentary allies of the agricultural interest fought to keep out cheap imports of wheat in order to maintain relatively high prices for their own produce, while industrialists campaigned for the removal of import controls, arguing that cheaper bread would improve the living standards of their workers without the need to increase wages. In short, urban manufacturers tended to favour free trade in food, while rural agriculturalists were 'protectionists'. The manufacturers won this battle, and agricultural workers continued to flock into the towns which offered more lucrative (if not more healthy) work opportunities.

Case study: 3.1

The decline of manufacturing industry

In the eighteenth century, Britain was the first country to experience an industrial revolution. Its initial competitive advantage was based on the exploitation of key raw materials, notably coal, but this was reinforced by British inventions, like the steam engine. In the second half of the nineteenth century Britain's economic pre-eminence was eroded by competition from overseas, as new sources of raw materials were opened up by improvements in transport, and other countries adopted industrial techniques. But the number of workers employed in manufacturing industry continued to increase; between 1921 and 1951 it rose by 1.5 million, to 8.3 million (38 per cent of workers). Traditional industries like coal mining and iron and steel-making were now supplemented by the domestic manufacture of consumer goods like household appliances and motor cars. A strong manufacturing base was held to be important, not least because Britain's industrial strength had helped it to survive two global conflicts. Also, it was felt that the country's prosperity depended on its ability to sell its goods in world markets.

However, since the mid-1960s Britain's manufacturing industry has declined sharply. In part, this was caused by improved wages and living standards, which meant that Britain found it more difficult to compete with overseas producers in an increasingly 'globalised' economy. Successive governments tried to prop up manufacturing industry through subsidies; even the Conservative governments of 1979–97 resorted to this method to some extent, although Thatcherites objected to the practice on principle. A more relaxed attitude to manufacturing evolved not least because it was most unlikely that the nation would ever face 'total war' on the previous models of 1914–18 and 1939–45; if the UK ever became embroiled in a global conflict, it was likely to be decided by a rapid exchange of nuclear weapons rather than a concerted and prolonged productive effort from industry.

By 2000 manufacturing accounted for less than 15 per cent of employment. Some industries saw a truly spectacular decline; textiles, which had employed over a million people in the 1970s, fell to below 200,000. Meanwhile, the services sector had rapidly increased; around three-quarters of the working population was employed in concerns like banking, retail and tourism. This change in occupational patterns had profound political consequences, not least because the service industries did not lend themselves so easily to trade union activity as did the old techniques of mass production. Another consequence was that the UK's import bill no longer matched the value of its exports. This chronic trade deficit was partly offset by the 'invisible' earnings of the financial sector, so that companies based in the City of London, which had always been powerful, now commanded the automatic respect of any political party with any hope of holding office. For many years before the 1997 general election, Labour had made a priority of proving that it could run the economy without injuring the interests of the City. It had come to share the Conservative view that the global market should decide whether or not the country continued to manufacture goods on a significant scale.

By the end of the twentieth century only about two per cent of Britain's workforce was engaged in agriculture, forestry or fishing. But until recently, farming has enjoyed an influence out of proportion to numbers, through the close relationship between the Ministry of Agriculture and the National Farmers' Union (NFU), who were part of a tight 'policy community' (see Chapter 18). The system of subsidies channelled through the European Common Agricultural Policy (CAP) was inappropriate for British conditions, since it was devised for the benefit of relatively inefficient farmers in other EU member states. Among its results, it offered payments to British farmers in return for removing a proportion of their land from productive use. This arrangement aroused some of the old public resentment towards the (much reduced) agricultural interest, especially when British industrialists were being told that they must compete in a global free market or face bankruptcy. The antagonism increased on both sides in the wake of outbreaks of the animal diseases BSE and foot and mouth, when farmers were accused of risking human health by cutting corners in their procedures. For their part, farmers resented the heavy-handed political response to their problems. Meanwhile the system of subsidies allowed vast supermarket chains to dictate low prices for agricultural produce, making farming an increasingly unattractive career option even for those who had been raised on the land.

After 1997 moves to ban hunting with dogs was seen by many rural dwellers as an attempt to interfere with their leisure activities after so much meddling with their economic interests. The issue led to the formation of the Countryside Alliance (1998), whose relationship with government is a far cry from the days of cosy post-war cooperation (see Chapter 18). Feelings were also aroused by the high tax on fuel, which hit isolated rural dwellers particularly hard, by the poor state of rural transport, and the disappearance of many village amenities like post offices. Yet despite the strong support for the Alliance, it soon became clear that the countryside was divided against itself on the subject of hunting. In part, this was because of a large influx of people who had prospered in the cities and migrated to the country in the hope of enjoying a more relaxed lifestyle without adopting any of the traditional rural pastimes.

Ethnicity

Until the post-war period Britain suffered relatively few ethnic tensions. Ill-feeling against Jews who had fled from persecution in Eastern Europe led to the passage of restrictive Aliens Acts in 1905 and 1919. But in the 1930s the British fascist leader Oswald Mosley (1896–1980) was unable to attract significant support for anti-Semitic policies, outside specific areas like the East End of London.

The generally relaxed British attitude towards immigrants owed something to the fact that its 'native' population was actually the product of the mingling

Table 3.2 The rising UK population, 1951–2001 (thousands)

Date	Total
1951	50 225
1961	52 709
1971	55 515
1981	56 352
1991	57 649
2001	58 789

Source: Office for National Statistics, www.ons.gov.uk

of peoples from all over Europe, throughout the centuries. However, anti-Irish sentiment was strong in some areas, and the arrival of (more conspicuous) black and Asian immigrants in the second half of the twentieth century created new social tensions. The problem was self-reinforcing, because it was natural for newcomers to congregate in specific areas (as the British did themselves when they settled abroad), and this option became more attractive when immigrants encountered the hostility of many white people. Faced with discrimination at work, and relatively limited educational opportunities, most immigrants were restricted in their choice of housing. Taken together, these factors meant that immigrants tended to live in the most deprived areas. The arrival of an immigrant family in a particular street was often taken by its existing white residents as a sign that the area was 'declining'. In turn this fuelled additional hostility towards the immigrants.

It is often implied in the popular press that UK politicians have been inactive in the face of mass immigration. In fact restrictions have been imposed by legislation of 1962, 1968, 1971 and 1981. The automatic right to settle in Britain is now virtually restricted to people with at least one British grandparent. However, since the 1990s public attention has switched to the asylum system, which allows the right of residence to people who have a well-founded fear of persecution in their home countries. Politicians of both main parties have freely spoken of 'bogus' asylum seekers, who are really economic migrants in search of better living standards. Despite legislation of 1965, 1968 and 1976 aimed at improving race relations, 'playing the race card' continued to be regarded as a respectable electoral tactic in some quarters. In 1978, for example, Margaret Thatcher undoubtedly won support by expressing sympathy with those who thought they were being 'swamped' by immigrants.

The official statistics do not support such provocative rhetoric. At the time of the 2001 census 87.5 per cent of respondents described themselves as 'White British' (see Case study 3.2). Only 3.6 million out of 58.8 million UK residents had been born outside the European Union (EU). Recent opinion polls show that the overwhelming majority of immigrants and their children feel British. Some ethnic groups could even be accused of being more British than the British, like the middle-class Indians lampooned in the BBC comedy show *Goodness Gracious Me*. Many immigrants from India and their children have excelled in education, and are joining professions like medicine and the law in ever-rising numbers. By contrast Afro-Caribbean people, and people of Pakistani and Bangladeshi origin, have generally not fared so well. Jamaican 'Yardie' gangs have been associated with the rise in drug-related gun crime, not just in London but in provincial cities like Nottingham.

In recent years ethnic tensions (mainly in northern towns with high unemployment, like Blackburn and Burnley) have been exploited by the British National Party (BNP), which campaigns for an end to all immigration. The 1999 Macpherson Report (see Chapter 8) lifted the lid on 'institutional racism' within the Metropolitan Police Force. Prejudice was often unconscious, but this merely underlined its prevalence within society as a whole. In cities like Leicester (with an Indian population of over one quarter) race relations were generally amicable. But the problem was not confined to poor urban areas with significant ethnic minorities. Negative attitudes were also prevalent in prosperous places which were almost exclusively white.

There is evidence to suggest that attitudes towards ethnicity have changed since the Macpherson Report. For example, in March 2001 the Conservative leader

| Case study: | 3.2 |

Ethnicity in Britain

- In the 2001 census, 87.5 per cent of people living in England and Wales described themselves as 'White British'. The figure in Wales was 96 per cent.
- The proportion of people in England and Wales who described themselves as 'White Irish' was 1.2 per cent.
- The proportion of people describing themselves as 'Indian' was 2 per cent. In Leicester, the figure was 25.7 per cent.
- The proportion of people in England and Wales who described themselves as 'Black Caribbean' was 1.1 per cent. 0.9 per cent were 'Black Africans', and 0.2 per cent described themselves as 'Other Black'.
- 0.4 per cent of the population of England and Wales was of Chinese origin.
- In the regions of Yorkshire and Humberside, and the West Midlands, the proportion of people of Pakistani origin was 2.9 per cent.
- 'Other Whites' (i.e. those who were neither British nor Irish) made up more than 25 per cent of the population in Kensington and Chelsea.
- In the London borough of Tower Hamlets, more than a third of residents were of Bangladeshi origin.
- Several London boroughs (such as Lewisham and Lambeth) had more than 10 per cent of 'Black Caribbean' residents. A similar number (including Southwark and Newham) had more than 10 per cent of 'Black African' residents.

Source: 2001 census, Office for National Statistics, www.ons.gov.uk

William Hague claimed that Britain was in danger of becoming a 'foreign land'. He argued that he was referring to the growing influence of the EU, and certainly his remarks were less provocative than Thatcher's talk of being 'swamped' before the 1979 general election. Even so, Hague was widely criticised and subsequently modified his language. After the killing of a black teenager, Anthony Walker, in July 2005, there was a national outcry which suggested a new level of public sensitivity towards racially-motivated crime.

At the same time, a constructive debate had begun about the concept of multi-culturalism. At one time, this notion was taken to mean that immigrants should be encouraged to retain in full their former identities, regardless of their origin. This was contrasted to the ideal of 'integration', in which the immigrants would be required to conform to a British identity. The former Conservative cabinet minister Norman Tebbit talked of a 'cricket test', implying that the suitability of newcomers should be judged by their sporting loyalties. However, this argument merely raised serious questions about the nature of Britishness and exposed the extent to which English people had previously confused the concept with their own specific sense of nationhood: it could hardly be taken for granted, for example, that Scottish-born citizens would be enthusiastic supporters of the English cricket team. The most positive conclusion from the debate envisaged Britishness as an elastic concept, which could embrace people of varying cultures so long as they accepted the basic values of liberal democracy.

Gender

Traditionally, the major source of conflict in the area of gender has been discrimination against women. In this sphere there has been a spectacular change since the Victorian age, when women could not vote, lost their property on marriage and could be subjected to unpunished violence by their husbands. Yet despite dramatic improvements in all of these spheres, gender remains a serious source of social division in the UK. A particular grievance is the fact that women earn on average around 60 per cent of their male counterparts, despite legislation on equal pay (1970) and to outlaw sexual discrimination (1975).

If Britain were a genuine meritocracy, women would outnumber men in all powerful positions. Because of differential life-expectancy between the sexes there are more women than men (30 million compared to 28.5 million), and they consistently perform better in school examinations. But despite spectacular exceptions, like the career of Margaret Thatcher, most women are still prevented from putting their talents to full use. The usual rationale for this attitude is that most women will at some point face a choice between a full-time career and raising children. It is still not uncommon for employers to dismiss women who become pregnant, although they are likely to be punished for this practice by employment tribunals.

The enhancement of women's rights over the past century has certainly not resolved tensions. Rather, they have become more apparent as women have broken through the old restrictions which confined them to the 'private' world of the home while men monopolised public life. Women now find it much easier to escape from the expected role of subservient housewife, and they exercise their right to do so in

---

Case study: 3.3

How Britain has changed

- In 1981 men in paid employment outnumbered women by more than three million. By 2003 this gap had almost closed (12.8 to 12.7 million), though almost half of women were in part-time occupations.
- In 1970 the proportion of live births to unmarried women was less than 10 per cent. By 1993 this had risen to 32.2 per cent, and in 2003 it was 41.4 per cent.
- In 1911, the proportion of manual workers in Britain was around three-quarters. This had fallen to less than a half by 1981, and ten years later it barely exceeded a third.
- In 1971, just under half of households were owner-occupiers. By 2002, the proportion had risen to 69 per cent. In 1971, around a third of households lived in council accommodation. By 2002, the figure had declined to 14 per cent. This massive shift from rented accommodation to owner-occupation arose from the 'Right to Buy' policy imposed on councils by the first Thatcher government.

increasing numbers. The 2001 census found 5 million divorced or separated people, compared to 24 million who were married (or re-married); a significant majority of divorce petitions are filed by women. However, compared to 9 million households occupied by a married couple, in 2001 there were 1.6 million houses in which a lone parent was bringing up at least one dependent child. Lone parent households suffer from obvious economic disadvantages, and present an acute problem for policy-makers who recognise that childhood poverty and emotional disturbances can have a serious detrimental effect on future life chances. The Child Support Act 1991 was an attempt to ensure that both parents contributed to the maintenance of their children. But the difficulty of applying the rules with sensitivity to a wide variety of cases has caused additional friction between many divorced and separated couples.

A much-publicised question for Britons today is how to achieve a suitable 'work/life balance' (in itself a telling phrase, implying that work is not a part of 'real' life). Although this is a serious difficulty for members of both sexes, it is particularly pressing for women, many of whom have decided to abandon the idea of child-rearing in favour of nurturing their careers. In some high-profile cases, talented women have taken the opposite course. Such dilemmas are a by-product of successful campaigns which have given women the freedom to choose on issues like abortion. Many of these advances were won by the (liberal) feminist movement of the 1960s and 1970s. Ironically, one of the chief victims of these successful battles has been the feminist movement itself, which has lost its coherence as the most obvious abuses have been removed. But this is not to say that the battle for real equality has been won.

While most discussions of gender focus on the need for policies which will improve the life-chances of women (e.g. better childcare facilities allowing them to work full-time), there are also clear signs that many men are experiencing difficulties in the wake of the 'sexual revolution'. Recent spectacular stunts by the Fathers 4 Justice pressure group are a reminder to policy-makers that measures which help one constituency can damage the perceived interests of another (see Chapter 18).

David Beckham – a modern English icon (© AP/EMPICS)

Religion

The terrorist attacks of 11 September 2001 in New York and Washington, perpetrated in the name of Islam, brought the issue of religion back to the agenda of British politics. Like the rural/urban clash, this is an unwelcome echo of the past. Conflict between Protestants and Catholics was endemic between the sixteenth century Reformation and the removal of (most) anti-Catholic discrimination in 1829. Another intolerant law, which prevented Jews from sitting in the House of Commons, was repealed in 1858.

The more liberal climate of the Victorian period was a sign of genuine tolerance, because many policy-makers cared deeply about religion yet still agreed to extend civil rights to people whose beliefs they disliked. By contrast, the relaxed attitude of the twentieth century was fostered by general indifference towards religious faith. In 2001 more than 42 million people still described themselves as Christian, but for many people this was no more than a notional allegiance (see Table 3.3). Religious tensions persisted in towns like Liverpool and Glasgow, partly as an overspill from the conflict between Protestants and Catholics in Northern Ireland. But the civil unrest which erupted there in the late 1960s was a spectacular exception which proved the general rule. By that time few Britons on the mainland appreciated that religious discrimination could still create genuine outrage anywhere in the UK, and hostility towards Republican terrorism in Britain was all the greater because its roots were so little understood.

Popular misconceptions threatened to increase the inevitable tensions after the events of 11 September 2001. Islam is the fastest-growing faith in Britain; although the official census did not ask about religion before 2001, some estimates suggest that the number of British Muslims trebled over the last decade of the twentieth century. As Table 3.3 indicates, Muslims still represent a small proportion of the population (around three per cent). But in the wake of '9/11' there was always a danger of a backlash from people who equated Islam with violence (although very few people drew the same conclusion about Christianity when Catholics and Protestants were inflicting outrageous violence on each other in Northern Ireland). The issue inevitably became entangled with controversies over race relations and asylum. Several radical Islamic clerics have been given refuge in the UK because their views put their lives in danger at home, and press campaigns against several figures living in Britain have exploited racial tensions.

The terrorist attack on the London transport system in July 2005 brought these issues into sharp focus because three of the four suicide bombers had been born

Table 3.3 Religious affiliation in the UK, 2001

Christian	42 079 417
Muslim	1 591 126
Hindu	558 810
Sikh	336 149
Jewish	226 740
Buddhist	151 816
Other	178 837
No religion/not stated	13 626 299

Source: 2001 census, Office for National Statistics, www.ons.gov.uk

in Britain. There was further unrest in February 2006, during worldwide Muslim protests against the publication of some controversial cartoons by a Danish newspaper. Members of a small demonstration in London carried banners which condoned terrorist murders. The controversy revived memories of protests against Salman Rushdie's novel *The Satanic Verses* after its publication in 1988. In Britain, Rushdie's book was publicly burned; there were several deaths among protestors in other countries.

Unfortunately religious tensions can be accentuated by economic factors. The 2001 census found an unemployment rate of 14 per cent among Muslims (compared to 4 per cent for Christians). For the 16 to 24 age group, the rate was 22 per cent (11 per cent for Christians). The proportion of Muslims who described themselves as being in poor health was also double the rate for Christians. These factors, along with the Iraq War, help explain a sense of growing disenchantment among the ethnic minorities with both the Conservative and Labour parties.

Age

A major headache for British policy-makers today is the increasing proportion of elderly people in the population. For some years there have been predictions of a 'pensions crisis', as advances in medical science and a declining birth-rate have changed the balance of numbers between people in work and those over the retirement age. In 1971 the proportion of over-65s was 13 per cent; by 2003 this had risen to 16 per cent. More than 1.2 million people are now over 80. It is in this context that some commentators have urged a more relaxed attitude to immigration, since economic migrants are likely to be relatively young and vigorous. In 2006 the government accepted that the official retirement age (currently 65) would have to be revised over the next few decades.

In addition to this pressing economic problem there are also cultural tensions between members of different generations. As people live longer, they are more likely to be baffled and alienated by the leisure activities and attitudes of young people. Accelerating technological change has increased the cultural contrasts in recent decades, with relatively new innovations like the home computer and the mobile telephone creating suspicion and even fear among the elderly. Those who were born before the Second World War have also experienced an alarming change between the relative social solidarity of the 1940s and 1950s and the aggressive individualism of the years since 1980.

In the US retired people are regarded as a powerful political lobby. As yet, 'grey power' has not been exercised on a sustained basis in Britain. But the pensions issue is changing this situation, particularly because older people are most likely to vote. This fact has proved more potent than the frequent attempts to organise pensioners into a cohesive pressure group (see Chapter 18). Before the 2005 general election, the main parties engaged in something like an auction to attract the elderly. People aged over 55 constituted 35 per cent of the electorate in 2005 but, because they are more likely to vote than young people, 42 per cent of voters (see Chapter 17). In a work environment which increasingly values youth, 'ageism' (discrimination against older workers) is likely to induce forceful government intervention, as sexism and racism have done in the recent past. Pressure from older people who feel most vulnerable will also help to keep law and order issues high on the political agenda for the foreseeable future.

Economic divisions

For some commentators, the above discussion pays inadequate attention to the true cause of all the friction in British society. Influenced by the work of Karl Marx, they believe that the fundamental cause of all social division is economic. In their view, Britain is marked by significant economic inequalities; and until these are removed certain groups will continue to suffer discrimination and feel aggrieved. On this view, for example, hostility towards immigrants is really an expression of economic insecurity. A mass influx of foreigners, anxious to escape terrible poverty at home and willing to take on any available work, is alleged to present a threat to the livelihood of members of the existing population. Thus, by an unpleasant irony, foreigners who take low-paid jobs will be hated the most by their poor competitors, deflecting attention from the fact that all of them are being exploited by their common enemy – the employers. The same view of society would interpret the 'liberation' of women as a free gift to the capitalist system, since many female workers are part-timers who offer themselves as cheap labour even if they think that their wages provide a useful supplement to the family income.

Like feminism, the Marxist analysis of society is deeply unfashionable nowadays. This is not just because the (supposedly) Marxist regimes of Eastern Europe collapsed at the end of the 1980s. More important, it seemed that the key Marxist concept of class no longer provided a convincing explanation of social change in Britain, or indeed in other Western countries. Marx had predicted that the majority of workers would be increasingly exploited as **capitalism** moved from one crisis to the next. Instead, despite periodic economic recessions most people in work have enjoyed ever-improving living standards. Thanks to the introduction of cheap domestic appliances, most Britons today would find the daily life even of a well-paid worker in the Victorian era unimaginably tough. For example, as late as 1972 central heating had been installed in just over a third of British homes. Thirty years later, the proportion had soared to 93 per cent. There was a similar increase over that period in ownership of telephones (42 per cent in 1972, 98 per cent in 2002 – leaving aside mobile telephones, used in 75 per cent of households in 2002).

As we discuss in Chapter 17, social class still provides part of the explanation for voting behaviour and political commitment in general. But the situation has become much more complicated than it was in the earlier post-war period. Marxists, though, argue that in advanced capitalist societies there are only two classes – those who own and control the 'means of production' (the bourgeoisie), and those who have to sell their labour in order to survive (the proletariat). In Britain the official classification of occupational groups is linked to status within the overall workforce (see Table 3.4). This reflects the country's self image as a **meritocracy**. In general, the higher the social ranking, the greater the formal educational qualifications. It is now widely assumed, for example, that a university education is essential to anyone hoping to build a successful career in the managerial and higher professional occupations. But the list does not necessarily tally with public respect for the various activities; highly-educated

Capitalism: an economic, political and social system based upon the private ownership of property and the creation of wealth.

Meritocracy: a society in which the most powerful positions in all important spheres are allocated in relation to the ability of the candidates, rather than other factors such as birth, age, race or sex.

Table 3.4 Classification of social categories (used in official statistics)

1. Higher managerial and professional occupations (e.g. company directors, doctors and lawyers).
2. Lower managerial and professional occupations (e.g. nurses, journalists and junior police officers).
3. Intermediate occupations (e.g. secretaries).
4. Small employers (e.g. farmers).
5. Lower supervisory occupations (e.g. train drivers).
6. Semi-routine occupations (e.g. shop assistants).
7. Routine occupations (e.g. waiters, refuse collectors).
8. Long-term unemployed.

journalists (in the second group on the list) invariably feature near the bottom of any league table of popularity.

Other classifications rest on divisions between manual and non-manual labour (sometimes called 'white collar' and 'blue collar', respectively), and subdivide the manual category into 'skilled' or 'semi-skilled'. This reflects the old assumption that people who work with their hands earn less than 'brain workers'. But this no longer holds true; plumbers, for example, can earn considerably more than clerks in public service jobs. Until 1961, when a limit on their wages was removed, professional footballers would have ranked fairly low in any classification. Their current earning power and lavish lifestyles show how difficult it is to fit particular individuals into any list.

Soon after becoming Prime Minister in 1990, John Major promised that in the next decade the division between blue and white collar workers would be eroded further, so that Britain would become 'a genuinely classless society'. His remark is often misquoted as a promise to reduce economic inequality rather than to help undermine the traditional stereotypes associated with particular occupations. Even so, in a society where wealth is increasingly regarded as the key badge of status, the economic figures do suggest that Britain has a long way to go before it can be regarded a 'classless' in any meaningful sense (see Table 3.5).

When the figures in Table 3.5 are inverted, the extent of inequality in Britain becomes even more apparent. Thus in 2001 people in the bottom half of Britain's wealth league owned between them just five per cent of the wealth. Three quarters of the population own just one quarter of the wealth. The situation is even starker when house prices (which are open to wild fluctuations) are removed from the

Table 3.5 Distribution of Britain's wealth, 1976–2001 (including value of house)

	1976	1996	2001
Top 1 per cent owned	21%	20%	23%
Top 5 per cent owned	38%	40%	43%
Top 10 per cent owned	50%	52%	56%
Top 25 per cent owned	71%	74%	75%
Top 50 per cent owned	92%	93%	95%

Source: Inland Revenue, www.hmrc.gov.uk/

calculation. The most wealthy one per cent of Britons own a third of the non-housing wealth; the bottom half have to share just three per cent.

While there can be no dispute about the existence of substantial economic inequality in Britain, its effect on society as a whole is still controversial, reflecting continuing ideological divisions (see Chapter 15). For economic liberals like Thatcher, individuals are primarily motivated by the desire to improve the living standards of themselves and their families. The free market will decide who deserves the greatest rewards, and this acts as a spur to make ambitious people more productive. A more productive society benefits everyone within it; more jobs will be created, and even those who cannot find work of any kind can be guaranteed an income out of the proceeds. In keeping with these ideas, after Thatcher became leader in 1975 the Conservatives explicitly singled out 'aspiring' members of the working class as potential supporters. By contrast, social democrats believe that inequality is wrong in itself (outside modest limits). Among other effects, it denies anything like equal life-chances to those who are born into poor households. Thus the competition which is prized by economic liberals is rigged from the start, from the perspective of social democracy.

Poverty

The answer of the Blair governments to the problem of economic inequality has been difficult to square either with economic liberalism or with social democracy. On the one hand, before the 2001 general election Blair himself said that he had no difficulty with the fact that inequality had risen during his first term in office. But he had made **social exclusion** the subject of his first major speech as prime minister, and in 1999 he set a target of eradicating child poverty in Britain entirely by the year 2020. In part, this goal was to be met by helping lone parents to find paid work. But the system of taxation and state benefits would also have to be realigned to direct more assistance towards poor households with dependent children, thus offending against the economic liberal belief in the free market.

To some observers, poverty hardly exists in the UK today, compared to the situation at the beginning of the twentieth century (not to mention earlier times). Statistics relating to life expectancy illustrate this argument. Men born in 1901 could not expect to survive beyond the age of 45, while average life expectancy for women was 49. In 2002 the respective figures had risen to 76 and almost 80. This data is obviously a reflection of improvements in healthcare and discoveries like antibiotics; but it is also a reasonable indication that such benefits have been widely shared, otherwise high mortality rates among the poor would have had a greater effect in holding down the average. Nevertheless, the overall UK figures conceal significant disparities. For example, a female born in the London borough of Kensington and Chelsea in 2002 could expect to live to the age of 84, while her contemporary born in Manchester would die almost seven years earlier.

Clearly, absolute poverty has been greatly reduced since 1901. Very few Britons lack access to the basic amenities of life, like adequate food and shelter. But when commentators emphasise the continued existence of relative poverty they are pointing to a real dilemma for policy-makers. The general improvement over the last century or so has also led to a rise in demands among a more comfortable

Social exclusion: according to the government, 'social exclusion happens when people or places suffer from a series of problems such as unemployment, discrimination, poor skills, low incomes, poor housing, high crime, ill health and family breakdown. When such problems combine they can create a vicious cycle … Being born into poverty or to parents with low skills still has a major influence on future life chances'. (Source: www.socialexclusion.gov.uk)

Controversy: **3.1**

Unemployment and the 'undeserving' poor

Whatever measure of poverty one adopts, it is generally agreed that the lack of a job is the most significant indicator. In recent decades Britain has suffered two periods during which unemployment was around three million: 1982–87 and 1992–93 (see Chapter 2). These figures were bad enough by post-war standards, but they were disputed because the government repeatedly changed the method of calculation in ways which reduced the total. A similar problem in the 1930s had a lasting effect on many politicians, regardless of their party allegiance. The experience of post-war unemployment has been less formative, partly because benefit levels were relatively higher. Thus although there was outrage when the Conservative Chancellor Norman Lamont described high unemployment as 'a price well worth paying' for lower inflation, he was only expressing the private thoughts of many MPs of his generation. Attitudes towards the unemployed tend to change in line with economic prospects. During prosperous periods the public is generally hostile, but in a recession it is more sympathetic. Even if benefit levels remain the same, people seem to regard them as excessively generous when unemployment is low.

A constant factor amid these fluctuations is a distinction between the 'deserving' and 'undeserving' poor. Even during a recession many people assume that able-bodied individuals would be able to find work if they were sufficiently motivated. This attitude was concisely expressed by the Conservative minister Norman Tebbit, who told his party's 1981 conference that his father had 'got on his bike and looked for work' in the 1930s. This view – a lingering echo of the traditional Protestant work-ethic in Britain – explains why many members of the public are so ready to express hostility towards the unemployed when their own economic circumstances are reassuring enough to make them feel that there is no personal risk involved in a call for lower unemployment benefit. The first years of the twenty-first century have been such a period. In November 2004 the official number of unemployed was 1.38 million – lower than at any time since 1984, when comparable statistical methods were first adopted. Subsequently it edged upwards, but the publication of the monthly figures was no longer a key political event as it had been in the 1980s.

population, and those whose lifestyles would have aroused envy among the poor of 1901 can still be numbered among the ranks of the 'socially excluded' today because they enjoy much less than a full share of the technological and other advances over the period. For example, in 2001 more households (7 million) were in possession of two cars than those (6.7 million) who lacked a single vehicle. This indicator of economic inequality (in a society which regards a car as a necessity) was not a serious consideration back in 1901! In 1995 only 20 per cent of people regarded a home computer as a necessity for a child; four years later this proportion had more than doubled, to 42 per cent.

Relative poverty is officially defined as occurring when a household's income falls below 60 per cent of the national median (as opposed to the average). On this criterion, the Blair government estimated that child poverty doubled under Conservative rule between 1979 and 1997, to about 4.4 million. It claimed that its own policies had reduced the level by half a million by 2001. This was regarded as a reasonable start, but campaigning bodies like the Child Poverty Action Group pointed out that the government itself had embarked on its programme with a target of over a million during this period. According to the 2001 census there are around 12 million young people under 15 in the UK; if more than a quarter of these were suffering from relative economic deprivation the country was clearly a long way from the meritocratic goal of liberal democracy.

Sources of cohesion

As we noted above, the convenience of examining British society by means of its divisions should not blind us to the many sources of social cohesion. Not least of these is the general belief in the UK political system itself. The liberal democratic idea that power can change hands peacefully as a result of free and fair elections seems to be as strong as ever, even if fewer people feel inclined to vote. There is also a consistent level of support for such associated values as the right to freedom of expression. Overall, an optimistic observer could claim that Britain has become a pluralistic nation (see Chapter 1). On this view, the presence of diverse groups and the absence of serious friction between them is a sign of a healthy democracy in operation. Opinion poll evidence also reveals increasing tolerance for groups like homosexuals who have suffered in the past from serious discrimination in a variety of fields, as well as greater acceptance of ethnic minorities. It appears that these trends have been fostered by the growth of higher education, among other factors.

Citizenship

Citizenship: a status that bestows rights, and imposes obligations, on a person as a full member of a state.

The values of liberal democracy are associated with the notion of a common **citizenship**, in which the inhabitants of a country and their government are bound together by a widely-accepted framework of rights and responsibilities. Traditionally in Britain, individuals have been regarded as subjects of the Crown, and the institution of monarchy has been used to promote national unity (especially at times of crisis like the two world wars of the twentieth century). But even before the recent well-publicised problems of the royal family, critics were arguing that the monarchy was out of touch with the lives of modern Britons, harking back to the pre-democratic age of Empire. The idea of 'subjecthood' implied a passive, pseudo-religious obedience to monarchy and its symbols. By contrast, citizenship has always carried connotations of active independence, much more characteristic of a liberal democratic order.

The introduction by the Blair government of 'Citizenship' as part of the national curriculum implies a decisive move away from subjecthood. However, the break with the past has not been complete. When new applicants are accepted for citizenship, they still swear allegiance to the British Crown. More importantly, citizenship is normally associated with a codified constitution, laying down specific rights for individuals. Despite the passage of the Human Rights Act 1998, Britain still lacks a document of this kind (see Chapter 5).

One difficulty with applying the idea of citizenship to modern Britain is that in its fullest sense the concept seems best suited to relatively small-scale, pre-industrial

A street party for the Silver Jubilee of Elizabeth II, 1977 (© Colin Jones Topfoto)

societies. In a state like ancient Athens, for example, it was easy to accept that citizenship entailed duties to others as well as rights for oneself, since many citizens knew each other (by contrast, a recent study suggested that the average Briton would have fewer than 400 friends in their whole lives, and no more than 33 at any one time). In 'face-to-face' societies like Athens, participation in a democratic system meant far more than the periodic casting of votes for party candidates. Citizens attended decision-making assemblies, and could make their voices heard (equally, of course, women and slaves were denied the status of citizens in Athens).

Another problem identified by critics is that the idea of citizenship is undermined by significant economic inequalities. For example, individuals who can afford to work fewer hours will be able to inform themselves about current affairs, and to involve themselves in community activities more than low-paid workers who struggle to make ends meet or the long-term unemployed who often lack a sense of 'belonging'. Notoriously, the middle classes have been able to gain considerable benefits from the welfare state, while many of the less well-off have been unaware of their full entitlements. The idea of social exclusion implies that some individuals can be deprived of meaningful citizenship simply because they were born to the wrong parents or in the wrong neighbourhood.

Citizens or consumers?

Many of these considerations were used to criticise John Major's initiative of a 'Citizen's Charter'. First launched in 1991, the idea was intended to promote improvements in public service delivery, notably by making providers more accountable to the public. But critics could not fail to notice that it had been deliberately called the Citizen's Charter (i.e. the charter of the individual citizen), rather than the Citizens' Charter (i.e. a charter for people in a collective capacity). The poor, who are most dependent on the public services, would still be less likely to complain than the well-off individuals who in the last resort can 'opt out' and look for alternative provision in the private sector. To these critics, in short, the Citizen's Charter merely underlined the existence of a two-tier citizenship in Britain, reflecting the difference between the 'haves' and 'have-nots'. It also threatened to deflect critical attention away from politicians who set public service guidelines and budgets, to the people 'on the front line' who operate under constraints imposed from above. Thus while ordinary public service employees were being made more accountable, their political masters would be more likely to escape any blame. In this respect, the Citizen's Charter could be seen as another symptom of a shift from traditional notions of 'government' to a more ambiguous one of 'governance' (see Chapter 9).

In 1998 the Blair government re-launched the Charter programme under the less question-begging name 'Service First'. However, this was the only terminological revision of any significance. Users of public services were still referred to as 'clients' or 'customers'. In part, this reflected an assumption that the public services would become more efficient if they adopted the free-market outlook. Yet it also suggested that both of the main parties saw an intimate link between the exercise of 'citizenship' and economic activity. One might even suggest that they have come to see consumerism as the unifying principle which transcends the various divisions in British society. Before the 2005 general election, several senior Labour ministers urged that the consumerist leanings of most voters should be granted increasing recognition by policy-makers.

The results of the 2000–2001 'Citizen's Audit', a detailed survey funded by the Economic and Social Research Council (ESRC), underline the complex relationship between consumerism and citizenship. The survey found quite strong support for the basic propositions of citizenship in a liberal democracy (i.e. willingness to obey the law and pay taxes). But when respondents were asked about their political participation, the most significant changes since the last similar survey in 1984 were in categories which are characteristic of a consumerist society. The proportion of people who had boycotted a product soared from just four per cent to almost a third. In 1984, 30 per cent claimed to have contacted a politician, but the figure in 2000 was just 13 per cent. Over the same period, the proportion of respondents who had contacted the media more than doubled (from four to nine per cent).

Consumer: a person who purchases goods and services for their own use.

On this view, individuals might seem to have different interests arising from issues of gender, age, ethnicity, religion, etc. But their ultimate interest lies in securing or preserving a comfortable lifestyle; and they are increasingly likely to express their views by acting as **consumers**. This would hardly make Britain unique among liberal democracies. In the US – a society which is even more diverse than Britain – the idea of the 'American Dream' is a vital unifying principle. It is assumed that every American has the chance to rise to riches through individual effort, whatever the circumstances of his or her birth. But in the US electoral turnout is notoriously low, at least in part because large numbers of citizens do not feel that the main political parties come close to addressing their needs. We will return to this subject in later chapters (see, in particular, Chapters 15 and 18). But it can be argued that the confusion between consumerism and citizenship helps to explain why so many people who are either disillusioned with the affluent society or unable to share its fruits are increasingly disinclined to vote. It certainly helps to explain why the main political parties sound so similar, at a time when British society is actually more diverse than ever.

Conclusion and summary

In the 1950s the main social divisions in Britain were easily recognised. Most people could be categorised by their position within a well-defined class structure. Dress and accent were unmistakable external signs, and gave a reasonable indication of a person's outlook. The main political parties certainly thought that class was a reliable measure of social attitudes. Labour and the Conservatives pitched their main appeal to working- and middle-class people respectively, and in the 1950s they won more than 90 per cent of the vote between them at three out of four general elections.

As we have seen, class is still an important factor in Britain's political culture, but it is no longer a dominant consideration. There are, though, other sources of division. Some, like gender and ethnicity, remain high on the political agenda despite recent attempts to address them. Others, like the urban/rural divide and the age profile of the population are much more important now than they were in 1950.

It might have been expected that the political situation in Britain would have been transformed to reflect the fundamental changes of the past fifty years. For example, increasing social diversity lends weight to the argument for some form of proportional representation, which would encourage a proliferation of parties offering a much wider range of electoral choice. However, Labour and the Conservatives still dominate the scene, and third parties struggle to make a decisive impact. The argument of this chapter is that for the last two decades the main parties have worked on the assumption that the divisions within British society are not as important as the unifying factors. The chief among these is the widespread consumerist ethos, which the main parties compete to serve. Significantly, at the general elections of 1983 and 1987 Labour pitched its appeal to a variety of dissatisfied minority groups, hoping to assemble a winning coalition. This strategy failed comprehensively, so the party leadership embarked on the course which led to New Labour. At present, the parties see no reason to revise electoral strategies which are based on the perceived interests of the 'contented majority'. Apathy is something they can deal with; they will only be stirred to action in the unlikely case of an issue arising to unify the growing ranks of the disenchanted.

Further reading

In a fast-changing society like Britain, information about society and the economy can be out of date before it is published. Students are advised to keep a look out for survey results published in broadsheet newspapers. For example, an interesting study of 1000 people between the ages of 18 and 30 was published in *The Times* over the week beginning 13 September 2004. Newspapers, of course, are interested in themes which will provide eye-catching headlines, and most reports need to be treated with caution, for example by comparing them with other published findings.

There is a wide range of books which use statistical data to draw general conclusions about British society. A.H. Halsey and J. Webb (eds), *Twentieth Century British Social Trends* (London: Macmillan, 2000) includes discussions of all the major developments in a hundred years of radical change. See also H. Perkin, *The Rise of Professional Society: England Since*

1880 (London: Routledge, 1989). R. Lister's *Poverty* (Oxford: Polity Press, 2004) is an up-to-date study of that controversial subject, by a widely-respected observer. On ethnicity, see J. Solomos, *Race and Racism in Britain* (London: Palgrave, 3rd edition, 2003) and on gender, J. Lovenduski, *Feminising Politics* (Oxford: Polity Press, 2005).

K. Faulks, *Citizenship in Modern Britain* (Edinburgh: Edinburgh University Press, 1998) presents a strong argument against the economic understanding of citizenship. Some findings from the 2000–2001 'Citizen Audit' are summarised in C. Pattie, P. Seyd and P. Whiteley, 'Civic Attitudes and Engagement in Modern Britain', *Parliamentary Affairs*, Vol. 56, No. 4 (2003), pp. 616–33. A fuller analysis of the findings is in C. Pattie, P. Seyd and P. Whiteley, *Citizenship in Britain. Values, Participation and Democracy* (Cambridge: Cambridge University Press, 2004). The classic text on this subject, R.D. Putnam's *Bowling Alone. The Collapse and Revival of American Community* (London: Simon & Schuster, 2000) is well worth reading although its findings relate to the US.

Websites

Websites provide an essential source for the most up-to-date statistics. The most comprehensive source is the government's site, National Statistics Online (www.ons.gov.uk), which provides results from the 2001 census and many links to more detailed studies of social trends. The Department for Education and Skills website has a section on citizenship, www.Dfes.gov.uk/citizenship.

Chapter 4

The media and communications

Learning outcomes

After reading this chapter, you will:
- Be able to outline different approaches to the question of media influence, on voting behaviour and more general attitudes to political questions.
- Understand the role of political 'spin-doctors'.
- See that the relationship between the media and politicians has had important implications for liberal democracy in the UK.

Introduction

The relationship between politicians and the media is crucial to understanding British politics today. Voters are dependent on newspapers, television and the internet for information about current political developments. Coverage is increasingly extensive, particularly in the electronic media where special television channels are devoted to 24-hour news coverage, internet sites dealing with political issues have proliferated, and some politicians even publish internet 'blogs'.

Since the media is the prism through which almost everyone experiences UK politics, its performance is widely debated. Most people have a view about the quality of the media, and opinions tend to be polarised. Some attribute increasing public cynicism and apathy to the powerful influence of media organisations which have insufficient respect for politicians. Others claim that despite some irresponsible or frivolous exceptions the British media as a whole fulfils the invaluable function of holding politicians to account. On this view, politicians have brought themselves into disrepute, and continue to make matters worse for themselves by trying to avoid public-spirited journalistic scrutiny. Alternatively, it is also possible to argue that responsibility for recent negative publicity is shared in roughly equal measure. Opinion polls suggest that the public prefers politicians to journalists; but there is little to choose between their ratings, and both professions are deeply unpopular compared to people like doctors and teachers.

The debate over the nature and extent of media influence on democratic politics is complicated by the difficulty of measuring 'influence', whether for ill or good. We will return to this tricky question below. However, almost everyone is agreed that whether or not the media as a whole enables voters to take well-informed views on public issues, its freedom (within certain well-defined limits) is an essential component of a liberal democracy.

The UK media: not one, but many?

The media: newspapers, magazines, the radio and television considered as a group.

The press: the news media, including newspapers and magazines (radio and television news are sometimes included).

When we talk of **the media** and British politics, there is a danger of thinking that the word signifies a uniform body. Critics of particular media outlets are particularly liable to speak in this way. However, there are now numerous means of communication. In specific relation to politics, people can receive information from a wide variety of sources: newspapers, radio, television, the internet, etc. The obvious distinction is between printed sources, normally given the collective name of **the press**, and the ever-diversifying electronic media which first achieved a mass audience during the late twentieth century.

All of these various media compete for public attention; and only the outlets provided by the British Broadcasting Corporation (BBC) are publicly-owned (the BBC began as a private company in 1922, but became a chartered corporation four years later). Furthermore, although the BBC's Board of Governors has to pay close attention to the wishes of the government of the day, the Corporation has a long history of independence, particularly in its treatment of current affairs.

Superficially, this seems an ideal scenario for pluralism (see Chapter 1) in which individuals can easily access relevant information and a wide range of opinions on issues of public concern. However, this judgement is subject to important qualifications. First, although the press seems to be at a serious disadvantage compared to the situation before the advent of electronic media, its decline should not be exaggerated. When deciding on the main stories of the day, most television news programmes take their cue from the press. Newspaper journalists are frequently invited to elaborate their views on discussion programmes, and indeed many television and radio presenters also write for the press.

Second, the press is dominated by relatively few corporations, some of which have major shareholders with strong personalities and clear political agendas of their own. For example, the Australian-born Rupert Murdoch (now an American citizen) controls the *Sun*, *The Times*, the *Sunday Times*, and the *News of the World*. As well as accounting for around a third of national newspaper circulation, Murdoch's News Corporation has worldwide media interests, including the satellite broadcaster BSkyB, and the American television and cinema company Fox Entertainment, which in 2004 valued its assets at $31 billion and enjoyed annual revenue of $12 billion. Murdoch certainly does not impose a uniform editorial line on his various newspapers, but on certain subjects his opinions are well known and senior staff are unlikely to take a dissenting view. In particular, trade unions are unlikely to receive a favourable mention from Murdoch's stable of newspapers. In 1985 he broke the power of the printers' unions in the UK, with the wholehearted support of Margaret Thatcher. Murdoch is also a strong Eurosceptic and this position is reflected to varying degrees by his UK newspapers.

Despite its global operations, not even News Corporation can afford to be wholly complacent. The multinational media empire constructed by Murdoch's rival, Robert Maxwell, collapsed after the latter's mysterious death in November 1991, as a result of dubious and over-ambitious business dealings. But the massive resources of the media giants are a significant deterrent to would-be competitors. For example, the richest media outfits can offer the highest salaries to poach the best journalists, and engage in prolonged price-cutting wars against market rivals.

With nineteen British national daily and Sunday newspapers controlled by just eight individuals or organisations, it would be unrealistic to expect a wide range of opinions in their pages. But regardless of ownership there is a tendency for

---

Case study: 4.1

'Tabloids' and 'broadsheets'

Until recently, media commentators had a convenient way of distinguishing between Britain's national newspapers according to the size of their pages. The large-format 'broadsheets' included papers like *The Times*, the *Telegraph* and the *Guardian*. They were marked by extensive, detailed political coverage; commentary was provided by recognised experts who, while not exactly 'impartial', at least did justice to the complexity of key issues rather than presenting them as straightforward choices between good and evil. By contrast, tabloids like the *Sun,* the *Mirror* and the *Mail* aimed at the heart rather than the head. Assuming that their readers had little time to spare for the nuances of political debate, they spelled out their messages in down-to-earth language. The headline alone would usually be enough to inform the reader of the 'right' position to take on any issue.

For some broadsheet readers, the very inconvenience of the larger format was reassuring; the difficulty of turning the pages on crowded commuter trains symbolised the pains they were prepared to take in order to be well informed. However, in 2003 the broadsheet *Independent* newspaper began to print a tabloid edition. Its immediate popularity led some of its competitors to follow suit at a time when overall sales were in decline. In 2004 even *The Times* became tabloid-only.

Critics have linked this development to a more general trend towards 'dumbing down' in the media as a whole. Even the remaining broadsheets now report on the 'celebrity' gossip which has always characterised the tabloids. Coverage of political and economic issues is still extensive. But it can be argued that politics itself has been transformed by the tabloid effect, and Britain has entered the era of simplistic sound-bites and spin-doctors. The same old question can still be raised: have the politicians succumbed to the influence of the tabloids, or have they simply responded to the same public demand?

Table 4.1 Newspaper ownership and circulation, May 2005

Title	Proprietor	Circulation
The Times	Rupert Murdoch	685 448
Telegraph	Sir David and Sir Frederick Barclay	912 497
Guardian	Scott Trust	367 478
Independent	Independent Newspapers	262 004
Financial Times	Pearson	426 803
Sun	Rupert Murdoch	3 258 500
Mirror	Trinity Mirror	1 719 645
Star	Richard Desmond	850 936
Mail	Lord Rothermere	2 380 003
Express	Richard Desmond	926 438
Sunday Times	Rupert Murdoch	1 359 159
Observer	Scott Trust	453 197
Sunday Telegraph	Sir David and Sir Frederick Barclay	686 270
Independent on Sunday	Independent Newspapers	210 198
Mail on Sunday	Lord Rothermere	2 439 272
Sunday Express	Richard Desmond	912 089
News of the World	Rupert Murdoch	3 639 243
Sunday Mirror	Trinity Mirror	1 529 753
Sunday People	Trinity Mirror	941 026

Source: Data on circulation is from the Audit Bureau of Circulations Ltd, www.abc.org.uk

media outlets of any significance to approach public issues from a broadly similar perspective. Competition in the media focuses on two targets. Bare circulation statistics for the press, and audience figures for television and radio, constitute one obvious reference-point. But a great deal also depends on the nature of the audience. Most of the media is dependent on advertising revenue. Above all, advertisers want to reach free-spending individuals rather than the poor or the thrifty. Hence, for example, a magazine which is purchased by a small but affluent group is likely to be in a healthier financial state than a mass-circulation newspaper that appeals primarily to the low-paid and unemployed.

The classic example of this phenomenon is the fate of the left-wing *Daily Herald*, which went out of business in 1964 despite a substantial readership. It was relaunched as the *Sun*, which was bought by Murdoch in 1969. Within a decade, a popular, Labour-supporting paper had been turned into socialism's most vocal press opponent. Ironically, Murdoch himself had been attracted by socialist ideas in his youth. Now he was a champion of the free market, and could claim that the fate of the *Herald* merely underlined the popularity of that position. But his critics replied that the operations of the free market prevented alternative viewpoints from securing a proper hearing.

Theories of media influence

While the effect of market forces on the mainstream British media undoubtedly tends to restrict the range of opinions covered, it is still possible to argue that the present situation satisfies the basic requirements of liberal pluralism. Debates on this subject are very difficult to resolve, because there is no agreement on the extent to which the media shapes public opinion, rather than merely reflecting existing views. Opinion polls, indeed, usually suggest that influence is slight. But even people who are aware of being influenced are often reluctant to admit that their choices have been swayed; and others will be genuinely unaware that their thinking has been affected. Thus people commonly claim to form their opinions on the basis of 'factual' reports on television rather than taking their ideas from the 'biased' press. However, there is a danger that these respondents have exaggerated the influence of television because moving pictures have a more vivid, immediate impact than the printed word, which might exert a more subtle influence. And as we have noted, television discussion programmes have their agenda shaped to a considerable extent by the content of newspapers.

There are three main theories on this subject:

1. *Reinforcement theory*. On this view, the media merely responds to existing demand. For example, in an ultra-competitive market a newspaper which advocated unpopular causes would quickly lose readers and revenue. The most that a media outlet can do is to give people additional reasons for what they believe already, as a result of other influences such as the views of parents and friends.

2. *Agenda setting*. This approach accepts that the media cannot change the way that people think on particular issues. But it argues that it can affect the political agenda by concentrating on specific subjects and avoiding others. Thus, for example, the general public might be hostile to corruption in all walks of life; but newspaper owners can direct their editors to focus attention on the misdeeds of politicians, rather than exposing dubious business practices which could lead to awkward questions about their own activities. At election-time the media can help to shape an agenda of salient issues which favour one party over another.

3. *Direct effects*. The most critical approach to media influence argues that it can directly affect the way people think about politics as well as setting the agenda. Gullible readers can be directed towards certain conclusions by means of selective or distorted reporting. But the same effect can be achieved in more subtle ways, by the use of value-laden terminology when addressing certain issues, parties or individuals.

The obvious difficulty with all such theories is that individual voters differ. Some people are never content with a single viewpoint; if their newspaper supports a particular policy, they will actively seek out a source which gives an opposing view. At the other extreme, some individuals accept what they hear or read without question. The overwhelming majority of people fall somewhere in between these poles. Thus our response to the rival theories will depend to a considerable extent on our assessment of the level of public knowledge of political issues. In turn, this has implications for the relative health of liberal democracy in the UK. Reinforcement theory tallies well with the pluralist approach, which argues that most people are rational enough to make political decisions after considering a range of proposals. To varying degrees, the agenda setting and direct effects models suggest a largely passive electorate, and are thus more compatible with an elitist approach.

As we have seen, empirical evidence on this subject is open to question and evades objective interpretation. For example, it was not until the time of the 1983 general election that a majority of *Sun* readers was able correctly to identify the political allegiance of that newspaper, despite its strong support for the Conservatives since the mid-1970s. On one level, this evidence could suggest that newspapers have a limited effect on partisan loyalties. But at the very least, it also indicates considerable potential for influence. If most *Sun* readers could not detect the clear pro-Tory bias of its news coverage, it is hardly likely that they would be fully conscious of any resulting change in their own views on parties or issues.

While the bias of the *Sun* should not have escaped anyone with basic political knowledge, some students of the subject concentrate on the more subtle manipulations of the media. In the mid-1970s the Glasgow Media Group (Glasgow University Mass Media Unit) began to study the language used in news reports, on television as well as in newspapers. Their most interesting finding was the extent to which even supposedly 'neutral' reports featured value-laden terms. Thus, for example, if trade union leaders were repeatedly described as 'making demands' (rather than a more neutral phrase, like 'offering proposals'), it was likely that they would forfeit public sympathy. The Group argued that there was an endemic bias against the left in the UK media. But their analysis actually revealed a deeper problem: that a neutral presentation of contentious issues is highly problematic, due to the inherent nature of language itself.

Although political influence is a highly complex phenomenon, there are at least three reasons for supposing that the 'direct effects' approach is the most persuasive. First, the media is very close to the advertising industry which works on the assumption that attitudes can be shaped by words and images. In most cases, advertisers try to manipulate potential customers into switching from one brand to another. These techniques have been borrowed by political parties in recent decades. It would be strange if media moguls with strong political agendas of their own had not been tempted to do the same thing.

Second, elements of the privately-owned press certainly behave as if they have a strong influence. Some of them make no secret of their party preferences, and in the run up to general elections many newspapers publish leading articles advising readers of the best way to use their votes. After the 1992 general election, which resulted in an unexpected fourth successive victory for the Conservatives, the *Sun* crowed that it had decided the contest. It had launched furious attacks on Labour, rather than offering readers positive reasons for staying loyal to the government. Newspapers also freely boast of their influence on subjects which lack a direct party political element.

Third, although analysis of voting behaviour can provide some insights into media influence, it is important not to overlook the extent to which the media tries to shape the general context in which elections take place. While elements of the press enjoy praising one party and abusing the other, for some media moguls the ideal situation would be a contest between parties which broadly agreed with each other in advocating policies that suited the interests of big business. It can be argued that, largely thanks to the influence of News International, this scenario had come about in the UK by the time of the 1997 general election. Murdoch's papers swung behind Labour after more than two decades of raucous support for the Conservatives. On one interpretation, the *Sun* and the *News of the World* had merely recognised a shift in public preferences, and supported Labour because they wanted to be on the winning side. However, it is debatable whether they would have done so had Labour not made special efforts to woo Murdoch in the period between 1992 and 1997. Certainly, the Murdoch press would not have endorsed Labour with such enthusiasm if the party had stuck to its 1992 policy of increasing income tax for high earners.

This third point seems to provide a decisive riposte to the view that the press can do no more than reinforce existing attitudes. While academics continue to debate the nature and extent of press influence, political leaders have been acting as if the influence is real and significant. Tony Blair, in particular, was prepared to risk antagonising Labour loyalists in his attempts to keep the Murdoch press happy; and successive Labour Home Secretaries have been anxious not to offend the *Daily Mail*, which consistently upholds a hard line on law and order. Labour's fear of the *Mail*'s influence over the news agenda as a whole is particularly telling, since that newspaper has continued to support the Conservatives. Thus the question of influence ends up looking like a hall of mirrors: whatever its direct impact on ordinary voters, the press enjoys considerable influence over political debate because politicians believe that it is influential.

The post-war media

Even those who continue to deny the reality of media influence have to accept that there has been a change in the attitude of journalists over recent years. They are far more inclined to be combative in their approach to politicians, whether in television interviews or in newspaper commentary. This development is significant in itself, suggesting that, whatever they might say about their role in public, journalists privately think that they enjoy more influence than ever before.

In an article in the *Political Quarterly* in 2002 (see Further reading), Steven Barnett identified four phases of British journalism since 1945. They are:

1. An *age of deference*, from the 1940s to the early 1960s. This period was marked by exaggerated respect among journalists, who acted as if politicians were bestowing great favours on themselves and their audience by agreeing to say a few words.

2. An *age of equal engagement*, between 1964 and 1979. The early 1960s were marked by increasing friction between the press and politicians, who were discredited by a succession of scandals. These events were exploited by young satirists who heaped ridicule on 'the establishment' in general. This context was sure to affect news journalists in turn, but at first they exercised restraint. In part this was because senior reporters had been groomed during the age of deference; the change could only be registered when they had been replaced by a new generation which had grown up laughing along with the satirists.

3. An *age of journalistic disdain*, emerging in the late 1970s as politicians themselves became more reliant on techniques derived from journalism and advertising. When people agree to market themselves like soap powder, they can hardly expect to be treated like heroic figures. Equally, one can argue that this period reflected the new dominance of the electronic media, with the printed press taking its tone from more aggressive television interviewers.

4. Barnett argues that we have now entered an *age of contempt*, in which journalists spend most of their time trying to trap politicians into damaging admissions (either about policy or, increasingly, their private lives), while politicians avoid giving straight answers. The result has been an increase in public cynicism about public life in general. This has created a vicious circle; sensing that the public attaches a low priority to politics, the media gives it less coverage and tends to focus on cynical **soundbites** and frivolities – the very things which helped to generate public contempt in the first place.

Soundbite: a short phrase that is easy to remember.

Significantly, on Barnett's chronology the 'age of contempt' began shortly after the then Conservative government had fired warning shots over press intrusion into the private lives of public figures. In December 1989 the Minister of State at the Home Office (and later Secretary of State for National Heritage), David Mellor warned the press that it was 'drinking in the last chance saloon' and that its existing system of self-regulation under the Press Council would be replaced by a more rigorous regime. Earlier that year a Home Office committee had been set up to inquire into the behaviour of the press. But these threats merely resulted in a revamped regulatory body, the Press Complaints Commission (PCC) which included representatives of the worst-offending newspapers. Mellor himself was forced to resign from the Cabinet in September 1992 after the tabloids revealed details of his own private life.

One can argue that Barnett's time-frame creates a misleading impression of unbroken decline in relations between the press and politicians, because it omits the period between the wars when the 'press barons', Lord Beaverbrook and Lord Rothermere, tried to bully the Conservative Party leadership into adopting their preferred policies on trade and the Empire. However, among other useful features it illustrates the complex relationship between the media, politicians and the broader context (what one might call 'the climate of opinion'). If journalists and politicians are now treated with contempt by the public, the history of their relationship suggests that they are almost equally to blame. The media might have taken the initiative by adopting a more hostile stance, but politicians have done themselves no favours in their response to this challenge.

New Labour and the media

Barnett's 'age of contempt' also embraces the period of political ascendancy for 'New' Labour. This is no coincidence. Although the Conservative governments led by Thatcher and John Major gave a high priority to relations with the media, for Blair's Labour Party the problem has been an obsession.

In the general elections of 1979, 1983 and 1987 Labour faced a hostile press, and on each occasion it lost heavily. Even before 1987 there were signs that the party was willing to adapt to the media environment rather than struggling to change it. During the election campaign of that year a special party political broadcast was devoted to improving the image of the then leader, Neil Kinnock. This was judged to be so successful that it was broadcast twice, depriving the party of the chance to explain its policies in more detail. When even this personalised approach failed to secure a Labour victory, the party made a more concerted effort to re-brand itself,

Table 4.2 Partisan support of daily newspapers, 1992–2005

Newspaper	1992	1997	2001	2005
Sun	Conservative	Labour	Labour	Labour
Mirror/Record	Labour	Labour	Labour	Labour
Star	Conservative	Labour	Labour	Not interested
Mail	Conservative	Conservative	Anti-Labour	Conservative
Express	Conservative	Conservative	Labour	Labour
Telegraph	Conservative	Conservative	Conservative	Conservative
Guardian	Labour	Labour	Labour	Labour (with misgivings)
The Times	Conservative	Eurosceptic candidates	Labour	Labour (with misgivings)
Independent	No preference	Labour	Anti-Conservative	Liberal Democrats
Financial Times	Labour	Labour	Labour	Labour

adopting a red rose as its symbol in order to distance it from traditional socialist images like the red flag. These symbolic gestures mirrored more substantive policy changes, driven through on the assumption that the electorate had become more Thatcherite since 1979.

A further electoral defeat in 1992 presented the party with an acute dilemma. It could either conclude that it had lost credibility with voters through its drive to secure more sympathetic media coverage – or that it should take further steps to win approval from the Conservative-supporting press. Kinnock's successor John Smith accepted that presentational changes had been necessary, but took the view that the party would win power next time round if it avoided factional disputes and waited for the Conservatives to inflict damage on themselves. Thus he satisfied neither 'traditionalists' nor the media-focused 'modernisers', even though the average Labour Party member regarded him with respect and affection.

When Smith died in 1994 the choice of his successor lay between two modernisers, Tony Blair and Gordon Brown. They were equally ambitious, and given the popularity of both men they were unlikely to split the modernising vote in a way which would allow a more traditional figure to win the leadership election. However, Brown was persuaded to leave the way clear for Blair. An important player in the manoeuvres leading up to this decision was Peter Mandelson, a former TV producer who had helped in Labour's rebranding after 1987. Mandelson was regarded as the archetype of a **spin-doctor** – a term which had been imported from America to identify political operators who tried to ensure favourable media coverage for their paymasters. Whatever Mandelson's precise role, his preference for Blair as leader was a typical spin-doctor's decision. On paper, the advantage actually lay with Brown in terms of seniority and experience. These factors were outweighed by the impression that Blair would look better on television.

New Labour strategists had considerable success in courting the press. At the 1992 election, only the *Daily Mirror* and the *Guardian* had been firm Labour supporters; most other daily newspapers backed the Conservatives. By polling day in 1997, the *Daily Star*, the *Independent* and, most significantly, the *Sun* had moved into the Labour camp. The remaining 'Tory press' was highly critical of John Major's record and offered the party only lukewarm endorsements. Twice as many people read a Labour-supporting paper in 1997 than had been the case in 1992. Only three daily newspapers endorsed the Conservatives in 2005 when *The*

Spin-doctor: someone who is employed to promote the image of a specific politician and party, hoping to generate positive publicity and to prevent the appearance of negative media stories.

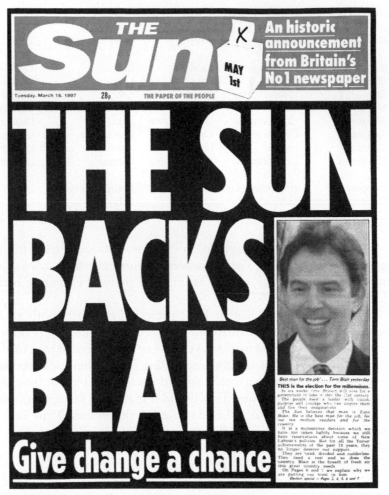

A timely conversion. The *Sun* dumps the Tories, 18 March 1997 (© PA/EMPICS)

Times, *Financial Times* and the *Sun* (all firm Tory supporters in the 1980s) once again backed Labour. A majority of *Sun* readers voted for Labour for the third election in a row (see Table 4.3). Coverage of the party's record and proposals on health and education was largely positive in the Labour-supporting press but it was criticised on the conduct of the war in Iraq and the issue of trust (see below).

The Blair governments and the media

Labour's crushing victory in 1997 should have given the party an ideal opportunity to take stock of its relationship with the media. Although the leadership had refused to make ambitious promises, the overwhelming scale of the win and symptoms of strong public enthusiasm offered extensive room for manoeuvre. In particular, newspapers like the *Sun*, which had been very influential during the Thatcher years, had reason to expect that their voices would carry less weight in Downing Street,

Table 4.3 Party supported by daily newspaper readers, 2005

Newspaper	Party supported by readers (%)		
	Con	**Lab**	**Lib Dem**
Sun	35	44	10
Daily Mirror	13	66	15
Daily Mail	57	24	14
Daily Express	44	29	20
Daily Star	17	53	13
Daily Telegraph	64	14	18
The Times	44	27	24
Guardian	7	48	34
Independent	11	38	43
Financial Times	36	34	23

Source: Ipsos MORI, www.ipsos-mori.com

compared to journals like the *New Statesman* which had been faithful to Labour through the bad times.

However, Blair had promised that the party would govern in the way that it had campaigned and this proved to be especially true of its treatment of the media. From their headquarters in the Millbank Tower near the Houses of Parliament, party operatives continued to 'rebut' potentially damaging stories at the first opportunity and to push out more positive publicity at the most favourable moment, either through deliberate 'leaks' or formal announcements. As in opposition, its approach was informed by the twin beliefs that the media was highly influential and instinctively hostile to the Labour movement and its aims. If anything, the years after 1992 had cemented these views. The harsh treatment of Major and his ministers by newspapers which had so recently advised their readers to vote Conservative suggested that New Labour could expect no mercy from its fair-weather media friends if it encountered trouble in office. The main lesson, according to the modernisers, was to avoid any concessions to 'Old' Labour views. Unless the party stuck rigidly to its new course it would allow elements within the media to combine both of their favourite habits – attacking a government and left-wing policies at the same time.

A key influence on Labour's strategy was Alastair Campbell, Blair's official spokesperson and later Director of Communications. Campbell was so close to Blair that some people regarded him as the real 'Deputy Prime Minister'. Unusually, although he was not a civil servant himself he was given authority over officials. A former tabloid journalist, Campbell had no illusions about the real motivations of his old colleagues. For all their talk of serving the public by holding governments to account, many journalists merely wanted to advance their personal interests by publishing sensational stories – whether true or not. Ironically, although Campbell often accused journalists of focusing on 'froth' and 'process' rather than issues of substance, an important part of his job was to ensure that the media had nothing worthwhile to report. Thus MPs and even senior ministers were warned to 'stay on message'; only the most reliable loyalists were allowed to address the media on behalf of the government.

'I don't think much of that poster, boss': Alastair Campbell, New Labour's communications supremo (© Matthew Polak/Sygma/Corbis)

Spinning into trouble

One problem with Campbell's approach was that over time he became a subject of media interest in his own right, even though he made it a rule that spin-doctors should never become part of a story. In a sense, his prominence was an important service to the government, since it often deflected hostile attention away from Blair. But his iron grip on official information led to allegations that Britain was governed by 'control freaks'. Ulterior motives began to be detected behind every announcement. Whatever their personal feelings about the government, many journalists felt that their profession was under attack. It was thus a matter of professional pride to cause the government as much trouble as possible, particularly at a time when the elected opposition parties were numerically weak in parliament.

The new emphasis on presentation was illustrated in the early days of the government, when several departmental information officers were removed, apparently for harbouring doubts about the New Labour project. A small army of 'special advisers' was brought into Whitehall; their number doubled, from 38 in 1997 to

87 by 2004 (with 29 attached to Downing Street). One of the special advisers, Jo Moore, sent an email suggesting that the terrorist attacks of 11 September 2001 presented an opportunity to 'bury' announcements which would otherwise have attracted adverse publicity. When the email was leaked Moore's immediate boss, the Transport Secretary Stephen Byers, refused to sack her. Eventually both resigned, but only after serious damage had been done to the image of the government as a whole.

It can be argued, indeed, that far from helping the government to fulfil a constructive mission, the obsession with 'spin' has presented the greatest threat to its popularity. It presents a unifying target for people who have been alienated from Labour for a variety of reasons. Byers was not the only minister to fall as a result of a press campaign. Mandelson himself was forced out twice – over allegations concerning his personal finances (December 1998) and his role in trying to secure passports for controversial businessmen (January 2001). When the Home Secretary David Blunkett stepped down in December 2004 because of a scandal in his private life and alleged misuse of ministerial powers commentators were strongly reminded of the Major era. Despite the Prime Minister's public declarations of support, Blunkett was compelled to resign because elements of the press persisted in publishing damaging stories. Blunkett's restoration to the Cabinet after the 2005 general election was thus a clear indication of Blair's true feelings towards the media. Equally, when Blunkett ran into new trouble over his financial dealings within a few months of his re-appointment, few media commentators were sad to see him emulating Mandelson with a second resignation (see Chapter 6).

Of these examples, the Mandelson case was the most instructive. Even after his second resignation he continued to enjoy Blair's personal support, and in 2004 he was nominated to the EU Commission, which made him far more powerful than he had been as a minister; and he remained a close adviser to the Prime Minister even at a distance. Clearly Blair thought that Mandelson's previous offences had been wildly exaggerated by a hostile media. But even if that were true, there was every reason to expect that he would continue to be a liability to the government as a whole, and to provide critics with a reason for questioning Blair's personal judgement. After the EU appointment it seemed that the best way of securing the Prime Minister's lasting favour was to become a media hate-figure.

Iraq, the BBC and the Hutton Inquiry

The Blair government always anticipated trouble from the newspapers, which have no duty to be impartial. But the BBC was a different matter. The Corporation is dependent on public funding through the licence fee, and the Home Secretary appoints the Board of Governors who in turn choose the BBC Director-General. As a public-service broadcaster it is supposed to be impartial in its political coverage. In practice, though, it has been criticised by Conservative and Labour governments, particularly at times of crisis such as the Falklands War (1982) and the American-led intervention in Iraq (2003). But even at the best of times there is an underlying tension in what appears to be an unequal relationship. Since the government can starve the BBC of funds by reducing the real value of the licence-fee – or in the last resort privatise it – the Corporation is arguably even more dependent on public approval than independent companies which are funded by advertising revenue or subscribers who pay to view.

This context explains why the BBC, rather than more openly critical newspapers like the *Daily Mirror*, bore the brunt of government anger after the Iraq war of 2003. Radio 4's *Today* programme carried a report by a BBC Defence correspondent, Andrew Gilligan, in which it was claimed that the government had distorted the threat from Iraq in the build-up to the conflict. In particular, Gilligan said that on the basis of an interview with a well-placed source it seemed probable that the government had known in advance that the regime of Saddam Hussein was in no position to threaten any British troops within 45 minutes of an order being given. Even so, the government had reported this threat in a dossier based on intelligence findings, which made the case for war to parliament and the public.

Gilligan's claim was broadcast very early in the morning, and was not repeated. Even so, it caused an uproar in Downing Street. Alastair Campbell demanded an apology for what he regarded as a slur on his integrity. After all, he had been involved in the process of compiling the published dossier. Meanwhile a search began for the source of Gilligan's story. Dr David Kelly revealed that he had spoken to Gilligan, although he felt that these conversations had not been accurately reported. Kelly was not a senior official in the Ministry of Defence, although he knew the situation in Iraq very well as a former UN weapons inspector. When it became clear that Kelly was indeed the source of Gilligan's remarks on the 45-minute claim, the government allowed him to face a parliamentary select committee without the usual high-level support. It was clear that Kelly felt painfully isolated, and once he had been exposed as Gilligan's source it was only a matter of time before the media started to hound him at home. When he was found dead in July 2003 most people accepted that he had committed suicide because of the strain.

The government immediately set up an inquiry under Lord Hutton, a senior Law Lord (see Chapter 8). It was open to members of the public, and although the proceedings were not televised the inquiry received intensive media coverage. Initially the government's critics were hopeful that Hutton would produce a damning report. However, Hutton had been given restricted terms of reference; and even within these limits he excluded many potentially awkward questions. This meant that his report, published in January 2004, was a surprise even to many of the government's supporters. Gilligan and the BBC were roundly criticised; by contrast, on the basis of Hutton's report an outside observer would have concluded that the government had behaved impeccably.

The immediate public response to the report was overwhelmingly hostile. Early polls suggested that nine voters out of ten regarded Hutton's investigation as a 'whitewash'. But no minister ever resigned as a result of actions taken in support of the Iraq war; the only front-bench casualties, Robin Cook and Clare Short, left the government because of their opposition to the conflict. Campbell left the government's service shortly after the Hutton Report, but it was clear that he would be brought back in some informal capacity whenever his old boss needed him. There were, though, more lasting departures from the BBC – Andrew Gilligan resigned, followed by the Director-General, Greg Dyke. Changes followed in the management structure of the Corporation, to tighten up the way it monitored its own output; the Board of Governors was to be disbanded in 2006, and its functions divided.

It is as difficult to draw 'objective' conclusions from the Hutton Inquiry as it is for the BBC to fulfil its duty to be truly 'impartial' at all times. However, the controversy sheds interesting light on many of the themes featured in this chapter, and some reflections seem beyond dispute:

- Whatever his merits as an investigative journalist, Gilligan can be seen as a product of the 'age of contempt'. In his original report, the claim that the government probably knew that it was distorting the case for war was added as a casual aside rather than a sensational revelation in itself. Clearly Gilligan, who had numerous Whitehall contacts, thought that the government would not be acting out of character if it misled MPs and the public on a vital issue.

- Alastair Campbell took a prominent role in compiling the government's dossier. In itself, this was remarkable; after all, Campbell was too busy with other activities to have much more than a layman's insight into the situation in Iraq, and he had neither been elected nor appointed to the civil service through the accepted process of selection. But as a seasoned tabloid journalist, it was hardly surprising that his input resulted in the production of sensational headlines by several newspapers.

- Throughout the controversy, the BBC Director-General Greg Dyke backed Gilligan and the Corporation's Head of News, Richard Sambrook. Yet Dyke was a long-term Labour supporter, whose appointment had aroused criticism because he had recently donated money to the party. Even if he had not held his senior position within the BBC, it is likely that Dyke would have been very doubtful about the case for war. However, his conduct suggests that institutional loyalties can have a marked effect on decisions, even those that are taken at high personal cost. By telling contrast, Dyke's predecessor John (later Lord) Birt was originally a Tory appointee who was far less popular at the BBC but ended up as a trusted adviser of the New Labour government.

- There were other intimate links between New Labour and the BBC. For example, the chairman of the Corporation's board of governors, Gavyn Davies, was the husband of Sue Nye, political secretary to Gordon Brown. Davies also resigned after the Hutton Report.

- Advance news of the inquiry's findings were leaked to the *Sun*. Significantly, of all national newspapers the *Sun* had been most supportive of the Iraq intervention, even at the outset when public opinion was opposed. The source of this leak was never identified, even though he or she would have been as easy to unmask as the late Dr Kelly. To the outsider, the leak appeared to be yet another repayment of a debt that the government felt it owed to Rupert Murdoch and News International. Later the *Sun* was told the date of the 2005 general election long before any other newspaper.

In the medium term the Hutton Report did the government few favours. It was still difficult to say who was most to blame for the death of Dr Kelly – the media, or the politicians. People who had consistently opposed the intervention in Iraq tended to harden their views rather than change them. Fears that the BBC would tone down its criticisms of government decisions on a range of issues seemed to be misplaced. Before long it had screened a documentary series which suggested that the British and US governments habitually exaggerated security threats for their own ends.

| Controversy: | 4.1 |

Does the media help or hinder the democratic process?

For	Against
The media ensures that the electorate is well informed on key issues.	The media distorts and over-simplifies key issues.
The media provides important insights into the character of political leaders.	The media is obsessed with personalities, usually focusing on irrelevant characteristics.
The media provides citizens with a vital means of participation between elections.	With its endless opinion polls and phone-in shows, the media distracts the electorate from more direct and effectual forms of participation.
The media is the voice of the people, and can keep politicians informed about changes in the public mood.	The media is unrepresentative of real public opinion, and pressurises politicians to take decisions which are contrary to the national interest.
The media holds governments to account when the parliamentary opposition is weak.	Unlike an elected opposition, the media can ask awkward questions without facing the prospect of holding office and having to take tough decisions. Its irresponsible tactics encourage voters to dismiss all constructive opposition as 'weak'.
Owners of newspapers and other media organs are successful business-people who can offer useful advice to elected politicians.	Media moguls enjoy too much influence as it is. They might pose as champions of the national interest, but their only concern is to make money. They should never be invited to Downing Street.

Even on the worst interpretation of the government's actions over the war on Iraq it could be argued that something important had been gained over the course of the twentieth century. In 1914 millions of Britons had enlisted in what turned out to be a world war, anxious to participate in a quarrel which few of them understood. In 2003, by contrast, a government with a crushing parliamentary majority felt unable to commit a few thousand of its citizens into battle without making the most of the intelligence reports at its disposal. There were no official inquiries into the causes of the First World War. From this perspective, it might be concluded that in one important respect the media 'age of contempt' is preferable to a time of excessive deference.

The media might be selective in its interests, but it clearly retains the potential to be a force for good. It is very doubtful whether the Live Aid concert of 1985, and associated charitable efforts to relieve poverty in Africa, could have happened without it. In 2005 a campaign spearheaded by the television chef Jamie Oliver forced the government to devote more funding to nutritious school meals. Although much of the media's output would have horrified the politicians who oversaw the foundation of the BBC as a public corporation in 1926, they would have glimpsed some slender grounds for optimism.

Politics and the internet

The political significance of the internet is increasing. The Blair governments have a strategy for e-government under which government departments and related agencies are required to publish material online. These sites are excellent resources for students of politics (the Cabinet Office E-government website is www.cabinetoffice.gov.uk/e-government/). Some government services can also be accessed online: more than two million people filed their tax self-assessment forms electronically in 2006, for example.

The new media, of which the internet is a key part, poses a challenge for the old media as citizens can now access easily a phenomenal amount of information online rather than having to rely on the press. Most old media outlets have responded to this by developing their own news websites. The BBC news website recorded a large increase in 'hits' (some 45 million in total) during the 2005 general election campaign whereas viewing figures for election coverage on BBC television news have fallen over the last decade. Newspaper circulation has similarly fallen during recent general election campaigns. The internet is largely unregulated – a positive for those concerned about press censorship, but a concern when the internet opens the way for criminal activity. The government and political parties have also recognised the importance of the internet as a source of information on political developments by putting official information (e.g. policy papers and press releases) on their websites. The Hutton Inquiry broke new ground by releasing scores of confidential government documents on its website.

The internet also provides a mechanism for political participation by ordinary citizens. This is evidenced by the growth of political 'blog' sites produced by independent commentators – albeit, many of them written by people connected to the 'Westminster village'. Few of these sites offer much to students of politics – http://ukpollingreport.co.uk/blog/index.php and www.politicalbetting.com/ are honourable exceptions for those interested in opinion polling – but some (e.g. http://5thnovember.blogspot.com) offer irreverent insights into the activities of the political elite. Recent general elections have also seen the emergence of sites offering 'guidance' on how to vote (e.g. www.whoshouldyouvotefor.com). Pressure groups and new social movements also use the internet to publicise their causes and mobilise citizens. However, there is as yet little evidence to suggest that the internet has had a significant effect on either voting behaviour or the campaign strategies of the main parties.

Conclusion and summary

A free media is a necessary, but not a sufficient, component of a democratic society (see Controversy 4.1). That is, when the media is under the control of the state there can be no free expression in a meaningful sense. Equally, though, there is no guarantee that a media which is entirely (or mainly) in private hands will allow (let alone actively encourage) the free expression of the full range of public opinions. The familiar argument that the public gets the media it deserves can only arise from a naïve faith in the free market. Despite the availability of new media forms like the internet (see Case study 4.2), false opinions backed by money have a far better chance of reaching a significant audience than any view – however logical or insightful – which is given to the world unaided. Ironically, far from being a danger to democracy the state-funded BBC remains the most reliable defender of minority viewpoints in Britain today.

Although scholars dispute the extent of direct media influence on voting behaviour, that an important influence exists is indisputable – even if the only people who are directly influenced are the politicians themselves. Awareness, one might say 'fear', of the media's power has helped to shape the range of policy options offered to the public at election-time. According to pluralist theory, a free media ought to widen the choice for voters; but this promise has not been borne out in practice.

The relationship between politicians and journalists has changed considerably in recent years. The media was quite deferential until the 1970s, but is now openly combative. In part, this is a result of the emergence of television, which encouraged interviewers to act like public inquisitors. The balance of power has shifted so dramatically that people who would formerly have sought a career in politics now plump for the media, even though journalists are among the least popular members of society. If the media has begun to drain talent away from public service in this fashion, that alone would be enough to raise questions about its real value to the democratic process.

Further reading

The best scholarly introductions to this subject are C. Seymour-Ure, *The British Press and Broadcasting since 1945* (Oxford: Blackwell, 2nd edition, 1996), R. Negrine, *Politics and the Mass Media in Britain* (London: Routledge, 1994) and J. Whale, *Politics and the Media* (London: Fontana, 1980). J. Curran and J. Seaton, *Power without Responsibility: the Press and Broadcasting in Britain* (London: Routledge, 2003) is a critical account. M. Cockerell, *Live from Number 10: The Inside Story of Prime Ministers and Television* (London: Faber and Faber, 1988) includes a wealth of anecdotes and insights about the developing relationship between the media and politicians. Invaluable recent articles include R. Kuhn, 'The Media and Politics', in P. Dunleavy, A. Gamble, R. Heffernan and G. Peele (eds), *Developments in British Politics 7,* (London: Palgrave, 2003), pp. 140–60, and J. Stanyer, 'Politics and the Media: A Breakdown in Relations for New Labour', *Parliamentary Affairs*, Vol. 56, No. 2, (2003), pp. 309–21. S. Barnett, 'Will a Crisis in Journalism Provoke a Crisis in Democracy?', *Political Quarterly*, Vol. 73, No. 4 (2002), pp. 400–8 is a forcefully-argued contribution to the debate. On the Hutton Inquiry, see W.G. Runciman (ed.), *Hutton and Butler: Lifting the Lid on the Workings of Power* (Oxford: Oxford University Press, 2004) and S. Rodgers (ed.), *The Hutton Inquiry and its Impact* (London: Politico's, 2004)

Published studies of recent general elections invariably offer useful studies, for example J. Bartle, R. Mortimore and S. Atkinson (eds), *Political Communications: The General Election Campaign of 2001* (London: Frank Cass, 2002) and M. Scammel and M. Harrop, 'The Press: Still for Labour, Despite Blair', in D. Kavanagh and D. Butler, *The British General Election of 2005* (London: Palgrave, 2005), pp. 119–45. R. Shannon, *A Press Free and Responsible: Self-Regulation and the Press Complaints Commission 1991–2001* (London: John Murray, 2001) is a comprehensive account of the battle to preserve press freedom at a time of growing public unease concerning intrusions on privacy. A fascinating insight into the sleazier side of the media can be gained from T. Bower, *Maxwell. The Final Verdict* (London: HarperCollins, 1996). Memoirs by political journalists may also be consulted; see, for example, J. Cole, *As it*

Seemed to Me: Political Memoirs (London: Weidenfeld & Nicolson, 1995) and A. Marr, *My Trade. A Short History of British Journalism* (London: Pan, 2005).

Websites

Most national daily and Sunday newspapers have websites that contain full electronic versions of their print editions. The best coverage of the media and politics is found in the media section of the *Guardian* http://media.guardian.co.uk/. Circulation figures are published by the Audit Bureau of Circulations www.abc.org.uk. Details on the organisation of the BBC are at www.bbc.co.uk/info/.

The Department for Culture, Media and Sport www.culturc.gov.uk is the responsible government department and Ofcom www.ofcom.org.uk the independent regulator for the communications industry. The Press Complaints Commission site www.pcc.org.uk includes details of a code of practice for the press. The Hutton Inquiry site www.the-hutton-inquiry.org.uk/ set new standards for government transparency by releasing hundreds of documents.

Part 2
Constitution and institutions

Chapter 5

The constitution

Learning outcomes

After reading this chapter, you will:

- Understand the traditional features and sources of the UK constitution.
- Have an insight into the factors which have undermined the traditional constitution.
- Be able to evaluate Labour's reform programme since 1997.

Introduction

The UK constitution is often regarded as a dry subject, only suitable for discussion among academics or political obsessives. Constitutional experts only intrude upon everyday life when they are invited to speculate on television about the latest crisis to affect the monarchy. In itself, this attitude tells us something important about British political culture. It reflects a feeling given eloquent expression by the poet Alexander Pope: 'For forms of government let fools contest/Whate'er is best administered is best'. Other countries have made a great fuss about constitutional arrangements. The Ancient Greeks regarded the makers of constitutions with veneration, and the philosopher Aristotle conducted an intensive study of the various systems of his time. Eighteenth century revolutionaries in America and France debated endlessly about constitutional arrangements. But this has not been the British way. The UK constitution has *evolved*, thanks to countless practical decisions which have served the public interest rather than following some abstract ideas.

This benign view of the UK constitution has never won universal acceptance. For many years critics have claimed that unplanned evolution has left the country with outdated institutions, fitted for a living museum rather than a nation which hopes to prosper in a fast-changing modern world. The 1997 general election gave these critical voices new prominence, and by no stretch of the imagination could the constitution now be described as dry and academic. This chapter includes many themes which are also mentioned elsewhere, but this only underlines the relevance of constitutional debate throughout the subject-matter of UK politics.

The uncodified constitution

Aristotle believed that a constitution was integral to the way of life of any political society. A more precise definition would be that it is an authoritative set of laws, rules and practices specifying how a state is to be governed and the relationship between the state and the individual. It provides a framework for the political system, establishing the main institutions of government, outlining their powers and the relationship between them. It also determines where 'sovereignty' – the ultimate decision-making power – resides within the state.

A distinction is frequently drawn between *written* and *unwritten* constitutions. In a written constitution, the main rules and principles governing the state are enshrined in constitutional texts with special status. In an unwritten constitution, such rules are found in convention or tradition. The British constitution is usually classed as unwritten, because the UK has no single constitutional document. This makes the country unusual among liberal democracies; only Israel and New Zealand are in the same position. By contrast, the written US constitution dates back to 1787 (though it has been subject to various revisions). Many of the constitutions of Western Europe were rewritten after the Second World War; for example, the present French constitution was introduced in 1958.

The British constitution is certainly highly flexible. In 1940, for example, the British War Cabinet decided after only the briefest of discussions to propose a union of the UK state with France, which was then on the brink of surrender to Nazi Germany. Only the refusal of the French government thwarted this dramatic deal. Yet it is too simplistic to describe the UK constitution as 'unwritten'. A more accurate word is *uncodified*. This is because, in practice, all constitutions contain a mixture of written and unwritten rules. A written constitution is not a detailed instruction manual, but rather a reference point for a political system which is subject to change. Thus the US constitution includes judicial decisions and conventions as well as the written constitutional text; a strong presidency, for example, is alien to the original spirit of the constitution. By the same token, some of the most important rules governing political activity in the UK are written down, in the form of Acts of Parliament or judicial rulings; but some distinction must still be made because the UK lacks a single, formal constitutional document (see Analysis 5.1).

Analysis: **5.1**

Codified and uncodified constitutions

Advocates of a codified constitution for the UK claim that it would be an essential guarantee of liberal democracy. To live under a written constitution is taken as a badge of active citizenship. However, there are arguments on both sides. It is worth remembering that the Weimar Republic, introduced in Germany after the First World War, had a codified liberal constitution. While the Nazi regime of Adolf Hitler was not exactly a product of the Republic, its liberal principles did nothing to prevent its rise to power.

In codified constitutions, the powers of executive, legislature and judiciary may be clearly laid down in a single authoritative document. There will usually be provisions for amending the constitution, depending on circumstances; but the provisions will be 'entrenched', requiring more than a simple vote in the legislature before they can be altered. The basic rights of citizens are identified, in a way which allows them to claim protection against the state. Political disputes may arise within the state; but unless a fundamental issue of principle is at stake the parties to the quarrel will at least abide by mutually recognised rules.

Supporters of uncodified constitutions like the UK argue that they are flexible enough to meet sudden emergencies (whereas constitutional changes in a country like the US can only take place after a cumbersome and time-consuming process). Because emergencies do arise, countries with codified constitutions can find themselves having to bend the rules, thus undermining the whole idea of a formal constitutional document. They also argue that the accumulated wisdom of the past is the best guide to present conduct. The founders of the US constitution might have been extremely wise; but it is against all probability that more wisdom was contained in that generation than in the combination of all their successors. Finally, codified constitutions place enormous influence in the hands of unelected judges, like the US Supreme Court, which can overrule politicians if their laws do not accord with constitutional principles. Elected politicians might make mistakes, but at least they can be held to account by the public. If their decisions are wrong they should be rectified at a general election rather than being nullified by a group of people who are also capable of making mistakes, and who might be utterly unrepresentative of public opinion.

Sources of the UK constitution

In the absence of a single codified document, there are five principal sources of the UK constitution:

1. Statute law.
2. Common law.
3. Conventions.
4. Authoritative works.
5. Law of the European Union (EU).

Statute law: law derived from Acts of Parliament and subordinate legislation.

1. *Statute law*. **Statute law** is created by parliament. Legislative proposals (Bills) become Acts of Parliament and enter into law when they have been passed by

both Houses of Parliament, and have received the Royal Assent (which they do automatically, now that the UK is a constitutional monarchy). They are implemented by the executive and enforced by the courts.

Under the doctrine of parliamentary sovereignty (see below), parliament is the supreme law-making body in the UK. It can repeal or amend any existing statute. But some Acts of Parliament have greater constitutional significance than others. For example, a succession of statutes (1832, 1867, 1884, 1885, 1918, 1928, 1948 and 1969) gave the vote to all adults. The Parliament Act of 1911 formally established the superiority of the House of Commons, and the UK joined the European Economic Community (EEC) under the terms of the European Communities Act 1972. Since Labour came to office in 1997 several key constitutional statutes have been passed, such as the Scotland Act 1998 which created a Scottish Parliament, the Human Rights Act 1998 which incorporated the European Convention on Human Rights into UK law, and the House of Lords Act 1999 which removed most hereditary peers from the upper chamber.

Common law: law derived from decisions in court cases and from general legal custom.

2. *Common law.* Where there is no clear statute law, the courts interpret and clarify the legal position. Such rulings become part of the **common law**, and take precedence over earlier decisions. However, parliament retains the right to supersede common law through further Acts of Parliament.

The common law also includes customs and precedents that have been accepted over time. The most important of these are the Crown's **prerogative powers**, including the right to declare war and negotiate treaties; to dissolve parliament; and to appoint government ministers and judges. These powers remained in the hands of the monarchy despite two revolutions in the seventeenth century. Since then they have passed to government ministers, who exercise them in the name of the Crown. Thus the Prime Minister declares war, decides the timing of general elections and appoints ministers. The monarch will usually be consulted, but this is purely formal. There is some debate about whether the monarch could still refuse to allow a dissolution of parliament, if a workable government could be formed from the existing House of Commons. But such a move would be highly controversial, and it is now assumed that the Royal Family should be 'above politics'. Even the Queen's Birthday Honours list is under the control of government ministers. Ultimately the Prime Minister is more powerful than any British monarch since the seventeenth century, because his or her control over parliament is direct, whereas the monarch could never be totally confident of its support.

Prerogative powers: discretionary powers of the Crown that are exercised by ministers.

3. *Conventions.* Conventions are rules or norms that are considered to be binding. The UK constitution is regarded as flexible because some of its key elements are based on long-standing conventional practices.

Convention: an established norm of political behaviour that is considered binding, but which lacks a firm basis in law.

One important **convention** is that the Prime Minister should be a member of the House of Commons. In 1940, when Neville Chamberlain resigned as Prime Minister, an important body of opinion believed that his successor should be the Foreign Secretary, Lord Halifax. If Halifax had pressed his case with energy, he might have been chosen. But he hesitated, partly because he felt that the national leader during wartime should be a member of the elected House. Winston Churchill took the position instead. In 1963 another peer, the Earl of Home, was able to become Prime Minister because he was able to renounce his title under the terms of the newly-passed Peerage Act. As Sir Alec Douglas-Home he quickly gained a seat in the Commons through a conveniently-called by-election.

The flexible nature of the UK constitution would be tested if a general election did not produce a clear winner. Such an outcome is called a 'hung parliament'. By convention, though, the monarch must ask the leader of the largest party if he or she is able to form a workable government. If the largest party is unable to govern, the monarch will ask other leaders whether they can form an administration. If these efforts fail, a new general election will be called. The last time this happened was in February 1974, when Labour's Harold Wilson eventually formed a government even though his party won fewer seats than the Conservatives. A new general election was called in October of the same year.

Convention also governs the circumstances in which governments or ministers should resign. The convention of collective responsibility means that ministers ought to stand down if they do not accept a policy position agreed by the Cabinet. In 2003 Robin Cook and Clare Short both resigned because they disagreed with the government's position on war in Iraq. The convention of individual ministerial responsibility means that a minister should resign if serious mistakes are made within their departments – even if they played no part in the mistaken decision.

In reality, though, these conventions have rarely been followed. In 1982 the Foreign Secretary, Lord Carrington, and two of his junior ministers resigned because they were held to be partly responsible for the Argentine invasion of the Falklands Islands. However, in this grave crisis Carrington and his colleagues took responsibility on themselves to appease the mood in the country; their own role in precipitating the invasion was arguably less than that of the Prime Minister Margaret Thatcher who had authorised cuts in defence spending which left the islands vulnerable to attack. In recent years many ministers have refused to stand down even when they have clearly made mistakes. If they subsequently step down, it will be because the Prime Minister has decided they must go. The convention of collective ministerial responsibility was stretched in the 1990s, when John Major struggled to keep order within a Cabinet which was profoundly split over Europe. Several ministers made it clear that they disagreed with the Prime Minister's approach, either by leaking their private thoughts to journalists or by making 'coded' speeches of dissent. They were not sacked, because the Prime Minister's position was weak.

4. *Authoritative works.* There are a number of established legal and political texts which are accepted as works of authority on the UK constitution. Such texts have no *formal* legal status, but are regularly consulted as reliable guides to the workings of institutions and of the political system in general. The best-known of these is Erskine May's *Treatise on the Law, Privileges, Proceedings and Usage of Parliament* (first published in 1844 but regularly updated). It is regarded as the 'Bible' of parliamentary practice, and is used by the Speaker and other senior officials.

5. *European Union law.* When the UK parliament passed the European Communities Act 1972 it accepted that EEC (now EU) law would take precedence over UK statute law if there was a conflict between the two. There was a general recognition that this development would have a radical effect on the British

constitution. However, parliament retained the power to repeal the legislation and the UK has opted out of some EU policies, notably the single currency (see Chapter 12).

Main principles of the UK constitution

There are five main building blocks of the traditional UK constitution:

1. Parliamentary sovereignty.
2. The rule of law.
3. A unitary state.
4. Representative government.
5. Membership of the European Union.

The first four have evolved over many centuries; the fifth is a relatively recent development.

Parliamentary sovereignty: the doctrine that Parliament is the supreme law-making authority in the UK.

1. *Parliamentary sovereignty*. The doctrine of **parliamentary sovereignty** is the key element of the UK constitution. That is, the Westminster parliament is regarded as the supreme law-making institution. The doctrine has three main elements:

   - parliament can legislate on any subject it chooses;
   - Acts of Parliament cannot be overturned by any other authority;
   - no parliament can bind its successors, meaning that any piece of current legislation may be repealed by a future parliament.

   In practice, though, parliament is not in control. The legislative and executive branches of the UK government *are fused*. The executive, or government, is composed of members of the two Houses of Parliament; in countries like the US which have a constitutional separation of powers, the executive is excluded from the legislature (or has only token representation), and has to bargain with members of the legislature in order to secure the passage of laws. By contrast, the UK government is normally in a dominant position in the House of Commons, through the whipping system of party discipline and its control over the legislative timetable. In turn the Commons has far more power than the House of Lords, unlike the situation in the US where the Senate is genuinely regarded as an upper chamber.

   In most other liberal democracies, laws which have significant constitutional implications cannot be passed simply by securing a majority in the legislature; such laws are said to be entrenched. There are no such safeguards in the UK. The executive-dominated House of Commons does not even need to secure the consent of the House of Lords, under the terms of the Parliament Acts of 1911 and 1949 which confined the power of the Lords to a period of delay. The executive can also take decisions, like declarations of war, without consulting parliament. This is because the executive in parliament has inherited many of the powers which were once 'royal prerogatives' under the control of the monarch. When wars are declared the government will normally accept demands for a recall of parliament; but this is by no means automatic. Parliament is also able to both establish and abolish subsidiary authorities, like local government, as these do not enjoy special constitutionally-protected status.

There are, though, significant external constraints on the executive. British power and prestige declined steeply during the course of the twentieth century, greatly reducing the scope and reach of parliamentary decisions. More recently, membership of the European Union has raised important constitutional questions. EU law takes precedence over Acts of Parliament if they come into conflict. Laws can be made inoperative if the courts hold them to breach the terms of the Human Rights Act 1998, which incorporated the European Convention on Human Rights into UK law (see Chapter 8).

However, the main restrictions on the executive are informal conventions and traditions of behaviour. Governments regularly claim a mandate for certain policies which have featured in their election manifestos. These may or may not have been important issues during the campaign; but normally questions of constitutional significance will be extensively discussed. It is recognised that some issues are so important that they cannot be implemented without a referendum,

'I don't know who writes these terrible scripts': The Queen reads out the government's legislative programme (© Tim Graham/Getty images)

and that a government will abide by the result even though this infringes the sovereignty of parliament. While no parliament can bind its successors, it would be very difficult, for example, for a future government to abolish the Scottish Parliament without getting popular consent through a new referendum (see Chapter 18).

The rule of law: a system of rule where the relationship between the state and its citizens is governed by the law.

2. *The rule of law*. **The rule of law** is a crucial principle in all liberal democracies – a guarantee against the arbitrary exercise of power. It ensures that all citizens of a state are to be treated equally and impartially. When they are charged with offences against the law they can expect a fair trial from an independent judiciary – a principle which dates back to Magna Carta, signed by King John in 1215. Although errors can be made in the judicial process, there are procedures for overturning wrongful verdicts. Citizens can also expect to obtain redress from the state if any of its servants have acted unlawfully. On the other hand, certain laws are designed to protect individuals from unlawful activity by their fellow-citizens. The state is expected to maintain an adequate police force to enforce these laws; the police should also be impartial in their work, disregarding irrelevant factors like ethnicity, gender or social status (see Chapter 8).

The principle of impartial law-enforcement highlights a characteristic constitutional anomaly in the UK, which Labour attempted to redress after its re-election in 2001. The head of the judiciary, responsible for all key appointments, was the Lord Chancellor; yet this Cabinet minister was not strictly independent at all, being appointed by the Prime Minister. Furthermore, the Lord Chancellor was also Speaker of the House of Lords, making him an important member of the legislature. Thus the Chancellor belonged to all three branches of government, making it likely that he would be subject to conflicts of interest. From the perspective of constitutional theory this situation was bizarre (or dangerous, depending on the observer's outlook). Yet it could be argued that in a perverse way the system actually guaranteed a high level of independence, because the legal profession would never tolerate an appointee who tried to interfere with their traditional practices. However, the second Blair government decided to address the anomaly, with distinctly mixed results. Its attempts to abolish the office of Lord Chancellor were thwarted by the resistance of the House of Lords and the post remains. However, the Lord Chancellor's constitutional powers have been significantly reduced by the Constitutional Reform Act 2005 (see Chapter 8).

Critics have argued that the rule of law is under threat in the UK for other reasons. Historic rights, like trial by jury, have been overturned at times of crisis: 'Diplock courts' where a judge sits without a jury were introduced to deal with terrorist cases in Northern Ireland in 1973 (the UK government is to abolish Diplock courts in Northern Ireland in 2007). The terrorist attack on New York in September 2001 was also cited as a reason for new restrictions on civil rights, even though this took place on foreign soil. Detention without trial, which was also used in Northern Ireland during 'the Troubles', and in the rest of the UK during the Second World War, is a clear breach of traditional liberties. However, the UK government argued that the terrorist threat made it necessary in specific instances, provoking a debate which goes to the heart of liberal democratic principles.

Controversy:	5.1

Terrorism and the rule of law

Activities by terrorists with a political motivation constitute a formidable challenge to liberal democracies. Such states uphold the idea that all political disputes must be resolved by dialogue rather than violence. At most, people with a grievance may resort to peaceful civil disobedience if the democratic process cannot satisfy their demands. Yet if their actions infringe the law, they can expect to be punished by the courts under their usual procedures.

However, the potential threat from terrorism today has changed the terms of debate. On the one hand, it can be argued that people who kill and maim have put themselves outside the protection of liberal procedures, so that traditional understandings of the rule of law should be set aside to deal with them. An alternative view is that many terrorists have the explicit aim of undermining liberal democracy. If their actions can provoke arbitrary acts, like imprisonment without trial, they will have won a kind of victory. A more practical objection, with particular relevance to the UK, is that several miscarriages of justice occurred in the 1970s, when the country was faced with a terrorist campaign by Irish Republicans. Although trial by jury was maintained on the mainland, suspects were convicted on flimsy evidence because of a prevailing atmosphere of panic and a thirst for vengeance. This precedent could hardly inspire public confidence in any future government which declared that certain people had to be detained because of evidence which could not be publicised due to security considerations. More radical critics argued that governments have a vested interest in suspending traditional liberties, and that it was quite possible for ministers to create a lasting sense of panic which would transform a temporary suspension of the rule of law into a permanent arrangement.

Unitary state: a homogeneous state in which power is concentrated at the centre.

3. *A unitary state.* The UK is composed of four constituent nations: England, Scotland, Wales and Northern Ireland. It is far from being united, in respect of culture, language or tradition (see Chapter 11). Yet the UK is commonly regarded as a **unitary state**, not least by the lawmakers at Westminster. A unitary state is highly centralised, with the dominant power located in national institutions. Certain powers might be delegated to subnational or local levels, but they are not protected by constitutional safeguards. Thus in 1985 the Thatcher government was able to abolish the Greater London Council (which had been created by another Conservative administration in 1963) and six metropolitan counties. By contrast, in federal systems power is shared between national and regional governments. Federal constitutions grant specific powers to the different tiers of government. In the UK, the word 'federal' is now widely regarded in a negative light with Eurosceptics associating federalism with the construction of a European polity. Yet when ministers devised constitutions for other countries within the old British Empire, the federal principle was often followed, for the good reason that it maximised the sense of self-government for people who would have resented centralised power.

The component nations of the UK came together in different ways. Wales was conquered by England, while both Scotland and Ireland joined the Union through negotiated agreement. England and Wales became closely integrated for most administrative purposes; but the Welsh language has survived, and the strong tradition of Welsh religious dissent was recognised in the disestablishment of the Church of England in 1920. Scotland retained its own legal and judicial systems. The Irish Free State formally seceded from the union in 1922, after further bloodshed. The north of Ireland, which remained within the union, retained separate institutions and a highly distinctive style of politics.

A classic unitary state exhibits a high degree of both centralisation and standardisation, with all parts of the state being governed in the same way. The UK never fitted this model. It is more accurate to describe it as a **union state**, reflecting the political and cultural variations which remained after the different countries came together. Defenders of this arrangement claimed that it was far more flexible than a formal federation, allowing 'asymmetrical' institutional development to reflect local circumstances. Thus there has been a Secretary for Scotland since 1885, but a similar post for Wales was not created until 1964, in response to an upsurge in Welsh nationalism. The devolved institutions established in 1999 in Scotland, Wales and Northern Ireland differ from each other (see Chapter 11). While critics argued that **devolution** on this scale signalled the end of the United Kingdom, supporters of the move could claim that it merely underlined the flexible nature of the union state.

4. *Representative government.* Although universal adult suffrage is a relatively recent development, the principle of representation is as old as the House of Commons (which dates back to 1265). Over the centuries the importance of the representative principle has strengthened, with the development of political parties and the supremacy of the Commons over the Lords. From the constitutional monarchy of the late seventeenth century the UK system evolved into a form of liberal democracy. The legislative and executive branches are fused rather than separate. Government takes place through parliament under a constitutional monarchy. Ministers are politically accountable to parliament, legally accountable to the Crown and must face the electorate at least every five years.

By the mid-nineteenth century, the British political system was one of cabinet government. Cabinet was the key policy-making body, but even if certain ministers sat in the House of Lords it was understood that a government could not survive without a workable majority in the Commons. A century later, considerable powers had been accumulated by the Prime Minister, who was now rather more than 'first among equals'. But even in the era of prime ministerial government, no-one could hold that office without enjoying the support of a majority of the people's representatives, or being able to win a parliamentary seat. The government is still held to be accountable for its actions, although tight party discipline makes it very unlikely that a government with a sizeable parliamentary majority will lose the confidence of the Commons. It will be judged on its record at a general election, which cannot be called more than five years after the previous contest.

5. *Membership of the European Union.* As we noted earlier, membership of the EU has important consequences for the UK constitution. EU regulations do not need explicit parliamentary endorsement before they become binding, and the UK courts apply EU law directly. If questions of interpretation arise, they are referred to the European Court of Justice (see Chapter 12).

Union state: a state in which the component parts are culturally distinct and, despite a strong centre, are governed in different ways.

Devolution: the transfer of decision-making authority from central to subnational government.

Controversy: **5.2**

The traditional constitution

Defenders of the traditional UK constitution claim that:

- It is flexible enough to accommodate social and political change.
- It provides government which is strong but accountable to the public.
- The rule of law guarantees the rights of the individual against the state.
- The constitution has evolved in response to genuine needs, and has stood the test of time.

Against this, critics argue that:

- There are inadequate constitutional controls over the executive.
- The system is over-centralised, leaving local government at the mercy of the centre.
- Non-democratic institutions, such as the monarchy and the House of Lords, have survived.
- Individuals are still treated as subjects, rather than citizens, and their rights can easily be overridden.

The UK government does not enjoy sole policy-making power in many important areas. EU policy competence has increased significantly since the single market programme was launched in the mid-1980s. The EU now has exclusive policy competence in trade, agriculture and fisheries. Responsibility for issues such as regional policy, working conditions and environmental policy is shared between the EU and its member states. The Council of Ministers, in which representatives of national governments negotiate legislative proposals, increasingly takes its decisions by qualified majority voting. But unanimity is still required for the most sensitive issues, like taxation or treaty changes.

The constitution under pressure

Although there were many important changes to the UK constitution in the first half of the twentieth century, these were rarely accompanied by a sustained debate about the fundamental nature of the constitution itself. This only became a regular feature of political discourse in the 1960s, as part of a more general inquest into the reasons for the decline of the UK, which was now too obvious to ignore. Unease was expressed by commentators outside parliament, but senior politicians from both main parties (e.g. Labour's Richard Crossman and the Conservative Lord Hailsham) added their voices.

The Establishment: the most influential people in a country, especially those with a similar social background who support the status quo.

The constitution was coming under pressure for a variety of reasons. The central state was forced to recognise the growing strength of nationalism in Scotland and Wales; unrest in Northern Ireland threatened to produce a civil war. A decline in social deference produced a new, more critical approach to the British **Establishment**, including the monarchy. But the main focus of attention was the state. Critics argued that, since the Second World War, it had taken on too many functions and had become 'overloaded' (see Chapter 2). In the process, too much power had accumulated in the hands of a single person – the Prime Minister. Lord Hailsham warned that the UK was in the process of becoming an **elective dictatorship**.

Elective dictatorship: a situation in which an elected government, and particularly the Prime Minister, is able to act without fear of constraint by other institutions.

The impact of Thatcherism

Ironically, Hailsham himself was a member of the government which brought many of these fears to a head. Margaret Thatcher herself was far from radical in her view of the constitution; for example, in 1975 she opposed the use of a referendum to settle the question of UK membership of the EEC. But her determined opposition to the ideas of the post-war 'consensus' led her to attack many established institutions (see Chapter 2). Her most startling innovation was to abolish the Greater London Council and six other metropolitan authorities. The surviving local authorities were subjected to regular reforms, progressively reducing them to the status of service deliverers. Many of their functions were allotted to unelected 'quangos' and other agencies, leading to a loss of political accountability.

At the centre, Thatcher was accused of politicising the civil service. Whitehall bureaucrats had been regarded as a key element of the constitution, acting as impartial servants of the public whatever party happened to be in power. But since the 1960s they had been undermined along with other members of the 'Establishment'. Mrs Thatcher saw them as a drain on the public purse, who only stirred themselves into action when their own interests were under threat. Her direct impact can be exaggerated; it was still possible for old-style 'mandarins' to win promotion. But the ethos of the civil service was transformed. Instead of advising ministers from the perspective of Britain's long-term interests, senior civil servants became much more willing to see things from the point of view of their political masters, who lived from one election to the next, in the constant expectation of being shuffled to another post.

Thatcher's appetite for conflict and change extended beyond Whitehall and local government. The trade unions, which had been drawn into an uneasy partnership with post-war governments, were excluded from Downing Street and subjected to a series of reforms. Their opposition to Thatcher's aims was predictable. But the Prime Minister also clashed with the Church of England, which criticised the social effect of her economic policies. Teachers, academics, doctors, lawyers and even the police were antagonised by attempts to make them more 'business-like'.

In the 1980s there were also growing concerns about civil liberties. In part, this was due to technological advances which made it much easier for the state to keep its own citizens under surveillance. But Mrs Thatcher's rhetoric increased fears that these instruments would be put to extensive use. She regarded socialists as little better than traitors, and even moderates who did not share her views were dismissed as appeasers. The search for internal enemies came to a head during the year-long miners' strike (1984–85), for which the government had made extensive preparations. At that time freedom of movement was restricted, and the traditional independence of Britain's police forces was overridden.

Thatcher's battle against established institutions had several ironic consequences. In some respects she carried out her promise to reduce the scope of central state activity; for example, her governments returned many nationalised industries to the

Case study: 5.1

Thatcherism and the monarchy

The emergence of Britain's first female Prime Minister when a woman, Elizabeth II, also occupied the throne turned out to be something less than a happy coincidence. The real source of friction was ideology rather than gender; but when it became clear that Buckingham Palace and Downing Street were not in full accord it was natural for the media to adopt its familiar tactic of focusing on personalities rather than principles. The Thatcherite ethos, with its heavy emphasis on hard work and thrift, was as antipathetic to the concept of monarchy as a socialist could ever be. Mrs Thatcher also offended the Queen with her attitude to the Commonwealth, which she regarded as an irritating talking-shop. The battle for the Falklands was very much Thatcher's war, and no-one could have drawn any other conclusion from the victory celebrations despite the fact that the Queen was Commander-in-Chief of the armed forces.

The imperfect sympathy between the Prime Minister and the Queen provided an opportunity for republicans within the media, notably the Australian-born Rupert Murdoch, to chip away at the ties between Conservative voters and the throne. A useful source of grievance was the cost of the extended royal family, although the right-wing press kept silent about more spectacular examples of government profligacy and celebrated the privatisation of public utilities at a fraction of their true market value. Thus the monarchy had been softened up even before the domestic problems of the Prince of Wales and his siblings hit the headlines.

private sector. However, in other respects state responsibilities increased (and even the privatised utilities were still subject to state regulation). The inescapable problem for Thatcher was that her authority derived from her position within the central state. Judging by her attendance records she had limited respect for parliament, but she could not achieve her aims without it.

The main effect of Thatcher's premiership was to expose the lack of accountability in the UK constitution. Her own electoral success brought the first-past-the-post system into discredit, since she implemented radical changes without coming near to securing a majority of the votes cast. Elsewhere, the 'hiving-off' of state functions eroded the chain of responsibility which formerly ended with departmental ministers. Quangos still disbursed taxpayers' money, but if abuses were exposed their leaders, rather than the ministers who appointed them, would lose their jobs (see Chapter 9). The resignations of Lord Carrington and his colleagues in 1982 proved to be an honourable exception. By the end of the Thatcher years it was much more likely that a minister would resign because of a personal indiscretion than through some professional failing. In turn, this development led to a new media interest in the private lives of senior politicians. During the 1990s the Major government came to be regarded as the epitome of financial and moral iniquity, the embodiment of 'sleaze'. Having served Thatcher's purposes – and, almost uniquely, escaped her reforming impulses – parliament now suffered the consequences. Although most long-established institutions were damaged in the 1980s and 1990s, parliament's reputation probably fell further than the others.

New Labour and constitutional reform

Throughout its history, the Labour Party had tended to regard constitutional reform as a distraction from important business. The experience of Thatcherism changed its outlook. Eighteen years of unavailing struggle against policies which enjoyed only minority support was a sharp reminder of the importance of mediating institutions, like local government, between the individual and the central state. Tactical considerations also played a part. If Labour showed new interest in the constitution it could hope to pick up support from the pressure groups (like Charter 88) which were springing up to defend civil liberties and to agitate for radical constitutional reforms. Tony Blair and Liberal Democrat leader Paddy Ashdown worked together to develop a joint approach on major constitutional issues such as devolution. By the mid-1990s, New Labour was advocating a liberal constitutional reform agenda of devolution, a strengthening of civil liberties, reform of the House of Lords and greater freedom of information. This was very different to the socialist perspective Labour had embraced in the early 1980s which proposed the abolition of the House of Lords, the nationalisation of the Bank of England and withdrawal from the European Community.

At the 1997 general election Labour promised to satisfy these demands. Its manifesto commitments covered four main themes:

- Rights.
- Modernisation.
- Democratisation.
- Decentralisation.

The result of the 1997 general election apparently gave it a suitable mandate for change, especially since the Conservatives made much of their opposition to devolution during the campaign. But Labour's landslide victory was also a source of temptation. Between 1979 and 1997, for understandable reasons, the party had developed an 'oppositionist' mentality. Now that power had fallen into its hands in such a dramatic fashion, the party leadership suddenly woke up to the possibility of using the weapons they had inherited from the Conservatives, rather than decommissioning them as they had intended.

The detail of Labour's constitutional reforms is discussed in the relevant chapters (see also Table 5.1). The reform of the House of Lords is assessed in Chapter 7, the Human Rights Act 1998 in Chapter 8, devolution in Chapter 11 and electoral reform in Chapter 16. For the present purpose it is most convenient to provide an overview, under the headings of 'core' and 'optional' reforms. The core reforms are the ones in which Labour had invested the greatest political capital prior to the 1997 general election; the optional agenda consists of changes which the government could have postponed without serious loss of credibility.

Core reforms

In 1997 Labour won 56 out of 72 Scottish seats at Westminster, and 34 of the 40 constituencies in Wales. In a landslide year it was hardly surprising that these tallies

Table 5.1 New Labour's constitutional reforms

Area	First Blair government (1997–2001)	Second Blair government (2001–5)	Third Blair government (2005–)
Devolution	Creation of: • Scottish Parliament with legislative and tax-raising powers • Welsh Assembly with secondary legislative powers • Northern Ireland Assembly and power-sharing executive • Regional Development Agencies in English regions	2002 White Paper on elected regional assemblies in England; but 'no' vote in referendum in north east (2004) Northern Ireland Assembly suspended (2002–) Changes to role of Scotland Office and Wales Office	Government of Wales Bill 2005 proposes a strengthening of the powers of the Welsh Assembly
Parliament	House of Lords Act 1999 removes all but 92 hereditary peers	Parliament fails to approve any of seven options for House of Lords reform (2003)	
Rights and judiciary	Human Rights Act 1998 incorporates European Convention on Human Rights into UK law Freedom of Information Act 2000	Derogation from Article 5 of Human Rights Act (2001–5) Freedom of Information Act comes into force fully (2005) Constitutional Reform Act (2005) reforms the office of Lord Chancellor, sets up Judicial Appointments Commission and paves the way for a Supreme Court Creation of Department for Constitutional Affairs (2003)	
Electoral reform	New electoral systems for devolved administrations, European Parliament and elected mayors Jenkins Report on electoral reform for Westminster (1998)		Government of Wales Bill 2005 proposes changes to Additional Member System Single Transferable Vote to be used for Scottish local elections from 2007
Participation	Referendums on devolution in Scotland, Wales (1997) and Northern Ireland (1998) Referendum on elected mayor of London (1998) Political Parties, Elections and Referendums Act 2000 regulates conduct of parties, elections and regulations	Trials of alternative voting methods (e.g. at 2004 European Parliament elections)	Proposed referendum on EU Constitution postponed after 'no' votes in France and the Netherlands (2005)

should be the best return the party had ever achieved outside England. Scotland and Wales had suffered badly during the Thatcher–Major years, losing much of their traditional manufacturing industry. Scotland had also been used as a guinea-pig for the poll tax; and under John Major the lack of Conservative legitimacy in Wales had been underlined by the choice of two English MPs, with English seats, to serve as Secretaries of State for Wales. It was natural for the government's opponents in those countries to hope for reform from Labour, despite the unsuccessful devolution experiment of the late 1970s. At the same time, Labour strategists knew that a second failure would fuel an upsurge of support for the Scottish Nationalists and Plaid Cymru.

Devolution was thus an immediate priority for the new government, and referendums were held in both Scotland and Wales almost before the dust had settled from the 1997 general election. The resulting Scottish Parliament and Welsh Assembly reinforced the idea of the UK as a union state (see Chapter 11). The Westminster parliament retains the right to repeal the legislation, and certain powers have been retained. Thus the Scottish Parliament can change the UK rate of income tax, but only by three per cent. Both Scotland and Wales kept their Secretaries of State in London, but in a Cabinet reshuffle in June 2003 they were combined with other posts. Labour's attempts to dictate the leadership of the Welsh party betrayed its hope that the new institutions would be more obedient than autonomous. Ultimately, though, it had to accept meaningful devolution as a necessary price for control at Westminster.

Another core reform was the establishment of the Greater London Authority and an elected mayor of London. Although the party had fared badly since 1979 in the south-east of England, it had retained its enclaves in the capital itself; and the proposals would reverse the abolition of the Greater London Council (GLC), a Conservative decision which Labour activists regarded as purely vindictive. For Labour, there was a most unwelcome reminder of the GLC in the election of its last leader, Ken Livingstone, as London's first mayor – as an independent candidate in 2000 and as the official Labour candidate in 2004. As in Wales, the Labour party fought hard before accepting this consequence of its own reforms.

Labour's 1997 election manifesto also included commitments to incorporate the European Convention on Human Rights into UK law; to introduce a Freedom of Information Act; and to reform the House of Lords. The first of these promises was fulfilled by the Human Rights Act 1998 (see Chapter 8). In opposition, Labour had promised that the incorporated Convention would represent a minimum guarantee of human rights and indicated that it would build further on that framework. However, in the wake of the September 2001 terrorist attacks in the US, the UK government used its right to derogate from the provisions in the Convention relating to detention without either trial or deportation procedures. The UK was the only country to respond to 11 September in this way, raising the question of whether the government had truly accepted a culture of rights, rather than exploiting the issue to discredit the Major government. Critics have argued that the government ought to have devised its own Bill of Rights, specifically applicable to the British context, rather than importing a document whose meaning was often necessarily vague.

The government did introduce a Freedom of Information Bill, which passed in 2000. It gave individuals a greater right of access to personal information held on them by a range of public bodies. However, the Act disappointed radical reformers, and marked a retreat from principles set out in a 1997 White Paper. The full provisions of the Act came into force at the beginning of 2005; it remains to be seen whether it will affect significantly the tradition of secrecy in government dealings.

If New Labour had not taken some action over the Human Rights Convention or freedom of information, its credibility with the civil rights lobby would have been destroyed. Even more pressing was the need to carry out a reform of the

Treasury documents on Britain's exit from the ERM in 1992, when Norman Lamont was Chancellor, were later released under the Freedom of Information Act (Photograph by John Stillwell/PA/jd) (© John Stillwell/PAjd/EMPICS)

House of Lords, which was a long-standing target for party activists. However, as recounted in Chapter 7, the reform of the Lords turned into a fiasco. Ostensibly, the reason was that no parliamentary consensus could be formed behind any of the proposed reforms. But it was difficult to avoid the conclusion that the government simply lacked the political will to satisfy demands even for a partly-elected upper chamber.

Optional reforms

The Labour government of 1997–2001 got off to a dramatic start, with the announcement that interest rates would in future be set by the Monetary Policy Committee of the Bank of England. Far from being a manifesto commitment, this move was a surprise even to some ministers. While it was welcomed by many economists, the decision is best seen in the context of the existing shift from 'government' to 'governance' (see Chapter 9). It was unlikely that future Chancellors of the Exchequer would refuse to take the credit if interest rates helped to secure the twin goals of sustainable economic growth and low inflation. However, there would now be someone else to blame if these targets were not met.

The government also promised a referendum on the electoral system, and after the election it set up a Commission to investigate alternatives. However, the result of the 1997 general election made a referendum (let alone a completed reform) into an option rather than a necessity. Blair had conducted lengthy negotiations with the Liberal Democrat leader, Paddy Ashdown, about the introduction of a proportional voting system. In hindsight, it is clear that he was insuring himself against the possibility of a hung parliament, in which he would need Lib-Dem support. Labour had always been divided on the attractions of proportional representation, and reform lost its attractions when first-past-the-post had spoken so decisively in favour of the party. Despite a well-argued report by the Jenkins Commission, the government ditched any plan for a referendum.

In its 1997 manifesto Labour committed itself to referendums on regional government in England. This was the English equivalent of devolution for Scotland and Wales, and looked like a 'win-win' scenario for Labour. The manifesto recognised that demand for elected regional assemblies varied in different parts of the country; and the areas of highest demand tended to be those, like the north-east, where voters had stayed loyal to Labour through the Thatcher–Major years. It came as a shock to the central party when, in November 2004, a referendum in the north-east rejected the proposal. But the seven-year gap between the original promise and the calling of a referendum suggested a lack of political will on the government's part; and from the outset it had been stressed that the regional assemblies would have very limited powers.

To the general public, the most baffling of Labour's reforms was the proposed abolition of the office of Lord Chancellor. This was the oldest position in government, dating back to 605AD. Yet it had come to symbolise the oddity of the UK constitution, since the holder of the post was simultaneously a member of the executive (as a Cabinet minister) and the legislature (as Speaker of the House of Lords), as well as being head of the judiciary. A decision by the European Court of Human Rights in 1999 suggested that the existence of such a multi-faceted figure was in itself a contravention of the Convention on Human Rights; and since this had just been incorporated into UK law through the Human Rights Act 1998 the continued existence of the Lord Chancellor might have caused grave embarrassment. However, there were also growing demands for reform amongst the judiciary and legal commentators, which might have been a more potent factor in prompting government action.

Whatever the motives behind it, the attempt to abolish the Lord Chancellor turned into another constitutional fiasco (see Chapter 8 for details). The plans were obviously drawn up in haste, as a by-product of a Cabinet reshuffle. It was not even realised that legislation would be required to abolish the ancient post. A year later, the House of Lords agreed that the present Lord Chancellor, Lord Falconer, would no longer appoint judges or sit in a judicial capacity himself. But although Falconer headed a new Department of Constitutional Affairs, replacing the old Lord Chancellor's Department, he was still lumbered with the old title.

For the Conservatives, the affair of the Lord Chancellor finally exposed the government as a group of constitutional vandals. On the other flank, radical reformers lamented the lack of any coherent agenda for modernisation. It seemed that the government only took effective action when its hand was forced by tactical necessities. Even then, in cases like devolution and the Human Rights Act it seemed uneasy with the practical effects of its own handiwork. But when it acted on its own initiative it tended to botch the job. According to these critics everything would have been different if Labour had set out with a worked-out programme of change, culminating in a written constitution.

A new constitutional settlement

The changes introduced by the Blair government add up to the most significant programme of constitutional reform in modern British history. Commentators have rightly talked of a new constitutional settlement replacing the traditional constitution. Many of the institutions and processes associated with the traditional constitution have been affected by New Labour's reforms. Acts creating the Scottish Parliament and Welsh Assembly, and incorporating the European Convention on Human Rights into British law can be regarded as marking a further codification of the UK constitution as they set out in statute law important principles regarding the relationship between institutions and between the state and its citizens.

However, New Labour's reforms can also be seen as evolutionary rather than revolutionary. The Blair governments have not developed an overarching vision of their new constitutional settlement: they have not, for example, introduced a single codified constitution. Reform has also happened in a piecemeal fashion and remained incomplete into Blair's third term. Proposals for a second stage of reform of the House of Lords stalled during the second term and plans for elected regional assemblies were put on ice after the 'no' vote in a referendum in the north-east.

The main principles of the UK constitution outlined earlier in this chapter have been adapted rather than overturned. The Blair governments have consciously steered clear of making direct challenges to these principles. Devolution and the Human Rights Act 1998 have important implications for the sovereignty of the Westminster parliament. But the relevant legislation has sought to safeguard the central position of the doctrine of parliamentary sovereignty within the constitutional settlement. The Scotland Act 1998, for example, makes it clear that the Westminster parliament remains sovereign and retains the power to make laws for Scotland. It also retains the right to repeal the Act and abolish the Scottish Parliament – although this would be highly contentious. In practice, however, Westminster has accepted that it should not legislate on matters devolved to the Scottish Parliament so parliamentary sovereignty no longer means that Westminster has real power to make law across the UK. Devolution has also clarified the UK's status as a union state in which the component nations of the Union are governed in different ways.

The Human Rights Act 1998 also preserves parliamentary sovereignty by dictating that if the courts find legislation to be incompatible with the European Convention on Human Rights, that legislation is not automatically struck down but it is left to parliament to decide on amendments. The Human Rights Act strengthened the rule of law by clarifying and expanding the rights of citizens in statute law. But parliamentary sovereignty allows the government to restrict the rights granted by these Acts, for example by getting a temporary derogation (2001–2005) from Article 5 on the right to liberty and security after the 9/11 terrorist attacks. As we have seen, the government response to the terrorist threat has been to restrict civil liberties. The Constitutional Reform Act 2005 paves the way for a new Supreme Court but this body will not be able to overturn Acts of Parliament.

Criticisms of New Labour's reforms

The post-1997 reforms have been subject to criticism from two main perspectives:

1. A conservative critique which holds that New Labour has damaged the traditional British constitution.
2. A liberal critique which argues that New Labour's reforms have been too timid.

Both perspectives claim that the reforms introduced by the Blair governments have been incoherent. Changes, they argue, have been introduced without the reference point of an overarching constitutional vision and without sufficient thought to their consequences.

1. *The conservative critique.* The conservative critique argues that the pre-1997 traditional constitution needed only pragmatic reform that would respect its underlying principles and gradual evolution. It argues that New Labour's reforms have damaged the fabric of the constitution so that its component parts no longer form a coherent and effective whole. Reforms have also brought about new constitutional problems: devolution has left questions about the status of England unanswered while the Human Rights Act has extended the political role of the judiciary.

   This conservative critique was most associated with the Conservative Party before the 1997 general election. At that time, the Conservatives opposed Scottish and Welsh devolution, electoral reform, reform of the House of Lords and the incorporation of the European Convention of Human Rights into domestic law. But the Conservatives have since changed their position on some of these issues, accepting devolution and supporting a more radical reform of the upper house than the government.

2. *The liberal critique.* New Labour's reforms grew out of a liberal agenda for constitutional change that was also supported by the Liberal Democrats, pressure groups such as Charter 88 and many political commentators. But by the end of Blair's first term, many of these (including the Liberal Democrats) were unhappy with what they saw as the government's limited ambition. They were critical of the absence of vision and the timidity of the constitutional reforms. The reforms were neither sufficiently coherent nor sufficiently radical. The hopes of liberal reformers that the Blair governments would bring about a more democratic House of Lords, proportional representation for Westminster, elected regional assemblies in England, a more effective means of holding the executive accountable, and the abolition of many quangos, were frustrated.

Despite the important constitutional developments since 1997, the issue played a limited role in the 2005 general election campaign. Since plans for regional assemblies in England had stalled, New Labour had little to propose. It promised to complete its reforms of the House of Lords, to strengthen the powers of the Welsh Assembly, revisit the issue of the devolution of power to English regions and cities, and review the operation of the new electoral systems operating in the UK. The Conservatives pledged that in future purely English issues would be decided by English MPs (see Chapter 11). Both of the opposition parties promised to strengthen parliament, in order to check the power of the executive. The biggest divergence was on the subject of civil liberties. The Conservatives wanted to review the Human Rights Act 1998 while the Liberal Democrats expressed forceful opposition to Labour's identity card scheme. As usual, the Liberal Democrats advanced the case for proportional representation for Westminster, which the Conservatives oppose.

Conclusion and summary

The UK constitution has undergone radical changes since 1979. This could be seen as a tribute to its boasted flexibility, since society has also been transformed and it would have been absurd if uncodified conventions and traditions had prevented a degree of modernisation. However, there is plenty of scope for arguing that instead of keeping pace with social change, the UK constitution has been altered primarily to suit the interests of the two main parties. The crucial point here is that while other institutions have been forced to adapt to the wishes of successive governments, the House of Commons has barely been touched. Almost the only change which threatened to curb the already over-mighty executive came at the beginning of the Thatcher years, when the select committees were strengthened (significantly enough, by a minister, Norman St-John Stevas, who was dismissed before his reforms had bedded down). (See Chapter 7)

While Thatcher was an inadvertent constitutional reformer, the Blair government came to office with an ambitious agenda for change. Judged by the record of any previous government, its achievements were highly impressive. But the picture is far less positive when compared with its own intentions. Ultimately the value of a reform programme depends upon the practical results, in terms of government effectiveness and the position of the individual in relation to the state. Despite devolution, it would be difficult to say that there has been any marked change in either of these respects. Indeed, thanks to the government's response to 11 September, many UK citizens feel that traditional understandings of the rule of law are under threat. Labour's 1997 manifesto claimed that UK government was 'centralised, inefficient and bureaucratic'. Few would claim that things were very different by the end of its second term.

Further reading

Detailed texts on the traditional UK institution include V. Bogdanor (ed.), *The British Constitution in the Twentieth Century* (Oxford: Oxford University Press, 2004), R. Brazier, *Constitutional Practice. The Foundations of British Government* (Oxford: Oxford University Press, 3rd edition, 1999). P. Hennessy, *The Hidden Wiring: Unearthing Britain's Constitution*

(London: Orion, 1996) is a shorter introduction and R. Brazier, *Constitutional Reform: Reshaping the British Political System* (Oxford: Oxford University Press, 2nd edition, 1998) a short assessment of the reform agenda. V. Bogdanor, 'Constitutional Reform', in A. Seldon (ed.), *The Blair Effect* (London: Little, Brown, 2001) is an excellent survey of the first Blair government's reforms. N. Johnson, *Reshaping the British Constitution* (London: Palgrave, 2004) is a full and critical assessment. A. King, *Does the United Kingdom still have a Constitution?* (London: Sweet and Maxwell, 2001) is a thought-provoking survey. Lengthier treatments are provided by R. Blackburn and R. Plant (eds), *Constitutional Reform: The Labour Government's Constitutional Reform Agenda* (Harlow: Longman, 1999) and D. Oliver, *Constitutional Reform in the UK* (Oxford: Oxford University Press, 2003).

Authoritative studies of specific areas of the constitution include V. Bogdanor, *The Monarchy and the Constitution* (Oxford: Clarendon Press, 1997) and V. Bogdanor, *Devolution in the United Kingdom* (Oxford: Oxford Paperbacks, 2001).

Websites

The Department for Constitutional Affairs www.dca.gov.uk/ has responsibility for rights, the legal system, reform of the House of Lords and electoral administration. The monarchy has also gone online: www.royal.gov.uk contains information about the current role of the monarchy and offers the chance to email the Queen.

There are authoritative discussions of recent developments on the site by the Constitution Unit, based in University College, London at www.ucl.ac/constitution-unit. Particularly useful are the 'Monitor' newsletters and the summary assessments of constitutional reform under the Blair governments. The Democratic Audit www.democraticaudit.com/ is an independent research unit that has produced audits of democracy in Britain, including constitutional reform. Charter 88 has been the most influential pro-constitutional reform pressure group. Its website www.charter88.org.uk/ includes updates on recent developments and campaign material. Other groups with an interest in constitutional reform include the Electoral Reform Society www.electoral-reform.org.uk/ and the civil liberties group Liberty www.liberty-human-rights.org.uk/.

Chapter 6

The core executive

Learning outcomes

After reading this chapter, you will:

- Be able to evaluate where power lies within the core executive.
- Appreciate the resources that are available to the Prime Minister.
- Understand the role played by the Cabinet and government ministers.
- Be able to assess the relationship between ministers and civil servants.

Introduction

The executive is the dominant branch of British government, taking major decisions on issues of public policy and exercising significant control over the legislative process. The core executive includes the Prime Minister, the Cabinet and its committees, the Prime Minister's Office and the Cabinet Office. The Prime Minister is generally held to be the most important figure in British politics but their power is not fixed and is subject to important constraints. The Cabinet takes relatively few decisions but much work is done within its committees. This chapter explores where power lies within the core executive and assesses Tony Blair's premiership.

The core executive model

Cabinet government: executive power is vested in the Cabinet whose members exercise collective responsibility.

Prime ministerial government: executive power is vested in the Prime Minister who is the dominant figure in the Cabinet system.

An enduring question in the study of British politics has been whether the UK has a system of **Cabinet government** or **prime ministerial government**. Those who favour the cabinet government classification note that the British constitution provides for collective government exercised by senior ministers. In *The English Constitution* (1867), Walter Bagehot described a system of Cabinet government in which the Prime Minister was 'first among equals' but far from an all-powerful figure. Proponents of the prime ministerial government perspective point to the growth in the powers of the Prime Minister and diminished position of Cabinet in the twentieth century. In an essay introducing a 1963 edition of Bagehot's classic text, Cabinet minister Richard Crossman argued that the Prime Minister was the most powerful actor and determined policy with limited reference to the Cabinet.

Core executive: those organisations and actors who coordinate the activities of central government.

An alternative approach to the Cabinet government versus prime ministerial government debate has emerged in the last decade or so. This is the core executive model developed by political scientists such as Martin J. Smith (*The Core Executive in Britain*, Palgrave, 1999). The **core executive** is defined as those organisations and actors who coordinate the activities of central government. It includes the Prime Minister and his or her advisers, the Cabinet and ministerial committees, the Prime Minister's Office and Cabinet Office, and senior civil servants particularly those in the Treasury. The core executive approach argues that the long-running debate on whether Britain has either prime ministerial government or Cabinet government is flawed. Power is not inevitably located in one or the other; instead it is shared between actors who are mutually dependent. The decline in the influence of the Cabinet does not inevitably mean that the Prime Minister is dominant. The key actors in the core executive all have resources but to achieve their goals they need to cooperate and exchange these resources with each other. The core executive is fragmented as it consists of a range of institutions and actors forming overlapping networks. Power is based on dependence not command.

However, the core executive approach recognises that the Prime Minister has considerable resources at his or her disposal. They have powers of patronage, chair the Cabinet, lead a political party and have a high profile in the life of the nation. But the resources available to the Prime Minster are not fixed; how they are utilised depends on a number of variables. These include external factors (e.g. policy success, parliamentary majority, government popularity) and the strategies of resource exchange (e.g. the leadership style) adopted by the Prime Minister. Cabinet ministers also have resources. Most head a government department, giving them authority and policy knowledge. They may also enjoy support within their party and policy success. Departmental civil servants are also significant actors, having detailed knowledge and experience as well as links across the Whitehall network.

A Prime Minister needs the support of Cabinet ministers and officials to achieve their objectives. Smith contends that Margaret Thatcher's downfall became inevitable when she failed to recognise her dependence on the support of Cabinet ministers at a time when her government ran into difficulties. By contrast, John Major navigated the difficult waters of his premiership as he recognised that the Prime Minister needs the support of other actors within the core executive. Huge parliamentary majorities and a concentration of resources in 10 Downing Street strengthened Tony Blair's position but his uneasy relationship with Chancellor Gordon Brown has been a key feature of his premiership.

The Prime Minister

The title of 'Prime Minister' has been bestowed on the holder of the office of First Lord of the Treasury since 1730 with Sir Robert Walpole (1721–42) generally recognised as its first recipient. Commanding the support of the House of Commons and Cabinet, he was able to stamp his imprint on the activities of the government. The role and powers of the Prime Minister (PM) expanded from the mid-nineteenth century when the operation of central government was formalised, government activity mushroomed and the Prime Minister took over many of the prerogative powers of the monarch. However, the powers of the Prime Minister have never been set out in statute law. Tony Blair believes that 'it is not possible to precisely define them' while former Prime Minister Herbert Asquith felt that 'the office of Prime Minister is what the holder chooses and is able to make of it'.

A basic job description of the office would run along the following lines:

> The Prime Minister is head of the government, providing political leadership within the Cabinet system and the country at large. Specific tasks include the appointment and dismissal of government ministers; presiding over the Cabinet and its committees; advising the monarch on many civic and church appointments; deciding the date of general elections, and representing the United Kingdom in the international arena.

Of the eleven post-war premiers, Tony Blair is the only one not to have had previous ministerial experience. He was the youngest to become PM (43) with Churchill the oldest, beginning his second term in office a few days short of his 77th birthday. Churchill, Callaghan and Major are the only ones not to attend university.

The Prime Minister is appointed by the monarch but the choice is usually straightforward as convention dictates that the leader of the largest party in the House of Commons should be invited to form a government. The last occasion when there was some contention occurred when the February 1974 election produced a hung parliament. Conservative leader Edward Heath was given time to explore an alliance with the Liberals before Harold Wilson was invited to form a minority government. The PM requires the continued support of Parliament to stay in office and is also accountable to it. He or she fields questions in the Commons at Prime Minister's Questions every Wednesday for thirty minutes. They are also obliged to make statements to the House on major developments. However research conducted by Patrick Dunleavy and others shows a decline in Prime Ministerial engagement with parliament. The incidence of speeches and votes by Prime Ministers has fallen with the PM often present only for major set-piece events.

The Prime Minister has considerably more resources at his or her disposal than other Cabinet ministers, but they do not give him or her great autonomy. The distribution of power within the core executive creates the potential for prime ministerial predominance but there are also institutional constraints on this (see Table 6.1).

Case study: 6.1

Post-war Prime Ministers

Clement Attlee, Labour (1945–51)

Attlee was the first Labour Prime Minister to lead a majority government, one that created the modern welfare state. He was a low-key but astute leader of a Cabinet of political heavyweights. Died in 1967.

Winston Churchill, Conservative (1951–55)

Voted the greatest Briton in a recent BBC poll, Churchill's reputation as leader was forged during his first spell as Prime Minister (1940–45) during the Second World War. Back in Downing Street, Churchill concentrated on international affairs and allowed Cabinet ministers to shape important parts of domestic policy. Dogged by ill-health, he resigned in 1955. Died in 1965.

Sir Anthony Eden, Conservative (1955–57)

Eden earned a great reputation at the Foreign Office but as Prime Minister led his country to national humiliation at Suez (1956), and kept the Cabinet in the dark on much of the planning of the Anglo-French invasion. He resigned in the following year on the grounds of ill-health. Died in 1977.

Harold Macmillan, Conservative (1957–63)

Dubbed 'Supermac' during a period of economic growth, Macmillan's aristocratic demeanour belied a ruthless streak apparent when he sacked six Cabinet ministers in the 1962 'night of the long knives'. Resigned after prostate surgery. Died in 1986.

Sir Alec Douglas-Home, Conservative (1963–64)

A surprise choice as Conservative leader, the Earl of Home renounced his peerage on becoming Prime Minister and won a parliamentary by-election. He became the only post-war Prime Minister to return to a Cabinet position when taking the post of Foreign Secretary in 1970. Died in 1995.

Harold Wilson, Labour (1964–70 and 1974–76)

A technocrat and party man, Wilson had a reputation for putting party unity before principle. He suspended the doctrine of collective responsibility to allow Cabinet ministers to campaign on opposing sides in the 1975 referendum on EEC membership. His sudden resignation in 1976 still provokes conspiracy theories. Died in 1995.

Edward Heath, Conservative (1970–74)

Heath retreated from his free market agenda in the face of economic and industrial relations problems, but did not face significant dissent from his Cabinet. He achieved his main ambition by securing British entry into the EEC. Died in 2005.

James Callaghan, Labour (1976–79)

Callaghan was the only person to hold all four major offices of state in the twentieth century. The 'Lib–Lab pact' sustained his government in office until defeated in a vote of confidence in 1979. Died in 2005.

Margaret Thatcher, Conservative (1979–90)

The most controversial of post-war Prime Ministers, Thatcher was a conviction politician who gave her name to a New Right ideology. In her first term in office she set the agenda despite having few ideological allies in the Cabinet. But her increasingly dogmatic approach angered Cabinet ministers who withdrew their support when she failed to secure victory in the first ballot of the 1990 Conservative leadership election.

John Major, Conservative (1990–97)

Castigated by his critics as a grey man lacking a 'big idea', but he survived as leader of a deeply-divided party for six and a half years by recognising his dependence on the support of senior Cabinet colleagues.

Tony Blair, Labour (1997–)

The architect of New Labour, Blair saw effective political communications as essential. Centralised power in Downing Street but allowed Chancellor Gordon Brown significant autonomy in economic and social policy. Blair enjoyed high opinion poll ratings in his first term but these waned after he took Britain to war in Iraq.

The power of the Prime Minister is also dependent on factors such as effective leadership and a favourable political climate. The main resources available to the Prime Minister are:

- Powers of patronage.
- The authority of the office.
- Party leadership.
- Public standing.
- Policy-making input.
- The Prime Minister's Office.

Patronage

The Prime Minister is charged with making a range of Crown and public appointments including senior positions within the civil service, military, intelligence and security services, judiciary and Church of England plus positions in the public sector (e.g. Chairman of the BBC) and chairs of key committees of inquiry (e.g. the Hutton Inquiry). Though the PM receives advice on the suitability

Ranking prime ministerial performance

Given the proliferation of league tables in many areas of public life, it is no surprise that UK academics have followed their American counterparts by ranking the performances of heads of the executive branch. A 2004 survey by MORI and the University of Leeds saw 139 political scientists and historians rate the success in office of twentieth century Prime Ministers on a scale of 0 to 10. The results were:

Position	Prime Minister	Party	Period in office	Mean score
1	Clement Attlee	Lab	1945–51	8.34
2	Winston Churchill	Con	1940–45, 1951–55	7.88
3	David Lloyd George	Lib	1916–22	7.33
4	Margaret Thatcher	Con	1979–90	7.14
5	Harold Macmillan	Con	1957–63	6.49
6	Tony Blair	Lab	1997–	6.30
7	Herbert Asquith	Lib	1908–16	6.19
8	Stanley Baldwin	Con	1923–24, 1924–29, 1935–37	6.18
9	Harold Wilson	Lab	1964–70, 1974–76	5.93
10	Lord Salisbury	Con	1895–1902	5.75
11	Henry Campbell-Bannerman	Lib	1906–8	5.01
12	James Callaghan	Lab	1976–79	4.75
13	Edward Heath	Con	1970–74	4.36
14	Ramsay Macdonald	Lab	1924, 1929–31, 1931–35	3.73
15	John Major	Con	1990–97	3.67
16	Andrew Bonar Law	Con	1922–23	3.50
17	Neville Chamberlain	Con	1937–40	3.43
18	Arthur Balfour	Con	1902–05	3.42
19	Alec Douglas-Home	Con	1963–64	3.33
20	Anthony Eden	Con	1955–57	2.53

Source: Ipsos MORI/University of Leeds, www.ipsos-mori.com

A note of caution is required: Attlee's position at the top of the table owes something to the preponderance of Labour supporters (57 per cent) among those surveyed. The 12 per cent of respondents who identified themselves as Conservatives placed Thatcher first. The characteristics rated most important for prime ministerial success were leadership skills (chosen by 64 per cent), sound judgement (42 per cent), good in a crisis (24 per cent), decisiveness (22 per cent) … and luck (22 per cent).

of candidates from people in those fields, it is almost inevitable that political considerations will be particularly significant. Recommendations for most of the honours bestowed by the Crown emanate from Downing Street. Prime Ministers have used the honours system to acknowledge the support of loyal MPs and reward (or entice) wealthy individuals making large donations to their political party. The system has been reformed in recent years so that more honours are given to members of the general public and individuals can nominate people via the Downing Street website. But higher awards are still coloured by party politics.

Table 6.1 Prime ministerial resources and constraints

Resources	Constraints
1. Patronage	
Appoints ministers	Senior colleagues have claims for inclusion
Reshuffles Cabinet	Desirability of ideological balance
Dismisses ministers	Danger of dismissed ministers emerging as rivals for leadership
2. Authority in the Cabinet system	
Chairs Cabinet meetings	Requires Cabinet support on major issues
Determines outcome of Cabinet discussions	Senior ministers have authority and may
Holds bilateral meetings with ministers	challenge PM's preferred policy
Appoints members of Cabinet committees	Ministers have departmental resources
Restructures central government	Not involved in detailed policy-making in Cabinet committees
3. Party leadership	
Leader of largest party in House of Commons	Support of party is not unconditional
Elected by MPs and party members	Possibility of backbench rebellions
4. Public profile	
High public profile	Unpopularity undermines authority
Communicator-in-chief for the government	May become focus of media criticism
Speaks for nation in times of crisis	
Represents UK on world stage	
5. Policy-making Input	
Directs government policy and sets agenda	Lacks time and detailed knowledge
Has authority to get involved in any policy area	Lacks resources provided by a government department
Political rewards of policy success	May be associated with policy failure
6. Prime Minister's Office	
Provides independent advice and support	Prime Minister's Office has limited resources
Helps PM to direct policy	Other departments have own interests

Source: Adapted from M. Garnett and P. Lynch, *AS UK Government and Politics* (Deddington, Philip Allan Updates, 2nd edn, 2005, pp. 271–3)

In the political domain, the most significant awards are peerages because hereditary peerages (until the 1999 reforms) and life peerages have entailed membership of the House of Lords. Prime Ministers have used these patronage powers to alter the party balance within the upper House in their favour. Blair thus created a large number of Labour peers before embarking on reform of the Lords. An independent Appointments Commission now makes recommendations on non-party appointments to the Lords, but the PM retains the power to make party nominations. Like his predecessors, Blair has used his power to create peers to offer ministerial positions to allies such as Lord Irvine and Lord Adonis who were not MPs.

The Prime Minister's most significant patronage powers cover the appointment and dismissal of government ministers. This gives the PM a clear advantage over his colleagues for it is he or she who determines their career path. The Conservative Party gives its leader a free hand in appointing Cabinet ministers but a Labour Prime Minister forming their first Cabinet after a spell in Opposition must choose from those MPs elected to the shadow Cabinet. This tied Blair's hands in 1997 but not in 2001.

In theory the Prime Minister can create a Cabinet in their own image, promoting allies and excluding MPs whose views do not tally with theirs. In practice, the PM's choice is constrained. A Prime Minister should be wary of overlooking senior party figures – including those who have in the past been, or could in future become, rivals for their job. In such cases, US President Lyndon Johnson noted that 'it is probably better to have him inside the tent pissing out, than outside the tent pissing in'. John Major included both of his opponents in the 1990 Conservative Party leadership election, Michael Heseltine and Douglas Hurd, in his Cabinet. Similarly Blair included his 1995 leadership rivals John Prescott and Margaret Beckett. Some politicians are of such standing within the party that they become near-automatic choices for Cabinet and may be able to negotiate their preferred post. In a 1995 meeting in the Granita restaurant in London, press reports suggest that Gordon Brown agreed not to stand against Blair in the Labour leadership contest in return for assurances that he would become Chancellor, exercise significant influence over social policy and that Blair would eventually step down and back a Brown leadership bid. But the precise details of the deal are disputed, notably by allies of the two.

Ideology also colours decisions on Cabinet formation. A Cabinet that excludes members of one wing of a party may be more united but may fuel backbench discontent. In the early 1980s, Thatcher included both 'dries' and 'wets' in her Cabinet but ensured that monetarists held the key economic posts. Major included pro-Europeans and Eurosceptics but sought to prevent either from establishing the upper hand. Blair has appointed ministers allied to himself and Gordon Brown plus some with 'old' Labour sympathies (notably Prescott). Finally, the Prime Minister's choice depends on the pool of talent within their party. Some MPs may be considered too old or inexperienced; others may simply not be up to the job.

Cabinet reshuffles are used to promote allies and successful ministers, demote underachievers and dissenters, and freshen up the government. The ability to dismiss ministers is a powerful weapon in the Prime Minister's armoury but can backfire. A botched reshuffle can raise questions about the Prime Minister's judgement, expose divisions and draw attention to policy failures. Macmillan's sacking of a third of his Cabinet in 1962 (the 'night of the long knives') damaged his standing. Sacked or demoted ministers may also make damaging criticisms as in the case of Norman Lamont who claimed in his 1993 resignation speech that the Major government was 'in office but not in power'. But failure to act can be perceived as weakness: Major was accused of not being ruthless enough in dismissing ministers such as Secretary of State for National Heritage, David Mellor who became embroiled in sex and financial scandal.

Authority in the Cabinet system

The office of Prime Minister gives its holder authority within the Cabinet system. As chair of the Cabinet, the Prime Minister can steer discussions so that their preferred option prevails. The Prime Minister determines the agenda of Cabinet meetings. Potentially difficult issues can be kept off the agenda and dealt with instead in committee or bilateral discussions. The Prime Minister can also control the information presented to ministers by determining the issues and papers brought before Cabinet. The 2004 Butler inquiry found that crucial papers on weapons of mass destruction in Iraq were not placed before the Cabinet (see Controversy 6.1, page 119). It is the Prime Minister who determines which ministers speak in Cabinet, in what order and at what length.

Cabinet discussions rarely end in formal votes. It is the Prime Minister who determines the course of action: this need not be the preferred option of the majority of Cabinet. But this does not give the Prime Minister licence to do as he or she wishes against the advice of colleagues. A Prime Minister who is perceived to be too dominant (or indecisive) will weaken their own position. Ministers also have resources within the core executive. A determined minister may be able to frustrate the Prime Minister's wishes, particularly if they are able to forge an alliance with like-minded ministers. But the Prime Minister should provide a sense of direction and purpose. They also decide the membership, chair and remit of Cabinet committees where much detailed policy work occurs. Committees can be created to examine issues the Prime Minister wants to prioritise though they will not have time to dictate proceedings at committee level.

The Prime Minister can restructure central government by creating or merging government departments. Blair boosted the role and resources of the Prime Minister's Office. The Prime Minister also holds the title of Minister for the Civil Service so is responsible for its organisation and management. Thatcher, Major and Blair all carried out extensive reforms of the civil service (see Chapter 9).

Party leadership

Being leader of the largest party in the House of Commons gives the Prime Minister additional authority. Those with a working majority are well-placed to enact their legislative programme. But rebellions by backbench MPs have become more frequent in the last forty years and can derail government policy. Blair suffered sizeable rebellions on war in Iraq, university tuition fees and foundation hospitals in his second term.

Both Labour and Conservative leaders are currently elected by a combination of MPs and party members. (As the only candidate, Michael Howard was declared Conservative leader in 2003 without recourse to a vote of party members. Proposals to reduce the role of members were blocked in 2005.) This gives the leader added legitimacy. But a party's support for its leader is not unconditional. Thatcher was forced to resign when she failed to muster sufficient support from Conservative MPs in the 1990 leadership contest. Major resigned as Conservative leader (but not as Prime Minister) in 1995, calling a leadership contest that he hoped would strengthen his position. He secured a 218 to 89 vote victory over John Redwood but one-third of the party failed to support him thus leaving his authority in doubt. Few Prime Ministers have enjoyed a more dominant position within their party than Blair. He took Labour from the political wilderness and continued the reform of the party organisation in a way that enhanced the leader's power. But the war in Iraq damaged his standing in the party. Few Labour candidates highlighted Blair's leadership during the 2005 election campaign.

Public standing

The media spotlight on the Prime Minister has intensified so that they have become the communicator-in-chief for the government, articulating government policy and speaking on behalf of the nation during times of crisis. Blair makes frequent statements from outside Number 10, holds monthly media sessions and appears before the Commons Liaison Committee. High opinion poll ratings further strengthen the Prime Minister's hand; poor ratings may persuade MPs that a change of leader is required. Though a divisive figure, Thatcher was widely regarded as a determined leader with a clear agenda. This was a profitable image early in her premiership but thereafter she was regarded as dogmatic and unbending. Blair enjoyed high poll ratings during his first term but excessive 'spin' and war in Iraq lost him the trust of many voters.

Policy-making input

The Prime Minister's authority is not confined to specific fields of government policy. Rather, they have overall charge of government strategy and establish the general tenor of domestic and foreign policy. Thatcher and Blair set out broad goals which they expected departmental ministers to act upon. Economic and foreign affairs are areas in which a Prime Minister is especially likely to take an active interest. The Chancellor and Foreign Secretary are important actors in their own right but the Prime Minister tends to be proactive in setting objectives and coordinating policy given the importance of these areas. The Prime Minister also takes the lead role in times of crisis. Blair took direct charge of the government response to the 2000 fuel blockade, the 2001 foot-and-mouth outbreak and 9/11 terrorist attacks on New York and Washington.

The Prime Minister can also choose to play an active role on issues of particular interest to them. Prime ministerial involvement can make a significant difference, pushing a policy up the agenda or forcing a department to change trajectory. Thatcher was a hands-on politician who intervened in a wide range of domestic policy including local government, education and health. Policy successes such as privatisation strengthened her position but failures such as the poll tax (which she championed) undermined her. Major's key initiatives were the Northern Ireland peace process and the Citizen's Charter. The latter brought some improvement in public services but failed to enthuse voters. Blair's personal initiatives have come largely in foreign affairs (e.g. Kosovo) and Northern Ireland though he has also taken a keen interest in education. Surprisingly he showed only limited interest in constitutional reform, allowing Cabinet committees to fill in the details.

The Prime Minister's Office

There is no Prime Minister's department in British government. Within 10 Downing Street, however, lies the Prime Minister's Office which has grown in importance in the last twenty years. In 2004 it had a staff of 190 made up of both career civil servants and politically-appointed special advisers. As Blair pointed out to the House of Commons Liaison Committee in 2002, this is considerably fewer than assist the German Chancellor or French Prime Minister.

The Prime Minister's Office provides support across the range of prime ministerial responsibilities. Following the 2001 reorganisation, it contains three main directorates headed by special advisers: Policy and Government, Communications and Strategy, and Government and Political Relations. The latter handles relations with the Labour Party and the general public. The Policy and Government Directorate provides policy advice and coordinates the development and implementation of policy across government departments. It provides the Prime Minister with an alternative source of policy advice to that which he receives from Cabinet ministers and includes chief advisers on foreign policy and the European Union. Sections within the directorate deal with honours and appointments, Prime Ministerial visits and relations with parliament.

The Communications and Strategy Directorate oversees policy presentation. It contains three units: the Press Office, the Strategic Communications Unit and the Research and Information Unit. The first of these is important given the heightened media focus on the Prime Minister and New Labour's awareness that the government needs to get its message across effectively. Bernard Ingham and Alastair Campbell, press officers to Thatcher and Blair respectively, were skilled communicators and influential members of the prime ministerial inner circle. The Press Office deals with the media on a day-to-day basis. Briefings to the press used to take place through the 'lobby system' in which statements made by officials from Number 10 could not be attributed. The system is now more open: transcripts of daily press briefings appear on the Number 10 website and the Prime Minister holds 'on-the-record' monthly question and answer sessions with the media. Ministers are required to consult Number 10 before releasing information to the media, but Brown's advisers have promoted his views to the detriment of government unity. The Strategic Communications Unit takes a longer-term perspective on how to get the government's message across. The Research and Information Unit prepares briefings for Number 10.

The Cabinet Office

The bolstering of the Prime Minister's Office has strengthened the PM's position within the core executive. There may be no formal Prime Minister's department, but the restructured Prime Minister's Office is a good approximation of one. Many of the activities of the Cabinet Office (which is physically connected to Number 10) have also been brought within the Prime Minister's remit. It was created in 1916 to provide support for the Cabinet. The key unit is the Cabinet Secretariat which regulates business by circulating papers, preparing the agenda and drawing up the minutes of meetings. It also coordinates policy work on issues that bridge the interests of several departments and acts as a facilitator where disputes between departments arise. The Head of the Home Civil Service (Sir Gus O'Donnell since 2005) is head of the Secretariat and attends Cabinet meetings as Secretary of the Cabinet.

The Economic and Domestic, Defence and Overseas, and European secretariats each provide advice to the Prime Minister and coordinate the work of the Cabinet in policy areas that fall within the remit of more than one government department. The Civil Contingencies Secretariat is charged with improving the UK's resilience against disruptive challenges (e.g. disease or terrorist attack). Created after the 2001 foot-and-mouth epidemic, it identifies potential domestic threats and oversees contingency planning. The Joint Intelligence Committee (JIC) provides ministers with intelligence assessments in defence, security and foreign affairs. It includes senior officials from relevant government departments and the heads of the Secret Intelligence Service (MI6, responsible for foreign intelligence work), the Security Service (MI5, responsible for domestic intelligence work) and Government Communications Headquarters (GCHQ). The chairman of the JIC has direct access to the Prime Minister and heads the Security and Intelligence Secretariat within the Cabinet Office.

The Cabinet Office has taken on other roles under Blair including policy delivery and public service reform. Three units responsible to the Prime Minister were created early in Blair's second term in office: the Prime Minister's Delivery Unit is charged with achieving targets set for departments by the centre; the Strategy Unit develops longer-term policy; and the Office of Public Service Reform is responsible for pushing forward the Prime Minister's reform agenda in education, health, transport and so forth. Other units include the Regulatory Impact Unit (charged with cutting red tape) and the Office of the e-Envoy (responsible for e-government). The Blair government has also sought advice from outside government by setting up task forces (some 300 in total since 1997) and appointing policy 'Tsars' to examine issues ranging from drug misuse to pensions. Following the 2004 Phillis Report, overall responsibility for government communications was transferred to a senior civil servant based in the Cabinet Office.

Leadership style

The core executive model recognises that power is dynamic rather than static. The ability of the Prime Minister to exercise their resources depends on the structural factors assessed above but also on context and agency. Context concerns the circumstances of the time: a Prime Minister enjoying the support of the Cabinet, a large parliamentary majority and high opinion poll ratings will be in a stronger position than an unpopular Prime Minister heading a divided party. A healthy economy and policy success will also empower the Prime Minister whereas recession and policy failure will weaken their position. Unforeseen problems can undermine the Prime Minister's position: when asked what he feared most, Harold Macmillan replied 'events, dear boy, events'.

Agency refers to the actions of political actors – in this case, the leadership style of the Prime Minister. Thatcher was a self-styled 'conviction politician' who imposed her vision and political will on her government, taking a hands-on role in decision-making. She would often announce her decision before Cabinet had chance to discuss the issue in question. Important decisions were taken in Cabinet committees where allies had been placed or in meetings of like-minded ministers and political advisers (e.g. the economist Alan Walters). Thatcher's skilful management of the Cabinet early in her premiership enabled her to cement her authority when she had few ideological allies. But in her third term Thatcher's dogmatic approach exasperated ministers. Economic problems, the poll tax, divisions on Europe and low opinion poll ratings contributed to her downfall. But Thatcher was in part

Margaret Thatcher leaves Downing Street after losing the support of her Cabinet and parliamentary party (© Ken Lennox/Mirrorpix)

the author of her own fate: by ignoring the concerns of ministers she alienated colleagues whose support she ultimately needed. When Thatcher was vulnerable, ministers utilised their own resources and denied her their unequivocal support.

Major adopted a more collegial style. His approach was closer to that of Harold Wilson: both led a divided Cabinet and prioritised short-term deals over medium-term strategy. Cabinet exercised greater influence over the direction of policy. Major's critics depicted him as a weak leader who lacked vision and became overwhelmed by events. He certainly made mistakes and was damaged by policy failures. But Major's management of his Cabinet was sufficient to keep him in office without ever appearing totally secure. By giving some ground to Eurosceptics while working closely with pro-European ministers such as Heseltine and Kenneth Clarke, he lessened the chances of a serious rival emerging.

Blair as prime minister

Tony Blair's period in office has prompted much commentary about changes in the balance of power within the core executive. Seasoned observers depict Blair as an especially powerful Prime Minister. Peter Hennessy describes Blair's as a 'command premiership' driven by 'what Tony wants' while Michael Foley and Labour MP Graham Allen argue that the Blair period has seen the emergence of a 'British presidency'. Blair himself believes that a 'strong centre' is essential for effective government. His special adviser Jonathan Powell reportedly told senior civil servants in 1997 that Blair would replace a 'feudal' system in which departmental 'barons' enjoyed significant autonomy with a 'Napoleonic' system directed from Number 10.

Blair has had little time for Cabinet, as Robin Cook noted in his diary entry for 7 March 2002:

A British presidency?

Michael Foley argues in *The British Presidency* (Manchester University Press, 2000) that the office of British Prime Minister has become more 'presidential'. He claims that the 'presidentialisation' of the post of Prime Minister has created not a pale imitation of the United States Presidency but a 'de facto British Presidency'. Two concepts are identified as central to this development: 'leadership stretch' and 'spatial leadership'. The former refers to the greater emphasis placed on personalised leadership and communications; the latter points to the creation of a sense of distance between the Prime Minister and his or her government and party. The political and media spotlight falls on the Prime Minister to a far greater extent than any other minister – the Prime Minister thus becomes communicator-in-chief for the government and spokesperson for the nation. They claim to represent the public interest and make populist criticisms of the failure of government organisations (e.g. Blair's claim that public sector and civil service lethargy in policy delivery left 'scars on my back'). British election campaigns have also become more akin to their American counterparts in their focus on the leader.

Foley's is an important contribution to debates on Prime Ministerial power but his thesis has been criticised by adherents to the core executive model. They claim that the core executive is characterised by relationships of dependency rather than command – the resources available to the Prime Minister have increased but they still face significant constraints. Richard Heffernan argues in 'Why the Prime Minister cannot be a President: Comparing Institutional Imperatives in Britain and America', *Parliamentary Affairs*, Vol. 58, No. 1 (2005), pp. 53–70 that institutional factors prevent a Prime Minister becoming a President. So, the Prime Minister is indirectly elected, is accountable to the legislature and is head of a collegial executive. But a British Prime Minister also has greater resources than a US President given the former is leader of a political party and the British constitution allows for executive dominance whereas the separation of powers is a guiding principle of the US constitution.

> A momentous event. A real discussion in Cabinet. … Tony does not regard Cabinet as a place for decisions. Normally he avoids having discussions in Cabinet until decisions are taken and announced to it. (*The Point of Departure*, Pocket Books, 2004, p. 115)

Blair prefers to formulate policy and review progress through informal get-togethers with ministers and advisers. The press dubbed this 'sofa government'. The number of Cabinet committees has expanded though some meet infrequently. This informality, the absence of proper records of some meetings and the corresponding neglect of formal Cabinet committee structures has been rebuked by former Heads of the Civil Service Richard Wilson and Robin Butler. The latter's criticisms were contained in the Butler Report on the use of intelligence on Iraq's weapons of mass destruction (see Controversy 6.1). The Hutton Inquiry that preceded it also shone some light on the prevalence of informal meetings and the influence of senior advisers and officials. Blair has also made greater use of bilateral meetings with individual ministers in which he undertakes a policy 'stock-check' and sets new goals. In *The Powers Behind the Prime Minister* (Harper Collins, 2001), Kavanagh

Controversy: **6.1**

Collective government and the war in Iraq

The 2004 *Review of Intelligence on Weapons of Mass Destruction* (HC 898) chaired by Lord Butler was critical of the way in which decisions were taken within the core executive prior to the launch of the war in Iraq in 2003. In the year before the war, Iraq featured as a specific item on the Cabinet agenda on 24 occasions when the Prime Minister, Foreign Secretary or Defence Secretary gave a verbal briefing on developments. But there was little collective discussion in Cabinet and ministers did not have access to key papers. [These included the unamended text of the intelligence on Saddam Hussein's weapons of mass destruction and the Attorney General's initial thoughts on the legality of war.] Without papers being circulated in advance, Butler believed that Cabinet ministers would have not been able fully to 'bring their political judgement and experience to bear on the major decisions for which the Cabinet as a whole must carry responsibility' (paragraph 610).

Nor was the Cabinet Committee machinery used fully: the Defence and Overseas Policy Committee did not meet to discuss Iraq. However, 25 informal meetings between key ministers and military officials were held between April 2002 and March 2003. Changes within the Cabinet Office had had adverse effects. The transfer of the Cabinet Secretary's intelligence role to a new Security and Intelligence Committee had undermined coordination. The combination of two key posts in the Cabinet Secretariat – the Head of the Defence and Overseas Secretariat and Head of European Affairs – with the posts of Prime Minster's advisers on Foreign Affairs and European Affairs respectively meant an excessive concentration of decision-making at the top.

Paragraph 611 offered the sharpest criticism of the Blair style of government and is worth quoting in full:

> We do not suggest that there is or should be an ideal or unchangeable system of collective Government, still less that procedures are in aggregate any less effective now than in earlier times. However, we are concerned that the informality and circumscribed character of the Government's procedures which we saw in the context of policy-making towards Iraq risks reducing the scope for informed collective political judgement. Such risks are particularly significant in a field like the subject of our Review, where hard facts are inherently difficult to come by and the quality of judgement is accordingly all the more important.

The government issued its response to the Butler Report in March 2005 (CM 6492). It claimed: 'The Prime Minister recognises the importance of Cabinet discussion'. Small groups discussing operational military planning and diplomatic strategy would in future operate formally as an ad hoc Cabinet committee. But the government defended the current structure of the Cabinet Office and Cabinet Secretariat.

and Seldon report that Blair held 783 such meetings in his first 25 months in office whereas Major held 272 in the equivalent period.

To achieve a strong centre, Blair has bolstered the Prime Minister's Office, increased the number of special advisers and reorganised the Cabinet Office. He aims to command swathes of government policy from Downing Street as well as improve policy coordination and delivery. Administering policy directives set by Number 10 has become a primary task of civil servants working in the core executive. The creation of the Delivery Unit and Strategy Unit reflect Blair's desire for 'joined-up' government directed from the centre.

These developments have increased the resources available to the Prime Minister but others have had the opposite effect, making it more difficult for the PM to impose his will. The transfer of competences to the devolved administrations, the European Union and Bank of England has removed some policy responsibilities from the core executive. The Blair governments have also been unusual for the extent of the Chancellor of the Exchequer's influence. Blair has granted Gordon Brown unparalleled influence in economic and social policy. Brown chairs the influential Economic Affairs and Public Expenditure Cabinet committee. But the relationship between the two has been fraught, often because of personal ambition though policy differences have also emerged. Brown jealously guarded the Treasury's position as arbiter of the five economic tests for British entry to the single currency, frustrating Blair's hopes of entry.

In his first two terms in office, Blair enjoyed a number of advantages: large parliamentary majorities, a strong position within his party and a largely quiescent Cabinet. But he faced large-scale rebellions by Labour MPs on Iraq, foundation hospitals and tuition fees in his second term, and saw his opinion poll ratings fall. Although Labour won a third term in office in 2005, a reduced parliamentary majority limited Blair's room for manoeuvre and his government suffered its first legislative defeat on the Terrorism Bill. Blair's announcement that he would step down during his third term also weakened his authority. Preparations for an eventual handover to Brown were stepped up in 2006 with the Chancellor given greater scope to speak for the government on a range of domestic and international policies.

Despite the finger pointing, the relationship between Tony Blair and Gordon Brown is one of mutual dependence (© Graeme Robertson/Getty Images)

The Cabinet

The Cabinet system consists of a number of bodies. At the apex is the Cabinet itself, a body consisting of senior government ministers. Below it is a network of committees that report to the Cabinet. Ad hoc meetings of ministers and advisers occur regularly as do bilateral meetings between the PM and ministers. The Cabinet government perspective holds that executive power is vested in a Cabinet whose members exercise collective responsibility. But the political importance of the Cabinet has waned in the modern era to the extent that it now has only a limited role in decision-making. Though the term 'Cabinet government' is of limited explanatory value today, it would be wrong to write off the Cabinet as a 'dignified institution' with little influence.

In the twentieth century, the Cabinet averaged some twenty members. The Cabinet appointed after the 2005 election had 23 members. It contained six women, one fewer than the record set in 2001, and Baroness Amos became only the second black Cabinet minister (Paul Boateng had been the first in 2002). Most Cabinet ministers are heads of government departments. Those heading the main offices of state – the Treasury, Foreign Office and Home Office – plus major spending departments such as health, education and social security are permanent fixtures in the Cabinet. Other posts are recent creations: the Secretary of State for International Development was first appointed to the Cabinet in 1997. Ministers tend to remain in post for longer in the senior Cabinet positions as, for most, this will mark the pinnacle of their career (see Table 6.2). Cabinet ministers must be members of Parliament, to which they are politically accountable. Most are drawn from the House of Commons though the Lord Chancellor (for the moment) and Leader of the House of Lords must be members of the upper house. The last member of the Lords to hold one of the main offices of state was Lord Carrington, Foreign Secretary from 1979 to 1982.

The work of the Cabinet is governed by convention rather than statute law. But authoritative guidance for ministers is contained in the *Ministerial Code*. This was made public in 1992 (when it was known as *Questions of Procedure for Ministers*) and can be viewed on the Cabinet Office website. It includes guidance on ministers' relationships with parliament, the civil service and their constituencies. The *Ministerial Code* specifies that legislative proposals must receive prior approval from the Treasury and government law officers. If a proposal covers the work of another department, the lead minister should seek views on draft proposals. The detailed content of material entering the Cabinet system is largely determined by government departments which also follow guidelines set out by the Cabinet Office.

The Cabinet's main functions are:

- Registering and ratifying decisions taken elsewhere in the Cabinet system.
- Reaching or endorsing final decisions on major issues.
- Settling disputes between government departments.
- Determining government business in parliament.

The *Ministerial Code* states that the main business of the Cabinet system is discussion of major issues that engage the collective responsibility of government and the final resolution of disputes between government departments. The Cabinet

Table 6.2 Cabinet posts in the Blair governments (examples)

Post/policy area	First Blair government (1997–2001)	Second Blair government (2001–05)	Third Blair government (2005–)
Prime Minister	Tony Blair	Tony Blair	Tony Blair
Chancellor of the Exchequer	Gordon Brown	Gordon Brown	Gordon Brown
Home Secretary	Jack Straw	David Blunkett (2001–04) Charles Clarke (2004–05)	Charles Clarke (2005–06) John Reid (2006–)
Foreign Secretary	Robin Cook	Jack Straw	Jack Straw (2005–06) Margaret Beckett (2006–)
Education (Education and Employment, 1997–2001; Education and Skills, 2001–)	David Blunkett	Estelle Morris (2001–02) Charles Clarke (2002–04) Ruth Kelly (2004–05)	Ruth Kelly (2005–06) Alan Johnson (2006–)
Health	Frank Dobson (1997–99) Alan Milburn (1999–2001)	Alan Milburn (2001–03) John Reid (2003–05)	Patricia Hewitt
Environment (Environment, Transport and the Regions, 1997–2001; Environment, Food and Rural Affairs, 2001–)	John Prescott (also Deputy Prime Minister)	Margaret Beckett	Margaret Beckett (2005–06) David Miliband (2006–)
Transport (Environment, Transport and the Regions, 1997–2001; Transport, Local Government and the Regions, 2001–2; Transport 2002–)	John Prescott (also Deputy Prime Minister)	Stephen Byers (2001–2) Alistair Darling (2002–05; also Secretary of State for Scotland)	Alistair Darling (2005–06) Douglas Alexander (2006–) (Both also Secretary of State for Scotland)
Trade and Industry	Margaret Beckett (1997–98) Peter Mandelson (1998) Stephen Byers (1998–2001)	Patricia Hewitt	Alan Johnson (2005–06) Alistair Darling (2006–)

itself takes relatively few decisions though most major issues are discussed by it or reported to it. Most decisions are initiated and concluded in ministerial standing committees, in bilateral meetings or in correspondence between departments. Cabinet acts as a clearing-house for policy, registering or ratifying decisions that have been taken elsewhere. Ministers are discouraged from re-opening issues on which a decision has already been reached. The Cabinet's ability to decide policy is constrained by the infrequency of meetings, its size and the detailed nature of much policy. It is impractical for 23 ministers to engage in detailed discussion of complex issues. Ministers are primarily concerned with their departmental remit and have little time to get to grips fully with other complex issues.

The agenda for Cabinet meetings is determined in advance by the Prime Minister and Cabinet Secretariat. Most sessions include oral reports on parliamentary business and developments in domestic and foreign affairs though time for discussion is limited. The Prime Minister will not want lengthy debate on their favoured course of action but nor is it in their interest for ministerial discontent to fester. Where proposals emanating from a particular department are on the agenda, the appropriate Secretary of State will introduce the item. The Prime Minister sums up the discussion and announces the final outcome. Ministers can advise and warn but the Prime Minister takes the final decision. The Cabinet takes fewer decisions and meets less often than in the recent past. Lengthy discussions on major issues of the day were commonplace thirty years ago but are now infrequent. Cabinet normally met twice per week in the 1950s, now it meets once a week (on a Thursday morning) when parliament is in session. Under Blair meetings usually last for an hour, compared to two hours under Major, though some have been concluded in thirty minutes.

Government policy is often settled with little or no discussion in Cabinet. The final decision on the poll tax was taken by a ministerial committee and only briefly discussed in Cabinet on the day of Heseltine's resignation. Only two other senior ministers were consulted on Blair and Brown's 1997 decision to hand responsibility for setting interest rates to the Bank of England. Nor was the proposed abolition of the office of Lord Chancellor brought before Cabinet.

The *Ministerial Code* states that decisions should where possible be reached in committee or through bilateral agreements and only referred to the Cabinet when disputes have not been resolved. Such appeals may require the Cabinet to decide between the competing claims (e.g. for policy responsibility or resources) of departments. The Cabinet's decision is final. But disputes are not always resolved satisfactorily. In the Westland affair, Secretary of State for Defence, Michael Heseltine resigned from the Cabinet in 1986 in protest at Thatcher's decision that Cabinet would not hear his appeal against a ministerial committee decision on

First among equals? Tony Blair and the Cabinet in 2001 (© Topham/PA)

the award of a defence contract to an American rather than European helicopter manufacturer. Secretary of State for Trade and Industry, Leon Brittan subsequently resigned when it emerged that he had instructed a civil servant to leak information detrimental to Heseltine's case.

Cabinet committees

As we have seen, much detailed decision-making in the core executive occurs within Cabinet committees. The Prime Minister determines their membership and terms of reference. Ministerial standing committees form the layer immediately below the Cabinet in the Cabinet system hierarchy. The most important tend to be:

- Domestic Affairs (DA).
- Economic Affairs, Productivity and Competitiveness (EA).
- Public Services and Expenditure (PSX).
- Defence and Overseas Policy (DOP).
- Legislative Programme (LEG).

Some standing committees delegate detailed work to ministerial sub-committees: a sub-committee on International Terrorism, for example, reports to the Defence and Overseas Policy Committee. Blair reduced the total number of Cabinet committees from 61 to 44 in 2005, of which 21 were standing committees (see Table 6.3). The Prime Minister chaired a total of 15 committees including those on Anti-Social Behaviour, European Union Strategy and Public Services Reform which reflected Blair's own political priorities. He had chaired just four standing committees the year before the 2005 election The change was presented as a response to criticism of Blair's preference for informal over formal decision-making mechanisms. Other senior ministers also chair standing committees. Deputy Prime Minister John Prescott chaired five after 2005 and stood in for the Prime Minister on seven others. The Chancellor chairs the important Economic Affairs, Productivity and Competitiveness and Public Services and Expenditure committees.

Ad hoc committees are also created to examine particular issues. Some have a short lifetime; others sit for the life of the government. The number of sub-committees and ad hoc committees has grown since 1997. Among those meeting in 2005 was an ad hoc committee on the 2012 London Olympics bid. Whereas standing committees are primarily made up of Cabinet ministers, sub-committees and ad hoc committees include junior ministers. The Joint Consultative Committee on Constitutional Reform set up in 1997 was unusual as it included Liberal Democrat MPs but it was little used after Paddy Ashdown stood down as Liberal Democrat leader. Official committees staffed by departmental civil servants shadow their ministerial counterparts

Blair holds frequent meetings of small groups of ministers, advisers and officials. As we have seen, this 'sofa style' has been widely criticised. But a reliance on small groups is not unusual. When such groups meet regularly with the same membership they are sometimes referred to as a 'kitchen Cabinet' or 'inner Cabinet', though no such institution exists officially. Harold Wilson came closest to formalising such arrangements when he established an 'inner Cabinet' to handle the 1968–69 sterling

Table 6.3 Cabinet committees, 2005

Ministerial standing committees and sub-committees	Chairman	Deputy chairman
Anti-Social Behaviour (ASB)	Prime Minister	Deputy Prime Minister
Asylum and Migration (AM)	Prime Minister	Deputy Prime Minister
Civil Contingencies (CCC)	Home Secretary	
Constitutional Affairs (CA)	Deputy Prime Minister	
Sub-committees:		
Electoral Policy (CA(EP))	Deputy Prime Minister	
Freedom of Information (CA(FoI))	Secretary of State for Constitutional Affairs	
Parliamentary Modernisation (CA(PM))	Leader of House of Commons	
Defence and Overseas Policy (DOP)	Prime Minister	Foreign Secretary
Sub-committees:		
International Terrorism (DOP (IT))	Prime Minister	Home Secretary
Protective Security and Resilience (DOP(IT)PSR)	Home Secretary	
Iraq (DOP(I))	Prime Minister	Foreign Secretary
Conflict Prevention and Reconstruction (DOP(CPR))	Foreign Secretary	Secretary of State for International Development
Domestic Affairs (DA)	Deputy Prime Minister	
Sub-committees:		
Ageing Policy (DA(AP))	Secretary of State for Work and Pensions	
Children's Policy (DA(CP))	Secretary of State for Education and Skills	
Communities (DA(C))	Foreign Secretary	
Legal Affairs (DA(L))	Secretary of State for Constitutional Affairs	
Public Health (DA(PH))	Deputy Prime Minister	
Economic Affairs, Productivity and Competitiveness (EAPC)	Chancellor	
Energy and the Environment (EE)	Prime Minister	Deputy Prime Minister
Sub-committee:		
Sustainable Development in Government (EE(S))	Minister of State for Environment, Food and Rural Affairs	
European Policy (EP)	Foreign Secretary	
European Union Strategy (EUS)	Prime Minister	Foreign Secretary
Housing and Planning (HP)	Prime Minister	Deputy Prime Minister
Legislative Programme (LP)	Leader of House of Commons	
Local and Regional Government (LRG)	Deputy Prime Minister	
Sub-Committee:		
Local Government Strategy and Performance (LRG(P))	Minister for Communities and Local Government	
National Health Service Reform (HSR)	Prime Minister	Deputy Prime Minister
Public Services and Expenditure (PSX)	Chancellor	

Table 6.3 Cabinet committees, 2005 (continued)

Ministerial standing committees and sub-committees	Chairman	Deputy chairman
Sub-committee: Electronic Services (PSX(E))	Chief Secretary	
Public Services Reform	Prime Minister	Deputy Prime Minister
Regulation, Bureaucracy & Risk (RB)	Prime Minister	Chancellor
Sub-committees: Panel on Regulatory Accountability (RB(PRA))	Prime Minister	Chancellor / Chancellor of the Duchy of Lancaster
Public Sector Inspection (RB(I))	Chancellor of the Duchy of Lancaster	
Schools Policy (SP)	Prime Minister	Deputy Prime Minister
Science (SI)	Secretary of State for Trade and Industry	
Serious and Organised Crime and Drugs (SOC)	Prime Minister	Deputy Prime Minister
Welfare Reform (WR)	Prime Minister	Chancellor
Restructuring of the European Space and Defence Industry (MISC 5)	Secretary of State for Trade and Industry	
Animal Rights Activists (MISC 13)	Home Secretary	
Universal Banking (MISC 19)	Secretary of State for Work and Pensions	
Olympics (MISC 25)	Foreign Secretary	
London (MISC 26)	Minister for Communities and Local Government	
Efficiency and Relocation (MISC 30)	Chief Secretary	

Source: Cabinet Office, http://www.cabinetoffice.gov.uk/cabsec/index/index.htm

crisis. 'War Cabinets' of senior ministers and military officials meet at times of conflict. This was the case in the 1982 Falklands War, the 1999 conflict in Kosovo and the 2001 war in Afghanistan. Iraq was discussed regularly in Cabinet in the build-up to the war but detailed decisions on the campaign were taken by the 'war Cabinet'.

Ministerial responsibility

In theory, the Cabinet is a united body as it is made up of members of the same party who stood on an agreed manifesto at the general election. However, the sense of unity is undermined by departmental and personal rivalries. Ministers fight for the interests of the government department they represent. Departments provide ministers with authority and expertise which they hope to strengthen by winning additional money and influence over policy. In negotiations on spending, ministers may act primarily as departmental chiefs rather than members of a collegiate body.

Collective responsibility

Collective responsibility: the convention that ministers are responsible collectively for government policy and should resign their post if they cannot support a key element of it.

The necessity of unity for the smooth functioning of the executive is made apparent by a key convention of cabinet government, that of **collective responsibility**. All government ministers assume collective responsibility for decisions made in the Cabinet and its committees, regardless of whether they had opposed the policy or not been consulted about it. Once policy has been settled, ministers should support it or tender their resignation. Two Cabinet ministers (Robin Cook and Clare Short), and two junior ministers (John Denham at the Home Office and Lord Hunt at Health) left the government in 2003 because they disagreed with policy on Iraq (see Table 6.4). Ministers must also keep the details of discussions in the Cabinet system secret, ostensibly to ensure that sensitive information does not enter the public domain but also to hide divisions. Finally, collective responsibility requires the government as a whole to resign if it is defeated in a vote of confidence in the House of Commons. The last time this happened was in 1979 when James Callaghan's Labour government fell after losing a vote on Scottish devolution.

Despite being the first principle of conduct set out in the *Ministerial Code*, collective responsibility has been eroded. It was suspended temporarily during the 1975 referendum on the European Economic Community when Wilson allowed ministers to campaign for either a 'yes' or 'no' vote on an issue that divided the Labour Party. Ministers have also been allowed to vote in different ways on 'free votes' in the House of Commons (e.g. on fox hunting). Recent political history has seen ministers who disagree with government policy often stay in post and make noises about their dissatisfaction in public. This was the case with 'wets' in Thatcher's first administration and Eurosceptics in Major's Cabinet. Clare Short remained in the Cabinet for two months after publicly criticising the war with Iraq before resigning. But Prime Ministers have also ridden roughshod over the convention of collective responsibility by taking decisions with little reference to the Cabinet. Heseltine, Nigel Lawson and Howe all blamed Thatcher's contempt for Cabinet when resigning. Short and Mo Mowlam similarly complained about Blair's failure

Table 6.4 Ministerial resignations: collective responsibility (examples)

Date	Minister	Post	Reason for resignation
1985	Ian Gow	Minister of State, Treasury	Opposed Anglo-Irish Agreement
1986	Michael Heseltine	Secretary of State for Defence	Opposed defence procurement decision ('Westland affair')
1989	Nigel Lawson	Chancellor of the Exchequer	Opposed conduct of economic policy
1990	Sir Geoffrey Howe	Leader of the House of Commons	Opposed conduct of European policy
1995	John Redwood	Secretary of State for Wales	Leadership challenge
1996	David Heathcote-Amory	Paymaster General	Opposed policy on Europe
2000	Peter Kilfoyle	Under-Secretary of State, Defence	Opposed general direction of government policy
2003	Robin Cook	President of the Council and Leader of the House of Commons	Opposed policy on war with Iraq
2003	John Denham	Minister of State, Home Office	Opposed policy on war with Iraq
2003	Lord Hunt	Minister of State, Department of Health	Opposed policy on war with Iraq
2003	Clare Short	Secretary of State for Overseas Development	Opposed policy on Iraq

to consult Cabinet. Finally, the requirement for secrecy has been undermined by ministers revealing details of Cabinet discussions in published diaries (e.g. Richard Crossman, Barbara Castle, Tony Benn and Robin Cook) or by leaking information to the media.

Individual ministerial responsibility

Individual ministerial responsibility: the convention that ministers are responsible to parliament for the policy of their department, the actions of officials working within it, and for their own personal conduct.

According to the convention of **individual ministerial responsibility**, ministers are accountable to parliament for the policies they pursue, for their own conduct and the conduct of civil servants within their department. They must answer questions about the policy and activities of their departments on the floor of the House and in Select Committees. The *Ministerial Code* states that ministers have a duty to give parliament 'as full information as possible' and 'not to deceive or mislead parliament and the public'. Ministers are also expected to follow the seven principles of public life set out by the Committee on Standards in Public Life in 1995: selflessness, integrity, objectivity, accountability, openness, honesty and leadership. But the convention of individual ministerial responsibility is imprecise resulting in a lack of constitutional clarity about the circumstances when ministers should resign. Ministerial resignations may result from a range of circumstances including health worries, a desire for a less stressful lifestyle or the chance of a more lucrative career (though these may conceal political reasons for leaving). Resignations on the grounds of individual ministerial responsibility fall into four main categories, although in practice they often overlap (see Table 6.5):

- Mistakes made within the department.
- Policy failure.
- Political and media pressure.
- Personal misconduct.

The textbook example of a minister resigning because of mistakes made by civil servants is more than fifty years old. Agriculture minister Sir Thomas Dugdale resigned in 1954 ostensibly over mistakes made by civil servants regarding the compulsory purchase of land in the Crichel Down case. But he did not fall on his sword without political pressure being applied. The norm is that ministers are not obliged to resign if misjudgements can be traced to the actions (or inaction) of civil servants rather than to ministers directly. In cases such as the sale of arms to Sierra Leone (1998–99), official inquiries pointed to errors by officials and thus allowed ministers to deny direct responsibility. The BSE inquiry was critical of ministers and civil servants but those ministers accused of misleading the public had left office long before the publication of the Phillips Report in 2000.

Confusion over the responsibility of ministers and civil servants was apparent in the controversy provoked by the 1996 Scott Report on the sale of arms to Iraq by British companies in the late 1980s. It found that ministers (assisted by civil servants) had misled parliament by concealing a change in government policy on arms sales. Despite the criticism, no minister resigned. Instead the government held that ministers were only culpable if they 'knowingly' misled parliament. They could not be held accountable for operational decisions taken by officials of which ministers had no knowledge.

Table 6.5 Ministerial resignations: individual ministerial responsibility (examples)

Date	Minister	Post	Reason for resignation
1963	John Profumo	Minister of War	Misled parliament about sexual relationship with call-girl
1967	James Callaghan	Chancellor of the Exchequer	Devaluation of sterling (became Home Secretary in reshuffle)
1972	Reginald Maudling	Home Secretary	Financial misconduct
1982	Lord Carrington (and two others)	Foreign Secretary	Misjudgements made before the Argentine invasion of the Falkland Islands
1983	Cecil Parkinson	Secretary of State for Trade and Industry	Extra-marital affair
1986	Leon Brittan	Secretary of State for Trade and Industry	Authorised leak of confidential letter
1988	Edwina Currie	Under-Secretary of State, Health	Errors of judgement on public health issue
1992	David Mellor	Secretary of State for National Heritage	Financial dealings and extra-marital affair
1994	Neil Hamilton and Tim Smith	Minister of Corporate Affairs, Board of Trade and Minister of State, Northern Ireland	'Cash for questions'
1995	Jonathan Aitken	Chief Secretary to the Treasury	Launched libel trial
1996	David Willetts	Paymaster General	Misled parliament
1998	Ron Davies	Secretary of State for Wales	Allegations about personal conduct
1998	Peter Mandelson	Secretary of State for Trade and Industry	Failed to disclose loan
2001	Peter Mandelson	Secretary of State for Northern Ireland	Allegations of abuse of office
2002	Stephen Byers	Secretary of State for Transport	Policy problems and misled parliament on departmental management
2002	Estelle Morris	Secretary of State for Education and Skills	Policy problems and self-criticism
2004	Beverly Hughes	Minister of State, Home Office	Misled parliament
2004	David Blunkett	Home Secretary	Allegations of abuse of office
2005	David Blunkett	Secretary of State for Work and Pensions	Failed to consult committee on private sector job

The creation of Next Steps agencies which deliver public services but have an arms-length relationship with Whitehall departments has further muddied the waters (see Chapter 9). Following a series of prison escapes, Home Secretary Michael Howard sacked Derek Lewis, the Chief Executive of the Prison Service in 1995. Howard was ultimately responsible for policy but pinned the blame on Lewis who was responsible for the day-to-day operational management of prisons but had seen his room for manoeuvre constrained by Howard's interventions. It is worth noting that the distinction between operational and policy issues is not new: in the days before Next Steps agencies, Northern Ireland Secretary James Prior did not resign after a mass escape from the Maze prison in 1983.

A classic example of ministerial resignation in response to policy failure occurred when Foreign Secretary Lord Carrington and two junior ministers resigned following the Argentine invasion of the Falkland Islands in 1982. Yet Defence Secretary John Nott remained in office. Inconsistency is also apparent in the cases of two Chancellors, James Callaghan and Norman Lamont. Callaghan resigned after the devaluation of sterling in 1967 but Lamont survived sterling's exit from the ERM in 1992. Resignations on the grounds of policy failure are the exception rather than the norm. Home Secretary Charles Clarke refused to resign in April

2006 when it became clear that the Home Office had failed to deport – or record the location of – foreign nationals who had been released after serving prison sentences. Clarke accepted responsibility but, contrary to the convention of individual ministerial responsibility, argued that he should remain in post so that he could rectify mistakes. Blair supported Clarke's reasoning initially but then sacked him in a Cabinet reshuffle in May 2006.

Ministerial resignations often result from cumulative pressure rather than a single incidence of failure. The Prime Minister, House of Commons, political party or media can all apply pressure on ministers they perceive to be under-performing. The resignations of Stephen Byers and Estelle Morris in 2002 fall into this category. Byers endured failures in the transport system, disputes between advisers and civil servants in the Department for Transport, Local Government and the Regions (DTLR) – on which matter he gave an 'incorrect understanding' to the Commons – and an adverse press. Morris claimed that she resigned because she felt she was not up to the job of Secretary of State for Education (she later took a job in higher education but returned to government as a junior minister in 2005). Feminists praised her honesty but Morris had earlier pledged to resign if government targets on literacy and numeracy were not met. Failure to provide full and accurate information to parliament or the public led to the resignations of David Willetts, Beverly Hughes and David Blunkett.

Personal misconduct caused several ministers in the Major and Blair governments to stand down. Allegations of financial 'sleaze' or abuse of office often bring about a resignation. Neil Hamilton and Tim Smith resigned in 1994 when the 'cash for questions' scandal blew up. Peter Mandelson was twice obliged to leave the Blair Cabinet, firstly when details of an undisclosed loan emerged (1998) and then when it was suggested that he misused his position by speaking to the immigration minister about obtaining British citizenship for an Indian businessman Srichand Hinduja (2001). A subsequent inquiry on the latter exonerated Mandelson but the case illustrated that a minister is unlikely to remain in office if the Prime Minister considers media publicity too damaging or has lost faith in a minister. David Blunkett also resigned from the Cabinet twice, in 2004 and 2006, having fallen foul of the *Ministerial Code* (see Case study 6.2).

In today's liberal social climate, sex scandals do not automatically trigger resignation. Cecil Parkinson resigned in 1983 when his former secretary Sarah Keays made damaging accusations about his conduct during an affair that produced a daughter. Robin Cook and John Prescott later stayed in post when their extra-marital affairs were exposed. A minister's chances of survival again depend upon the Prime Minister's view on whether the minister made serious errors of judgement. John Major can consider himself fortunate that his affair with Edwina Currie while both were junior members of the Thatcher government was not revealed during his prime ministerial 'back to basics' campaign which the press interpreted as an attempt to restore traditional moral values.

Case study: 6.2

The fall and fall of David Blunkett

David Blunkett is one of two Cabinet ministers to have resigned from the Blair government on the grounds of individual ministerial responsibility, be given a second chance in Cabinet only to be forced to resign again (Peter Mandelson is the other). Blunkett resigned his post as Home Secretary in December 2004 after allegations emerged about the relatively short time it took for the approval of a visa for a nanny, Leoncia Casalme, employed by his ex-lover Kimberly Quinn. When an email from Blunkett's office to immigration officials saying 'no favours but slightly quicker' in relation to the visa application came to light, Blunkett stood down. An independent inquiry chaired by former civil servant Sir Alan Budd found a 'chain of events' linking Blunkett to a change in the decision on Mrs Casalme's application. Budd did not find conclusive evidence that Blunkett had directly intervened to fast-track the application. It was the suggestion of improper use of office not his sexual relationship with a married woman that brought about the resignation.

Six months after returning to the Cabinet as Secretary of State for Pensions, Blunkett resigned again in November 2005. While out of the Cabinet, Blunkett had been a director of DNA Bioscience, a company that had won contracts from the government. He broke the *Ministerial Code* by failing to consult the Independent Advisory Committee on Business Appointments, which former ministers must approach before taking a post in the private sector within two years of leaving office, when taking the position.

Ministers and departments

The British government contains more than one hundred ministers. Senior ministers hold the rank of Secretary of State, sit in the Cabinet and head government departments. Below them in the hierarchy come Ministers of State then Parliamentary Under-Secretaries who have specific responsibilities within their departments. Ministers perform a number of roles. The most significant is policy leadership. Some ministers (e.g. Howard and Blunkett at the Home Office) have clear agendas and push through major reform programmes. But few ministers have the time or knowledge to play a hands-on role across their brief so tend to concentrate on policy initiation and selection. Within their departments, ministers set strategic objectives but leave many management decisions to senior civil servants. Ministers also act as departmental representatives in the core executive, European Union and parliament.

Government departments are the primary administrative units of central government. They are located in the Whitehall area of London – hence the usage of the term 'Whitehall' to describe the bureaucratic apparatus of central government – although civil service posts are being relocated to the English regions. In major departments a Cabinet minister (normally a Secretary of State) is the political head and the Permanent Secretary is the most senior civil servant. Departments are organised according to function (i.e. the policy area they are responsible for, such as health) or the sections of society they serve (e.g. those receiving social security benefits). The work of some departments (e.g. the Ministry of Defence) covers the whole of the UK but some (e.g. the Department for Work and Pensions) cover England, Scotland and Wales but not Northern Ireland. On matters devolved to the Scottish Parliament, central government departments are responsible for England and Wales only (e.g. the Department for Education and Skills). The functions of government departments include providing policy advice to ministers, managing public spending and fostering relations with interested parties. Whitehall departments also oversee the provision of public services though responsibility for much day-to-day policy delivery has been transferred to semi-autonomous executive agencies (see Chapter 9).

Governments often restructure departments and reallocate responsibilities to reflect their priorities or the preferences of senior ministers. Responsibility for transport was subsumed within the Department for the Environment, Transport and the Regions in 1997 to reflect the policy interests of John Prescott, was then shifted to a Department of Transport, Local Government and the Regions in 2001, before becoming a separate department in 2002 (see Table 6.2). The Treasury is the most important department in Whitehall. It controls public spending and other departments require its approval to undertake major new financial commitments. Under the Comprehensive Spending Review, the Treasury sets firm spending limits for each government department over a three-year cycle. This has allowed the Chancellor to mould policy development in high-spending departments such as health and social security. Treasury monitoring also occurs through Public Service Agreements which spell out delivery targets agreed with departments.

The civil service

Civil servant: an official employed in a civil capacity by the Crown.

Government departments are staffed by **civil servants**, career administrators who are responsible to the Crown. The number of full-time civil servants was reduced from 732,000 in 1979 to below half a million in the mid-1990s before rising to 554,000 in 2004. Following the Gershon Report on civil service efficiency, the Blair government announced plans to cut some 80,000 jobs and transfer others. The civil service is structured along hierarchical lines in which posts range from junior positions (e.g. clerks) to those in the 3000-strong senior civil service.

The civil service has traditionally operated according to four principles: impartiality, anonymity, permanence and meritocracy. As civil servants serve the Crown rather than the government of the day, they are expected to be politically impartial. Anonymity means that individual civil servants should not be identified as the author of advice to ministers. All civil servants must sign the Official Secrets Act and keep government information secret. Civil servants may be called before parliamentary committees where, under the 'Osmotherly rules' drawn up by a civil servant in 1980, they give evidence 'on behalf of ministers and under their directions'. Permanence means that civil servants stay in their posts when there is a change of government.

The British civil service is unusual in that civil servants are not political appointments but are made on merit. Government departments have traditionally been staffed not by experts (in, say, law or economics) but by generalists appointed on merit. Recruitment through competitive examinations and interviews was put in place by the 1854 Northcote–Trevelyan Report and remained little changed for almost 150 years. Two important changes have occurred in the last two decades. First, more outsiders have been recruited from the private sector: many chief executives of Next Steps agencies were brought in from private companies rather than promoted from within. A drive to recruit people with specialist skills and experience in finance, IT, communications and policy has been launched. Second, efforts have been made to increase diversity in the senior civil service. Into the 1980s, senior ranks were largely made up of white, middle-class men who had a public school and Oxbridge education. By 2004 women made up 28 per cent of the senior civil service and ethnic minorities 3 per cent.

These principles have come under strain in recent years as concern has grown that the civil service is being politicised and its neutrality undermined. There are suggestions that senior civil servants felt to be out of sympathy with government policy have fared less well in promotions than those perceived to be more amenable. Given the greater emphasis on policy presentation, ministers expect civil servants to publicise policy achievements. The boundary between legitimate civil service work and party political activity is not clear, but such actions could be deemed as justifying rather than simply reporting policy. Civil service impartiality is more obviously threatened when civil servants are asked to undertake research on proposals from opposition parties so that ministers can discredit them.

Civil service anonymity has also been eroded. Sensitive information has, on occasion, been leaked by civil servants. Foreign Office clerk Sarah Tisdale was jailed for six months for leaking information about the deployment of cruise missiles but a year later a jury cleared Clive Ponting, a senior civil servant in the Ministry of Defence, of breaking the Official Secrets Act 1911 by revealing details of the 1982 sinking of the Argentine cruiser, the *General Belgrano*. David Shayler revealed information about MI5's covert activities in the late 1990s. He claimed to be acting in the public interest but was jailed for six months in 2002 for breaking the Official Secrets Act. Of greater significance is the willingness of ministers to allow civil servants to be named and identified as being responsible for mistakes or misjudgements. Chief executives of Next Steps agencies have faced tough questioning by parliamentary committees. The 2003 suicide of Dr David Kelly, an expert on Iraq's weapons of mass destruction at the Ministry of Defence, served as a warning about the dangers of apportioning blame. The Freedom of Information Act has also brought about the release of policy advice produced by civil servants.

The permanence of the civil service has been undermined by the hiving off of policy implementation responsibilities to executive agencies with their own management and pay structures. As we will see in Chapter 9, new methods of management, market-testing, contracting-out and recruitment from the private sector have ended the traditional model of a unified, hierarchical civil service in which officials have a 'job for life'.

Special advisers

Special adviser: a temporary political appointment made by a minister.

The prominence of **special advisers** has also impacted upon the role and status of civil servants. Their number increased from 38 under Major to 87 under Blair in 2004, 29 of whom worked for the Prime Minister compared to three under Major. Special advisers are not career civil servants but political appointments made by ministers. They fall into two main categories, policy advisers and media advisers (spin-doctors). Special advisers are permitted to convey instructions and commission work from civil servants. Two special advisers in Number 10 – Chief of Staff Jonathan Powell and press officer then Director of Communications Alastair Campbell – have been allowed to exercise management control over civil servants. David Hill was not afforded this authority when he replaced Campbell in 2003. Advice from Treasury civil servants was routinely channelled through Brown's Chief Economic Adviser Ed Balls (1997–2005). The Blair governments' use of media advisers rather than civil servants to communicate government policy has also created tensions. This was most apparent at the DTLR where the differences between Jo Moore, media adviser to Secretary of State Stephen Byers, and Martin Sixsmith, the civil servant in charge of communications, cost all three their jobs in 2001–02.

The Committee on Standards in Public Life (2000) concluded that the increased influence of special advisers had not brought about the politicisation of the civil service. But it did recommend a new Code of Conduct and a limit on numbers. A 2001 House of Commons Select Committee on Public Administration investigation also felt that special advisers need not threaten the civil service but recommended improved accountability and clarity in funding. Both committees pressed for a Civil Service Act to set out the constitutional framework within which the civil service operates. A Civil Service Code setting out the duties of civil servants came into force in 1996 but critics believed that it did not spell out fully the relationship between ministers and civil servants. The government finally produced a draft Civil Service Bill (Cm 6373) in 2004. It proposed that special advisers should not authorise expenditure, issue orders to civil servants or discharge any statutory power. Two special advisers at Number 10 would be exempt. Advisers would still be able to commission work from civil servants. The draft Bill did not give the Civil Service Commissioners greater powers to guard against the politicisation of the civil service. Their role remains that of ensuring that appointments are made on merit.

Civil servants and ministers

The civil service is active throughout the policy-making process, consulting with interested parties, formulating options, providing advice to ministers, drawing up legislation and overseeing the policy implementation. Government departments build up networks of contacts with interest groups within their policy field. The Department of Transport, for example, has lines of communication with producer, consumer and promotional groups including the motor industry, multinational oil companies, road users groups, local authorities and the environmental movement. Concerns arise if some groups are perceived to enjoy a privileged relationship. The old Ministry of Agriculture, Food and Fisheries (MAFF) was accused of reflecting the interests of producers (the farmers) rather than those of consumers. MAFF's record in protecting consumer interests in cases such as salmonella in eggs and BSE in cattle was poor. In 2001, agriculture was subsumed in a new Department for the Environment, Food and Rural Affairs (DEFRA) which was expected to take fuller account of the interests of consumers and the environment.

Civil servants in Whitehall provide ministers with policy advice – although as we will see in Chapter 9, the vast majority of civil servants are involved in the delivery of services and work in executive agencies. The 'Westminster Model' perspective is that civil servants advise but it is ministers who decide and are accountable to Parliament. The relationship is less clear cut in practice because ministers and civil servants each have resources. The contacts with interest groups that civil servants forge, their greater experience and expertise plus their control over information give them an advantage over ministers. Civil servants can thus steer ministers towards the options they feel are most practicable and affordable.

Concerns that civil servants had too great an influence in the policy process were aired by critics from the left and the right in the 1970s and 1980s. On the left, Tony Benn's diaries reveal his fears that his radical agenda was being frustrated by the institutional conservatism of the civil service. The New Right complained that civil servants were maximising their own resources rather than promoting efficiency and enterprise. The BBC comedy *Yes Minister* depicted memorably the power-struggle between Whitehall mandarin Sir Humphrey Appleby and the minister James Hacker whose proposals he sought to frustrate. Since the mid-1990s the balance appears to have shifted in favour of ministers. Special advisers appointed by ministers provide an alternative source of policy advice to department civil servants. The civil service has also been fragmented by the creation of executive agencies and its culture changed by the introduction of new managerial techniques. Senior civil servants now spend less time on frontline policy and more on departmental management.

Some government departments develop a strong ethos that informs the policy advice presented to ministers. The Foreign and Commonwealth Office has a pro-European outlook that Thatcher in particular disapproved of. By contrast the Treasury appears institutionally sceptical about British membership of the European single currency, reinforcing Brown's own doubts. It had supported ERM membership in the late 1980s but Treasury documents released in 2005 assessing Sterling's exit on Black Wednesday in 1992 revealed doubts about fixed exchange rates and criticism of the actions of politicians. Ministers may find it difficult to force through changes in policy that run against the grain of thinking in their department, but successive Conservative ministers managed to overturn the interventionist ethos of the Department of Trade and Industry and instil a *laissez-faire* outlook.

The role of the civil service in the implementation stage of the policy-making process has also changed. Since the mid-1980s much of its policy implementation role has been transferred from Whitehall to semi-autonomous Next Steps agencies. Government departments oversee the policy delivery records of these bodies but leave the day-to-day administration to them.

Conclusion and summary

Two countervailing trends are apparent in the contemporary core executive: central-isation and fragmentation. Resources have been further concentrated at Number 10 thereby increasing the potential for prime ministerial predominance. Blair's quest for a 'strong centre' has seen the Prime Minister's Office strengthened and Number 10's role in policy-making and delivery extended through bilateral meetings with ministers and the creation of the Strategy Unit and Delivery Unit within the Cabinet Office. Cabinet plays only a limited role in decision-making; many decisions are reached in informal meetings of an inner circle of ministers and advisers. The strengthening of the centre has improved the support available to the Prime Minster in the absence of a formal Prime Minister's department. But the neglect of formal mechanisms for decision-making, the influence of special advisers and an excessive focus on government communications have raised concerns about the health of British democracy. As the Butler Report implied, one need not hold an idealised view of collective government to have concerns about the absence of checks and balances at the centre. A culture in which a coterie of advisers and ministers tell a Prime Minister what they think he or she wants to hear is not conducive to good government.

The second trend evident in the core executive is fragmentation. Blair may appear a more dominant Prime Minister than many of his predecessors but he has allowed (sometimes to his regret) Chancellor Gordon Brown to set the agenda in economic and social policy as well as extend Treasury control of departmental spending. The Blair governments have also transferred policy competences away from the core executive to bodies such as the Scottish Parliament, Welsh Assembly and European Union. Interest rates were a prominent concern of Thatcher and her Chancellors but these are now determined by the Bank of England's Monetary Policy Committee. As Chapter 9 will examine, the fragmentation of the civil service and emergence of new forms of governance has weakened the centre's capacity to dictate policy. The Cabinet Office's remit on 'joined-up government' has only addressed this partially. The same chapter will also explore the impact of globalisation. A Prime Minister in the early twenty-first century enjoys greater resources within the core executive but his predecessor one hundred years before took decisions that impacted upon the lives of hundreds of millions of people living in the British Empire. Definitive verdicts on where power lies within the core executive are thus elusive. The resources available to the Prime Minister vary over time according to the institutional practices prevalent within the core executive, the leadership style of the Prime Minister and the wider political environment.

Further reading

P. Hennessy, *The Prime Minister. The Office and its Holders since 1945* (Penguin, 2001) offers an accessible account of the development of the office of Prime Minister. M. Smith, *The Core Executive* (Palgrave, 1999); M. Smith, 'Prime Minister and Cabinet', in J. Fisher, D. Denver and J. Benyon (eds), *Central Debates in British Politics* (Longman, 2003), and R. Rhodes and P. Dunleavy (eds), *Prime Minister, Cabinet & Core Executive* (Palgrave, 1995) introduce the core executive model. R. Heffernan, 'Prime Ministerial predominance? Core Executive Politics in the UK', *British Journal of Politics and International Relations*, Vol. 5, No. 3 (2003), pp. 347–72 is also worth consulting. The 'British Presidency' thesis is developed in M. Foley, *The British Presidency* (Manchester University Press, 2000). R. Heffernan, 'Why the Prime Minister cannot be a President: Comparing Institutional Imperatives in Britain and America', *Parliamentary Affairs*, Vol. 58, No. 1 (2005), pp. 53–70 offers a critique. D. Kavanagh and A. Seldon, *The Powers Behind the Prime Minister* (Harper Collins, 2001) and M. Burch and I. Holliday, 'The Prime Minister's and Cabinet Offices: An Executive Office in all but Name' *Parliamentary Affairs*, Vol. 52, No. 1 (1999), pp. 32–45 examine the Downing Street support network.

On Blair as Prime Minister, see M. Burch and I. Holliday 'The Blair Government and the Core Executive', *Government and Opposition*, Vol. 39, No. 1 (2004), pp. 1–21, and P. Hennessy, 'Rulers and Servants of the State: The Blair Style of Government 1997–2004', *Parliamentary Affairs*, Vol. 58, No. 1 (2005), pp. 6–16. Two accounts by journalists offer interesting insights: A. Rawnsley, *Servants of the People* (Penguin, 2001) and J. Naughtie, *The Rivals* (Fourth Estate, 2002). A. Seldon, *Blair* (Free Press, 2005) is the most detailed biography. R. Cook, *The Point of Departure* (Pocket Books, 2004) is a revealing diary by a former Cabinet minister.

Introductory texts on the Cabinet include S. James, *British Cabinet Government* (Routledge, 1999) and M. Burch and I. Holliday, *The British Cabinet System* (Harvester Wheatsheaf, 1995). The role of ministers is explored in D. Marsh *et al.*: 'Reassessing the Role of Departmental Cabinet Ministers', *Public Administration*, Vol. 78, No. 2, 2000 and V. Bogdanor, 'Ministerial Accountability', *Parliamentary Affairs*, Vol. 50, No. 1, 1997. On government departments, see D. Kavanagh and D. Richards, 'Departmentalism and Joined-up Government', *Parliamentary Affairs*, Vol. 54, No. 1 (2001), pp. 1–18. P. Hennessy, *Whitehall* (Pimlico, 2001) is the best study of the civil service. M. Stanley, *How to be a Civil Servant* (Methuen, 2004) provides an insider guide to the role. On civil service reform, see R. Rhodes, 'New Labour's Civil Service: Summing-up Joining-up', *Political Quarterly*, Vol. 71, No. 2 (2000), pp. 151–66 and V. Bogdanor, 'Civil Service Reform: A Critique', *Political Quarterly*, Vol. 72, No. 3 (2001), pp. 291–9.

Websites

The 10 Downing Street website www.number-10.gov.uk/ provides transcripts of the Prime Minister's speeches and of daily press briefings but includes little on the Prime Minister's Office. The Cabinet Office website www.cabinet-office.gov.uk/ has detailed information on the Ministerial Code, Cabinet committees and the civil service. The www.direct.gov.uk/ was set up as part of the e-government strategy. It includes an A–Z of central government with links. On the civil service, the Cabinet Office site www.civilservice.gov.uk/ and the companion site to Martin Stanley's book *How to be a Civil Servant* www.civilservant.org.uk/ cover the organisation and its reform.

Chapter 7

Parliament

Learning outcomes

After reading this chapter, you will:

- Be able to summarise the main functions of the House of Commons and the House of Lords.
- Understand the effect of the 'fusion' between executive and legislature in the UK.
- Be in a position to assess recent proposals for reform in the light of public dissatisfaction with Westminster politics in general.

Introduction

For most democratic theorists, the nature and status of the legislative body in any political system is a primary consideration. While the executive and judicial branches of government play crucial roles in their respective spheres, the legislature is the *creative* element of any constitution. It is essential in a representative democracy that the law-making body should broadly reflect public opinion, and its members should be directly accountable to voters in case they fail to discharge this function.

The British Houses of Parliament based in the Palace of Westminster are among the best-known symbols of democratic government. However, this familiarity reflects the relative longevity of representative British institutions, and the nation's former position at the centre of a worldwide empire, rather than the success of today's parliament as a legislature. It can be argued, indeed, that the prominence of

Westminster as a political icon has become an obstacle to a realistic understanding of the legislature within the uncodified British constitution. From the viewpoint of liberal democracy the House of Commons is at best a curious anomaly; at worst, critics portray it as a travesty of constitutional principle, a mere rubber-stamp for decisions taken by the executive. The so-called 'upper chamber', the House of Lords, is even more difficult to defend, since even after recent reforms its members are not accountable to the general public through elections.

Few observers nowadays argue that the UK parliament is working well, when judged against the expected functions of a healthy legislature. Some go so far as to speak of a crisis of democratic institutions, which is fostering apathy among the British public. Thus while discussions of this subject still need to focus on the alleged failings of parliament and on proposals for reform, the situation cannot be understood without some explanation of the fact that while almost every aspect of public life in Britain has been subjected to radical change in recent years, the House of Commons has emerged almost unscathed.

The House of Commons

In assessing the role of the elected House of Commons in the British political system, five main features stand out:

- accountability;
- representation;
- debating;
- passing legislation;
- recruitment of leaders.

The order in which the various functions are treated below does not necessarily reflect their relative importance, but has been chosen to evaluate the performance of today's House of Commons. At the outset, though, it is useful to note a possible tension between the role of the Commons as a pool of potential ministers (the 'recruitment' function) and the other listed roles.

In most liberal democracies the executive and the legislature are strictly separated, as in the US and France. In these states, politicians who become heads of government tend to have served their apprenticeship by performing executive functions at lower governmental levels (e.g. as state governors or city mayors) rather than by winning a reputation in a legislative assembly. In Britain, by contrast, convention dictates that all ministers must be members of one of the two Houses. Defenders of this arrangement can cite examples like Winston Churchill, who used the Commons as a platform to hold government to account even during the 1930s when his own party was in power, and went on to become a great Prime Minister. But Churchill's abilities were untypical, as were the dangers Britain faced at that time. In 'normal' times, and for MPs on the government side with the usual ambition to be recruited into ministerial office, there is an obvious tendency to opt for a loyal party vote in the Commons even when personal conscience and the views of constituents suggest a different course of action.

Accountability

The most dramatic episodes in parliamentary history are examples of holding the executive to account. In the seventeenth century parliament was a focus for successful resistance against two monarchs, Charles I and James II. At a more mundane level, governments during the nineteenth century regularly fell because of parliamentary votes, sometimes on what now seem to be trivial issues. A more recent example came in 1940, when the Prime Minister Neville Chamberlain resigned after losing the support of a significant number of MPs, even within his own party, as a credible war leader.

While it is not impossible to imagine the House of Commons today flexing its muscles as it did in the Victorian era, this could only happen in unusual circumstances. Two examples illustrate the point. In March 1979, the Labour government was defeated in a parliamentary 'vote of confidence', forcing the Prime Minister James Callaghan to call an early general election. But this was the result of Callaghan's miscalculations rather than a renewed burst of vitality from MPs. Labour had governed, either with a slender overall majority or depending for survival on the support of minority parties, during five years of economic difficulty and industrial unrest. Callaghan was advised that he was likely to win if he called an election in the autumn of 1978, but it was doubted whether Labour would secure a healthy majority. Callaghan held on in the hope that circumstances would improve. As it turned out, his government was hit by a new outbreak of strikes ('the winter of discontent'), and it lost the support of nationalist parties when it failed to secure devolution for Scotland and Wales (see Chapter 11). The vote of confidence in 1979 merely put the government out of its misery; had the Commons returned to the unruly days of the nineteenth century Callaghan would have been forced to call an election much earlier.

Another example came in July 1993. John Major's Conservative Government was beaten in a crucial vote on the Maastricht Treaty, but made the issue into a matter of general confidence on the following day and won by 38 votes. The government's supporters argued that there was, in fact, a clear majority in the Commons in favour of the Treaty, and that the initial defeat was the result of unprincipled manoeuvres by Labour and Conservative rebels. However, by July 1993 the Conservatives had already lost public confidence as a result of Britain's departure from the European Exchange Rate Mechanism (ERM); by June 1993 they were more than 20 per cent behind Labour in the opinion polls. It can be argued that on this occasion the government scraped through *because* of its unpopularity. Realising that they might lose their own seats if a general election was called, the Conservative 'Eurosceptic' rebels returned to the fold and cast loyal votes once the issue had been made into a question of 'confidence'.

Perversely, then, instead of following the will of the people and using their votes to topple a government which is generally disliked, MPs are most likely to launch effective rebellions on important issues when they feel in no danger of triggering a general election which might cost them their seats. The main reasons for this dramatic change since the nineteenth century are the rise of political parties, and the professionalisation of politics. MPs who rebel on crucial issues are putting at risk their chances of future promotion to ministerial office, which was a secondary concern to most of their nineteenth century forebears. Since the majority of votes in

Case study: 7.1

Party whips

Whips are MPs (in the Commons) or peers (in the Lords) who are appointed to ensure obedient voting from their party's parliamentary supporters, using threats or flattery as the occasion demands. Although they have often been accused of accumulating personal information in order to force would-be rebels into line, they have a genuine need to know if certain MPs have troubles (such as alcoholism) which might affect their voting or suitability for service in responsible positions. They can also help to defuse difficult issues by keeping their leaders informed about the party mood.

A three-line **whip** is an instruction to an MP to attend and vote, signalled when an item of business in the weekly programme is underlined three times. Single and double underlining mean that attendance and voting is less important. If an MP is deprived of the whip, he or she is no longer issued with these instructions, which amounts to being expelled from the parliamentary party. This sanction is not always as effective as party leaders would like; Michael Foot lost the Labour whip for two years in the 1960s but went on to lead his party, while Harold Macmillan's similar punishment in the 1930s did not prevent him from becoming a Conservative Prime Minister. More recently, eight Tory MPs were deprived of the whip in 1994, and a further MP resigned in protest; but the Major government needed all the votes it could get, and the eight 'whipless wonders' were enticed back into the fold before the 1997 general election. The Labour MP George Galloway was expelled by his party in 2003, for outspoken comments about the Iraq war. At the next election he stood as a candidate for a new party, 'Respect', and won the seat at the expense of a government supporter.

Previous behaviour need not be a handicap in certain situations. Within months of being denounced from the Labour front bench, the former Conservative MP Robert Jackson was warmly welcomed by the government Chief Whip when he decided to defect in January 2005. By contrast, in the weeks before the 2005 general election the Tory MP Howard Flight, who had never been in trouble before, lost the party whip and his parliamentary seat as the result of a verbal gaffe on the subject of public spending cuts.

general elections are cast for party labels rather than for individuals, MPs know that open dissent even in a popular cause is unlikely to save their seats if they precipitate a general election in adverse circumstances for their parties. They might even lose the confidence of their constituency workers, and be deselected as official candidates. By contrast, in the nineteenth century many MPs regarded parliamentary attendance as a burden rather than a privilege; and if continued membership really mattered to them, they knew that their chances of success rested more on their independent wealth and standing in their constituencies rather than the favour of party workers.

The parliamentary opposition

The largest party not included in the government is known as the official 'Opposition'. Its leader is paid an additional salary from public funds, in recognition of the fact that democracy can only thrive when there is a potential alternative government in existence. The very architecture of the House of Commons is confrontational, inviting the expectation of rival parties with very different ideas about how the country should be run.

One of the most familiar clichés in British politics is the idea that the opposition has a duty to oppose. But in normal circumstances it is also fated to lose. Opposition can be enjoyable when the government has no overall majority in the Commons (or is actually in a minority, as Labour was for much of the 1974–79 period). But when the opposition is faced with a crushing government majority, hope can only be kept alive by the prospect of splits within the government ranks, and/or consistent opinion poll findings which suggest that the period of purgatory will end at the next general election. Perhaps there will also be the occasional by-election to provide concrete evidence of an upsurge in support.

Between 1997 and 2005, the Conservative opposition had none of these reasons to be cheerful. For the most part its opinion poll ratings remained at around 30 per cent; the Liberal Democrats won by-elections, but there were no Conservative gains. The Conservatives were led in opposition by politicians with very different qualities, but none proved capable of seriously discomfiting Tony Blair (although William Hague's supporters argued that he often 'won' televised confrontations at Prime Minister's Question Time). The one big issue which might have been exploited by an opposition determined to oppose – the war on Iraq – rebounded against the Conservatives because both Iain Duncan Smith and Michael Howard had initially expressed effusive support for the government's policy.

Any official opposition today is faced with daunting handicaps, reinforcing the argument that the UK now has a dominant party system (see Chapter 13). The government can depend upon the support of a highly-trained civil service. It controls the parliamentary timetable, and can shape the news agenda to its own advantage by choosing the best moment to publicise its concrete achievements (by the same

Tony Blair makes his point at PMQs, to the obvious delight of John Precott and Gordon Brown (© PA/TopFoto)

Types of legislatures

The leading scholar on the British parliament and member of the House of Lords, Lord Norton of Louth has developed a three-fold typology of legislatures:

1. *Policy-making legislatures.* These are legislatures that can modify or reject legislative proposals made by the executive. They can make amendments to government proposals on the floor of the assembly or in committee, can veto government Bills and members can put forward alternative Bills. The US Senate is an example of a policy-making legislature but relatively few parliaments enjoy this level of influence.

2. *Policy-influencing legislatures.* These are legislatures that can modify or reject legislative proposals from the executive but are unable to develop extensive legislative proposals of their own and substitute them for government sponsored Bills. These legislatures thus have only modest influence over policy and react to government proposals rather than taking the lead in formulating policy. Many West European legislatures fall into this category.

3. *Legislatures with little or no influence.* These are legislatures that are unable to modify or veto legislative proposals from the executive. They are unable to formulate any meaningful alternative policy proposals of their own. Examples are found in one-party states where the legislature meets infrequently and simply rubber-stamps proposals made by the executive.

The UK parliament is a policy-influencing body. The House of Commons and House of Lords can vote against government Bills and approve amendments of their own, but the executive controls the parliamentary timetable and enforces party discipline. Private Members Bills have little prospect of success.

Source: P. Norton, 'The House of Commons', in B. Jones, D. Kavanagh, M. Moran and P. Norton, *Politics UK*, *5th edition*, Box 17.1, p. 389 (Longman, 2004: Harlow)

token, it can 'bury bad news' by releasing damaging information when the media's attention is focused elsewhere). Even Prime Minister's Question Time is normally an unequal battle, since the incumbent always has the last word.

None of this, however, was much help to John Major in his second term (1992–97). Even before Tony Blair became Labour leader in 1994 the Conservatives looked beaten and divided, and Blair made the most of his opportunity, often contriving to look and sound more 'prime ministerial' than Major himself.

The situation between the general elections of 1992 and 1997 might be regarded as a conclusive answer to anyone who thinks that active parliamentary opposition in Britain is futile. Equally, though, it can be argued that the circumstances in those years were misleading. The Conservatives had lost their vital reputation for economic competence because of sterling's enforced exit from the Exchange Rate Mechanism (ERM) in September 1992, just six months after the party had won a fourth consecutive general election. This accentuated existing Conservative divisions over Europe, which were being stoked up by the former Prime Minister Margaret Thatcher. Major had succeeded Thatcher because he showed none of her crusading zeal. Although the change undoubtedly helped the Tories to win (against most expectations) in 1992, when events subsequently turned against the party his assets began to look like handicaps. If this was not enough, after Blair became Labour leader and accepted many Conservative reforms Major was deprived of his final refuge – an opposition that could be depicted as extreme.

The lack of a clear ideological distinction between the two main parties (see Chapter 15) is a new development in the democratic era. William Hague, Iain Duncan Smith and Michael Howard all tried to appeal to the 'core' Conservative constituency by exaggerating the remaining policy differences. David Cameron, who took over at the end of 2005, enjoyed one important advantage over his predecessors – divisions within the Labour Party were now serious enough to ensure that the Prime Minister could be defeated even on key policy votes. This meant that on some issues the Conservatives were in a position to embarrass the government, either by helping the rebels or offering support to the Prime Minister at his time of need. For the first time since 1997, it was no longer possible to dismiss the official Opposition as an irrelevance, and Conservative proposals won a more respectful hearing from the media as a result. Even so, the suspicion remained that the new situation owed far more to government mistakes than to the independent efforts of the opposition.

'Low level' accountability

Government supporters in the House of Commons might be willing to vote against their leaders. But they are unlikely nowadays to use their 'nuclear option' of forcing their own party out of office. However, parliamentary accountability can still be exercised in ways which do not involve a formal vote. For example, if party whips detect a high level of opposition to a particular measure, the government can withdraw or revise it rather than cause ill-will by exerting pressure on MPs.

Controversy:	7.1

Accountability without democracy?

Disturbingly for those who prize Britain's democratic institutions, it can be argued that non-elected institutions are now more effective in holding the executive to account.

The media routinely justifies its activities by appealing to the public interest. Especially since 1997, while the parliamentary opposition has been dwarfed by Labour's majority, the media has claimed to be the most effective monitor of the government's conduct (see Chapter 4).

The judiciary has become more active in recent years, risking conflict with successive governments by ruling that ministers have exceeded their legal powers. This judicial activism has developed further since the passage of the 1998 Human Rights Act (see Chapter 8), and because of the increasing amount of 'delegated' legislation (where the scope of ministerial power is not clearly defined in Bills passed by parliament).

Vigilance from the media and the judiciary can obviously be beneficial to a liberal democracy. The remaining questions are whether these institutions can compensate for shortcomings in the performance of elected representatives – and whether they perform their enhanced roles in a responsible fashion. At best, the situation may be likened to a vehicle whose tyres and bodywork are in reasonable condition, but the brakes have malfunctioned.

This occurred in 1994, when the Major government dropped plans to privatise the Post Office even though it had made the sell-off the centrepiece of its legislative programme for that session. Even the Blair government, with its impressive parliamentary majority, watered down proposals to allow new 'super-casinos' before the 2005 general election, and afterwards allowed a free vote on proposals concerning restrictions on smoking in public places. Its position had become more vulnerable thanks to the election, in which its overall majority was cut to 67.

Even if backbench MPs feel reluctant to bring down a government, they can still secure the departure of an individual minister – even one who enjoys the full backing of the Prime Minister. Again, this proved to be the case on several occasions during the Major years; but it also happened under Thatcher even though her governments enjoyed much larger majorities in the Commons. In 1986, for example, the Secretary of State for Trade and Industry, Leon Brittan, left the Cabinet as a result of pressure from Conservative backbenchers. The departure in 1990 of Thatcher herself could be cited as the most spectacular recent example of backbench power, though she and her admirers tend to blame her enforced withdrawal on the 'treachery' of Cabinet colleagues. The leadership election which brought her premiership to an end was foreshadowed by a highly-critical speech from the backbenches by Sir Geoffrey Howe, who had just resigned from the government having served alongside Thatcher since 1979.

Select committees

Another way in which the executive can be made accountable to MPs is through select committees (not to be confused with standing committees, which scrutinise specific pieces of legislation). These bodies, which have become more prominent since they were reformed in 1979, oversee a wide range of government activities (though their remits do not always coincide exactly with those of individual departments). The membership generally reflects the party balance in the Commons. However, prolonged service on the committees can generate conflicting loyalties. Since a unanimous report is likely to carry maximum weight, members have a vested interest in striking compromises across party lines, to the displeasure of their whips. Over time, they can become more expert in their chosen subject than ministers who usually have short tenures in a specific office. Select committee members who have relinquished their ambitions for further promotion are particularly dangerous in these circumstances; they are likely to enjoy the public exposure which follows a controversial committee report, and will not easily be dissuaded by the whips from speaking out.

The select committees have wide powers to summon witnesses and to examine restricted documents. However, the secretarial support available to members is limited; the 42 committees in 2003 could only draw on the services of around 150 staff. Certain witnesses (particularly civil servants) have been notably unhelpful, only appearing at all if their ministers approve and rarely saying much of interest when they do turn up. Even when they reach conclusions embarrassing to governments, committee findings can simply be ignored. The oldest and best-respected of the bodies, the Public Accounts Committee (which dates back to parliament's mid-Victorian heyday) can criticise excessive government expenditure, but has no right to pass judgement on the policies themselves.

Controversy: 7.2

'Sleaze' and the interests of MPs

When most MPs enjoyed private means and regarded politics as something of a hobby, it was taken as a matter of course that they would have extensive financial interests outside the House. One reason for the eccentric business hours of parliament was the assumption that busy people would have to attend to other matters during many 'normal' working hours. The new dominance of 'professional' politicians, with fewer outside interests, is thus one reason why reform of the parliamentary timetable since 1997 could be contemplated. But it also coincided with a rise in media attention to the business interests of politicians.

In 1975 a Register of Interests was introduced, in which all members of the Lords and Commons declared their financial dealings. In the 1990s a series of scandals were exposed, including several instances where MPs were accused of having asked questions in parliament in return for cash. Under pressure, in October 1994 Prime Minister John Major set up a Committee on Standards in Public Life under a judge, Lord Nolan. In the following year the committee recommended that MPs should make full disclosures of their financial dealings, including the sums involved. The government accepted most of the proposals, despite some furious opposition from its own backbenchers who resented the imputation that all MPs were potentially corrupt and required special monitoring to make sure that they were behaving. Nolan's seven principles of public life – selflessness, integrity, objectivity, accountability, openness, honesty and leadership – were more relevant to the qualities expected of a saint than of a legislator in tune with the modern world.

A Commissioner for Parliamentary Standards was appointed, who would work with a new parliamentary select committee on Standards and Privileges. But the second holder of the post, Elizabeth Filkin (1999–2002) was effectively sacked because she took the job too seriously, issuing several critical reports which embarrassed the government. Thus MPs ended up with the worst of both worlds; if they lost the support of the executive for one reason or another they could be punished under regulations which were excessively intrusive, but they stood accused of trying their best to evade them. So much for 'selflessness, integrity' and all the rest!

Despite these institutional limitations, the potential power of the select committees is significant enough to provoke a more devious response from governments of both main parties. A favourite tactic is to interfere with the membership. A precedent was set in 1992 when the outspoken Conservative Nicholas Winterton was removed, on dubious grounds, as chairperson of the Health Committee. Labour was less successful in its attempts to prevent Gwyneth Dunwoody from retaining the chair of the select committee on Transport. But in May 2002 an attempt to reduce the power of the whips over select committee membership was defeated in the Commons.

Significantly, the then Leader of the House of Commons, Robin Cook, was the only Cabinet minister to support this plan. When Cook resigned over Iraq in the following year the select committees lost an important champion. Another setback for the system was the uncomfortable appearance of the weapons expert Dr David Kelly before the Foreign Affairs Committee, just a few days before his apparent suicide on 18 July 2003. Some observers felt that he had been treated with unnec-

The Education Select Committee interrogates the Secretary of State (Charles Clarke), January 2004 (© Topham/PA)

essary brutality by committee members who were more interested in publicising their own work than in holding the executive to account.

Perhaps the best testimony to the growing importance of the select committees is Blair's decision to appear for televised question sessions before the Liaison Committee, which brings together all of the committee chairpersons. The relatively serious nature of the questioning on these occasions has been favourably contrasted with the atmosphere at the weekly Prime Minister's Question Time. For the moment, though, the select committees remain a pale shadow of their US congressional counterparts. Further strengthening of their powers and resources would be an

Table 7.1 House of Commons Select Committees, 2006

Administration	Office of the Deputy Prime Minister
Armed Forces	Procedure
Constitutional Affairs	Public Accounts
Culture, Media and Sport	Public Administration
Defence	Quadripartite (export controls)
Education and Skills	Regulatory Reform
Environmental Audit	Science and Technology
Environment, Food and Rural Affairs	Scottish Affairs
European Scrutiny	Standards and Privileges
Finance and Services	Statutory Instruments
Foreign Affairs	Trade and Industry
Health	Transport
Home Affairs	Treasury
International Development	Welsh Affairs
Modernisation of House of Commons	Work and Pensions
Liaison	
Northern Ireland	

important facet of a Commons revival, and both the Conservatives and the Liberal Democrats advocated changes in their 2005 party manifestos. But on their own the committees are unequal to the task of executive scrutiny.

Representation

The House of Commons consists of 645 MPs, elected from single-member constituencies on the basis of universal suffrage among adults over 18. The geographical nature of representation is supposed to ensure that individual MPs can be identified as the exclusive representatives of their constituents, as opposed to the multi-member arrangements produced by proportional representation systems (see Chapter 16).

In performing their various roles MPs can represent their constituents in two distinct ways. First, they are expected to act as advisers and advocates even for local people who have voted for rival candidates. Thus, when a constituent has a plausible grievance against a public authority, conscientious MPs will take up the case in the relevant quarter, for example writing to ministers or even raising the matter in the House of Commons. MPs often find themselves called upon to act like social workers, helping their constituents with housing problems, social security benefits or disputes with the local health services. Some MPs can win enviable local reputations for this time-consuming aspect of their work, though this is rarely sufficient to save them when their party becomes unpopular at the national level.

MPs may also represent the opinions and interests of their constituents in parliamentary votes. Strictly speaking, those who allow their votes to be dictated by constituency opinion rather than following their personal wishes are acting as **delegates** rather than mere **representatives**; they might deserve their place in the Commons because they are particularly eloquent in expressing the views of their constituents, but as far as voting is concerned their places could be taken by remotely-controlled computers. This delegate view of representation has rarely been advocated in British politics – at least, not outside the left of the 'Old' Labour Party. MPs are far more likely to cite the eighteenth-century politician Edmund Burke, who argued that representatives are chosen because of their personal qualities rather than their obedience to anyone else's opinion, and that if voters dislike their decisions they can always choose another representative at the ensuing election.

Delegate: a representative who is under instructions to vote in a particular way.

Representative: someone who is chosen to take part in decision-making and to make up his or her own mind after hearing the evidence.

However, it can be argued that the overwhelming majority of MPs today are indeed delegates – but the opinions they follow are those of their party leaders rather than the majority of their constituents. Although rebellions against the party line happen more frequently than most critics suppose, they rarely result in a defeat for the governing party. Thus even on controversial policies like the war on Iraq and the introduction of university tuition fees, the Blair government was able to secure majority support, although the first was deeply unpopular even when MPs believed that Saddam Hussein was able and willing to deploy weapons of mass destruction, and the second was a breach of a manifesto promise. After the crucial second reading of the Bill to introduce tuition fees, 72 Labour MPs voted against the government, but the measure still went through by five votes. Concerted appeals by Tony Blair and Gordon Brown persuaded a few MPs to swallow their misgivings, in the knowledge that a full-scale rebellion could bring down the government and trigger an election, while exposing damaging divisions within the party ranks.

Philip Cowley has demonstrated that members of the 2001–2005 parliament were the most rebellious since the Second World War, and the trend continued after the 2005 general election. The Blair government actually lost an important House of Commons vote, in November 2005 on proposals to allow the detention of terrorist subjects for up to 90 days. The vote, which saw a government defeat by 322 to 291, was a considerable blow to the Prime Minister, since he had invested some of his personal authority in the outcome. The defeat reflected both the government's reduced majority after the 2005 general election, and the extent to which a significant group of Labour MPs was now prepared to defy the party leadership (and the majority of voters, according to opinion polls). In February 2006 the government also had to make important concessions before introducing an Education Bill. Despite the concessions, 52 Labour MPs persisted in their opposition. On the crucial second reading the government only secured a majority thanks to Conservative support or abstentions. This was almost as embarrassing as a defeat, and further undermined Blair's authority.

While the evidence of backbench mutiny is impressive, it has to be seen in context. Most governments gradually accumulate a phalanx of rebels who are prepared to rebel out of a mixture of disappointed ambition and genuine ideological disagreements. Yet there were times after 1997 when it appeared that Tony Blair was actively seeking to maximise discontent, by introducing policies which were directly antagonistic towards long-established Labour positions on key questions like civil liberties and the public services. If the same proposals had been introduced by a Conservative government, it is likely that the overwhelming majority of Labour MPs would gladly have opposed them. Over education, even the ultra-loyal Deputy Prime Minister, John Prescott, openly voiced his concern. It is certainly difficult to use evidence from this unusual period to contest the general proposition that MPs are becoming more obedient.

Are MPs socially representative?

Apart from the active ways in which MPs represent their constituents, they can also be judged on the extent to which they are socially 'representative', as individuals. In seeking to explain the recent unpopularity of politicians, critics have focused on their apparent remoteness from the 'real world'. Particular concern has been raised about the under-representation of women, although the number has increased from 60 after the 1992 general election to 128 in 2005 (see Table 7.2 and Chapter 16). Despite Labour's high-profile efforts to address this imbalance, the number of female candidates for the party actually decreased between 1997 and 2001, from 155 to 148. There was an increase in 2005, but only to 166 out of 627 Labour candidates; and attempts to enforce all-women shortlists are still highly controversial, despite being made legal under the 2002 Sex Discrimination (Election Candidates) Act. All the major parties are now committed to increasing black and Asian representation. There was a record number of ethnic minority candidates in 2005 (113) but the new House of Commons still included only 15 black and Asian MPs.

Parliament is deeply unrepresentative in other respects. The fact that in 2001 there were only five MPs under the age of 30 could perhaps be interpreted as a

Table 7.2 Women candidates and MPs, 1983–2005

Year	Conservative		Labour		Lib Dem		Total women MPs
	Candidates	MPs	Candidates	MPs	Candidates	MPs	
1983	40	13	79	10	75	0	23
1987	46	17	92	21	105	2	41
1992	59	20	138	37	144	2	60
1997	66	13	155	102	139	3	120
2001	93	14	148	95	140	5	118
2005	123	17	166	98	145	10	128

Note: 'Total women MPs' includes MPs from other parties.

Source: Data from various House of Commons research papers

good thing, suggesting that maturity is still prized in politics if not (for example) in the business world or the media. But the fact that even Labour could muster no more than 51 MPs (12 per cent of their total) who had once been manual workers was a glaring anomaly. In the party of the ordinary working man, there were now almost as many lecturers (49) as manual labourers. Manufacturing industry might have been declining in Britain for many years, but not to this extent. Meanwhile the Conservatives and the Liberal Democrats could boast only one MP each from a background in manual work. After the 2005 general election, almost a third of MPs had attended a public school, compared to about 7 per cent of the population as a whole. Among Labour MPs, the proportion of public school products was 18 per cent.

Certain trades can justify their excessive representation because of the nature of their work. Thus there is an over-abundance of lawyers, and even within that narrow category of economic activity barristers (33) were massively over-represented in 2001 compared to solicitors (35), when these figures are related to their respective numbers in the world of work. More troubling, perhaps, is the number of MPs who have never seriously considered any other career than politics. The number of MPs from the main parties who were classed as having been 'politicians or political organisers' before entering the Commons was 66 in 2001 – more than 10 per cent of the overall membership of the House.

While all of the main parties now acknowledge the importance of increasing the representation of women and the ethnic minorities, little is ever said about the mismatch between the previous occupations of MPs and the world outside Westminster. This evidence exposes the superficial nature of the debate about social representation. Women and members of the ethnic minorities will be made more welcome in future only insofar as they fit the socio-economic profile of existing MPs. By contrast, manual workers tend to be unwelcome regardless of gender or ethnicity. It can be argued that this half-hearted approach to the representativeness of the Commons explains why electoral turnout has continued to fall even though there is now a broader range of candidates in other respects.

In any case, the argument about social representation seems to be based on a mistake. By definition, politicians *are* unrepresentative of society as a whole. A cynic would say that their interest in politics in itself makes them deeply unrepresentative!

Beyond this, it can be asked whether a nation's representatives really ought to be 'representative' in the social sense. An ideal democracy would produce legislators who are drawn from the highest-calibre members of all important social groups and economic occupations. By contrast, to be truly 'representative' the legislature would have to include a healthy proportion of the uninterested or unintelligent, along with a sprinkling of convicted criminals. As it is, the life of a politician is becoming increasingly unattractive, ensuring that although the current imbalances in terms of gender and ethnicity may be redressed in future, many MPs will be chosen from the ranks of narrow political obsessives and opportunists, regardless of their origins.

Debating

It is usually argued that, whatever its other limitations, parliament provides the nation with a grand forum for debate on important occasions. In May 1940, for example, some MPs were able to set aside partisan loyalties and speak from the heart when the future of Britain hung in the balance. In October 1971, after a six-day debate, MPs approved the terms of membership of the European Economic Community (EEC) negotiated by Edward Heath's government. Despite high tension between Labour and Conservatives and that time, a total of 130 MPs from both parties either abstained or voted against their leaders (tellingly, there were more than twice as many Labour rebels even though the Conservatives decided not to impose the whip on their members). The debates on the Falklands War in 1982, the Westland Affair (1986), and the Maastricht Treaty (1993), are also remembered as dramatic occasions, although only the last-named took place after the television cameras had been allowed into the Commons (November 1989; continuous radio broadcasts began in 1978).

Nowadays, aficionados can watch parliamentary proceedings all day long on a special digital TV channel. However, most people will only ever catch a glimpse of the Commons chamber when snippets from Prime Minister's Question Time are included in the evening news bulletins. In part, the lack of interest in parliamentary activities can be attributed to the media, which prefers to secure its own 'scoops' through set-piece studio interviews with the leading players. However, it does seem that the sense of drama has been leaking away from the chamber for other reasons. One indication of the decline can be registered in the virtual disappearance of MPs who were widely regarded as great 'House of Commons men', i.e. people who were steeped in respect for the procedures of the House, even when (like Enoch Powell, 1912–98) they were prepared to use venues outside Westminster to express their iconoclastic views on a range of issues. Nowadays 'elder statesmen' who could command an audience by virtue of their long-learned experience of debate tend to accept a seat in the House of Lords at the first general election after the end of their ministerial careers. In this respect perhaps the most telling moment was the retirement of Tony Benn (born 1925, first elected in 1945) at the 2001 general election. Although still vigorous and determined to influence public debate, Benn realised that his membership of the Commons was a drawback rather than an asset; he declared that he was leaving the Commons 'to go into politics'.

We argued above that a recovery of parliamentary accountability is not impossible, even under the present system; and the same is true of the quality of debate. However,

The prototype of Prime Minister's Question Time? (© ArenaPAL/Topfoto)

in both cases a revival is difficult to foresee in the absence of changes which go far beyond the kind of institutional tinkering which has been on offer in recent years (see below).

Passing legislation

In theory, the UK parliament has a free hand in passing legislation. No parliamentary decision can be binding on its successors, so that (for example) if so minded, MPs could repeal all legislation relating to Britain's membership of the EU or even abolish the monarchy. In this sense, one could claim that parliament is still the 'sovereign' body in the UK and argue that this is entirely proper since the House of Commons is directly elected by the British people.

In practice the situation is very different. The government (or executive), rather than parliament itself, is responsible for almost all the laws which are passed by parliament. Instead of being a law-*making* body in any meaningful sense, the UK legislature is expected to *legitimise* government decisions. In itself, this has the potential to conflict with the responsibility of holding government to account. Yet it is debatable that parliament performs even this truncated role very successfully. There are signs that the public increasingly regards the passage of legislation as no more than the first stage of the process – and not just because much of today's legislation is poorly drafted and soon requires amendment.

The legislative process

On paper, proposals laid before parliament are faced with a formidable obstacle-course before they become law. The government discloses its programme at the beginning of a parliamentary session, in the Queen's Speech which is delivered from the throne but written by ministers, reflecting the fact that although the monarch is technically head of state she enjoys far less power than the average president. A lengthy debate follows, which gives the government some idea of the level of opposition. When there is either a minority government, or one with a slender majority, the votes at the end of these debates will give some indication of its chances of survival.

Even before the Queen's Speech the government will normally have consulted groups which have a particular interest in the legislation. At an early stage in its deliberations it may issue a **Green Paper**, setting out the various arguments and inviting further comment. A **White Paper** indicates that the government has made up its mind, and the document usually forms the basis of a subsequent **Bill**.

Green Paper: a document published by the government setting out various options and inviting comment.

White Paper: a government document setting out detailed proposals for legislation.

Bill: A proposed piece of legislation that is yet to complete the legislative process.

Extensive consultation before a Bill is introduced ought to satisfy most critics of representative democracy. However, in the UK the process is likely to be inadequate, for a variety of reasons. Sometimes there is a real need for action in a particular area, and the government genuinely has limited time for talking. More often, the government will only consult with favoured organisations ('insider groups' – see Chapter 18). This is because it will have promised action to its supporters both inside and outside parliament, and is simply not prepared to listen even to constructive objections. This explains the fate of the community charge (or poll tax), which seemed watertight to most Conservative supporters before implementation but soon proved to be unworkable. Inadequate consultation can also occur because most ministers are keen to make a mark in their present posts. As such, they will tend to exaggerate the level of support for their ideas, and to discount any criticisms as the product of 'biased' thinking.

Whip: an instruction to vote issued to MPs by political parties.

Whips: party officials responsible for ensuring maximum turn out by for parliamentary votes.

Once consultation is over and the Queen's Speech has been approved, Bills are introduced in accordance with a timetable prepared by the government's 'business managers' – that is, the **whips** and the Leader of the House of Commons, in consultation with other ministers. Often there will not be time to complete the programme, so Bills have to be ranked according to the government's priorities. Contentious Bills might be left to the end of the session. In the last session before a general election, a government might announce a series of Bills which have no chance of being enacted, in order to publicise their main intentions if they are re-elected. Both the Major and Blair governments took this approach with identity cards (in 1997 and 2005 respectively). Equally, the government might decide to introduce its most controversial proposals at an early stage, in the hope of breaking any resistance to the remainder of its programme.

Act: A legislative proposal which has cleared every stage in the legislative process and enters into law.

Bills can either be introduced in the Commons or the Lords; normally controversial legislation goes to the Commons first. The full process of Bill to **Act** is outlined in Case study 7.2.

Private Members' Bills

The discussion so far has been based on the assumption that a successful Bill will normally be sponsored by the government of the day. This is slightly misleading – but only slightly. Early in each session MPs wishing to introduce a Bill of their own take part in a ballot. Twenty names are chosen at random. Some of those selected will be hoping at the very least to win some publicity for a cherished cause; others may

Case study:	7.2

The passage of a Bill

A Bill originating in the House of Commons will go through the following stages in the legislative process:

First reading: Usually a simple announcement of a Bill's title and the date for the second reading. At this stage the bill is not even printed in full; the proposer lays a printed 'dummy Bill' before the House.

Second reading: The general principles of the Bill are debated by the whole House, followed by a vote. The minister responsible for the Bill outlines its provisions and explains its purpose; the relevant opposition spokesperson replies. After contributions from backbenchers on all sides, the debate is wound up by frontbenchers, with the government having the last word. Governments are rarely defeated at this stage, but the debate usually sets the tone for the rest of the process. After second reading a vote is held on a 'programme motion' (without debate). This is a recent innovation, which sets limits on the amount of time for debate in committee. Until 1997 the government could call a vote at any time to impose a 'guillotine', bringing debate to a close. However, these decisions were contentious in themselves, leading to accusations that the government was trying to prevent the proper scrutiny of its proposals. The new procedure was supposed to be more 'consensual', allowing MPs from all sides a say in drawing up the timetable. However, critics have claimed (with justification) that it simply tightens government control over the scrutiny process.

Committee stage: Most Bills are then scrutinised by a standing committee, which reflects the overall composition of the House. The amount of time taken varies, sometimes stretching over a number of weeks (though the members only meet at specific times). For example, in 2003 the government's Hunting Bill was scrutinised by a standing committee in 27 sessions, for a total of 77 hours. At any one time several standing committees will be at work, in different committee rooms at Westminster. Normally consisting of between 16 and 50 MPs, the standing committee debates each clause of the Bill and considers amendments. Often these will be introduced by the government itself, to close loopholes in the original Bill which have come to light in previous debates. Sometimes, though, a new and contentious proposition might be introduced. For example, although the 1989 Local Government Act was mainly about the provision of council services, at committee stage the responsible minister, Michael Howard, introduced a new clause which attempted to stop councils 'promoting' homosexuality. As Section 28 of the Act this amendment became one of the most unpopular measures taken by the Conservatives governments of 1979–97, and was repealed by the Blair government.

Report stage: When the committee has completed its deliberations its decisions are reported back to the full House. More amendments can be considered at this stage.

Third reading: This takes place immediately after the Report stage. Normally by this time the opponents of the Bill will have accepted that further resistance is futile, although on particularly contentious matters dissenting MPs will want to put their objections on record once again.

If the Bill passes its third reading, it is sent to the Lords where it undergoes the same process (except that the committee stage is usually open to all members of the upper house rather than a 'representative' sample as in the Commons). If it is amended there, it returns to the Commons where the changes are considered (not the Bill as a whole). A compromise is usually reached to iron out any differences between the two Houses, so that the Bill can be presented for the *Royal Assent*. This final formality – it has not been refused for 300 years – makes the Bill into law.

Sometimes, though, the two Houses find it impossible to compromise, as in the case of the 2004 Hunting Bill. In these situations governments can utilise the provisions of the 1949 Parliament Act, which ensures that in most circumstances the will of the Commons must prevail. The only way in which the Lords can prevent a Bill from becoming law is if they reject a Bill which has passed its second reading within thirteen months of parliament being dissolved for a general election (see below).

have entered the ballot under instruction from the whips, having no bright ideas of their own to suggest. They will soon be bombarded with proposals, from pressure groups and lobbyists of all kinds. Often such groups will provide ready-drafted Bills, to save the member the trouble of asking an expert to compose the text.

A devious MP might try to curry favour with ministers by sponsoring a proposal which the government would like to see on the statute book but lacks the time (or

---

Case study: **7.3**

Parliamentary weapons for the backbencher

In addition to Private Member's Bills, there are several other ways in which backbenchers can hope to win publicity for a cause:

Questions to ministers: Apart from Prime Minister's Question Time, which now lasts for 30 minutes on Wednesdays, having been split into two quarter-hour sessions until 1997, there are other regular sessions during which MPs can question departmental ministers. As well as oral questions on the floor of the House, backbenchers expect answers to written questions; ministerial responses are published in the official parliamentary record, *Hansard*.

Early Day Motions (EDMs): Backbench MPs can make a point by putting down a statement in the form of a motion, which is supposed to be for discussion on 'an early day'. In practice, the subjects are rarely discussed, let alone voted on; indeed, the serious EDMs are usually advanced by MPs who feel that they have no chance of gaining a hearing through more orthodox channels. On these occasions, they are attempts to gauge parliamentary opinion; if the motion attracts any support it will be available until the end of the session to MPs who want to sign it. Some MPs use EDMs to express support for constituency matters (and even to give public backing to their local football team).

Adjournment debates: At the end of a day's official business MPs (chosen by ballot) have half an hour to raise an issue of interest to them, often concerning constituency matters. A minister from the relevant department will reply to the debate, after other interested MPs have contributed.

Ten-minute rule Bills: MPs who lose out in the ballot for the right to introduce a Private Member's Bill can plead for their cause for ten minutes before the beginning of official business on specific days. These Bills have even less chance of success; but they give another fleeting chance of winning publicity.

the political courage) to offer open support. In the 1960s several measures of social reform became law because the Home Secretary, Roy Jenkins, supported them even though he knew that members of his own party had mixed feelings. Alternatively, the government might decide that a particular Private Member's Bill is so popular with parliament and the public that it should throw its weight behind it. Either way, Private Member's Bills have virtually no chance of success unless they enjoy at least the benevolent neutrality of the government. Constraints of time mean that most Bills are 'talked out' by determined opponents. Their chances are equally dim if they are uncontentious, because Bills will fail unless enough MPs feel sufficiently motivated to turn up for the debate. Case study 7.4 presents a rather unusual case history; but it illustrates the difficulties faced even by a Private Member's Bill that enjoys substantial cross-party support.

Case study: 7.4

Hunting – the history of a Private Member's Bill

Between 1992 and 1995 three Private Member's Bills were introduced by Labour MPs hoping to outlaw hunting. They all ended in failure. However, in its 1997 manifesto Labour offered hope to campaigners by promising a free vote on the subject. Any anti-hunting MP who was successful in the private members' ballot could therefore be certain of 'benevolent neutrality' from the incoming government.

In March 1998 a Bill sponsored by Labour's Michael Foster gained its second reading in the Commons. However, the hunting lobby had already reacted to the new political climate, organising a mass protest rally in Hyde Park in July 1997. Foster's Bill was 'talked out' by its parliamentary opponents on third reading. In the summer of 1999 Tony Blair revealed on television that he would like to see a ban introduced before the next election. Evidently the government still wanted to secure this result by means of a Private Member's Bill, which might reduce any direct political damage. However, Blair's remark made it difficult to avoid a more direct commitment. In 2000 a new Bill was introduced by the Home Office minister Mike O'Brien. The major difference from the previous proposal was that MPs could opt for a compromise, allowing hunting with hounds to continue under licence. When this formula was rejected by the Commons, the Bill as a whole was thrown out by the Lords. Under the provisions of the Parliament Act of 1949 the bill lapsed when Blair called a general election for June 2001. The new Bill had been introduced too late in the parliament to ensure its success.

After Labour had been re-elected Blair clearly still hoped for a compromise. But by this time it was clear that the Commons would settle for nothing less than an outright ban. A game of 'ping-pong' ensued, with the Commons passing a new Bill and the Lords rejecting it. At length, in November 2004 the Commons Speaker Michael Martin declared that the terms of the Parliament Act had been satisfied, and the Bill was given the Royal Assent. The ban came into force in February 2005. For the opponents of hunting, however, the saga had only completed its first phase. The Countryside Alliance launched an unsuccessful legal challenge to the Parliament Act itself, and also tried to overturn the legislation by appealing to the Human Rights Act 1998 (see Chapter 8). In the 2005 general election, the Countryside Alliance campaigned against several pro-hunting MPs, and claimed to have played a decisive role in several seats.

Recruitment of ministers

Despite occasional excitements like the Hunting Bill, for most backbench MPs the legislative routine allows little opportunity for independent thought or action. Sometimes the whips will be knocking at an open door, asking their colleagues to vote for measures which they already support wholeheartedly. But on other occasions MPs will be forced to troop into the voting lobbies against their consciences. For many (particularly those new to the House) this way of life is only worthwhile because they hope to be plucked one day from the backbenches and given ministerial office, perhaps leading one day to Downing Street. There are, after all, plenty of government positions to fill. By law, the number of paid ministerial jobs is fixed at 109, and some of these posts are taken by members of the House of Lords. Even so, it is hardly irrational for new MPs to expect office after being elected to represent the governing party.

In the past, skilful orators had reason to hope that a well-received debut (a 'maiden speech') followed by some well-timed debating interventions was the best way of embarking on the fast-track to promotion. This is probably still true; Tony Blair and Gordon Brown both attracted favourable attention through their early performances in the 1983–87 parliament, when Labour was in opposition and hungry for fresh talent. However, politicians who fail to shine in the unique atmosphere of the Commons can be more optimistic about their prospects today than at any time in the recent past, as the importance of the chamber diminishes.

The most obvious short-cut to ministerial office is only available to long-standing personal friends of the Prime Minister. Lord Falconer, the Lord Chancellor appointed in 2003, had once been Blair's flat-mate; his predecessor Lord Irvine had been Blair's head of chambers when he was a barrister. Neither had made a strong impression in the House of Commons, for the very good reason that they had never been elected to sit there. This phenomenon was nothing new, though in these cases it allowed commentators to scoff about 'Tony's cronies'.

Those who cannot boast of personal friendship with powerful ministers need not despair. Unthinking loyalty to one's party might not be enough to secure one of the great offices of state, but reliable MPs have a much better chance of rising than trouble-makers, who are often offered unimportant posts to keep them quiet (though they usually find it difficult to win further promotion even if they perform well). A blemish-free voting record is the ideal qualification for a junior whip, whose job is to instil the same degree of loyalty in others. In recent times this was the first step on the ladder for several prominent figures, notably John Major.

However, ambitious new MPs are best advised to demonstrate their attributes through media appearances. The ability to defend party policy (and to attack rivals) on radio or television is at least as important today as a sharp parliamentary debating style; and although the skills are closely related, the crucial difference is that physical appearance is presumed to make much more impact on television than in the Commons chamber. This was a key factor in persuading senior figures in the Labour Party to prefer Blair over Brown before the 1994 leadership election. The journalist Boris Johnson became one of the best-known Conservative MPs after chairing the comedy programme *Have I Got News For You*; only a handful of viewers can have known anything about his beliefs or his parliamentary prowess. As well as helping politicians to rise within established parties, a high media profile can win them seats as independent candidates, as in the case of the former BBC reporter Martin Bell in the Tatton constituency in 1997. It is equally important to build up strong and favourable contacts within the media. The dullest of new MPs will be regarded as 'rising stars' if a couple of friends in national newspapers describe them in this fashion.

The House of Lords

The current dissatisfaction with MPs has cast an ironic light on the position of the House of Lords. For more than a century the upper house has been regarded very much as the lesser one; the last Prime Minister with a peerage was the third Marquess of Salisbury who left office in 1902. The sharp decline of the Lords in the following decades was marked by the passage of two Parliament Acts (1911 and 1949), which effectively removed its power of veto. After 1949, the Lords could merely delay the passage of most legislation for a maximum of thirteen months. Another crucial landmark was the Life Peerages Act 1958. This measure promised to enhance the quality of the House of Lords, since the new life peers owed their membership to their own achievements rather than the circumstances of their birth. However, there was a danger that the Act would make the Lords less distinctive, because many of the life peers had previously been MPs. In 1963 the Conservative government of Harold Macmillan also passed the Peerage Act, allowing ambitious politicians to renounce inherited titles which would otherwise make them ineligible for a seat in the Commons. This legislation was quickly utilised by the 14th Earl of Home, who reverted to Sir Alec Douglas-Home in order to succeed Macmillan as Prime Minister (1963–64). After a further stint as Foreign Secretary (1970–74), Home rejoined the Lords, but this time as a life peer.

In combination, these measures made the House of Lords into a 'revising' chamber. Leaders of the House of Lords, like Viscount Whitelaw (1983–88), believed that peers should only persist in their opposition to a Bill in the last resort. The role of the Lords, in Whitelaw's view, was to give the Commons a chance to reconsider legislation which had not been thought through properly. Superficially this was a modest ambition; but it implied that the Commons could not be relied upon to give adequate scrutiny to Bills. The effect of the Life Peerages Act 1958 had been to make the Lords into something like a retirement home for former ministers, who could bring their accumulated wisdom and experience to bear when the Commons had been over-hasty. Significantly, ennobled politicians forgot much of their previous partisanship when they were 'kicked upstairs'; although there was a whipping system, debates were far more polite and non-affiliated peers ('cross-benchers') often exercised a decisive influence in votes.

Supporters of the Lords could argue that it performed a valuable role in a liberal democracy, even though few people would have designed it in its existing form. However, when Labour took office in 1997 it was committed to radical changes. The main objection to the unreformed Lords was the continued numerical dominance of hereditary peers. Of 1290 members of the Lords in November 1999, only 478 were life peers (though there were also 27 law lords – see Chapter 8 – and 26 bishops). By no means all of the hereditary peers who made up the majority of the upper house were Conservative supporters. But during the Thatcher years Labour had been infuriated by the sudden appearance at Westminster for crucial votes of many peers who only seemed to attend debates when the government was struggling to push through controversial legislation (e.g. on the poll tax in 1988). The behaviour of these so-called 'backwoodsmen' made it easy to portray the survival of unelected peers as an offence against democratic principles; and, perhaps, the Blair government was the more eager to act against them because this was one way of giving satisfaction to its radical supporters.

Parliamentary reform

Reform of the House of Lords

In 1998 the Blair government published a White Paper, *Modernising Parliament: Reforming the House of Lords*. This envisaged the removal of all hereditary peers after a transitional period. In future, new members of the House would be appointed by an independent commission, rather than the Prime Minister.

However, when a Bill was passed in 1999 this proposal had been watered down after a deal with the leader of the Conservative peers, Lord Cranborne. Ninety-two hereditaries – elected by their fellow peers – were allowed to remain, pending the report of a Royal Commission (see Table 7.3). Headed by the former Conservative minister Lord Wakeham, members were hand-picked in the expectation that they would plump for a wholly-appointed Lords. However, it decided that the best long-term solution was an upper house with a mixed composition, including an elected element which might be chosen through proportional representation on a regional basis. The House would retain its existing powers (or lack of them). The changes

TIMELINE 7.1

Parliamentary reform since 1900

1911	Parliament Act, replaced House of Lords veto over legislation with the power to delay passage of Bills by 2 years
1949	Second Parliament Act, reduced House of Lords delaying power to 1 year
1958	Life Peerages Act, introduced women peers, and allowed the appointment of peers whose titles could not be inherited
1963	Peerage Act, allowed holders of hereditary peerages to renounce their titles
1978	Radio broadcasts of House of Commons became permanent
1979	Reform of select committee system in House of Commons
1986	Televised coverage of House of Lords became permanent
1989	Televised coverage of House of Commons became permanent
1995	Establishment of Committee on Standards and Privileges following Nolan Report on Standards in Public Life
1999	House of Lords Act, reduced the number of hereditary peers in the House of Lords to 92, pending further reform
2002	Changes to hours of sitting of House of Commons

Table 7.3 Membership of the House of Lords, 1999 and 2006

	October 1999 (before the House of Lords Act came into force)	March 2006
Peers by type		
Hereditary peer	759	92
Life peer	518	580
Law lord	27	27
Archbishop/bishop	26	26
Total membership	1330	725
Peers by party affiliation		
Conservative	471	205
Labour	179	206
Liberal Democrat	72	74
Cross-bench	353	190
Other	138	38

Note: Figures for party affiliation exclude peers on 'leave of absence'.

Source: House of Lords, www.parliament.uk/about_lords/membership.cfm

had not been implemented by the time of the 2001 general election, but Labour promised that if re-elected it would broadly follow the Commission's guidelines.

In February 2003 the Commons voted on a series of options. Blair himself still favoured a wholly-appointed House, and the Labour whips intervened on his behalf (although the votes were supposed to be free). Even so, the proposal proved the least popular among MPs and was heavily defeated by 323 to 245. By this time many Conservatives had swung behind the idea of a fully-elected House, the option which was also favoured by many Labour backbenchers and by the Liberal Democrats. The government struggled to face down these demands, and its normal overwhelming majority was slashed to just three on a proposal that the elected element should total 80 per cent of the new House (a vote on a wholly-elected House was lost by 17).

The government's opposition to a significant elected element was ironic, given that the main argument against the old House of Lords was its lack of democratic credibility. Indeed Blair's speeches on the subject revealed that the government was fearful of an elected upper house with more credibility than the Commons, particularly if it were based on proportional representation. At the 2004 Labour Party conference the Lord Chancellor Lord Falconer, who himself symbolised the extent of prime ministerial patronage, as an unelected minister and favoured friend of Blair, promised a 'once and for all' reform of the Lords early in the government's third term. However, while promising to make the resulting House of Lords more 'representative', it seemed clear that he had no wish to satisfy the demand of the party, which was to make it as 'democratic' as possible. The issue was given low priority in the party's 2005 manifesto which stated that the remaining hereditary peers would be removed but that the government would again try to find a consensus on the composition of the upper house.

Meanwhile the half-reformed Lords continued to invite the Commons to think again on a range of issues, most notably hunting (see Case study 7.4). During the 2001–2005 Parliament, the number of government defeats in the Lords was four times the figure for the whole eighteen years of Conservative government under

Thatcher and Major. The use of the Parliament Act in November 2004 to force through a hunting ban was only the third time that this legislation had been put into operation, and the Speaker's decision to apply it was immediately challenged by the pro-hunting lobby. By 2005, Labour was the largest party in the House of Lords but fell well short of a majority. Reflecting the government's frustration, the 2005 Labour manifesto promised a limit of 60 sitting days for the consideration of most Bills in the Lords and a review of conventions in the upper house. In February 2006, while the government was engaged in a new struggle with the Lords over anti-terror legislation, the Lord Chancellor indicated that ministers were now prepared to accept the introduction of an elected element in the House of Lords. This announcement was probably part of the government's preparations for the replacement of Blair with Gordon Brown, who was more enthusiastic about an elected upper chamber.

Reform of the Commons

While the Labour government was determined to reshape the House of Lords, the radical impetus was strangely lacking where the House of Commons was concerned. In Labour's 2005 general election manifesto, it merely congratulated itself on having changed the Commons by promoting more women MPs. The contrasting attitude to reform is easily explained. In opposition, politicians thunder against the dominance of the executive in the Commons. But once they win office – especially if they do so with the backing of an overwhelming majority – the procedures which seemed anti-democratic before the election invariably appear in a far more attractive guise.

Thus, in 1996 Labour's Shadow Leader of the Commons, Ann Taylor, pledged the party to reforms which would make the Commons a far more effective check on the executive. A new select committee on Modernisation was set up after the 1997 election to produce reform proposals. However, although the Modernisation Committee was far from idle, it concentrated on matters like changes to the parliamentary working day. This was serious enough for MPs with young families – since the institution continues to be dominated by men, it is hardly surprising that its hours of business are uncongenial to women. In October 2002 the Commons voted to bring their sittings on Tuesdays and Wednesdays forward by three hours, from 2.30pm to 11.30am, and to clock off at 7pm rather than 10pm to compensate. They would finish at 6pm on a Thursday. Ironically, though, within a few months many MPs were complaining that the changes actually made their lives more stressful! Their old lunchtimes were now disrupted, and the truncated Thursday session meant that some MPs started going back to their constituency homes on the Wednesday evening. There was a suspicion that the main impetus behind the reforms was that key votes would now take place early enough to meet the deadlines of the press and the electronic media.

In January 2005 MPs voted to restore the 10pm finish on Tuesdays, and to lengthen the Thursday sitting by meeting an hour earlier. The traditional long summer break from the end of July to October is now interrupted by two weeks of sittings in September; but this can be no great hardship since the holiday begins earlier in the month of July. Thus even the drive to modernise working hours has faltered.

Robin Cook, Leader of the Commons from 2001 to 2003, favoured more radical changes which promised to increase accountability rather than improving working conditions or suiting the convenience of the media. In particular, it was proposed that select committees would be strengthened; as well as receiving greater staff support, they would be allowed to scrutinise Bills before they were introduced. But despite the government's proud declaration of 'a mandate to modernise' Cook was able to make little meaningful progress against the opposition of the whips and other ministers. In June 2004 the Modernisation Committee decided that the Commons would become more 'welcoming' to members of the public if MPs were no longer allowed to refer to them as 'strangers' during debates. This innovation was suggested at a time when security at the House was actually being tightened in the face of terrorist threats and intrusions from campaigners (see Chapter 18); the newly 'welcoming' Palace of Westminster was now surrounded by huge concrete blocks designed to thwart attackers using bombs in cars or lorries.

Conclusion and summary

For all its democratic symbolism, parliament is clearly in need of major reforms. It might have acted as an effective legislature in the nineteenth century, but increasingly that period looks like a freakish exception to the general rule of executive dominance. In the past the unelected monarch provided a focal point of opposition for politicians hoping to restrain the over-mighty executive. The fact that the source of power has changed – and that many MPs dream of one day taking the premiership – does not mean that parliament should no longer perform the checking role it once discharged with reasonable success.

As this chapter has shown, the obstacles to change are the power of the Prime Minister who must command a majority in the Commons, and the deterrent effect of strong party discipline among MPs. It almost seems that successive governments have regarded near-dictatorial powers as a sacred trust which must be transmitted to their successors, whether or not the ruling party changes. Even unpopular governments which looked very likely to lose the next election, like those headed by James Callaghan and John Major, have made little or no effort to change things in order to make life easier for themselves after returning to opposition.

Almost the only viable argument in favour of executive dominance is that government is a complicated and wide-ranging business, often requiring rapid decisions with some guarantee of implementation. The same point is raised against proponents of proportional representation, which is likely to give rise to coalition governments (see Chapter 16). Objective students of the present situation should consider whether the deficiencies in parliamentary accountability really are outweighed at the present time by more effective and rational decision-making.

Further reading

R. Rogers and R. Walters, *How Parliament Works* (Harlow: Pearson Education, 5th edition, 2004) is an invaluable guide for students and practitioners alike. M. Rush, *Parliament Today* (Manchester: Manchester University Press, 2005) is a good introduction. Though somewhat dated, J. Garrett's *Westminster: Does Parliament Work?* (London: Gollancz, 1993) remains a very useful account by a frustrated insider. Philip (now Lord) Norton has produced several accessible articles and books on this subject, notably *Parliament in British Politics* (London: Palgrave, 2005). P. Ridell, *Parliament under Blair* (London: Politico's Publishing, 2000) assesses the impact of the Blair government. D. Shell, *The House of Lords* (London: Prentice-Hall, 2nd edition, 1992) is a good, but dated, introduction to the upper house.

On parliamentary reform, see P. Norton, 'The House of Commons: the Half Empty Bottle of Reform', in P. Norton (ed.) *Parliaments and Pressure Groups in Western Europe* (London: Frank Cass, 1999). A summary of more recent reform initiatives is P. Cowley and M. Stuart, '"Modernising" the House of Commons', *Politics Review*, Vol. 12, No. 4 (2003), pp. 2–4. It is difficult to publish academic commentaries fast enough to keep pace with the meandering course of Lords reform, but N. Baldwin, 'Reforming the Second Chamber', *Politics Review*, Vol. 11, No. 3 (2002), pp. 8–12, makes sense of its early stages. M. Russell, *Reforming the House of Lords: Lessons from Overseas* (Oxford: Oxford University Press, 2000) is a comparative study. Most aspects of parliament and the reform process in particular are covered in a special issue of *Parliamentary Affairs*, Vol. 57, No. 4 (2004).

An invigorating account of backbench disobedience is P. Cowley, *The Rebels: How Blair Mislaid his Majority* (London: Methuen, 2005). On women in the Commons, see S. Childs, *New Labour's MPs: Women Representing Women* (London: Routledge, 2004) and J. Lovenduski and P. Norris, 'Westminster Women: the Politics of Presence', *Political Studies*, Vol. 51, No. 1 (2003), pp. 84–102. G. Brandreth, *Breaking the Code: Westminster Diaries, 1992–97* (London: Weidenfeld & Nicolson, 1999) provides an insider view of the work of the whips at a particularly difficult historical juncture.

A lively, affectionate study of the parliamentary mind-set is provided by P. Riddell, *Honest Opportunism: How we get the Politicians we Deserve* (London: Indigo, 1996). Those with a more jaundiced view of our legislators will find plenty of support for their pessimism in D. Leigh and E. Vulliamy, *Sleaze: The Corruption of Parliament* (London: Fourth Estate, 1997). Some fascinating insights into New Labour's true commitment to modernisation can be gleaned from the late Robin Cook's memoir, *The Point of Departure* (London: Simon & Schuster, 2003).

Websites

By far the best resource for students of parliament is the official website www.parliament.the-stationery-office.co.uk. This provides links to sites for the House of Commons and the House of Lords, giving concise introductions to parliamentary procedure and recent reforms. It also provides access to the official record of debates (Hansard) and even contact addresses for MPs and peers. www.politics.co.uk features many useful links to articles with more critical content. The Department of Constitutional Affairs is responsible for reform of the Lords and includes full details of recent reform proposals at www.dca.gov.uk/constitution/holref/holrefindex.htm.

Three sites on the activities and behaviour of MPs can be recommended. Philip Cowley's website www.revolts.co.uk provides a comprehensive analysis of backbench rebellions; the Public Whip www.publicwhip.org.uk/index.php provides details of the voting records of MPs since 1997, and They Work For You www.theyworkforyou.com/ has a search facility for everything each MP has said in the House of Commons since 2001.

Chapter 8

Law and the judiciary

Learning outcomes

After reading this chapter, you will:

- Understand the importance of the judiciary and police to an understanding of British governance.
- Be able to evaluate recent debates about the role and nature of the judiciary, and their constitutional implications.
- Understand recent changes and controversies affecting the British police force.

Introduction

In most courses on British politics, law and order and the judiciary have been treated as something of an 'optional extra'. In itself this tells us something about traditional understandings of the British system of government, in which the judiciary and the police force have been regarded as 'above politics'.

This approach was always highly misleading, and is no longer tenable. Law and order was a central political issue long before February 1993 when Tony Blair promised to be 'tough on crime and tough on the causes of crime'. But as other subjects of controversy have declined, political leaders now spend much of their time trying to drum up support on questions like the level of recorded crime and police numbers. Meanwhile, critics continue to focus on the social backgrounds and attitudes of individual judges and police officers.

At the same time the relationship between the (appointed) judiciary and elected politicians has become increasingly strained. Senior judges frequently complain about undue interference from politicians. But in their turn they find themselves under almost constant attack, not just from politicians but also from sections of the media. Friction between government and the police has been less severe, but several Home Secretaries have been given rough receptions from police conferences in recent years. In this chapter we examine the reasons for these tensions in the context of constitutional change, and discuss other issues involving the British judiciary and police force.

The judicial system in the UK

Justice in Britain is administered through a complex network of courts which have evolved over many centuries. There are important variations between the systems in the component parts of the UK. For convenience we will follow the usual practice and focus on the system in England and Wales.

Most minor criminal cases – those leading to sentences of six months' imprisonment or less on conviction – are heard in magistrates' courts. There are more than 700 of these courts in England and Wales, staffed by around 29,000 magistrates (also known as Justices of the Peace or JPs). This office dates back to the reign of Richard I in the twelfth century. Most magistrates are part-time and unpaid, appointed by influential local figures who in turn are selected by the Lord Chancellor. The magistrates in some large urban areas are paid ('district judges' who were formally known as 'stipendary' magistrates). Magistrates sit without a jury, in panels of between two and seven members. Most of them have no legal training, because their judgements are supposed to reflect the 'common sense' of the local community. They can, though, draw on technical advice from legally-trained officials. Nearly 97 per cent of cases in England and Wales (over four million annually) are dealt with in this way.

Magistrates send more serious criminal cases for trial before a judge and jury at the local Crown Court. There are more than 60 of these in England and Wales, including the Central Criminal Court in London (better known as the Old Bailey). More than half of the defendants plead guilty before the case opens, so that the proceedings only concern the appropriate sentence. Appeals against Crown Court verdicts are heard by senior judges sitting in the Criminal Division of the Court of Appeal. When an important point of law has been raised and needs clarification, the Appeal Court can give leave for a further appeal, to the judicial committee of the House of Lords. This committee consists of specially-appointed Lords of Appeal in Ordinary, chosen for their experience and knowledge. At present there are twelve of these judges (see Table 8.1 below).

Criminal cases concern offences technically committed against the Crown. *Civil* cases concern disputes between private parties, and most of these are dealt with by separate institutions. The great majority of civil cases are heard in the County Courts, of which there are 260 in England and Wales. More complicated cases go to the High Court (based at the Royal Courts of Justice on the Strand in London) which is divided into three branches (the Queen's Bench, Chancery and Family Divisions) depending on the nature of the case. Appeals from these courts are heard in the Civil Division of the Court of Appeal; and, as in criminal cases, further appeals may be heard in the Lords.

The Queen's Bench contains an Administrative sub-division which hears cases brought by individuals or organisations against ministers who are alleged to have exceeded their statutory powers. There is obvious potential here for clashes between politicians and judges. More mundane cases of alleged maladministration by government departments are heard by a wide variety of independent tribunals. These hearings, usually held in public, are usually quicker (and cheaper) than more formal courts. Most of the tribunals have a heavy workload; for example, in 2003 the Immigration Tribunal received more than 100,000 cases relating to immigration.

Ombudsman: an independent official who investigates complaints made against the government by citizens.

Citizens seeking redress against departmental decisions can also write to their MPs requesting a ruling from Parliamentary Commissioners for Administration (PCAs), or '**Omdudsmen**' as they are more popularly known. Government proposals which are likely to prove controversial, such as the siting of new roads and power stations, can be examined by public inquiries.

Judicial review and the Human Rights Act 1998

In the US, the nine Justices of the Supreme Court are able to rule that legislative acts are unconstitutional, and thus null and void. Since Britain lacks a codified constitution, not even the most senior judges can strike down Acts of Parliament in this way. However, they do have the power of **judicial review**, which can force ministers to change the way in which they implement legislation. Under this procedure, judges appraise the decisions of a minister against the letter of the relevant legislation. If the wording is unclear, they are required to interpret the intentions of parliament at the time that it was passed. To this end, they can consult the written record (*Hansard*) to see what was said by the proposers of the measure. However, in practice they will be using their own judgement, deciding what parliament *ought* to have meant when it passed the legislation.

Judicial review: the review of the legality of ministerial decisions by the courts.

In recent years judicial review has been exercised more widely and, it seems, more willingly. There are several contributory factors:

- The importance of judicial review was underlined in 1980s when the courts were asked to pronounce on controversial new legislation, notably on industrial relations.

- Also beginning in the 1980s, successive governments have proposed reforms which members of the **judiciary** have interpreted as attempts to undermine their independence. This has made them less likely to give ministers the benefit of the doubt in any dispute.

Judiciary: the branch of government responsible for the interpretation and enforcement of laws though the courts.

- Legislation has become increasingly complicated in recent decades, allowing ministers wider scope for discretion which in turn might be open to legal challenge.

- Judges have come to see themselves as custodians of civil liberties, in the face of encroachments by successive governments.

- The new willingness of judges to take their side against government has encouraged would-be applicants for judicial review to come forward when other sources of redress have been exhausted.

Thus to a considerable extent judicial activism is self-reinforcing; the more active the judges, the more likely it is that they will be called upon to take part in political controversies. The effect has been remarkable. In the early 1970s there were fewer than 200 judicial reviews every year. By 1985 there were more than 1000 applications, and in 1998 the figure exceeded 4500. In one of the best-publicised cases, the former editor of *The Times* newspaper, Lord Rees-Mogg, challenged the right of parliament to ratify the Maastricht Treaty. His case was rejected by the High Court in July 1993, but Lord Justice Lloyd stressed that it had been a proper subject for review. In November 2004, the Countryside Alliance announced its intention to challenge the constitutional propriety of the 1949 Parliament Act which allows the House of Commons to over-ride the Lords (see Chapter 18).

The judiciary fought many bruising battles against the Conservative governments in the 1990s, and relations with New Labour have been no better. This is despite an excellent start, when the Blair government passed the Human Rights Act (HRA) in 1998 (see Case study 8.1). This legislation incorporated into British law the European Convention on Human Rights. The UK had been a co-signatory of the Convention in

Case study:	8.1

The Human Rights Act 1998

The Human Rights Act 1998 incorporated the rights set out in Articles 2 to 12 and Article 14 of the European Convention on Human Rights. It did not incorporate Article 13 – providing the right of effective redress to people whose rights under the Convention had been breached – because the government believed the Human Rights Act itself met this requirement.

The Convention rights incorporated in the Human Rights Act 1998 are:

- Article 2. Right to life
- Article 3. Freedom from torture
- Article 4. Freedom from slavery and forced labour
- Article 5. Right to liberty and security
- Article 6. Right to a fair trial
- Article 7. No punishment without law
- Article 8. Right to respect for private and family life
- Article 9. Freedom of thought, conscience and religion
- Article 10. Right to freedom of expression
- Article 11. Freedom of assembly and association
- Article 12. Right to marry and found a family
- Article 14. Freedom from discrimination

The Act also includes the three articles of the First Protocol to the Convention:

- Protection of property
- Right to education
- Right to free elections

1951, but until 1998 British citizens seeking protection under its terms had to apply for a ruling from the European Court of Human Rights (ECHR) at Strasbourg when all other avenues had been exhausted. By the time of the 1997 general election the legal profession in general, including many senior judges, was in favour of a Human Rights Act which would allow such cases to be heard in the UK.

The HRA was a radical change, the lasting implications of which have yet to be worked out (the Act only came into full force in October 2000). But in theory, at least, it gave a further boost to judicial activism. All new legislation has to be tested against the HRA before it receives the Royal Assent. But any UK law judged to be incompatible with the terms of the HRA would become impossible to enforce. Ministers either have to appeal against the judgement to the House of Lords or revise the legislation to make it compatible. Between 1998 and 2003 judges found against the government on 15 occasions (five of these verdicts were subsequently reversed by the Lords).

In the wake of the attacks in New York and Washington in September 2001 the Blair government took advantage of its right to opt-out of specific terms of the HRA

Human rights or national security? A dilemma for policy-makers after the attack in London on 7 July 2005 (© Getty Images)

in order to pass new anti-terrorist legislation which seemed likely to contravene Article 5 (see Case study 8.1). No other European government took this step, despite the general sense of danger throughout the West. Critics could argue that the government's decision made a mockery of the HRA as a whole, since the provisions on liberty were central to the original Convention. Many of the other terms were vague and even contradictory. Thus, for example, the press was deeply concerned about the right to privacy, which seemed to endanger its lucrative practice of celebrity-hounding. Any restrictions on such reporting would seem to conflict with the right to freedom of expression which is also enshrined in the Convention. In practice, judges seemed willing to side with privacy rather than the press. The HRA has helped several celebrities to win substantial damages from intrusive publications (see Chapter 4).

After the attacks on the London transport system in July 2005, the HRA came under additional scrutiny. Although government ministers had initially claimed that the impact of the HRA had been limited, at the time of writing (June 2006) it is clear that many senior figures now consider the Act to have been a mistake. For their part the Conservatives promised to repeal the legislation.

Who are the judges?

Whatever its other merits, the British judiciary could not be rated as the most democratic of the country's institutions. It epitomises the traditional 'Establishment' – male, white, affluent and well furnished with friends in high places. Britain's judges are appointed by politicians, rather than elected; and the decisive voice in all important appointments rests with the Lord Chancellor, an unelected member of the House of Lords who is chosen by the Prime Minister.

As the list of current Lords of Appeal in Ordinary makes clear (see Table 8.1), the senior ranks of the judiciary are dominated by Oxbridge-educated men who are over the legal retirement age for other professions (in fact judges do not have to retire until 75). In 2004 Baroness Hale of Richmond became the first woman member, and the same year saw the appointment of Linda Dobbs as the only representative of the ethnic minorities among more than 100 High Court judges. These

Table 8.1 The Lords of Appeal in Ordinary, 2006

Name	Year of birth	University
Lord Bingham of Cornhill	1933	Oxford
Lord Brown of Eaton-Under-Heywood	1937	Oxford
Lord Carswell	1934	Oxford and Chicago
Baroness Hale of Richmond	1945	Cambridge
Lord Hoffman	1934	Cape Town and Oxford
Lord Hope of Craighead	1938	Cambridge and Edinburgh
Lord Mance	1943	Oxford
Lord Nicholls of Birkenhead	1933	Liverpool and Cambridge
Lord Rodger of Earlsferry	1944	Glasgow and Oxford
Lord Saville of Newdigate	1936	Oxford
Lord Scott of Foscote	1934	Cape Town and Oxford
Lord Walker of Gestingthorpe	1938	Cambridge

Lord Falconer, Secretary of State for Constitutional Affairs and Cherie Booth, judge, human rights lawyer and wife of Tony Blair (© Peter MacDiarmid/Reuters/Corbis)

are exceptions that only underlined the nature of the previous rules. Women still account for only 8 per cent of all senior judges; but even on that showing they are faring better than members of the ethnic minorities, regardless of gender.

In October 2004 the Lord Chancellor, Lord Falconer, and the Lord Chief Justice, Lord Woolf, endorsed proposals which were intended to help redress the balance. The main recommendation was to relax the qualifications needed for a judicial post, allowing judges to be appointed at an earlier stage in their legal careers. In theory this fast track approach might help to create a senior judiciary which is more representative of society as a whole. But at the same time the Attorney General Lord Goldsmith was warning that young barristers were starting their careers with debts of up to £20,000, threatening to make the legal profession into 'the preserve of the privileged and wealthy'.

It might be thought that the social background of senior judges is of limited importance for most people, since they are most likely to come into contact with magistrates who are fairly representative of the local community. But the law is a hierarchical profession, which takes its tone from the top. If the senior judiciary became more socially representative it might be less easy to criticise its judgements in future; whenever the tabloid press finds fault with a court decision it almost invariably tries to back its argument by giving reasons for thinking that the legal profession must be 'out of touch' with ordinary people. Another attempt to make the law seem more accessible began in November 2004, when it was announced that some High Court cases would be televised on an experimental basis.

Are judges biased?

Worries about the social composition of the senior judiciary are not new. In the first edition of his classic book *The Politics of the Judiciary* (Fontana, 1977), John Griffiths argued that although judges drawn predominantly from the upper classes were not necessarily biased in a party-political sense, their rulings were characterised by an unconscious conservatism (in the sense of favouring the *status quo*). Two well-known cases involving local authorities certainly suggest a distaste for political radicalism. In 1976 the newly-elected Conservative Tameside council reversed a decision by its Labour predecessor to convert local grammar schools into comprehensives. The Labour Secretary of State for Education, Fred Mulley, ordered the council to press ahead with the comprehensive scheme, taking his authority from the Education Act 1944 which allowed him to overrule the local authority if he were satisfied that its actions were 'unreasonable'. Mulley's intervention was challenged by the council, whose defiance was backed by the Court of Appeal and the House of Lords.

In the Tameside case it could be argued that Mulley had indeed overstretched the terms of the 1944 Act, and that in electing a Conservative council the local voters had registered their opposition to comprehensive education. As such, the higher courts could claim that they were fighting on the side of local democracy against the power of the central state. In 1981 they had the chance to strike again in the same general cause. Labour had won the Greater London Council (GLC) elections, partly because of a promise to reduce fares on London public transport. One Conservative-controlled borough objected. The High Court upheld the GLC's policy, but this verdict was subsequently reversed by the Court of Appeal and the Lords. The flimsy justification for this ruling was the statutory requirement that the Council should provide transport on an 'economic' basis. Comparing this decision with the Tameside case, critics drew the conclusion that senior judges only choose to fight on behalf of local democracy when the central government is controlled by Labour.

During the 1980s there were several examples of conservative decisions by the judiciary, particularly on trade union matters (see Controversy 8.1). In 1985 one important case went against the Thatcher government. Clive Ponting, a senior civil servant, was acquitted on a charge of breaking the Official Secrets Act, having leaked details relating to the sinking of the Argentine vessel *General Belgrano* during the Falklands War. However, this blow against the power of the state was landed by the jury, which had defied the judge's firm direction that they should equate the 'public interest' with the political needs of the government.

Controversy: 8.1

The courts and the Wapping dispute

During the 1980s the courts found no serious fault with any of the government's repeated measures to constrain trade union power. In one celebrated case, they showed an inclination to extend the terms of the legislation. In 1986 SOGAT 82, a print-workers' union, was fined after its members had picketed a newspaper distribution company owned by the media magnate Rupert Murdoch. The dispute with Murdoch had been triggered by his decision to move the printing of *The Times*, *Sun* and other newspapers to modern premises in Wapping, East London, allowing him to sack many of the printers. The Court of Appeal ruled that the distribution plant was an entirely separate company from Murdoch's News International, and that SOGAT's actions were instances of illegal 'secondary picketing'. The ruling helped Murdoch to win the dispute, which was seen as a final blow to old-style union action after the defeat of the miners' strike in the previous year.

But earlier discussions of conservative judicial bias looked highly ironic in 1998, when an Appeal Court judgement was set aside because one of the judges was accused of being too radical. The former Chilean dictator Augusto Pinochet had been arrested in London on the application of the Spanish government, which wanted him extradited to face charges relating to his period in office. The High Court ruled in Pinochet's favour, but this judgement was overturned by 3–2 in the Court of Appeal. It transpired that one of the majority, Lord Hoffman, had an indirect interest in the work of the pressure group Amnesty International. This was held to invalidate the verdict, and the case was heard again. This time the Appeal Court ruled that the final decision should lie with the Home Secretary, who eventually allowed Pinochet to return to Chile.

One of the judges who found Hoffman's position untenable was Lord Hutton, who in 2003–2004 became famous for presiding over the inquiry into the circumstances surrounding the death of the weapons inspector Dr David Kelly. At the time of his appointment Hutton was hailed as a fearless judge who would seek the truth no matter where it led. But during the inquiry, he stuck rigidly to an interpretation of his brief which would allow him to avoid any criticism of the government's conduct. By contrast, he was merciless in his treatment of the BBC. Hutton (born 1931, educated at public school and Oxford) thus reverted to a type which seemed to be

| Analysis: | 8.1 |

Judicial independence

From the perspective of democracy and governance in contemporary Britain, the story of relations between politicians and the judiciary in recent years is salutary. The increasing salience of law and order on the electoral agenda has encouraged politicians to make ambitious promises about a crackdown on crime. In doing so, they have forgotten that they would need cooperation from a legal profession which prides itself on its independence. Even if they were generally in favour of harsher punishments and stern ministerial decisions on issues like asylum, senior judges would feel inclined to think twice if they perceived that they were being bullied. The idea that tougher measures were needed implied that previous judicial decisions had been too soft. It was little wonder that judges began to dig in their heels when the debate on law and order hotted up after Tony Blair and Michael Howard began their verbal jousting on home affairs in 1993.

Reformers have tended to forget that the British ideal of judicial independence was an inspiration to the founders of the US constitution. The founding fathers formalised the principle by separating the three branches of executive, legislature and judiciary. But British judges have traditionally felt that they could assert their independence without written constitutional provisions. On this argument, whenever British judges have sided with governments they have done so without feeling constrained by the fact that the Lord Chancellor who appointed them was also a member of the executive and the legislature. On their own view, they were merely upholding the impartial rule of law. Even the more cynical argument that judges come from a social background which predisposes them towards maintenance of the *status quo* cannot be used against them so easily, at a time when the main political parties seem intent on devising penal policies to attract votes rather than to tackle the problem of crime.

dying out – the safe lawyer brought in to make sure that a public inquiry could be held without undue embarrassment to the existing government. Previous appointments (Sir Richard Scott, who reported in 1996 on the sale of arms to Iraq, and Sir William Macpherson (see below)) proved less fortunate for the powers that be. It is not the fault of judges that they are invariably chosen to perform such duties; but the publicity surrounding public inquiries does add urgency to the task of making the senior ranks of the judiciary more representative of British society as a whole.

The judges in rebellion

The idea that a Law Lord could be accused of left-wing bias was not as startling in 1998 as it might have been ten years before. The Thatcher governments were rarely challenged by the judiciary, but the situation under her successor John Major was very different. Ministerial decisions were often overturned in the courts. Major's last Home Secretary Michael Howard (1993–97) was particularly unfortunate in this respect. Although he was an experienced barrister, he fell foul of several high profile rulings on his use of the powers of deportation and exclusion. The courts also ruled against his attempts to increase the sentences imposed on the child-murderers of the toddler James Bulger, a ruling confirmed subsequently by the European Court of Human Rights.

A cynical observer could trace the new restive mood to the attempt by the Thatcher government in 1989–90 to push through a radical reform of the legal profession. The main proposal was to abolish the distinction between barristers (who argue cases in court) and solicitors (who prepare the cases for the barristers). If implemented, this might have reduced the costs of litigation and speeded up the judicial process. However, it was fiercely resisted by the barristers; and judges, who are recruited from the ranks of the barristers, were equally determined to uphold the dignity of their profession. Although they succeeded in watering down the proposals, members of the legal profession understood that this skirmish was likely to be the first of many. If they had expected Thatcher to spare them out of gratitude for their help in her battles with other vested interests, they had been sadly mistaken.

Under Major the new conflict between judges and politicians was diverted into different fields. If the government could not reform the traditional career structure of the legal profession, it could try to undermine the ability of judges to exercise their own discretion in sentencing convicted criminals. In 1994 Home Secretary Michael Howard introduced mandatory sentences for certain categories of repeat offenders. Spurred on by the Law Lords, the House of Lords watered down this legislation. While Labour was promising to be 'tough on crime, tough on the causes of crime', it seemed as if the supposedly conservative judges were now isolated on the liberal side of the argument about penal policy.

After the fall of the Conservative government in 1997, senior judges found themselves in the unusual position of attacking Labour ministers from the left. The Lord Chief Justice, Lord Woolf, had been a feisty critic of Howard, and continued his campaign against Labour Home Secretary, David Blunkett. In March 2004 he attacked Labour for its plans to streamline the appeals procedure for failed asylum seekers. This came after the High Court had ruled against Blunkett's policy of denying benefits to asylum seekers who failed to apply on arrival. Woolf also lambasted the

Table 8.2 Britain's top judges and law officers, 2006

Judges		
Title	**Appointed**	**Duty**
Lord Chancellor and Secretary of State for Constitutional Affairs	Lord Falconer of Thoroton (born 1951, appointed 2003)	Head of judiciary; responsible for judicial appointments.
Lord Chief Justice of England and Wales	Lord Phillips of Worth Matravers (born 1938, appointed 2005)	Head of the judiciary in England and Wales and the criminal branch of Court of Appeal
Master of the Rolls	Sir Anthony Clarke (born 1943, appointed 2005)	Heads civil branch of Court of Appeal; Head of Civil Justice
President of the Queen's Bench Division	Sir Igor Judge (born 1941, appointed 2005)	Head of Criminal Justice
President of the Family Division	Sir Mark Potter (born 1937, appointed 2005)	Heads Family Division of High Court
Chancellor of the High Court	Sir Andrew Morrit (born 1938, appointed 2000)	Heads Chancery Division of High Court
Government law officers		
Title	**Appointed**	**Duty**
Attorney General	Lord Goldsmith (born 1950, appointed 2001)	Chief legal adviser to the government and acts as the government's barrister in legal case; also head of the Crown Prosecution Service and Director of the Serious Fraud Office
Solicitor General	Mike O'Brien (born 1954, appointed 2005)	Acts as deputy to the Attorney General
In Scotland, the relevant officials advising the Scottish Executive are the Lord Advocate (Colin Boyd) and the Solicitor General (Charles Mullin).		

Source: Department of Constitutional Affairs, www.dca.gov.uk/judicial/senjudfr.htm

government for allowing the prison population to rise to nearly 75,000 (a record). This reflected the view of many judges that, contrary to Howard's favourite slogan, prison does not work as an effective means of protecting the community in the long term. But in voicing this opinion Lord Woolf aroused serious displeasure in the Home Office.

Woolf retired as Lord Chief Justice in 2005 and was succeeded by Lord Phillips of Worth Matravers (see Table 8.2). Reforms to the office will see Lord Phillips play a wider role, hearing the most important appeals in civil and family as well as criminal law, and continuing to set sentencing guidelines. The Constitutional Reform Act 2005 states that the Lord Chief Justice represents the views of the judiciary in England and Wales to parliament and to ministers, and can make written representations to parliament on matters relating to the judiciary. The Lord Chief Justice also takes over the judicial functions of the Lord Chancellor, becoming President of the Courts in England and Wales (see below).

New Labour's constitutional reforms

While the judges were at loggerheads with the Blair government over specific policies, a new controversy erupted on the subject of constitutional reform. The government believed that the position of Lord Chancellor had become increasingly anomalous. He sat in the Cabinet, presided over the House of Lords, and as head of the judiciary was responsible for the key judicial appointments. As such, he was at once a member of the executive, the legislature and the judiciary, making a mockery of the liberal constitutional principle that these branches of government should be divided. The office could even be held to contravene the terms of the Human Rights Act 1998, which decrees that trials should be conducted by an 'independent and impartial tribunal'.

In June 2003 it was announced that the then Lord Chancellor, Lord Irvine of Lairg, would be standing down as part of a wider government reshuffle. He was replaced by Lord Falconer of Thoroton who was, like Irvine himself, a close friend of the Prime Minister. But the proposed changes went further. It was envisaged that Falconer would be the last Lord Chancellor, and hold that title only for a transitional period. He would no longer act as a judge, and his powers of judicial patronage would be handed to an independent appointments commission. A Department for Constitutional Affairs was to take over many of the functions of the Lord Chancellor's Department. Finally, the judicial committee of the House of Lords would be replaced by a Supreme Court, sitting outside parliament. The existing Law Lords would join this court, and would no longer be entitled to vote in the House of Lords itself. The overall effect would be to reaffirm the principle of a separation of powers, and was regarded in some quarters as an early step towards a written constitution for the UK.

Reform along these lines had long been advocated by expert observers of the judicial scene. However, the announcement aroused a furore. It seemed that ministers had only realised at the last minute that the post of Lord Chancellor, which dated back to the seventh century, could not be abolished without legislation. The impression of another botched job – at a time when the government had destroyed the old House of Lords without a clear idea of a replacement (see Chapter 7) – lent weight to the argument that traditional institutions were being thoughtlessly reformed to appease Labour's radical supporters. It was reported that a new American-style Justice Department had been considered, only to be rejected by Blunkett because it would have cut into his Home Office empire.

After protracted manoeuvres, the Constitutional Reform Act was passed in 2005. The government had retreated from its plan to abolish the post of Lord Chancellor. Falconer kept the title of Lord Chancellor but the office was reformed with its judicial functions transferred to the Lord Chief Justice who becomes President of the Courts in England and Wales. For the first time, the Act enshrines in law a duty on ministers to respect the independence of the judiciary (see Analysis 8.1). It bars them from

The Attorney General and the invasion of Iraq

The difficult relationship between the law and politics was illustrated by the controversy surrounding the treatment of advice given to the government by the Attorney General, Lord Goldsmith about the legality of the invasion of Iraq under international law. The Attorney General is the chief legal adviser to the government.

During the 2005 general election campaign, it emerged that the Attorney General had amended his advice on the legality of the invasion of Iraq in the days leading up to the invasion by American and British forces. In a lengthy written answer to parliament on 7 March 2003, Goldsmith stated unequivocally that the invasion of Iraq was legal under international law, citing the combined effect of United Nations resolutions 678, 687 and 1441 as grounds for military action. The latter was particularly important as it stated that Iraq would face 'serious consequences' if it failed to 'comply with its disarmament obligations'.

However, in an unpublished document sent to the Prime Minister ten days before his submission to parliament, the Attorney General stated that the 'language of resolution 1441 leaves the position unclear'". He outlined a number of difficulties of interpretation and stated that 'the safest legal course would be to secure the adoption of a further resolution to authorise the use of force'. This earlier document only came to light because of a leak to the media.

The main points of controversy included: (i) Blair's perceived failure to inform the Cabinet and parliament of the reservations expressed in the Attorney General's initial assessment, and (ii) whether the Attorney General had been put under political pressure to amend his legal advice. Downing Street responded by noting that technically the Attorney General had not changed his advice on the legality of the invasion because he had not reached a firm conclusion in his first, unpublished memo. However, if the initial assessment had been released at the time, it would have been more difficult for the government to secure the support of parliament for the war.

seeking special access to judges. An independent Judicial Appointments Commission will recommend candidates for judicial positions to the Lord Chancellor. The Act also establishes an independent Supreme Court which will take over the judicial role of the House of Lords and whose members would be appointed by an independent body. But the failure to find an appropriate building for the Supreme Court has delayed its launch.

Meanwhile, the role of the Attorney General – the chief legal adviser to the government – was placed in the spotlight by the controversy over Lord Goldsmith's advice to the government on the legality of the invasion of Iraq (see Controversy 8.2). The case once again illustrated the uneasy relationship between politics and the law.

The police

Respect for the police force is an essential ingredient of any democratic society, which rests on the voluntary consent of its citizens. In popularity polls, the British police always rank highly among public servants. Their familiar dark blue uniforms are a source of reassurance to most people. However, they have aroused suspicion

Case study:	8.2

Crime in England and Wales

The importance of law and order as an electoral issue means that official crime statistics are subjected to close scrutiny. In 2003–2004 the police recorded 5.9 million crimes in England and Wales. However, the British Crime Survey (BSC) which focuses on the experience of people rather than police activity, produced an estimate of 11.7 million crimes. The government hailed this as a success, pointing out that the BSC figure had declined by 36 per cent since 1995. However, the BSC excludes certain categories of crime, including shoplifting and crime against young people. At least it was beyond dispute that the level of police detection was very low. The official 'clear-up' figure for 2003/4 was just 1.4 million crimes.

Source: Home Office

and even hatred in some sections of the community, who feel that they do not enforce the law impartially.

The key role of the police as defenders of a free society has led critics to demand that they be subject to democratic controls. But a workable system has proved elusive. Currently there are 43 police forces in England and Wales: until 1964 there were more than 200. (For the situation in Northern Ireland, see Case study 8.3.) Nominally, police forces are supervised by police authorities, composed of magistrates, local councillors and other prominent local figures. The councillors have a majority on the authorities, despite attempts by recent governments to turn the balance towards non-elected nominees. But in practice the authorities have little control over the conduct of the forces. This lies with the Chief Constables, who are responsible to the Home Secretary. The reality of the situation was brought home in 2004 when Home Secretary Blunkett ordered the suspension of the Chief Constable of Humberside in the wake of adverse findings in a report into a notorious murder case at Soham, Cambridgeshire. The police authority in Humberside wanted to keep their Chief Constable, and as local people their opinion should have carried weight. But Blunkett was bound to get a compromise on his own terms, because the power of the Home Secretary to suspend Chief Constables had been verified by the Police Reform Act 2002.

In November 2004 the Blair government issued a White Paper, *Building Communities, Beating Crime*, including several proposals to improve links between the police and local people. The police would be made more accessible, and their numbers increased by 12,000 from the current 140,000. The government also aimed to recruit 20,000 additional Community Support Officers, who lack many of the powers of ordinary police officers but are presumed to have a reassuring effect on local people. At the same time, the government was encouraging the use of Anti-Social Behaviour Orders (ASBOs), introduced by the Crime and Disorder Act 1998 to address the problem of persistent 'low level' crime.

The White Paper suggested that some of the existing 43 police forces could be amalgamated. In 2006 the government announced proposals for the merger of forces which would reduce the number of police forces to 24. The government ruled out a unified national police force, but some critics claimed that this was already happening by stealth. A National Policing Plan had already been introduced, by the 2002 Police Reform Act. There are good operational reasons for closer cooperation between forces on complex operations against terrorism and organised crime and for the establishment of national databases to track down criminals who do not restrict their operations to a single area. Yet the lingering suspicion of a national force is not just based on respect for traditional demarcations. During the miners' strike of 1984–85, when local forces were closely coordinated through the National Reporting Centre (NRC), critics alleged that the police were being used to impose the will of a particular government rather than upholding the rule of law. There is also a danger that a nationwide force will blur the lines of political responsibility. Even the present system opens the possibility that Chief Constables can be used as convenient scapegoats by Home Secretaries when things go wrong. In reality, police shortcomings can be caused by inadequate resources supplied by central government – and, ironically, officers complain that the paperwork demanded by Whitehall initiatives absorbs much of the time that could be spent on detection.

Miscarriage of justice: a situation in which someone is punished by the courts for a crime when the evidence is insufficient to secure a conviction.

The police themselves have often been criticised for the irresponsible exercise of power. During the 1970s, for example, there were several high-profile prosecutions (such as the cases of the Birmingham Six and the Bridgewater Four) which were subsequently exposed as **miscarriages of justice**. In 1986 the responsibility for deciding whether or not to prosecute was taken away from the police and given to a **Crown Prosecution Service (CPS)**, staffed by solicitors under an independent Director of Public Prosecutions. The police were also vulnerable to criticism because they investigated alleged abuses within their own ranks. The Police Complaints Authority (PCA) established as a result of the Police and Criminal Evidence Act (1984), was not independent enough for the liking of some observers, particularly when it investigated deaths in police custody. It was replaced by an Independent Police Complaints Commission (IPCC) which began work in April 2004. In 1993 two non-police members were added to Her Majesty's Inspectorate of Constabulary (HMIC) which investigates the efficiency of the police.

Crown Prosecution Service (CPS): an independent body which advises the police on possible prosecutions, reviews cases submitted by them, determines what charges are to be faced and prosecutes cases in court.

| Case study: | 8.3 |

The Police Service of Northern Ireland

The importance of consent to the effective operation of a police force was illustrated by the findings of the Patten Commission which examined policing in Northern Ireland after the 1998 Good Friday Agreement. In a society almost evenly divided by religion, the existing Royal Ulster Constabulary (RUC) was predominantly Protestant. Its very name implied that members were committed to the union between Britain and Northern Ireland. If this were not enough to deter Catholics from joining, would-be recruits were often intimidated by Republican paramilitaries.

The Patten Commission recommended the replacement of the RUC with a Police Service of Northern Ireland, which was duly established in November 2001. The new force is committed to equal recruitment from both communities.

The police and society

After the 1981 riots a senior judge, Lord Scarman, compiled a wide-ranging report into the underlying problems of Britain's inner cities. Although the riots had numerous causes, some of the worst outbreaks took place in areas marked by tension between ethnic minorities and the police.

Scarman recommended a new emphasis on more sensitive 'community policing'. He also urged a recruitment drive among ethnic minorities, along with an attempt to root out existing discrimination in police ranks. But although the government acted on many of Scarman's findings, concrete progress was slow. By 2004 less than 3 per cent of police came from the ethnic minorities. The government set a target of 7 per cent by 2009, while London's Metropolitan Police was aiming at no less than 26 per cent by the same date (from 10 per cent in 2004).

The Metropolitan Police had reason to be particularly sensitive on this issue in 2004, since five years earlier they had been the subject of one of the most critical reports in British history. The Macpherson Report of 1999 identified 'institutional racism' within the force (see Analysis 8.2). It seemed that the Metropolitan Police, at least, were all too representative of one unpleasant element of society. Previously, the HMIC had also emphasised the problem of sexism in the ranks. In 2004 women accounted for 20 per cent of police officers. The government aimed to raise the proportion to 35 per cent. The question remains whether such moves would be sufficient to overcome the so-called 'canteen culture' which had shaped attitudes among so many generations of police. In this context the suicide attacks in London on 7 July 2005 presented a serious test of police attitudes.

Analysis:　　　　　　　　　　　　　　　　　　　　　　　　　　　　**8.2**

Institutional racism

In April 1993 a black teenager, Stephen Lawrence, was murdered in Eltham, South London. When no charges were brought in the case, the victim's family began to campaign for an official inquiry into the police investigation. The calls were resisted until 1998, when the Labour Home Secretary Jack Straw appointed a former High Court judge, Sir William Macpherson, to examine the conduct of the Metropolitan Police. When he reported in the following year Macpherson found that the investigation into Lawrence's death had been highly incompetent. More seriously, he also found that the force was tainted with 'institutional racism'. In other words, there was a pervasive culture within the Metropolitan Police which meant that officers discriminated against members of the ethnic minorities, whether they were victims of crime or suspected criminals. The collective attitude of the police might reflect unconscious bias rather than malevolent prejudice. But this implied that the police were not alone in their unacceptable attitudes. Rather, it could be argued that they merely reflected prevailing attitudes in society as a whole.

Macpherson listed 70 recommendations, most of which were accepted. Among other things, in future new recruits were to be screened to see if they betrayed signs of racism. But progress would have to be monitored closely, since Macpherson was revisiting much of the territory which had been examined by Lord Scarman nearly two decades earlier, apparently to limited effect. There were fears of a backlash against the findings of the report, which were attacked in some quarters as examples of so-called 'political correctness'.

Conclusion and summary

It is a key principle of liberal democracy that the police and judiciary should be seen as impartial enforcers of the law, rather than the servants of existing governments. Traditionally, supporters of the British system of government have claimed that it satisfies this requirement even in the absence of a codified constitution.

Relations between government and law enforcers have become more problematic in Britain since the 1970s. During the Thatcher years police and judges were often accused of pandering to the government's will. But since the beginning of the 1990s there have been frequent clashes, between successive Home Secretaries, the police and the judges. In part, this friction has arisen because politicians have made ambitious electoral promises about crime and punishment. Their attempts to exert greater control have been helped by a widespread sense that neither the judiciary nor the police are democratically accountable, or representative of society as a whole. For their part, judges and police could argue that in spite of several damaging episodes in recent decades they remain much more popular than the peoples' elected representatives.

Attempts are being made to change the social composition of the police and the judiciary. It seems fair to say that the police are less independent now than they were 30 years ago, and it is likely that the trend towards a national force (in practice if not in name) will continue. By contrast, the judiciary have become more conscious of their role as independent watchdogs of traditional British liberties. Senior judges continue to resist changes which they find unpalatable, and once Labour's constitutional reforms have been fully implemented their position may be strengthened even further.

Further reading

Although his central thesis is now almost 30 years old, J.A.G. Griffith's *The Politics of the Judiciary* (London: Fontana, 5th edition, 1997) is still the most incisive general work on this subject. On recent reforms, see S. Prince, 'The Law and Politics: Rumours of the Demise of the Lord Chancellor have been Exaggerated', *Parliamentary Affairs*, Vol. 58, No. 2 (2005), pp. 248–57, and S. Prince, 'The Law and Politics: Upsetting the Judicial Apple-Cart', *Parliamentary Affairs*, Vol. 57, No. 2 (2004), pp. 288–300. Judicial review is explored in A. Le Sueur, 'The Judicial Review Debate: from Partnership to Friction', *Government and Opposition*, Vol. 36, No. 1 (1996), pp. 190–210. A lively account of the judiciary based on interviews with leading legal figures is C. Banner and A. Deane, *Off With Their Wigs! Judicial Revolution in Modern Britain* (London: Imprint Academic, 2003).

On the Human Rights Act 1998, see the article by the former Lord Chancellor, Lord Irvine – D. Irvine, 'The Human Rights Act: Principle and Practice', *Parliamentary Affairs*, Vol. 57, No. 4 (2004), pp. 744–53. For academic assessments, see I. Loveland, 'Incorporating the European Convention on Human Rights into UK Law', *Parliamentary Affairs*, Vol. 52, No. 1 (1999), pp. 113–27 and the special issue of *Political Quarterly*, Vol. 68, No. 2 (1997). Students should also consult D. Beetham, I. Byrne, P. Nogan and S. Weir (eds), *Democracy under Blair: A Democratic Audit of the United Kingdom* (London: Politico's, 2002), for an appraisal of the judicial system and the police against exacting criteria of democracy and human rights. On the police, R. Reiner's *The Politics of the Police* (Oxford: Oxford University Press, 3rd edition, 2001) is an accessible and comprehensive account.

Websites

The websites for the Department for Constitutional Affairs (www.dca.gov.uk) and the Home Office (www.homeoffice.gov.uk) provide internal and external links for students in search of up-to-date information on judicial and police matters. Latest developments in the field of human rights can be consulted on the website of the pressure group Liberty (www.liberty-human-rights.org.uk). The Human Rights Act can be read in full on www.hmso.gov.uk/acts/acts1998/19980042.htm; the Macpherson Report is available on www.archive.official-documents.co.uk/document/cm42/4262/4262.htm

Part 3

Multi-level governance

Chapter 9

The changing state

After reading this chapter, you will:

- Be able to identify the main features of the move from government to governance.
- Appreciate the major issues raised by the development of the quango state.
- Be able to evaluate the significance of new forms of governance for the UK state.

Introduction

For much of the twentieth century, the United Kingdom was one of the most centralised of liberal democratic states. The Westminster Model of government was one in which power was concentrated at the centre. The doctrine of parliamentary sovereignty dictated that no other body could challenge parliament's legislative supremacy. The fusion of the executive and legislative branches meant that a governing party commanding a majority in the House of Commons had significant control over the policy-making process. Aside from local government which was relatively weak, there was no tier of government beyond the centre in Great Britain.

A major theme of this book is the decline of the Westminster Model as both a description of the British political system and an explanatory framework. In Chapter 6 we saw how the core executive model of resource exchange has greater explanatory value than long-running debates about prime ministerial versus Cabinet government. This chapter examines the changing role of the state focusing on the transition from an era of government in which formal institutions were the dominant actors to governance in which a range of public bodies, private organisations and specialist agencies are involved in policy-making. Particular attention will be paid to the reform of the civil service, the enhanced role of quangos and regulatory agencies, and the impact of globalisation.

Government to governance

Government: decision-making through formal institutions and rules.

Governance: decision-making by multiple actors in networks.

The changing nature of the UK state is encapsulated by the notion of a shift from **government** to **governance** (see Table 9.1). Government involves decision-making through formal institutions and rules; it is hierarchical with clear lines of control and accountability. Governance refers to the role of multiple non-state actors and networks in decision-making. It is characterised by fragmentation rather than centralisation, interdependence rather than hierarchy, regulation rather than command. Governance requires bargaining and cooperation between actors working within the same or linked policy fields whereas government involves clear lines of command and control. The key developments in this transition from government to governance have been:

- The separation of policy-making and policy implementation functions within central government.
- The emergence of an enabling or regulatory state which oversees the provision of public goods by a range of actors rather than providing them directly.
- The introduction of market forces and private sector management practices in public administration.
- The diffusion of decision-making from the centre to supranational and sub-national bodies.

Table 9.1 Government to governance

Government – the Westminster Model	Governance
The centre	
Parliamentary sovereignty	Intergovernmental relations
Cabinet or prime ministerial government	Resource exchange in the core executive
Ministerial accountability to parliament	Distinction between accountability and responsibility
Hierarchical civil service	Division between policy advice and policy implementation functions
Significant state role in the provision of public goods	Enabling state and regulatory state
Sub-national politics	
Unitary state	Multi-level governance
Scottish Office and Welsh Office	Scottish Parliament and Welsh Assembly
Local government	Local governance
External relations	
Sovereign nation state	Pooling of sovereignty
Intergovernmental cooperation	European integration
World of nation states	Globalisation

These trends have been apparent in central government, local government, the welfare state and the European Union (EU). Reform of the civil service has seen the creation of semi-autonomous executive agencies responsible for policy implementation, the **market-testing** of activities and the rise of a new managerial culture. Local authorities have lost functions to quangos and agencies, have been required to put contracts for service delivery out to tender and are subject to a comprehensive inspection regime. Within the welfare state, schools and hospitals have been given greater responsibility over their day-to-day running but are also subject to inspection and central intervention. As we will see in Chapter 12, the EU's legislative and regulatory roles have been extended.

Market-testing: the policy that activities provided by public bodies should be tested to see if they could be provided more efficiently by the private sector.

Changing attitudes towards the state

In the period of consensus politics (1945–70) Labour and the Conservatives were broadly agreed that the state should play a leading role in the economy and welfare provision. The state had an ownership role in nationalised industries such as coal, electricity and the railways which were run as public corporations under state direction. Other forms of state intervention included public subsidies (e.g. regional aid and funding for companies in financial difficulties), the regulation of monopolies, laws on the environment and so forth. Within the welfare state, the National Health Service (NHS) also had a centralised system of management which gave local hospitals and general practices limited room for manoeuvre.

The Thatcher governments 'rolled back' the state's role in economic management and the provision of public goods. They enhanced the position of the market by privatising nationalised industries, opening up contracts for the delivery of public goods to private sector competition and using private sector funding for public projects. The New Right was hostile to bureaucracy believing that it was monolithic, inefficient, poorly managed, averse to enterprise, and prone to expansion. It offered a similar critique of the welfare state claiming additionally that it had fostered a dependency culture in which individuals come to rely on state benefits and have little incentive to seek employment.

The reforms implemented by the governments of John Major and Margaret Thatcher amounted to a new vision of the state. The state lost its monopoly status in the provision of public goods: many services would still be funded by the state but they would be delivered by the private sector, voluntary groups, specialist agencies or the family unit rather than by central government or local authorities. American New Right theorists David Osborne and Ted Gaebler encapsulated the change in *Reinventing Government* (Addison Wesley, 1992) where they wrote of a 'reinvention of government', the purpose of which was to 'steer' rather than 'row'. Conservative minister Nicholas Ridley used the term 'enabling authority' to describe the role of local councils who no longer provided all aspects of services such as housing and education directly, but funded them and set a framework in which private companies, voluntary associations and quangos delivered local services. Similar trends in the civil service and the welfare state amounted to the development of an **enabling state**.

Enabling state: a state that sets the framework for the provision of public goods by a range of bodies.

It would be wrong, however, to claim that New Right ideology was the sole or primary factor in the development of policies such as civil service reform or privatisation. Pragmatic political considerations – for example, raising revenue to finance tax cuts, or winning the next election – were often more significant. Nor did Conservative attempts to roll back the state always succeed. The Thatcher and Major governments were unable to achieve significant reductions in public spending as cuts in some areas were countered by increases in others. The higher unemployment that resulted from the contraction of manufacturing industry increased the social security bill. Public spending increases were also evident in defence and law and order. These were prioritised by the neo-conservative branch of Thatcherism which saw a strong state as essential to uphold the authority of the government and protect traditional values. As we will see below, privatisation and the transfer of functions from Whitehall or local authorities to semi-autonomous agencies transformed rather than ended state involvement. In place of state provision of public goods emerged a regulatory state of government-created regimes in which service providers were required to meet particular targets.

The Citizen's Charter

The Citizen's Charter introduced by the Major government in 1991 provides a good example of changing conceptions of the role of the state. It also shows that Major was not persuaded by New Right ideologues: they wanted to roll back the state further through an extensive privatisation of the welfare state whereas Major wanted to make the state provision of public services more responsive to those using them. The Citizen's Charter treatment of citizens as consumers or customers did fit the neo-liberal emphasis on the individual but it was government that set performance targets for services. The Charter aimed to improve public service performance through market-testing and greater competition, the setting of performance targets and the publication of league tables. The latter brought greater transparency, allowing people to compare the performances of providers of public goods (e.g. on hospital waiting times, school exam results or the punctuality of trains) and encouraging poor performers to explain how they would improve. Good service providers would be rewarded by the award of a Charter Mark. The Citizen's Charter spawned a series of specific charters such as the Patient's Charter and Passenger's Charter.

The Citizen's Charter was much derided at the time as a big idea that failed to take off. The fate of the Cones Hotline seemed symbolic. This was a telephone service which motorists could contact to complain when motorway lanes were cordoned off without good reason, but in three years it received only a few hundred calls at a disproportionate cost and was closed down. In retrospect the launch of the Citizen's Charter can be seen as a significant step in the development of the state given the endurance of its methodology of consumerism and accountability for public service provision through performance targets and league tables. The Blair government relaunched the Charter as Service First but it maintained most of its key features, the main change resulting from this makeover being greater consultation with users.

The Bank of England

The Bank of England is the UK's central bank. It is responsible for ensuring monetary and financial stability; its key functions include setting interest rate levels and issuing banknotes. The Bank was nationalised in 1946 but the Blair government granted it operational independence in 1997. Decisions on interest rate levels have been taken by the Bank's Monetary Policy Committee (MPC) since then. This removed a potentially significant economic tool from the Chancellor of the Exchequer, as, prior to 1997, decisions on the level of interest rates could have been decided by political considerations (e.g. the desirability of a pre-election rates cut) as well as economic ones. The Chancellor does retain a significant role under the new system for it is he or she who sets an overall target for inflation. The MPC then has to judge the interest rate level required to meet that target. The Chancellor also appoints four of the nine members of the MPC; three other members (the Governor of the Bank of England and two Deputies) are appointed by the Crown. A Treasury representative is present at MPC meetings and takes part in discussions, but cannot vote. Minutes of the monthly meetings of the MPC are published.

New Labour and the state

New Labour accepted the broad thrust of the changes to the civil service, local government and welfare state introduced under the Conservatives. Few of the reforms in these areas were undone and where policies were changed (e.g. the move to Service First or the abolition of the NHS internal market), these were not so comprehensive as to mark a return to the *status quo ante*. New Labour's main concern when it came to the role of the state was with constitutional reform (see Chapter 5). Here the trends of fragmentation and the dispersal of functions away from the core executive were developed. This was most apparent in the case of devolution with policy competences transferred to devolved administrations in Scotland, Wales and Northern Ireland (see Chapter 11). This restricted the core executive's authority to make policy that had UK-wide application. The decision to grant the Bank of England operational independence to set interest rate levels also reduced the policy-making resources of the core executive (see Case study 9.1).

Table 9.2 Government task forces and ad hoc advisory groups, 2005 (examples)

Task force	Government department
Commission for Africa	Department for International Development
Commission on Boundary Differences and Voting Systems	Department for Constitutional Affairs
Food in Schools Management Group	Department of Health
Inter-Faith Forum on Teenage Pregnancy	Department of Health
Live Music Forum	Department for Culture, Media and Sport
Manufacturing Forum	Department of Trade and Industry
Race Equality Advisory Panel	Home Office
The Pension Commission	Department for Work and Pensions

Source: Data taken from Cabinet Office Public Bodies database, www.knowledgenetwork.gov.uk/ndpb/ndpb.nsf/0/8AC8284830318568802570AD0044C876?OpenDocument

Fragmentation and centralisation have gone hand-in-hand. Blair believed that the centre would have to strengthen its capacity to coordinate and steer if New Labour were to reform public service delivery. Fragmentation in the core executive and the delivery of public goods was to be addressed through 'joined-up government'. This involved centralisation with Number 10 playing a strategic role in directing and coordinating policy-making and policy-delivery across Whitehall. As we saw in Chapter 6, special units charged with coordinating cross-cutting policies and ensuring policy delivery report directly to the Prime Minister. The Treasury has similarly stepped up its efforts at coordination. Several hundred ad hoc policy review bodies and taskforces offer policy expertise (see Table 9.2).

New Labour has sought to tackle social and economic problems through a 'third way' that does not resort to either the centralised bureaucracy of the welfare state of the post-war settlement or a neo-liberal approach that looks only to market solutions (see Chapter 15). It has built up the role of markets by extending the Private Finance Initiative, which uses private finance to fund public projects (see below), and promoting managerial change, but has advocated partnership between public, private and voluntary actors. The regulatory state has been extended with the centre setting more performance targets, offering rewards for institutions that perform well but intervening when they fail. Service delivery agencies are expected to pay greater attention to the needs of service users.

Reform of the civil service

The principles under which the civil service operated in the early 1980s were not radically different from those of the 1880s. Previous attempts at reform such as the 1968 Fulton Report did not produce the scale of change envisaged at the time. The reorganisation of the civil service under the Conservative governments of 1979–97 did, however, bring about dramatic changes in the organisation and culture of the civil service. Influenced by New Right ideology, they viewed the civil service as inefficient, badly-managed and resistant to change.

The main themes in the reform of the civil service have been:

• The separation of policy-making and policy implementation functions.
• The creation of semi-autonomous executive agencies.
• The introduction of market-testing and private finance.
• The introduction of managerial practices used in the private sector.

The defining moment in the reform process was the publication of the 1988 'Next Steps' report by Sir Robin Ibbs, the head of the Efficiency Unit. It claimed that the civil service was failing to provide effective policy advice or deliver quality services. The Next Steps report recommended that the civil service should be broken up as it was too large to be managed as a single organisation. The reforms that followed separated its policy-making and policy implementation roles. Government departments continued to provide policy advice but responsibility for the implementation of policy and delivery of public services was transferred to newly-created executive agencies (sometimes known as Next Steps agencies).

Agencification

Executive agencies are staffed by civil servants but led by specially-appointed chief executives with overall managerial responsibility. The relationship between agencies and their parent government departments are set out in framework documents which spell out the division of responsibility and lines of communication. Agencies have to meet performance targets determined in Whitehall. By 1997, 138 executive agencies had been created although the number then fell to 86 in 2005 as agencies were privatised or merged. Three-quarters of civil servants work in Next Steps agencies or in departments such as HM Revenue and Customs that operate along Next Steps lines. Executive agencies vary greatly in their size and scope (see Table 9.3). The largest are Jobcentre Plus which delivers benefits and provides advice to the unemployed through a network of local offices (with 76,000 staff) and the Prison Service (45,000) which manages prisons in England and Wales.

Official reviews suggest that executive agencies have been generally successful in achieving efficiency savings and improving service. The UK Passport Service and Driver and Vehicle Licensing Agency (DVLA) have, for example, reduced the time it takes to get a passport or driving licence. But there have been high profile problems. The Child Support Agency (CSA) has underperformed chronically since its creation in 1994. Designed to collect payments from absent fathers (or mothers) who refuse to contribute to the costs of raising their children, the CSA has consistently failed to meet performance targets, built up a huge backlog of cases and provoked large numbers of complaints. A restructuring that gave ministers greater powers of oversight and a simplification of the system for calculating maintenance payments did not improve matters greatly. There was a major dispute in 1997 between Home

Table 9.3 Executive agencies, 2004 (examples)

Next Steps agency	Parent department	Staff numbers
HM Court Service	Department for Constitutional Affairs	9420
HM Land Registry	Department for Constitutional Affairs	7930
Army Training and Recruitment Agency	Ministry of Defence	3920
Defence Procurement Agency	Ministry of Defence	3790
Ministry of Defence Police and Guarding Agency	Ministry of Defence	6010
Criminal Records Bureau	Home Office	340
HM Prison Service	Home Office	45280
UK Passport Service	Home Office	2450
Companies House	Department for Trade and Industry	1110
Driver and Vehicle Licensing Agency	Department of Transport	6000
Driving Standards Agency	Department of Transport	2130
Highways Agency	Department of Transport	1930
Office for National Statistics	HM Treasury	3450
Child Support Agency	Department for Work and Pensions	10570
JobCentre Plus	Department for Work and Pensions	76760
Pension Service	Department for Work and Pensions	17790

Source: Cabinet Office, civil service statistics for staff in post 1 April 2004, www.civilservice.gov.uk/management_of_the_civil_service/statistics/index.asp

Secretary Michael Howard and Derek Lewis, chief executive of the Prison Service over who was responsible for a series of escapes from prison. The relationship between the Home Office and agency was later changed to make ministers more clearly accountable to parliament for prisons policy.

Marketisation

Marketisation: the extension of market mechanisms into government and the public sector.

The role played by the private sector in central government has been extended. Market-testing was introduced into the civil service in 1991. It required that the activities of government departments and executive agencies (e.g. IT services) were examined to ascertain whether the private sector could deliver services more efficiently and economically than 'in-house' providers. By 1995, over £2 billion of activities had been market-tested producing savings of £800 million. Some executive agencies, including Her Majesty's Stationery Office, have been privatised. But market-testing has also brought problems. The failure of IT systems provided by the private sector in the Child Support Agency caused long delays and cost millions of pounds. The Blair government ended the requirement that activities are market-tested but regular reviews of service provision have continued.

The Blair governments have made extensive use of Public Private Partnerships (PPPs). These are formal agreements between government bodies (e.g. government departments, agencies and local authorities) and the private sector to deliver or manage public goods. The most controversial form of partnership is the **Private Finance Initiative (PFI)** which allows for private sector funding of large scale projects providing public goods. Here a private company undertakes an infrastructure project and often delivers the associated service for a specified period of time, normally 30 years. But government pays for the services and pays a premium

Private Finance Initiative (PFI): a policy promoting the use of private sector funding for the provision of public goods.

Controversy: 9.1

PFI and the Skye Road Bridge

The Skye Bridge which opened in 1995 has been one of the most contentious Private Finance Initiative (PFI) projects. The bridge linking the Isle of Skye with the mainland was built by a commercial group funded by US investors and run by Skye Bridge Limited. It cost £39 million to construct, £12 million of which came from central government. The money would be recuperated through a toll imposed on users of the bridge. Motorists staged a 'can pay, won't pay' campaign from the outset and the Scottish Executive signalled its unease in 2000 by freezing the toll at £11.40 for a return trip. The Executive bought back the bridge from its owners in 2005 and abolished the tolls. This cost the Executive £27 million but it calculated that it would have had to pay £18 million in subsidies over the remaining years of the franchise if tolls were frozen at the 2000 rate.

Time will tell whether the Skye Bridge proves part of a wider trend of PFI failure or remains a one-off. But the Department of Health is concerned about the costs of PFI schemes in the NHS (e.g. a proposed £1 billion refurbishment of St Bartholomew's hospital in London) given the level of debts already accrued by NHS Trusts.

to cover the financial risks taken by the company. PFI was introduced by the Major government in 1992 but took off under New Labour: by the end of 2004, contracts for 677 PFI projects had been signed to a total value of £43 billion. The largest were transport projects such as the redevelopment of the London Underground, the Channel Tunnel rail link and the Birmingham Northern Relief Road (a toll road that runs parallel to the M6 in the Midlands). The most common were hospital infrastructure projects. The government claims that PFI brings increased public investment, delivered efficiently, without undermining its tight fiscal stance. But critics argue that the projects do not provide value for money as the borrowing costs are high (see Controversy 9.1).

New public management

The 1988 Next Steps Report aimed to transform the culture of the civil service by instilling a more professional approach to management. Central to this was the introduction of management techniques used in the private sector. These included efficiency drives to ensure value for money, clear lines of managerial responsibility, the measurement of performance against specific targets, and responsiveness to consumer demands. This managerial revolution and emphasis on market mechanisms are collectively known as the **new public management**.

New public management: the emphasis on market mechanisms and private sector managerial practices in government organisations.

The new managerial culture has permeated both executive agencies and government departments. Executive agencies have significant discretion in the management of their finances and the pay and working conditions of their employees. Many agency chief executives are recruited from the private sector through open competition rather than promoted from within the civil service. Government departments have also been given greater discretion regarding their internal organisation. The Senior Civil Service, the top echelon of 3000 policy-makers in Whitehall, was created in 1995 with open competition and written employment contracts the norm. Recruitment from the private sector, fast-track promotions, the recruitment of specialists (e.g. in IT, finance, management and communications) and efforts to improve diversity within the civil service have developed further under New Labour.

A reduction in the size of the civil service was another plank of the Conservative strategy of improving efficiency and professionalism. The number of civil servants fell from 732,000 in 1979 to 500,000 in 1997. Numbers rose under the Blair government to reach 554,000 in 2004. Following the 2004 Gershon Report on efficiency savings, the government announced that 104,000 civil service posts would be cut and another 20,000 relocated to the English regions.

The Blair governments have adopted a pragmatic approach to civil service reform, accepting the majority of the Conservative reforms and promising further improvements. The 1999 White Paper *Modernising Government* identified efficient public service delivery, coordination, innovation, and diversity as New Labour's priorities. By 2004, Blair's vision was of a smaller core civil service with a clearer sense of purpose, greater recruitment from the private sector and more effective leadership within departments.

Reform concerns

These reforms have provoked concerns that the civil service's traditional principles of impartiality, anonymity and permanence have been undermined. The separation of the policy advice and policy implementation functions of the civil service has brought fragmentation and problems of effective control. The creation of Next Steps agencies has also blurred the lines of accountability. It is not clear whether agency chief executives or government ministers should be held ultimately responsible for policy failures. Ministers have used this confusion to avoid being held accountable for problems. Critics claim that market forces and private sector management practices have undermined the public service ethos of the civil service. They also point to problems created by the contracting out of services to the private sector (e.g. in IT provision) and to the long-term costs associated with PFI schemes.

The quango state

Quango: a quasi-autonomous non-governmental organisation which takes decisions on how public money should be spent but which has significant autonomy from government and is not directly accountable to it.

The creation of executive agencies responsible for the implementation of government policies is an example of a restructuring of the state that has brought about an increase in the number and role of specialist agencies. Executive agencies differ from the other agencies discussed in this section as they operate within the terms of framework documents drawn up by their parent government department and their staff are civil servants. The agencies discussed below are known as **quangos**, an acronym for 'quasi-autonomous non-governmental organisations'. Quangos are non-departmental bodies (i.e. they have significant autonomy from government departments), are not directly accountable to ministers or local councils, and their staff are neither civil servants nor local government officials. The broad remit and budgets of many of these organisations are, though, set by central government. Quangos are thus funded by the taxpayer but are not democratically accountable to parliament or the electorate.

The presence of quangos within the UK state is not a new phenomenon. The Arts Council for England, which determines how £400 million of public funding is distributed among projects in music, the theatre, dance and the visual arts, was created in 1946. But the last thirty years have seen an expansion in the scope and number of agencies. The Thatcher and Major governments abolished some quangos (e.g. nationalised industries) but created more (e.g. regulatory agencies). The Blair governments have not reduced the number of quangos or made them more democratic despite pledging to do so while in Opposition. Instead it has added to the proliferation of such bodies by establishing new agencies with responsibilities for health, training, housing and regional development.

The definition and measurement of quangos is disputed. The government prefers to use the term non-departmental public body (NDPBs) to describe agencies funded by the state to develop, manage and provide public goods but which are neither elected nor controlled directly by central government (see Table 9.4). The Cabinet Office identifies four main types of NDPB:

- *Executive NDPBs* are established by statute and are responsible for administrative, regulatory or commercial functions. They have their own staff and budget. There were 211 executive NDPBs in 2005.

- *Advisory NDPBs* provide expert advice to ministers. Their staff and budget come from the sponsor government department. There were 458 advisory NDPBs in 2005.
- *Tribunal NDPBs* have quasi-judicial power in particular fields of law. Their staff and budget come from the sponsor government department. There were 42 of these bodies in 2005.
- *Independent monitoring board NDPBs*, formerly known as 'boards of visitors',

Table 9.4 Non-departmental public bodies, 2005 (examples)

NDPB	Status	Role
Arts Council England	Executive NDPB	Distribute funding for the arts in England
Competition Commission	Executive NDPB	Investigate mergers, monopolies and the regulation of utilities
Employment Tribunals (25 offices)	Tribunal NDPBs	Resolve disputes between employees and employers over employment rights
Environment Agency	Executive NDPB	Manage English and Welsh waterways and prevents their pollution
Health and Safety Commission	Executive NDPB	Ensure that risks to health and safety in the workplace are properly controlled
House of Lords Appointments Commission	Advisory NDPB	Make recommendations on appointment of non-party political life peers
Independent Police Complaints Commission	Executive NDPB	Supervise or conduct inquiries into complaints against the police in England and Wales
National Lottery Commission	Executive NDPB	Grant and enforce licenses to run the National Lottery
Office of the Information Commissioner	Executive NDPB	Supervise and enforce the Data Protection Act 1998 and the Freedom of Information Act 2000
Primary Care Trusts (302 in England)	NHS Bodies	Improve the health of their communities, and provide integrated services
Qualifications and Curriculum Authority	Executive NDPB	Maintain the national curriculum and associated exams
Regional Development Agencies (8 in England)	Executive NDPBs	Develop economic development strategies for their regions
Serious Organised Crime Agency	Executive NDPB	Prevent and detect serious and organised crime in England and Wales
UK Sport	Executive NDPB	Foster participation and excellence in sport

Source: Data taken from Cabinet Office Public Bodies database, www.knowledgenetwork.gov.uk/ ndpb/ndpb.nsf/0/8AC8284830318568802570AD0044C876?OpenDocument

are responsible for prison inspections. They are funded by the sponsor department and numbered 151 in 2005.

This Cabinet Office typology of quangos is based on a minimalist approach that is rejected by other observers. The official figures presented above count the 302 Primary Care Trusts in England as one NHS Body and do not include an array of other bodies. So the official definition does not extend to quangos such as City Academies, public corporations (e.g. the BBC) or government taskforces (e.g. the Better Regulation Taskforce). This is because they have different appointment processes and have looser links to government departments.

Stuart Weir and Wendy Hall in 1994 provided a more accurate picture of the extent of the quango state in *EGO-TRIP* (Democratic Audit Paper no. 2, 1994), identifying 5521 quangos most of which operated at local level and were excluded from the government's tally of NDPBs. The 2001 House of Commons Public Administration Select Committee Report *Mapping the Quango State* also adopted a broad perspective when identifying more than 5000 state funded bodies that provided public goods at local level, employing some 60,000 people. In contrast, the Cabinet Office database of public bodies recorded a fall in the number of NDPBs from 1128 in 1997 to 910 in 2005. This reflected the merger of some bodies but is largely accounted for by the transfer of departmental sponsorship from central government to the devolved administrations.

The extension of the quango state raises concerns for democrats, notably:

• Patronage and the process of appointments to quangos.
• The lack of openness in the way quangos conduct their work.
• The accountability of quangos to elected bodies.

Table 9.5 Appointed members of public bodies (2001–2003)

Parliament (the reformed House of Lords)	690
Board members of executive and advisory non-departmental bodies, public corporations, etc. (central and devolved government)	21 901
Task forces, ad hoc advisory bodies, policy reviews	1 895
The courts (the judiciary throughout the UK; lay JPs, etc., except for district court service in Scotland)	29 338
Members of NDPB tribunals (not of social security and employment tribunals, etc.)	11 572
NHS (health authorities, primary care trusts, NHS trusts, other NHS bodies, commissions and tribunals)	4 591
Local public spending bodies (registered social landlords, training and enterprise bodies, board members of higher and further education institutions)	47 647
Local partnerships (statutory and on local authority initiative)*	75 000 (est.)
Prison service (members of Boards of Visitors)	2 002
School governors**	381 500

* Members are elected to a few neighbourhood regeneration boards alongside appointed and co-opted members

** Includes parent governors who are elected to governing bodies alongside other categories of member

Source: House of Commons Select Committee on Public Administration, 4th Report, *Government by Appointment: Opening up the Patronage State*, 2002–2003, p. 9, www.parliament.uk/parliamentary_committees/public_administration_select_committee.cfm

The House of Commons Public Administration Select Committee 2003 Report *Opening up the Patronage State* notes that hundreds of thousands of posts in public bodies such as quangos, the lower courts and the welfare state are filled by appointment (see Table 9.5). Until the 1990s ministers and civil servants were responsible for many of these appointments. Following recommendations from the Nolan Committee on Standards in Public Life, a post of Commissioner for Public Appointments was created. He or she monitors appointments to many quangos and insists that they should be made on merit. Many posts are advertised in the national press: a glance at the 'Society' supplement of the *Guardian* on a Wednesday gives a good idea of the number and type of positions. More women and ethnic minorities have been appointed in recent years but they remain under-represented. But ministers retain the final say on appointments to many national bodies while appointments to most local quangos escape serious scrutiny. Transparency is also lacking: not all quangos issue annual reports and few hold public meetings although government departments conduct periodic reviews and parliamentary select committees can scrutinise their work.

The freedom from government control and partisan politics enjoyed by some organisations can be a good thing – the BBC (a public corporation) and the Electoral Commission being cases in point. But the transfer of decision-making power from elected politicians to quangos has exacerbated the democratic deficit, particularly at local level. Central government has done little to democratise the quango state but the Welsh Assembly has taken a lead by scrapping some quangos and bringing their functions under the control of the Assembly government.

The local quango state

The trends we have identified in this chapter – the hiving-off of functions to specialist agencies, the creation of an elaborate regulatory framework, the introduction of markets and private capital, and a managerial culture – have also changed the character of local government and the welfare state (see Chapter 10). Local councils have lost functions to quangos and are subject to a comprehensive inspection regime. The Audit Commission is one of the most important bodies in the regulatory state as it carries out inspections of some 11,000 public bodies including local authorities and their services, plus the NHS. It publishes information on their performance and assesses whether they are delivering value for money. The government then rewards the best performing local authorities by granting them greater discretionary powers but penalises those that fare badly by subjecting them to central intervention.

In education, local authority control over schools has been weakened. Governors and head teachers play a greater role in the day-to-day running of their schools. The Blair governments have encouraged schools to specialise in particular subjects and established city academies which are state-funded but run independently by private companies or faith-based groups. Schools under local authority control are subject to regular inspection by the Office for Standards in Education (OFSTED). Special management teams are sent into schools with poor records and the worst are closed down. National targets for examination passes and class size are set by the centre.

The Thatcher and Major governments separated the purchaser and provider roles within the NHS by creating an internal market. This was a quasi-market in which district health authorities and general practices purchased healthcare from hospitals. Hospitals and general practices were given greater freedom to run their own affairs, the former as self-governing NHS Trusts and the latter as GP fund holders. The Blair government abolished the quasi-market but established foundation hospitals (in England) which have greater budgetary and managerial discretion. Compulsory competitive tendering in the NHS saw contracts to provide services such as cleaning and catering won by private companies. The role of the market is also apparent in the use of the Private Finance Initiative to fund the renovation of hospitals and delivery of healthcare. As we have seen, the NHS is also subject to inspection by the Audit Commission and the publication of performance league tables. The government sets national targets for reducing deaths from cancer and heart disease, for example.

Few would argue that greater transparency in public services is undesirable. But the methods for achieving this have been questioned. Setting national performance targets and producing league tables allows for comparisons between different providers of health and education, but the data that is used is often flawed. The first Blair government focused on reducing hospital waiting lists but hospitals could manipulate waiting lists by undertaking simple operations rather than more costly or complex ones. The government then turned its attention to waiting times. School heads also complain that league tables do not pay sufficient attention to factors such as the relative deprivation of their catchment area.

The regulatory state

Regulatory agency: an independent organisation created by government to regulate an area of public life.

Central government has played a regulatory role in the British economy and society over many years. **Regulatory agencies** responsible for working conditions and pollution control first appeared in the nineteenth century. Local authorities have long had regulatory powers, for example in public health and planning. Quasi-judicial bodies such as employment and immigration tribunals are also well-established features of the British legal system. But self-regulation has been the norm in many areas of economic and social life.

The number of regulatory agencies has increased in the last thirty years or so, producing a 'regulatory state'. Rather than acting as owner or sole provider of public goods, the state has transferred these functions to the private sector or to semi-autonomous agencies. The state has limited its role to that of regulator by creating regulatory regimes to ensure appropriate levels of performance. The alternative title of 'contract state' is also used to describe the system in which central and local government fund the provision of some services which are delivered by private companies that compete for contracts.

Privatisation and regulation

Privatisation: the transfer of state-owned bodies to the private sector often through the sale of shares.

The **privatisation** of public corporations and the accompanying creation of regulatory agencies in the 1980s and 1990s is a prime example of the expansion of the state's regulatory role. The nationalisation programme of Clement Attlee's Labour governments (1945–51) had given the state responsibility for the provision of public goods such as energy, public transport, utilities and some manufactured goods. Most of the nationalised industries were swept away by the privatisation programme of the Thatcher and Major governments. Privatisation changes the balance between the public and private sectors by reducing the size of the public sector through the extension of the free market and private sector. Broadly defined, it includes the breaking of monopolies (e.g. the deregulation of bus services) and the private provision of public goods (e.g. through competitive tendering or the Private Finance Initiative). But the most significant form of privatisation was the sale of public corporations to the private sector between 1979 and 1997. This brought significant sums of money into the Treasury although there were costs involved such as the wiping of debts of some industries and advertising campaigns. It also extended the number of shareholders although most shares ended up in the hands of City institutions.

The largest privatisations took the form of stock market flotations in which shares in the new companies were offered to individual and corporate buyers, usually at prices below their market value. Among the industries sold in this way were nationalised corporations such as British Petroleum, British Airways and British Telecom plus publicly-owned utilities like water, gas and electricity. The privatisation of British Rail involved the sale of franchises – a licence to provide a service for a set time period – to private companies while the rail infrastructure was owned by a new company, Railtrack. Privatising public utilities such as water, gas and electricity posed particular problems as they are natural monopolies in which it is difficult to introduce competition. The operational functions of gas and electricity utilities (e.g. ownership of generators and pipelines) were separated from their supply and service activities which were taken over by regional companies.

Privatisation transformed the role of the state in the former nationalised industries but did not end it completely. In some cases the government retained a 'golden share'

The Ufton Nervet crash 2004: safety on the railways was seriously questioned after privatisation (© Richard Austin/Rex Features)

Table 9.6 Privatisation and the regulatory state

Company	Date of privatisation	Regulatory agency
British Telecom	1984	Office of Telecommunications (OFTEL)
British Gas	1986	Office of Gas and Electricity Markets (OFGEM) – replaced the Office of the Gas Regulator (OFGAS) in 2000
Water companies (10)	1989	Water Services Regulation Authority – replaces the Office of Water Services (OFWAT) in 2006
Regional electricity companies (12)	1990	Office of Gas and Electricity Markets (OFGEM) – replaced the Office of Electricity Regulation (OFFER) in 2000
National Power and Power Gen (electricity generators)	1991	Office of Gas and Electricity Markets (OFGEM) – replaced the Office of Electricity Regulation in 2000
Railtrack (railway infrastructure)	1996	Strategic Rail Authority – until 2005 when many of its functions were transferred to the Department of Transport's Rail Group
Railway operating companies	1995	Office of Rail Regulation – replaced the Office of the Rail Regulator in 2004

giving it the right to block developments (e.g. takeovers) deemed contrary to the public interest. The European Court of Justice ruled in 2003 that the government must give up its golden share in the British Airports Authority. The main development was the change in the role of the state from owner to regulator. Privatisation did not create truly private companies accountable only to their shareholders but hybrid companies over which the state still exercised some control. Regulatory agencies with statutory powers were created to ensure that privatised companies acted in the public interest (see Table 9.6). These bodies have the power to set a pricing formula which may cap price increases or force reductions and promote competition by breaking up monopolies.

Although they have no direct role in the provision of services, the regulators manage the rules of the game under which privatised companies operate. The Office of Telecommunications (OFTEL) forced British Telecom to reduce prices, improve the standards of its service to customers, and open up its telecommunications infrastructure to competitors in the telephone, mobile 'phone and internet markets. The energy regulator OFGEM ended regional monopolies in domestic gas and electricity supply by requiring competition between supply companies. But the effectiveness of regulatory agencies is open to question. Those regulatory bodies responsible for the railways failed to force real improvements in the rail infrastructure (see Controversy 9.2). A wider concern is that regulatory agencies may grow too close to the bodies they oversee and thus share similar views on what is best for the sector. Studies from the USA speak of 'regulatory capture' in which a regulatory agency becomes 'captured' by the bodies they are responsible for and lose sight of their duty to prioritise the interests of citizens and consumers.

Rail privatisation

The railways provide the main example of a failed privatisation. When British Rail was privatised in 1996, ownership of the rail infrastructure was transferred to Railtrack, a company floated on the stock market, and franchises for eighteen passenger services awarded to private train-operating companies. Responsibility for regulation of the railways was split between two regulators, the Office of the Rail Regulator and the Office of Passenger Rail Franchising. Train services showed little improvement or got worse while chronic under-investment in the rail network (e.g. tracks and signalling) was a factor in a number of serious train accidents. Leadership and clear lines of responsibility were obviously lacking.

Railtrack made a series of heavy losses and required government funding to stay afloat. In 2001, the Secretary of State for Transport, Stephen Byers decided to end the subsidy as he believed that Railtrack was incapable of solving the problems of the industry. This forced Railtrack into administration and left its shareholders with limited compensation. Responsibility for the railway system and timetabling was then transferred to a new not-for-profit company Network Rail. Government involvement was extended when the Strategic Rail Authority was wound up in 2005 and the Department of Transport regained control of national rail strategy. The system for issuing franchises for train operators was also changed: the number of franchises was reduced and more account taken of the past record of operators when franchises were awarded. The renamed Office of Rail Regulation remained as an independent regulator and took over responsibility for rail safety from the Health and Safety Executive.

Other regulatory bodies

Aside from privatisation, the shortcomings of self-regulation have also prompted the government to establish regulatory agencies. A number of food safety scares arose in the 1990s, notably the spread of Bovine Spongiform Encephalopathy (BSE) in cattle. After a damning report by a public inquiry into BSE, the Food Standards Agency was set up in 2000 to ensure that food production met stricter public health standards. The credibility of self-regulation in the City of London financial markets was also undermined by scandals such as the mis-sale of endowment mortgages and pensions. The Financial Services Authority was established to regulate banking, insurance and mortgage services.

The expansion in the number of agencies also reflects a belief that some areas of life should be subject to regulation at arms length from the government. Scientific and medical advances are a case in point, with the Human Fertilisation and Embryology Authority regulating human cloning and the National Institute for Clinical Excellence (NICE) responsible for licensing new medicines (see Case study 9.2). Regulation has also increased in sport where UK Sport and others promote participation and the Olympic Delivery Authority is responsible for preparations for the 2012 Olympic Games in London. Finally, the EU also has a significant role in regulating British society, particularly in environmental policy and working conditions.

Case study: 9.2

NICE work? Regulating NHS treatments

The National Institute for Health and Clinical Excellence (NICE) is an independent body responsible for developing clinical guidelines and for recommending the use of new and existing medicines in the National Health Service in England and Wales. Guidelines and new technologies are referred to NICE by the Department of Health and Welsh Assembly. In licensing drugs and treatments, NICE takes account of both clinical evidence (how well do they work?) and economic evidence (do they offer value for money?). The House of Commons Health Select Committee and the World Health Organisation have been critical of the lack of transparency of NICE's decision-making process.

With NICE appraisals of new medicines taking up to 14 months, there is pressure on Primary Care Trusts and government ministers to make promising new drugs available to those in need as quickly as possible. Fast-track appraisals are expected to be used in less complex cases. Controversy arose over the availability of the drug Herceptin in 2005. Although it had been licensed for late stage breast cancer it had not been approved by NICE for the treatment of early stages of the disease. With Herceptin being provided to patients it might benefit by some Primary Care Trusts but not others, the Secretary of State for Health, Patricia Hewitt intervened to fast-track use of the drug and warn Trusts that they should not refuse to provide it on the grounds of cost if the drug had been recommended by a consultant. Critics argued that Hewitt's intervention had undermined NICE's independence.

Decisions made by NICE also have important financial implications for the NHS. NICE estimated that its 2005 decision that statins which reduce levels of cholesterol should be prescribed for people at risk of heart attack or strokes would cost the NHS up to £82 million per year. Five years earlier, NICE ruled that the drug beta interferon should not be given to every NHS patient with multiple sclerosis as it would not give good value for money.

Multi-level governance

So far this chapter has concentrated on the transfer of functions outwards from the core executive to semi-autonomous agencies and the private sector. But functions have also been transferred from the core executive downwards to subnational bodies and upwards to supranational institutions. Devolution has seen legislative authority on issues such as health, education and economic development delegated by Westminster to devolved bodies in Scotland, Wales and Northern Ireland. The powers of the devolved administrations and the implications of devolution for British politics are explored in detail in Chapter 11. The EU has extensive policy competences. It is the lead actor in areas such as agriculture and trade; even fields where policy competence is shared between the EU and its member states, qualified majority voting often applies meaning that individual states cannot veto legislative proposals.

The term 'multi-level governance' describes this dispersal of decision-making authority across different tiers of government. The development of multi-level governance has changed the role of the state. Nation states remain key actors in

EU policy-making but they do not monopolise the decision-making process because other actors (e.g. the European Parliament and European Commission) have significant resources (e.g. legislative or regulatory authority). EU membership has also limited the policy autonomy of the core executive and fostered policy networks of subnational, national and supranational actors. In EU regional policy, the devolved administrations and local authorities engage directly with the European Commission thereby limiting central government's ability to act as a 'gatekeeper' between the supranational and subnational tiers of government. The impact of EU membership is assessed more fully in Chapter 12.

The multi-level governance perspective captures the transfer of policy-making authority from the centre to subnational and supranational tiers of government. However, it exaggerates the extent to which this has eroded the capacity of both central government and the nation state. Legislation establishing the devolved administrations safeguards the supremacy of the Westminster Parliament and the centre is the dominant actor in institutions established to coordinate inter-governmental relations (i.e. relations between the UK government and devolved administrations). Nation states take the leading role in 'history-making decisions' within the EU (e.g. Treaty reform) and the autonomy enjoyed by supranational institutions is limited.

Globalisation

Globalisation is one of the most pervasive buzzwords in contemporary political analysis, but its character and impact are disputed. It refers to a widening and deepening interconnectedness between peoples and societies in many forms of activity. The boundaries between the domestic and the international have become blurred: politics within the nation state is influenced increasingly by transnational forces. The following are key trends associated with globalisation:

- The development of a global economy.
- The increased importance of international organisations.
- The development of global communications.
- The permeability of state boundaries.
- The development of a global culture.

The emergence of a global economy is central to the concept of globalisation. This global economy is characterised by the free movement of capital and the dominant position of multinational corporations. The liberalisation of capital movements, banking and financial markets has allowed billions of pounds worth of financial transactions to daily occur across national boundaries. Currencies, investments and markets are interconnected: significant movement in the value of the dollar or of shares in Tokyo may have knock-on effects across the developed world. Multinational corporations such as BP, Ford and Siemens are key players in the global economy, investing in countries beyond their home state and expanding their market share. Their turnovers, even profits, dwarf the Gross National Product of many Third World states. But they are still subject to the laws and regulations of their home state and others.

The starting point of the era of globalisation is often put at the 1960s as this was when the political significance of the trends mentioned above became apparent. However, sceptics point out that volumes of international trade and capital flows were higher in the late nineteenth century than they were in the late twentieth century. Mass migration is not a new phenomenon either.

Economic globalisation

Two claims made frequently about economic globalisation are firstly, that it has put in place a dominant neo-liberal economic paradigm and secondly, that nation states have been rendered near helpless by global market forces. Both claims are made by adherents of a hyperglobalist perspective which holds that the era of the sovereign nation state has ended. Many neo-liberals welcome globalisation as the logical conclusion of the triumph of global capitalism whereas many on the left view economic globalisation as a malevolent force that has exacerbated the divide between rich and poor. Hyperglobalists identify important trends but exaggerate their implications. Policies to promote financial liberalisation, free market competition, reform of welfare states and counter-inflationary strategies have been put in place in many liberal democratic states. But national governments also continue to protect privileged sectors of their economies and their distinctive welfare regimes.

Economic globalisation has been a constraint on the actions of British governments. Sterling's exit from the Exchange Rate Mechanism in 1992 offered a vivid illustration of how the financial markets limited the Major government's room for manoeuvre. But it has not restricted the autonomy of British governments as much as is sometimes claimed. Considerations about foreign investment, capital movement or currency rates have not, for example, been the final determinants of UK policy on the single currency. Recent British governments have been more comfortable with economic globalisation than have their French counterparts. Both Conservative and New Labour governments have incorporated the rhetoric of globalisation into their discourse in a positive way, presenting it as a justification for their economic policies rather than an obstacle to their realisation.

Technological developments in communications and transport have been critical to the advance of globalisation. The spread of the internet has enabled instantaneous worldwide networking and transactions. It and media organisations such as CNN have spread Western popular culture so that young people in every continent are attuned to American fashion, film and music. Globalisation has promoted cultural interaction but has not eradicated local cultures and values. Indeed local cultures often undergo a renaissance in response to the spread of homogeneous global brands. The internet also illustrates the permeability of state boundaries. It is not easy for governments to block international communications and almost impossible for them to close their borders to migration or terrorism. These are global problems that require a coordinated international response. They also impact upon domestic politics: national security and asylum were two of the most important issues in Britain's 2005 general election campaign.

International organisations

The number of international organisations has mushroomed to more than 250 as states look to global or regional cooperation on economic, security and environmental issues (see Table 9.7). The most significant are those able to issue authoritative decisions that are binding on their member states (e.g. the EU). The UK is a permanent member of the Security Council of the United Nations, giving it the right to veto proposed resolutions. It is also a founding member of the North Atlantic Treaty Organisation (NATO), the major post-war defence organisation, and the G8 group of the leading economic states.

International trade is an area in which the autonomy of the British government is notably curtailed. Trade negotiations are conducted by the EU while the World Trade Organisation (WTO) is responsible for regulating international trade. It requires states to abide by WTO trade agreements and issues binding decisions when resolving disputes about tariffs and other barriers to free trade. It ruled in 2003 that tariffs imposed by the US on steel imports were unfair and allowed the EU to reciprocate by imposing tariffs on some US goods. President George W. Bush removed the steel tariffs to prevent the trade dispute from escalating.

The International Monetary Fund (IMF) acts as a bank for national central banks, issuing loans to aid states experiencing economic difficulties but requiring in turn that the recipient states introduce economic reforms. When the Callaghan government received a £2.3 billion loan from the IMF in 1976 following a run on sterling, it was required to cut public spending and tighten monetary policy. Public sector strikes followed but the IMF had played an important role in developing an economic framework that would be taken up enthusiastically by the Thatcher governments. The IMF also issues annual reports on the major economies although these do not require national action.

Those sceptical of claims made about the significance of globalisation note that the key economic and political developments are occurring at regional rather

Table 9.7 International organisations (examples of bodies of which the UK is a member)

International organisation	Year founded	No. of members	Functions
United Nations (UN)	1945	191	Promote peace and security, development, humanitarian aid, etc.
International Monetary Fund (IMF)	1945	184	Issue loans to states experiencing balance of payments problems
World Bank	1945	184	Economic assistance to developing states
North Atlantic Treaty Organisation (NATO)	1949	26	Defence alliance (originally against Soviet Union)
European Union (EU)	1958	25	Economic and political integration; originally named the European Economic Community (EEC)
G8	1975	8	Discuss economic strategies of the leading economies; originally named the G6
World Trade Organisation (WTO)	1995	148	Promote and regulate global free trade; successor to the General Agreement on Trade and Tariffs (GATT) of 1947

than global level. Economic and political integration is most advanced in Europe where the 25-member European Union has supranational authority and extensive policy competences. The EU's 'Lisbon process' economic reforms and its common immigration policy are intended to address the challenges of globalisation. In world trade, the EU is best viewed as a regional actor in competition with trading blocs in North America and Asia-Pacific rather than as a part of a truly global economy. As we will see in Chapter 12, the EU has also had a significant impact on British politics and the UK political system.

Live 8 and the Make Poverty History campaign brought global issues onto the national agenda (© David Fisher/Rex Features)

The scope of international law expanded in the second half of the twentieth century and now covers human rights and crimes against humanity. The UK (but not the USA) ratified the 1998 treaty establishing the International Criminal Court. The UK is also a signatory to international protocols such as the Kyoto accord on climate change which is binding upon its signatories – but not on those like the USA that did not ratify it. One of the most high profile cases of international law seen in British courts in recent years was that concerning former Chilean military dictator General Augusto Pinochet. The House of Lords ruled in 1999 that Pinochet could be extradited from Britain to face charges under international law prohibiting torture. He was subsequently spared extradition from the UK on the grounds of ill health but later faced charges in Chile.

International non-governmental organisations (INGOs) have also grown in number and significance with groups such as Amnesty International operating at a global level. UK government departments such as the Department for International Development work closely with the Red Cross and Oxfam. The impact of development issues on British politics was also apparent in the Make Poverty History campaign and 2005 Live8 concerts.

The 'hollowing out' of the state?

The final section of this chapter examines the impact of the move from government to governance by assessing two competing perspectives on the 'hollowing out' of the state. In work such as 'The Hollowing Out of the State', *Political Quarterly*, Vol. 63, No. 1 (1994), Rod Rhodes argues that the developments outlined in this chapter have eroded the autonomy of central government, which has seen its functions dispersed to supranational bodies, subnational institutions and a large number of specialist agencies. Rhodes's 'differentiated polity' perspective is challenged by David Marsh, Martin Smith and David Richards in 'Unequal plurality: towards an Asymmetric Power Model of British Politics', *Government and Opposition*, Vol. 38, No. 3 (2003), where they note that although governance has undermined the Westminster Model, the state has been reconstituted rather than fundamentally transformed. Central government retains significant resources.

Rhodes describes the UK state as a 'differentiated polity', the main features of which are as follows.

1. The hierarchical form of government that was a key feature of the Westminster Model has been replaced by a looser form of governance in which self-organising networks enjoy significant autonomy from the state. There is no 'sovereign actor' in contemporary British politics: governance is 'governing without government'.

2. The differential polity is fragmented and segmented. Although many of Rhodes's key works were written before Scottish and Welsh devolution, he had already identified intergovernmental relations – interactions between interdependent government units such as central government, local authorities, the EU and specialist agencies – as a key feature of the era of governance. The centre does not enjoy a monopoly of power but engages in bargaining with other authoritative actors.

3. Centre–local relations are, Rhodes claims, characterised by power-dependence rather than command. Different tiers of government have their own resources, are interdependent and their relationship is one in which resources are exchanged.

4. The core executive is segmented as it consists of various actors and networks which have their own resources. Decision-making is not the preserve of the Prime Minister or Cabinet; it is instead characterised by bargaining within and between networks.

5. Policy networks are a defining feature of the policy-making process (see Analysis 9.1). They take different forms ranging from loose issue networks whose membership fluctuates to closed policy communities which consist of small, tightly integrated groups. Policy networks set the agenda and the rules of the game by determining which actors should participate in the policy process, defining their role and privileging certain actors. Power-dependence and resource exchange between public bodies and private interests are key features. With the creation of executive agencies, government departments are no longer at the heart of policy networks.

Analysis: 9.1

Policy networks

The concept of policy networks is an influential one in the study of policy-making. The policy networks perspective claims that the nature of the relationship between government and pressure groups varies across policy fields. There is no one simple model that explains policy-making across all areas of public policy: power is dispersed across a large number of relatively autonomous networks in the era of governance. At one end of the policy networks spectrum are issue networks which are relatively open and contain a large number of actors (government departments, agencies and pressure groups) who move in and out of the network as the policy focus shifts. Policy communities are located at the other end of the spectrum. These are much tighter, closed groupings containing a smaller number of actors. Government departments and insider groups enjoy privileged status and have a relationship of dependency.

A concern raised about the policy networks approach is that it underplays the capacity of central government to steer or even control the policy process. Conservative and New Labour governments have, for example, acted to open up some closed policy communities. The health policy community was dominated by the Department of Health and professional bodies such as the British Medical Association (representing general practitioners) and royal colleges (representing consultants). The Thatcher governments sought to reduce the influence of health professionals by creating a new layer of NHS managers who would make policy decisions while the Blair governments have required Primary Care Trusts to consult with their local communities. In agriculture, bodies representing the interests of food producers (farmers) enjoyed a privileged relationship with the Ministry for Agriculture Food and Fisheries (MAFF) while bodies representing consumer interests had only outsider status. Following a series of food safety scares, the Blair Government replaced MAFF with a new Department for the Environment, Food and Rural Affairs in which consumer interests would be more readily heard and set up a new regulatory body, the Food Standards Agency.

6. The state is being 'hollowed out' as functions are transferred away from the core executive: upwards to the EU, downwards to subnational bodies and outwards to quangos and the private sector.

Rhodes argues that the hollowing out of the state has in turn generated a number of problems.

1. A fragmentation of decision-making. Services are delivered not by central or local government alone but by a combination of public bodies, actors from the private and voluntary sectors and specialist agencies. Effective policy-making and policy implementation requires coordination but the absence of a single authoritative body makes this less likely. In short, central government has seen its capacity to steer reduced.

2. A greater likelihood of policy disasters (see Analysis 10.1, page 229). Policy disasters are major failures in public policy that are attributable to serious shortcomings in the policy-making process. The number of policy disasters has increased in recent years. Some such as the problems in the Child Support Agency or the controversy over the cost of the Millennium Dome are illustrative of the dangers of agencification and insufficient regulation of relationships with the private sector.

3. A weakening of accountability. Fragmentation has eroded lines of democratic accountability, notably the principle that ministers are accountable to parliament for decisions or actions taken within their department. It is not always clear whether a minister in a central government department or the chief executive of a Next Steps executive agency is accountable for the actions of an agency. A prime example was the 1997 dispute between the Home Secretary, Michael Howard and the chief executive of the Prison Service, Derek Lewis over who was accountable for a series of escapes by prisoners. Lewis was sacked. The government distinguishes between policy, for which the minister is accountable, and operation (or management) where responsibility has been delegated to agency chief executives. Yet the distinction between accountability and responsibility is far from clear cut and challenges parliament's status as the institution primarily responsible for scrutinising and legitimising policy.

Traditional forms of accountability have been undermined but new forms have also emerged. Centrally-determined performance targets, systems of audit and regulation, and the production of league tables are used to hold semi-autonomous agencies accountable for their record in delivering public goods. Here, an agency is no longer accountable simply to an institution further up the policy-making hierarchy but upwards to ministers, downwards to consumers of public services and outwards to groups within the policy network.

A reconstituted state

The impact of governance and claims that the state has been hollowed out are disputed. Marsh, Smith and Richards have written persuasively of a 'reconstituted' rather than hollowed-out state. They agree with much of Rhodes's critique of the Westminster Model but dispute his interpretation of the extent to which new forms of government have undermined the capacity of the centre. Their 'asymmetric power model' asserts that the relationship between central government and other actors is asymmetric as the former has a unique set of resources (e.g. the state bureaucracy, authority and substantial tax-raising powers).

Marsh, Smith and Richards agree that the core executive is segmented but argue that relations of resource exchange are asymmetric: in other words, the Prime Minister enjoys significant advantages even if he or she does not have a monopoly over decision-making. They also note that key elements of the British political tradition remain intact, notably a Whitehall culture that 'government knows best'. Ministers and civil servants continue to view British politics in terms of parliamentary sovereignty and resist attempts to open their world to greater scrutiny. Actors in the core executive are still the most important in policy-making. The resources they possess are much greater than those of other actors. As we will see in the following chapter, central government has been able to restructure local government and curtail its discretionary powers. Government departments are also the most significant actors in policy networks because they have the greatest resources; the most influential interest groups are those with close relationships with government departments.

Developments under the Blair governments add weight to claims that central government has sought to reassert its position in response to the dispersal of resources to other actors. As we have seen, Blair has extended Number 10's control over public policy by promoting 'joined-up government' and setting targets for policy implementation and service delivery. Special government units and taskforces have been established to promote coordination in cross-cutting policy areas populated by an array of networks. The Treasury has also enhanced its coordinating role through the Comprehensive Spending Review process and use of Public Service Agreements. The scope of the state has expanded in some ways, such as the increase in the number of civil servants and the extension of regulatory regimes.

New Labour has not restored the state's ownership role (only responsibility for the railways infrastructure has been brought back under government control) and government intervention in the economy is far less pronounced than in the early post-war period. But the New Labour government does still play an important role in steering the economy and society, notably through its policies on macroeconomic stability, competitiveness and training, and social justice.

Conclusion and summary

In the last three decades, the role of the state has undergone significant change. State intervention in the economy and society was commonplace in the post-war period but by the end of the twentieth century the state was in retreat. Government has given way to governance as decision-making functions were transferred from the core executive to supranational bodies, subnational institutions and a large number of specialist agencies. The major trends in this era of governance were the separation of policy-making and policy implementation functions, the development of an enabling or regulatory state which oversees the provision of public goods by a range of actors rather than providing them directly itself, and the introduction of market forces and private sector practices into public service delivery.

The move from government to governance has placed the Westminster Model under severe strain. It no longer offers the optimal explanatory framework for understanding British politics. But claims that the British state has been hollowed out and the autonomy of central government all but ended are exaggerated. The centre has sought both to defend its policy-making autonomy and enhance its capacity to coordinate the delivery of public goods.

Fragmentation and centralisation have gone hand-in-hand under the Blair governments. New forms of governance have also challenged the Westminster Model's understanding of representative democracy by which ministers are held accountable to parliament for policies that were made and then implemented by their departments. The transfer of functions from government departments to executive agencies has blurred the lines of accountability. The expansion of the quango state has also widened the democratic deficit, particularly at local level, raising concerns about accountability, transparency and patronage. But new forms of accountability have emerged in a regulatory state which measures the performance of bodies responsible for delivering public goods. Finally, the development of multi-level governance has had both negative and positive consequences for British democracy. Devolution has brought decision-making closer to the people of Scotland and Wales, and opened up new avenues for participation. But the transfer of policy competences to the EU has reduced the scope for effective scrutiny and accountability.

Further reading

D. Richards and M. Smith, *Governance and Public Policy in the UK* (Oxford: Oxford University Press, 2002) is the best text on the changing state. The reform of the civil service is examined in D. Richards, *The Civil Service under the Conservatives, 1979–97* (Brighton: Sussex Academic Press, 1997). A. Massey and R. Pyper, *Public Management and Modernisation in Britain* (London: Palgrave, 2005) is a good introduction to the new public management.

Rod Rhodes has been particularly influential in the study of governance. R. Rhodes, *Understanding Governance: Policy Networks, Governance, Reflexivity and Accountability* (Buckingham: Open University Press, 1997) brings together some of his most important work. His 'The New Governance: Governing without Government', *Political Studies*, Vol. 44, No. 4 (1996), pp. 652–67 is a good starting point. R. Rhodes, 'The Hollowing Out of the State', *Political Quarterly*, Vol. 65, No. 2 (1994), pp. 138–51 is a key article and I. Holliday, 'Is the British State Hollowing Out?', *Political Quarterly*, Vol. 71, No. 2 (2000), pp. 167–76 an important response. D. Marsh, D. Richards and M. Smith, 'Unequal Plurality: towards an Asymmetric Power Model of British politics', *Government and Opposition*, Vol. 38, No. 3 (2003), pp. 306–32 challenges Rhodes's differentiated polity model. Their major works on central government include D. Marsh, D. Richards and M. Smith, *Changing Patterns of Governance in the United Kingdom: Reinventing Whitehall* (London: Palgrave, 2001). D. Osborne and T. Gaebler, *Reinventing Government* (Harlow: Addison Wesley, 1992) is an influential New Right perspective on the changing state.

The quango state is mapped by S. Weir and W. Hall, *EGO-TRIP* (London: Democratic Audit Paper no. 2, 1994) and D. Lewis, *The Essential Guide to British Quangos 2005* (London: Centre for Policy Studies, 2005). On accountability, see P. Norton, 'Regulating the Regulatory State', *Parliamentary Affairs*, Vol. 57, No. 4 (2004), pp. 785–99 and in the same volume, M. Flinders, 'MPs and Icebergs: Parliament and Delegated Governance', (pp. 767–84). S. Jenkins, *Accountable to None: the Tory Nationalization of Britain* (London: Penguin, 1995) is a readable critique of the extension of the quango state under Thatcher and

Major. The regulatory state is examined in M. Moran, 'The Rise of the Regulatory State in Britain', *Parliamentary Affairs*, Vol. 54, No. 1 (2001), pp. 19–34. V. Bogdanor (ed.), *Joined-Up Government* (Oxford: Oxford University Press, 2005) assesses the Blair governments' efforts to address fragmentation in central government. On policy disasters, see the special issue of *Parliamentary Affairs*, Vol. 56, No. 3 (2003).

I. Bache and M. Flinders (eds) *Multi-Level Governance* (Oxford University Press, 2004) includes essays on the UK and EU. Introductions to globalisation include J. Baylis and S. Smith, *The Globalisation of World Politics* (Oxford University Press, 2001) and D. Held, *The Global Transformations Reader* (Polity, 2003). The hyperglobalist perspective is presented in K. Ohmae, *The End of the Nation State* (HarperCollins, 1996).

Several official publications can be recommended. The Cabinet Office publication *Public Bodies 2005* provides full details of NDPBs in the UK. Independent studies include the House of Commons Public Administration Select Committee, *Mapping the Quango State*, 5th Report, 2000–2001, HC 367 and its *Governing by Appointment: Opening up the Patronage State*, 4th Report, 2002–2003, HC 165-I. J. Macleavy and O. Gay, *The Quango Debate*, House of Commons Research Paper 05/30, 2005 is a useful summary.

Websites

The Cabinet Office website www.cabinetoffice.gov.uk is a valuable source of information on civil service reform, executive agencies and non-departmental public bodies. The easiest way to navigate is to follow the sitemap at www.cabinetoffice.gov.uk/sitemap. Reports from the House of Commons Public Administration Select Committee are available at www.parliament.uk/parliamentary_committees/public_administration_select_committee.cfm. The quango state has also been mapped by the Democratic Audit www.democraticaudit.com/british_democracy/index.php. Most executive agencies, quangos and regulatory bodies have websites but their quality varies greatly. Executive agencies mentioned in this chapter include the Child Support Agency (www.csa.gov.uk), the Prison Service (www.hmprisonservice.gov.uk). Quangos include the Arts Council (www.artscouncil.org.uk) and regulatory bodies OFGEM (www.ofgem.gov.uk), the Financial Services Authority (www.fsa.gov.uk), NICE (www.nice.org.uk) and the Audit Commission (www.audit-commission.gov.uk). Websites of international organisations referred to in this chapter include www.un.org, www.imf.org and www.wto.org.

Chapter 10

Local government to local governance

Learning outcomes

After reading this chapter, you will:
- Be aware of the structure and internal organisation of local government.
- Be aware of the functions and financing of local government.
- Understand the move from local government to local governance.

Introduction

There are compelling reasons why a liberal democratic state such as the United Kingdom should have a robust system of local government. In a country of 59 million people, central government does not have the capacity to handle all the functions associated with the modern state so the centre decentralises some decision-making power to local bodies. There are strong normative arguments for granting local decision-making powers to democratic bodies such as elected local councils. Pluralists argue that power should be dispersed among different tiers of government rather than concentrated at the centre. Decentralisation is beneficial as it puts decision-making closer to the people: local authorities are better able to recognise and meet the needs of local communities. They also provide opportunities for people to participate in local politics.

Government to governance

Local government: a system in which elected local authorities are responsible for the provision of many local services.

The term **local government** refers to the 500 or so local authorities in the UK. Elected local councillors make up the local council within these authorities, taking decisions on behalf of the citizens and communities they represent. Local government in the UK is weaker than in many other liberal democracies. It is not afforded constitutionally protected status meaning that central government can – and often does – change the structure and powers of local government with little recourse to local opinion. Local councils have no power of general competence but can only act within the powers specified by law. If they overstep their powers, councils can be challenged in the courts. Much of the legislation affecting local government did, historically, give councils extensive discretionary powers that allowed them to set their own priorities and adopt different policies. Councils also have the power to levy local taxes. But the financial and policy discretion afforded to local authorities by the centre has declined.

For much of the twentieth century local government was the predominant actor in local service delivery with responsibility for education, housing, social care, policing, etc. This position has been eroded over the last thirty years as the autonomy (or discretionary power) afforded to local authorities has been reined in by the centre. Central government has extended its control over local government activity by taking over some of its functions, transferring others to non-elected agencies and putting in place an inspection regime which penalises councils that fail to meet nationally-determined targets. The centre has also tightened its grip on local government finance so that it controls much of the money paid to local authorities.

Local governance: a system in which a range of bodies and networks are involved in the provision of local services.

The last two decades have also seen a move away from local government, in which elected local authorities provided most local services directly (e.g. education and housing), to **local governance** in which a range of bodies are involved in decision-making at local level. These bodies include specialist agencies or quangos (e.g. foundation schools), local partnerships, voluntary bodies and private companies. The emergence of local governance has necessitated a rethinking of the proper role of local authorities and the nature of local democracy.

The structure of local government

The most significant post-war reorganisation of local government in England and Wales took place in 1974 (see Timeline 10.1). It introduced a two-tier system in which the functions of local authorities were divided between two levels of local government. In England, different arrangements were put in place for the major urban conurbations and the rural shire counties. Six metropolitan councils were established in the major urban areas of the West Midlands, South Yorkshire, West Yorkshire, Tyne and Wear, Greater Manchester and Merseyside. They were major strategic bodies with responsibility for transport, policing and strategic planning. Below the metropolitan council tier were 36 metropolitan districts responsible for big-spending local services such as education, personal social services, housing and leisure.

TIMELINE 10.1

The development of local government

1888	Local Government Act establishes two-tier system of county councils and borough councils in rural England and Wales
1894	Local Government Act creates urban and rural district councils
1963	London Government Act creates Greater London Council and 32 London boroughs
1973	Local Government Act creates two-tier system of local government in urban areas and shire counties of England and Wales (comes into effect in 1974)
1980	Local Government Planning and Land Act introduces Compulsory Competitive Tendering (CCT)
1984	Rates Act introduces rate-capping
1985	Local Government Act abolishes Greater London Council and six metropolitan councils (came into effect in 1986)
1988	Local Government Finance Act replaces domestic rates with community charge (poll tax) and business rates with national non-domestic rates
	Education Act allows schools to 'opt-out' of local authority control
1992	Local Government Finance Act replaces community charge with council tax
1995–1998	Forty-six unitary authorities created in England. Two-tier systems of local government replaced by unitary authorities in Scotland and Wales
1999	Local Government Act replaces CCT with Best Value
2000	Local Government Act requires local authorities to select one of three models of political management; CCT replaced by Best Value
	First elections to Greater London Authority and Mayor of London
2001–2002	Referendums on directly elected mayors held in 30 local authorities; 11 vote 'yes'

The names and division of labour between the two tiers was different in rural areas. Here, 47 county councils in England and Wales were responsible for education and social services in addition to the strategic functions such as policing and transport handled by the metropolitan councils. A total of 333 district councils were responsible for housing, leisure and other services. To further confuse the picture, the English and Welsh shires also have a lower tier of parish councils that run such things as village halls, allotments and cemeteries.

Different arrangements applied in London and Scotland. In London, the Greater London Council (GLC) had been established in 1965. It had strategic responsibilities similar to those of the metropolitan councils, although the Inner London Education Authority (ILEA) was responsible for education across the capital. Thirty-two London boroughs, plus the City of London Corporation, provided those services delivered by the metropolitan districts in other urban areas. Local government in Scotland was reorganised in 1975 with the creation of nine regional councils and 53 district councils.

The post-1975 pattern of local government was more uniform and streamlined than the diverse patchwork of authorities that had been in place for the previous hundred years. The number of local authorities was greatly reduced, the 333 district councils in England replacing more than a thousand bodies. But the reorganisation was criticised for transferring strategic functions to larger authorities and redrawing traditional boundaries.

Unitary but not uniform

The structure of local government has been altered by central government in three waves since the mid-1970s. This has produced a more fragmented pattern. Nor is it clear that the restructuring of local government has had a positive effect on the performance of local councils.

Left-wing Labour administrations in the GLC and metropolitan counties frustrated the Thatcher governments' efforts to control local authority spending and taxation. The centre responded by abolishing the GLC and the six metropolitan councils in 1986; ILEA was abolished in 1990. Some of their responsibilities shifted to the London boroughs and the 36 metropolitan district councils (now known as metropolitan authorities), but others were transferred to unelected agencies. Major urban areas now had only a single tier of local government and London became the only major West European capital city without a large strategic authority.

The Major government proposed a further reorganisation of local government, its aim being the creation of a substantial number of unitary authorities (i.e. a single tier of local government) in Great Britain. It established an independent commission (to examine the case for all-purpose unitary authorities in England). Having encountered significant local opposition to change, the commission recommended fewer changes than the government had envisaged. The resulting picture was an uneven one: 46 unitary authorities were established in England by 1998, leaving a two-tier structure of 34 county councils and 238 district councils elsewhere. Historic names such as Rutland, which had been abolished in 1974, returned to the local government map but only four county councils – Avon, Berkshire, Cleveland and Humberside – disappeared. Reorganisation in Scotland and Wales was dictated by ministers. This produced a more coherent outcome as 22 unitary authorities were created in Wales and 32 in Scotland, but there was controversy over the lack of consultation.

A third reorganisation followed under the first Blair government. It was centred on the capital where the Greater London Authority (GLA) was set up. It consists of two elements: a 25-member Greater London Assembly elected by the Additional Member System (see Chapter 16) and a directly elected executive mayor. The GLA has strategic responsibility in areas such as transport, economic development, policing and planning. These functions are carried out by agencies (e.g. Transport for London) accountable to the mayor. The mayor sets the budget (some £4 billion) and determines policy; the Assembly scrutinises these and makes recommendations. The mayor's powers are limited, evidenced by the failure of Ken Livingstone – who was elected in 2000 as an independent and 2004 as Labour candidate – to persuade the government to drop its preference for a Public–Private Partnership to finance the redevelopment of the Underground. His main initiative was a congestion charge for drivers entering central London. Five parties won seats in the 2004 Assembly election: Conservative (9 seats), Labour (7), Liberal Democrat (5), Green (2) and UKIP (2). A further round of local government reorganisation is expected during the third term Blair government and is predicted to see a return to the unitary authority model.

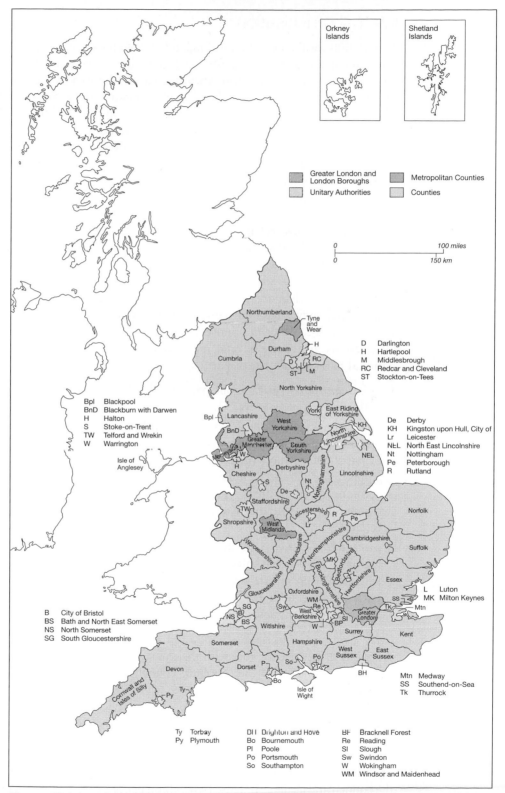

Figure 10.1 Local government in England, counties and unitary administrations, 1998 (Produced by ONS Geography GIS & Mapping Unit, 2003) © Crown copyright. All rights reserved. Licence number 100030901.

Internal organisation

The 21,000 local councillors in England and Wales are elected for four-year terms. The simple plurality system for single member seats but where more than one councillor is to be elected from a ward, a variant known as the 'block vote' is used. In a ward electing three councillors, an elector can vote for three candidates; the top three candidates are elected without any redistribution of votes.

Councillors undertake a number of functions such as contributing to local policy-making or scrutinising council activity, and representing the interests of their constituents. A 2004 survey found that 70 per cent of councillors in England and Wales were male, 96 per cent were white and 39 per cent had retired from full-time employment. If representation is taken to imply that a group should be a microcosm of wider society, then councillors are not representative of their communities or those who are most reliant on council services. Most councillors do not receive a salary for their local authority work; allowances have increased but are not equivalent to the average wage.

In the early post-war period, political party involvement in local politics was limited in non-urban areas. Many councillors stood as independents, concealing any affinity they may have had with the major parties. Around half of all councillors were returned to office unopposed. The situation has changed dramatically. Almost all elections are contested and more than 90 per cent of councillors represent a national party. A number of party systems exist at local level:

- *Dominant-party systems*: one party has held a majority of seats and ran the local authority for many years.
- *Two-party systems*: most seats are held by two parties. These may alternate in power, form minority administrations or work together in coalition. The nature of party competition varies: Labour–Conservative duopoly is the norm in many county and district councils, but Labour–Liberal Democrats competition is common in urban areas. No single party had overall control of 131 of the 410 councils in England and Wales in 2005 so coalitions or informal agreements were required.
- *Multi-party systems*: council seats are divided between three or more parties, making majority rule unlikely. Parties must cooperate to run the local authority and transfers of power are frequent. The Greens, the United Kingdom Independence Party, Respect and the British National Party have all won council seats in England in recent years.

Party groups meet to discuss policy and agree their positions. Councillors may face sanctions if they do not vote with their party. The influence of party groups reached its apex in Labour-run metropolitan councils in the 1980s when major decisions were taken by senior party figures away from the council chamber.

Local government officers provide policy advice to councillors and implement council decisions. In many councils, policy work is conducted within service departments (e.g. social services) and central departments (e.g. finance) that are staffed by officials and headed by a chief officer who has professional experience in that area. Most authorities have a chief executive who has overall responsibility for the work of the council and its departments. Two million people are employed in local government in the UK, more than the total number working for central and regional government.

Decision-making by committee was the norm in local government in the twentieth century. Committees handled decision-making in areas in which councils provided services. They included councillors from both the ruling group and other parties, thus allowing discussions on alternative proposals but also lengthening the time it took to make policy. Nor was decision-making as transparent as this implies for key decisions were often taken by small groups behind closed doors. Committee work did allow councillors to concentrate on those areas in which they had professional experience. But it also produced compartmentalisation whereby councillors and officials concentrated on their areas of interest rather than focusing on the bigger picture.

Elected mayors

Interest in the idea of elected mayors grew in the 1990s. Conservative Secretary of State for the Environment Michael Heseltine had long been interested while key New Labour politicians such as Tony Blair were also drawn to it. In office, the Blair government proposed a separation of the executive and scrutiny functions of local authorities. Council leaders would take strategic decisions while the remaining non-executive councillors scrutinised their activities. It was hoped that this would professionalise local government, provide stronger community leadership and improve accountability. The Local Government Act 2000 duly required councils with a population of over 85,000 to introduce one of three models of political management:

- A directly elected mayor with a cabinet.
- A directly elected mayor with a full-time council manager.
- A cabinet with an executive leader chosen by councillors.

Councils were required to consult with local citizens when reaching a decision on which model to adopt. Binding referendums were to be held if a council recommended one of the options involving a directly elected mayor. They could be called by the council or by local citizens presenting a petition supported by 5 per cent of the local population. The government's preferred model was the directly elected mayor and cabinet. It believed that elected local mayors would become the key political actors in their communities, taking policy initiatives, setting the budget and taking executive decisions. Direct election would also give the mayor added legitimacy and a higher profile. Supporters pointed to the effective political and economic leadership provided by mayors in American cities, but UK elected mayors pale in comparison given the limited powers of their local authorities. It is also worth noting that elected mayors are not the same as, and do not replace, civic mayors whose role is largely ceremonial.

Under option one, the mayor would appoint his or her own cabinet while under option two, much policy and financial power would reside with an appointed council manager who was responsible to the mayor. Established players in local government were wary of the mayoral options, fearing that their influence would be diminished further.

Referendums on elected mayors were held in 30 authorities (excluding London) in 2001–2002, just three of which produced a turnout above 40 per cent. Only

Table 10.1 Mayoral elections

	Local authority	Mayor	Party affiliation	Turnout (%)
May 2002	Doncaster	Martin Winter	Labour	27.1
	Hartlepool	Stuart Drummond	Independent	28.8
	Lewisham	Steve Bullock	Labour	24.8
	Middlesbrough	Ray Mallon	Independent	41.3
	Newham	Sir Robin Wales	Labour	25.5
	North Tyneside	Chris Morgan	Conservative	42.3
	Watford	Dorothy Thornhill	Liberal Democrat	36.1
October 2002	Bedford	Frank Branston	Independent	25.4
	Hackney	Jules Pipe	Labour	26.3
	Mansfield	Tony Egginton	Independent	18.5
	Stoke-on-Trent	Mike Wolfe	Mayor 4 Stoke	24.0
June 2003 (by-election)	North Tyneside	Linda Arkley	Conservative	30.9
May 2005	Doncaster	Martin Winter	Labour	54.5
	Hartlepool	Stuart Drummond	Independent	51.0
	North Tyneside	John Harrison	Labour	61.4
	Stoke-on-Trent	Mark Meredith	Labour	50.8
October 2005	Torbay	Nicholas Bye	Conservative	24.0
May 2006	Hackney	Jules Pipe	Labour	34.0
	Lewisham	Steve Bullock	Labour	33.8
	Newham	Sir Robin Wales	Labour	34.5
	Watford	Dorothy Thornhill	Liberal Democrat	39.2

eleven of these referendums produced votes in favour. Ten authorities then adopted the elected mayor with cabinet model and one, Stoke on Trent, the mayor with council manager option. Independent (i.e. non-aligned) candidates triumphed in five of the eleven mayoral elections held between 2002 and 2003 (see Table 10.1). In Middlesbrough, former police chief Ray Mallon (known as 'Robocop' for his zero-tolerance approach to crime) won. Stuart Drummond (better known as 'H'Angus the Monkey', Hartlepool United's club mascot) was victorious in Hartlepool in 2002 and was re-elected in 2005. Torbay moved to the mayor and cabinet model in 2005 but electors in three authorities voted against the mayoral model in referendums held in 2004–2005.

Attempts by the centre to persuade authorities in big cities such as Birmingham to adopt the mayoral model failed. Frustration at the limited progress and Deputy Prime Minister John Prescott's preference for elected regional assemblies saw the second-term Blair government tone down its support for elected mayors in large urban areas (or 'city-regions'). Following the north-east referendum 'no' to a regional assembly, the government is expected to launch another concerted push for elected mayors. Research by the (pro-mayoral) New Local Government Network suggests that elected mayors have a higher public recognition rating than other local politicians but have yet to stamp their policy imprint on local politics.

The cabinet with executive leader model was chosen by 316 local authorities, 82 per cent of the total number. Here the council leader is indirectly-elected by councillors which in practice, means that the leader of the largest political group becomes council leader. He or she shares executive power with a cabinet of up to nine councillors selected from the majority party or the ruling coalition. Old-style

Monkey business: Stuart Drummond (aka H'Angus the Monkey) was twice elected mayor of Hartlepool (© David Davies/PA/EMPICS)

decision-making by committees may have ended, but the cabinet and executive leader model was the preferred option as it was the closest to the existing pattern of informal inner cabinets consisting of the council leader and the chairs of committees.

Under each of three models, the main functions of non-executive councillors (i.e. 'backbenchers' who were not members of the cabinet) were to scrutinise the activities of the council executive and propose policy or budgetary amendments. Much of the scrutiny work would be done in specialist committees, but the strength of the party groups acts as a bulwark against over-zealous scrutiny by members of the ruling party. The government also expected non-executive councillors to devote more time to their roles as community representatives.

Authorities with populations under 85,000 were permitted to introduce 'alternative arrangements' that meant slimming down the existing committee system rather than adopting one of the executive models. Of the 86 councils concerned, 56 opted for a system in which the full council established the policy agenda and budget, supported by up to five policy committees which were accountable to scrutiny committees.

Functions of local authorities

Local authorities are responsible for many of the services that citizens utilise on a regular basis (see Table 10.2). These include:

- Education: primary and secondary schools, nurseries, youth services and adult education.
- Social services: residential care and care in the community.
- Housing: public housing, redevelopment, services for the homeless.
- Highways: road building and maintenance (except motorways and trunk roads), traffic regulation and road safety (e.g. speed limits).
- Public transport: bus services, licensing of taxis, etc.
- Planning: strategic planning (e.g. redevelopment), decisions on planning applications.
- Environmental health: refuse collection, recycling, pollution control, health and safety inspections of commercial premises.
- Leisure and culture: public libraries, arts, leisure centres, parks.

In its heyday in the late nineteenth and early twentieth centuries, local government provided many of the public services associated with the modern state. These included public housing, primary and secondary education, public health, policing and the supply of water, gas and electricity. But local government's service provision role has declined over the last half century. The nationalisation of public utilities in the 1940s saw local authorities lose functional responsibility for the provision of water, electricity and gas. The creation of the National Health Service (NHS) in 1948 ended local authority ownership of most hospitals.

The focus of this section is on the changes to local government's service provision role introduced by the Thatcher, Major and Blair governments. A number of trends are evident, mirroring those found in the central state (see Chapter 9):

Table 10.2 Local government in England and Wales – who does what?

	Metropolitan councils	Unitary authorities	County councils	District councils
Education	*	*	*	
Housing	*	*		*
Strategic planning	*	*	*	
Local planning	*	*		*
Transport	*	*	*	
Highways	*	*	*	
Social services	*	*	*	
Leisure	*	*		*
Libraries	*	*	*	
Environmental health	*	*		*
Refuse collection	*	*		*

Source: Adapted from Local Government Association, 'Local Government Structure', http://www.lga. gov.uk/Briefing.asp?lsection=761&id=SXCEEC-A77F5AD1&ccat=120

- The transformation of local authorities into 'enabling authorities' which oversee the provision of services by other bodies rather than providing them directly themselves.
- The move from local government to local governance with local services being delivered by a variety of bodies including quangos, voluntary organisations and private companies.
- The increased role of market forces and the private sector in local service delivery.
- The changing nature of local accountability. Local elections used to be the main way in which councillors were held to account for the quality of local services. Now service providers must meet targets and are subject to inspection by regulatory bodies.

Education is the single largest item covered by central government grants to local authorities. The Education Act 1944 stated that local councils would be Local Education Authorities with responsibility for the provision, management and staffing of primary and secondary schools. Responsibility for polytechnics and higher education colleges was removed from local authorities in the early 1990s and transferred to new agencies. The Education Act 1988 allowed state schools to opt-out of local authority control, subject to approval by a ballot of parents, and become 'grant maintained schools' funded directly by central government. Conservative expectations of a revolution in schooling were frustrated as only 5 per cent of some 25,000 schools 'opted out' before Labour ended the grant-maintained status.

Local authority discretion in the schools that do fall under their auspices has declined. Legislation introduced by Conservative and Labour governments has given governors and head teachers a greater role in the day-to-day running of their schools, including control over their own budgets. Labour pressed for comprehensive secondary education in the 1970s; New Labour has allowed schools to hold parental ballots on academic selection. It has also encouraged schools to specialise in particular subjects and created state-funded but independently-run city academies. Schools under local authority control are subject to regular inspection by the Office for Standards in Education (OFSTED), which provides another example of the development of the regulatory state (see Chapter 9). Schools with poor academic or disciplinary records may be forced to introduce 'special measures' or be closed down.

Housing was a major function of local authorities in the 1950s, when councils were required to build new homes to meet local needs. The Thatcher governments gave council tenants the right to buy their homes at a discounted price. This removed more than two million houses from local authority control; Housing Action Trusts were created to manage public-owned housing. Councils also faced restrictions on borrowing money to repair houses or build new ones. The Blair governments encouraged councils to transfer ownership of their housing stock to 'registered social landlords' (e.g. housing associations set up by councils), subject to approval in residents' ballots. Housing associations do not face the same restrictions on borrowing money. By the end of the decade, the number of houses owned by registered social landlords is likely to exceed that of council houses.

Local authorities are responsible for *personal services* to the elderly, children and young people, and those with mental health problems. They provide services such as residential and day care, help in the home (e.g. meals on wheels) and child protection. This is one of the few areas in which government legislation has extended rather than reduced the role of local authorities. Since the 1990s, social workers employed by local councils have been responsible for assessing requests for residential care and providing care in the community.

Local authority involvement in *economic development* has also expanded. This has resulted from both central government pressure (the Local Government Act 2000 required local authorities to promote economic development), the role of the European Union (which provides funding for regeneration projects directly to local authorities) and local initiatives. Councils have become leading actors in networks – which include businesses, chambers of commerce, training bodies and voluntary agencies – that seek to promote investment and employment. But vocational training is now controlled by specialised agencies (learning and skills councils) rather than local authorities. Local authority led regeneration has been particularly evident in areas that suffered from the decline of manufacturing industry, such as South Wales and North East England. Public–private partnerships have also revitalised *public transport* systems, funding new tram networks in cities such as Manchester and Nottingham. Indeed, much local public transport is often operated by private companies. Some councils have considered introducing congestion charges (see Controversy 10.1).

Local authority involvement in *policing* has diminished. Police services are controlled by police authorities which enjoy significant autonomy. Councillors once

Controversy:	10.1

Congestion charging

Congestion charging is one of the most controversial examples of policy innovation by local government. The most significant scheme is that introduced by the Mayor of London and Greater London Authority in February 2003. Drivers of private vehicles entering a defined 'central zone' between 7.00am and 6.30pm on weekdays would be charged an initial £5 per day. This was raised to £8 in 2005 and the zone was extended westwards. Cameras read the registration numbers of cars entering the zone and check it against a database. Non-payers face a standard £100 penalty. Various categories of people and vehicles are entitled to discounts, including people living within the congestion charging zone, disabled drivers, taxis and motorcycles.

The scheme aimed to tackle the worst city centre congestion and air quality in the UK by encouraging people to use buses, rail and the tube rather than their cars. Much of the money raised by the charge would be used to improve public transport. Before the charge was introduced, the average speed in London was 11 miles per hour and drivers in London spent more than half their time in queues. The charge has had a significant effect as traffic fell by 18% and vehicle emissions by 12% in its first year. But charging has not been welcomed universally. Only half of Londoners support it and small businesses claim to have lost trade.

The Transport Act 2000 allowed local authorities to introduce congestion charging at their discretion. A number of councils have given it serious consideration, but few have taken the plunge. Durham City Council introduced a £2 charge to enter part of the city in 2002. The City of Edinburgh Council proposed charges for entering an outer cordon and inner cordon but its plans were rejected by a margin of three to one in a local referendum in 2005.

made up a majority of members serving on committees which held chief constables accountable, but no longer do so. The merger of local police forces will also erode the connection between the police and local authority boundaries. Local tax bills include precepts charged by police and fire services. These sums are collected by local government but are then paid directly to the relevant authorities. Local authorities are responsible for *civil defence* and are required to draw up emergency planning arrangements to deal with terrorism, disease and so forth.

From provider to enabler

Enabling authority: a local authority that sets a framework in which a range of bodies provide local services but which does not provide many of these services itself.

The Conservative vision was of local authorities as **enabling authorities** that set the strategic priorities for services and set out a framework for competition between would-be service providers, but would no longer be universal service providers themselves. This mirrored the emphasis on government acting as an enabler or regulator that underpinned changes occurring at the centre such as the reform of the civil service. This perspective challenged the traditional view of local democracy by focusing not on the interests of local government but on those of local citizens who, as consumers of local services, wanted more efficient and economical services. Service providers would be held accountable through contracts and charters, while councillors remained accountable to the electorate for strategic and budgetary decisions. Rather than providing services directly, local authorities now organise, supervise, regulate and fund the provision of services by other competing bodies. The Conservatives argued that this amounted to decentralisation of power to the citizen, but it took interventionist measures to bring this about.

Compulsory competitive tendering: the policy that public bodies are required to open up contracts for service provision to the private sector.

Compulsory competitive tendering (CCT) was introduced in 1980 then extended in 1988 and 1992. It required local authorities to put contracts for service provision out to tender, meaning that council departments had to compete with outside contractors for the right to provide services such as refuse collection, leisure facilities and so forth (see Case study 10.1). The contract would be awarded to the lowest bidder. Conservatives supported CCT as it brought about the separation of local authorities' previous roles as both a purchaser and provider of services, tackled the monopoly status of local government services and weakened trade union influence. In-house bids were successful in many large contracts, but the CCT process had forced local authorities to make efficiency savings so that they could compete with the private sector. It was also expected to improve the efficiency of service provision, but critics argued that savings were made at the expense of quality and working conditions.

Under New Labour, CCT was replaced by Best Value in 2000. Councils were no longer forced to put contracts out to tender, but were required to obtain best value. Local authorities had to conduct regular reviews of their services to ensure that 'continuous improvement' was underway. They and their services were also subject to inspections at least once every five years by the Audit Commission or specialist inspectorates such as OFSTED. Where inspections revealed significant failings, central government had wide-ranging powers to intervene. This could include requiring local authority departments to comply with specific recommendations, or the removal of 'failing' services from local authority control. New Labour's 'stick and carrot' approach also included incentives for the best performers. Authorities

Case study: 10.1

Recycling

Recycling is an issue that illustrates the nature of multi-level governance in the UK and the potential for policy innovation in local government. Local authorities are at the forefront of efforts to increase recycling in Britain as they are responsible for waste management. In shire counties where two-tiers of local government remain, district councils are responsible for the regular collection of household waste, but county councils provide waste disposal sites. Since the introduction of Compulsory Competitive Tendering, private companies have won many of the contracts to collect and dispose of domestic refuse.

Local authorities are required to meet targets for recycling set by central or subnational government. The Department for the Environment, Food and Rural Affairs set a series of targets for councils in England in its Waste Strategy 2000, rising from 25 per cent by 2006 to 33 per cent by 2015. The European Union has also developed a waste management strategy.

Facilities such as 'bottle banks' have been provided by local authorities for a number of years. The Household Waste Recycling Act 2003 now requires English local authorities to collect at least two separate recyclable materials (e.g. paper, glass, cans and plastics) from households by 2010. Kerbside collections of recyclable material are provided for four out of five households. More innovative approaches include charging for excess waste, encouraging home composting and providing cash prizes for environmentally friendly households. In 2003–2004, the recycling rate for household rate was 17.7 per cent. There were significant differences in local authority performance: Lichfield recycled or composted 46 per cent of household waste but Liverpool City Council only 4 per cent.

Sources: Department for the Environment, Food and Rural Affairs, 'Summary of Local Authority Performance Against Statutory 2003–04 Performance Standards for Recycling and Composting' (2005) www.defra.gov.uk/environment/waste/index.htm; Local Government Association, 'Ten Easy Ways to Prevent Waste' (2005) www.lga.gov.uk/Publication.asp?lSection=0&id=SX1283-A7828682

demonstrating excellence in a particular area could be selected as 'Beacon Councils' which would serve as models for other councils.

A new inspection regime, Comprehensive Performance Assessment (CPA), was introduced in 2002. Key services are inspected and their performance, plus the overall performance of councils, ranked according to five categories ranging from poor to excellent. This allows league tables of local authority performance to be produced. The incentives for high achievers are greater: councils rated as excellent in priority service areas (e.g. education, social care and transport) receive 'additional freedoms' such as more discretion in spending. Those rated good or better will face 'lighter touch' inspections in future. Poor performers again face having special management teams sent in to address their shortcomings. In 2004 two-thirds of councils were rated 'excellent' or 'good'; only Kingston upon Hull was rated 'poor'. The number of inspections has now been reduced and greater emphasis placed on the views of service users.

Local government finance

Local government expenditure accounts for 26 per cent of all public spending in England and Wales, or £84 billion in 2005–2006. Of this, £35.0 billion was spent on education, £16.9 billion on social services and £12.5 billion on the police and fire services. Funding for local authorities comes from three main sources:

- Grants from central government (£44 billion in 2005–2006 or 52 per cent of local authority funding).
- Local taxation on domestic properties, i.e. the council tax (£21 billion or 25 per cent).
- Local taxation on business properties, i.e. the national non-domestic rate (£18 billion or 21 per cent).

Local authorities have limited financial autonomy. Only the council tax is under the direct control of local authorities but levels are subject to capping by central government. The percentage of local authority finance controlled by councils themselves has fallen over the last twenty years. In 1989–90, the last year of the old rates system, central government provided 41 per cent of local government finance while councils raised the rest through taxes on domestic and business properties. The fall in the ratio of contributions from local citizens is significant as it means that large increases in council tax bills are needed to provide relatively small sums of money. To fund a 1 per cent increase in spending in areas not covered by government grants, a local authority would have to increase the council tax by 4 per cent. Local authorities thus have less discretion in spending, forcing them to make difficult decisions about how money should be allocated. A spending increase in one area will necessitate higher council tax bills (which may, in any case, be capped) or cuts in another budget heading.

Changes to the way in which central government provides grants to local authorities have also eroded local authority autonomy. Prior to 1979, funding from the centre came largely in the form of lump sum payments which local author-ities could then decide how to distribute. But the Thatcher governments moved towards targeted funding, making greater use of specific grants earmarked for particular purposes (e.g. teachers' pay). A system of central targets and penalties for overspending councils was also put in place.

The Revenue Support Grant is the largest source of local authority income. Since 1990, central government has determined its level by reference to a Standard Spending Assessment (SSA). This is the centre's assessment of how much each individual local authority must spend to reach a 'standard level of service' in major local services. Calculations are made on the basis of indicators ranging from the total population of the area to the numbers of pensioners and primary school children who live there. When the SSA total figure has been calculated, the government estimates the amount raised by local taxation and provides the remaining sum itself through the Revenue Support Grant. Councils are told how much they will receive in the autumn and must inform the government of their proposed rate of council tax by March. The SSA system has been heavily criticised within local government for its insensitivity to local differences and for the further erosion of their ability to focus spending on particular areas.

From 2006–2007, funding for schools will be taken out of the Revenue Support Grant and be paid as a Dedicated Schools Grant by the Department for Education and Skills. The government will also replace annual grants from the centre with three year settlements.

Local taxes

The domestic rates were the main local tax until 1990. Paid by the head of household, the rates were based upon the value of a property (its 'rateable value') and took no account of the number of people resident within it. As a tax on property rather than individuals, this produced some anomalies. A single old age pensioner living in a large house would pay the same amount as a family in a neighbouring property even though they made less use of local services. Businesses also paid rates based on the value of their properties (e.g. shops or factories). The 1980s and 1990s brought significant change in local government finance.

The Thatcher government sought to curb local authority spending and revenue-raising. The Rates Act 1984 gave the Secretary of State for the Environment the power to 'rate-cap' individual local authorities, that is limit the revenue they can raise through local taxes by setting a ceiling on the level of the rates. This power was used selectively in its early years when Labour-controlled authorities were its main victims, but it was universally applied from 1992 to 1999. Most councils now cap themselves by setting their budgets at the limit imposed by the centre. The Local Government Act 1999 ended universal rate-capping although the centre reserved the power to place a ceiling on council tax levels. The Blair government did not use these powers until 2004 when five local authorities had their council tax levels capped.

The major reform of the Thatcher period was the Local Government Finance Act 1988. It had three main elements:

- The replacement of the domestic rates with a personal 'community charge'.
- The replacement of the business rates with a centrally-set 'national non-domestic rate'.
- The introduction of a Revenue Support Grant allocated on the basis of a central government Standing Spending Assessment.

The community charge, commonly known as the 'poll tax', was supposed to make local authorities more accountable for their spending decisions (see Analysis 10.1). The Conservative case for the poll tax argued that under the rates system, the burden of local taxation fell on too few shoulders. Half of the electorate did not pay the domestic rates and a further one in six was entitled to rebates reducing their rates bills. Only 34 per cent of the adult population paid the full rates. The Thatcher government believed that the poll tax would increase local accountability as all citizens would have to pay something. If they deemed that high community charges were not producing efficiency and quality in local services, electors could remove overspending councils through the ballot box. This was not what happened in practice. When they received higher than predicted poll tax bills, voters blamed the Thatcher government rather than their local council. The centre retained its powers to set a ceiling for the levels of local tax bills (now known as 'charge capping'), but

Policy disasters – the poll tax

A policy disaster is a significant and very costly failure of government policy which has major political repercussions and is widely perceived to be disastrous. Such a policy would clearly fail to meet the objectives set for it and would produce a chain of events that make the situation far worse than would be the case if alternative policies had been pursued.

In the last twenty years, policy failures have appeared to occur more frequently and to be more costly than in the past. Examples include the BSE crisis, Britain's unhappy period as a member of the European Exchange Rate Mechanism and the poll tax. The prevalence of policy failure is sometimes attributed to an overly centralised system of government that does not allow for sufficient consideration of policy within the core executive or parliament. In the case of the poll tax, ministers who were convinced of its ideological merits ignored warnings from the Treasury that it would prove costly. Conservative MPs who were concerned about the possibility of large bills for their constituents and the perceived unfairness of the poll tax proposed changes (e.g. linking it to the ability to pay) but these were defeated in the House of Commons. Nor were local authorities, who warned of difficulties in collecting the poll tax, consulted properly.

The Thatcher government's objectives when introducing the poll tax included greater local accountability and control of local authority spending. But the situation was made worse rather than better. People blamed the government rather than their local council for large poll tax bills, forcing it to both 'charge cap' authorities proposing sizeable poll tax bills and increase VAT to pay for additional funding for local councils. Ministers had lost control of events. The political damage caused by the poll tax debacle added to the pressure that forced Thatcher's resignation in 1990. All three candidates who stood in the second ballot of that year's Conservative leadership election promised to scrap the poll tax. It was eventually replaced by the council tax in 1993.

this undermined its claim that the new tax made councils more accountable for local taxation.

Implementation problems also bedevilled the poll tax. It proved difficult for local authorities to collect, notably because of a campaign of civil disobedience under which people refused to pay the tax or dropped off the electoral register in an attempt to avoid detection. The poll tax was widely perceived to be unfair and regressive as it bore no relation to ability to pay. Riots in London preceded its introduction in England and Wales in April 1990. (The poll tax had been introduced a year earlier in Scotland, where a revaluation of the rates was due, but Northern Ireland retained the rates.) The government responded to criticism from Conservative MPs who feared that middle-class voters would desert the party in protest at the tax by providing transitional relief to local authorities in order for them to keep poll tax bills low. This negated one of the aims of the tax, namely a reduction in spending. In 1991, the government also increased VAT to fund a reduction in poll tax bills.

One of John Major's main priorities on winning the 1990 Conservative leadership election was to find an alternative to the poll tax. The council tax was duly introduced under the Local Government Finance Act 1992 and came into effect the following year. It is a hybrid local tax that combines a property element and a

Rioting greeted the introduction of the poll tax in England 1990 (© Mirrorpix)

personal element. The level of the council tax is determined according to the value of a property, with properties allocated to eight different 'bands'. It is paid by the head of household rather than by all adults living in the property, but there is a 25 per cent reduction for single-member households. Councils can also create discounts or exemptions. Although no tax can be considered popular, the introduction of the council tax did not provoke significant protest from political elites or the electorate.

Successive higher than inflation increases in council tax rates – notably an average 12.9 per cent increase in 2003–2004 – provoked fresh controversy. The average bill for a Band D property in England with two adult residents was £1,214 in 2005–2006 compared to £568 in 1993–94. In 2004 the Blair government set up an independent inquiry, chaired by Sir Michael Lyons, to examine local government funding. It would look at reform of the council tax, the balance between central and local funding and the wider role of local government (see Controversy 10.2).

Business rates used to be set by local authorities but their replacement, the national non-domestic rate (often known as the uniform business rate), is set by central government. Councils collect it, but revenues are paid into a central fund and returned to local authorities by the government according to their populations. The new tax removed an established method of raising revenue away from local authorities and transferred it to the centre. Councils are now permitted to increase the national non-domestic rate by 1 per cent per annum for up to five years.

Other sources of revenue

Local authorities supplement their income from grants and local taxes in a number of ways. Councils are permitted to set discretionary charges for many of the services they provide. Most apply charges for services such as leisure facilities, meals on

Controversy: 10.2

Council tax revaluation

When the council tax was introduced in 1993, residential properties were placed into one of eight bands (with 'band A' the lowest and 'band H' the highest) based on their value in 1991. Since then, property prices have increased dramatically and a revaluation of house values in England is needed so that council tax bills reflect the price of properties.

The increase in property prices does not mean that houses will automatically be placed in a higher council tax band. It is the relative value rather than absolute value that is significant: if the value of all properties had increased by the same rate since 1991, all houses would stay in the same bands. This of course has not happened as property hot spots have seen above-average increases, particularly in the south-east of England. A council tax revaluation took place in Wales in 2004. Some 58 per cent of houses stayed in the same band and 8 per cent moved down. But a third of houses have moved up one or more bands. In property hot spots such as Cardiff (62 per cent) and Wrexham (52 per cent) the proportion was higher. A ninth band was created for the costliest properties.

This does not imply that the same scenario will be repeated in England. But ministers were concerned about the political costs of big increases in council tax bills for large numbers of householders. Revaluations of property values under the old domestic rates system had been shelved in the 1970s and in the 1980s the Thatcher government pushed ahead with the poll tax in Scotland rather than face a revaluation. A year before the council tax revaluation in England was due to begin in 2006, the government announced that this would be postponed and the revaluation issue added to the remit of the review of local government finance being conducted by Sir Michael Lyons. The decision has the virtue of allowing a fuller consideration of local taxation, e.g. the differential between council tax bills across bands with top band properties currently paying only three times more than those in the bottom band. Sceptics believed that the government had found a convenient way of passing the buck. Press reports suggested that the new round of inspections would take the presence of conservatories and even pleasant views into account when determining house values.

wheels and car parking, but levels vary. An authority that wants to cut congestion may, for example, impose prohibitive fees for car parking in a city centre and operate a park-and-ride scheme.

Councils also collect rent from tenants living in local-authority owned housing but the sale of council houses in the 1980s reduced the scope for revenue-raising. Faced by cash shortages and restrictions on borrowing, many councils sold off assets in the 1980s and 1990s. This produced unintended consequences: the sale of playing fields reduced people's opportunities to participate in sport at a time when government was emphasising the importance of regular exercise to combat child obesity.

The EU has been an important source of funding since the late 1980s when the sums available through its Structural Funds were increased. Poorer regions of the UK (e.g. Merseyside) were eligible for large sums from the European Regional Development Fund; others won grants from the European Social Fund. Roadside signs indicating that a new road has been paid for by EU funding are a familiar site in parts of the UK.

The most controversial form of revenue-raising to emerge in recent years is the Private Finance Initiative (PFI). This has been open to local authorities since New Labour came to power and has been used to fund infrastructure projects such as the building of new schools and transport systems (see Chapter 9). In PFI schemes, the private sector provides the finance for large scale construction projects and provides the associated services for a set period (usually more than 20 years). The local authority pays for the services over this period and also pays a premium to cover the financial risks taken by the company. Supporters of the scheme claim that it has brought much needed investment but its critics argue that PFI projects are more expensive and put off unpalatable costs until a later date.

Local government in a multi-level polity

The relationship between central and local government is inevitably imbalanced and has often been strained in recent years (see Analysis 10.2). Central government controls the main part of local authorities' revenue through the Revenue Support Grant, keeps tight control over local authority spending and taxation and has put in place an extensive inspection system for local authority performance. Legislation from the centre has also altered dramatically the structure and functions of local government. The discretion that local authorities have to determine their own spending priorities and introduce policy initiatives has waned, but they are still able to make political decisions that impact upon the daily lives of citizens.

In the early post-war period, the centre adopted a hands-off approach to local government that allowed councils considerable leeway in how they spent general

Analysis: 10.2

Centre–local relations

Academics have developed a number of models to explain the relationship between central and local government. Among the most influential have been:

1. *The partnership model.* This saw central and local government as partners. Central government afforded local authorities significant financial and political discretion, consulting with them on matters of mutual interest. Centralisation in the 1980s weakened the utility of this perspective.

2. *The agency model.* This views local authorities as mere agents of central government, implementing policies determined at national level with little scope for discretion. This model encapsulates the centralising trends of the last two decades but downplays the limited room for manoeuvre that local authorities still have in spending and implementing policy.

3. *The power-dependence model.* This recognises that both central and local government have resources and engage in a process of bargaining. Central government controls legislation and much local finance, but local councils have influence as elected bodies and key players in local policy networks. This model has been developed by Rod Rhodes, notably in his book *Beyond Westminster and Whitehall* (London: Allen & Unwin, 1988).

grant funding. Intervention by the centre in the terrain of local government was infrequent and was preceded by consultation. Relations worsened in the 1980s when Conservative governments sought, first, to control public expenditure by reining in local authority spending and second, to redefine the role of local authorities by transferring some of their functions to the centre, to specialist agencies or to the private sector. Labour-controlled authorities resisted government efforts to control local spending and limit their policy discretion, but the centre responded through legislation and ministerial diktats that abolished the metropolitan counties, restructured and capped local taxation, and required councils to open up contracts for service provision to the private sector.

New Labour's election victory in 1997 brought a limited rapprochement in centre–local relations. Local authorities welcomed the positive tone on localism and a greater willingness to engage in dialogue. The emphasis on a leadership role for councils in their communities and promises of greater autonomy for the best performing councils suggested a brighter future for local government. But the Blair governments have kept a tight grip on local authority finances, established a comprehensive inspection regime, intervened when councils failed to meet targets set by the centre but left the local quango state largely untouched.

Local authorities reacted to the increased intervention of the centre by strengthening their lobbying efforts at national level. The Local Government Association, created in 1997 from an amalgamation of existing bodies, provides a more professional national voice for the interests of local authorities in their collective dealings with the centre. It also offers valuable advice to councils on implementing new legislation and adopting best practice.

Local authorities are also better represented in Brussels. Many councils employ specialist staff to handle relations with the EU; some maintain offices in Brussels, either individually or jointly with neighbouring authorities. This focus on the EU reflects both the expansion of EU funding opportunities and the significance of EU legislation (see Chapter 12). Grants from the EU are paid direct to local authorities, enabling recipients to pursue economic regeneration projects that might otherwise be beyond their means. But central government has tried to maintain its control over local authority spending by setting conditions for the provision of matching funding from the centre.

Many of the directives implemented by local authorities on issues such as water quality, public procurement or health and safety in the workplace originate from the EU. Local authorities thus lobby the European Commission in order to secure funding and influence legislative proposals. When local authorities are concerned about policy emanating from central government (as in the 1980s and 1990s) they may look to the Commission to introduce alternative legislation. But they are far more likely to achieve results when they have the active support of the UK government. Although local authorities compete with each other for funding, engagement in EU policy-making has encouraged pan-European cooperation on issues of mutual concern. Lobbying by organisations representing sub-national governments was, for example, a factor in the creation of the EU Committee of the Regions in 1993, in which UK local authorities are represented.

The local quango state

Elected local authorities are just one element in a complex network of bodies involved in service provision at local level. Local government in which decisions are taken by elected local authorities has been replaced by local governance in which a plethora of unelected or indirectly-elected agencies also make decisions on the allocation of resources at local level. Whereas local government was characterised by decision-making by a hierarchical authority, local governance involves greater flexibility, fluid boundaries and interdependent relationships between councils, agencies and private companies.

Unelected specialist agencies, known as quangos, are a major feature of local governance (see Chapter 9). The House of Commons Public Administration Select Committee's 2001 Report *Mapping the Quango State* identified more than 5000 bodies providing public services operating at local level (see Table 10.3). This 'local quango state' includes foundation schools, registered social landlords, NHS trusts and primary care groups. The number of staff employed by these bodies (some 60,000 people) is almost three times higher than the total number of elected councillors.

Many quangos perform important functions in an efficient and non-partisan manner, but the extent of the local quango state has raised concerns about the

Table 10.3 The local quango state

Higher education institutions	166
Further education institutions	511
Foundation schools	877
City technology colleges	15
Training and enterprise councils (England)	72
Local enterprise councils (Scotland)	22
Career service companies (Scotland)	17
Registered social landlords (England)	2074
Registered social landlords (Wales)	92
Registered housing associations (Scotland)	255
Registered housing associations (Northern Ireland)	40
Housing action trusts	4
Police authorities (England and Wales)	41
Joint police boards/unitary police authorities (Scotland)	8
Health authorities (England and Wales)	99
NHS trusts (England and Wales)	373
Primary care groups (England and Wales)	434
Primary care trusts (England and Wales)	40
Health boards (Scotland)	15
Special health boards (Scotland)	8
Acute NHS trusts (Scotland)	14
Primary care trusts (Scotland)	13
Integrated acute and primary care trust (Scotland)	1
Health and social services trusts (Northern Ireland)	19
Health and social services councils (Northern Ireland)	4
Health and personal social services boards (Northern Ireland)	4
Advisory committees on JPs (UK)	119
Dartmoor Steering Group (Ministry of Defence)	1
Total	5338

Source: Select Committee on Public Administration, *Mapping the Quango State*, 5th Report 2000–01, HC 367, Table 6. www.publications.parliament.uk/pa/cm200001/cmselect/cmpubadm/367/36702.htm

health of local democracy. The Committee on Standards in Public Life has produced guidelines on appointments, but there is limited scrutiny of ministerial decisions on who should serve on quangos. The lack of local accountability, transparency and scrutiny of decisions taken by quangos has aggravated the democratic deficit in local government. Not all quangos issue annual reports, few hold public meetings and their chief executives are not required to explain their decisions to elected local representatives.

The centre has encouraged local authorities to develop partnerships with voluntary bodies and private companies in order to deliver economic, social and environmental redevelopment. This is known as the 'new localism'. Partnership is seen as a means of overcoming the problems of fragmentation in policy areas where multiple agencies have overlapping responsibilities. There is great diversity in the character of these networks and partnerships across local authorities and policy fields. In drawing up plans to tackle crime, a local authority will engage with the police but also with agencies and pressure groups that aim to improve access to legal advice, tackle social exclusion (e.g. long-term unemployment or poor housing), address health problems (e.g. drug dependence) and so forth. Public–Private Partnerships and PFI have raised private sector money for capital spending on projects supported by local councils.

Devolution and local government

The creation of devolved institutions in Scotland and Wales in 1999 has had important implications for local government in those nations. Local government is among those policy competences devolved from Westminster to the Scottish Parliament and National Assembly for Wales. They provide Revenue Support Grant funding to local authorities in their respective nations and set targets for service delivery. The devolved bodies can also restructure local government and redefine its responsibilities. Legislation passed by the Scottish Parliament will introduce the single transferable vote for local elections in Scotland from 2007 (see Chapter 16). The devolved bodies also have responsibility for policies that are mainstays of local government activity (e.g. education and economic development) and oversee the work of a series of quangos. The three largest quangos in Wales were merged with their home departments in 2004 to become part of the Assembly government administration.

In England, the Major government created Government Offices for the Regions to handle the implementation at regional level of policy developed by various Whitehall departments. New Labour then bolstered regional government by setting up Regional Development Agencies (RDAs) in the English regions in 1999 (see Chapter 11). These are unelected agents of central government charged with promoting economic development; they have limited budgets and follow targets set by ministers. The RDAs are scrutinised by unelected Regional Assemblies made up of local councillors and community representatives.

Local authorities were wary of Labour's plans for elected regional assemblies – as they had been of directly elected mayors. Although regional assemblies would have only limited executive powers, their proposed roles in economic development, planning and housing threatened to squeeze further local authority influence in the already crowded world of subnational governance. The government's insistence that assemblies could only be established in areas where wholly unitary local government has been instituted also threatened the continued existence of county councils in some parts of England. The 2004 'no' vote in a referendum on an assembly for the north-east of England halted the momentum. The 2005 Labour manifesto made no mention of elected assemblies, proposing instead greater powers for RDAs.

Local democracy

The move from local government to local governance has important implications for notions of local democracy. The predominant view in the twentieth century saw elected local councils as the main expression of local democracy and as a bulwark of a pluralist system. Local councillors were afforded principal actor status as they were elected by and accountable to citizens. There was widespread agreement among political elites that local councils were best placed to provide education, housing and other local services and should be allowed significant autonomy in expenditure and policy-making so that they could respond to local needs.

Although attractive to pluralists, this vision of local democracy had its limitations. Participation in local politics was limited with turnout in local elections lower than for general elections, averaging only 40 per cent at the end of the twentieth century. The party politicisation of local politics since the 1970s lessened the focus on purely local matters. Local service provision was also questioned as both public expenditure and local taxes increased without matching improvements in service efficiency or quality. Scandals in Westminster city council in the 1980s and Doncaster council at the start of this century damaged the reputation of local politicians. The Committee on Standards in Public Life found little evidence of corruption in local government but recommended an ethical framework for councillors which New Labour enacted in 2000.

Reforms introduced by the Thatcher, Major and Blair governments have necessitated a new perspective on local democracy. Elected councils are no longer directly responsible for the provision of core local services. They are just one part, albeit a crucial one, in a world of local governance inhabited by a plethora of public and private actors. The spread of the quango state has exacerbated the democratic deficit in local government. But government ministers claim that the systematic inspection of local authority performance has introduced greater transparency, made councils more responsive to those using their services and forced them to rectify their shortcomings.

Initiatives aimed at increasing participation in local politics have had mixed results. Councils have been encouraged to pilot new forms of voting such as all-postal ballots and e-voting. Turnout increased in most cases, but still remains low. The centre also promoted new ways of involving local citizens in decision-making, including the creation of 'citizens' juries to discuss policy proposals and the use of local referendums. But turnout in local referendums, notably on elected mayors, has been low. Some authorities have conducted interesting experiments in direct democracy, for example Milton Keynes held a referendum on council tax levels in 1999 and Edinburgh a vote on congestion charging in 2005, but these do not amount to a fundamental overhaul of local democracy.

Conclusion and summary

Local government is in a healthier position today than it was twenty years ago, but it remains structurally weak. New Labour has restored some discretionary powers to local authorities and promoted community leadership. But the twin trends of centralisation (i.e. central government intervention through legislation and control of local expenditure) and fragmentation in local service delivery (i.e. the transfer of functions from elected councils to non-elected agencies) have not been reversed. Ministers have encouraged local communities to play a more active role in tackling issues at grassroots level, but UK local authorities cover larger territories than is the case in many European states meaning that decisions are not taken particularly close to the people they affect. The next reorganisation of local government may scrap district councils and create larger unitary authorities and 'city regions', perhaps with elected mayors. The continued absence of constitutional safeguards for local government also leaves local authorities in the UK in a more parlous position than its counterparts in most other Western liberal democracies.

Further reading

The most comprehensive textbook is D. Wilson and C. Game, *Local Government in the United Kingdom* (London, Palgrave, 3rd edition, 2002). T. Byrne, *Local Government in Britain* (London: Penguin, 2000) and J. Chandler, *Local Government Today* (Manchester: Manchester University Press, 3rd edition, 2002) are also solid introductions to the topic. J. Stewart, *The Nature of British Local Government* (London: Palgrave, 2000) is of value for more advanced readers. R. Leach and J. Percy-Smith, *Local Governance in Britain* (London: Palgrave, 2001) reflects the move from local government to governance.

G. Stoker and D. Wilson (eds), *British Local Government into the 21st Century* (London: Palgrave, 2004) is an excellent supplement to the textbooks, analysing developments in local government under New Labour. T. Travers, 'Local and Central Government', in A. Seldon and D. Kavanagh (eds), *The Blair Effect 2001–05* (Cambridge: Cambridge University Press, 2005), pp. 68–93 examines policy in the second Blair government.

Case studies of the operation of local government in parts of the UK include T. Travers, *The Politics of London* (London: Palgrave, 2003) and A. McConnell, *Scottish Local Government* (Edinburgh: Edinburgh University Press, 2004). C. Copus, *Party Politics and Local Government* (Manchester: Manchester University Press, 2004) is a detailed study of local party politics. D. Butler, A. Adonis and T. Travers, *Failure in British Government: The Politics of the Poll Tax* (Oxford: Oxford University Press, 1994) is the definitive study of the poll tax policy disaster. R. Rhodes, *Beyond Westminster and Whitehall* (London: Allen & Unwin, 1988) and his *Control and Power in Central–Local Government Relations* (London: Ashgate, 2nd edition, 1999) offer sophisticated theoretical approaches.

Websites

Most local authorities have their own websites, but they vary in quality. Among the best are the London borough of Brent www.brent.gov.uk/, Leicester City Council www.leicester.gov.uk/ and Surrey County Council www.surreycc.gov.uk. The Office of the Deputy Prime Minister www.odpm.gov.uk is responsible for local government in England. Its website includes information on government policy and funding. The Audit Commission www.audit-commission.gov.uk/ provides detailed data on local authority performance. The Direct Government gateway www.direct.gov.uk/Dl1/Directories/LocalCouncils/fs/en provides links to local authority websites. Arrangements for the government of London are detailed at www.london.gov.uk/.

Information on council tax bands is published by the Valuation Office www.voa.gov.uk/; the tax is being reviewed by the Lyons Inquiry www.odpm.gov.uk/odpm/lyonsinquiry_lg_funding.htm

The Local Government Association www.lga.gov.uk is a lobbying organisation representing the interests of English and Welsh local authorities. Its website has information on developments in local government, plus facts sheets on local government structure and elections. The New Local Government Network is a think tank that looks to promote local leadership and revitalise local communities. Its website www.nlgn.org.uk includes a number of useful papers, particularly on directly elected mayors. Material from the Local Government Chronicle is available from www.lgcnet.com but a subscription is required.

Chapter 11

Devolution

Learning outcomes

After reading this chapter, you will:
- Appreciate the development of the multinational United Kingdom.
- Be aware of powers of the devolved institutions in Scotland, Wales and Northern Ireland.
- Understand the impact of devolution on the UK and its component nations.
- Be able to evaluate the character of the post-devolution state.

Introduction

The creation of devolved institutions in Scotland, Wales and Northern Ireland – and the prospect of regional assemblies in some English regions – has added a new tier of government to the UK's multi-level polity. The devolution settlement implemented by the Blair government gave new institutional expression to the distinctive character of the four component parts of the multinational UK state. But devolution has been asymmetric: each nation is governed in a different way. Devolution has also radically changed the traditional constitution, requiring new procedures to manage relations between the nations of the UK and reform of central government. The new arrangements have bedded down without major incident, but the process of devolution has not yet reached its final destination and problems remain to be ironed out.

The Union

The integration of the four nations of the UK was uneven: they joined the Union at different times and under different circumstances. England completed its conquest of Wales in 1536, forcibly imposing rule from London. Despite forcible Anglicisation, Wales retained its distinctive identity and culture, particularly in terms of language (though Welsh was in decline by the mid-twentieth century) and religion (with Nonconformism a major issue in Welsh politics until the 1920s). The 2001 census found that 28 per cent of people in Wales could speak, write or understand Welsh.

Scotland was an independent state before joining the Union under the 1707 Act of Union. This was an international treaty negotiated between the two states by which Scotland would be governed by a sovereign parliament at Westminster but preserved its separate legal, education and local government systems plus the Presbyterian Church. Scottish civic identity thus endured. Though key decisions were thereafter made in London, Scottish distinctiveness was recognised through special administrative arrangements at the centre.

Ireland joined the Union in 1800 through an Act of Union after centuries of English and Scottish settlement. The Union was a troubled one as Catholic grievances fuelled a popular Irish nationalism in the south whereas Protestant settlers in Ulster identified with the Crown. The 'Irish Question' dominated politics at Westminster in the late nineteenth and early twentieth centuries. By the 1880s over 80 of Ireland's 101 seats in the House of Commons were held by Nationalists. Led by Gladstone, the Liberal Party presented Home Rule as the optimal means of both accommodating Irish nationalism and preserving the Union. But three Home Rule Bills (1886, 1893 and 1913) fell in the face of resistance from Conservatives and Liberal Unionists. The onset of the First World War averted serious unrest in Great Britain although the 1916 Easter Rising in Dublin was crushed by British troops.

Negotiations between the British government and Irish republicans led to the 1920 Government of Ireland Act which partitioned Ireland. Twenty-six counties in the south – all with a substantial Catholic majority – were granted self-government and under the 1921 Anglo-Irish Treaty became the Irish Free State, a dominion within the Commonwealth. It became the Republic of Ireland in 1949. Six counties in the north of Ireland that had a Protestant majority exercised their right under the 1920 Act to remain part of the UK as Northern Ireland. Northern Ireland was governed by a devolved parliament at Stormont until direct rule from London was imposed in 1972 as the security situation worsened.

The union state

Unitary state:
a culturally and politically homogeneous state in which all parts are governed in the same way from a powerful centre.

Forty years ago textbooks on British politics described the United Kingdom as a **unitary state,** that is one exhibiting high levels of centralisation, standardisation and homogeneity. Power was concentrated at the centre and subnational institutions were weak; policy was implemented in the same way throughout the state and there were few economic, political or cultural differences within the UK. This was an accurate characterisation to the untrained eye. Parliamentary sovereignty and executive dominance of the House of Commons concentrated power in London, local government was weak and sub-state nationalism had made little impact. But the unitary state concept did not adequately convey the peculiarities of the UK state. Politics was different in the Celtic nations – Northern Ireland had a separate parliament, Scotland its own legal and local government systems, and Scotland and Wales were subject to specific administrative arrangements. British identity provided a common bond between the peoples of the UK. Rather than replacing other identities, it enabled the Welsh and Scottish to retain their own distinctive cultures and identities while also sharing an overarching British civic identity. Britishness was constructed around symbols of the UK state such as the monarchy, parliament and Empire, but these were in decline by the early 1960s. Identity was a particularly contentious issue in Northern Ireland where many Catholics identified with the Republic of Ireland rather than the UK.

The rise of sub-state nationalisms brought fresh academic thinking on the nature of UK territorial politics. Michael Hechter focused on a core-periphery divide in British politics: political and economic elites in the south-east of England exploited resources in the Celtic fringe. Jim Bulpitt characterised the UK as a 'dual polity' in which local elites were afforded relatively free rein on mundane matters so that the political elite in London could concentrate on issues of 'high politics' such as the economy and foreign affairs. Stein Rokkan and Derek Urwin developed a typology that distinguished between unitary and union states (see Analysis 11.1). Whereas unitary states were highly integrated, union states were multinational states in which political and cultural differences persisted. The UK was a **union state**: its component nations came together in different ways and retained some distinctive features.

Two types of **devolution** have been found in the UK: legislative and administrative. Legislative devolution involves the creation of separate parliaments with legislative power and has been the norm since 1999. Legislative devolution also existed in Northern Ireland in the Stormont period (1921–72). Prior to 1999, administrative devolution was the norm for the UK union state. Here Scottish and Welsh interests were catered for through distinctive procedures at Whitehall and Westminster but Scotland and Wales were denied their own parliaments.

The Scottish Office was established as a government department in 1885, the Welsh Office in 1964 and the Northern Ireland Office in 1972. The relevant Secretaries of State normally had a Cabinet seat; only the post of Secretary of State for Scotland was consistently awarded to a constituency MP from the nation in question. The territorial ministries were responsible for a range of government activities (e.g. agriculture, education, health, local government) in their respective nations but had only limited influence within Whitehall. They both represented their nation's interests in central government and implemented government policies in their respective territories. By the 1980s, critics depicted the Scottish Office as an agent of a hostile Conservative government rather than an effective lobbyist for Scotland.

In the House of Commons, the Scottish Grand Committee and Welsh Grand Committee discussed matters in these nations. They contained all MPs representing Scottish and Welsh constituencies respectively. Special standing committees considered legislation applying to Scotland and Wales. Departmental select committees on Scottish affairs and Welsh affairs were created in 1979 to keep the work of the territorial ministries under review. A Northern Ireland Select Committee was established in 1995. Scotland and Wales were over-represented in the Commons having more

Union state: a state in which cultural differences survive the union of different areas and parts of the state are governed differently, but which has a strong political centre.

Devolution: the transfer of decision-making authority by central government to subnational government.

Analysis: 11.1

Unitary and union states

A typology developed by Stein Rokkan and Derek Urwin distinguishes between a *unitary state* and a *union state*:

> The unitary state (is) built up around one unambiguous political centre which enjoys economic dominance and pursues a more or less undeviating policy of administrative standardisation. All areas of the state are treated alike, and all institutions are directly under the control of the centre.
>
> The union state (is) not the result of straightforward dynastic conquest. Incorporation of at least parts of its territory has been achieved through personal dynastic union, for example by treaty, marriage or inheritance. Integration is less than perfect. While administrative standardisation prevails over most of the territory, the consequences of personal union entail the survival in some areas of pre-union rights and institutional infrastructures which preserve some degree of regional autonomy and serve as agencies of indigenous elite recruitment.

An alternative typology, based on the extent of regionalism found in European Union states, distinguishes between three types of unitary state:

- *Regionalised unitary states* have directly-elected regional assemblies enjoying legislative powers or significant autonomy from the centre.
- *Decentralised unitary states* have only unelected regional bodies created by central government to carry out administrative functions.
- *Centralised unitary states* have no elected regional assemblies. Subnational government is weak.

In this perspective the UK is now considered a regionalised unitary state whereas prior to devolution it was a centralised unitary state.

Source: S. Rokkan and D. Urwin, 'Introduction: Centres and Peripheries in Western Europe', in S. Rokkan and D. Urwin (eds), *The Politics of Territorial Identity: Studies in European Regionalism* (Sage Publications, 1982), p. 11

MPs per head of population than England. Scotland, Wales and Northern Ireland also enjoyed higher levels of public spending per head of population than England, in part because of the greater incidence of social deprivation.

England is the largest of the UK's four nations with a population of 49 million (83.5 per cent of the total UK population). Scotland has a population of 5 million, Wales almost 3 million and Northern Ireland 1.6 million. Significant regional disparities exist within the UK. Cities such as Manchester, Birmingham and Leeds are thriving regional centres but wealth and influence are concentrated in the southeast of England. Many central government, financial and media institutions are located in London. Economic and social conditions are better in the prosperous middle-class areas surrounding London than in poorer areas in the north of England,

Wales, Scotland and Northern Ireland – though some inner city London boroughs are among the poorest in the UK. After prospering in the nineteenth century, areas such as Glasgow, Lancashire, the Black Country, south Wales and Belfast suffered economic and social deprivation as manufacturing industry declined dramatically in the second half of the twentieth century. Poverty, unemployment and poor health are more pronounced in these areas, necessitating higher levels of welfare spending by central government.

Towards devolution

Studies of the road to devolution taken by Scotland and Wales focus on three main factors:

1. The development of sub-state nationalism in Scotland and Wales.
2. The changing attitudes of elite actors, particularly political parties.
3. The changing economic and political environment.

Sub-state nationalism

Popular support for nationalist parties increased in Scotland and Wales in the 1960s and 1970s at a time when the UK state and economy were under strain. But Labour and the Conservatives were divided on the issue and proposals for devolution failed. Popular support for devolution underwent a revival in the 1980s and 1990s, with a changing context (e.g. further European integration) again a factor. This time devolution also secured strong elite support, particularly in the Labour Party (see Timeline 11.1).

Plaid Cymru and the Scottish National Party (SNP) promoted their respective national cultures and sought greater political autonomy. Political and economic change brought opportunities for the nationalists. They were beneficiaries of voter dissatisfaction with the performance of the main parties and the limited modernisation of the British state. Retreat from Empire and entry into the European Economic Community (EEC) posed questions about British identity at a time when Scottish and Welsh popular culture was blossoming. The UK's relative economic decline also fuelled sub-state nationalism; the SNP argued that the discovery of North Sea oil made an independent Scotland economically viable. There were tensions within the nationalist parties, however. The SNP experienced internal disputes over the optimal strategy for achieving independence and its place on the left–right political spectrum. Cultural issues were problematic for Plaid Cymru as some members emphasised Welsh language issues while others urged a broader appeal.

The rise of sub-state nationalism posed difficult questions for Labour and the Conservatives. Conservative leader Edward Heath signalled in 1968 that his party would create a Scottish Assembly, despite opposition from Scottish Tories. The pledge was not implemented by the Heath government (1970–74) which introduced local government reform instead. Mrs Thatcher steered the Conservatives towards implacable opposition to legislative devolution after her 1975 leadership victory.

TIMELINE 11.1

Scottish and Welsh devolution

1885	Creation of Scottish Office
1925	Plaid Cymru founded
1934	Scottish National Party formed following merger of National Party of Scotland (formed 1928) and the Scottish Party (1932)
1944	SNP wins its first Westminster seat at Motherwell by-election
1964	Creation of Welsh Office
1966	Plaid Cymru wins its first Westminster seat at Carmarthen by-election
1974	October general election: SNP wins 30.4 per cent of vote and 11 seats; Plaid Cymru wins 10.8 per cent of the vote and 3 seats
1978	Parliament passes legislation on Scottish and Welsh devolution
1979	Scottish devolution referendum produces 51.6 per cent 'yes' vote, but fails to meet requisite threshold of support of 40 per cent of the Scottish electorate. Only 20 per cent support devolution in Welsh referendum
1989	Scottish Constitutional Convention set up. Conservative government introduces poll tax in Scotland, a year before England and Wales
1993	White Paper sets out (limited) new powers for Scottish Office
1995	Scottish Constitutional Convention issues blueprint for a Scottish Parliament with legislative and tax-varying powers
1997	New Labour wins general election and issues devolution White Papers. Devolution approved in referendums in Scotland (74 per cent 'yes' on Scottish Parliament, 64 per cent 'yes' on tax-varying powers) and Wales (50.3 per cent 'yes')
1999	Devolved bodies begin operating after first elections. Labour–Liberal Democrat coalition takes power in Scotland; minority Labour administration in Wales
2000	Alun Michael resigns as Welsh First Secretary and is succeeded by Rhodri Morgan who subsequently forms a Labour–Liberal Democrat coalition. Death of Scottish First Minister Donald Dewar; Henry McLeish replaces him
2001	McLeish resigns as First Minister and is succeeded by Jack McConnell
2003	Second elections to the Scottish Parliament and Welsh Assembly. Labour–Liberal Democrat coalition formed in Scotland; Labour governs alone in Wales
2005	*Better Governance for Wales* White Paper proposes more powers for the Welsh Assembly

Labour had focused historically on class politics; it was committed to a redistribution of resources to produce common minimum standards of welfare provision. In the 1970s, Labour's electoral dominance in Scotland and Wales came under threat from the nationalists. Two broad camps developed in the Labour Party. Opponents of devolution, such as future leader Neil Kinnock, feared that it would undermine the equitable provision of public services and break-up the Union. Supporters believed it would bolster support for Labour in its heartlands and reduce the nationalists' appeal.

Harold Wilson took some of the heat out of the issue in 1969 by setting up a Royal Commission on the Constitution. Its 1973 Kilbrandon Report favoured an elected Scottish Assembly. The Callaghan government (1976–79), which was reliant on support from the Liberals in the House of Commons, introduced Bills establishing assemblies in Scotland and Wales. But legislation would not come into force unless devolution was approved in referendums in Wales and Scotland. Furthermore, MPs backed a parliamentary amendment stipulating that the Scottish Assembly must win the support of at least 40 per cent of the total Scottish electorate. The Welsh referendum produced a decisive 'no': only 20 per cent of those who voted backed devolution. In Scotland 51.6 per cent of those who voted supported devolution, but only 32.8 per cent of the electorate had voted 'yes'. The proposal was thus defeated as the 40 per cent threshold was not reached. The Callaghan government soon fell and was replaced by a Conservative administration opposed to devolution.

Elite conversion

Support for devolution regained momentum in the late 1980s, particularly in Scotland. The Conservatives won four general elections between 1979 and 1992 but saw their already low level of support in Scotland and Wales decline still further. Power was concentrated in Whitehall as the Thatcher governments appeared unsympathetic to Scottish distinctiveness, notably when imposing the poll tax in Scotland a year before England. The free market, individualist ethos of Thatcherism ran counter to a Scottish political culture supportive of state intervention and community politics. The decline of manufacturing industry and restructuring of the public sector had a disproportionate impact as relatively high numbers of Scots were employed in these sectors or relied on welfare benefits. European integration also boosted the devolution cause: the European Community actively involved sub-national bodies in decisions on Structural Fund spending in poorer regions. Regions in other member states gained more autonomy and became adept at lobbying in Brussels. Local actors in the UK (e.g. councils, businesses and trade unions) argued that greater autonomy was an essential step towards economic regeneration.

The Major governments (1990–97) sought belatedly to bolster declining support for the Union by granting the Scottish Office limited new powers, but were unable to turn the pro-devolution tide. The Conservatives supported legislative devolution for Northern Ireland but were the only mainstream party to oppose devolution to Scotland and Wales at the 1997 election, warning that it would create constitutional anomalies and hasten Scottish independence. The Tories were seen as pro-English and were heavily defeated, failing to win a single seat in Scotland and Wales. Following the referendums, the Conservatives dropped their opposition to devolution and promised to work constructively within the new institutions while challenging the perceived shortcomings of the devolution settlement.

Labour's conversion to devolution was crucial to the prospects for a Scottish Parliament. Influential figures like John Smith (Labour leader, 1992–94) saw devolution as a key part of constitutional modernisation. Support for devolution also put Labour at the heart of political debate in Scotland, notably in the Scottish Constitutional Convention. This was a non-governmental body established in 1989 by leading figures from Scottish politics and civil society to develop a blueprint for a Scottish Parliament. The Liberal Democrats also took part, but the Conservatives and the SNP did not. The Convention's proposals ultimately mirrored Labour's preferred option of a parliament with legislative and tax-raising powers.

Tony Blair maintained Labour's support for devolution but overruled the Scottish Labour Party by insisting on a two-question referendum that asked electors to endorse both the parliament and its tax-varying powers. Labour's 1997 election manifesto proposed devolution referendums in Scotland and Wales; a Scottish Parliament with legislative and tax-varying powers and a Welsh Assembly with secondary legislative powers; and elected assemblies in some English regions. The Liberal Democrats also supported a Scottish Parliament. Within the SNP, gradualists who viewed devolution as a stepping-stone to independence had achieved ascendancy over fundamentalists who viewed it as an unwelcome distraction. Plaid Cymru supported devolution but sought greater autonomy for the proposed Assembly.

The Blair government detailed its proposals in two White Papers before calling referendums for September 1997. The Scottish referendum produced large 'yes' votes on both the creation of a Scottish Parliament (74.3 per cent) and on tax-varying powers (63.5 per cent). Support for the Parliament in all 32 local authority areas (two areas opposed tax-varying powers) on a turnout of 60 per cent gave it added legitimacy. The convincing outcome reflected the development of a cross-party consensus on devolution over the previous decade.

The Welsh devolution referendum produced a wafer-thin majority as 50.3 per cent voted 'yes' and 49.7 per cent 'no'. On a turnout of 50.1 per cent, less than a quarter of people in Wales had voted for devolution. The result revealed a divided Principality. Eleven local authority areas voted in favour of devolution and eleven against. Those areas voting 'no' were (with the exception of Pembrokeshire) located in the east of Wales and had closer connections with England than areas voting 'yes' which were located in west Wales and contained a higher proportion of Welsh speakers. There was no popular consensus on the merits of devolution and the Welsh Labour Party was divided. A low-key referendum campaign overshadowed by the death of Diana, Princess of Wales did little to boost interest.

Devolution in Scotland and Wales

Labour's devolution settlement is asymmetric: each of the devolved institutions has different powers and distinctive features. The Scottish Parliament has legislative and tax-varying powers whereas the Welsh Assembly has only secondary legislative powers. They started life in temporary homes in Edinburgh and Cardiff, before moving to new – and in the case of Scotland, vastly over-budget – buildings at Holyrood and Cardiff Bay.

The Scottish Parliament

The Scottish Parliament has 129 members (MSPs) elected by the Additional Member System (AMS). Seventy-three MSPs (57 per cent of the total) are elected in single-member constituencies using the simple plurality system; the remaining 56 MSPs (43 per cent) are 'additional members' chosen from party lists. They are elected in eight multi-member regional constituencies each of which elects seven 'additional members' using the list system of proportional representation. These seats are allocated to parties on a corrective basis so that the distribution of seats reflects better the share of the vote won by the parties (see Chapter 16). Elections are held every four years.

Debate on the floor of the Scottish Parliament (© James Fraser/Rex Features)

It has primary legislative powers in a range of policy areas including law and order, health, education, transport, the environment and economic development (see Table 11.1). Westminster no longer makes law for Scotland on these matters. The Parliament passed over 60 Acts in its first four years. The Scotland Act 1998 places a number of limits on the Scottish Parliament's legislative powers. It specifies a number of policy areas in which the Scottish Parliament has no legislative authority. These 'reserved powers' remain the sole responsibility of Westminster. They include the UK constitution, economic policy, foreign policy and relations with the European Union (EU). The Act also states that Westminster remains sovereign in all matters, but has chosen to exercise its sovereignty by devolving legislative responsibility to a Scottish Parliament without diminishing its own powers. Westminster retains the right to override the Scottish Parliament in areas where legislative powers have been devolved. It may also legislate to abolish the Scottish Parliament, though an attempt to do so would be hugely controversial.

The Scottish Executive draws up policy proposals and implements legislation passed by the Parliament. The First Minister, usually the leader of the largest party at Holyrood, heads the Executive and appoints the cabinet. The cabinet appointed after the 2003 elections had 11 members, seven of whom headed executive departments. Ministers exercise statutory powers, issuing secondary legislation and making public appointments for example. They are accountable to the Scottish Parliament.

The Parliament is funded by a block grant from the UK Treasury, totalling £21 billion pounds in 2005. The Executive and Parliament determine how this money will be allocated. The size of the grant is determined by the 'Barnett formula'. This is an automatic formula agreed in 1978 by which public spending is allocated to Scotland, Wales and Northern Ireland based on spending levels in England. The Scottish Parliament has tax-varying powers: it can raise or lower the rate of income tax in Scotland by up to 3 per cent (i.e. three pence in the Pound), but has yet to use this power. It also decides the basis of local taxation in Scotland.

Table 11.1 Powers of the devolved institutions

Institution	Powers
Scottish Parliament	Law and home affairs Economic development (including industry, administration of EU Structural Funds, inward investment and tourism) Agriculture, fisheries and forestry Education and training Local government Health Social work Housing Environment Transport Culture and sport Research and statistics Tax-varying power of plus or minus 3 pence in the Pound
National Assembly for Wales	Economic development (including industry, administration of EU Structural Funds, inward investment and tourism) Agriculture, fisheries and forestry Education and training Local government Health Social work Housing Environment Transport Culture, the Welsh language and sport
Northern Ireland Assembly	Economic development (including industry, administration of EU Structural Funds, inward investment and tourism) Agriculture, fisheries and forestry Education and training Local government Health and social services Housing Environment Transport Planning Sport and the arts Tourism
Reserved Powers (remain the responsibility of Westminster)	Constitution of the UK Defence and national security Foreign policy including relations with the European Union Fiscal, economic and monetary systems Common market for UK goods and services Employment legislation Social security Transport safety and regulation Some areas of health (e.g. abortion) Media and culture Protection of borders

The Scotland Act 1998 signalled that the number of MPs sitting for Scottish constituencies at Westminster should be reduced, ending Scotland's over-representation. The Blair government subsequently endorsed the Scottish Boundary Commission's recommendation that the number constituencies be reduced from 72 to 59 at the 2005 general election. Constituency boundaries for Westminster and Holyrood are no longer coterminous.

The Welsh Assembly

The Welsh Assembly, properly known as the National Assembly for Wales, has 60 Assembly Members elected by the AMS. Forty members are elected in single-member constituencies using the simple plurality system; the remaining 20 are elected in five multi-member constituencies by the list system of proportional representation. Elections are held at fixed four-year terms.

The Assembly is considerably weaker than the Scottish Parliament: it has only executive and secondary legislative powers, not primary legislative power. It determines how legislation passed by Westminster on a range of Welsh issues should be implemented. If Westminster leaves significant scope for interpretation, the Assembly can play an important role in determining policy in Wales. But if Westminster legislation is tightly drawn, the prospects for Assembly initiative are reduced. The 1998 Government of Wales Act specified the policy areas in which the Assembly has executive power. They include education, health, transport, the environment and economic development (see Table 11.1). Funding comes from a Treasury block grant (£11 billion in 2005) determined by the Barnett formula. The Assembly decides how to allocate this money and can alter the basis of local taxation but does not have tax-varying powers.

The Welsh Assembly government formulates and implements policy. Originally called the Administration of the National Assembly for Wales, it was renamed in 2001. The First Minister (initially known as First Secretary of the Assembly) heads the Assembly government and appoints the cabinet. The current nine-member cabinet has eight departmental ministers. The First Minister is normally the leader of the largest party in the Assembly.

Scottish and Welsh devolution in action

Devolution has confirmed the distinctive nature of party systems in Scotland and Wales. Both have multi-party systems in which four main parties score more than 10 per cent of the vote. Support for Labour is higher in Scotland and Wales than many English regions, the Conservative vote is lower and nationalist parties are firmly established. Differential voting patterns have also developed as electors vote differently in elections to the devolved assemblies than in general elections. Support for Labour has been lower in elections to the devolved assemblies than in the preceding general elections, while the SNP and Plaid Cymru performed better in elections to the devolved assemblies than in comparable general elections. But devolution has posed strategic problems for the nationalists. A fall in their support in the 2003 elections and questions about the 'gradualist' strategy provoked tensions in the SNP and led to John Swinney's resignation in 2004. Alex Salmond returned as leader even though he had a seat at Westminster not Holyrood.

The Labour, Conservative and Liberal Democrat parties in Scotland and Wales have been granted more autonomy since devolution. They select candidates, determine their own policy priorities and conduct election campaigns with relatively little interference from London. This has afforded greater influence to Labour activists and trade unionists. They tend to oppose 'New Labour' policies such as foundation hospitals, making policy divergence from the UK party line more likely. Tensions between the UK and subnational parties have emerged, notably in the 1999 Welsh Labour Party leadership election in which Blair's favoured candidate Alun Michael received heavy-handed backing from London.

The Alternative Member System has helped to increase the representation of smaller parties in the devolved assemblies. No party won an absolute majority of votes or seats in Scotland or Wales in the 1999 elections. Labour was the largest party in both bodies with the nationalist parties forming the main opposition. The Conservatives were third placed in both contests but relied heavily on list seats; the Liberal Democrats were fourth. In Scotland, Labour and the Liberal Democrats quickly agreed a joint programme and formed a coalition government. Labour

Table 11.2 Elections to the Scottish Parliament, 2003

	Constituency contests		Regional lists		
	Share of vote (%)	Seats won	Share of vote (%)	Seats won	Total seats
Con	16.6 (+1.1)	3 (+3)	15.5 (+0.1)	15 (−3)	18 (+0)
Lab	34.6 (−4.1)	46 (−7)	29.3 (−4.3)	4 (+1)	50 (−6)
Lib Dem	15.4 (+1.1)	13 (+1)	11.8 (−0.6)	4 (−1)	17 (+0)
SNP	23.8 (−4.9)	9 (+2)	20.9 (−6.5)	18 (−10)	27 (−8)
Green	0.0 (+0.0)	0 (+0)	6.9 (+3.3)	7 (+6)	7 (+6)
Scottish Socialist	6.2 (+5.2)	0 (+0)	6.7 (+4.7)	6 (+5)	6 (+5)
Others	3.4 (+1.7)	2 (+1)	8.9 (+3.3)	2 (+0)	4 (+3)

Note: figures in brackets refer to change since 1999.

Source: The Electoral Commission, www.electoralcommission.org.uk/

Table 11.3 Elections to the Welsh Assembly, 2003

	Constituency contests		Regional lists		
	Share of vote (%)	Seats won	Share of vote (%)	Seats won	Total seats
Con	19.9 (+4.1)	1 (+0)	19.2 (+2.7)	10 (+2)	11 (+2)
Lab	40.0 (+2.4)	30 (+3)	36.6 (+1.2)	0 (−1)	30 (+2)
Lib Dem	14.1 (+0.7)	3 (+0)	12.7 (+0.3)	3 (+0)	6 (+0)
Plaid Cymru	21.2 (−7.2)	5 (−4)	19.7 (−10.8)	7 (−1)	12 (−5)
Others	4.8 (+0.1)	1 (+1)	11.8 (+6.7)	0 (+0)	1 (+1)

Note: figures in brackets refer to change since 1999.

Source: The Electoral Commission, www.electoralcommission.org.uk/

initially formed a minority administration in Wales but entered a 'partnership' with the Liberal Democrats in November 2000.

Labour was returned as the largest party in the 2003 elections in Scotland and Wales. In Scotland, Labour suffered a net loss of six seats and the SNP eight; the Scottish Greens and Scottish Socialist Party made gains (see Table 11.2). Labour and the Liberal Democrats formed a coalition government with a majority of five. Labour fared better in Wales where it made a net gain of two seats to take 30 of the 60 seats in the Assembly (see Table 11.3). With the Presiding Officer and his deputy Plaid Cymru and Independent members respectively, Labour had a technical majority. This disappeared in 2005 when Labour AM Peter Law left the party to sit as an independent.

A new politics?

The optimism felt at the opening of the new institutions waned as the early years of devolution brought controversy and disappointment. In the first year of devolution, there was much talk of a 'new politics' different in style from Westminster's adversarial politics. Post-devolution politics in Scotland and Wales has been more consensual, inclusive and transparent. There is a different atmosphere in the devolved assemblies: they have different procedures and most politicians have no experience of Westminster. Women are better represented in the devolved assemblies than at Westminster thanks to a 'zipping' system that alternates men and women on the candidate lists in 'list' seats. Women constituted 50 per cent of the Welsh Assembly and almost 40 per cent of the Scottish Parliament in 2003.

Devolved politics have not been immune from controversy. Scottish First Minister Henry McLeish resigned in 2001 after allegations emerged about payments he received from the lease of a constituency office while an MP at Westminster. Mike Gorman, Liberal Democrat Deputy First Minister in Wales, and Scottish Conservative leader David McLetchie were also forced from office after campaigns by a media that now focuses on devolved politics. An independent inquiry was critical of the costs involved in the building of the new Scottish Parliament building at Holyrood.

The Scottish Executive initially adopted a low-key programme but lost its major figure when the popular First Minister Donald Dewar died in October 2000. Henry McLeish won the Scottish Labour leadership election and became First Minister. His administration began to carve out an agenda different from that of the UK Labour government, notably on tuition fees and free care for the elderly. Following McLeish's resignation, Jack McConnell was elected unopposed as Labour leader and became Scotland's third First Minister in three years. Neither McLeish nor McConnell were well known figures outside Scotland when they became First Minister. Tensions within the Labour–Liberal Democrat coalition have been more evident since 2003. Labour MSPs have been unhappy with some policies favoured by the Liberal Democrats, notably the single transferable vote (STV) for local elections, while some Liberal Democrat fear that being in coalition undermines the party's distinctiveness.

Alun Michael never enjoyed the full confidence of his party during his spell as leader of a minority Labour administration. A dispute over Treasury provision of

Case study: 11.1

Strengthening the Welsh Assembly

The Richard Commission was set up by the Welsh Assembly in 2002 to assess the case for reform of the Assembly's powers and structure. Its 2004 Report proposed that the Assembly be given primary legislative powers in those policy areas in which it currently has secondary legislative powers. It also recommended increasing the size of the Assembly to 80 members and moving to the single transferable vote system.

Rather than supporting the Richard Report, First Minister Rhodri Morgan and Secretary of State for Wales Peter Hain preferred an evolutionary development of the Assembly's powers but rejected major reform of the electoral system. The UK government set out its plans in the 2005 *Better Governance for Wales* White Paper and the ensuing Government of Wales Bill 2005. There would be a clearer separation between the work of the Assembly and the Assembly Government, plus a bar on candidates standing for both constituency and list seats. The key proposal is for a three stage increase in the legislative powers of the Assembly:

1. The use of Westminster legislation to give the Assembly maximum discretion or 'framework powers'.
2. The transfer of functions to the Assembly in policy areas where it already has secondary legislative powers. This has already happened on issues such as university tuition fees and animal health.
3. Subject to approval in a referendum, the granting of primary legislative powers to the Assembly in areas where it currently has secondary legislative powers. The Assembly would not, though, have tax-varying powers.

The UK government suggested that the Assembly's new structure and powers should be allowed to bed down for the 2007–2011 term before a referendum is held.

matching funding for EU spending in Wales led to his resignation in February 2000. Rhodri Morgan was elected Labour leader and became First Minster. He agreed a Labour–Liberal Democrat partnership in November 2000 then led a minority Labour administration after the 2003 elections.

In 2004 the Richard Commission, an independent inquiry established by the Assembly, issued its report proposing that the Assembly be given primary legislative powers in policy areas where it exercised secondary legislative powers (see Case study 11.1). It also recommended an increase in the size of the Assembly (to 80) and replacing the AMS electoral system with the single transferable vote system of proportional representation. Neither the Assembly Government nor the UK government endorsed the Report fully. The UK government's 2005 *Better Governance for Wales* White Paper proposed a widening of the Assembly's existing secondary legislative powers (e.g. by giving it greater discretion to tailor Westminster legislation). In time the Assembly might also gain primary legislative powers, subject to approval in a referendum.

Policy divergence

Devolution has enabled administrations in Scotland, Wales and Northern Ireland to adopt policies which differ from those pursued by the UK government in England (see Table 11.4). The Scottish Executive has, for example, introduced free long-term personal care for the elderly and abolished tuition fees for university students. The Welsh Assembly has less scope to alter policy but has taken initiatives in education by abolishing school league tables and piloting a Welsh Baccalaureate. These changes were unlikely to have occurred if Westminster had retained responsibility. The devolved administrations have also chosen to allocate resources differently. The Scottish Executive agreed a three-year pay settlement with teachers and the Welsh Assembly government froze prescription charges.

Differential policy can be seen as a healthy consequence of devolution as the devolved bodies react to the particular concerns of their electorates. They have also been 'policy laboratories', testing policies (e.g. the creation of a Children's Commissioner in Wales and Scotland's ban on smoking in public places) that are then rolled out elsewhere. But policy divergence may cause concern if it produces significant anomalies or widens disparities in welfare provision. Can the National Health Service be regarded as a truly 'national' body when pensioners in Scotland are entitled to free long-term personal care that is not available to the elderly in England, or when less strict waiting list targets contribute to longer waits for operations in Wales? Devolution is not the only factor: decentralisation (e.g. greater

Table 11.4 Examples of policy divergence

Country	Example of political divergence
Scotland	Free long-term personal care for the elderly
	Abolition of up-front tuition fees for university students
	Abolition of fox hunting
	Abolition of ban on 'promoting homosexuality' in schools (i.e. repeal of Scottish equivalent of 'Section 28')
	Abolition of feudal system of land tenure
	Three year pay settlement for teachers
	Freedom of Information Act with fewer restrictions than UK equivalent
	Introduction of STV for local government elections from 2007
	Ban on smoking in public places takes effect before ban in England
Wales	Abolition of school league tables
	Abolition of 'Sats' tests for 7, 11 and 14 year-olds
	Creation of 22 local health boards
	Piloting of Welsh Baccalaureate in 19 schools and colleges
	Freeze on prescription charges and free prescriptions for people aged under 25 and over 60
	Free bus travel for pensioners
	Free school milk for children under seven
	Establishment of Children's Commissioner
Northern Ireland	Abolition of school league tables
	Free fares for the elderly
	New package for student finance
	Establishment of Children's Commissioner

autonomy for hospitals) will inevitably reveal differences in standards and raise questions about the equity of 'postcode lotteries'. The Scottish Executive increased fees for English students attending Scottish universities to stem the rise in applications from English students hoping to escape top-up tuition fees. But the extent of divergence should not be exaggerated. Important forces promote convergence in policy frameworks (e.g. the civil service, EU law and UK-wide policy communities in health) while the devolved administrations have limited budgets.

Policy divergence might undermine the principle of equal rights (particularly social rights) for UK citizens. But devolution has enhanced democracy and accountability in the UK by bringing decision-making closer to the people. No longer are Scots ruled by a Westminster governing party that only a small minority voted for. The devolved administrations represent a wider range of opinion and have more women members. The Scottish Parliament has encouraged public participation by opening proposed legislation to wider consultation than is the case at Westminster. But turnout fell at the 2003 elections in Scotland (to 49.4 per cent) and Wales (38.2 per cent).

AMS has produced more proportional election results but tensions between constituency and list members over the distribution of constituency work have been apparent. The UK government has established a Commission on Boundary Differences and Voting Systems (the Arbuthnott Commission) to assess electoral arrangements in Scotland, where four electoral systems will be in use by 2007. It will also examine the use of different boundaries for Westminster and Scottish Parliament elections. The 2005 *Better Governance for Wales* White Paper proposed that candidates should no longer be able to stand for both a constituency and regional list seat.

Survey evidence suggests that devolution is the preferred constitutional option for a majority of voters in Scotland and Wales. Surveys conducted for the Economic and Social Research Council (ESRC) found that support for devolution has solidified in Wales: only one in five people oppose devolution whereas a plurality favour an Assembly with powers similar to those of the Scottish Parliament. But voters have been disappointed by the limited impact of the devolved bodies. Scottish Attitudes Surveys show that the percentage of Scots naming the Scottish Parliament as the institution with most influence over Scottish affairs fell from 41 per cent in 1999 to 17 per cent in 2003.

England

England has little tradition of regional government, being governed as a single entity from Westminster and having elected local (rather than regional) authorities for much of its history. Nor do most parts of the country have a strong regional identity. Some that do, notably Cornwall, find themselves subsumed into larger administrative units (see Figure 11.1). The Major government established a new regional infrastructure by setting up ten Integrated Regional Offices in 1994. Two main factors accounted for this: first, a desire to rationalise the regional organisation of government departments, the health service and regional quangos, and, second the EU's emphasis on regional action as seen in its provision of funding for poorer regions.

Figure 11.1 Government office regions in the UK, as at 3 August 1998 (Produced by ONS Geography GIS & Mapping Unit, 2003) © Crown copyright. All rights reserved. Licence number 100030901.

The Blair governments maintained this functional **regionalisation** (i.e. the creation of regional administration by the centre) by setting up Regional Development Agencies (RDAs) in eight English regions in 1999. Another was created for London. RDAs are unelected agencies of central government charged with promoting economic development, have limited budgets (totalling £2 billion), are required to draw up a regional economic strategy and are accountable to ministers. Regional chambers (also known as 'assemblies') act as regional planning bodies and are involved in the production of regional sustainable development frameworks. In terms of membership, 70 per cent of members of regional chambers are local councillors; the other 30 per cent are drawn from sectors such as education, business and trade unions.

New Labour was also committed to a democratic **regionalism**, its 1997 manifesto containing a commitment to establish elected regional assemblies in areas where support was confirmed in a referendum. Divisions on the issue within the party slowed progress and the attention shifted to elected mayors (the Mayor of London and Greater London Authority are examined in Chapter 10). The 2002 White Paper *Your Region, Your Choice: Revitalising the English Regions* (Cm. 5511) set out plans for regional assemblies with 25–35 members elected every four years by the Additional Member System. They would be relatively weak bodies having few executive powers and limited budgets. In economic development, assemblies would fund and make appointments to the RDAs. On planning, housing and culture and tourism, they would take over from quangos the responsibility for allocating resources and developing regional strategies. Funding would be provided by Treasury block grants though assemblies would also be able to raise funds by adding a precept to council tax bills.

Assemblies would be established only if two conditions were met: (i) the replacement of the two-tier system of local government with one of unitary authorities throughout the region, and (ii) the proposed assembly had been approved in a regional referendum. The first referendum took place in the north-east in November 2004. A government consultation exercise suggested that popular support was highest in the north-east where a campaign for an assembly was supported by local businesses, trade unions and politicians. But the referendum produced a 78 per cent 'no' on a turnout of 48 per cent. Reasons for the decisive 'no' vote included:

- The cost to local taxpayers of an assembly.
- Opposition to the creation of another tier of government.
- Doubts about the usefulness of the assembly given its limited powers.
- Concern from local councillors about the creation of unitary authorities.
- The 'yes' campaign's inability to translate a strong regional identity into support for an assembly.

The 'no' vote signalled the end of the road for Labour's plans for elected regional assemblies. Referendums planned for the north-west and Yorkshire and Humberside were abandoned. The 2005 Labour manifesto made no mention of elected assemblies, the government turning its attention to local government reform instead. For the medium term, the pattern in England is likely to remain one of functional regionalisation rather than democratic regionalism driven by popular pressure for autonomy.

How will a revival of English identity find political expression? (© Mirrorpix)

The 'English question' also encompasses questions about the representation of English interests at Westminster and Whitehall (see below). In recent years English identity has undergone an intellectual renaissance – seen in the plethora of books on Englishness – and popular revival, evidenced by public displays of the St George Cross since the 1990s (e.g. Euro96) and during the 2006 World Cup. Surveys show that the number of people in England describing themselves as 'English rather than British' has risen. But the predicted English nationalist backlash against inequities in the post-devolution polity has not arrived. The English have accepted Scottish and Welsh devolution without much complaint and do not support regional assemblies or an English parliament in large numbers.

Changes to UK government

Inter governmental relations: relations between the UK government and the devolved administrations.

Devolution necessitated new procedures for handling relations between central and subnational government (i.e. **inter-governmental relations**), and changes to the operation of central government. It is important for central and subnational governments to cooperate, share experiences and iron out difficulties in policy areas where competences are shared. On social inclusion, for example, the UK government is responsible for social security but devolved bodies make policy on employment and training. Intergovernmental relations have proceeded smoothly, in part because Labour holds power in London, Edinburgh and Cardiff and the devolved administrations initially adopted a cautious approach to policy divergence.

Concordats: formal agreements between UK government departments and the devolved administrations.

A number of formal mechanisms for intergovernmental relations have been put in place. These have developed pragmatically and have yet to be fully tested. **Concordats** set out the rules governing the relationship between central government departments and the devolved administrations. On EU policy, for example, the UK government consults the devolved administrations on policy in the EU but once the UK government's single negotiating position has been settled, the devolved bodies are bound by it.

Discussions between UK government ministers and ministers from the devolved administrations on policy in devolved matters are conducted in the Joint Ministerial Committee (JMC). It can also be used to resolve policy disputes. JMC sessions are not meetings of equals; the UK government is acknowledged as the main player. Ideas are also exchanged in the British–Irish Council, a more equitable but less powerful body created under the Good Friday Agreement. The Judicial Committee of the Privy Council is the final arbiter in case of legal dispute about institutional competences. It has only been called upon in a handful of cases.

Whitehall

The UK civil service remains a unified service. Most civil servants who worked in the old territorial ministries were transferred to the devolved institutions, aiding continuity and informal contacts. But they owe their loyalty to the administration for which they work so poor relations between governments could cause tensions between civil servants in London and Edinburgh.

Once the devolved administrations began operating, the (renamed) Scotland Office and Wales Office were no longer responsible for formulating or implementing policy, their primary function being to represent their nation's interests in Whitehall. They ceased to exist as separate departments in June 2003 when they became part of a new Department for Constitutional Affairs. The posts of Secretary of State for Scotland and Secretary of State for Wales were combined with other portfolios. So Alistair Darling was Secretary of State for Transport and Secretary of State for Scotland. The government argued that the limited workload of the territorial ministries no longer justified separate cabinet posts. The post of Secretary of State for Northern Ireland was unchanged as its workload is larger. The holder acts as a broker in negotiations in the Province and has responsibility for security. If the Assembly and Executive are suspended, the Northern Ireland Office is responsible for the execution of policy.

A number of government departments (e.g. the Department of Health) now spend much of their time on policy for England. Responsibility for the English regions rested with the Office of the Deputy Prime Minister, where John Prescott had a strong interest, then the Department for Communities and Local Government.

Westminster

MPs at Westminster can no longer ask parliamentary questions to the Secretaries of State for Scotland and Wales on solely devolved matters. The remit of the three Select Committees for Scottish, Welsh and Northern Ireland Affairs has also been adapted. The Standing Committee on Regional Affairs has been revived as a forum for discussions on the English regions. 'Sewel motions' enable the Scottish Parliament or Northern Ireland Assembly to delegate responsibility for legislating on devolved matters back to Westminster on a case-by-case basis. The 1999–2003 Scottish Parliament utilised the Sewel convention on more than 40 occasions. This has been interpreted as a weakening of the Parliament's role, but it is often convenient for it to allow Westminster to ensure uniformity on technical matters, for example giving gay couples in Scotland the same partnership rights as those in England. The Welsh Assembly depends on Westminster to pass primary legislation which it then implements. Critics complain that Westminster has not taken a consistent line on the leeway it is prepared to afford the Assembly and often ignores requests to introduce measures as Wales-only Bills.

West Lothian Question: why should MPs representing Scottish constituencies be permitted to vote on English matters at Westminster when English MPs cannot vote on matters devolved to the Scottish Parliament?

The most controversial issue is the **West Lothian Question** (see Controversy 11.1). It asks why MPs representing Scottish constituencies at Westminster should be permitted to vote on purely English matters (e.g. local government in England) when English MPs have no say over matters devolved to the Scottish Parliament. The question was first raised by Tam Dalyell, MP for West Lothian, in the 1970s and has yet to be fully answered. Four main solutions have been proposed:

1. A reduction in the number of MPs from Scottish constituencies, ending the over-representation of Scotland at Westminster. The number of Scottish MPs was reduced from 72 to 59 at the 2005 general election but their role has not been re-assessed.

2. A ban on MPs representing Scottish constituencies from voting on legislation on English matters (e.g. health or education in England). This is the position of the Conservative Party but has been rejected by Labour.

3. The creation of elected assemblies with limited executive functions in the English regions. This was the policy of the Blair government but was shelved after a 'no' vote in a referendum on a north-east regional assembly in 2004.

4. The creation of an English parliament to handle English 'domestic' issues. This is supported by some Conservative MPs; critics fear that it will break-up the Union.

None of the proposed solutions is unproblematic: indeed, the 'answer' may create more problems than the 'question'. It is worth recalling that there have always been anomalies in the British constitution. There was no 'Belfast question' when Northern Irish MPs (albeit only 12 of them) voted on English matters during the Stormont period.

Controversy: 11.1

The 'West Lothian Question'

The 'West Lothian Question' asks why MPs representing Scottish constituencies at Westminster should be able to vote on English 'domestic' matters when English MPs cannot vote on equivalent matters devolved to the Scottish Parliament. It thus questions: (i) House of Commons procedures for dealing with legislation that applies only to England, or to England and Wales; (ii) the role of Scottish MPs in the House of Commons; and (iii) the relationship between Scottish MPs and their constituencies given that MSPs are responsible for handling grievances that arise on matters devolved to the Scottish Parliament.

The first substantial post-devolution cases of the 'West Lothian Question' arose in 2003. In June, John Reid, MP for North Hamilton and Belshill, was appointed Secretary of State for Health. This drew criticism from some English commentators who complained that Reid was responsible for bringing forward legislation on foundation hospitals in England, a policy that would not apply in his own Scottish constituency.

More significantly, the votes of MPs representing Scottish constituencies were then crucial in securing government victories on Bills establishing foundation hospitals and providing for differential university tuition fees in England. A majority of MPs representing English constituencies opposed both foundation hospitals and tuition fees; if Scottish MPs had been barred from voting, the government would have been defeated.

Date	Division	Vote (for–against the government)	Result if Scottish MPs had been barred from voting
19 November 2003	Health and Social Care (Community Health and Standards) Bill (Division 381)	302–285	258–268
27 January 2004	Higher Education Bill (Division 38)	316–311	270–290
31 March 2004	Higher Education Bill (Division 123)	316–288	269–270

The Conservatives propose a Bill certification system ('English votes for English laws') in which the Speaker would certify relevant Bills (or certain clauses) as 'English-only'. MPs representing Scottish constituencies would not be permitted to vote on these Bills, though they could participate in debates. The sole Conservative MP in Scotland and many SNP MPs already abstain on some English legislation

The proposal is not without difficulties. Scottish MPs who voted (both for and against) on foundation hospitals and tuition fees noted that the Bills contained clauses relating to Scotland. Even if they had not, they also claimed that English-only legislation on health spending would still impact upon public spending in Scotland and tuition fees would have a knock-on effect on Scottish universities (e.g. increased applications from English students). Labour claims that the Conservative plan would create different classes of MP and could prevent a government without a majority in England from enacting its legislative programme.

Funding

Barnett formula: a formula used to determine relative levels of public spending in the component nations of the UK.

The devolved administrations are funded by block grants from the UK Treasury the size of which is settled by the **Barnett formula**. This formula, agreed in 1978, translates changes in public spending in England into equivalent changes in the block grants for Scotland, Wales and Northern Ireland, calculated on the basis of population. Under the formula Scotland, Wales and Northern Ireland receive more public spending (some 20 per cent) per head of population than England. Critics in both the Labour and Conservative parties claim that this amounts to an English subsidy of the other nations of the UK. But the detailed operation of the Barnett formula is complex and opaque: despite their favourable allocation and real terms increases in funding since 1999, Scotland and Wales have seen their relative share of public spending squeezed. Labour has no plans to introduce an alternative to Barnett; a government committed to change would find it both complex and controversial.

The devolved administrations have little scope to distribute large sums of money between policy areas. The Scottish Parliament has yet to use its tax-varying powers; indeed Labour has issued campaign pledges not to do so. Even if it were to raise income tax by the permitted maximum of 3 per cent, this would raise only an extra £650 million (the block grant is £20 billion). MSPs from across the political spectrum support an extension of the Parliament's financial powers, ranging from control over VAT to full fiscal autonomy. The latter would give the Scottish Parliament full responsibility for taxation and spending in Scotland, ending its reliance on a Treasury block grant. This would greatly enhance its powers but would make it more difficult for the Executive to sustain current levels of spending on health, education and so forth.

Northern Ireland

Northern Ireland has long been treated as a 'place apart' by British politicians and political scientists, the former imposing special arrangements for its government and the latter employing different analytical techniques. The inter-communal tensions between unionists and nationalists are the primary factor in Northern Irish politics, and management of these the main goal of the UK government. The main political divide in Northern Ireland is that between unionists and nationalists. In general terms, unionists want Northern Ireland to remain part of the UK whereas nationalists favour a united Ireland or, as a minimum, closer links with the Republic. Unionists identify themselves as British and tend to be Protestant whereas nationalists see themselves as Irish and tend to be Roman Catholic. Both traditions have extreme fringes that are prepared to use violence to achieve their goals. Loyalists have engaged in sectarian and paramilitary attacks to defend the Union; republicans view armed struggle as a legitimate means of forcing British withdrawal.

Communal tensions colour everyday life in Northern Ireland: unionists and nationalists tend to live and work in different areas, attend different schools, socialise with people from their own community and read different newspapers. Each community attaches great importance to its history and traditions: marches

War or peace? A loyalist street mural in Belfast (© Mirrorpix)

by the Protestant Orange Order or the display of the Irish tricolour are steeped in symbolism. Catholics currently make up 40 per cent of the Northern Ireland population.

Civil rights protests against discrimination faced by Catholics gave way to violence in the late 1960s. The Royal Ulster Constabulary (RUC), a police force made up largely of Protestants and distrusted by many Catholics, struggled to contain the violence and in 1969 the British army was sent to restore order. Terrorist groups such as the republican Provisional Irish Republican Army (IRA) and Irish National Liberation Army (INLA), plus loyalist paramilitary groups such as the Ulster Defence Association (UDA) and Ulster Volunteer Force (UVF) carried out attacks. With the security situation deteriorating, the Heath government introduced direct rule from London, but 'the Troubles' continued. Only in the 1990s did the peace process succeed in reducing the violence by which time more than 3500 lives had been lost. The Provisional IRA has been on ceasefire since 1994 (save for an interlude in 1996–97) as have some of the loyalist paramilitaries. But dissident groups have carried out sporadic attacks, the most brutal being the Real IRA's Omagh bombing that killed 29 civilians in 1998.

Communal divisions also underpin representative politics in Northern Ireland. Elections are contested between unionist and nationalist parties; the main electoral issue is the constitutional status of Northern Ireland. But differences exist within the unionist and nationalist blocs. The Ulster Unionist Party (UUP), led by Sir Reg Empey since 2005, supports the Good Friday Agreement and has sought to foster a civic unionist identity. Its main challenger in the unionist bloc is the Democratic Unionist Party (DUP). Led by Ian Paisley since its formation in 1971, it has a strong Protestant ethos. The DUP opposes the Good Friday Agreement and has opposed sharing power with Sinn Fein.

The Social Democratic and Labour Party (SDLP) favours a greater role for the Republic in the affairs of Northern Ireland. Formed in 1970 and led by Mark Durkan since 2001, it is committed to bringing about constitutional change through exclusively peaceful means. Its main rival within the nationalist bloc is Sinn Fein, a republican party led by Gerry Adams. Sinn Fein is the political wing of the Provisional IRA, whose armed struggle it supported. In the 1990s the leadership of Sinn Fein embraced the political process ahead of the armed struggle ('the ballot rather than the bullet') but the party retains links to the IRA. The Alliance Party and Women's Coalition operate in the centre ground but have had limited support.

Direct rule and devolution

Northern Ireland has always been governed differently from the rest of the UK. Between 1921 and 1972 it was the only part of the UK to have a devolved parliament with legislative and executive powers. This period of rule by the Stormont parliament and executive highlighted the problems of majoritarian democracy in a divided community. Dominated by unionist politicians, Stormont pursued policies that discriminated against the minority Roman Catholic population in representative politics (by gerrymandering constituencies) and social affairs (where Catholics experienced poorer housing and higher unemployment).

Direct rule: the government of Northern Ireland through special arrangements at Whitehall and Westminster.

With the Troubles escalating, the British government suspended the Stormont parliament and imposed **direct rule** from London in 1972. The Northern Ireland Office was created to administer the Province; the Secretary of State and junior ministers were drawn from the UK governing party rather than parties from Northern Ireland. The Northern Ireland Constitution Act 1973 stated that the constitutional status of Northern Ireland is conditional on the consent of the people of Northern Ireland. It will remain a part of the UK for so long as that is the wish of a majority of the people of Northern Ireland. A huge majority supported the constitutional status quo in a referendum largely boycotted by nationalists in 1973. Surveys since then show that a majority want Northern Ireland to remain part of the UK.

The lack of input from Northern Ireland politicians, the leeway afforded to civil servants in policy-making and the limited scrutiny of Northern Irish issues at Westminster – where policy was made through Orders in Council rather than primary legislation – created a democratic deficit. The main British political parties have tended not to contest elections in Northern Ireland. The Conservatives had a formal alliance with the Ulster Unionists at Westminster until 1974; all formal ties between the two were revoked after the Anglo-Irish Agreement. There is a Northern Ireland branch of the Conservative Party but it enjoys little support from its UK parent party. Its best electoral performance came in 1992 when it polled 5 per cent of the vote. Labour finally agreed to allow people resident in Northern Ireland to become party members in 2003 having been threatened with legal action, but the party has not set up constituency associations in the Province. At Westminster,

Labour and the Conservatives have also tried to keep the constitutional status of Northern Ireland out of mainstream British party competition. When in power, both parties have supported power-sharing devolution though Labour advocated a 'united Ireland by consent' when in opposition in the 1980s.

Since direct rule, successive British governments have been committed to **power-sharing devolution**. Devolved institutions would be constructed so as to ensure that representatives of the unionist and nationalist communities shared power: there would be no return to majoritarian rule. A variety of initiatives were tried and failed. One of the most significant was the 1974 Sunningdale Agreement which proposed a power-sharing executive and Council of Ireland but collapsed when unionists held a general strike.

Power-sharing devolution: a system in which decision-making authority is devolved to institutions that have special arrangements to ensure cross-community representation and support for key policies.

The search for peace

Another failed initiative in the early 1980s prompted a changed approach by the British government. The 1985 Anglo-Irish Agreement gave the Republic of Ireland a formal role in the search for a settlement by establishing a consultative intergovernmental body and recognising that the Republic represented the interests of Catholics in Northern Ireland. Unionists resisted the Agreement and progress faltered. But the peace process was revived in the late 1980s and early 1990s (see Timeline 11.2). Various factors were significant:

- Changes in the strategies pursued by political parties in Northern Ireland.
- Changes in the strategy of the British government.
- Changes in the wider environment, notably a rethinking of Irish identity, the end of the Cold War and the election of President Bill Clinton in the USA.

In 1988, John Hume and Gerry Adams began talks that persuaded the Sinn Fein leadership that they could achieve a change in Northern Ireland's constitutional status through the political process. Senior figures in Sinn Fein were already concluding that the armed struggle had produced a stalemate and that representative politics offered the best prospect for advancing their goals. Pressure from the Clinton administration on both Irish republicans and the two governments helped open up the space for Sinn Fein's participation in the peace process. Sinn Fein was admitted to multi-party talks in 1997 once the IRA had restored its ceasefire and a Commission chaired by US Senator George Mitchell had established principles of non-violence that included the total disarmament of paramilitary organisations.

The British government was also modifying its position. Secretary of State for Northern Ireland Peter Brooke announced in 1990 that Britain has 'no selfish strategic or economic interest in Northern Ireland'. With the Cold War over, UK concerns about Irish neutrality and Sinn Fein rhetoric about revolutionary change were in abeyance. The British government now presented itself as a neutral facilitator in the search for a political settlement. It also opened secretive Back Channel communications with the IRA. The British and Irish governments set out parameters for an agreement in the 1993 Downing Street Declaration and the 1995 Framework Document. The latter signalled that an agreement would have three strands: power-sharing devolution in Northern Ireland; the relationship between the north and south of Ireland; and the relationship between the British and Irish governments.

TIMELINE 11.2

The Northern Ireland peace process, 1988–2005

1988	Talks between SDLP leader John Hume and Sinn Fein leader Gerry Adams begin
1990	Secretary of State for Northern Ireland declares that Britain has 'no selfish strategic or economic interest in Northern Ireland'. Secret Back Channel communications between British government and IRA
1991–92	Talks between main constitutional parties
1993	Downing Street Declaration issued by Prime Minister John Major and Taoiseach Albert Reynolds
1994	IRA announces ceasefire; loyalist paramilitaries follow suit
1995	UK and Irish governments issue Framework Documents. David Trimble becomes UUP leader. Bill Clinton's first visit to Belfast
1996	Mitchell Commission issues Principles for Non-Violence, including total decommissioning of paramilitary weapons. Multi-party talks between parties reach stalemate. IRA ceasefire ends
1997	New Labour government elected. IRA ceasefire restored. Sinn Fein enters multi-party talks, DUP withdraws from them
1998	Good Friday Agreement on power-sharing devolution, cross-border bodies, etc. Approved in referendums in Northern Ireland and the Republic. David Trimble selected as First Minister, Seamus Mallon as Deputy First Minister (they take office in 1999). First Assembly elections: UUP and SDLP are the main representatives of the unionist and nationalist communities. Real IRA bomb Omagh
1999	Power formally devolved to Northern Ireland Assembly in December. Executive includes two Sinn Fein ministers
2000–01	Assembly and Executive temporarily suspended on three occasions as dispute over decommissioning continues. IRA puts some arms 'beyond use'
2002	Assembly and Executive suspended in October. Reform of Police Service of Northern Ireland
2003	Second Assembly elections see DUP and Sinn Fein emerge as main unionist and nationalist parties
2005	IRA declares an end to conflict and puts its weapons 'beyond use'

Unionist parties did not change their positions as dramatically as Sinn Fein. But UUP leader David Trimble was eventually prepared to accept Sinn Fein participation in a devolved executive and the creation of weak North–South bodies if they formed part of a settlement that bolstered Northern Ireland's place in the Union and brought about full decommissioning of IRA arms. This meant the amendment of Articles 2 and 3 of the Irish Constitution (which referred to the 'national territory' as constituting the whole of Ireland) and a republican commitment to the principle that Northern Ireland's status should not change without the consent of a majority of its people.

The Good Friday Agreement

The year 1997 brought a Labour election victory and Sinn Fein entry into multi-party talks that culminated in the 1998 Good Friday Agreement (officially titled 'the Belfast Agreement'). Consent is again a key principle: there would be no change in

Consociationalism and the Good Friday Agreement

In the 1970s, Dutch political scientist Arend Lijphart developed a model of consociational democracy for divided societies. It is most suited to deeply divided societies that are in transition for consociationalism requires elite negotiation, accommodation and compromise. Four main principles underpin consociational agreements:

- *Executive power-sharing*: power is shared by representatives of significant communities in the executive branch.
- *Segmental autonomy*: each community regulates its own internal affairs; the equality and autonomy of communities is protected by law.
- *Proportionality*: elections take place under proportional representation and government posts are shared in proportion to representation in the legislature. Public spending and posts in the public sector may also be allocated on a proportional basis.
- *Veto rights*: the minority group has the right to veto proposals which they believe violate their basic interests.

The internal arrangements for the government of Northern Ireland set out in the 1998 Good Friday Agreement follow these principles. They are designed to promote consent and accommodation between unionists and nationalists, while protecting their basic interests and identities. First, power in the Northern Ireland Executive is shared between representatives of the main communities in a 'grand coalition'. The main unionist and nationalist parties hold ministerial posts in the Executive, which is headed jointly by a First Minister and Deputy-First Minister drawn from the two blocs in the Assembly.

Second, the Agreement legitimises and affords equal respect to British and Irish identities in Northern Ireland. It also calls for a tailor-made Bill of Rights to supplement the European Convention on Human Rights and obliges the UK government to create a Human Rights Commission.

Proportionality is also built in to the Agreement. Elections to the Assembly take place under the single transferable vote system in 18 multi-member constituencies. STV was believed to encourage cross-community vote transfers (e.g. from the pro-Agreement SDLP to the pro-Agreement UUP), though this remains the exception rather than the norm in Northern Ireland. Ministerial posts in the Executive are allocated to parties in proportion to their strength in the Assembly. The d'Hondt rule is used to determine the order in which posts are allocated. Proportionality rules also apply to Assembly committees.

Finally, controversial legislative proposals must pass special procedures in the Assembly, 'parallel consent' (i.e. majority support from both unionists and nationalists) and also a 'weighted majority' (i.e. 60 per cent support from Assembly members present). Assembly members are obliged to designate themselves as 'unionist', 'nationalist' or 'other' for this purpose.

Some critics of the Good Friday Agreement argue that its consociational features have institutionalised and frozen existing ethnic divisions. Rather than encouraging citizens of Northern Ireland to see themselves as members of a single community, it has legitimised the unionist–nationalist divide and done little to address sectarianism. Some academics favour alternative models of conflict resolution that encourage inter-group accommodation by rewarding political parties that win cross-community support, or actively promote social change in order to end sectarianism.

the constitutional status of Northern Ireland without the consent of the majority of its people. The Republic amended its constitution to remove its territorial claim over Northern Ireland. Parity of esteem is another defining principle: the Agreement recognises the legitimacy of both unionist and nationalist identities and includes provisions on equality and human rights.

Consociationalism (i.e. power-sharing) is the key principle underpinning the arrangements for devolution in Northern Ireland (see Analysis 11.2). A 108-member Northern Ireland Assembly has primary legislative power in a range of policy areas including economic development, agriculture and education (see Table 11.1). Its responsibilities are similar to those of the Scottish Parliament but it does not have tax-raising powers and the Agreement states that the UK government may devolve responsibility for policing and justice to the Assembly in future.

The Assembly is elected by the single transferable vote (STV), a system of proportional representation in which electors rank candidates standing in multi-member constituencies (see Chapter 16). This system ensures that a wide range of opinion is represented in the Assembly. Parallel consent (i.e. cross-community support) and weighted majorities are required on controversial issues. The Agreement also ensures that both unionists and nationalists are represented within the Northern Ireland Executive. It is headed jointly by a First Minister and Deputy First Minister elected from the unionist and nationalist blocs in the Assembly. UUP leader David Trimble became First Minister in 1999; Mark Durkan replaced Seamus Mallon as Deputy First Minister in 2001. Ministerial posts in the Executive Committee are allocated on a proportional basis according to party strength in the Assembly. Four parties were represented in the first Executive Committee: the UUP (4 ministers), SDLP (4), DUP (2) and Sinn Fein (2).

The Agreement also established north–south, east–west and intergovernmental bodies. The Northern Ireland administration and Irish government cooperate on cross-border issues in a North–South Ministerial Council which has some executive powers. The British–Irish Council offers an arena for the exchange of ideas and policy cooperation in a number of areas. Its members include sovereign states (the British and Irish governments), devolved administrations (from Scotland, Wales and Northern Ireland), and Crown Dominions (the Isle of Man and Jersey). A British–Irish Intergovernmental Conference is a forum for formal discussions on Northern Ireland matters between the two governments.

Finally, the Agreement established an independent commission on policing (the Patten Commission) which recommended major changes to the RUC, now remodelled as the Police Service of Northern Ireland. Provision was made for the early release of prisoners and political parties pledged to use their best endeavours to bring about the decommissioning of weapons held by paramilitary groups.

The Agreement won overwhelming approval in referendums in Northern Ireland (71 per cent 'yes') and the Republic (94 per cent). Only a narrow majority of unionists supported it. Pro-agreement parties won 80 of the 108 seats in the first Assembly elections, where the UUP and SDLP came first and second. Vote transfers turned a majority of first preference votes for 'anti-Agreement' unionists (the DUP and smaller parties) into an overall majority for 'pro-Agreement' unionists (the UUP and Progressive Unionist Party) in the Assembly. Most vote transfers, however, stay within the same communal bloc (e.g. UUP to DUP, SDLP to Sinn Fein).

Table 11.5 Elections to the Northern Ireland Assembly

	1998		2003	
	First preference vote (%)	Seats	First preference vote	Seats
Unionist				
Ulster Unionist Party	21.3	28	22.7	27
Democratic Unionist Party	18.1	20	25.7	30
Progressive Unionist Party	2.6	2	1.2	1
United Kingdom Unionist Party	4.5	5	0.8	1
Other unionists	2.9	3	0.5	0
Nationalist				
Social Democratic and Labour Party	22.0	24	17.0	18
Sinn Fein	17.7	18	23.5	24
Others				
Alliance Party	6.5	6	3.7	6
Women's Coalition	1.6	2	0.8	0
Independent (K. Deeny, West Tyrone)	–	–	0.9	1

Devolution has been dogged by problems such as Orange Order parades, paramilitary activity and, most importantly, decommissioning. The IRA did not fully decommission its arms nor declare explicitly that its conflict was over until 2005. This ran counter to the letter and spirit of the Agreement – but so did the actions of other parties to the Agreement, albeit less spectacularly. The British government has suspended the devolved institutions and re-imposed direct rule on four occasions. The longest period of suspension began in October 2002.

Most of the main actors remain committed to the key tenets of the Good Friday Agreement, but differences between the UUP and the nationalist bloc on its full implementation are deep-rooted. Unionist support for the Agreement has fallen significantly. Opinion polls show that a majority of unionists now oppose the Agreement, believing that it had given ground to nationalists and republicans but failed to deliver on key unionist demands. The UUP has suffered serious divisions since 1998: Trimble faced numerous leadership challenges, three UUP Assembly members defected to the DUP in 2003 and the Orange Order severed its ties with the party. The anti-Agreement DUP has overtaken the UUP as the main representative of the unionist party. It was the largest party in the 2003 Assembly elections, held while the Assembly was suspended (see Table 11.5). It benefited from discontent with the operation of the Agreement among unionist voters and a feeling that the UUP had made too many concessions to republicans and had not defended unionist interests vigorously. DUP success continued in the 2005 general election when it won nine seats and the UUP just one. Trimble lost his Westminster seat and resigned as UUP leader to be replaced by Sir Reg Empey.

The 2003 and 2005 elections confirmed a 'hollowing out' of the pro-Agreement centre. The DUP leapfrogged the UUP to become the biggest unionist party, the non-sectarian Alliance Party and Women's Coalition lost support, and Sinn Fein confirmed its position as the main nationalist party. Many nationalist voters now

Table 11.6 Preferred long-term policy for Northern Ireland (%)

Long-term policy	Protestant	Catholic	All
Remain part of the United Kingdom	85	24	59
Reunify with the rest of Ireland	5	47	22
Independent Northern Ireland	6	15	11
Other/don't know	4	15	9

Source: Northern Ireland Life and Times Survey 2004, www.ark.ac.uk/nilt/2004/Political_Attitudes/
NIRELAND.html

viewed Sinn Fein as the best representative of their community, believing that it had extracted concessions from the unionists and UK government. It also had a more effective party organisation than the SDLP.

These developments cast further doubt on the chances of Agreement being implemented in full. The IRA's September 2005 decision to end its terrorist campaign and put all of its weapons beyond use was a highly significant development, marking the apparent culmination of efforts to bring the divisive issue of decommissioning to a conclusion. But there was no swift resumption of devolution as unionists waited for definitive evidence that the IRA was no longer involved in criminal activities – IRA members had been blamed for a high profile murder and a major bank robbery the previous year. Senior DUP politicians cast doubt on the verdict of General John de Chastelain's independent decommissioning body that the IRA had disarmed. This illustrated the depth of mistrust on both sides that make it difficult for the DUP and Sinn Fein to work constructively in a new Executive.

The Agreement nonetheless still offers the best prospect of political stability. Continued direct rule is the likeliest alternative, though all major Northern Ireland parties now favour some form of devolution. Other scenarios are unlikely. A return to devolution minus North–South bodies and some aspects of power-sharing (favoured by the DUP) will not gain cross-community support. Scottish and Welsh devolution make the full integration of Northern Ireland into the UK (favoured by some on the unionist fringe) unlikely. An independent Northern Ireland is barely viable. A united 32 county Ireland is a possibility in the longer term but as a decisive majority of Protestants support Northern Ireland's place in the Union, it would fail the key test of consent (see Table 11.6). Furthermore, only around a half of Catholics favour a united Ireland.

The post-devolution polity

Devolution has created new a new relationship between the UK's component nations. It offers further institutional recognition of the distinctiveness of these nations but reflects also their desire to remain part of a multinational UK state. Rather than enforcing a coherent blueprint, devolution has been asymmetric: the nations of the UK are each governed in different ways. The post-devolution UK no longer comfortably fits the centralised, homogeneous norm of a unitary state. But neither has it been transformed into a federal state in which power is constitutionally divided between autonomous institutions.

Federalism: a
form of government
in which the
constitution divides
decision-making
authority between
national and regional
tiers of government.

In *Devolution in the United Kingdom* (Opus, 2001), Vernon Bogdanor characterises the post-devolution UK as 'quasi-federal' UK. It has some federal characteristics but also retains some of the features of a unitary state. The legislation creating devolved institutions thus established a formal division of powers between central government and the devolved bodies, but Westminster remains sovereign as it limits the powers of the devolved institutions and can overrule or abolish them. When Gladstone sought to recognise the multinational character of the UK state by devolving power to a legislative assembly in Ireland in the late nineteenth century, constitutional theorist A.V. Dicey argued that there could be no halfway house between the parliamentary sovereignty and separatism. More than a century later, Labour's devolution settlement has arguably taken the UK into this middle ground. Westminster remains sovereign but this no longer amounts to full supremacy over policy across the UK. Though sovereignty has formally been delegated rather than devolved, Westminster has accepted that it will not impose legislation in areas devolved to the Scottish Parliament. The power to legislate on matters affecting Scotland is divided between parliaments in Westminster and Holyrood.

The prospects of an alternative model of territorial management emerging have receded. There looks to be no going back to the pre-1999 system of administrative devolution for Scotland and Wales. Any attempt to weaken or remove the Scottish Parliament or Welsh Assembly would be highly controversial given that the decision to create these bodies marked an acceptance that Scotland and Wales have a (limited) right of self-determination. A strengthening of the Welsh Assembly is more likely than its abolition and, despite the long suspension of devolved institutions in Northern Ireland, key actors in the peace process are committed to devolution.

Table 11.7 National Identity in England, Scotland and Wales
Respondents were asked to choose how they would describe themselves from the options presented below

Identity	1997	2003
England		
English not British	7	17
More English than British	17	19
Equally English and British	45	31
More British than English	14	13
British not English	9	10
Scotland		
Scottish not British	23	31
More Scottish than British	38	34
Equally Scottish and British	27	22
More British than Scottish	4	4
British not Scottish	4	4
Wales		
Welsh not British	17	21
More Welsh than British	26	27
Equally Welsh and British	34	29
More British than Welsh	10	8
British not Welsh	12	9

Source: J. Curtice, 'Devolution and Britishness', *ESRC Devolution Briefing No. 35*, August 2005, Table 3, www.devolution.ac.uk/Briefing_papers.htm

A federal UK is presented as a solution to some of the anomalies of the devolution settlement by commentators from across the political spectrum – notably the Liberal Democrats, but also some enthusiasts for an English parliament. In a federal UK, Westminster would be a federal parliament handling issues such as the economy, constitution and foreign policy, while 'domestic' issues such as health and education would be devolved to legislative assemblies in England, Scotland, Wales and Northern Ireland. But the dominance of England, with 85 per cent of the UK population, is a major obstacle to a viable federal model.

Despite the siren warnings of the Conservatives in the 1990s, devolution appears to have lessened the prospects for Scottish and Welsh independence – although significant numbers of Scots favour this option. The number of people describing themselves as 'primarily' Scottish, Welsh or English rather than 'primarily British' has risen (see Table 11.7). But the increase is not dramatic and most people see themselves as having dual identities, i.e. being British as well as Scottish, Welsh or English.

Conclusion and summary

Devolution has already brought about radical change in UK territorial politics, but the new asymmetric settlement is characterised by the same flexibility and pragmatism that has been a hallmark of the British political tradition. There have been no major confrontations between the devolved bodies and the UK government, in part thanks to this pragmatic adaptation and the coincidence of Labour holding office in London, Edinburgh and Cardiff. The House of Lords Select Committee on the Constitution warned in 2003 that tensions might not be so readily resolved or suppressed when parties of a different political hue gain power. It recommended that existing formal and informal mechanisms for intergovernmental relations be put on a firmer footing.

Nor has devolution reached a natural conclusion: as former Secretary of State for Wales, Ron Davies pointed out, devolution is a 'process not an event'. The Scottish Parliament has bedded in most readily, but major changes to its electoral system are already being mooted. The limitations of the Welsh Assembly are apparent. The UK government has added higher education to the list of devolved areas, but the Richard Commission's recommendation that the Assembly be granted primary legislative powers has not won great political or popular support. Regional assemblies in England look unlikely. The main parties in Northern Ireland support devolution, but differ in their interpretation of the Good Friday Agreement. Devolution has also posed some as yet unanswered questions about the operation of central government. Despite the creation of the Department for Constitutional Affairs, responsibility for the devolution settlement is split across Whitehall. An answer to the West Lothian Question remains elusive, the Barnett formula survives in the absence of easy alternatives while the full implications of policy divergence remain uncertain. The creation of the devolved institutions marked the 'end of the beginning' for the multi-level UK polity; crucial steps in the next phase of its development are only now being contemplated.

Further reading

V. Bogdanor, *Devolution in the United Kingdom* (Oxford: Opus, 2001) concentrates on the historical context of devolution, but offers the clearest analysis of its anomalies. Useful introductions include C. Pilkington, *Devolution in Britain Today* (Manchester: Manchester University Press, 2002) and M. O'Neill (ed.), *Devolution and British Politics* (Harlow: Longman, 2004). The Constitution Unit publishes an annual 'State of the Nations' survey of devolution including A. Trench (ed.), *Has Devolution made a Difference? The State of the Nations 2004* (London: Imprint Academic, 2004). R. Weight, *Patriots* (London: Palgrave, 2003) is an excellent account of national identity in modern Britain.

Analytical accounts of pre-1999 territorial politics include M. Hechter, *Internal Colonialism* (London: Routledge, 1975) and J. Bulpitt, *Territory and Power in the United Kingdom* (Manchester: Manchester University Press, 1983). J. Bradbury, 'The political dynamics of sub-state regionalisation', *British Journal of Politics and International Relations*, Vol. 5, No. 4 (2003), pp. 543–75 provides a theoretical approach to devolution.

On Scotland, P. Lynch, *Scottish Government and Politics* (Edinburgh: Edinburgh University Press, 2nd edition, 2006) is a good introduction to the new structures while G. Hassan and C. Warhurst (eds), *Tomorrow's Scotland* (Edinburgh: Lawrence and Wishart, 2002) examines the new Scottish politics. On devolution in Wales, see K. Morgan and G. Mungham, *Redesigning Democracy: The Making of the Welsh Assembly* (Cardiff: Seren, 2000). R. Hazell (ed.) *The English Question* (Manchester: Manchester University Press, 2006) and J. Tomaney and J. Mawson, *England: The State of the Regions* (London: Policy Press, 2002) explore the governance of England.

There is a substantial literature on Northern Ireland. Good introductions include J. Tonge, *Northern Ireland: Conflict and Change* (Harlow: Longman, 2nd edition, 2002) and P. Dixon, *Northern Ireland. The Politics of War and Peace* (Palgrave, 2001). J. McGarry and B. O'Leary, *Explaining Northern Ireland* (Oxford: Oxford University Press, 1995) offers an advanced analysis of the conflict. Detailed studies of the Good Friday Agreement and beyond include J. Tonge, *The New Northern Irish Politics?* (London: Palgrave, 2004) and M. Cox, A. Guelke and F. Stephen (eds), *A Farewell to Arms? Beyond the Good Friday Agreement* (Manchester: Manchester University Press, 2nd edition, 2005).

Websites

Students of devolution are well served by the internet. The Constitution Unit publishes detailed Quarterly Monitoring Reports on devolution www.ucl.ac.uk/constitution-unit/research/devolution/devo-monitoring-programme.html. The ESRC's Devolution and Constitutional Change Programme website www.devolution.ac.uk/ includes publications from a number of academic research projects on devolution.

The devolved institutions all have informative websites: the Scottish Parliament www.scottish.parliament.uk/ and Scottish Executive www.scotland.gov.uk/; the Welsh Assembly www.wales.gov.uk./; the Northern Ireland Assembly www.ni-assembly.gov.uk. The Department for Communities and Local Government has information on the English regions www.odpm.gov.uk/ and the Northern Ireland Office details on the peace process www.nio.gov.uk.

Information on Scottish politics is available at www.scottishpolitics.org/; Welsh politics at the Institute of Welsh Affairs www.iwa.org.uk/index.htm, and 'the Troubles' in Northern Ireland from the CAIN website http://cain.ulst.ac.uk/index.html.

Chapter 12

The UK and the European Union

Learning outcomes

After reading this chapter, you will:

- Understand the historical development of the European Union and the role played by its major institutions.
- Be aware of the policies pursued by successive British governments towards the EU.
- Be able to evaluate the impact of EU membership on British politics and the political system.

Introduction

The United Kingdom joined the European Economic Community – later to become the European Union (EU) – in 1973. Since then the EU has enlarged to 25 members and has extended its policy competences considerably. Member states form a single European market of 450 million people. Within the EU the UK has often been considered an 'awkward partner' wary of deeper political and economic integration. Domestically, the UK's relationship with the EU remains a major issue that has caused divisions between and within the main political parties. EU membership has also required the British state to adapt some of its practices and procedures.

The development of the European Union

Supranational: an institution or organisation which has decision-making authority independent of its member states.

Intergovernmental: an institution or organisation based on cooperation between nation states.

Economic and Monetary Union (EMU): a project creating a single currency, central bank and common monetary policy for its members.

Following the Second World War (1939–45), West European states engaged in closer political and economic cooperation to aid their reconstruction and prevent future war. France was the driving force, putting forward the 1950 Schuman Plan that proposed the creation of a European Coal and Steel Community (ECSC). France, West Germany, Italy, Belgium, the Netherlands and Luxembourg ('the Six') duly set this up in 1952. As a **supranational** body with its own policy-making authority, budget and law, the ECSC differed from **intergovernmental** bodies (e.g. the Council of Europe created in 1948) in which states cooperated voluntarily and could veto proposals.

Further integration followed when the Six signed the 1957 Treaties of Rome establishing the European Economic Community (EEC) and the European Atomic Energy Community (EURATOM). These organisations began operating in 1958. The institutions of the EEC were modelled on those of the ECSC. The EEC's early achievements included the creation of a Common Agricultural Policy (CAP) in 1962 and a customs union in 1968, the latter involving the removal of internal tariff barriers and establishment of a common external tariff. Integration stalled in 1965 when President de Gaulle precipitated the 'empty chair crisis' by withdrawing French representatives from the Council of Ministers in protest at proposals to strengthen supranationalism. The 1966 'Luxembourg compromise' resolved the conflict by confirming the veto power of member states, placing them in the ascendancy.

Global economic crisis contributed to a drop in the pace of integration in the 1970s. Ambitious plans for **Economic and Monetary Union** (EMU) made at the 1969 Hague summit were abandoned. But there were also advances. The first direct elections to the European Parliament (EP) were held in 1979, the year in which

Analysis: 12.1

EEC, EC and EU

The EU has had a bewildering number of official titles since the European Economic Community (EEC) was founded in 1958. The three main organisations (the EEC, ECSC and Euratom) were collectively known as 'European Communities'. The 1965 Merger Treaty created one Council, one Commission, one European Court of Justice and one Assembly (later renamed the European Parliament) for the three organisations.

The Maastricht Treaty created a new organisation, the European Union which is built upon three pillars. The first is the European Community, as the EEC was now renamed – that is, its institutions, laws and policies. Community laws and methods do not apply in the second pillar (the Common Foreign and Security Policy) and third pillar (Justice and Home Affairs) where intergovernmental procedures were used. The European Union does not have a legal personality but is founded upon the existing EC and the Maastricht Treaty. If ratified, the EU Constitutional Treaty would give the EU legal personality by merging the EC and EU, ending the distinction between the two.

In this chapter, the term EU is used except where a contrast is being drawn between the Community method and intergovernmentalism, or where it is historically inaccurate.

the European Monetary System (EMS) was established. Its main element was the Exchange Rate Mechanism (ERM), a currency grid in which the values of member currencies were fixed against each other. The EEC also enlarged with the UK, Ireland and Denmark joining in 1973, Greece in 1981 then Spain and Portugal in 1986.

Single market to single currency

Integration moved up a gear in the mid-1980s as member states pressed for further economic integration to improve Europe's competitive position. This, plus Franco-German plans for institutional reform, was supported by an activist Commission led by Jacques Delors. The Single European Act (SEA) was agreed in 1985 and came into effect in 1987. Its centrepiece was the creation of a Single European Market (SEM) by the end of 1992. The SEM is an area without internal frontiers in which the free movement of goods, services, persons and capital is ensured. Three main forms of barrier – physical, technical and fiscal – were to be removed. The removal of physical barriers required the abolition of custom checks at internal borders. For technical barriers, the principle of 'mutual recognition' meant that goods meeting minimum standards in one member state could be freely traded in another. Qualifications would also be accepted across the EC. New VAT procedures were introduced in an attempt to remove fiscal barriers.

The SEM proved a major success though progress in some areas was slower than anticipated. It also gave new impetus to the integration process as France, Germany and the Commission pressed for a greater EC role in social policy, freedom of movement for workers and EMU. Meanwhile the end of the Cold War, reunification of Germany and collapse of communist regimes in eastern Europe overturned prevailing assumptions about the security of Europe. In twin Intergovernmental Conferences (IGCs) in 1990–91, member states thrashed out proposals for EMU and political union.

The Maastricht Treaty, properly known as the Treaty on European Union, was agreed in 1991 and came into force in 1993. It created a European Union comprised of three pillars: (i) the existing EC with responsibility for the SEM, trade, agriculture and so forth, (ii) an intergovernmental pillar on Common Foreign and Security Policy (CFSP) and (iii) an intergovernmental pillar on Justice and Home Affairs (JHA). Decision-making in the second and third pillars was conducted by national governments who retained veto rights, with little input from the Commission or European Court of Justice. The Maastricht Treaty also stated that a single European currency was to be established by 1999 at the latest.

Britain won two Treaty exemptions. First, an opt-out from Stage III of EMU meant that the UK would not have to join the single currency automatically. Instead, the UK Parliament would decide at a future date whether or not to participate. Second, the UK was alone in refusing to sign the Social Agreement (often referred to as the 'Social Chapter') that extended cooperation in social policy, believing that it would increase costs for British companies.

Ratification of the Treaty proved difficult. It was rejected in a Danish referendum in 1992, narrowly approved in France and subject to a tortuous parliamentary ratification in Britain. A 'yes' vote was ultimately secured in a second Danish vote and the Treaty came into force in 1993. The EU spent the remainder of the 1990s

Enlargement:
the admittance of
new members into
an international
organisation.

engaged in both 'deepening' (further integration, notably EMU) and 'widening'
(**enlargement**).

Deepening and widening

Maastricht set out a three-stage transition to EMU. Stage I, the completion of the
SEM, was underway. In Stage II member states would engage in greater economic
coordination. Stage III would then see the creation of an independent European
Central Bank (ECB), the irrevocable fixing of exchange rates and the replacement
of national currencies with the single currency (the euro). It would begin in 1999
for those states meeting specified 'convergence criteria' – low inflation, low interest
rates, sound public finances (levels of government debt) and ERM membership. The
targets appeared tough but the Treaty allowed for flexibility if states were moving
in the right direction.

Turmoil in the ERM with the exit of the UK and Italy (1992) and the widening of
the bands of permitted currency fluctuation (1993) raised doubts about the viability
of EMU. The ERM subsequently stabilised but some states had to cut welfare
spending or engage in creative accountancy to meet the convergence criteria. Eleven
states – Austria, Belgium, Finland, France, Germany, Ireland, Italy, Luxembourg, the
Netherlands, Spain and Portugal – formed the 'first wave' of states joining the euro
on 1 January 1999. Only four unambiguously met the criteria. Britain, Denmark
and Sweden opted out; Greece did not meet the criteria but joined in 2001. Euro
notes and coins entered circulation on 1 January 2002 and national currencies
ceased to be legal tender the following month.

Budgetary discipline was to be ensured by the Stability and Growth Pact which
allows sanctions to be imposed on euro-zone states that failed to reduce excessive
deficits. But political pressure saw France and Germany avoiding fines despite
persistent breaches of the 3 per cent ceiling on budget deficits. Helmut Kohl's centre-
right government in Germany was a leading supporter of the Pact but his centre-left
successor Gerhard Schroeder sought to loosen the spending restrictions it imposed.
The strict criteria were officially relaxed in 2005 despite central bank opposition.

The accession of Austria, Finland and Sweden to the EU in 1995 proceeded
smoothly, but the eastward enlargement of the Union was a far more ambitious
project. Twelve central and eastern European states applied for membership in the
early 1990s, having been freed from one-party rule and Soviet influence in 1989.
The 1993 Copenhagen European Council agreed three main criteria for their
membership: a liberal democratic political system, a functioning market economy
and acceptance of the *acquis communautaire* (the body of existing EU law). Meeting
these criteria was sometimes painful as it necessitated major political, economic and
administrative reforms in the applicant states.

Ten states eventually joined the EU in 2004: Cyprus, the Czech Republic, Estonia,
Hungary, Latvia, Lithuania, Malta, Poland, Slovakia and Slovenia (see Figure 12.1).
A proposal for the re-unification of Cyprus was defeated in a referendum meaning
that Northern Cyprus, which has had a separate administration since Turkish
military intervention in 1975, did not join the EU. The eight post-communist
member states are often viewed as a homogenous bloc. US Defense Secretary Donald
Rumsfeld, for example, drew a contrast between 'Old Europe' (notably France and

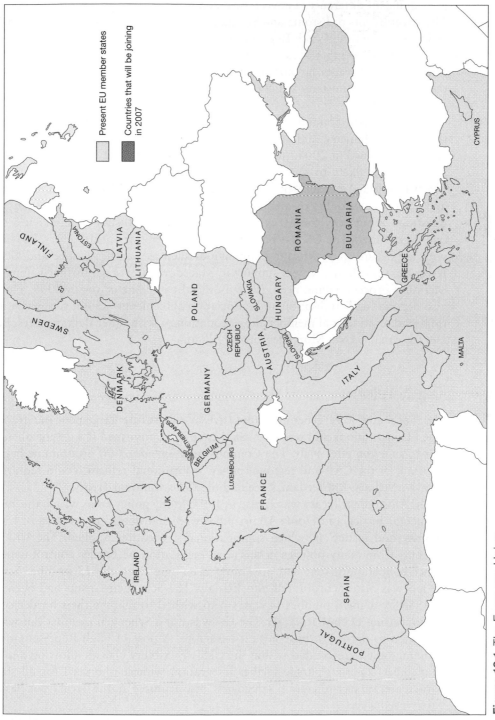

Figure 12.1 The European Union

Germany) which opposed the 2003 invasion of Iraq and 'New Europe' (the post-communist states and some West European states) which were supportive. But there are significant differences between post-communist states on socio-economic issues. The governments of Estonia and Slovakia take a free market position whereas those of Hungary and the Czech Republic are more interventionist. Slovenia will become the first 'new' member state to join the single currency in 2007. On institutional reform, Poland wants favourable terms for large member states (e.g. on voting in the Council of Ministers) while the other new members try to protect the interests of smaller states.

Two more post-communist states, Bulgaria and Romania, are scheduled to join the EU on 1 January 2007. Their reform programmes lagged behind those of the states who joined in 2004. Accession talks with Turkey and Croatia began in 2005 but neither is likely to join for at least a decade. Turkey applied to join in 1987 but was rejected because of concerns about its political system, weak economy and poor human rights record. Despite political and economic advances in Turkey, questions about how the EU could accommodate a Muslim state, albeit a secular one, were raised. The UK has been a strong supporter of Turkish entry, but in states with large Turkish or Muslim communities such as Austria, France and Germany fewer than one in five voters support it. Macedonia is a stage further behind in the accession process having been granted official candidate status in 2005. The EU is also negotiating Stabilisation and Association agreements – closer ties which may in time lead on to formal membership negotiations – with other Balkan states, Bosnia-Herzegovina, Serbia, Montenegro, and Albania.

Treaty reform

Member states were generally supportive of eastward enlargement but recognised that EU institutions and policies would have to be reformed if a 25-member Union was to function effectively. The Commission's *Agenda 2000* programme began the overhaul of the CAP and regional policy. Institutional reform would require three Treaty revisions: Amsterdam, Nice and the Constitutional Treaty.

The Amsterdam Treaty was agreed in 1997. Many policy areas within the intergovernmental Justice and Home Affairs pillar were transferred to an 'area of freedom, security and justice' in which supranational procedures applied. The UK gained opt-outs from many policies in this area. Legislation on border control issues (e.g. police cooperation) that had previously been agreed by the 13-member Schengen Group was also incorporated into EU law. The Schengen Group had been set up in 1985 by a small number of states who wished to remove their border controls without using EC law to do so. The UK was not a Schengen member but was now permitted to opt-in to those laws it wished to. A post of High Representative and planning unit were created within the CFSP. Flexibility clauses allowing a majority of member states to pursue further integration without the need for all states to participate, subject to certain safeguards, also featured in the Treaty but have been barely used since.

Agreement on institutional reform had to wait until an ill-tempered European Council meeting at Nice in 2000. The Nice Treaty set out changes to **qualified majority voting** (QMV) – a procedure in which states are allocated a certain number

Qualified majority voting: a voting system in the Council of Ministers in which decisions require a specified majority of votes, with votes allocated to member states according to their size.

of votes according to their size (see below) – and the size of the Commission and EP that would come into effect after enlargement. Its main policy innovation was a European Security and Defence Policy (ESDP) under which the EU would develop a common defence policy and have the capacity for autonomous, but limited, military action.

The Nice Treaty did not come into force until 2003 after a second referendum in Ireland reversed an initial 'no' vote. By then preparations for further Treaty reform were underway as few states were satisfied with the Nice Treaty. A Convention on the Future of Europe chaired by former French President Giscard d'Estaing produced a draft constitution which was then discussed by member states. For a while it appeared that agreement would not be possible as Spain and Poland refused to compromise on voting arrangements. A change of government in Spain cleared the way for a deal and the EU Constitutional Treaty – often referred to as the 'EU Constitution' or 'European Constitution' – was signed at the 2004 Dublin European Council (see Controversy 12.1).

The major institutional reforms set out in the EU Constitution are:

• The creation of a full-time President for the European Council, serving a two-and-a-half year term, and an EU Minister for Foreign Affairs.

Controversy: 12.1

The UK and the EU Constitution

The Blair government downplayed the significance of the EU Constitutional Treaty by claiming that it was largely a tidying-up exercise that brought existing Treaty provisions within a single document. Blair stated that it did not 'alter the fundamental constitutional relationship' between Britain and the EU – Parliament has, for example, long accepted the primacy of EU law. Ministers argued that it set out clearly the limits of the EU's powers and states that powers not explicitly conferred upon the EU remain with member states. The Constitutional Treaty's main purpose was to ensure that a 25-member EU worked effectively, hence changes in the functioning of the Commission, Council and EP. Britain had retained its veto on tax, social security, defence and foreign policy and its budget rebate. Extensions of QMV would be largely limited to technical areas or policy fields where other member states might frustrate British interests. Large states such as the UK would also be beneficiaries of new QMV procedures that took greater account of population. Provisions on enhanced cooperation would allow some member states to pursue further integration in new policy areas while others stand aside.

Eurosceptics argued that the Constitutional Treaty marked another step on the road to 'a country called Europe'. The proposed creation of a President of the European Council, an EU Foreign Minister and a European Public Prosecutor would take the EU closer to statehood. The EU would gain legal personality; the Constitution and EU law would have clear primacy over national law. The Charter of Fundamental Rights would become legally-binding rather than just declaratory. QMV would replace unanimity in 15 areas and be the norm in 24 new areas. Some Eurosceptics drew comfort from the inclusion of a secession clause allowing member states to leave the Union. Finally, casual observers may be surprised by the Foreign Office's claim that a Treaty consisting of some 230 pages plus a further 286 pages of Annexes amounts to a 'simplified Treaty which is easier to read and understand'.

- A 'team Presidency' system for the Council of Ministers to replace the current system in which member states take it in turns to hold the Presidency for a six month term.
- A 'dual majority' system of QMV under which legislative proposals will need the support of 55 per cent of member states representing 65 per cent of the EU's population. This will end the current system under which states are allocated votes according (roughly) to their population.
- The extension of QMV to 15 more areas of EU activity.
- A clearer definition of the competences of the EU and its member states.

The EU Constitution cannot come into force unless approved by all member states. Fifteen had ratified it by mid-2006, but referendums in France and the Netherlands, two of the EU's founder members, produced 'no' votes in the previous year. Many voters in France opposed economic liberalisation; those in the Netherlands supported it but were unhappy with the Dutch contribution to the EU budget. Economic reform was dividing member states. On one side are states such as the UK, Ireland and Slovakia that are supportive of an 'Anglo-Saxon' model of flexible labour markets, deregulation and competition. On the other are states like France, Germany and Poland which favour the 'European social model' of regulated markets, higher social standards and greater protection for workers.

Many observers pronounced the Constitution dead but EU leaders refused to sign the death certificate, putting it into cold storage instead. Some of the reforms proposed in the Constitution will still be put in place as they require intergovernmental agreement rather than Treaty amendments. An EU Minister for Foreign Affairs, diplomatic service and even changes to voting weights could all come into effect without the Constitution.

The institutions of the European Union

The EU's institutional architecture is unique as it includes intergovernmental bodies in which national governments meet (the Council of Ministers and European Council) and supranational bodies with their own authority (the European Commission, the European Parliament and European Court of Justice). The balance of power between the institutions has changed over time and remains fluid, though national governments tend to be the most powerful actors.

The European Commission

The European Commission is the EU's primary executive arm though it also has legislative functions. It has both a political role, carried out by the College of Commissioners, and a bureaucratic role, carried out by staff working in its Directorates General and Services. But the image of the Commission as a super-bureaucracy is problematic as only 22,000 people work there, fewer than in some British local authorities. It acts in the general interest of the Union and is independent of member states.

The President of the Commission is nominated by national governments but is independent of them. He or she is appointed by a qualified majority vote of states in the European Council. The nominee then seeks the approval of the EP in a majority vote. The President and other Commissioners serve a five-year term. They swear an oath to serve the EU and do not act as national representatives. The President allocates portfolios within the College of Commissioners (although deals are often brokered between governments), can reshuffle posts and may demand the resignation of a Commissioner. The President provides leadership within the organisation but needs the support of key member states if they are to exert influence over the integration process. Delors (1985–94) was the most influential President of recent years, steering the Community towards EMU and political union. Jacques Santer (1994–99), Romano Prodi (1999–2004) and José Manuel Barroso (2004–) have been relatively low key figures, focusing on reforming the Commission's working practices.

Commissioners are nominated by member states though the Commission President is consulted. Former Labour minister Peter Mandelson is the British national on the Barroso Commission. The Commissioners meet collectively in the College of Commissioners to finalise legislative proposals and discuss developments. The EP votes to approve the College as a whole but cannot veto individual Commissioners. Each Commissioner is assigned a policy portfolio. Before 2004, the five largest states (Germany, France, Britain, Italy and Spain) nominated two Commissioners. Now each member state nominates one to give a total of 25. If ratified, the Constitutional Treaty will reduce the size of the College to 18 from 2014. The Commissioners are supported by officials working within 23 Directorates-General responsible for specific policy areas. A network of several hundred committees aid the policy process by bringing in outside experts.

Co-decision: a legislative procedure in which the Council of Ministers and European Parliament share legislative authority.

The Commission has the sole right to initiate draft legislation in most areas of EC activity. When drafting proposals, the Commission often acts on requests from member states. If it gains EP backing on issues decided by **co-decision**, the Commission may be more inclined to launch ambitious initiatives. In the ensuing negotiations between EU institutions, it also acts as a persuader and broker. In the 1980s and early 1990s the Commission acted as a 'motor of integration', using a favourable political climate (e.g. the backing of key member states and the greater role for the Commission necessitated by the SEM) to enhance its position. But declining support for integration and poor management within the Commission have since diminished its authority.

The Commission executes and administers EU legislation. Member states have delegated rule-making powers on technical and administrative matters (e.g. CAP price and supply measures) to it. The Commission acts as a regulatory body in the SEM and competition policy, where it has the power to break-up monopolies. It is also the 'guardian of the Treaties', referring states or companies that infringe EU law to the European Court of Justice. But the Commission's limited resources force it to rely on national bureaucracies to monitor the implementation of EU legislation. Additionally, the Commission oversees EU expenditure and collects revenue but its financial management record has been criticised by the Court of Auditors. Concerns about the fraudulent use of some EU funds prompted the EP to stage a vote of no confidence in the Commission in 1999. Though it survived the vote, the Santer Commission was damaged and the College resigned *en masse* months later. Reform of the Commission's management and administration, including the creation of independent agencies, gathered pace but critics still bemoan its performance. Finally, the Commission represents the EU on the world stage, notably in trade negotiations.

The Council of Ministers

Government ministers from member states take decisions on EU legislation in the Council of Ministers, also known as the Council of the European Union. The Council is the EU's main legislative body though it shares legislative power with the EP in many policy areas and must await legislative proposals from the Commission. It has greatest autonomy on foreign, security and defence policy and is also responsible for coordinating the broad economic policies of member states.

The Council consists of nine sectoral bodies dealing with specific areas of EU activity. The General Affairs and External Relations Council, consisting of foreign ministers, is the most significant as it deals with foreign affairs and sensitive matters. It meets monthly as does the Economic and Financial Affairs Council (Ecofin) made up of national finance ministers. The Agriculture and Fisheries Council handles the largest area of EU expenditure. Preparatory work is mainly carried out by national delegations headed by a Permanent Representative. These delegations meet weekly in the Committee of Permanent Representatives (COREPER). COREPER I handles issues such as the Single European Market, COREPER II deals with sensitive issues such as those coming before the General Affairs Council.

Member states take turns to hold the Presidency of the Council of Ministers for a six-monthly term. This involves chairing meetings and acting as spokesperson for the EU. States holding the Presidency seek to put their stamp on the work of the Council but will face criticism if they pursue their own interests at the expense of consensus. The UK last held the Presidency in 2005. If ratified, the Constitutional Treaty will introduce a new system in which groups of three states share the Presidency for 18-month terms.

Intensive negotiations occur within the Council as member states try to broker agreements while defending their national interests. Some three-quarters of issues are settled in working groups at the foot of the Council hierarchy, others in COREPER. For the 15 per cent or so of issues that reach the ministerial councils, decisions are reached under **unanimity** or Qualified Majority Voting according to the policy area in question. In the former, a proposal fails if a single member state deploys its veto (abstention is not counted as a veto). Unanimity now applies only to major or sensitive policies.

Unanimity: a system of voting in which any member state can veto a proposal.

QMV means that the Council should not be regarded as a purely intergovernmental body. It now applies to most areas of EC activity. Member states are allocated a number of votes according to their population (see Case study 12.1). Prior to eastward enlargement a qualified majority was 62 out of 87 votes (i.e. 71 per cent), 26 votes constituting a blocking minority. The Nice Treaty weighting of votes came into force in 2004. Proposals require:

- A 'double majority', that is support from a majority (or sometimes two-thirds) of member states; plus
- A qualified majority of 232 votes out of 321 (i.e. 72.3 per cent).

Case study: 12.1

Qualified majority voting

The weighting of qualified majority voting (QMV) votes in the Council of Ministers is determined according to the population of the member states. The allocation is decided by political bargaining rather than mathematics with those resulting from the Nice Treaty proving particularly contentious. As the table below shows, there were clear winners and losers. Though comfortably the EU's largest state, Germany has the same number of votes as the three other 'large states'. Spain and Poland held out for a settlement that gave them a disproportionately large share of votes. The Union's 'micro-states' have far more votes than a strict population-based formula would give them.

Member state	QMV votes	Population (millions)	Population per votes (millions)
Germany	29	82.53	2.85
France	29	59.90	2.07
United Kingdom	29	59.65	2.06
Italy	29	57.89	2.00
Spain	27	42.35	1.57
Poland	27	38.19	1.41
Netherlands	13	16.26	1.25
Greece	12	11.04	0.92
Portugal	12	10.47	0.87
Belgium	12	10.40	0.87
Czech Republic	12	10.21	0.85
Hungary	12	10.12	0.84
Sweden	10	8.98	0.90
Austria	10	8.11	0.81
Denmark	7	5.40	0.76
Slovakia	7	5.38	0.77
Finland	7	5.22	0.75
Ireland	7	4.03	0.58
Lithuania	7	3.45	0.49
Latvia	4	2.32	0.58
Slovenia	4	2.00	0.50
Estonia	4	1.35	0.38
Cyprus	4	0.73	0.18
Luxembourg	4	0.45	0.11
Malta	3	0.40	0.13
TOTAL	**321**	**456.81**	–
States joining in 2007			
Romania	14	21.71	1.55
Bulgaria	10	7.80	0.78
TOTAL in 2007	**345**	**486.32**	–

Source: population figures from *Eurostat Yearbook 2004* at http://epp.eurostat.cec.eu.int/

Concerns among large states that their importance would not be reflected by the above allocation were partially addressed by the Nice Treaty. A qualified majority is achieved if a minimum of 232 votes is cast in favour *and* a majority of member states approve the measure. In addition, a member state may ask for confirmation that the votes in favour represent at least 62 per cent of the total population of the EU. If this is not to the case, the decision will not be adopted.

- A Council member may additionally request that the qualified majority represents at least 62 per cent of the EU population.

The Constitutional Treaty proposed further changes from 2009, replacing weighted votes with a 'double majority' system that concentrates on population. A qualified majority would be defined as at least 55 per cent of member states, comprising at least 15 in total and representing at least 65 per cent of the EU population. A blocking minority would have to include at least four states.

QMV is an efficient way of reaching decisions in a 25-member Union. But it poses problems if member states regularly find their interests frustrated, particularly if these are keenly felt or reflect the democratically-expressed wishes of their citizens. The EU prefers to avoid such problems so strives for consensus where possible; relatively few decisions have to be taken by a formal vote. Voting records are not made public.

The European Council

The European Council is the meeting place of the heads of government (and in the case of France and Finland, heads of state) and foreign ministers of EU member states. The Commission President and Vice-Presidents also attend. It meets at least twice per year, in June and December, with additional sessions on particular issues (e.g. employment) often held. Meetings are chaired by the member state holding the Presidency of the Council of Ministers. If the Constitutional Treaty comes into force, an individual will be chosen by the European Council to serve a two-and-a-half year term as President.

Since its inception in 1974, the European Council has strengthened the role of member states in major decisions and curtailed the Commission's agenda-setting ability. The European Council is a political rather than legislative body. Though

EU leaders gather at the Hampton Court summit during the 2005 UK Presidency (© AFP/Getty Images)

it does not make legislation, except in special circumstances, it has become the EU's main strategic body. Summit meetings are major events in the EU calendar, discussing high profile issues and determining the Union's direction. The European Council also acts as a 'court of appeal' on unresolved issues, launches initiatives and stages final negotiations on Treaty change. It has special responsibility for decision-making on foreign policy and the economic situation in the EU.

The European Parliament

The European Parliament is the EU's only directly-elected institution. It is based in three locations: Strasbourg (where most plenary sessions are held), Brussels (where committee meetings are held) and Luxembourg (where the Secretariat is based). It meets in monthly plenary sessions, except in August, but much of its work is done in twenty standing committees. There are 732 members (MEPs) with seats allocated to member states in very approximate relation to their population.

Direct elections to the EP have been held at fixed five-year intervals since 1979. All member states use some form of proportional representation. Citizens vote for candidates from national parties though many stand on platform agreed by like-minded parties across the Union. MEPs sit in political groups based on ideology rather than nationality. The European People's Party and European Democrats (EPP–ED), a centre-right grouping, replaced the Party of European Socialists (PES) as the largest group in 1999. British Labour MEPs sit in the latter; Conservative MEPs are allied to the former although David Cameron promised to take them out of the EPP–ED because of its federalist ethos.

The EP's powers have expanded significantly since the SEA. It shares legislative power with the Council of Ministers, though it cannot initiate legislation. The EP's influence varies according to the legislative process being used. There are three legislative routes:

- *The assent procedure*. This is used in limited circumstances, for example to approve the accession of new member states, and requires that the EP hold a simple majority vote.
- *The consultation procedure*. Here, the EP is asked for its opinion on a legislative proposal, but the Council and Commission are not obliged to take account of it.
- *The co-decision procedure*. This gives the EP greater influence as it can amend and block proposed legislation. Co-decision requires three readings of legislation in the EP, allows the EP to negotiate amendments with the Council in a conciliation committee, and gives it an absolute veto. This makes it more difficult for the Council to ignore the EP in inter-institutional negotiations.

The EP shares budgetary authority with the Council. It can exert influence over EU spending by requesting amendments to the draft EU budget and can (as in 1998) refuse to discharge the final budget. The Parliament also oversees Commission and Council activities by questioning their members and monitoring their actions. As we have seen, the EP votes to approve the Commission President and the College of Commissioners as a whole after staging public hearings. Unease among MEPs about the conservative views of Rocco Buttiglione, the nominee for Commissioner for justice and security, saw the EP flex its muscles in 2004. President-elect Barroso backed down, Buttiglione withdrew his nomination and Latvia also changed its nominee before the College was approved. The EP can also censure and dismiss the entire Commission. EP action on financial mismanagement triggered the resignation of the Santer Commission in 1999.

Supporters of the EP regard the increase in its legislative and scrutiny powers as the optimum means of addressing the EU's **democratic deficit**. This refers to the transfer of policy competences from national governments, accountable to national legislatures and electorates, to the EU in which the main executive body (the Commission) is not directly elected and decision-making in the Council is not open to public scrutiny. However, critics note that the EP enjoys neither the authority nor the legitimacy of national parliaments. Turnout in EP elections is low (averaging 45.7 per cent in 2004) and few citizens are aware of its role.

Democratic deficit: an erosion of democratic accountability that occurs when decision-making authority is transferred from institutions that are directly accountable to elected bodies to ones that are not.

The European Court of Justice

The European Court of Justice (ECJ), located in Luxembourg, is the EU's judicial body. It consists of 25 judges, one from each member state. Complex cases may be handled by eleven or more judges, but many are considered by just three to five. The ECJ upholds Community law, ensuring that it is applied fully and uniformly. It decides cases involving member states, EU institutions, businesses and individuals. The Court also hears requests from national courts for preliminary ruling on matters of Community law. ECJ decisions have had an important impact on the integration process, extending the EU's policy competences and the powers of its supranational institutions. Another body, the Court of First Instance was set up in 1989 to take on some of the ECJ's caseload.

Interpreting the European Union

The EU has some of the characteristics of an international organisation and some of a federal state, but fits the classic definition of neither. In international organisations (e.g. the United Nations) and regional trade bodies (e.g. the North American Free Trade Area), nation states cooperate voluntarily in areas of mutual concern but retain extensive veto rights. The EU, however, has supranational elements such as its own budget, institutions with independent authority, such as the Commission and a body of law that has primacy over national law.

In federal states, the constitution divides power between two autonomous tiers of government, the federal (i.e. national) government and state (i.e. subnational) governments. Some features of the EU suggest a federal system, even a nascent federal state. The EU has some elements comparable to a federal system. The Treaties set out the powers held by different levels of government, giving the EU sole decision-making competence in some policy areas and shared power in others. The EU has its own system of law and budget. EU citizens have rights under the Charter of Fundamental Rights and are directly represented in the EP. But the powers of the Commission and EP are not equivalent to those of the executive and legislature of a sovereign state. Member states are represented in the European Council and

Council of Ministers where inter-state bargaining determines the direction taken by the EU. National governments retain substantial decision-making authority on taxation, health, education and foreign policy. Although European integration has brought about change in the political systems of member states, they retain many of their distinctive features. Finally, citizens still identify primarily with their nation state rather than the EU.

Integration theory

Neo-functionalism: a theory of integration that highlights the role played by supranational bodies and interest groups.

Inter-governmentalism: a theory of integration that focuses on the dominant role played by national governments.

Two main theories explaining European integration have emerged in the political science literature, **neo-functionalism** and **intergovernmentalism**. Neo-functionalism was prevalent in the 1950s and 1960s. It held that interest groups and supra-national bodies were the key actors in the integration process. Integration is dynamic: cooperation in one area (e.g. coal and steel) produces 'spillover' into other fields (e.g. trade). Neo-functionalists assumed that political and economic elites would then transfer their loyalties to supranational bodies. The theory fell out of favour in the 1970s when national governments reasserted their authority, but was revived by scholars arguing that the Commission and business interests were responsible for pushing for the Single European Market and EMU.

Intergovernmentalism affords leading actor status to nation states: they determine the development of the EU by agreeing to cooperate in areas of mutual benefit but defend their sovereignty in other areas. This perspective argues that EMU came on the EC agenda because key member states saw it as being in their national interest, its precise make-up being decided through inter-state bargaining. Liberal intergovernmentalism notes that prior to such negotiations, governments form their policy preferences in response to pressures from groups and institutions in the national arena. Critics argue that intergovernmentalism downplays the influence of supranational bodies and is more suitable in explaining 'history-making decisions' than routine policy formation.

Multi-level governance: an approach that highlights the roles played by supranational, national and subnational institutions in decision-making.

Academics were tiring of debates between neo-functionalists and intergovernmentalists by the 1990s and looked instead to frameworks that reflected the diversity and complexity of EU decision-making. **Multi-level governance** is one such approach. It recognises that a range of actors are involved in EU decision-making, their relative importance varying according to the policy areas concerned. National governments remain the most important players for they have authority in major policy areas and are the main players in crucial decisions such as Treaty change or defence. But they do not monopolise decision-making. Supranational bodies like the Commission have their own authority and are the most important actors in technical policy areas such as the SEM. Subnational governments also play a role in decision-making, particularly in federal states such as Germany.

Britain and the European Union

The UK rejected invitations to become a founder member of both the ECSC and EEC because first Clement Attlee's Labour government then Anthony Eden's Conservative administration feared the loss of sovereignty it would entail. Policy-makers of the time saw Britain operating in 'three circles', the Commonwealth, the 'special relationship' with the USA and intergovernmental cooperation in Europe. They supported free trade rather than a customs union with Britain forming the European Free Trade Association (EFTA) in 1960. Pro-European commentators argued that Britain 'missed the bus', losing out on a chance to shape the EEC from within. But it would be dangerous to assume that had it joined at the outset, Britain could have imposed its own agenda on the 'Six'.

Harold Macmillan's Conservative government applied for EEC membership in 1961. The change in policy was a result of a number of factors. The Commonwealth was of declining significance for Britain: trade with Commonwealth states had fallen and Britain's leadership within the organisation was being challenged. This mirrored the UK's waning influence in world affairs, as witnessed by the 1956 Suez debacle when American pressure curtailed British military action in Egypt. The EEC was developing successfully by the early 1960s, raising fears that Britain would be left

TIMELINE 12.1

The UK and European integration

1950	Attlee government rejects invitation to participate in ECSC
1955	British delegate withdraws from the Spaak Committee discussions on the creation of the EEC
1957	Treaty of Rome establishes the EEC
1960	Britain and six other states form EFTA
1961	Macmillan government applies for EEC membership
1963	De Gaulle vetoes British membership application
1967	Wilson government launches 2nd membership application; it is again vetoed by de Gaulle
1970	EEC begins membership talks with Britain (now led by Heath government)
1971	EEC membership negotiations concluded and ratified by Parliament
1973	Britain joins the EEC
1975	67 per cent 'yes' vote in referendum on renegotiated membership terms
1984	Fontainebleau summit settles the British budgetary question
1985	Thatcher government agrees to the Single European Act
1989	Thatcher's 'Bruges speech' rejects EMU and political union
1990	Britain joins the ERM
1991	Major government agrees to the Maastricht Treaty; Britain has 'opt-out' on EMU
1992	Britain leaves the ERM
1993	Maastricht Treaty ratified despite Eurosceptic rebellions in House of Commons
1997	Blair government agrees to Amsterdam Treaty but rules out joining euro until five economic tests are met
2000	Blair government agrees to Treaty of Nice
2003	Blair government announces that five economic tests for euro entry have not been met
2004	Blair government agrees to EU Constitutional Treaty

behind. Macmillan saw EEC membership as essential to Britain's modernisation. Crucially, he also came under pressure from the Kennedy administration which made it clear that Britain would only remain America's main ally in Europe if it entered the Community.

The 1961 membership application is sometimes presented as a *volte face* in British policy. But in reality the government hoped to secure some of its traditional objectives within the EEC. Britain did not abandon its opposition to supranationalism, but hoped to more effectively promote its vision of an intergovernmental EEC and defend its sovereignty from within the EEC. The US would remain the major strategic ally and special arrangements for Commonwealth trade were negotiated. However, de Gaulle vetoed the application in 1963 citing Britain's Atlantic rather than European outlook. Labour Prime Minister Harold Wilson reapplied in 1967 for similar reasons and met the same fate.

Membership negotiations proved successful under Edward Heath's Conservative government in 1970–71, by which time de Gaulle had left office. Heath was the most pro-European of British Prime Ministers and had been chief negotiator at the time of the 1961 application. Now the UK secured a number of concessions but on joining the EEC in 1973 soon gained a reputation as an 'awkward partner'. Wilson extracted further concessions in 1974–75, but discontent about the size of the UK contribution to the EEC budget remained. He called a referendum on continued membership in 1975, largely to appease a divided Cabinet, which produced a decisive 'yes' vote.

Thatcher and Major

Margaret Thatcher's Conservative government continued efforts to reduce Britain's budget contributions and reform the CAP, her bruising campaign eventually bearing fruit at the 1984 Fontainebleau summit. Attention was by then turning to the SEM with Britain a leading proponent as the removal of barriers to free trade dovetailed with the Thatcherite commitment to the free market. Thatcher duly signed the SEA despite her hostility to the institutional reforms it entailed. By the late 1980s Thatcher was a staunch opponent of further integration, opposing the Social Charter and EMU which she viewed as anathema to the free market and national sovereignty. Thatcher's uncompromising attitude, expressed memorably in a 1988 speech in Bruges which rallied Conservative Eurosceptics, provoked divisions within her Cabinet that contributed to her own downfall in 1990.

John Major had been instrumental in taking Britain into the ERM in the final weeks of Thatcher's premiership. On becoming Prime Minister, he promised a more constructive approach in the EC but was determined to preserve sovereignty in key areas and resist pressure to join a single currency. He presented the Maastricht Treaty as a good deal for Britain: the UK had an EMU opt-out, had not signed up to the Social Agreement and had ensured intergovernmental cooperation on foreign policy and immigration. Sterling's forced exit from the ERM on 'Black Wednesday' in 1992 undermined Major's position and fuelled Eurosceptic opposition to EMU (see Case study 12.2). But Major maintained his non-committal 'wait and see' policy believing that it was in Britain's interest to decide on EMU entry only when the economic situation at the launch of Stage III was clear.

'Yes but no': Mrs Thatcher began her spell as Conservative leader (1975–90) as a pro-european, but ended it as a Eurosceptic (© Mirrorpix)

Major found it increasingly difficult to rally his party behind an agreed position on Europe and influence the direction of European integration at a time when Britain's minimalist approach left it in a minority in the EU. British policy became more Eurosceptic in tone and substance. Major threatened to veto institutional reform and pursued a policy of non-cooperation (blocking proposed legislation) after the EU banned British beef exports during the BSE crisis. His vision of a flexible Europe in which states could opt-out of new areas of EU activity won little support.

The Blair governments

New Labour came to power in 1997 promising to play a positive, leading role in the EU. Within weeks, the Blair government had agreed the Amsterdam Treaty. On institutional reform, Blair accepted greater use of QMV in both the Amsterdam and Nice Treaties but continued to defend unanimity on issues of 'vital national

Case study: | 12.2

'Black Wednesday' 1992

The 16th September 1992 ('Black Wednesday') was one of the dramatic and significant days in contemporary British politics. It was the day on which sterling was forced out of the Exchange Rate Mechanism. For months, sterling had been close to the bottom of the permitted bands of fluctuation. Media reports on the morning of 16 September that Germany wanted sterling to be devalued forced its value down, forcing the Major government to intervene by buying Sterling on the foreign exchange markets (at a cost of £3.7 billion) and twice raise interest rates (from 10 per cent to 12 per cent and then 15 per cent). The measures were unsuccessful and the government was forced to suspend sterling's membership of the ERM. It would not rejoin.

The events had long-term repercussions. The Conservative Party's reputation for economic competence was shattered and its opinion poll ratings plummeted, barely recovering since. Britain's position in the EU was also affected: relations with Germany were damaged and Eurosceptic opposition to the single currency was reinforced. Treasury papers show that soon after Black Wednesday civil servants judged the 1990 decision to join the ERM to have been a mistaken one made for political reasons without due consideration to the impact of German unification, moves towards EMU and the state of the British economy. But such verdicts were made with the benefit of hindsight – in 1990, the main parties, financial institutions, businesses and trade unions supported ERM entry. John Major and Norman Lamont recognised subsequently the political damage and short-term economic pain that ERM membership caused, but argued that it was the key factor in squeezing inflation out of the British economy.

interest' such as taxation, Treaty change and defence. In negotiations on the EU Constitution, Britain proposed a greater role for the European Council and national parliaments. During the 2005 UK Presidency of the EU, Blair accepted a reduction in the size of the British budget rebate in return for a future review of EU spending (see Controversy 12.2).

The government signed up to the Social Agreement (now properly called the Social Chapter) at Amsterdam but has opposed the further extension of EU competence in social policy. Britain was a main architect of an EU employment strategy that balanced labour market flexibility with effective social protection, echoing Blair's domestic 'third way'. But Blair has been frustrated by the slow pace of economic and welfare reform in other member states. He supported the 'Lisbon Agenda' measures which aimed to make the EU the most competitive and 'knowledge-based' economy in the world by 2010. But at the half-way point of this ten-year plan, economic growth in the euro zone was sluggish, unemployment high and the targets of 20 million extra jobs and annual economic growth of 3 per cent appeared over-ambitious.

At Amsterdam, the government maintained Britain's traditional opposition to supranational authority in foreign and defence policy. But Europe's relative inaction during the conflict in Kosovo convinced Blair that the EU must develop a more effective defence and security role. The 1998 Anglo-French St Malo initiative signalled Britain's new willingness to support a greater EU defence role. Britain became an agenda setter, supporting the Nice Treaty provision for a European

Controversy: 12.2

The UK and the EU budget

During its Presidency of the EU in 2005, the UK came under intense pressure to give up its budget rebate during negotiations on the EU budget for 2007–13. The rebate was worth 66 per cent of the UK's net contribution to the EU or some £3.6 billion per annum, a figure which would increase to £5 billion as the overall EU budget grew. It had been secured by Margaret Thatcher in 1984 at a time when the UK was the third poorest member of the EEC but one of the biggest net contributors to its budget. She argued that the UK deserved special treatment as it is not a beneficiary of payments made under the CAP.

By 2005 the UK was the second highest contributor to the EU budget but also one of the wealthiest member states. If payments are measured against national wealth, the UK was the fourth largest net contributor behind the Netherlands, Sweden and Germany. If the rebate remained untouched, the European Commission calculated that the UK would become only the ninth largest contributor. The proportion of the EU budget spent on agriculture had, meanwhile, fallen from 70 per cent to 40 per cent since 1984.

A deal was reached at the eleventh hour at a European Council meeting in Brussels in December 2005. The overall EU budget for 2007–13 will rise to 862 billion euros (£592 billion) – only 1.045 per cent of the EU's combined gross national income. The UK gave up 20 per cent of its rebate, a total of 10.5 billion euros (£7 billion) over the seven-year period, but the rebate would nonetheless rise to £4.3 billion per annum. Blair claimed the deal meant that the UK would pay its fair share towards the cost of enlargement while maintaining a sizeable rebate. He also secured agreement that the European Commission would hold a full review of its spending commitments in 2008. But critics in the UK warned that the review might not produce the reforms Blair hoped for as member states will be able to veto proposed changes, allowing France to block CAP reform. If he had not given ground, Blair risked lasting damage to British relations with key allies.

Security and Defence Policy. This allowed the EU to deploy rapid reaction forces in conflict prevention and crisis management situations where NATO chose not to act. But divisions between member states during the build-up to the US-led invasion of Iraq in 2003 damaged Britain's standing and hit hopes that the EU could develop a common policy.

In October 1997 Chancellor Gordon Brown announced that Britain would not join the single currency during Labour's first term in office. But the government supported British membership of the euro zone if the economic conditions were right (see Controversy 12.3). Labour had no constitutional objection to entry though it would hold a referendum to seek popular approval for any Cabinet decision to join. Brown set five 'economic tests' against which entry would be judged:

- Sustainable convergence between the British economy and those of the euro zone.
- Sufficient economic flexibility.
- The impact on investment in the UK.

Controversy: 12.3

The UK and the euro

Supporters of EMU claim that British entry would bring a number of benefits including an end to exchange rate uncertainty and the elimination of transaction costs for travellers and companies trading within the EU. The UK could expect to enjoy the low inflation and low interest rates that the European Central Bank has helped bring about in the euro zone. Staying out of the euro is not cost-free. The EU accounts for the majority of British imports and exports. Non-participation might have an adverse effect on inward investment and reduce Britain's influence in the EU.

Opponents note the loss of monetary sovereignty that EMU membership would entail – decisions on interest rate levels would be taken by the independent ECB in the light of the needs of the euro zone as a whole, not just the UK. Should the UK experience localised economic difficulties, the government would have few economic options available to it so downturns might be more severe. The Stability and Growth Pact also restricts levels of public spending. Eurosceptics argue that the UK economy is robust enough to flourish outside the euro and Britain has strong trading relations with non-EU countries (notably the USA).

In its 2003 report on the five economic tests, the Treasury concluded that the UK economy had not sufficiently converged with those of the euro zone. The comparatively high level of home ownership in the UK means that high interest rates in the euro zone could destabilise the British housing market. Nor was the UK economy judged flexible enough to withstand economic problems in the euro zone. The employment and foreign investment tests were not met though they would be once greater convergence had been achieved. The financial services test was met with the City of London prospering outside the euro zone. Though the Treasury's verdict was negative, the reports argued that progress was being made and that euro entry under the right conditions would be beneficial. But Gordon Brown appears unwilling to gamble on euro entry when Britain is enjoying a period of low inflation and economic stability.

- The impact on financial services.
- The impact on employment.

Detailed targets were not specified, allowing the government also to take account of the bigger political picture. Should the tests be met and a referendum 'yes' vote secured, the changeover to the euro could be achieved within two years. A decision on whether the economic tests had been met was not taken until June 2003 when Brown announced that the Cabinet had agreed that Britain was not yet ready to adopt the euro. The Treasury released eighteen studies concluding that only one of the five economic tests (financial services) had formally been met. During the 2005 election campaign Blair and Brown suggested that euro entry in Labour's third term was unlikely.

Despite the appearance of rational decision-making, policy on EMU has been shaped primarily by political considerations and by the strained relationship between Blair and Brown. Brown has been cautious about EMU, wary of the impact membership would have on a British economy enjoying low inflation and increased public spending. Blair is instinctively more positive, viewing EMU entry as essential to full British engagement in the Union.

An 'awkward partner'

In a key study of British policy in the EU, Stephen George described Britain as *An Awkward Partner* (Oxford University Press, 3rd edition, 1998). George is not claiming that Britain is the only country to fight for its national interest, but notes that it is less enthusiastic about integration than most member states and more likely to hold a minority position. Successive British governments have been wary of or hostile to proposals for further integration. Rather than having a long-term vision they have often acted pragmatically, reacting to proposals rather than setting the agenda. Britain prefers intergovernmental cooperation to supranational authority, the SEM to EMU and incremental reform of EU procedures to political union.

British influence has been less pronounced than that of other large member states, notably France and Germany. The Thatcher and Major governments did not set the agenda on EMU but reacted to proposals from other states by trying to slow the pace of integration or minimise its impact. This is not to say that Britain is unimportant in big EU decisions. The UK was an influential supporter of the SEM though it proposed a minimalist approach to institutional reform. The Blair government has also been an influential player in EU defence, immigration and social policy. But the UK has not forged durable alliances with like-minded states across a range of issues, developing instead a series of one-off agreements with member states on single issues. The Blair governments established bilateral links as a basis for joint initiatives, for example with France on defence policy, Germany on social policy and Italy on tackling illegal immigration.

A series of domestic factors explain why Britain has been an 'awkward partner'. The first concerns the historical development of the UK. As we will see below, key principles of the British constitution such as parliamentary sovereignty are of enduring significance and are often seen as being challenged by European integration. Other European states experienced major upheavals in the twentieth century; for them, EU membership was part of their modernisation and was not perceived as a threat to national identity. Political economy is also important. British elites did not want to be drawn into exclusively regional relationships, looking instead to strategic relationships with the Commonwealth and the United States. They have rarely departed from a global economic outlook, favouring free trade and open markets, for much of the last two hundred years.

The remainder of this chapter will explore four further factors in more detail:

1. The debate about British sovereignty.
2. The impact of the EU on the British state.
3. Disputes between and within the main political parties.
4. The relatively low levels of public support for European integration.

Sovereignty

Sovereignty:
ultimate decision-making authority.

The **sovereignty** implications of European integration feature prominently in British debates, but sovereignty is a contested concept. It has an internal and external dimension. Within the UK, the doctrine of parliamentary sovereignty, states that Westminster has final legal authority. National sovereignty refers to the right of

Sovereignty

An institution is generally understood to be sovereign if it has final legislative authority and can act without undue external constraint. There are three interlinked facets of sovereignty: the state dimension, the constitutional dimension and the popular dimension. Each figures in British debates about the EU and European integration has impacted upon all three.

The state dimension recognises that sovereignty is the bedrock of the modern nation state and that sovereignty has both an internal and external dimension. Sovereignty is territorially-bounded (i.e. the sovereign has supreme authority within defined physical borders) and concerns the core functions of the modern state (economic management, defence, law and order, etc.). It is also a guiding principle of the international system: states are the main actors in international affairs and engage in cooperation through treaties. But international organisations recognise that the state has exclusive rights of jurisdiction over its own citizens within its territory.

The constitutional dimension concerns the location of sovereign authority within the state. The supremacy of parliament is a cornerstone of the British constitution, establishing that parliament has the right to legislate on any subject of its choosing, that legislation made by parliament cannot be overturned by any higher authority and that no parliament can bind its successors. Finally, the popular dimension concerns the relationship between state and society, claiming that the sovereign authority derives its legitimacy from the consent of the political community.

national governments to make laws that apply within their territory free from interference from other states. A distinction between *de jure* and *de facto* sovereignty is also helpful. The *de jure* account links sovereignty with authority – the right to make law – whereas the *de facto* account couples it with power and autonomy – the ability to act without undue interference.

Eurosceptics often define sovereignty in zero-sum terms, as ultimate decision-making authority: a state either has absolute authority or it does not, there can be no middle ground. Sovereignty may be voluntarily delegated when a state signs an international treaty (e.g. to join NATO) or creates a new legislature (e.g. the Scottish Parliament) within its boundaries. But European integration is qualitatively different because, Eurosceptics argue, the EU's supranational institutions have authority independent of the member states, whose laws and interests they can override.

Sovereignty is not just a legal concept for Eurosceptics as they believe that European integration has had a detrimental impact on British democracy and nationhood. Critics argue that the bond between political elites and the people has been weakened as electors are unable to use the ballot box to remove from office decision-makers in Brussels. Eurosceptics also claim that legitimate authority is vested in the nation state as people identify with national institutions not the EU, particularly in the UK where parliament is an important symbol of Britishness. They differ on how sovereignty might be restored. The Conservative Party favours opt-outs from policies it opposes and a renegotiation of the treaties to repatriate some competences to national governments and weaken the EU's supranational elements. The United Kingdom Independence Party (UKIP) calls for the UK to withdraw from the EU. It believes that the EU cannot be reformed from within to meet British interests and that only by leaving can the UK governments act freely.

Pro-Europeans define sovereignty in terms of effective influence and a practical capacity to act. Britain has 'pooled' or shared sovereignty with other EU member states. EU membership has, they argue, enhanced sovereignty by enabling the UK to achieve policy objectives such as the SEM that it could not have brought about independently. As a member of a strong EU, Britain also has greater influence in world affairs. This perspective rejects a zero-sum definition of sovereignty as supreme authority. In an interdependent world, nation states are 'porous', their autonomy constrained by developments that do not respect national boundaries such as economic globalisation, migration and environmental degradation. Even if Britain were to leave the EU, it could not regain full, unfettered control over all aspects of public policy.

The EU and British sovereignty

EU law has primacy over domestic law: in cases of conflict, domestic law must be amended so that it complies with EU legislation. The European Communities Act 1972 gave future Community law legal force in the UK and denied effectiveness to national legislation which conflicts with it. This was illustrated in the 1990 *Factortame* case. The 1988 Merchant Shipping Act prevented non-British citizens from registering fishing boats as British in order to qualify for the UK's quota under the Common Fisheries Policy. But the House of Lords, following a ruling from the ECJ, ruled that the Act was incompatible with Community law and should be 'disapplied'. Compensation was later paid to those fishermen affected by the 1988 Act.

The supremacy of Community law would appear to undermine parliamentary sovereignty as it implies that Parliament cannot legislate on any subject of its choosing and legislation made by parliament can be overturned by another authority. But parliamentary sovereignty is not rendered meaningless because parliament retains ultimate legislative authority. It retains the right to withdraw from the EU by repealing the 1972 European Communities Act, although the UK would have to enter difficult negotiations with other member states to finalise the terms of withdrawal.

EU membership has impinged on sovereignty in other ways. Member states do not have the right of veto in those policy areas where QMV applies. One safeguard, the Luxembourg Compromise, has fallen into disuse. The extension of EU competences has impacted upon the capacity of states to pursue independent policies. Parliament and the electorate have little opportunity to hold EU decision-makers accountable.

British governments have often spoken of defending national sovereignty but, in practice, have been willing to cede authority to achieve their key objectives. They have thus treated sovereignty as executive autonomy (the capacity of governments to achieve policy objectives) which might be enhanced in the EU.

Analysis: **12.3**

Europeanisation

The term Europeanisation is used by political scientists examining the impact of EU membership on the policies and institutions of its member states. It is generally held to refer to the adaptation of politics in the domestic arena in ways that reflect the policies and procedures of the EU. But Europeanisation is a complex process that takes a variety of forms. 'Top-down' Europeanisation occurs when EU legislation brings about enforced change in national policy. This is most apparent in areas where the EU has extensive policy competences, though governments have some autonomy in deciding how EU directives should be transposed into national law. The various opt-outs and opt-ins negotiated by British governments have also placed limits on 'top-down' Europeanisation in the UK.

But Europeanisation can also take the form of an interaction between states and the EU as national governments export or 'upload' their policy preferences to the Union. The Thatcher governments were able to export existing British deregulatory practices to other member states through the EU's Single European Market project, to the benefit of UK companies. The Blair governments have also sought to export their 'third way' social policy agenda through the Union's Lisbon process.

The EU and the UK polity

Europeanisation:
the impact of
EU policies and
procedures on
government and
politics in EU
member states.

Membership of the EU has brought about changes in British policies and institutions, though this **Europeanisation** of the UK polity has not been uniform or as dramatic as the term suggests. The impact of European integration on UK policy varies from sector to sector according to the extent of EU competence and the distinctiveness of the British approach. In areas such as trade and agriculture where the EU has exclusive competence, British policy has been extensively Europeanised. Since the SEM much of the legislation on the standards of goods and services emanates from Brussels. Government departments and local authorities implement these laws while the British courts enforce them by hearing cases under EU law.

Although procedures have been adapted, EU membership has not brought about a major reorganisation of central government. The 'Whitehall ethos' of centralised decision-making remains largely intact; emphasis is placed on the effective coordination of policy. The main departments involved in developing British policy in the EU are the Prime Minister, the Cabinet Office and the Foreign Office. The Prime Minister shapes the key objectives of British policy and attends European Council meetings. In this respect, membership has strengthened the position of the Prime Minister. But Cabinet divisions on European policy undermined Thatcher and Major's position, while Blair ceded significant responsibility for policy on the euro to the Treasury.

The European Secretariat, based in the Cabinet Office, coordinates policy and ensures that government departments fall in line with the agreed negotiating position. The Secretariat has been more closely integrated into the policy-making machinery at 10 Downing Street under Blair, particularly with the appointment of Sir Stephen Wall as its head and the Prime Minister's Adviser on Europe. A ministerial standing committee on European Policy chaired by the Foreign Secretary develops Britain's policy position in the EU. A Cabinet committee on European Strategy was created in June 2003 to formulate the government's position on the Constitutional Treaty, EMU entry and improve policy presentation.

The Foreign and Commonwealth Office (FCO) takes the lead diplomatic role in negotiations in the EU. The Foreign Secretary attends European Council meetings and key meetings of the Council of Ministers, as well as taking charge of many ministerial discussions. The FCO plays a strategic role in forging alliances in the EU and a coordinating role in instructing the UK Representation (UKRep). UKRep consists of staff seconded from government departments to assist in EU negotiations and UK policy formulation. Its head, the Permanent Representative, holds regular meetings with FCO officials and the head of the European Secretariat to clarify the British position.

The Treasury keeps a tight rein on EU-related expenditure through the EUROPES system which prevents government departments from bypassing domestic spending constraints by using EU funds. This tough approach has periodically caused conflict between the Treasury and other bodies, for example in a dispute over the payment of EU regional funding that forced the resignation of Welsh First Minister Alun Michael in 2000. The Treasury has also staked a lead role in determining policy on EMU, setting the five economic tests and assessing whether they have been met. Most government departments have units responsible for EU matters. EU legislation forms a large part of the workload of the Department of Trade and Industry and the Department for the Environment, Food and Rural Affairs. But the extension of EU competences means that departments such as the Home Office are also involved in EU policy-making. Interest groups have responded by switching some of their lobbying efforts to Brussels.

Though Whitehall has sought to maintain centralised policy-making, European integration has been a factor in the development of multi-level governance in the UK. Local authorities and the devolved administrations are responsible for implementing EU legislation in their respective areas of competence. But this is not simply a top-down relationship. Pressure from local and regional elites for the UK to gain maximum benefit from Structural Funds and promote their interests more effectively within the EU fuelled demands for regionalism in the 1980s and 1990s. The Major government responded by creating Government Offices for the Regions in England; Labour cautiously embraced English regionalism. Poorer regions of the UK such as Northern Ireland, Cornwall and Merseyside received EC regional funds in this period. The European Commission actively encouraged the participation of local and regional actors in decision-making and in institutions such as the Committee of the Regions. Many local authorities and regions have offices in Brussels to lobby on their behalf and report on policy developments. Yet central government retains a gatekeeper role in the relationship between English regional and local government and the EU by ensuring that it controls policy-making and expenditure.

Devolution brought a closer fit between the UK state and the EU's multi-level system. It also forced a reworking of the centralised process by which Britain's EU policy is settled. The EU has competence in many policy fields devolved to the Scottish Parliament, Welsh Assembly and Northern Ireland Assembly, but responsibility for Britain's relations with the EU is 'reserved' to Westminster. The devolved administrations are consulted on British policy and have had some input (e.g. on environmental policy) but once the UK government's single negotiating line has been settled, they are bound by it. The arrangements have operated smoothly to date, largely because Labour is in power in London, Edinburgh and Cardiff. But tensions between different tiers of government on EU matters occur frequently in states such as Germany and may arise in future in the UK on issues such as fishing quotas and regional funding.

Finally, Parliament debates major developments in the EU but finds it difficult to maintain effective scrutiny of the huge volume of EU legislative and policy proposals (over 1000 a year). The latter task falls to the House of Commons European Legislation Committee and three European Standing Committees. Ministers should not normally agree to EU legislation until Parliament has had a chance to scrutinise the proposals.

Political parties and Europe

Britain's relationship with the EU has been an issue that the main political parties have found difficult to manage. The UK has not developed the strong elite consensus on the benefits of European integration apparent in most other member states. Labour and the Conservatives have instead often taken contrary positions, one adopting a sceptical position critical of the pro-European outlook of the other. But the issue of Europe has also caused divisions within the two main parties when integration is viewed as challenging their ideology or self-image. These divisions have proved difficult for their leaders to contain or manage. Nor have they found Europe an issue that can be exploited easily for electoral purposes.

British politics is adversarial in character. The simple plurality electoral system and two-party dominance of the House of Commons encourages parties to take opposing positions on key issues. Differences of principle have been evident on Europe, notably in the early 1980s. The gap between Labour and Conservative positions has widened since 1997. Conservative policy has become more Eurosceptic while Labour has adopted more integrationist positions on defence, immigration and institutional reform – but its support in principle for euro membership has not been translated into action. For the most part, the Labour and Conservative leaderships have shared a vision of British membership of a free-trading, intergovernmental EU. But they highlight differences of detail or degree for tactical reasons: accusing your rival of failing to serve the national interest may bring political reward. So, Labour was largely supportive of the Maastricht Treaty but voted against it as the Major government had not signed the Social Chapter. Unable to rely on Labour support, Major was thus forced to confront Eurosceptics in his own party to get the legislation through parliament.

Parties' European policies are also shaped by their ideology and strategic interests. Divisions on Europe are not always easy to locate on the left–right axis where the left favours economic interventionism and the right the free market. In the 1980s, Nigel Lawson, Sir Geoffrey Howe and Mrs Thatcher disagreed on the ERM and EMU despite their shared commitment to neo-liberal economics. Instead, divisions can usefully be plotted on a sovereignty–interdependence axis where pro-Europeans are willing to pool sovereignty and Eurosceptics defend it.

Labour and the Conservatives have swapped positions on Europe. From the early 1960s to the late 1980s, the Conservatives proclaimed themselves the 'party of Europe'. They were the first to apply for EEC membership (1961) then secured entry (1973). There was a close fit between the free trade and free market outlook of the Tories and the EC. The signing of the Maastricht Treaty (1992) proved the high-water mark for pro-European Conservatism. **Euroscepticism** escalated thereafter as European integration was seen as a threat to national sovereignty and Thatcherite economics.

Euroscepticism: scepticism or hostility to key elements of the EU and integration process.

Labour opposed the 1961 application but the Wilson government launched its own unsuccessful entry bid six years later. The leadership supported membership in principle but opposed the EEC entry terms agreed by the Tories in 1971–72 before settling for minor concessions when back in office. Labour moved to the left after its 1979 election defeat, calling in its 1983 manifesto for withdrawal from an EEC depicted as a capitalist club that would frustrate the party's socialist 'alternative economic strategy'. This marked the pinnacle of Labour Euroscepticism.

Under the leadership of Neil Kinnock, later to become an EU Commissioner, Labour's ideology moved closer to the 'European social model' favoured by other West European social democratic parties. Many in the labour movement who had viewed the SEM with suspicion now looked favourably on EC social and regional policy. The shift in the party's European policy also enabled Labour to reposition itself as a modernised and moderate party. From the late 1980s, Labour leaders have believed that in an era of globalisation, efforts to make the British economy more competitive whilst ensuring social protection for the poorest in society must be pursued in a European context.

Intra-party divisions

The Labour and Conservative parties are coalitions of opinion on Europe, containing convinced pro-Europeans and Eurosceptics as well as pragmatists. MPs opposed to the official line tend to stay in the party as there are disincentives to leave: resigning the whip deprives them of access to parliamentary resources while the electoral system discourages them from setting up minor parties that are unlikely to prosper. This creates problems of party management. Party leaders hoping to develop a clear European policy often meet resistance from within their own ranks and have to fall back on a lowest common denominator position upon which most in the party can agree. This is especially true if the governing party has only a slim parliamentary majority. Major's 'wait and see' position on EMU was designed to hold the centre ground in the Conservative Party but it did not stem Eurosceptic dissent.

Most Conservative MPs supported EEC entry in the 1960s and 1970s, though some on the right such as Enoch Powell warned against the loss of sovereignty. Europe re-emerged as the main fault-line in the party in debates on the Maastricht Treaty in 1992–93. Many Tories previously supportive of the SEA felt that its provisions on EMU and political union, rendered Maastricht a 'Treaty too far'. Eurosceptic resistance culminated in 46 Tory MPs voting against the Bill ratifying the Treaty at third reading, forcing Major to hold a vote of confidence. Conflict on Europe dogged the remainder of his premiership: eight rebel MPs had the whip temporarily removed in 1994 (and one resigned it) then John Redwood responded to Major's 1995 invitation to his critics to stand against him in a leadership contest by launching a Eurosceptic campaign that garnered 89 votes. Tensions in the Cabinet between pro-European ministers (e.g. Kenneth Clarke and Michael Heseltine) and Eurosceptics (e.g. Michael Howard and Michael Portillo) also made life difficult.

Europe was the decisive issue in the 1997 and 2001 Conservative leadership elections in which Clarke was defeated by his Eurosceptic rivals, first William Hague then Iain Duncan Smith. Few pro-Europeans have since held positions of influence. Conservative policy became more Eurosceptic as the centre of gravity within the party shifted. Some 85 per cent of members voting in a 1998 ballot backed Hague's policy of ruling out euro membership for two parliaments. Iain Duncan Smith, Michael Howard and David Cameron all then ruled out joining the euro. The Conservative position is summed up by its phrase 'in Europe, not run by Europe'. It opposed the European Constitution, favours a renegotiation of some Treaty provisions to limit the powers of supranational institutions, and seeks the repatriation of some policies (e.g. fishing) from Brussels. It is not clear how a future Conservative government would persuade other member states to renegotiate the Treaties in a way that afforded Britain special treatment. Dissent within the party has abated, though some Conservative Eurosceptics favour withdrawal from the EU.

Serious divisions occurred in the Labour Party in the 1970s and early 1980s. Most of the Labour movement opposed the terms under which Britain joined the EEC but the leadership supported membership in principle. Yet 69 Labour MPs defied a three-line whip to vote for entry. To limit the damage, Wilson called a referendum on continued membership (1975) in which Cabinet ministers took opposing sides. Hopes that the 67 per cent 'yes' vote would settle the issue were frustrated. A 1980 Labour conference vote endorsing a policy of withdrawal prompted some pro-European MPs to quit and establish the Social Democratic Party.

Labour's subsequent pro-European conversion was relatively smooth. Pro-European John Smith defeated Eurosceptic Bryan Gould in the 1992 leadership contest, though 66 Labour MPs would vote against the Maastricht Treaty. The Blair governments' support for euro membership in principle, when the conditions are right, has not provoked the level of dissent seen in the Conservative Party in the 1990s. Failure to meet the five economic tests has hidden the scale of anti-euro sentiment in the party. The Labour European Safeguards Committee, which opposes both EU membership and the euro, is relatively small. But anxiety about the constraints on future policy imposed by the ECB and Stability and Growth Pact is evident on the soft left. For pragmatists, Brown's successful anti-inflation strategy makes euro membership less attractive.

'Europe' as an election issue

The main parties have found Europe a difficult issue to exploit for electoral advantage. As taking a clear position risks exposing intra-party divisions, party leaders have often put forward compromise positions and downplayed the issue. But voter concern about the pace of European integration has increased and the gap between Labour and Conservative positions widened. The Conservatives saw Europe as a potential vote winner at the 1997 and 2001 elections as their policies on the EU and the euro were more in tune with public opinion than Labour's. Yet they did not deliver substantial electoral reward. Voters amenable to the Conservative message were wary of the divisions within the party in 1997, particularly as Major issued a public rebuke to Tory Eurosceptics who rejected the 'wait and see' position on the euro in their election addresses.

Europe was the number one issue in the Conservative's 2001 election campaign, the party pledging to 'keep the Pound'. Opposition to the euro helped the Conservatives win back support from minor Eurosceptic parties, but did not secure them sufficient support in target seats to make inroads into Labour's majority. Europe did not rank among the top ten concerns of voters. Eurosceptic themes proved most popular with elderly voters and those without university degrees but for young and professional voters, reinforced the caricature of the Conservatives as extreme and 'out of touch'. Europe barely featured in the 2005 election campaign, in part because Blair

---

Analysis: **12.4**

Euroscepticism

The term 'Eurosceptic' became widely used in debates on the Maastricht Treaty. But it is problematic as it is imprecise, being used in popular discourse to describe both *principled* opposition and *qualified* opposition to European integration and the EU. The term may be employed in a narrow sense where a sceptic is a person who doubts the truth or value of a generally held idea or belief. Here a Eurosceptic will doubt the wisdom of certain EU policies and practices but may not oppose EU membership or European integration *per se*. But the label is also applied to convinced opponents of both European integration and the EU. Such people are sometimes described as 'Europhobe' but they would argue that opposition to the EU does not automatically equate with a dislike of Europe or of cooperation between European countries.

Alex Szczerbiak and Paul Taggart employ a distinction between 'hard Euroscepticism' and 'soft-Euroscepticism' in the comparative study, A. Szczerbiak and P. Taggart (eds), *Opposing Europe: The Comparative Politics of Euroscepticism* (Oxford University Press, 2 vols, 2006). Hard Euroscepticism refers to parties that oppose the European integration project as embodied in the EU, i.e. in which powers are transferred to supranational institutions. Soft Eurosceptic parties are not opposed to the European integration project in principle, but express qualified opposition to current or planned EU policies. This might be because EU policies are felt to be at odds with the national interest or the party's ideology.

In the British case, UKIP are the main exponents of hard Euroscepticism as they oppose most key aspects of the European integration project as currently conceived and propose withdrawal from the EU. The Conservative Party has adopted a soft Eurosceptic position since 1997, opposing some existing EU policies (e.g. the Common Fisheries Policy) and the trajectory plotted for the EU by the Constitutional Treaty. Critics suggest that if other member states refuse to accede to demands made by a future Conservative government for the renegotiation of EU Treaties, then some Tories might view withdrawal as the logical response.

It is worth noting that the term 'pro-European' is also a vague one. In the British context, relatively few pro-Europeans favour a federal EU state. The position held by most pro-Europeans is that the long-term political and economic advantages of constructive engagement with the integration process will outweigh any short-term costs associated with the transfer of policy competences to the EU.

had neutralised a major cause of contention by promising a referendum on the EU Constitution.

Minor parties also compete for the Eurosceptic vote (see Analysis 12.4). The Referendum Party, established by millionaire businessman Sir James Goldsmith in 1994, contested the 1997 election. Its rhetoric was strongly Eurosceptic though its proposed referendum would have offered voters a choice between a 'federal Europe' and an 'association of sovereign states' but not withdrawal. It won 3 per cent of the votes in seats it contested but was wound down shortly afterwards. This left UKIP, formed in 1993, as the main vehicle for populist right-wing Euroscepticism. Campaigning for withdrawal from the EU, it saw three MEPs elected in 1999 but came to prominence in the 2004 European elections when it won 16 per cent of the vote and 12 seats in the EP. The candidature of former television presenter and Labour MP Robert Kilroy-Silk increased the party's profile but his leadership ambitions were thwarted and he left UKIP the following year. UKIP won only 2 per cent at the 2005 general election, a result that reflected the party's internal difficulties and the low profile of Europe as an election issue.

Public opinion

Public support for EU membership and further integration has long been lower in the UK than other member states (see Table 12.1). British citizens are also less knowledgeable about the EU than their continental European counterparts. A number of explanations may be offered. First, the EU has a negative symbolism as integration is judged in terms of a loss of sovereignty and a threat to national identity. Surveys indicate that national identity is stronger in the UK than elsewhere in the EU and identification with Europe weaker. Second, the Union's shortcomings

Table 12.1 British public opinion and EU membership

Question: If there were a referendum now on whether Britain should stay in or get out of the European Union, how would you vote?

Year	Stay in (%)	Get out (%)
1977	47	42
1980	26	65
1983	36	55
1987	48	39
1990	62	28
1991	60	29
1992	52	35
1993	46	39
1994	52	36
1996	44	40
1997	49	35
1998	47	40
1999	51	41
2000	49	44
2001	48	43
2003	49	41

Source: Ipsos MORI, www.ipsos-mori.com

are more prominently aired than its successes. The British public are poorly served by media coverage of the EU – opinion polls show a majority of voters want better quality information. Newspapers such as the *Sun* and *Daily Mail* offer their readers a diet of populist Eurosceptic stories on EU inefficiency and bureaucracy, while *The Times* and *Daily Telegraph* take a more considered Eurosceptic position. The *Daily Mirror* is the main pro-European tabloid; the *Guardian*, *Independent* and *Financial Times* are also largely supportive. Voters also get information from television. Here too a 2005 report commissioned by the BBC criticised its news coverage of the EU for being over-simplistic.

Parliament has been the main arena in which debate on Britain's relationship with the EU has been conducted. Here party managers can put pressure on potential rebels to toe the line. But debates on Europe have been put into the public domain by dissenters eager to publicise their case. Various Eurosceptic groupings have been established since the late 1980s. Some, such as the Bruges Group (a cross-party body, though largely made up of Conservatives) and Labour Against the Euro emerged in the parliamentary arena; others were set up by companies (e.g. Business for Sterling) or wealthy individuals (e.g. the Democracy Movement). Party managers have often taken a relaxed attitude towards these groupings, hoping that they will release pressure building within the party. But Eurosceptic groups have widened the terms of debate by promoting the option of withdrawal from the EU which is rarely aired in parliament.

The Blair governments had proposed to hold referendums on the EU Constitutional Treaty and on UK membership of the euro. The former had been scheduled for 2006 but was postponed indefinitely after the 'no' votes in France and the Netherlands. The prospects of the latter receded after the Treasury's 2003 verdict that the economic tests had not been met. Referendums would have pushed debate on Britain and Europe firmly into the public arena. They would have been contested by cross-party campaigns, but with the 'yes' campaigns including most Labour and Liberal Democrats MPs and the Conservatives being the main participant in the 'no' campaign.

Table 12.2 British public opinion and the euro

Question: If there were a referendum now on whether Britain should be part of a single European currency, how would you vote?

Year	In favour (%)	Against (%)
1994	33	56
1995	29	60
1996	23	60
1997	25	60
1998	31	54
1999	31	53
2000	25	60
2001	28	57
2002	31	53
2003	30	56
2004	26	61
2005	26	57

Adapted from: Ipsos MORI, www.ipsos-mori.com

Victory for a government-backed 'yes' campaign would have been far from assured. Opinion polls in the last decade have shown consistently that a majority of voters are opposed to joining the euro; fewer than a third are in favour (see Table 12.2). More people favour continued British membership of the EU than oppose it, but polls conducted on the EU Constitution showed a plurality against it. The voting intentions of many of those surveyed are, however, not fixed: significant numbers might be persuaded to change their views.

Conclusion and summary

This chapter has examined 'Britain in Europe' (the positions adopted by British governments in the EU) and 'Europe in Britain' (the impact of European integration on British politics). The Blair governments have been more pro-European and more influential than their predecessors, shaping the EU agenda on social policy, defence and immigration. But New Labour's defence of the national veto in sensitive areas and reticence on joining the euro place them closer to the traditional British inter-governmental approach than to the integrationist position of other West European social democratic parties. Despite claims by Eurosceptics that the Constitutional Treaty invests the EU with more state-like attributes, it did not advance the integrationist process as much as Euro-enthusiasts in other member states had hoped. EU enlargement and the waning of Franco-German influence suggest that Britain will not be as isolated as in the past.

Blair's aim of increasing public support for European integration has not borne fruit, in part because of the timidity of his efforts but also because of the prevalence of Euroscepticism in British political culture. The British state has experienced a limited Europeanisation: it is a multi-level polity in which decision-making competences are shared between supranational, national and subnational institutions. Devolution has brought about a closer fit between the British polity, the EU and other member states. But institutional factors such as the enduring importance of sovereignty, the simple plurality electoral system and divisions between and within the main political parties on the EU continue to underpin British 'awkwardness'. More effective national and EU-level scrutiny of EU legislative proposals is required if the democratic deficit is to be bridged.

Today's British policy-makers are faced with a similar strategic question to that which faced their predecessors some fifty years before: is it in the national interest to position the UK closer to the United States or Western Europe? Blair's answer – that Britain should seek to bridge the two as America's main ally in Europe – is consistent with the approach adopted by most post-war governments. But, as the war in Iraq illustrated, being between Europe and America is not always the most comfortable position.

Further reading

The best introduction to Britain's relationship with the EU is A. Geddes, *The European Union and British Politics* (London: Palgrave, 2004). D. Baker and D. Seawright (eds), *Britain For and Against Europe* (Oxford: Clarendon Press, 1998) has essays on the attitudes towards Europe of political parties, business, trade unions and the media. Three historical perspectives can be recommended: J. Young, *Britain and European Unity* (London: Palgrave, 2nd edition, 1999), S. George, *An Awkward Partner: Britain in the European Union* (Oxford: Oxford University Press, 3rd edition, 1998) and H. Young, *This Blessed Plot: Britain in Europe from Churchill to Blair* (London: Papermac, 1999). A. Gamble, *Between Europe and America: the Future of British Politics* (London: Palgrave, 2003) is a compelling analysis of the strategic choices facing the UK.

There is a large number of textbooks on the EU, including D. Dinan, *Ever Closer Union* (London: Palgrave, 2nd edition, 2005) and I. Bache and S. George, *Politics in the European Union* (Oxford: Oxford University Press, 2nd edition, 2006). S. Hix, *The Political System of the European Union* (London: Palgrave, 2nd edition, 2005) is more advanced but rewarding.

The 'awkward partner' debate is covered in J. Buller, 'Britain as an Awkward Partner: reassessing Britain's Relations with the EU', *Politics*, Vol. 15, No. 1 (1995), pp. 33–42 and S. Wilks, 'Britain and Europe: an Awkward Partner or an Awkward State?', *Politics*, Vol. 16, No. 3 (1996), pp. 159–67. On sovereignty, see N. Nugent, 'Sovereignty and British Membership of the European Union' *Public Policy & Administration*, Vol. 11, No. 2 (1996), pp. 2–18. The Europeanisation of the UK polity is explored in S. Bulmer and M. Burch, Organizing for Europe: Whitehall, the British State and European Union', *Public Administration*, Vol. 76, No. 4 (1998), pp. 5–67, and A. Forster and A. Blair, *The Making of Britain's European Foreign Policy* (Harlow: Longman, 2002).

Divisions within the Conservative Party are explored in D. Baker, A. Gamble and S. Ludlam, 'Sovereign Nations and Global Markets: Modern British Conservatism and Hyperglobalism', *British Journal of Politics and International Relations*, Vol. 4, No. 3 (2002), pp. 399–428, and Labour divisions in A. Gamble and G. Kelly, 'The British Labour Party and Monetary Union', *West European Politics*, Vol. 32, No. 1 (2000), pp. 1–25. Two collections bringing together arguments on Britain and the EU are useful: M. Holmes (ed.), *The Eurosceptical Reader* (London: Palgrave, 2002) and D. Leonard and M. Leonard (eds), *The Pro-European Reader* (London: Palgrave, 2002). A. Forster, *Euroscepticism in Contemporary British Politics* (London: Routledge, 2002) traces the development of Eurosceptic ideas. British policy on the euro is examined in A. Blair, *Saving the Pound?* (Harlow: Longman, 2002).

Websites

The European Union's official website contains a wealth of information on EU policies, institutions and current developments. Its homepage http://europa.eu.int/index_en.htm provides an introduction to the work of the EU plus links to the sites of the EU institutions, information on the EU's policy activities and current legislation. The websites of the main EU institutions have further information on their structure and work:

The Council of Ministers http://ue.eu.int/showPage.ASP?lang=en.

The European Commission www.europa.eu.int/comm/index_en.htm.

The European Parliament www.europarl.eu.int/news/public/default_en.htm.

The European Court of Justice http://curia.eu.int/en/index.htm.

Eurobarometer surveys of opinion can be found at http://europa.eu.int/comm/public_opinion/index_en.htm. The EU's Bulletin of the European Union is a useful source of information on the recent activities of the EU institutions. Independent sites covering EU developments include EU Observer www.euobserver.com and European Voice www.europeanvoice.com.

On UK policy, the Foreign and Commonwealth Office site http://www.fco.gov.uk contains a section devoted to Britain and Europe which includes an overview of policy, government documents and ministerial speeches. Different positions in the British debate on Europe can be explored through the websites of pro-European groups such as the European Movement www.euromove.org.uk/ and Eurosceptic groups such as the Bruges Group www.brugesgroup.com.

Part 4
Political parties

Chapter 13

UK party systems

Learning outcomes

After reading this chapter, you will:
- Be able to explain the development of the Westminster party system.
- Understand how the classification of party systems in the UK has become more complicated since the introduction of elections to the European Parliament and devolved institutions.
- Recognise the impact of different voting systems.

Introduction

In an ideal world of pluralist democracy, there would be a wide range of political parties all of which had a realistic chance of gaining at least token representation in the legislature. Such a situation would reflect the fact that people enjoying freedom of thought and expression are likely to hold divergent opinions on key issues, and to form association with others of a like mind. Indeed, if everyone did think alike on the most important issues, some people would still feel inspired to compete for the right to represent their fellow citizens, and find some grounds for arguing amongst themselves. In these circumstances, it is inevitable that political parties will develop (see Chapter 14).

Students hoping to gain an insight into the political culture of any society will be rewarded by a close study of the patterns of party competition. But they are well advised to do more than simply count the number of parties which contest elections with a chance of forming a government – which is the usual way of classifying a party system. For example, the UK and the US are traditionally regarded as having two-party systems. But this does not necessarily mean that a large proportion of citizens are deprived of a meaningful choice. It could be the case that the main parties are coalitions in themselves, flexible enough to represent a majority of voters. However, Western societies are becoming increasingly diverse, and voters seem to be more selective nowadays. In this context, it is relevant to ask whether two-party systems are really sustainable, and if their survival (particularly in media presentation of political choices) has become a factor in the recent decline of political participation in countries like the US and the UK.

History of a two-party system

Party: an organisation of people with common political beliefs which competes in elections in an attempt to win power or influence.

Institutionalised **party** conflict in Britain dates back to the seventeenth century and the division between 'Tories' (who supported the full exercise of the Royal prerogative) and 'Whigs' (who favoured a limited or 'constitutional' monarchy). These labels survived through the eighteenth century, but continuing competition was only marginally related to principle after the 'Glorious Revolution' of 1688–89. That settlement was a clear victory for Whig principles, since it established that the monarch could not rule without parliament. After the succession of the Hanoverian dynasty in 1714 some Tories continued to flirt with the restoration of the Stuarts, who were associated with strong monarchical rule. But even if either of the Jacobite rebellions of 1715 and 1745 had succeeded, it is unlikely that the role of parliament would have been reduced. Thus at this time the clash between Whigs and Tories was little more than a faction-fight between retinues of 'ins' and 'outs'.

Meaningful party conflict resumed towards the end of the eighteenth century, in the wake of the French Revolution. Few Whigs advocated a similar upheaval in Britain, but many of them did favour a rationalisation of the electoral franchise and a redistribution of seats to reflect the rising population of cities like Manchester and Birmingham. The Tories, by contrast, preferred to leave things as they were. This battle closed with the passage of the Great Reform Act (1832), which satisfied the demands of most Whigs. In response, the Tories became even more self-conscious in their resistance to change in 'Church and State', and adopted the new name of 'Conservatives'. Yet the Whigs were scarcely radical; many of them believed that the Reform Act had 'perfected' the constitution. Thus in the years after 1832 a rising young Tory, William Gladstone, was able to join the Whigs without feeling that his views had changed very much.

Party system: the set of political parties in a political system, and their interactions.

Thus Britain entered the era of mass parties after a second extension of the franchise in 1867 (see Chapter 16) with a recognisable **two-party system**. That is, although party identification was still fairly loose and informal – and defections from one camp to the other were not unusual – parliament was dominated by a governing party and an opposition which had a realistic expectation of forming an administration in the near future (see Analysis 13.1). The oratorical combat between the Liberal Gladstone and the Conservative Disraeli dominated exchanges in the House of Commons for many years. Gladstone formed four governments, only retiring in 1894 at the age of 84; Disraeli was Prime Minister on two occasions. In

The classification of party systems

The most familiar way of defining party systems is to look at the number of parties which have a realistic chance of participating in a government, rather than the number of organisations that nominate candidates at elections. In *one-party* states, like China or Zimbabwe, elections are meaningless because opposition candidates are either banned or elections are rigged to ensure 'victory' for the government. But it is also possible to identify *dominant-party* systems, where there are no such restrictions but one party almost always wins. Thus in Sweden the Social Democratic Labour Party was in office for all but two of the years between 1951 and 1993, while the Congress Party governed India without a break for thirty years after the country's independence in 1947.

In *two-party* systems only the government and the main opposition party has a realistic chance of winning power (the classic example is the United States, where Congress is dominated by the Republicans and the Democrats, and independent candidates for the presidency rarely win a single vote in the electoral college). A variant of this situation is a *two-and-a-half-party* system, in which third parties regularly win sufficient representation to have a potential effect on the overall outcome.

In *multi-party* systems, there might be more than two parties with substantial support, or competition between the two leading parties might be so close that neither is able to form a government without help from one or more of the minor parties. In either case, the outcome of elections in multi-party systems is almost invariably a coalition government.

Party systems are closely related to the electoral system in operation. Thus the simple plurality (or first-past-the-post) electoral system is associated with two-party systems, while more proportional systems like the Additional Member System (AMS) and the Single Transferable Vote (STV) foster multi-party systems and coalition governments (see Chapter 16).

an era of mass-production as well as mass parties, the idolisation of these parliamentary giants was exploited in a wide range of memorabilia, ranging from portraits to dinner-plates. The railways ensured the rapid distribution of party publicity, and took leaders like Gladstone on nationwide campaigns to address large crowds of partisan supporters who were rallied by increasingly sophisticated constituency organisations.

However, the dominance of the Conservatives and the Liberals did not mean that they were the only parties which mattered. From the 1880s until 1918 Irish Nationalists, demanding Home Rule for their country, could depend on a parliamentary strength of more than 80 MPs. For both main parties the support of this phalanx was well worth having; the trick, though, was to woo the Nationalists without having to adopt policies which might split their own supporters. Gladstone's decision to embrace Home Rule in 1885 alienated senior Liberals, including Joseph Chamberlain who had been one of the first politicians to understand the importance of professional organisation in the new political environment. Chamberlain joined the Conservatives, who promptly added 'Unionist' to their title in order to emphasise their opposition to Home Rule.

" DOCTORS DIFFER ! "

DR. WILLIAM G. "I WARN YOU, MR. BULL, YOUR CONSTITUTION IS BEING SERIOUSLY IMPAIRED BY THAT—A-PERSON'S TREATMENT."
DR. BENJAMIN D. "MY DEAR MR. BULL, YOUR CONSTITUTION IS PERFECTLY SAFE IN MY HANDS."

Gladstone and Disraeli, gladiators in a two-party battle (reproduced with the permission of Punch, Ltd.)

The situation became even more complicated when the Labour Representation Committee, the forerunner to the Labour Party, was established in 1900. Initially Labour cooperated closely with the Liberals. But it was always likely that an organisation dedicated to securing parliamentary representation for working people would establish its independence – and equally probable that this development would create serious complications for its longer-established rivals. The Representation of the People Act 1918, which finally abolished property qualifications and extended the franchise to all males aged 21 and over (and to women over 30) opened the prospect that Labour might become the single dominant force in British politics. The payment of MPs, which began in 1912, made parliamentary service into a potential career rather than a part-time hobby for the rich. Without undue reliance on hindsight, it can be argued that the emergence of Labour in this context forced the Conservatives and the Liberals into a life-and-death struggle, to see which would survive as the main challenger to a party which made up in numbers for the relative poverty of its grass-roots activists.

On the face of it, the odds were stacked against the Conservatives, who relied heavily on a declining aristocracy. Yet, as Disraeli had understood, many members of the working class were deferential towards aristocrats, while they regarded the Liberal Party as the representative of directly-antagonistic business interests. Also, the Conservatives since 1832 had grown accustomed to survival in an unpromising context; Disraeli's acceptance of reform in 1867 was only the most spectacular example of the party's ability to take pragmatic decisions when survival was at stake. However, after 1918 the most important reason for Conservative success was a disastrous feud between the two leading Liberals, Herbert Henry Asquith (Prime Minister, 1908–16) and David Lloyd George (Prime Minister, 1916–22). The schism was not healed until Asquith's death in 1928, by which time the Liberals had been reduced to just 40 MPs.

Despite the precipitate Liberal decline in terms of seats, the period between 1922 and 1931 was a genuine respite from the familiar two-party pattern. The classic three-party split came in 1923, when the main parties were divided by little more than 1.2 million votes out of an electorate of 21.2 million (see Table 13.1). Although the Conservatives won the most seats, Labour formed its first (minority) government with support from the Liberals. This new symptom of friendship between progressives across party lines might have formed the basis for a dominant and lasting anti-Conservative coalition. But the Liberals had no intention of dissolving their historic identity in return for a junior partnership with Labour. The main consequence of the short-lived 1924 Labour government was to bring the Liberals into further discredit among opponents of socialism, for having made the party of the working class look like a respectable organisation capable of running a government without triggering a social revolution. Further defections from the Liberal ranks led to a dismal performance by the party in the 1924 general election. Asquith's death removed the main obstacle to unity amongst remaining members, and Lloyd George's inspired leadership ensured a revival in 1929. But a second minority Labour government, elected in that year, collapsed in the face of an economic crisis in 1931. In the apparent need for national unity the Liberals split again, and both factions were dwarfed by the other parties. Between 1931 and 1974, their percentage vote only crept into double figures on one occasion (1964).

During the 1950s the two-party system seemed impregnable. In 1951 the two giants received almost 97 per cent of the UK vote between them (and although it lost the 1951 election in terms of seats, Labour won 200,000 more votes than the Conservatives, from an electorate that had swollen to 34.6 million). At the next two elections (1955 and 1959) their combined share exceeded 90 per cent. In 1964, when the Liberals broke through into a double-figure vote share, the party won only 9 out of 630 seats; all of the remainder divided between Labour and the

Table 13.1 Share of the UK vote for the three main parties, 1922–1931 (%)

	1922	1923	1924	1929	1931
Conservative	38	38	48	38	55
Labour	29.5	30.5	33	37	32
Liberal	29	29.6	17.6	23.4	11.7

Note: For 1931, figures for Labour and Liberal are collated from supporters and opponents of National Government.

Conservatives. Two years later the Liberals won three more seats; but their vote fell back to 8.5 per cent. In 1970 the respective tallies were 6 seats and 7.5 per cent of the UK vote.

The decline of the two-party system

Things began to change with the two general elections of 1974, for two reasons of comparable importance (see Analysis 13.2). The first was that the electorate was growing disillusioned with both main parties. Labour's Harold Wilson had come to office in 1964 promising a radical, modern approach to the economy; but these hopes were quickly dashed as his Government fought to maintain the value of sterling. By 1970, Britain was afflicted by a double curse: rising inflation and (relatively) high

| Analysis: | 13.2 |

'Catch-all' parties and the two-party system

Some commentators argue that a two-party system is a major influence in support of moderate policies. On this account, if a party wants to keep its place in government, or as the main Opposition, it will be forced to seek 'the middle ground' of political opinion in the country. It will devise policies which appeal to a significant number of people, while avoiding alienating important groups (and even trying to detach a few 'converts' from what might be regarded as the opposite camp).

An excellent example of a 'catch-all' party in this mould was the Conservative Party between 1945 and 1975. The 'One Nation' politics espoused by leaders like Harold Macmillan and Edward Heath were based on the view that the nation's internal differences could be reconciled, provided that the elected government was prepared to act as an 'honest broker'. However, the Heath government (1970–74) was dogged by persistent opposition from the unions, and when the Prime Minister appealed for support from the electorate in February 1974 he was snubbed. Many Conservatives believed that he had gone much too far in his attempts to conciliate, and that if anything the party now put the interests of the unions above the needs of the business community.

Between the late 1970s and mid-1980s, the UK was still dominated by two parties; but neither could have been described as 'moderate' by post-war standards. Mrs Thatcher made no attempt to conciliate groups which she regarded as 'enemies within'. This strategy proved successful, not least because Labour became for some years a 'sweeping-up party' which tried to stitch together a coalition of voters who had different reasons to dislike Thatcherism. The Social Democratic Party (SDP) tried to cash in on this desertion of the 'middle ground', but its attempt proved premature.

Labour under Neil Kinnock (1983–92) and the Conservatives under John Major (1990–97) tried unconvincingly to adopt the 'catch-all' role, mainly because both leaders were distracted by powerful party factions hoping to force them to left or right. Tony Blair's 'New' Labour was a determined attempt to fulfil the promise of the SDP, and the success of the strategy was marked by election victories deep into 'natural' Conservative territory. However, there was always a danger that one day it would mirror the fate of 'One Nation' Conservatism, by making too many compromises with the traditional enemy and conclusively alienating its original supporters.

The Gang of Four began their attempt to break the two-party system by launching the SDP. From left to right: Roy Jenkins; Dr David Owen; Bill Rodgers; Shirley Williams (© D. Gaywood/Rex Features)

unemployment. The Conservatives led by Edward Heath returned to office in 1970, but their record was comparably poor. Despite their tarnished images Wilson and Heath led their respective parties into the elections held in February and October 1974, offering little change from the policies which had apparently failed. It is little wonder that many voters were beginning to look around for a third option. For more than a decade, the two main parties had both been vulnerable to a Liberal revival at by-elections which provided ideal opportunities for the public to register its dissatisfaction outside Scotland and Wales, where nationalist parties offered additional options.

The second reason for the decline of the two-party system was the phenomenon known as 'class dealignment' – the erosion of the link between socio-economic factors and voting behaviour (see Chapter 17). In particular, this development troubled Labour strategists who could no longer depend on instinctive loyalty from the traditional working class. It was not merely a question of giving this constituency new reasons for voting Labour; social mobility was diminishing the size of the constituency itself. This underlying problem contributed to the strains felt by Labour during the 1970s, culminating in the 1979 electoral defeat which was soon recognised as being far more important than the bare voting figures suggested (in fact, with almost 38 per cent of the vote Labour's performance in 1979 was only slightly worse than it had been in February 1974, when the party had been able to form a minority government).

The victory of Margaret Thatcher's Conservatives had several important effects on the party system. The first of these came in 1981, with a conscious attempt to 'break the two-party mould', by a group of Labour defectors led by the former Cabinet ministers Roy Jenkins, David Owen, Shirley Williams and Bill Rodgers. The so-called 'Gang of Four' had become increasingly disillusioned with Labour's official policy on a range of issues, notably its anti-European stance. They founded the Social Democratic Party (SDP), and fought the 1983 election in alliance with the Liberals. The combined Alliance vote in 1983 was 7.78 million – less than 700,000 behind Labour. However, the impact of the simple plurality electoral system (or first-past-the-post) minimised the parliamentary effect of this achievement; the Alliance only returned 23 MPs, compared to 209 for Labour. Its impotence at Westminster provided vivid (if spurious) support to the claim of its opponents, that a vote for the Alliance was 'a wasted vote'. Thus the attack on the two-party mould only reinforced the potency of the idea that only Labour or the Conservatives could form a government. After another disappointing result in 1987, the two Alliance parties merged and in 1989 adopted the name 'Liberal Democrats'.

Another notable effect of Thatcherism was a new and lasting polarisation of the UK in a geographical sense. The Conservatives owed their four successive victories to a virtual monopoly of the south-east of England outside London – an area which gave them 170 seats in 1987. Labour was equally entrenched in (generally declining) inner-city constituencies. Even more startling was the Conservative decline in Scotland and Wales. In Scotland the party won 22 seats in 1979, but none at all in 1997, when it also lost the last of the 14 Welsh constituencies it had held back in 1983. The 2001 Conservative comeback in these countries amounted to the recapture of a single Scottish seat. It fared no better in Scotland in 2005, although it did take two Welsh seats. By contrast, after the 2001 election Labour held 55 out of 72 Scottish seats, and 34 of 40 in Wales. Boundary changes before the 2005 general election helped to reduce Labour's tally to 41 seats in Scotland, and it lost 5 Welsh seats. But despite these losses, as far as Westminster politics was concerned Scotland and Wales unquestionably had dominant-party systems.

The UK party system since 1997

These figures underline the danger of over-simplification in assessments of the UK party system. Leaving aside the anomaly of Northern Ireland (see below), the country is characterised by a series of mini-party systems rather than presenting a uniform picture. In fact, even when the national and regional variations are screened out, there is plenty of room for debate about the nature of the UK party system as it stood after the 2005 general election. There are four possible arguments:

1. The mould has finally been broken, and Britain no longer has a two-party system. Although the Liberal Democrat vote only edged upwards in 2001, by less than two per cent, the party increased its parliamentary representation from 46 to 52. The trend was reinforced in 2005, when a more significant increase in its vote share (to 22 per cent) brought it 10 more seats. This implies that many voters no longer believe that a vote for the third party is a wasted vote; they are beginning to undermine the impact of the simple plurality electoral system through tactical voting. Before the 1997 election Tony Blair seriously discussed the prospect of a coalition with the (then) Liberal Democrat leader, Paddy Ashdown; even if the party does not overtake the Conservatives in the near future, there is every chance that some of its representatives will have to be included in a government. It is thus realistic to describe the UK as a 'multi-party system'.

Table 13.2 Combined vote share of Conservatives and Labour, 1974–2005 (%)

1974 (Feb)	1974 (Oct)	1979	1983	1987	1992	1997	2001	2005
75.0	75.0	80.8	70.0	73.1	76.3	73.9	72.4	69.4

2. The two-party system is alive and (reasonably) well. In 2001 the Liberal Democrats performed little better in terms of vote share than their Liberal predecessors did in October 1974, when they secured only 13 MPs. Even though the Conservatives ran a poor campaign under an unpopular leader in 2001, the Liberal Democrats did not even come close to challenging them for second place. The Liberal Democrats only edged upwards slightly in 2005, in a general election where they seemed well placed to attract the votes of disillusioned Labour supporters. Tactical voting is still unusual in a country where people are increasingly disinclined to vote at all, let alone to research the likely effects of a tactical switch. In the meantime, any distinctive policy proposals advanced by the Liberal Democrats will either be stolen by their rivals or subjected to attack from both flanks.

3. The UK is now a *two-and-a-half party system*, so far as Westminster is concerned (see Analysis 13.1). With 62 MPs after the 2005 general election, the Liberal Democrats are poised to take a central role in any future contest where the two main parties run each other close. This means that the party will be taken more seriously as at least a potential coalition partner, which in turn might have the effect of increasing its support.

4. It is possible to argue that the UK has become a *dominant-party system* since 1979, even if the life-cycle for the dominant parties has been relatively short (see Analysis 13.1). In a genuine two-party system the leading opposition group should have a reasonable expectation of winning power at the next election. By contrast, the Conservatives were easily re-elected in 1983 and 1987, and despite problems over the poll tax and the deposition of Thatcher they still managed to win in 1992. After the belated swing of the pendulum, Labour's victories in 1997, 2001 and 2005 were long regarded as foregone conclusions (see Table 13.3). Although the party's majority in 2005 was only 67, compared to 166 in 2001, there were no early signs that its conduct in office during this third term would mark a significant change from previous trends.

The fourth possibility – that Britain now has a dominant-party system – is particularly serious It might be argued that recent results have been produced by unusual circumstances, rather than initiating a lasting new pattern of party competition. Yet the political culture of the UK – with no codified constitution to rein in the ambitions of a government – encourages winning parties to claim that they have won unequivocal mandates to rule, even though they invariably fall well short of an overall majority vote. Under the 'Westminster Model', successive governments have exhibited some of the features of what Lord Hailsham called an 'elective dictatorship', however slender their parliamentary majorities. Governing parties are tempted to ignore the opposition parties in parliament, and to make key bureaucratic appointments with a view to cementing their power, oblivious to the

Table 13.3 Overall majorities after recent general elections (% vote share in brackets)

1979 Conservative	1983 Conservative	1987 Conservative	1992 Conservative	1997 Labour	2001 Labour	2005 Labour
43 (43.9)	144 (42.4)	102 (42.3)	21 (41.9)	179 (43.2)	166 (40.7)	67 (36.1)

possibility that the weapons they forge might be used against them when they return to Opposition. In short, governments in a dominant-party system tend to overlook the key distinction between rule in the interest of a party, and administration in the interest of the nation as a whole.

Almost the only crumb of comfort to be derived from the record of dominant parties is that their behaviour usually brings about their own downfall. During their years of uncontested power, both the Conservatives and Labour have shown a tendency to waste much of their energies on internal faction-fighting, and to become embroiled in allegations of 'sleaze'. These have also been features of dominant parties in other countries (e.g. the Japanese Liberal Democratic Party, which was in power continuously between 1945 and 1993, and the Italian Christian Democrats which enjoyed a similar lease of office. Both eventually collapsed amid allegations of corruption).

The view that the UK now has a dominant-party system is supported by a growing body of evidence. But most commentators still opt for the second argument, concluding that although the vote-share of the two main parties has fallen almost continuously since the early 1970s, Britain retains a two-party system (see Table 13.X). The traditional 'mould' came closest to breaking in 1983, but the circumstances then were unusual because the formation of the SDP attracted heavy (and usually favourable) press coverage. However, an increasingly volatile (and apathetic) electorate makes political predictions unusually hazardous today. After the 1992 general election produced a fourth consecutive Conservative majority, some reputable commentators argued that the party had become dominant in the UK; yet only five years later its survival as a significant force in British politics was open to question.

The only firm conclusion to be drawn from the example of party competition in the UK is that it illustrates the strong bias of the simple plurality electoral system against third parties. However, this might become irrelevant to British conditions if the Liberal Democrats continue their recent gradual progress and turn out to hold the balance of power in any forthcoming election. Even then, given their addiction to the two-party battle it is not impossible that Labour and the Conservatives will bury their old squabbles and forge an anti-Liberal coalition!

Party systems in Scotland and Wales

As we have seen, the pattern of party competition at Westminster in recent years would provide a highly misleading impression of the contests in Scotland and Wales. The introduction of devolved institutions, elected by the Additional Member System (AMS), has underlined this point, and also illustrates the distorting effect of simple plurality compared to the true levels of party support in those countries (see Table 13.4).

Table 13.4 Distribution of seats in Welsh Assembly and Scottish Parliament, 2003

Wales		Scotland	
Party	Seats	Party	Seats
Labour	30 (+2)	Labour	50 (−6)
Plaid Cymru	12 (−5)	SNP	27 (−8)
Conservative	11 (+2)	Conservative	18 (+0)
Lib Dems	6 (+0)	Lib Dems	17 (+0)
Other	1 (+1)	Greens	7 (+6)
		Scottish Socialists	6 (+5)
		Independents	4 (+3)

Note: Figures in brackets refer to change since 1999.

The results show several interesting variations from the outcome in recent Westminster elections. First, although the Conservatives only held four parliamentary seats in Scotland or Wales after the 2005 general election, the devolved institutions (which they initially opposed) have given them a chance to re-establish a significant elected political presence, showing that their continuing support had been masked by the simple plurality system rather than disappearing as the bare figures suggested. Second, Labour is by no means as dominant under AMS as it would seem from the Westminster situation. Third, in Scotland the new voting system has given a significant voice to parties which stand little chance of gaining representation at Westminster. It seems likely that the system will encourage a form of 'split-ticket' voting – i.e. in elections to the devolved institutions voters will have more incentive to vote for minority party candidates, while continuing to choose between the major UK parties in general elections.

Even without the effects of the voting system, the multi-party competition in Scotland and Wales is enlivened by the presence of popular nationalist parties which have little chance of making a significant impact at Westminster. At present their prospects of forming administrations in Scotland or Wales are fairly remote; and Labour seems to prefer the Liberal Democrats as a coalition partner in both countries. However, in Wales Labour decided to form a government on its own after the 2003 election, despite falling short of an overall majority.

The party system in Northern Ireland

The example of Northern Ireland shows that the exchange of simple plurality for proportional representation (PR) does not always mean the replacement of a two-party system by a multi-party fight. But that is only because Northern Ireland was multi-party even before STV was used in the 1998 Assembly elections. In Northern Ireland the main cleavage between parties has been based on culture and religion rather than class, resulting in a very different pattern of competition (see Chapter 11). The Ulster Unionists (UUP) and Democratic Unionists (DUP) are predominantly Protestant, while most of the Catholic vote is divided between the Social Democratic and Labour Party (SDLP) and Sinn Fein. The parties on each side differ

Table 13.5 Share of votes for the main parties in Northern Ireland 1997–2005 (%)

Party	1997 Westminster	1998 Assembly	2001 Westminster	2003 Assembly	2004 European Parliament	2005 Westminster
DUP	13.6 (2)	18.1 (20)	22.5 (5)	25.6 (30)	32 (1)	33.7(9)
Sinn Fein	16.1 (2)	17.6 (18)	21.7 (4)	23.5 (24)	26.3 (1)	24.3 (5)
UUP	32.7 (10)	21.3 (28)	26.8 (6)	22.7 (7)	16.6 (1)	17.7 (1)
SDLP	24.1 (3)	22 (24)	21 (3)	17 (18)	15.9 (0)	17.5 (3)

Note: Figures in brackets refer to seats won.

in their approaches to the long-running political problems of Northern Ireland. The DUP was opposed to the 1998 Good Friday Agreement which the UUP accepted. On the catholic side the SDLP has always been in favour of a peaceful transition to a united Ireland while Sinn Fein is the political wing of the Irish Republican Army (IRA), which, after several ceasefires, ordered its supporters to end their armed struggle in July 2000.

Until the implementation of direct rule from Westminster in 1972, Northern Ireland had a dominant-party system. The UUP was genuinely popular among the protestant majority, but it reinforced its position by the creative drawing of electoral boundaries. Change has been almost continuous since 1972, but the transformation has been dramatic since the Good Friday Agreement. The position of the UUP and the DUP has been almost exactly reversed; the UUP vote has fallen from 32.7 per cent in 1997 to a low of 16.6 per cent in 2004, while the DUP climbed from 13.6 per cent to 33.7 per cent in 2005. The position of the SDLP has deteriorated in a similar fashion *vis à vis* Sinn Fein. Since 1997 the combined share of the two main Protestant parties has actually increased, although the Catholic population has been rising faster (see Table 13.5).

The willingness of voters to defect from the 'respectable' Northern Ireland parties towards politicians who were once dismissed as extremists is an ironic by-product of an initiative which was carefully designed to bolster moderation. The STV system in itself is an effective way to secure representation for a wide range of parties, but the final mix in the Northern Ireland assembly was supposed to include a strong contingent from smaller moderate groupings (notably the non-sectarian Alliance Party), which had previously lost potential support because they had little chance of picking up seats under simple plurality. Furthermore, the UK government ensured that the NI executive formed after the 1998 elections was a 'Grand Coalition', containing members of all four main parties. However, this arrangement soon proved unworkable, mainly due to the obstructive attitude of the DUP. Although the 2003 Assembly elections eventually went ahead, the institution had been suspended since October 2002 and the newly-elected representatives had nowhere to sit (though they did continue to draw their salaries). The results of recent Northern Ireland elections thus show that although electoral systems are an important factor in determining political outcomes, they can be outweighed by other considerations.

The 'effective number of parties'

An alternative way of identifying the number of significant political parties operating in a political system is to measure the 'effective number of parties' (ENEP). This is calculated on the basis of shares of the vote won in general elections. It is a weighted indicator that arrives at a final figure by giving larger parties more weight than smaller ones. In a system where two main parties have equal vote shares, the effective number of electoral parties will be 2.0. For UK general elections between 1945 and 1970 the effective number of electoral parties averaged 2.39, but rose to 3.18 for the period 1974–2005, confirming that a two-party system no longer operates in the national electoral arena.

The 'effective number of *parliamentary* parties' (ENPP) is calculated on the basis of the share of seats won in the legislature. In the UK it averaged 2.04 in 1945–70, increasing slightly to 2.23 across the period 1974–2005. This confirms that change in the legislature has been less pronounced than in general elections, and explains why the two-party system in the House of Commons has not been challenged significantly despite the fall in support for Labour and the Conservatives.

The table below illustrates the decline of the two-party system in the electoral arena but its resilience in the legislative arena:

Effective number of parties at UK general elections, 1974–2005

Year	Con vote (%)	Con seats	Lab vote (%)	Lab seats	Lib vote (%)	Lib seats	Others Votes (%)	Others seats	ENEP	ENPP
1974 (Feb)	37.9	297	37.2	301	19.3	14	5.6	23	3.13	2.25
1974 (Oct)	35.8	277	39.2	319	18.3	13	6.7	26	3.17	2.26
1979	43.9	339	36.9	269	13.8	11	5.4	16	2.87	2.15
1983	42.4	397	27.6	209	25.4	23	4.6	21	3.12	2.09
1987	42.3	376	30.8	229	22.5	22	4.4	23	3.08	2.18
1992	41.8	336	34.2	271	17.9	20	6.1	24	3.09	2.27
1997	30.7	165	43.4	419	16.8	46	9.3	29	3.21	2.15
2001	31.7	166	40.7	413	18.3	52	9.3	28	3.33	2.19
2005	32.2	197	35.2	355	22.0	62	10.5	32	3.61	2.51
Mean 1945–70	45.2	303	46.0	313	7.1	8	1.7	5	2.39	2.04
Mean 1974–2005	37.6	283	36.1	309	19.4	29	6.9	25	3.18	2.23

Notes: ENEP = effective number of electoral parties; ENPP = effective number of parliamentary parties. Liberal includes SDP/Liberal Alliance (1983–87) and Liberal Democrat (1992–). Northern Ireland MPs are included as 'Others'.

The effective number of parties varies across the regions of the UK. The variations are, though, most pronounced when we compare the effective number of parties in general elections with the figures which arise from elections to the devolved assemblies in Scotland, Wales and Northern Ireland. The use of proportional representation has given fuller expression to multi-party politics in the devolved assemblies, whereas the simple plurality electoral system used for Westminster elections gives Labour a clear majority of seats in Scotland and Wales.

Effective number of parties in Scotland, Wales and Northern Ireland

Election	ENEP	ENPP
Scotland		
Scottish Parliament 2003	4.59	4.28
Westminster 2005	3.82	1.98
Wales		
Welsh Assembly 2003	4.17	3.08
Westminster 2005	3.60	1.86
Northern Ireland		
Northern Ireland Assembly 2003	4.95	4.62
Westminster 2005	3.94	2.82

Technical note: To calculate ENEP, calculate the decimal vote share of all parties, square them and then add them together. Then divide 1 by the resulting number to get the ENEP figure. To calculate ENPP, calculate the decimal seats share of all parties, square them and then add them together. Then divide 1 by the resulting number.

UK parties and European elections

Observers looking for clues about the likely effect of a more proportional system of representation on the competition between parties at UK general elections ought to have been given an ideal opportunity in 1999, when for the first time UK representatives in the European Parliament were elected on a proportional basis. The results in 1999 and at the next poll in 2004 confirmed the expectation of a multi-party system (see Table 13.6).

However, it would be mistaken to see the Euro-elections as dress-rehearsals for PR elections to Westminster. Controversially, the Labour government plumped for a 'closed list' voting system, based on large regional constituencies. This method allows party leaders the maximum influence over the outcome, since the lists can be compiled in a way which excludes candidates with the mildest dissident inclinations. In itself, this aspect of the system did not increase the existing incentive for voters to turn out. In Great Britain, the 1999 turnout was a miserable 23.1 per cent. Five years later it jumped to 38.1 per cent, but this was at least in part because the poll took place on the same day as local elections, and all-postal ballots were held in

Table 13.6 Votes and seats, 2004 European Parliament elections (GB only)

Party	1999 vote (%)	1999 seats	2004 vote (%)	2004 seats
Conservatives	35.8	36	26.7	27
Labour	28.0	29	22.6	19
Lib Dems	12.7	10	14.9	12
UKIP	7.0	3	16.1	12
Green Party	6.3	2	6.3	2
SNP	2.7	2	1.4	2
Plaid Cymru	1.9	2	1	1
BNP	1.0	0	4.9	0
Others	4.8	0	6.1	0

Note: The number of seats was reduced from 84 in 1999 to 75 in 2004.

some areas. Even so, the UK is currently some way from the prospect of turnouts as low as this in general elections, whatever the voting system, and this ensures that parties with relatively small but highly-committed support can expect to do better than they would in the contest for Westminster seats.

The turnout in European elections since the first contest in 1979 has also been depressed because the election concerned an institution which relatively few voters knew or cared about. This meant that the results were of little value even as a glorified opinion poll. At most, it was a kind of opinion poll on the government's approach to the EU; but it would be suspect even for that purpose. In the context of 2004, the voters most likely to turn out were those who opposed closer integration with Europe (or favoured complete withdrawal). This explains the remarkable performance of the UK Independence Party (UKIP) – whose campaign was also given a sprinkling of celebrity stardust – and the poor showing of the Conservatives who, ironically, were not Euro-sceptical enough for this contest. In part, the low Labour vote might have reflected mid-term dissatisfaction with the government; but

Case study: 13.1

Party systems and local government

It is impossible to discern a single pattern in party conflict at local level. Rather, there are almost as many systems as there are councils in the UK. In some places a single party is so dominant that it approaches a one-party mini-state (this is particularly true of Labour in some inner-city areas of northern England, though in 2004 the party lost control of Leeds and Newcastle which it had run for 24 and 30 years respectively). Elsewhere, no single party is in control, and coalitions are patched together from a multi-party mix to suit local prejudices. Parties which are at loggerheads in some areas will readily form alliances in others if the arithmetic is right. In some places Independent councillors are in control (though often such candidates are really Conservatives in disguise).

Since councillors are elected by simple plurality, the wide diversity of party competition might suggest that electoral systems are not such an important influence after all. However, UK council contests are very different from general elections. First, councillors serve four-year terms but they are not elected at the same time; a proportion is elected every year. The tides of opinion which affect Westminster make regular and erratic sweeps over the local government landscape. Councillors can be punished for poor local services or rising council tax demands; but if their party is faring badly at national level even a spotless record of local achievement might not be enough to save them. This created tension within the Conservative Party in 1997, when the council and parliamentary elections were held on the same day. Many popular councillors felt that they had been dragged out of office by the irrelevant antics of Conservative MPs. Their sense of grievance was sharpened by the knowledge that successive Conservative governments had reduced the ability of local councils to take independent initiatives, making them even more vulnerable to swings of opinion on the national level.

One place which does not elect its representatives through simple plurality is London, where assembly members are chosen through AMS. In 2004 the result reflected a multi-party contest; the Conservatives led with 9 seats, followed by Labour with 7, the Liberal Democrats (5), the Greens (2) and UKIP (2). Labour's Ken Livingstone was elected Mayor in 2000 and 2004 through the Supplementary Vote system (see Chapter 16).

other factors were involved. The party actually increased its vote share in Wales, where Plaid Cymru fared particularly badly. The Liberal Democrats had the best reasons for satisfaction, since their vote increased almost everywhere compared to 1999. However, their share was still lower than it had been at the 2001 general election, and significantly below the level achieved by the party in 2005.

Conclusion and summary

When a governing party in the UK does badly in a contest like a local election, the invariable response is that things will be very different when the nation votes in 'the only contest that really matters' – i.e. the next UK-wide general election. Sometimes this bravado turns out to be justified, and it is true that many second-order elections are treated as a means of administering a 'painless' warning to a government which retains its underlying popularity.

However, while governments feel that it is relatively harmless to tinker with the electoral systems at subnational level, it is now valid to ask a question which would have seemed ridiculous in (say) 1955: 'What is the *real* UK party system?'. Until 1997 there could only have been one answer, despite the 'blip' resulting from the Alliance challenge in 1983. The recent revival of the Liberal Democrats as something more than a vehicle for protest votes has been enough to arouse speculation about genuine multi-party competition. But more importantly, since the introduction of PR for devolved assemblies and the European elections the underlying diversity of the UK electorate has been revealed.

The Westminster government still seems to regard rival institutions as strictly subordinated, like a glorified local government. Almost certainly it would have responded in the same way if regional government had been introduced in England, even if that, too, had resulted in multi-party competition. However, while the effect of elections in devolved institutions has been limited at Westminster, it is very likely to have impressed many members of the public who have been disillusioned with two-party competition since the 1960s. If subsequent reforms produce an element of the upper chamber elected by a form of PR, public demand for a system which will produce a closer reflection of party preferences is likely to become overwhelming.

Further reading

The classic work on party systems is G. Sartori, *Parties and Party Systems: A Framework for Analysis* (Cambridge: Cambridge University Press, 1976). P. Webb, *The Modern British Party System* (London: Sage, 2000) is an excellent advanced text. S. Ingle, *The British Party System* (London: Pinter, 3rd edition, 2000) is a highly readable and insightful account, although it also deals at length with party organisation and ideology. L. Robbins, H. Blackmore and R. Pyper (eds), *Britain's Changing Party System* (Manchester: Manchester University Press) includes some discussions which are still useful although the system has continued to change since the volume was published. Andrew Heywood's chapter, warning of the emergence of a dominant-party system, is particularly pertinent. R. Garner and P. Lynch, 'The Changing Party System', *Parliamentary Affairs*, Vol. 58, No. 3 (2005), pp. 533–54, and A. Russell, 'The

Party System: Deep Frozen or Gentle Thawing?', *Parliamentary Affairs*, Vol. 58, No. 2 (2005), pp. 351–65 take account of more recent developments.

Much of the literature on general elections includes assessments of the state of the party system. Particularly useful in this respect are P. Norris and C. Wlezein (eds), *Britain Votes 2005* (Oxford: Oxford University Press, 2005) and A. Geddes and J. Tonge (eds), *Britain Decides. The 2005 General Election* (London: Palgrave, 2005). The significance of electoral systems is assessed in P. Dunleavy, 'Facing up to Multi-Party Politics', in *Parliamentary Affairs*, Vol. 58, No. 3 (2005), pp. 503–32 and P. Dunleavy and H. Margetts, 'The Impact of UK Electoral Systems', in P. Norris and C. Wlezein (eds) *Britain Votes 2005* (Oxford: Oxford University Press, 2005), pp. 198–213.

Useful overviews of the various party systems within the UK include a selection of articles that have appeared in *Politics Review*. On the 2005 general election, see D. Denver, 'Four-Party Competition in Scotland', *Politics Review*, Vol. 15, No. 2 (2005), pp. 19–21; J. Bradbury, 'Labour Power under Pressure in Wales', *Politics Review*, Vol. 15, No. 2 (2005), pp. 16–18, and J. Tonge, 'DUP and Sinn Fein Triumph in Northern Ireland', *Politics Review*, Vol. 15, No. 2 (2005), pp. 10–13. On elections to the devolved assemblies, see D. Denver, '2003 Scottish Parliament elections: Messages for Unpopular Parties', *Politics Review*, Vol. 13, No. 2, (2003), pp. 28–31 and J. Bradbury, '2003 Welsh Assembly elections: Labour reclaims Power', *Politics Review*, Vol. 13, No. 2, (2003), pp. 22–6.

Websites

The official websites of British political parties contain details on their election results and policies. Richard Kimber's politics 'gateway' www.psr.keele.ac.uk/parties.htm provides links. The websites of the main parties in the UK are:

Conservative Party www.conservative-party.org.uk

Labour Party www.labour.org.uk

Liberal Democrats www.libdems.org.uk

Plaid Cymru www.plaid-cymru.wales.com

Scottish National Party www.snp.org.uk

British National Party www.bnp.net

Greens www.greenparty.org.uk

Respect www.respectcoalition.org

United Kingdom Independence Party www.independenceuk.org

Democratic Unionist Party www.dup.org.uk

Ulster Unionist Party www.uup.org/

Sinn Fein www.sinnfein.ie

Social Democratic and Labour Party www.sdlp.ie

Chapter 14

Party organisation

Learning outcomes

After reading this chapter, you will:
- Be able to explore different perspectives on the role of UK parties.
- Understand the organisation of the main political parties in the UK.
- Be able to evaluate the strengths and weaknesses of the rules governing party finance.

Introduction

Most commentators accept that political parties are an inevitable feature of liberal democracy. Yet in the UK today parties are often accused of bringing democracy into disrepute. Critics claim that they are more interested in 'playing party politics' than in addressing national priorities in a constructive way. Accordingly, while the proportion of voters prepared to turn out at elections has fallen sharply, there has been an even more spectacular decline in membership of the parties themselves.

In defence of UK parties, it can be argued that their plight merely reflects a more general tendency of people to disengage from traditional forms of voluntary activity. In particular, citizens are more inclined to throw their energies into single-issue pressure groups, which lobby MPs instead of putting themselves to the trouble of securing their own elected representatives (see Chapter 18). However, it is still worth asking whether there are respects in which the main political parties are responsible for their own predicament by mismanaging factors under their own control, like the scope for active participation allowed to their members, and the way in which they raise funds.

From cadre parties to mass parties

In the early years of party competition in the UK it would be wrong to say that politics was merely a game restricted to aristocrats. Some MPs came from relatively humble backgrounds, and people who lacked the vote could exert some influence over decisions by demonstrating in support of their favoured causes. However, even after the franchise was expanded by the 1832 Great Reform Act, non-aristocratic MPs usually owed their seats to aristocratic patronage. The loose political groupings of the eighteenth and early nineteenth centuries – the 'Whigs' and the 'Tories' – are best understood as **cadre parties**. They were associations of affluent individuals who joined together for specific political purposes, but retained enough independence to make new alliances (or to retire from public life) if circumstances changed.

Cadre party: a political party that develops from an elite in the legislature whose principal aim is to secure election for its candidates.

An alternative model of political organisation is a **mass party** – one which depends on a large membership to finance the party at national and local level, publicise its activities, run campaigns and recruit potential leaders. In the UK mass parties began to emerge after a further franchise reform, in 1867. This second Reform Act was pushed through by the Conservatives, under the leadership of Benjamin Disraeli. Against critics within the party who feared that reform would lead to revolution, he argued that the electorate was sure to be expanded soon anyway, to include members of the rising middle classes. The Whig Party had benefited from the 1832 Reform Act, winning the lasting loyalty of many new voters. By persuading the Conservatives to act against their instincts and push through a radical measure, Disraeli hoped that the rewards this time would go to his own party rather than the Liberals (the new name for the old Whig party).

Mass party: a political party with a mass membership, organised at national and local level, that develops outside the legislature.

The 1867 Reform Act did indeed improve Conservative prospects. But the effect was registered in both parties. More professional organisations were required in order to reach a larger electorate; and local bodies which emerged to work for the election of candidates needed coordination from the centre. A National Union of Conservative and Constitutional Associations was set up in 1867; a National Liberal Federation was established ten years later. While electoral fortunes depended largely on the campaigning energies of unpaid volunteers, the parties also began to appoint paid agents to oversee activities in individual constituencies and regions. Mass parties had arrived in the UK; bureaucracy and procedures to enforce discipline on what were still voluntary organisations was not far behind.

The functions of mass parties

Those who take a positive view of mass political parties in liberal democracies focus on six main functions:

1. *Representing opinion and building coalitions.* In liberal democracies, political parties try to win power through persuasion rather than violence. If they want to be successful at the national level, they must bring together and represent

sectional interests whose views are likely to diverge to some extent. Thus, unlike single-issue pressure groups (see Chapter 18) they can be unifying rather than divisive forces.

2. *Ensuring choice for voters.* Parties construct political programmes, featuring a range of alternative policy suggestions which they offer to voters at election time.

3. *Educating the public.* By communicating and explaining their policies to the electorate, parties raise the general level of public knowledge about key issues.

4. *Promoting participation.* Mass political parties are voluntary organisations which welcome new members, allowing them a chance to influence policy as well as helping to elect congenial representatives.

5. *Providing a channel of recruitment.* Through membership of a political party, citizens learn political skills and can maximise their chances of winning office at subnational, UK or EU level.

6. *Making leaders accountable.* Even if a party has an overwhelming parliamentary majority, its leaders should never forget their ultimate reliance on ordinary members, who can make their views known through recognised channels.

It is important to note that none of these points rest on the assumption that parties are composed of angelic public servants. The six functions could be regarded as benign by-products of a single-minded and self-interested quest for power by party members. However, critics of UK parties deny that they can even produce accidental benefits, arguing that:

- Far from enhancing national cohesion, parties exaggerate minimal disagreements and grievances for their own advantage.
- Parties try to restrict meaningful choice, monopolising media attention at election time and trying to strangle popular new movements at birth.
- Parties hinder public education, by concentrating on their favoured issues, belittling alternative views, and distorting statistical information.
- Parties only welcome the input of members who are prepared to play by the existing rules.
- Ambitious party members will only be selected as candidates for office if they support orthodox views and win patronage from senior party figures.
- Whether a party is in office or opposition, dissident members will be told to keep quiet in the interests of unity. As a result, action against unsatisfactory leaders will only be taken when the damage is already done.

Opponents and defenders of political parties tend to take polarised views, arguing that they either fulfil *all* or *none* of their expected roles. But other views are possible – for example, that they carry out some of the roles reasonably well, or most of them in part. Inevitably, assessments will depend to some extent on the expectations of the observer. Expectations of party performance in the UK are arguably higher at the beginning of the twenty-first century than ever before. In their defence, politicians can claim that the public makes unrealistic demands. However, the democratic process in Britain is heavily subsidised by taxpayers, who have a corresponding right to criticise if standards are perceived to be slipping. Equally, the most depressing reply to attacks on elected public servants is that 'the public gets the politicians it deserves'. Politicians cannot be immune from wider developments in society; but as elected representatives they have a responsibility to resist detrimental trends.

Conservative Party organisation

Whatever their electoral fortunes at any given time, the Conservatives provide the most convenient starting-point for a discussion of UK political parties. The party is regarded as the most successful democratic organisation of modern times, adapting to radical social and constitutional change since the advent of mass parties in the 1860s.

Leadership

Loyalty to the incumbent party leader is a key element of the traditional Conservative ethos. As an aristocratic organisation, the nineteenth-century party had an instinctive preference for hierarchy. The leader was expected to inspire his followers with attractive policies, but if anything it was more important that he should command personal respect. Ability was actively distrusted, unless it was combined with the right social background. Even Benjamin Disraeli could not be said to have risen to the leadership entirely through his merits; his father was well-connected and affluent. However, Disraeli was born a Jew and he did not go to public school. These factors contributed to the suspicion in which he was held by many of his colleagues long after he had proved himself to be an indispensable political asset.

On paper, the Conservative leader remains an all-powerful figure within the party, whether in government or opposition. There is no formal check on his or her powers over patronage, policy or party propaganda. In practice, though, the extent of a leader's power is related to popularity, and to the prospects for the party at any given time. If the Conservatives seem likely to win the next election, and the leader is respected by the general public, he or she will usually be able to silence

Table 14.1 Main party leaders since 1945

Conservative	Labour	Liberal/Lib Dems
Winston Churchill 1940–55	Clement Attlee 1935–55	Clement Davis 1945–56
Sir Anthony Eden 1955–7	Hugh Gaitskell 1955–63*	Jo Grimond 1956–67
Harold Macmillan 1957–63	Harold Wilson 1963–76	Jeremy Thorpe 1967–76
Sir Alec Douglas-Home 1963–4	James Callaghan 1976–80	David Steel 1976–88
Edward Heath 1965–75	Michael Foot 1980–3	Paddy Ashdown 1988–99
Margaret Thatcher 1975–90	Neil Kinnock 1983–92	Charles Kennedy 1999–2006
John Major 1990–7	John Smith 1992–94*	Sir Menzies Campbell 2006–
William Hague 1997–2001	Tony Blair 1994–	
Iain Duncan Smith 2001–3		
Michael Howard 2003–5		
David Cameron 2005–		

*Died in office

any parliamentary dissent. However, if the electoral prospects are doubtful and the leader's poll rating lags behind the party as a whole, even minor grievances can turn into crises of confidence. This explains the high wastage-rate of Conservative leaders since 1992, when the party's poll rating took a decisive downturn. In 1995 even the incumbent Prime Minister John Major only survived as leader because no convincing alternative candidate could be found when he submitted himself for re-election.

The Conservative leader's freedom of action is heavily constrained when the party is divided. Popular figures will usually have to be accommodated within the Cabinet or Shadow Cabinet, whether the leader likes them or not. In recent times, as the party has become increasingly influenced by ideological considerations (see Chapter 15), leaders have been forced to include opponents in their front-bench teams. Thus, for example, Thatcher had to give posts to leading critics of her economic policy even after she became Prime Minister in 1979. Between 1992 and 1997 John Major's moderate brand of Euroscepticism was drowned out by colleagues who either wanted closer ties with the EU or to withdraw completely (see Chapter 12).

Opinion poll fluctuations and party divisions are not the only factors behind the recent decline of Conservative leaders. Changes in society as a whole have also played a part. Sir Alec Douglas-Home succeeded Harold Macmillan in 1963 through what were termed 'the customary processes' of leadership selection. That is, senior party members made informal inquiries among their parliamentary colleagues about the suitability of the various contenders. In a new 'meritocratic' era this was widely regarded as outdated. A system of leadership election was introduced, and was used for the first time in 1965.

In itself, the introduction of formal rules for election has destabilised the position of Conservative leaders. Yet the various systems used since 1965 have compounded the problem (see Timeline 14.1). It can be argued that, far from improving the original prototype, the subsequent changes have been driven by short-term considerations. Thus a provision for annual elections was brought in to satisfy demand for

---

TIMELINE 14.1

Conservative leadership election rules

1965	Vote of MPs to fill leadership vacancy. In order to win on first ballot, candidate requires support of 50 per cent of MPs, and must enjoy a lead of at least 15 per cent over the runner-up. New challengers can emerge for a second ballot, in which the winner requires an overall majority. If this is not forthcoming the top two candidates proceed to a run-off in a third ballot
1975	Rules changed to allow annual challenges to incumbent leader. Challengers require only two nominees
1991	Rules on nomination of challengers tightened; now 10 per cent of MPs must demand an election
1998	Radical overhaul of rules. Now 15 per cent of MPs must call for a vote of confidence in the incumbent leader. If the leader loses he or she must resign. If more than two candidates contest the vacancy, a series of ballots are held by MPs until the field is reduced to two. The winner is decided by a ballot of all party members
2005	An attempt by the incumbent leader, Michael Howard, to push through a revision of the leadership rules was rejected by the party membership

Table 14.2 Conservative Party leadership election, 2005

First ballot of Conservative MPs	
David Davis	62
David Cameron	56
Liam Fox	42
Kenneth Clarke	38
Clarke is eliminated	
Second ballot of Conservative MPs	
David Cameron	90
David Davis	57
Liam Fox	51
Fox is eliminated	
Ballot of Conservative Party members	
David Cameron	134 446 (67.6%)
David Davis	64 398 (32.35)
David Cameron is elected leader	

a vote on Edward Heath's troubled leadership. Later, challenges to the incumbent leader were made more difficult to launch after contests in consecutive years (Sir Anthony Meyer in 1989 and Michael Heseltine in 1990, who both challenged Margaret Thatcher). In the 1990 contest, Thatcher secured 204 votes but fell four short of the 15 per cent lead needed for victory. After consulting Cabinet ministers – many of whom said she would lose – Thatcher resigned. John Major and Douglas Hurd then entered the second ballot against Heseltine, with Major declared the winner with 185 votes.

William Hague's *Fresh Future* reforms, introduced in 1998, were an attempt to assuage grassroots resentment against the parliamentary party which had just been crushed at the polls. The first trial of the system elevated Iain Duncan Smith to the leadership after a poll of party members. The success of the experiment can be measured from Duncan Smith's deposition two years later, without even fighting a general election. His successor Michael Howard was chosen without a contest – a process which was not unlike the informal system in place before 1965.

Although there was no significant rise in the Conservative vote under Howard's leadership at the 2005 general election, the party did improve its position at Westminster and it was felt that Howard had kept the party united. Even so, just before the election Howard took a conscious gamble with his authority, effectively removing the MP Howard Flight as an official candidate. Flight's offence was to have wondered in public about the real nature of Conservative plans for taxation. Many Conservatives shared his support for radical tax cuts, but that was not the party's stated policy.

When standing down immediately after the election, Howard recommended a change to the system for electing the leader, which would take the decisive voice away from the party members. His proposals, however, were rejected. In 2005 David Cameron won the leadership after a contest which was held to have improved the party's image. He came top of the second ballot of Conservative MPs (which Duncan Smith had failed to do in 2001) and beat David Davis by a two to one margin in the vote of party members (see Table 14.2). Only the passage of time would tell whether this meant that the new rules had proved themselves after an initial period of trial and error.

Case study: 14.1

The Conservative Party Board

Until 1998, the Conservative Party was divided into three sections; the parliamentary party consisting of MPs and peers; the professional party, consisting of paid officials with their headquarters in London; and the voluntary party, the National Union of Conservative Associations, which represented grassroots constituency members. After reforms proposed by William Hague in 1998, the three branches were united at the top in an overarching management Board. This promised to introduce more cohesion into the party. However, it did not make it more democratic. Of the 17 positions on the board, only five were open to election by ordinary party members. The proposals themselves (which included the new system of electing the party leader) won almost unanimous approval in a ballot of the whole party – but only a third of the members bothered to register their opinions.

The parliamentary Conservative Party

The decline of deference towards Conservative leaders has been particularly evident in the behaviour of the parliamentary party in recent years. Under Margaret Thatcher there were several rebellions, notably against the Community Charge or Poll Tax and plans to charge students for tuition fees. But problems came to a head under John Major. Opponents of the Maastricht Treaty almost brought the government down in July 1993. In the following year eight persistent rebels were deprived of the party whip, and another Conservative MP resigned the whip in protest. The original eight 'whipless wonders' were wooed back a few months later because of the government's perilous parliamentary position. They were back in the fold in time to vote in the leadership election of July 1995, called by Major in the hope that a resounding victory would force his critics to 'shut up'. The result gave him little respite: 111 MPs (from a full complement of 329) withheld their support; of these, 89 supported the challenger John Redwood who had been portrayed as an unruly extremist.

Backbench Conservative MPs have a well-established forum in which they can make their feelings known. The 1922 Committee provides the party leadership with a useful means of detecting unrest; the whips are in attendance to report on the mood. The leader is only allowed to address the Committee by invitation (and when the party is in office ministers are excluded from membership). Unlike most senior party officials the 1922 Chairperson is elected, and the result of the contest usually provides an insight into the balance of party factions. Backbench MPs can also influence the leadership through a variety of party committees which cover specific policy subjects.

Party members

The Conservatives are not unusual in having suffered a drastic decline in their membership. In 1953 a figure of more than 2.8 million was claimed. At that time, the local Young Conservatives were a lively element in the social scene of many

Table 14.3 Party membership, 1996–2005 (approximate figures)

Party	1996	2002	2005
Conservatives	250 000	330 000	254 000
Labour	400 000	280 000	210 000
Liberal Democrats	98 000	76 000	72 000

constituencies. By contrast, in the mid-1990s it was estimated that the membership had fallen below 400,000, and that more than half of the members were aged 66 or older (see Table 14.3). These findings were unlikely to improve the party's image; and yet they were publicised at the time when remaining members were blaming Conservative MPs for all their troubles, and demanding a greater influence over the choice of leader.

William Hague's response to these demands, the *Fresh Future* reforms of 1998, gave members the appearance of greater influence. But the reality was rather different. There was to be more consultation with members, through a new system of policy forums; but these groups were purely advisory and most of the key decisions were still taken by the leader and his close parliamentary allies. Ordinary members had an important say in the choice of their constituency candidates; but this has always been the case in a party where interference from the centre is usually resented. The central party has enjoyed some success in encouraging selection from a wider basis in terms of ethnicity, gender and sexual orientation; but before the 2005 election several prospective women candidates were deselected. Under David Cameron, the efforts to make candidates more 'representative' of society as a whole will be stepped up. It remains to be seen whether this initiative will overcome the traditional independence of individual constituency parties.

For grass-roots Conservatives the annual highlight is the party conference. These seaside gatherings used to be derided by critics as orchestrated rallies rather than serious political meetings. The motions were normally selected to avoid any searching examination of the party's record, and were almost invariably passed by general acclamation. The 'star performers' were those who could deliver the cheapest jibes against other parties. Until Heath succeeded Douglas-Home in 1965, the leader only bothered to attend the conference on the final day.

However, since 1979 Conservative conferences have become more interesting. In part, this is a product of principled division on issues like Europe. But although rousing receptions can still be orchestrated – Duncan Smith received standing ovations a few weeks before he was dumped by his party in 2003 – the audience is much more volatile than it used to be. During the 1990s dissenting speakers on Europe, like Lord Tebbit, could cause real embarrassment for the party leadership. In 1997, the hostility shown towards former ministers after Labour's landslide victory gave additional impetus to demands for reform. Ironically, though, the main influence over policy was exercised in October 1987, after the party had won a third election in a row. The audience at the 1987 conference showed symptoms of impatience that the proposed poll tax was to be introduced in stages, rather than all

Grass-roots Conservatives get over-excited at the 2004 party conference
(© Getty Images)

at once. Grass-roots Conservatives got their way, with calamitous results for their heroine, Margaret Thatcher.

Labour Party organisation

Since the publication of Robert McKenzie's classic study of *British Political Parties* in 1955, the Labour Party has been regarded as an organisation with democratic pretensions which contrast with its 'oligarchical' practices. That is, although the members have an important role in theory, the decisions that actually matter are taken by a small number of influential people. However, the party's procedures have undergone significant changes since the days of Clement Attlee, and the subject is well worth a new examination.

Leadership

Traditionally, Labour supporters have argued that their movement is far more important than any individual. Suspicion of Labour leaders was dramatically reinforced by the economic crisis of 1931, when the Prime Minister Ramsay MacDonald decided to stay at the head of a Conservative-dominated coalition and push through benefit cuts rather than resigning. Although he had played a vital role in making Labour a significant force in British politics, MacDonald had aroused misgivings through his apparent fondness for aristocratic society – hardly the kind of preference one would expect from a devoted servant of working-class interests. Other Labour leaders have found appeals for unity falling on deaf ears; Hugh Gaitskell encountered strong opposition over nuclear weapons and national-

The 'iron law of oligarchy'

In 1911 the German-born academic Roberto Michels (1876–1936) published *Political Parties: A Sociological Study of the Oligarchical Tendencies of Modern Democracy*. Michels argued that any large organisation will be run by a relatively small elite group (an 'oligarchy'). This observation – proclaimed by Michels to be an 'iron law of oligarchy' – is said to apply even to political parties which claim to be open and democratic. Whatever their original intentions, recruits into the leadership group will accumulate special knowledge which sets them apart from the rank-and-file who are incapable of action without direction from the top. This elite will pursue its own interests, presiding over a beguiled and benighted membership.

Michels' work preceded the 1917 Russian revolution, which lent spectacular support to his findings since the Bolshevik Party soon betrayed all of its democratic slogans. This book influenced Robert McKenzie's study of British political parties in the 1950s. More recent developments might suggest that Michels was unduly pessimistic in his portrayal of passive grass-roots party members. However, his analysis can still help to explain the behaviour of party leaders, who have been forced to adopt more creative tactics in order to convince their supporters that their input really matters, while retaining decisive power over policy-making.

isation, while in the 1970s grass-roots critics freely attacked James Callaghan and his Chancellor, Denis Healey.

However, the contrast with Conservative views of leadership can be exaggerated. As we have seen, despite the party's tradition of deference, Conservative leaders have often been criticised and occasionally deposed. If anything, Conservative members have exacted a heavier price for failure than their Labour counterparts. Since the Second World War there have been eleven Conservative leaders, compared to Labour's eight (and two of these died prematurely). Only two Labour leaders (Callaghan and Foot) have felt it necessary to resign shortly after a first electoral defeat, compared to four Conservatives (Douglas-Home, Major, Hague and Howard). In 1990 the mere prospect of defeat was sufficient to make Conservative MPs forget that Thatcher had led them to three consecutive victories, and they disposed of Duncan Smith before he had submitted himself to the judgement of the national electorate.

In theory, the formal powers of a Labour leader over patronage and policy-making are limited. In opposition, the front bench team is elected by the parliamentary party; the party conference is the sovereign policy-making body; and at other times the National Executive Committee (NEC) is responsible for day-to-day management. However, in practice most Labour leaders have been able to work around these constraints. Although the team members in a Labour Shadow Cabinet are chosen by MPs, the leader decides which positions they should occupy. When the party returns to power, the Shadow team must be retained at first (though a leader strengthened by electoral victory can take the opportunity to re-allocate their jobs). But after a decent interval he or she can drop any uncongenial colleagues, and bring in allies whether or not they are popular with their Westminster colleagues. Of course, a weak Labour Prime Minister will be subject to constraints when making personnel changes – but no more so than a Conservative counterpart. This point was illustrated vividly in 2004, when Tony Blair announced that he would only fight one more election as leader. Many observers believed that he had given a free licence to would-be parliamentary rebels, but his position was still stronger than that of John Major between 1993 and 1997.

The story is broadly similar where policy-making is concerned. Until the late 1950s Labour leaders could be confident of winning key votes on policy issues in the party conference, thanks to the consistent support of the biggest trade unions. The situation was more volatile for the next two decades, but the trouble usually arose when leaders deliberately challenged trade union interests (for example, when Gaitskell tried to remove the party's commitment to nationalisation, and when Harold Wilson flirted with reform of the unions themselves). Only in the late 1970s did the relationship between the leadership and the unions come close to breakdown, because the Callaghan government tried to combat an economic crisis through a mixture of spending cuts and pay controls – both of which were regarded by a more radical union movement as direct attacks on working-class interests.

One important result of the restless mood in Labour ranks was the introduction of a new system for electing the leader (and the deputy). Until 1981 the choice of leader had lain with Labour MPs. Afterwards the decision rested with an electoral college, in which the parliamentary party enjoyed no more influence than the grassroots constituency parties (30 per cent of the vote each), while the greatest share, of 40 per cent, was given to the trade unions. This arrangement reflected the fact that unlike the Conservative Party, whose members join a unified organisation, Labour is

| Controversy: | 14.1 |

Labour and the Militant Tendency

During the 1980s the battle for Labour's soul focused on the activities of the Militant Tendency, a small revolutionary Trotskyite group within the party which enjoyed the support of several high-profile councillors and MPs. The opponents of Militant argued that it contravened the party constitution, as a parasitic organisation which sought to hijack Labour and re-direct it to its own ends. The real controversy concerned Militant's ideas. Militant members rejected the 'orthodox' Labour view that 'socialism' could be secured by parliamentary methods. In their view, senior Labour politicians had always betrayed the party's historic commitment to socialist ideology; thus if Labour wanted to be true to its original ideas, 'revisionist' MPs were the people who deserved to be purged from the party (see Chapter 15).

The Militant Tendency never appeared likely to take over the party, as their opponents alleged; only a small handful of MPs sympathised with its aims. But even this tiny minority was capable of providing the Conservatives and their media allies with an easy propaganda target. As a result, Michael Foot and his successor Neil Kinnock both spent much of their energies trying to expel Militant members. In the short term their campaign merely drew further attention to the problem, exaggerating the extent to which Labour's parliamentarians were divided. But eventual success added greatly to the institutional strength of the Labour leadership, making it possible in future for the rank-and-file membership to allow 'heresy hunts' in a party which had previously prided itself on its broadly-based tolerance.

a federal party made up of various affiliated bodies (for example, trade unions and groups like the Fabian Society). But in the context of 1981 the effect of this 'democratisation' of the party was always likely to reinforce left-wing influence, since the constituency vote was largely controlled by radical activists.

The first leader to be chosen by the new electoral college, Neil Kinnock (1983–92), struggled to reassert the authority of his office. Several high-profile left-wing activists were expelled from the party in the mid-1980s after a prolonged campaign against the Militant Tendency (see Controversy 14.1). Although the purge failed to convince the public of Kinnock's prime ministerial potential, it did strengthen his position within the party. Labour's campaign for the 1987 general election was built around Kinnock's forceful personality. When the party lost that contest, and failed again in 1992, Kinnock stepped down. But far from weakening the position of Kinnock's successor, John Smith, the memory of four consecutive defeats strengthened the leadership role within the Labour Party, because most ordinary members were now prepared to suppress their differences in the common fight against Conservative rule.

Under Smith, the leadership reversed the previous trend of trying to resist grassroots reform and pushed through radical change from the top. The electoral college was revised, reducing the union vote from 40 to 33 per cent. But the most important change was the introduction of OMOV (One Member One Vote). In the past, union leaders had used their votes at party conferences without consulting their members. Although this was perfectly satisfactory to the party leadership when the unions were reliable allies, once the relationship soured it was regarded as a serious infringement of democratic principle. From 1993, union votes at conference would only be cast after a ballot of their members.

Despite these reforms, modernisers within the party believed that the process should have gone further. Tony Blair led a successful drive to revise Clause IV of the party's constitution. Blair had won the party leadership in 1994, securing a majority in each section of the electoral college, following Smith's sudden death (see Table 14.4). Although it was already clear that Labour would not reverse the major privatisations of the 1980s and 1990s, the end of the party's historic commitment to the principle of public ownership had far more than symbolic importance. Above all, it allowed Blair's allies to claim that their leader had made Labour 'electable' once again. Losing such a key battle was a crippling blow to the radical wing of the party, which was already being dismissed as 'Old Labour'.

Thus, whatever misgivings some party loyalists may have harboured regarding Blair's policies, by the time that he became Prime Minister the prestige of the Labour leader's office was arguably higher than it had ever been before. In the 1970s and 1980s dissent and intrigue against senior figures had been integral to the Labour

Table 14.4 Labour Party leadership election, 1994

	Parliamentary Labour Party (%)	Constituency party members (%)	Affiliated members (%)	Total (%)
Tony Blair	60.5	58.2	52.3	57.0
John Prescott	19.6	24.4	28.4	24.1
Margaret Beckett	19.9	17.4	19.3	18.9

The Labour Party élite dominates the stage (© AFP/Getty Images)

Party ethos. After a second election victory in 2001, Blair seemed invulnerable to any attack from within his own ranks – even from his ambitious Chancellor, Gordon Brown. Like the Conservative leader, the Labour incumbent can be challenged; but only with the backing of 20 per cent of MPs and after a vote from a special conference. The last challenge to an incumbent leader (under different rules) came in 1988, when Kinnock defeated Tony Benn. If Labour's rules had allowed just two MPs to trigger a leadership election, as the Conservatives did until 1991, even Blair would have lived in constant expectation of a challenge. As it was, he was able to force through highly controversial policies at home and abroad without a suggestion of a formal attempt to displace him.

There remains a possibility, though, that the stifled dissent of the Blair years might spill over dramatically after his departure. After all, Blair's authority ultimately arose from his party's desperation for an electoral victory. Three successive comfortable wins could breed the kind of complacency which undermined the position of Conservative leaders after 1987.

The parliamentary party

In the past, Labour MPs were associated with ideological disagreement and factional infighting. However, this image was always somewhat misleading. The most spectacular split, in 1931, was provoked by the leadership rather than MPs. Internal conflict also surfaced after 1955, when Clement Attlee was succeeded as leader by the social democrat Gaitskell rather than Anuerin Bevan, the hero of the left. However, despite continuing ideological differences during the 1970s the parliamentary party remained remarkably united in its voting. The conduct of Labour MPs between 1974–79, when their governments lacked a secure parliamentary majority, certainly presents a stark contrast with the antics of Conservative backbenchers in the 1992–97 parliament. And while the left has usually been associated with trouble-making, the split by those Labour MPs who formed the Social Democratic Party (SDP) in 1981 came from the other wing of the party.

The Parliamentary Labour Party (PLP) holds meetings which allow MPs to air their views, as Conservatives may do in their 1922 Committee. In recent times the PLP has been associated with obedience to the will of the whips, and to the party's 'spin-doctors' like Peter Mandelson and Alastair Campbell. In particular, the 102 women MPs elected in 1997 included some devoted loyalists; collectively they became known as 'Blair's Babes', even though their ranks included battle-hardened dissidents like Clare Short and Gwyneth Dunwoody. But MPs of both sexes were anxious to remain 'on message', willingly receiving instructions from party managers on what to say during media interviews. Even after the 2005 general election which seriously weakened his position, Blair received a warm reception from the first meeting of the new PLP.

Like the Conservatives, Labour has backbench parliamentary party committees covering specific subjects. But while the party is in government, independent-minded MPs have their best chance of making an impact through membership of select

Case study:	14.2

Parties and multi-level governance

Constitutional change has already affected the main UK parties to some extent. Ironically, the greatest impact has fallen on Labour, which pushed through devolution and allowed cities to elect mayors, should they choose to do so. In Wales, the Labour leadership failed in its attempts to stop Rhodri Morgan becoming Chief Minister (see Chapter 11). Denis Canavan stood successfully as an independent candidate for the Scottish Parliament after having been denied nomination by Labour. And in London, Labour prevented Ken Livingstone from running for mayor as the official party candidate. The result was a humiliating defeat for the party in the 2000 Mayoral election. The leadership had no alternative but to endorse Livingstone as its official candidate when he stood for re-election in June 2004. On the face of it, these misadventures look like serious blows for the 'control freaks' of the central party. But the most remarkable thing was not that such interference failed, but that it should have been attempted in the first place. There is no evidence that lasting lessons have been learned.

Devolution also caused serious tension between Conservatives north and south of the English border. Scottish Tories were at a serious disadvantage in the 1999 elections to the Scottish Parliament, having argued against devolution in the referendum less than two years earlier. Their traditional autonomy was strengthened, and they tried to disassociate themselves from the UK leadership as far as good manners allowed.

The presence of Liberal Democrats in the Scottish Executive since 1999, and (to a lesser extent) the party's inclusion in a coalition in Wales between 1999 and 2003, could only enhance the prestige of leadership positions in the UK party as a whole. Whatever the overall UK electorate might think, MPs and activists were now more inclined to regard the Liberal Democrats as a potential party of government. This may help to explain why Charles Kennedy was forced to resign as party leader in January 2006, when it was felt that he was not living up to the new expectations. In the longer term, it may increase the impetus towards tighter party discipline.

committees – provided, that is, that they do not take their independence so far as to launch damaging attacks on ministers (see Chapter 7).

Party members

Since Labour is a federal party, its members join affiliated bodies rather than signing up to a single organisation. For example, members can enrol in their local constituency parties, or join through a trade union. The link between Labour and the unions was regarded as an important handicap for the party in the 1980s. Since then the ties have been loosened, while union membership has declined steeply.

On the face of it, grass-roots Labour members enjoy more power today than ever before. The introduction of OMOV gave them individual votes in leadership ballots for the first time. The 1997 document *Partnership in Power* envisaged a two-year policy-making cycle, with policy commissions actively soliciting the views of the constituency members. Policy forums for ordinary members had been introduced under Kinnock back in 1990.

However, the extent to which these changes have really empowered Labour members can be disputed. Casting a single ballot in the leadership election gives members a feeling of participation, and although a single vote might not mean very much to the overall outcome, future contests might be closer than the 1994 poll which Blair won with 57 per cent (see Table 14.4). But some members clearly feel that they have lost influence on matters closer to home. The left-wing reform movement of the early 1980s had secured mandatory re-selection for parliamentary

---

Case study: | 14.3

New Labour's organisation

In the early 1980s Labour's organisation was regarded as highly inefficient, compared to the smooth-running Conservative election machine. The transformation of Labour's machinery is often credited to Peter Mandelson, appointed Director of Communications by Kinnock in 1985, and Alastair Campbell, a tabloid journalist who had also been close to Kinnock before becoming Tony Blair's press spokesperson in 1994. Their impact was symbolised by the move from Labour's old headquarters, Transport House on Walworth Road, to modern, well-equipped offices in the Millbank Tower, just a short distance from the House of Commons. While opinions differ about the real quality of Labour's campaigning, the 'Millbank Tendency' certainly helped to ensure that a united party image was conveyed to the media. Even before Labour returned to office in 1997, party strategists were being called 'control freaks'.

An important factor in the rise of 'New' Labour was the taming of the party's National Executive Committee (NEC). This key body, which among other things was responsible for authorising the party manifesto, used to be the forum for bitter and well-publicised squabbles. Under Smith and Blair, by contrast, it usually hit the headlines only when it took controversial actions to impose the leader's will on other elements within the party. In part this was due to structural changes; in 1997 the membership was increased from 29 to 32. Blair also appointed a Party Chair for the first time (previously this official had been elected and had a lower media profile).

candidates – whether or not they were sitting MPs. Although fear of being deselected in these votes fuelled the exodus of MPs into the SDP at this time, in fact the power was used quite sparingly by constituency members.

Now the power of deselection is more frequently associated with the central party, when it over-rides the wishes of local members. Several parliamentary candidates have been selected thanks to intervention from the NEC (which can veto potential dissidents) rather than any enthusiasm within the constituency. Defectors from the Conservative Party, like Alan Howarth and Sean Woodward, have been 'parachuted' into selection battles in certain constituencies with heavy NEC backing. Sometimes the sitting MP has been rewarded with a peerage for standing down shortly before an election, allowing the NEC to argue that it is too late to go through the usual selection formalities, and ensuring the selection of the candidate favoured by the national leadership. The overall effect of such manoeuvres can only be to deter any talented and ambitious recruits who would like to sit in parliament one day without having to give up the right to form an opinion for themselves. Compulsory all-women shortlists, imposed by the central party in order to change the composition of the parliamentary party, have also caused unrest, although they are now legal. In the 2005 general election Labour lost its safe seat of Blaenau Gwent in Wales because of local dissatisfaction with an imposed all-women shortlist.

Furthermore, although recent changes can be dressed up as democratic advances, the input of Labour Party members into policy-making can be exaggerated. The two-year policy process actually gives ample opportunity for the party to water down controversial suggestions from the grass-roots. The party leadership seems more impressed with the findings of non-party focus groups; indeed, it can be accused of paying more heed to the opinions of opponents than those of long-standing members who offer ideas which are at odds with the views of party leaders. In 2003 Blair launched a 'Big Conversation' with Britain as a whole, implying that a dialogue with his own party members was unlikely to generate satisfactory proposals. It is also difficult to see what room there is for grass-roots ideas to emerge as firm policy commitments while the party is in office, and decisions are taken daily by ministers in response to events, media pressures and the initiatives of rival parties.

For Labour members as for Conservatives, the annual gatherings for the party conference always used to be a highlight. But while the Conservative conference has become something more than the flag-waving rally of former years, many observers believe that the Labour conference has lapsed into an orchestrated, antiseptic ritual. In the past key decisions were cobbled together in smoke-filled rooms, by party leaders and union bosses who regarded the views of the average members as secondary considerations. However, at least the conference in those days had an element of drama – the most memorable occasion, perhaps, being 1981 when Denis Healey beat the left-wing candidate Tony Benn for the Deputy Leadership by less than one per cent of the electoral college vote. Nowadays the conference is more like a trade fair, a festival of corporate sponsorship in which many stalls are run by companies which formerly supported the Conservatives. In an astonishing contrast to the mid-1970s, when people who barracked Labour leaders were warmly applauded, in 2005 an 82-year-old activist was forced out of the hall by stewards when he expressed mild dissent during a speech by the Foreign Secretary, Jack Straw. The delegate, Walter Wolfgang, had originally come to Britain as a refugee from

Nazi Germany. After his ejection from the conference hall, he was questioned by police under anti-terrorist legislation.

Liberal Democrat organisation

Between 1950 and 1974, when Liberal representation in the Commons only once reached double-figures (in 1966), the party was regarded by many commentators as little more than an eccentric sect whose members only kept the flame alive because of some irrational tribal loyalty. The party conference, in particular, became an object of affectionate fun amongst media commentators; it was supposed to be the haunt of sandal-wearing, lentil-eating idealists who regularly passed motions on ethical subjects without the slightest hope of affecting policy at Westminster.

Growing disenchantment with the two main parties contradicted this image to some extent, though the personal scandal which engulfed the charismatic Liberal leader Jeremy Thorpe, and induced his resignation in 1976, was a serious setback. Thorpe ended up facing trial for conspiracy to murder, although he was acquitted. Under his successor, David Steel, the Liberals entered a short-lived pact which sustained James Callaghan's Labour Government. This was of dubious advantage to the party, and at the 1979 general election it was reduced to just 11 seats.

The party's prospects seemed to be transformed by the emergence in 1981 of the Social Democratic Party as an electoral ally which enjoyed strong media appeal. At that year's Liberal conference Steel told delegates to 'Go back to your constituencies and prepare for government'. The opinion polls at the time suggested that the two giants of post-war politics were about to be eclipsed by an alliance between the Liberals and the SDP. But from the beginning there were reasons for Liberal disquiet. In forming an entirely new party, the SDP's 'Gang of Four' had challenged preconceptions about the political landscape, promising to 'break the mould of British politics'. Yet in taking this course of action the Labour defectors who founded the SDP implied a criticism of the Liberal Party. After its long years in the wilderness, was it a suitable vehicle for the exercise of power? If ideology alone had been the deciding factor, the SDP leaders would have joined the Liberal Party, rather than founding their own organisation (see Chapter 15). The difference, rather, was one of ethos. Liberal activists had good reason to fear that a merger between the two parties would result in an SDP takeover, and the imposition of a very different approach to the business of politics and government. There was, in short, a part of the Liberal ethos which disliked the idea of compromise, which is inseparable from the exercise of power.

When the merger finally took place in 1988, after two disappointing general elections, it seemed that Liberal fears had been misplaced. The SDP had run out of steam, and far from being hijacked it looked as if the older party had performed a salvage operation on its Alliance partner. On a postal ballot of all members (probably little more than 60,000 at that time), the Liberal MP Paddy Ashdown became leader of the merged party, defeating another Liberal, Alan Beith.

However, some elements of the SDP lived on in the new party (which was briefly known as the Social and Liberal Democrats before adopting its present name). Its constitution attempted to strike a balance between the traditional Liberal commitment to grass-roots sentiment and the orientation towards strong leadership which was characteristic of the SDP. Thus the merger was not accepted unanimously, and the SDP leader David Owen was among those who refused to join. But the defectors did not all come from the same camp, and some prominent Liberals also decided to fight on under their old name. Paddy Ashdown, a dynamic character from a military background, was able to edge the Liberal Democrats towards the idea of cooperation with Labour. But he was acutely aware of the need to carry the membership with him at every step, and he was occasionally defeated in conference votes.

The Liberal Democratic conference is a more meaningful affair than either the Conservative or Labour Party gatherings. Votes on policy take place after intensive debates which are often marked by open dissent. For example, in 2003 a centrally-backed proposal to privatise the Royal Mail was described by a conference speaker as 'sinister'. Grass-roots members also enjoy a free hand in selecting parliamentary candidates, after an initial screening by the central party. The relative autonomy of constituency parties reflects the traditional Liberal focus on local issues. Free from central dictation, activists have tended to concentrate their fire on their chief local rivals, whether Conservative or Labour. This has allowed the main parties to accuse the Liberals of opportunism; instead of enforcing obedience to a specific line of policy, the national party has been prepared to tolerate a wide diversity of views in different parts of the UK.

After the Liberal Democrats gained 62 seats in the 2005 general election – the fourth consecutive contest in which their representation had increased – their leader Charles Kennedy announced a far-reaching policy review. The central party clearly hoped to reduce the influence of party activists over policy in the future. Kennedy had argued in 2001 that frontbenchers needed more freedom to suggest ideas in response to events. Accordingly, the party leader and his closest allies exercised decisive influence over the content of the 2005 manifesto.

These developments lent support to the 'iron law of oligarchy', in that senior Liberal Democrats demanded more central direction at a time when their party was gaining additional representation at Westminster (see Analysis 14.1). More significant evidence was to follow, as rumours began to circulate that Kennedy was suffering from a drink problem. The party leader was re-elected unopposed after the 2005 general election. But by the beginning of 2006, feeling among Liberal Democrat MPs was sufficiently strong to force Kennedy's resignation. One way or another, this was a result of the view that the Liberal Democrats were now serious rivals to the two main parties, instead of being a potential recipient of protest votes in general elections. Some of the party's MPs thought that they would have won more seats if Kennedy had performed better during the 2005 general election; others were worried that the subsequent election of the young and vigorous David Cameron as Conservative leader meant that Liberal Democrat progress would stall unless they chose a more dynamic leader themselves.

In 1976, the Liberal Party began to elect its leaders through a vote of the entire membership. Since the formation of the Liberal Democrat party its leaders have been chosen through the Single Transferable Vote (STV) system (see Chapter 16). When Kennedy won the leadership in 1999, only two nominees were required in order to stand. Since then the rules have been tightened. Leadership candidates have to be nominated by at least 10 per cent of the parliamentary party, plus 200 party

Table 14.5 Liberal Democrat leadership election, 2006

Leadership candidate	First round votes	Second round votes
Sir Menzies Campbell	23264 (45%)	29697 (58%)
Chris Huhne	16691 (32%)	21628 (42%)
Simon Hughes	12081 (23%)	–

members drawn from a minimum of 20 constituency organisations. In 2006 these provisions led to a three-cornered contest, between Simon Hughes, Chris Huhne and Sir Menzies Campbell, who emerged as a fairly comfortable victor (see Table 14.5). Although there were concerns about Campbell's age (64), he made it clear that he would exert strong leadership. Significantly, within a few days of his election he had persuaded party members to accept the proposal on Royal Mail privatisation, which they had found unacceptable three years earlier.

Party finance

For most of the period since 1945, the stock assumptions about British party finance have been that Labour is in the pay of the unions; big business has bought up the Conservatives; and the Liberals are permanently poverty-stricken. These views have been reinforced by the two main parties, who often accuse each other of bowing to their respective paymasters, and by the Liberals and Liberal Democrats, who have regularly denounced the reliance of their rivals on expensive advertising campaigns.

Trade unions and businesses are not the only source of party funding, of course. Membership subscriptions and voluntary fund-raising events have always played a role. But donations from wealthy organisations and individuals account for a significant proportion of party revenue, and inevitably their importance has grown

Case study: 14.4

The Political Parties, Elections and Referendums Act 2000

Labour's reforms dealt both with funding and spending. In future, parties had to make a public declaration of any donation worth more than £5,000 (nationally) or £1,000 (to a constituency party), whether the gifts came in the form of money or services. Donations from foreign individuals were outlawed, as were 'blind trusts' (which allowed recipients to claim that they knew nothing about the use to which money was put). Parties were required to declare their donations on a regular basis – quarterly at normal times, but every week during a general election campaign. After the 'loans for peerages' scandal of 2006, it became clear that the main parties were exploiting a loophole in the Act, since loans did not need to be declared.

At the same time, a cap was imposed on spending by the parties in their national campaigns. According to the spending formula, the limit for any party which contested all of the 646 UK seats in 2005 was £19,380,000, over the 365 days leading up to the election. These new regulations are overseen by the independent Electoral Commission.

as membership has declined. Arguing that such payments are rarely given without strings attached, critics have claimed that the influence of large donors over the parties is anti-democratic. The tendency of such party benefactors to receive honours, such as knighthoods and even peerages, is merely a symptom of a practice which suggests a major flaw in British political culture.

During the 1990s the Conservatives were tainted by several financial scandals. Labour came into office promising a new approach to politics, including a reform of party finance. The Committee on Standards in Public Life produced a report in 1998 which formed the basis of the Political Parties, Elections and Referendums Act (passed in November 2000).

Ironically, Labour's credentials for the task of cleaning up public life had already been undermined before the Committee on Standards compiled its report. Shortly after the 1997 election, it emerged that the motor-racing tycoon Bernie Ecclestone had donated £1 million to the party. It was alleged that this generous gesture affected Labour's decision to exempt Formula One racing from a ban on tobacco advertising, introduced soon after it returned to government. The incident certainly underlined Labour's success in attracting sponsorship from business-people (although it still depended on the unions for more than a quarter of its funding). After a media furore, Labour repaid the donation. But serious questions remained, particularly since Ecclestone had not previously been known for his sympathy with general Labour party aims. Shortly afterwards, further questions were raised about the lobbying activities of former Labour spin-doctors who promised privileged access to their clients. Firms which participated in Labour's Private Finance Initiative (PFI) also developed very close links to the government. Under the PFI, major public sector projects like schools and hospitals were constructed using private money, which would then be generously repaid by the taxpayer over many years (see Chapter 9). It was impossible to rule out the possibility that a relationship of mutual advantage could develop between certain firms and the governing party.

Allegations that policy influence could be bought in Britain continued after the passage of the Political Parties, Elections and Referendums Act 2000 (see Case study 14.4). Before the 2001 general election the Conservatives received a pledge of £5 million from a businessman, Stuart Wheeler. Wheeler was not interested in any material favours, but his donation made him an influential figure in subsequent leadership elections and on Conservative policy towards Europe. In its second term 'New' Labour was accused of changing its policies towards pub opening hours, casinos and electricity generation under pressure from various donors, including the corrupt US energy firm, Enron. After the 2005 general election, Blair gave a junior ministerial post to Lord Drayson, who had contributed £1 million to Labour funds

Table 14.6 Declared party spending in 2005 general election campaign

Party	Spending (£ million)
Conservative	17.85 (12.75)
Labour	17.94 (10.94)
Liberal Democrats	4.32 (1.36)

Note: Figures for 2001 are in brackets.

Source: Electoral Commission, 'Register of Campaign Expenditure', www.electoralcommission.org.uk

during 2004. Drayson's company, Powderject, had previously won a controversial government contract to supply smallpox vaccine. Another scandal broke in March 2006, when questions were raised about three Labour benefactors who had been nominated for peerages. The incident also suggested that the Act needed to be tightened in order to cover loans as well as 'gifts'.

Whatever its effect on fund-raising, the Act seemed at least initially to have fostered a more responsible attitude to spending (see Table 14.6). The combined expenditure of the three biggest parties in 2001 (before the legislation came into full force) was less than the £28.3 million spent by the Conservatives in 1997 (which left them almost bankrupt). But there was a significant increase for all three main parties in 2005. Even in 2001, obvious problems remained. The chronic unfairness of electoral spending remained; the Liberal Democrats were having to fund their campaigning on less than the annual wage of a premiership footballer, and their proportion of the spending was far less than their support (and membership, relative to their rivals) merited. The total amount spent by the three main parties in 2001 was less than the record transfer fee for a premiership footballer. In this respect, the 2000 Act revealed a party contest which was frighteningly vulnerable to concealed corruption; ironically, if electioneering were far more expensive it would be more difficult to buy influence, and it would be more likely that individuals or companies who contributed a significant proportion of a larger total might come under greater public scrutiny.

In the eyes of radical reformers, the 2000 Act could be no more than a staging-post towards the ideal situation, in which private funding of any kind is banned and the whole burden falls directly and openly on the taxpayer. After the 'loans for peerages' scandal of March 2006, Tony Blair announced that he had been converted to the idea of state funding, if cross-party agreement could be reached. There were, though, significant obstacles ahead. If parties were funded on the basis of their performance at the previous election – based on the percentage of votes cast rather than seats – it might be argued that the majority party would always be at an advantage. However, this is already the case, since governments can use taxpayers' money to publicise their policies between elections, and private companies naturally want to back the winning side. The main argument against state funding is that voters are reluctant to subsidise unpopular parties through their taxes. If their election funds were guaranteed in advance, parties would have no incentive to devise popular programmes, or (even more importantly) to recruit new members. But against this it can be argued that the current competition for private funds is one of the main reasons why parties have become unpopular in the first place.

Back to cadre parties?

As we have seen, the main trends in party organisation in the Labour Party and the Conservative Party over the last two decades have been:

1. *Democratisation* or, more accurately a veneer of democratisation. Party members have been given a number of rights including:
   - A role in the election of the party leader, as part of an electoral college in the

Labour Party and as the electorate in the second phase of the Conservative leadership election process.

- The right to voice in the candidate selection process.
- The right to participate in the policy-making process by making submissions to policy forums.
- The opportunity to vote on major changes in party policy, such as the abolition of Labour's Clause IV or David Cameron's 2006 statement of beliefs.

Analysis:	14.2

Beyond the mass party

The demise of both the nineteenth century cadre party and the twentieth century mass party required a rethinking of this typology which was developed by French political scientist Maurice Duverger in his classic work *Political Parties* (London: Methuen, 1954). Three alternative models of party organisation in the late twentieth century and beyond are of particular interest:

1. The 'catch-all party'. This model, developed by Otto Kirchheimer, claims that in the 1960s political parties abandoned their efforts to mobilise large social groups and downplayed their ideological conviction. Instead they sought to attract support where they could from a dealigned electorate and from interest groups by developing a broad appeal that is light on ideology and focuses on factors such as the qualities of their leaders. Party members have little influence. An exaggerated characterisation of this thesis presents parties as highly opportunistic and prepared to do whatever is required to win votes.

2. The 'electoral-professional party'. This model, developed by Angelo Panebianco, emphasises the role of professionals (e.g. campaign managers, opinion pollsters and spin-doctors) and the leaders they advise within modern political parties. These parties are primarily focused on electoral success and adopt a political marketing approach that emphasises personalities and issues rather than ideology. Again, party members have little influence over policy. The costs of running an election campaign mean that 'electoral-professional parties' rely heavily on donations from businesses and wealthy individuals.

3. The 'cartel party'. This model, associated with Richard Katz and Peter Mair, concentrates on the symbiosis between the state and political parties. Cartel parties enjoy access to state resources (e.g. state funding for parties and the resources available to MPs), have a clear advantage over parties that do not have such access. They also have a clear interest in maintaining this advantage and denying resources to competitor parties. An institutionalised relationship between political parties and the state may undermine the legitimacy of the political system if parties appear to be primarily motivated by the desire to monopolise state resources, and collude to ensure a favourable division of the spoils, neglecting their roles as representatives and mobilisers of different interests within civil society.

References: O. Kirchheimer, 'The Transformation of West European Party Systems', in J. LaPalombara and M. Weiner (eds), *Political Parties and Political Development* (Princeton University Press, 1966, pp. 177–200), A. Panebianco, *Political Parties: Organisation and Power* (Cambridge University Press, 1988), and R. Katz and P. Mair, 'Party Organisation, Party Democracy, and the Emergence of the Cartel Party', *Party Politics*, Vol. 1, No. 1 (1995) pp. 5–28.

2. *A strengthening of the position of the leader.* In practice, the rights of ordinary members are limited and real power has been concentrated further in the hands of the party leaders and their advisers. Ways in which the role of party members is limited and the authority of the leader enhanced include:

- Leadership rules make it difficult for the party leader to be removed – unless, as was the case with Iain Duncan Smith, they have lost the support of much of the parliamentary party.
- The central party organisation imposes controls over candidate selection (e.g. by drawing up lists of approved candidates).
- Key policy decisions are taken by the leader and his or her advisers; bodies such as policy forums and the party conference have, in effect, only advisory status.
- The leader and his or her advisers take the key strategic decisions about the conduct of election campaigns, with the leader acting as a communicator-in-chief for their party.

3. *A decline in party membership.* This means that parties have had to open up new avenues for funding and develop new campaign techniques that are less reliant on the activities of grassroots activists.

These developments have led some commentators to ask whether the era of mass parties is over (see Analysis 14.2). Britain's main parties are dominated by small groups of people associated with senior figures. In an ideal world party leaders would love to inspire an endless stream of new members. Apart from anything else, research shows that enthusiastic local members can sway sufficient votes to win closely-fought constituency battles. But parties can live with the reality of a relentless decline in membership, mainly because funds can be accumulated from other sources. In the final analysis, it is easier to meet the needs of a handful of rich donors than to formulate a policy programme which satisfies the conflicting hopes of grass-roots members and maintains their enthusiasm for campaigning on the doorstep. The introduction of state funding could accentuate this difficulty, unless the number of party members was made a key factor in deciding the amount of money which each party should receive.

The main development which has undermined the mass party is the rise of the media. When Michels put forward his 'iron law of oligarchy', communications technology was in its infancy. Now leaders can reach their target audience through television broadcasts, advertisements, email and telephone messages. A recent development is for parties to send mobile phone text messages, particularly to first-time voters. The same technology which makes a mass constituency membership less important also gives much more prominence to leaders. During election campaigns leaders can travel throughout the UK. But there is still no time to meet many members, so these tours are conducted mainly for the benefit of the media. Certainly leaders will spend much more time speaking to reporters, who may or may not vote for their party, than listening to the views of their ordinary supporters.

In place of mass parties, political scientists now refer to *electoral-professional parties* in the UK (see Analysis 14.2). Such organisations have no mass membership, and put most of their energies into securing the election of candidates by means of favourable media coverage. As a result, electoral-professional parties are engaged in almost continuous election campaigning. In a sense, the new situation is rather like a return to the old cadre parties, in a modern context. Like the old Whigs and Tories, Labour and the Conservatives have developed broadly similar policies, dictated by the perceived demands of their target voters in marginal seats rather than ideological considerations. Personalities, rather than principles, dominate debate; and rival contenders for leadership surround themselves with professional pundits, pollsters and spin-doctors who often generate factional disputes for want of more constructive tasks between elections. Infighting between personal followers was also strongly characteristic of eighteenth-century British politics.

Supporters of the Liberal Democrats consistently argue that their party is an exception to this trend. Overall, their members do have a more meaningful role in policy formulation, candidate selection and the choice of leader. This, it can be argued, is at least in part a reflection of liberal individualism; given their beliefs, it is unlikely that grass-roots members would remain within a party which was in the iron grip of the leadership. This continued interest in ideas is another respect in which Liberal Democrats differ from the other main parties.

However, it can be argued that the Liberal Democrats have only bucked the trend because they are untainted by the realistic prospect of power. It is hardly surprising that their members feel more involved; there are, after all, far fewer of them. The real test will come if the Liberal Democrats sustain their recent progress in terms of parliamentary seats, to the extent that they look very likely to become coalition partners in the UK government. The party has already become more centralised as a result of its encounter with the SDP – a party which was consciously devised as a vehicle for winning elections – and after the 2005 general election there were signs that it was hoping to ditch its more 'eccentric' (i.e. radical) policies for future elections. After the 2005 general election it acted swiftly and ruthlessly to depose a leader who seemed unlikely to take it much further. It was criticised for accepting a significant financial donation from a supporter based outside the UK; and subsequently it abandoned its distinctive pledge to increase income tax for high earners. Taken together, these developments made it more difficult to cite the Liberal Democrats as a contrast to its two main rivals.

Conclusion and summary

Whatever the future fortunes of the Liberal Democrats, there is plenty of evidence to support the view that Britain has entered an era of electoral professional parties. Both Labour and the Conservatives have introduced recent reforms which are supposed to encourage participation from their members; and both have tried to win new recruits. However, they are no longer mass parties in any meaningful sense. Membership rolls are falling, and not simply because Britons are becoming more selective when choosing spare-time pursuits. The main political parties still have their attractions for people with political ambitions, but they are no longer an obvious option for idealists. Returning to our six 'ideal' functions listed at the beginning of this chapter, it would be fairest to say that UK parties do carry all of them out to some extent; but that even on a sober assessment, the conclusion should be 'can do much better'.

Those who accept the accuracy of the 'iron law of oligarchy' will not be surprised by recent developments. Since they believe that all large-scale organisations are inevitably controlled by small cliques, in their view the mass party with real grass-roots participation could never have been more than a short-lived illusion. Despite all the talk of a crisis for parties, it is difficult to see what could be done to improve their prospects. With its fixation on personalities, its intolerance of ambiguity and its incessant demands for official statements, the media has been the main factor behind the decline of mass parties; and few observers expect a dramatic change in its working practices.

Further reading

The classic volume on this subject is R. McKenzie, *British Political Parties* (London: Heinemann, 1955). It is still well worth reading for its analytic framework, even though much has changed since the 1950s. S. Ingle, *The British Party System* (London: Continuum, 3rd edition, 2000) and J. Fisher, *British Political Parties* (London: Palgrave, 1999) are more recent books with comprehensive and insightful coverage. R. Garner and R. Kelly, *British Political Parties Today* (Manchester: Manchester University Press, 2nd edition, 1998) is also recommended. P. Webb, *The Modern British Party System* (London: Sage, 2000) offers a more advanced analysis. A special edition of *Parliamentary Affairs*, Vol. 58, No. 3 (2005) on the future of parties contains a number of important articles.

Since 1997 there has been a rash of material on New Labour. M. Russell, *Building New Labour. The Politics of Party Organisation* (London: Palgrave, 2005) and S. Fielding, *The Labour Party. Continuity and Change in the Making of New Labour* (London: Palgrave, 2002) are detailed studies. Shorter accounts include E. Shaw, 'The Control Freaks? New Labour and the Party', in S. Ludlam and M. Smith (eds), *Governing as New Labour* (London: Palgrave, 2003), pp. 52–69 and P. Seyd and P. Whiteley, 'New Labour and the Party', in S. Ludlam and M. Smith (eds), *New Labour in Government* (London: Macmillan, 2001), pp. 73–91. On the leadership, see T. Quinn, 'Electing the Leader: the British Labour Party's Electoral College', *British Journal of Politics and International Relations*, Vol. 6, No. 3, (2004), pp. 333–52. A comprehensive survey of the party was undertaken while Kinnock was beginning the reform process, by P. Seyd and P. Whiteley, *Labour's Grass Roots: the Politics of Party Membership* (Oxford: Oxford University Press, 1992). E. Shaw, *The Labour Party since 1945* (Oxford: Blackwell, 1996) is an accessible and thorough historical survey.

A. Seldon and S. Ball (eds), *Conservative Century: The Conservative Party since 1900*, (Oxford: Oxford University Press, 1994) is a massive volume covering almost every aspect of party history up to the mid-1990s. On the party's more recent problems, see M. Garnett and P. Lynch (eds), *The Conservatives in Crisis* (Manchester: Manchester University Press, 2003) and the *Political Quarterly* special edition, Vol. 75, No. 4, (2004). R. Kelly, 'The Party didn't work: Conservative Reorganisation and Electoral Failure', *Political Quarterly*, Vol. 73, No. 1 (2002), pp. 38–43 is a critical account. The Liberal Democrats have attracted less attention, but A. Russell and E. Fieldhouse, *Neither Left nor Right? The Liberal Democrats and the Electorate* (Manchester; Manchester University Press, 2004) and D. Dutton, *A History of the Liberal Party in the Twentieth Century* (London: Palgrave, 2000) are recommended recent accounts.

The Political Parties, Elections and Referendums Act 2000 and the debate on party funding is assessed in J. Fisher, 'Next Step – State Funding for the Parties?', *Political Quarterly*, Vol. 73, No. 4 (2002), pp. 392–9.

Websites

The main British political parties have websites containing details of their organisation:

Conservative Party, www.conservative-party.org.uk.

Labour Party, www.labour.org.uk.

Liberal Democrats, www.libdems.org.uk.

See the Further Reading in Chapter 13 for details of the websites of other UK political parties. For rules governing party finance and information on donors see the Electoral Commission www.electoralcommission.org.uk. Proposals for the further reform of party funding can be found on the website of the independent Power inquiry www.powerinquiry.org/research/index/php.

Chapter 15

Ideology and party competition

Learning outcomes

After reading this chapter, you will:
- Understand the nature of political ideology.
- Be able to evaluate the relationship between ideology and political practice.
- Appreciate recent ideological developments within the main British political parties.

Introduction

Ideology has an ambiguous status in the academic study of British politics. Often it is regarded as a sub-category of political theory rather than having any place within political science. It is difficult enough to present a definition of ideology that will command widespread acceptance, let alone to devise a 'scientific' method of assessing its precise impact on party competition and policy formulation.

However, no-one can seriously deny that ideas have *some* impact on participation in British politics, at all levels. Despite contemporary cynicism about politics, many people are inspired by their beliefs to vote, join political parties, demonstrate or stand for office. It is generally agreed that ideology is 'action-orientated'; it provides a rationale for policy ideas, and encourages people either to support or oppose them. Equally, ideas can also help us to understand a *decline* in participation. When parties seem to agree on most of the key issues, and merely exaggerate differences of detail in order to score points, sections of the electorate are likely to feel alienated from the political process.

Ideological conflict in Britain has certainly declined in recent years, from the 1970s and 1980s when the major parties were sharply divided. But this does not mean that we have experienced an 'end of ideology', as some commentators have supposed. On the view of ideology outlined in this chapter, it can never come to an end; even if all significant politicians agree in their underlying assumptions, those ideas will continue to reflect an ideological commitment of some kind. Students of politics will always have to take ideology into consideration, along with other factors such as economic and institutional change.

The nature of ideology

There are several contrasting definitions of ideology. The most familiar are outlined below.

1. *Ideology as objective thinking.* The word 'ideology' was first used by the French aristocrat Destutt de Tracy (1754–1836), during the French Revolutionary period. The early advances of empirical science persuaded de Tracy that human thinking could be purged of prejudice, superstition and self-interest. For him, ideology was a 'science of ideas' that would show people how to think objectively, trusting only the evidence of their senses.

2. *Ideology as a reflection of class interests.* The concept was revived by Karl Marx (1818–83) and his followers, but in a very different sense. For them, ideology was *distorted* thinking, the product of social conflict. They argued that the ideas of individuals are shaped by their position within the class system rather than by any objective 'truth'. In any era the ruling class is the group which holds the dominant economic power. It will generate ideas which justify its position, and will try to enforce these ideas on members of subordinate classes.

3. *Ideology as extremism.* Many commentators associate ideology with rigid or radical thinking. On this view, 'ideologues' are people who want the world to conform to their ideas. Their attachment to their favourite theory is so strong that they will continue to work on its behalf regardless of its impact on people. According to this view, Stalin, Mao and Hitler were typical ideologues, and their atrocities prove that ideology is always a very dangerous thing.

These three approaches to ideology are all useful to an extent. The problem is that all of them recommend the removal (or reduction) of political bias, while our purpose as students of politics is to understand its nature and influence.

Ideologies are best understood as belief systems which help us to make sense of the world. They can be compared to moral spectacles, though it is not so easy to put them on and take them off. The ultimate source of our political vision is the view we take of human nature. We regard significant political decisions as good or bad depending on whether they coincide with our ideas about the conditions under which human beings can thrive. So, for example, if we think that people are naturally aggressive we will tend to support strong measures to enforce the law. By contrast, if we believe that human beings are naturally cooperative, we may take the view that harsh laws cause social tension rather than curing it.

We might think that our own views are 'objective', based on a 'common sense' appraisal of the world as it really is. But although some ideas about human nature obviously make more sense than others, Destutt de Tracy was wrong to think that there could be a 'science of ideas'. One person's 'common sense' can seem dangerously irrational to someone else, and no-one has the authority to adjudicate between them.

On this basis we can provide a broad classification of ideologies. Despite the efforts of totalitarian regimes and other would-be agents of mind-control, no two individuals think exactly alike. While some commentators have searched for a logic underlying ideological thought, in practice people hold their views with different degrees of intensity, and they are often inconsistent. But there are sufficient similarities between the ideas of political actors for us to speak of relatively coherent ideological traditions, and to construct fairly cohesive ideological 'families'. We must make sure that the people we are evaluating really have enough in common to make it helpful for us to group them together. Sometimes this can involve a reassessment of common assumptions, and we might even decide that a political figure has been wrong to claim membership of a particular ideological family. We might conclude, for example, that a person who thinks of herself as a dedicated socialist really has much more in common with the liberal tradition. That is to say, people with strong political commitments are often the worst judges of their own beliefs.

The role of ideology

On this view, it is a mistake to confine the word 'ideology' to extreme political beliefs. All of us are to some extent 'ideologues'. That is, the judgements we all make about political issues ultimately arise from underlying beliefs about human nature, even if we are sometimes inconsistent, or reach 'illogical' conclusions because of muddled thinking or a lack of information about a particular policy and its likely impact.

If this is right, ideology undoubtedly deserves its place in the study of politics. However, the role of ideology has to be understood in the context of other political factors. After all, where do our ideas about human nature come from? We learn either from our own direct experiences, or from what we learn about the experiences of others. Whether we realise it or not, our thinking can be affected by watching the television, reading newspapers (see Chapter 4), or even by our day-to-day social interactions. If our experiences do not fit with our existing world view we might change our minds, either gradually or overnight in a kind of 'conversion'. Some people, for example, start off accepting that the world is imperfect, but end up hoping to change it for the better; others undergo the same process in reverse.

If ordinary voters find that circumstances affect their thinking, politicians face a much wider range of pressures. No successful British politician has been able to go through a whole career without making significant compromises. The process of winning selection for a parliamentary seat can affect their thinking. If they are elected they have to obey the party whips; if they are promoted to ministerial office they have to listen to the views of their colleagues or gauge the likely response from the public before they try to implement their most cherished schemes.

In short, 'Rab' Butler (1902–82), the former Conservative Chancellor of the Exchequer and Home Secretary, was right to describe British politics as 'The art of the possible'. It is difficult to generalise about the relative impact of ideas, events or institutions on political decisions because they all affect each other. It is often assumed that the influence of ideas varies according to circumstances. Commentators claim, for example, that the premiership of Margaret Thatcher (1979–90) was a period in which ideas were particularly important. But this view is slightly misleading. Certainly Thatcher herself was convinced that ideas were very important, and many voters supported her because she offered a clear alternative to the accepted political wisdom in Britain. But this is not to say that Thatcherism suddenly injected ideology into British politics. Rather, Thatcher and her supporters thought that the prevailing ideas before 1979 were wrong. Equally, as Prime Minister she often had to compromise, whatever her rhetoric might have suggested.

The best way of explaining the nature of political ideology in Britain is to provide a brief survey of modern British politics from the point of view of ideas. But first we need to provide some account of the competing ideological traditions. Commentators usually focus on three – conservatism, socialism and liberalism.

Conservatism

The Irish-born politician Edmund Burke (1729–97) is usually credited as the intellectual founder of conservative ideology. His *Reflections on the Revolution in France* (1790) argued in favour of gradual reform, rather than violent insurrection. According to Burke, human beings are creatures of passion and prejudice rather than cool calculation. Burke predicted that the French Revolution would prove his point. Instead of being a temporary measure to meet an emergency, violence would become part of the routine business of the new French government.

Burke, then, derived his opposition to revolution from his view of human nature. The denial that human beings are capable of rational conduct – or rather, that most people are incapable of acting rationally on a consistent basis – is a crucial element in Burkean conservatism. It is best described as a form of scepticism. Another aspect of conservatism is **elitism** – the view that power should be entrusted to a minority who, through training or natural ability, are rational enough to rule. Burke believed that aristocrats were best placed to provide this leadership. Their inherited wealth meant that they had no need to prepare for a life of labour, so their education could be devoted to grooming them for political office. Their wealth also gave them a vested interest in defending social stability. Talented people from more humble backgrounds could play some role in government, but their influence had to be kept within limits. Excessive mobility would disrupt a society which Burke compared to a living organism. On this view, individuals are interdependent – they cannot survive in isolation. As in an organism, every part of society is important. But the right balance between the parts has to be maintained, otherwise the organism will sicken and eventually die.

Elitism: the belief that power should be entrusted to a ruling minority.

Analysis: 15.1

'Left' and 'right' in UK politics

Like so many terms in the vocabulary of ideology, the distinction between 'left' and 'right' originated at the time of the French Revolution. The words are a convenient short-hand way of denoting political positions, and are still favoured in media discussions. They can also be used in visual depictions of ideological conflict in Britain, usually in the form of a 'spectrum' with the left wing of the Labour Party at one extreme and right wing Conservatives at the other. This spectrum is particularly helpful when people are asked to identify their own views on a scale of 1 to 10.

In 1968 the journalist and political economist Samuel Brittan called the division between left and right a 'bogus dilemma'. In reality, he argued, the two main parties stood for very similar policies in office, whatever they might say in opposition. In addition, some people could take 'right wing' views on topics like immigration while being 'left wing' on a subject like the welfare state.

The chief difficulty with 'left' and 'right' is that they are *relative* terms, dependent on circumstances. A person's views can be regarded as 'left-wing' at one time and 'right-wing' at another. Thus, for example, the Conservative MP and former Chancellor Kenneth Clarke was a 'centrist' within his party when he became an MP in 1970. But by the time of the 1997 general election he was widely regarded as being on the extreme left because of his views on European integration. On economic matters, if anything, over the years he had become more right wing!

For these reasons 'left' and 'right' have not been used in this chapter. The use made of ideological terms like 'conservative' and 'socialist' could be criticised for the opposite reason – for being *too* absolute and rigid, regardless of circumstances. However, the advantage of this approach is that it provides some yardsticks against which to gauge the changing ideas of political actors and parties, while analyses which continue to use 'left' and 'right' are built on shifting ground.

Allied to conservative scepticism about human nature is a support for *prescription*. In most circumstances people should prefer the tried and trusted policies of the past to any radical experiments. Individuals may not be reliably rational, but they are capable of correcting mistakes over time; and this process, rather than root and branch reform along the lines of some abstract political theory, is the proper business of politics. Conservatives pride themselves on their **empiricism**; they think that the best kind of government is the one which works best in practice. We have to be pragmatic – to make the best of what we find in an imperfect world. 'If it ain't broke, don't fix it' is a typical conservative maxim.

Empiricism: a belief in facts rather than theories.

Burke himself believed in a free market economy. Yet his support should be treated with caution, because he lived in the early stages of the industrial revolution, before the manufacturing process stimulated the growth of sprawling cities where many workers lived in anonymous poverty. One person who did reflect on industrial Britain was Benjamin Disraeli (1804–81: Prime Minister 1868 and 1874–80). While Burke believed in **paternalism** – the idea that the rich had a duty to help the poor, at least in 'deserving' cases – Disraeli extended that principle to include limited action by the state to improve working conditions. His greatest legacy in domestic politics

Paternalism: the belief that people in power should act in the interests of other people (often the poorest in society) and thereby limit the free choice of those people.

was the idea that the economic inequality of industrial society had created a Britain of 'Two Nations', whose inhabitants were alien to each other. In short, Britain was no longer an organic society.

Four additional points are worth making here. First, conservatives often deny that their ideas should be classed as an ideology. In their view all ideology is programmatic – the politics of the blueprint, usually based on unrealistic expectations about human nature. In other words, they adhere to the view noted above, that ideology is a form of extremism. But on the present interpretation, ideology should not be used as a kind of political insult. To be useful to students of politics, it should be taken as referring to underlying political bias of all kinds, whether or not this gives rise to a rigid set of policy ideas. Burkean conservatism is certainly different from other political belief systems, but not sufficiently so to make it unsuitable for classification as an ideology. Ironically, the assumptions which Burke regarded as entirely realistic are far removed from the dominant ideas in modern life, and if anyone was serious about restoring a conservative society on traditional lines he or she would probably have to resort to the violent methods which Burke deplored.

Second, since the social and political conditions which inspired conservative thought disappeared long ago, conservatism is often dismissed by its critics as a **reactionary** creed. But 'reaction' is one of those political insults which, on closer examination, proves to be meaningless. If it denotes a desire to restore the conditions of the past, anyone can become a 'reactionary' under certain circumstances. Today the term could be used to fit a fascist in Germany and a communist in Russia. In Britain, believers in large-scale nationalisation would have to share the label with people who think that the state should do nothing beyond keeping the peace at home and maintaining armies for possible action abroad. A more relevant charge is that conservatives have rarely expressed their views unless they feel that their view of the world is under threat. But this is an integral aspect of conservative ideology. When they are happy with things as they are, consistent conservatives simply see no reason to write at length on behalf of what they see as a common-sense view of the world. Unlike representatives of the other main ideologies, they see no purpose in working to improve human nature so that people can realise their true potential. In their view, human beings are and will always remain a very mixed bunch.

A third point is that conservatism seems to support the Marxist view that ideology is a reflection of class interest (see above). In this case, the class in question is obviously the aristocracy. Burkean conservatives would argue that on their own premises aristocratic rule is in everyone's interest. If aristocrats are best equipped to govern, they have a duty to do so whether they like it or not; after all, if they leave the task to others who lack their training, the result is likely to be bad government and social upheaval in which aristocrats will have the most to lose. This is highly characteristic of Burkean conservatism, which is a theory of responsibilities rather than rights (see Chapter 8). Yet there is a logical flaw in this argument. If human nature is as irrational as conservatives think, there is no reason to feel confident that many aristocrats will live up to their responsibilities. In theory, conservatism is more than simply a justification for the interests of a particular class. In practice, though, it was often used to defend people who evaded their responsibilities and took full advantage of their privileged social status.

Finally – perhaps most importantly – we must avoid the common mistake of assuming that any statement of principle put out by the Conservative Party is

Reactionary: opposed to political and social change.

Analysis: 15.2

Neo-conservatism

The controversy over the 2003 war on Iraq brought to wider notice a group of politicians who were close associates of the US President, George W. Bush. Happy to be labelled as 'neo'-conservatives, they had actively promoted the conflict and harboured even more ambitious designs for the re-shaping of the Middle East. In domestic affairs, their overall aim was the reaffirmation of traditional institutions, notably the family. They were also strong believers in the virtues of the free market.

Neo-conservatism is not exclusively a US phenomenon; the label was also applied to some New Right supporters of Margaret Thatcher, who upheld traditional moral values and also laid special emphasis on the family. However, the ideas are particularly suited to the US, where cultural norms and social institutions originally developed in a context of resolute individualism and suspicion towards the state. Thus the 'neo-cons' can pose as the guardians of a long-established American way of life. In the UK, by contrast, institutions evolved in a very different context, and in recent decades they have been undermined rather than strengthened by the market forces which neo-conservatives support. Thus the neo-conservative label is a source of confusion in the British context; people who associate themselves with this American tradition of thought have far more in common with Victorian liberals than with Edmund Burke.

inevitably a product of conservative ideology. To do so is to assert some kind of continuity between the thinking of Edmund Burke and the underlying beliefs of a group of people who (at the time of writing) are hoping to regain political power more than two centuries after his death. We have already noted the affinity between Burkean conservatism and a socio-economic order that barely survived him (although, of course, landed gentlemen continued to dominate politics for many years after 1800). We can also appreciate that particular party labels might persist for a variety of reasons, even if the original principles have been abandoned. So before we can say that any members of the Conservative Party today are distinctively conservative, we should examine their ideas in relation to other ideological traditions, to see whether any of them provides a better fit. The fact that Burke himself was a member of the Whig Party – the distant forerunner of today's Liberal Democrats – should be a sufficient warning against the automatic confusion of party labels with political belief systems.

Socialism

While conservatism reflects an aristocratic, largely rural society, modern socialism is a product of the industrial revolution. Robert Owen (1771–1858), whose *A New View of Society* (1813–14) is generally regarded as an early socialist tract, was actually a mill-owner who believed that the working class was being dehumanised by industrial capitalism. Karl Marx (1818–83), whose study of industrial capitalism led him to believe that he had discovered 'scientific' laws of historical development leading to an inevitable socialist revolution, was given financial and intellectual support by Friedrich Engels (1820–95), whose family fortune also came from manufacturing.

Although socialism has several variants, its core idea is that the character of human beings is environmentally determined. That is, people are decisively shaped by the circumstances in which they find themselves. The key to realising human potential is thus to create the right circumstances. Socialists believe that human beings can only fulfil their true potential in an environment which fosters cooperation. On this view, **capitalism** is unnatural because it creates a competitive environment for workers and employers alike. Instead of labouring together for the common good, workers spend their lives creating profit for their masters. They can take no pleasure from the productive process; in the Marxist term, they are alienated from the results of their own labour. This would be the case even if profits were being made from products which were socially useful. In practice, modern capitalism is biased towards the production of luxury items for anyone who can afford them.

Another key principle for socialists is **egalitarianism**. Economic inequality, they believe, prevents harmonious living. In particular, advanced capitalist society divides people into two classes; the owners of the 'means of production' (the **bourgeoisie**), and the working class (the **proletariat**). Under capitalism, the apparent interests of these two groups are diametrically opposed. The bourgeoisie owes its livelihood to the exploitation of the workers. Socialists argue that if the owners of the means of production understood their real interests they would give up their economic power, because only then could they escape from the degrading struggle for wealth which brings no spiritual satisfaction. Indeed, in some ways life is even more unsatisfactory for them, because the economic hardship of the workers creates a sense of solidarity which their bosses can never share. Unfortunately, their thinking is conditioned by capitalism, which makes them believe that competition is natural.

Thus socialists believe that human potential can only be fulfilled after the abolition of classes, and the destruction of private ownership of the means of production. But how is this to be achieved? This has been a divisive issue among people who nevertheless shared the distinctive socialist view of human nature. Marx and his followers believed that capitalism would have to be overthrown in a violent revolution. Although they recognised that capitalism had greatly increased the productive capacity of mankind, the system was doomed because of its own internal contradictions. Over time competition for new markets becomes increasingly frantic, and profits decline. Inefficient firms are forced out of business, thus swelling the ranks of a proletariat which faces ever-harsher working conditions. This new level of exploitation stimulates class consciousness among the workers: at last they realise where their true interest lies, they have the numbers on their side to confront the shrinking band of capitalists, and above all they are united. Once the revolution has been won, they will seize control of the state and use its power to abolish all productive private property. Production could then be geared to genuine need, and everyone will be happy to contribute their labour according to their abilities. Character traits which capitalists believe to be natural, such as selfishness, will disappear. There will no longer be any need for a coercive force like the state.

Although Marx's revolutionary doctrine won a small dedicated following in Britain, it represents only one strand of socialist thought. Earlier writers like Owen had thought that society could be transformed by peaceful means. In the year after

Capitalism: an economic, political and social system based upon the private ownership of property and the creation of wealth.

Egalitarianism: a political programme that aims to increase equality, based on the belief that people should be treated equally.

Bourgeoisie: in Marxism, the dominant class made up of owners of the means of production which exploits the proletariat.

Proletariat: in Marxism, a class of manual workers who need to sell their labour to earn money.

Marx's death (1883) a group of middle-class activists founded the Fabian Society, which preached a philosophy of gradual reform on socialist lines. The Fabians were tireless propagandists and statistical compilers, at a time when governments were badly informed. They believed that they could persuade influential people in central and local government to implement their policies without the necessity of violence.

Social democracy

The main point of dispute between the socialist revolutionaries and the 'gradualists' concerned the nature of class conflict. Marx and his followers believed that the bourgeoisie was incapable of making meaningful concessions, even to save itself. But the Fabians could point to peaceful reforms in the second half of the nineteenth century (notably under the premiership of Benjamin Disraeli) which improved working conditions. The parliamentary road to socialism was given added support in 1899, when the German socialist Eduard Bernstein (1850–1932) published *The Preconditions of Socialism*. This book can be seen as the founding document of social democracy, or 'revisionism'.

Bernstein argued that, contrary to Marxist theory, capitalism was showing itself to be highly adaptable. Far from stumbling from one crisis to the next, by the end of the nineteenth century it seemed as healthy as ever. Furthermore, bourgeois parliaments really had made meaningful concessions, extending the right to vote to members of the working class. Not only did Bernstein conclude that revolution was unnecessary; he even denied that a just society was incompatible with capitalism. Provided that they were subjected to state regulation, private enterprises could be allowed to stay in business.

Revisionism of one kind or another was always more popular than revolutionary Marxism within the British Labour Party. The last piece of the social democratic jigsaw was supplied after the Second World War by the economist and Labour MP Anthony Crosland (1918–77). His book *The Future of Socialism* (1956) argued that the clash between the owners of capital and the workers had been superseded by a technological revolution. Economic power was no longer a matter of ownership; it depended on expertise. Only skilled managers knew how to run modern factories. Their chief interest lay in the efficient working of their factories, so they could be trusted to improve conditions of employment and to avoid friction with the labour force. In these conditions, economic inequality was a less important consideration than 'equality of opportunity'. Crosland was a vocal advocate of comprehensive education, which (he hoped) would provide every child with an equal chance to join the professional managers who would hold the balance of power in a future society.

Social democrats continued to call themselves socialists. But to Marxists, they were nothing less than traitors to the working class. If we look again at the characteristic socialist view of human nature, we can appreciate the force of this point. Socialists believe that work in a capitalist economy is dehumanising, whether or not it is regulated by the state. Economic exploitation might be reduced by regulation, but it will continue to exist because capitalists cannot survive unless they pay their workers less than the full value of their labour. And even under the control of professional managers, firms will tend to produce goods which yield the highest profits, whether or not they satisfy any 'genuine' social need. At best, then, the capitalist system might give people a roughly equal chance of living equally degrading lives. More likely, economic inequalities will continue to ensure that the children of the rich take an unjustified share of the material spoils.

Ironically, it can be argued that the Marxists who supported the 1917 Bolshevik revolution in Russia were equally untrue to socialist doctrine. Marx argued that the prospects for socialism depended upon the emergence of working-class consciousness, and this could only happen in a fully-fledged capitalist society. By contrast, capitalism had barely developed in the Russia of 1917 – and it required active intervention from the state to help it take root. Although it took many years for the full horror of the Soviet Revolution to register with Western socialists, the initial bloodshed provided a welcome propaganda *coup* to the opponents of socialism in Britain and elsewhere. In turn, this made the peaceful, revisionist alternative much more attractive for people who wanted to build more equal and harmonious societies with the ballot box as their only weapon.

One intriguing point arising from this discussion is the ambivalent relationship between conservative thought and socialism. Conventionally, we assume that these ideologies are completely antagonistic. However, they have at least one common feature of considerable importance. They both assert that the well-being of society as a whole should override the interests of any individual. During the nineteenth century, traditional conservatives could join socialists in deploring the corrosive social effects of industrial capitalism. As a result, Victorian thinkers like John Ruskin (1819–1900) have been honoured by socialists and conservatives alike.

Liberalism

While socialism developed in reaction to the social impact of the industrial revolution, the origins of liberalism are more controversial. Marxists see it as an attempt to justify the rise to power and subsequent dominance of the bourgeoisie, which replaced the aristocracy as the ruling class as a result of the industrial revolution. But it can also be associated with the emergence of the Protestant religion (although for Marxists this is just another way of making the same point, because they regard Protestantism as a manifestation of bourgeois ideology).

Certainly liberal thought predates systematic socialist thinking. One of the classic texts, John Locke's *Two Treatises of Civil Government*, was published as long ago as 1690. Locke clearly belongs in the liberal tradition because of his emphasis on natural rights, given to individuals by God. Government, Locke argued, was only legitimate if it arose from the **consent** of the individual. On the basis of this contractual theory, Locke built a justification for the removal of any government which failed to protect the rights of its citizens. Although it would be wrong to see Locke himself as an early advocate of universal adult suffrage, many later democratic theorists enlisted his work in support of their ideas.

Consent: agreement or permission, although it can in practice be merely acquiescence.

At the core of liberal thinking is the concept of the free, rational individual. Government should be based on consent, reflecting the wishes of a rational people. Crucially, such a government should be *limited* in the scope of its activity, because rational individuals can be trusted to look after their own affairs for the most part. But there must be a framework of law to protect life and property from individuals who fail to understand the rational advantages of peaceful co-existence. Governments may levy taxation, but only with the free consent of their citizens. In the eighteenth century these liberal ideas were used by the American colonists during their rebellion against the British crown.

As a dissenter from the established Anglican church, John Locke argued passionately for religious toleration (at least for fellow Protestants). This element of liberal thought was given its finest expression by the Victorian philosopher (and briefly Liberal MP) John Stuart Mill (1806–73), in his tract *On Liberty* (1859). Mill believed that an individual should only be subject to interference when he or she caused harm to others. The obvious difficulty here was that 'harm' is in the eye of the beholder. For example, the very existence of non-believers in the world causes offence to fanatical followers of many religions. But Mill, like most secular-minded liberals, believed that his 'harm principle' would provide a guarantee of freedom of thought and speech to all 'rational' people like himself. This aspect of his thought is best characterised as an early example of **pluralism** – a belief, common to many liberals, that the expression of diverse opinions is the only way to promote the cause of truth.

Pluralism: the belief that a diversity of people and values is beneficial.

However, as a near-contemporary of Marx, Mill was troubled by the impact of the industrial revolution. In later life, indeed, he flirted with socialist economic ideas. This was an early symptom of the serious rift which opened up in the liberal ranks towards the end of the nineteenth century. Broadly speaking, after this time liberals could be divided into two distinct camps:

1. *'Laissez-faire' or neo-liberalism. Laissez-faire* liberalism is based on the idea that individuals are free so long as they are not subject to deliberate interference from anyone else. For *laissez-faire* liberals, the state exists merely to protect individuals from such interference, either to their lives or their property. If it goes beyond this role, the state itself becomes the main enemy to freedom. *Laissez-faire* liberals are particularly suspicious of any suggestion of an increase in state authority in the interests of society. In their view, 'society' does not exist: there are only individuals and their families, who should be left to pursue their own interests in their own way, provided that their actions do not prevent anyone else doing the same.

   In the second half of the twentieth century, *laissez-faire* ideas were revived, not just because of the obvious threat from totalitarian regimes like the Soviet Union but also because democratic governments in the West were taking a more active part in economic management. In *The Road to Serfdom* (1944), the Austrian-born economist Friedrich von Hayek (1899–1992) argued that this process would lead to the extinction of freedom if left unchecked. Among others, Hayek's ideas had a strong influence on Margaret Thatcher. To reflect the fact that *laissez-faire* ideas had been revised and updated in the modern context, Hayek and those who shared his views were described as neo-liberals.

2. *New liberalism.* Not to be confused with the advocates of neo-liberalism, *new* liberals envisage a far more positive role for the state. Their position arose in response to the poverty experienced by the majority of the population during the industrial revolution. Like all liberals, they had no objection to economic inequality. But they thought that people should at least be protected against the

Table 15.1 Typical attitudes of the main ideologies on key issues

Issue	*Laissez-faire* liberalism/ neo-liberalism	Social democracy/ new liberalism	Socialism	Conservatism
Economic competition	Natural to human beings and productive of prosperity and progress	Acceptable within limits	Destructive of human harmony and happiness	Natural to some, but likely to disturb social stability
Inequality of income	Morally acceptable; provides incentives to excel	Gap between rich and poor must not be too wide	Morally repugnant	Inevitable in any human society, but damaging if allowed to grow too wide
Welfare state	Acceptable as a 'safety net' for the poor; otherwise creates 'dependency culture' and destroys incentives	Relatively generous provision essential in a civilised society	Merely a prop to corrupt capitalist system	Necessary to prevent social discontent; reflects duty of rich to the poor
Law and order	Harsh punishment for those whose actions interfere with operation of free market	Punishment must include an attempt to reform criminals	Capitalist laws are merely devised to defend the existing economic order	All humans potentially evil. Punishment should fit the criminal as well as crime
Globalisation	A welcome development; people should have the opportunity of buying and selling in every market without restriction	In theory trade should be spread as widely as possible, but it should not result in exploitation at home or abroad	Closer links between the peoples of all nations are essential, but the profit motive can only divide human beings	We find it hard enough to understand our neighbours. Links of any kind with the wider world are likely to be unsettling

effects of unemployment which was no fault of their own, of ill health and of old age. They also argued that the state should provide at least a rudimentary education for all children, to give them a reasonable chance of developing into rational adult individuals.

This position was not so far removed from the social democratic ideas of Anthony Crosland. Like him, the new liberals were arguing for something like **equality of opportunity**. There was, though, a theoretical difference underlying this broad agreement on practical policies. The new liberals believed that equality of opportunity would guarantee that every individual had a realistic chance of fulfilling his or her potential through competition in a capitalist economy. That is, they were still committed to core liberal ideas concerning human nature. The social democrats, by contrast, still hankered after the harmonious, cooperative society which had fuelled

Equality of opportunity: equal access to the procedure by which an office or benefit is allocated.

Controversy: 15.1

Meritocracy and education

An excellent illustration of the way ideologies are constrained by the context in which they operate is provided by the idea of 'meritocracy', particularly in relation to schooling.

All three of Britain's main political parties claim to embrace 'equality of opportunity' – the idea that people should prosper according to individual merit, rather than the circumstances of their upbringing.

In practice, though, the concept gives rise to considerable difficulties to members of all the main ideological 'families'. Since socialists believe that economic inequality causes social friction, their own understanding of equal opportunities relates to the chances of living a worthwhile life in a harmonious, egalitarian society. Comprehensive education, in which children are taught in mixed-ability classes, thus has obvious attractions to socialists. But from the socialist point of view there remains a major difficulty in today's society arising from parental influence, which can give certain children a crucial advantage and leave them feeling that competition is better than cooperation.

Things are no easier for liberals or social democrats. *Laissez-faire* or neo-liberals argue that equality of opportunity is guaranteed when there are no deliberately-imposed barriers to individual advancement. Books like *Self-Help* (1859), by the journalist Samuel Smiles, showed that it was possible for individuals to rise through their own efforts in the Victorian period, long before the introduction of the modern welfare state. Yet many successful entrepreneurs have owed their prosperity to luck. *Laissez-faire* liberals might reply that individuals 'make their own luck'. But it is still the case that some individuals find it easier than others to be 'lucky', particularly if they have wealthy parents and attend public school alongside others with similar advantages.

Social democrats and new liberals have paid the most serious attention to this problem, since equality of opportunity is arguably their most important ideal. But they have fared no better. It has been judged politically impossible to abolish public schools, and the operations of the free market in housing are now reinforcing a 'two-tier' system even within state-run institutions, because wealthy parents can relocate to areas which will ensure that their children can attend the best comprehensive schools. Arguably, the recruitment of children into the best schools because of the location of their parents' house is even more difficult to justify than the previous system of selection by ability at the age of 11.

The obvious inequalities in educational opportunity in Britain cast serious doubts on the rhetoric of all the main parties, however sincere they might be in their efforts to raise standards across the board. In effect, they are now trying to devise policies which will convince a bare majority of the electorate that their children can enjoy something which would satisfy a very loose definition of the term 'equality of opportunity', while hoping that no-one will look too closely at the true implications of that phrase.

the original socialist vision. In other words, new liberals and social democrats could support the tentative beginnings of what became Britain's welfare state, without sharing the same hopes for the ultimate outcome of these policies.

Ideology and British political parties

After this brief survey of traditional British ideologies, we are in a position to assess the principles of the main parties. As we have seen, practical politics involves compromise, often on issues of crucial importance. So we cannot expect a perfect fit between an ideology and the stated principles of a particular party. But we ought to be able to draw conclusions about the general character of their ideas.

The Conservative Party and conservatism

When studying the impact of ideology on the political parties, we have to remember that these organisations are broad coalitions (otherwise, they would not have been so successful over the years). However, it is possible to make generalisations about the most influential ideas within each party at different times, and to trace the key developments.

Case study:	15.1

Michael Howard

In January 2004 the then Conservative leader Michael Howard published a 16-point list of his core beliefs, in the form of a newspaper advertisement. The points expressed the following ideas:

- Government should be limited.
- Inequality is not harmful to society.
- People want the best for their families.
- Freedom is necessary to human happiness and should be defended against all its enemies.
- People should enjoy equal opportunities.
- Politicians are the servants of the people.
- Individuals have a duty to look after those less fortunate than themselves.

Although many senior politicians talk about ideas, Howard's declaration was unusual in its scope. It was also consistent with the stances he had taken on a range of issues throughout his career. While some of these points are acceptable to traditional conservatives, their overall character in the context of the early twenty-first century can only be understood as a reflection of *laissez-faire* liberalism. In particular, Howard revealed a strong hostility towards the state, assuming that individual effort could produce greater efficiency and, in the final analysis, a more just society.

Howard stood down as Conservative leader after the 2005 general election, and his successor David Cameron expressed the view that government could be 'a force for good'. However, Howard's testament of ideological faith probably reflected the views of a majority of Conservative MPs at the time that Cameron took over the leadership. Despite superficial differences between Howard's ideas and Cameron's similar statement (entitled 'Built to Last'), it remained to be seen whether the new line in rhetoric would be reflected in specific policy proposals.

Party labels are adopted in specific historical circumstances, and subsequent developments can make them misleading, for reasons which must be explored. This is particularly true of the Conservative Party. When the Tory Party began to use the 'Conservative' label in the early 1830s, its supporters were trying to resist constitutional changes which they regarded as unacceptably radical. Their opponents, the Whigs, were arguing for a (limited) extension of the electoral franchise, and attacking the privileged position of the Anglican church. Resistance to these changes was based on the typical conservative argument that existing institutional arrangements worked perfectly well, so reform could only make things worse. This argument failed. However, the Whigs were themselves anxious to keep change within limits, and after their most notable victory, the Great Reform Act (1832) which extended the vote to comfortable middle-class property-owners, they claimed that the constitution was now perfect. But they had made it far more difficult to argue against further reforms. These duly arrived, in 1867 (inspired by the Conservative, Disraeli), then in 1885, 1918 and 1928, by which time almost all adults over 21 could vote.

From our earlier discussion, we can appreciate why these developments were deeply disturbing to traditional conservatives. At every step, the extension of the franchise took Britain further away from the ideal of benevolent rule by an aristocratic elite, and put the choice of governors in the hands of people who (according to conservative assumptions) were unfitted to participate in politics. There were further blows to the conservative world view in the constitutional crisis of 1910–11, which resulted in drastic reductions in the power of the House of Lords (see Chapter 7), and the First World War, which suggested that conservatives had good reason to distrust human nature but also left them struggling to provide any constructive visions for the future.

As we have seen, ideology is action-oriented. Taken together, the developments of 1832–1918 deprived Burkean conservatives of a positive rationale for political action. Remaining adherents were far more likely to withdraw from public life – or to revise their thinking in order to accommodate new realities. Traditional conservatives who remained in politics were most likely to gravitate towards new liberalism, which at least offered the chance of relative social stability and could be squared with Disraelian state paternalism. But the obvious home for new liberals was still the Liberal Party, which had carried through an ambitious programme of social reform in the years before the First World War. The Conservative Party looked doomed to extinction.

As it turned out, the Conservatives were able to take advantage of disastrous splits in Liberal ranks. They had already benefited from earlier Liberal divisions over Home Rule for Ireland. But the quarrel between the Liberal leaders Asquith and Lloyd George over the conduct of the First World War brought an end to that party's prospects of forming a government on its own. Ambitious young people who would otherwise have been happy to join the Liberals now regarded the Conservative Party as the obvious outlet for their talents, and as the main focus of opposition to Labour. The trend was not restricted to the young; Winston Churchill, who had defected from the Conservatives to the Liberals in 1904, decided to rejoin his old party 20 years later.

Thus the Conservative Party survived as an institution, but its name was now a source of confusion rather than an accurate indication of its ideological character. From 1918 (if not before) the majority of prominent Conservatives were, in fact, liberals of various kinds. For tactical reasons in the fight against Labour, the party might have been expected to embrace the *laissez-faire* strand of liberalism. After all, a creed which denied the very existence of 'society' presented the clearest possible contrast with socialism. Many of the grass-roots activists in the party did indeed adopt this position. But up until the mid-1970s, the leading members of the parliamentary party (like the ex-Prime Minister Edward Heath) were new liberals, who still accepted Disraeli's positive view of the state even if they had relinquished his vision of an hierarchical social order. To satisfy their more radical constituency supporters, the leaders often reflected *laissez-faire* ideas in their rhetoric. Thus, for example, the party campaigned in 1950 on a platform of freedom from government interference. But when it returned to office in 1951 it retained almost all of the welfare institutions established by the post-war Attlee government, and made little effort to reverse its programme of nationalisation. The leadership, at least, was able to give its support to the post-war 'consensus'.

In 1970 Heath came to office on much the same platform. His rhetoric had suggested a significant reduction in the role of the state, but this was never his intention. When his government foundered under the impact of high inflation and industrial disorder, the *laissez-faire* liberals within the party seized their opportunity. Thatcher's victory in the 1975 leadership election triggered off a prolonged debate between her supporters and those who remained loyal to Heath. Although this was strictly a dispute among liberals of different kinds, both sides claimed to represent 'true' conservative tradition!

Thatcherism and the New Right

The strength of Thatcher's convictions is reflected in the fact that, unusually among British politicians, her name is used as a shorthand ideological term. As we have seen, she was strongly influenced by the neo-liberal economist Friedrich von Hayek. A thorough-going individualist, she once declared that there was 'no such thing as society'. Yet she also supported a strong line on law and order and personal morality, urging a restoration of 'Victorian values' in place of the 'permissive' attitude to social matters which she and her supporters traced back to the 1960s.

It is often argued that these beliefs made Thatcherism an unstable – if not self-contradictory – ideological compound, arguing for the widest possible freedom in some spheres of conduct and heavy restraint in others. The impression of incoherence is increased by differences within the British New Right which supported Thatcher. Some believed that economic freedom was much more important than social stability, while others (the so-called neo-conservatives (see Analysis 15.3) reversed these priorities. These diverse groups coalesced in the Thatcher years and supported the Conservative Party because of their shared antipathy towards various elements of the post-war consensus, which Thatcher so openly attacked.

Whatever the logical status of the New Right, Thatcher's diverse disciples are best understood within the context of *laissez-faire* liberalism. Even the so-called neo-conservatives, who take much of their inspiration from the US, make the rational individual the focus of their thinking, and believe that the state should minimise its interference with the free market. And if the nature of Thatcherism is to be taken from the ideas of the Prime Minister herself, its place within the *laissez-faire* tradition is unmistakable. 'Economics are the method', she declared in 1981; 'the object is to change the soul'. If the state stepped back from economic interference,

The post-war 'consensus'

The framework of policies established by the Attlee Government is usually identified as the basis of a post-war 'consensus' which embraced all three of the major parties. Often this is characterised as a 'social democratic' consensus. This chapter suggests a slightly different interpretation. We can accept that the impulse behind the policies was *mainly inspired* by revisionist or social democratic principles, reflecting the beliefs of most senior Labour figures at the time. But Labour's programme of nationalisation, and the welfare state, could be endorsed from a variety of ideological perspectives. Parliamentary socialists could see these developments as first steps towards the ultimate goal of a cooperative society, in which the means of production would no longer be in private hands. New liberals welcomed the advances towards real equality of opportunity. In a perfect world they would have deplored the extent of nationalisation, but they could acquiesce given the fact that the nationalised industries were essential economic assets which had been struggling in the private sector. Social democrats, of course, would have had no such reservations about the encroachments of the state. Burkean conservatives – the few that still remained in the parliaments of 1945–51 – could welcome the element of paternalism and the implicit desire for a more stable society.

In other words, the post-war consensus can be regarded as a broad policy framework which was acceptable to all except revolutionary socialists and *laissez-faire* liberals. In turn, it is no surprise that these ideologies suddenly seemed much more attractive when the 'consensus' came under intolerable strain due to the economic difficulties of the 1970s (see Chapter 2).

she believed, individuals would be freed to take their destinies in their own hands. Mrs Thatcher thought that this new sense of personal liberation would in itself transform the moral outlook of most Britons, restoring something like the values which had made Victorian Britain so prosperous. However, there were bound to be people who continued to reject Victorian values to the extent of breaking the law; and the punishment of law-breakers was a proper role for the state. In this sense, Mrs Thatcher saw no contradiction in her support for 'the free economy and the strong state'; like the *laissez-faire* liberals of the nineteenth century, she thought that the state should crack down on criminal activity, which was incompatible with the efficient operation of the free market. The armed forces should also be provided with generous funds from the taxpayer, to defend Britain against the Communist Soviet Union. Thatcher regarded defence against non-communist states as a lower priority. Ironically, Thatcher-inspired defence cuts encouraged the Argentine regime to invade the Falklands Islands, resulting in the 1982 war, which, as a result of victory, greatly increased the government's popularity.

In office (1979–90) Thatcher was forced to compromise on numerous occasions, contrary to the image of the 'Iron Lady' who urged her supporters to 'think the unthinkable'. For example, in 1984 she was forced to abandon plans to charge tuition fees to university students, after protests from party supporters. However, this element of pragmatism reflected her awareness of opponents within her own party who were looking for an opportunity to bring her down, and (to a lesser extent) a recognition that her ideas were never accepted by a majority of voters.

David Cameron – the face of 'caring Conservatism'? (© Ray Tang/Rex Features)

Thus while Thatcherite thinking pointed to the scrapping of the welfare state, there was never any chance that institutions like the National Health Service (NHS) could have been abolished without stimulating widespread opposition. As it was, Thatcher overreached herself by introducing the Poll tax, which provoked a campaign of civil disobedience, a mass rally in London which turned into a riot, and a significant swing in the opinion polls towards Labour. Although disagreements about Europe helped to inspire the party revolt which ejected Thatcher from office in November 1990, the poll tax was a strong contributory factor to the background of discontent.

The Labour Party and socialism

We have seen that after the First World War the Conservative Party was regarded as the main focus of opposition to socialism in Britain. But was there really any socialism to oppose? Judging by Clause IV of the party's constitution, adopted in 1918, Labour was indeed committed to socialist goals. The clause pledged:

> To secure for the workers by hand or by brain the full fruits of their industry and the most equitable distribution thereof that may be possible, upon the basis of the common ownership of the means of production, distribution and exchange.

Yet this striking declaration of socialist aims had only been accepted as part of a deal to keep the party's intellectuals within the party fold. From the formation of the Labour Representation Committee (LRC) in 1900, real power lay with the trade union movement, whose primary aim was to secure the election of working men to parliament. In the party's early years most Labour MPs owed their seats to cooperation with the Liberal Party. When Labour formed its first (minority) government in 1923, far from storming Buckingham Palace the new ministers conformed to all the usual proprieties. During the General Strike of 1926, when a revolutionary situation really could have developed, the party's leaders hoped for a reasonable settlement as quickly as possible. And when capitalism seemed to be entering a final crisis after the Wall Street Crash of 1929, the second Labour government collapsed because it could offer no constructive alternative to orthodox capitalist economic management.

The post-war government (1945–51) of Clement Attlee presented Labour with its first real chance to prove that socialism could be achieved through parliamentary means. The government was elected by a landslide, swept into office by a widespread feeling that the time had come for a decisive change because the Conservatives had failed between the two World Wars. Labour's socialists still look back with nostalgia to these days. Throughout its six years in power after 1945 the government was faced with crippling economic difficulties. Even so, it took into state ownership gas, coal, iron and steel, the railways and the Bank of England. It also established the NHS, against strong opposition from the medical profession.

This was indeed a formidable policy programme. But did it really represent an advance towards socialism? Most of the government's acts of nationalisation targeted industries which had been failing in the private sector. Even the Conservatives had contemplated nationalising the railways, and the traumas of the privately-owned coal industry had triggered off the General Strike. If the Attlee government's programme of nationalisation had represented a preliminary shopping list, to be supplemented by profitable concerns in the chemical or light engineering industries, Labour would have proved that it was serious about the commitment enshrined in Clause IV. The party was re-elected in 1950 with a very slender majority and lost a subsequent election a year later. Had it secured a second landslide, it might have taken further radical action. But its room for manoeuvre would still have been restricted. Britain's post-war economic revival depended crucially on US assistance. A few months before the government's defeat in 1951 the Chancellor of the Exchequer Hugh Gaitskell imposed limited NHS charges to help pay for a massive defence rearmament programme. This was Britain's response to American demands during its war against Communism in Korea. The decision provoked the resignation from the Cabinet of the founder of the NHS, Aneurin Bevan, along with the future Prime Minister Harold Wilson.

After Labour returned to opposition, leaving Britain with a mixed economy and a welfare state which provided a guaranteed income for pensioners and the unemployed, the party was divided over the best way forward. The initiative in this dispute was taken by Hugh Gaitskell's supporters, who took a 'revisionist' or social democratic line. As we have seen, this position received powerful support in these years from Gaitskell's friend Anthony Crosland. When Gaitskell became leader in 1955 he tried to get rid of Clause IV, but without success.

By this time the alignment of ideological forces within the Labour Party had shifted. In the early days, the intellectuals tended to be attracted by socialist theory, and accused the Trade Unions of supporting the capitalist *status quo* if it allowed them to improve the standard of living of their members in relation to other workers. The revisionist argument reflected the fact that many of the next generation of Labour intellectuals, like Crosland and Gaitskell himself, only joined the party because the Liberals had no hope of forming a government on their own. Gaitskell's successor as leader, Harold Wilson, was another intellectual of this kind, having been a member of the Liberal Party at Oxford University. Wilson had sided with the Bevanite opponents of Gaitskell, but after the latter's death in 1963 he proved that the differences had been more about personality than any profound ideological disagreement.

Wilson's two stints as Prime Minister (1964–70 and 1974–76) were marked by struggles against economic difficulties more than the forward march of socialism. Whatever the preferences of Wilson himself, his second period in Downing Street coincided with a fuel crisis which undermined the social democratic assumption that growing prosperity would continue to fund a generous welfare state (see Chapter 2).

After Labour lost office in 1979, a bitter post-mortem took place on the party's recent record. The 'revisionists' were in retreat, and indeed four senior figures from that wing of the party left to establish the Social Democratic Party (SDP) in 1981. Under the leadership of Michael Foot (1979–83), it looked as if Labour might finally commit itself wholeheartedly to socialism. A movement to 'democratise' the party, headed by the former Cabinet minister Tony Benn, unseated several MPs for their insufficient commitment to socialist ideals, although the extent of this ideological witch-hunt was exaggerated by sections of the media. Benn himself came within a whisker of winning the party's deputy leadership.

Labour fought the 1983 election on a manifesto which was described as 'the longest suicide note in history'. In fact, it was no more radical than the party's successful policy platform of February 1974. The main difference was that this time it was widely assumed that if the party won, it would act on its promises. As a result, the 1983 general election was an occasion when the two main parties found that the charade which they had been acting out for so many years had suddenly become a reality. Conservatives had grown accustomed to attacking Labour's socialism, while recognising that the party's leaders presented no serious danger to capitalism. Meanwhile Labour had been fulminating against the Conservatives as hard-nosed apologists for greed and exploitation, while accepting that most of them were very agreeable parliamentary colleagues. Now, for the first time in post-war British history, the parties engaged in a bitter ideological battle. The conflict, though, was one-sided, mainly because the Conservatives could call on the support from outspoken elements of the tabloid press (see Chapter 4).

After Labour's crushing defeat in 1983 the process of ideological polarisation between the two main parties was brought to an end. Foot's successor Neil Kinnock embarked on the task of making his party 'electable' again. For Kinnock, that meant restoring the dominance in policy terms of the 'revisionist' or social democratic perspective. But although he ensured the defeat of socialist activists – many of whom had organised within the party as members of the Militant Tendency – he failed to convince the public that he was sufficiently 'prime ministerial' and under his leadership Labour lost two further elections. His successor John Smith (1992–94) belonged firmly in the social democratic tradition and the party was far keener to unite behind its leader that it had been in Kinnock's day. But Smith never had the chance to test the popularity of these ideas in a general election.

'New' and 'old' Labour

When Tony Blair was elected leader after Smith's sudden death in 1994 his first priority was to shed the ideological baggage of the past. Within a year he had succeeded where Gaitskell had failed, persuading his party to revise Clause IV of the party's constitution. The new draft of the clause spoke of a 'common endeavour' to ensure that individuals could realise their 'full potential' in a 'community' where:

> Power, wealth and opportunity are in the hands of the many not the few, where the rights we receive reflect the duties we owe, so that, freed from the tyranny of poverty, ignorance and fear, we may live together in a spirit of solidarity, tolerance and respect.

The new clause described Labour as 'a democratic socialist party'. This was a peculiar form of words. If the new clause proved anything, it was that Blair and his allies were not socialists of any kind. As we have seen, socialists believe that 'solidarity, tolerance and respect' are impossible to realise in a society dominated by capitalist ideas, because of the divisive nature of the profit motive. Blair's goal, by contrast, was to extend opportunities *within* capitalist society. This ambition could be squared with the social democratic tradition. However, Blair had gone out of his

John Prescott spells out 'New' Labour principles with the aid of a pledge card
(© TopFoto.co.uk)

way to avoid using that label. Instead, he began to talk about a 'third way' – an alternative to socialism and unrestricted capitalism. Yet revisionist social democracy was itself a 'third way' of this kind. Gradually it became clear that Blair's reluctance to associate himself with this tradition arose from ideological considerations. Blair disagreed with the social democratic emphasis on the redistribution of wealth to reduce social inequality. Instead, he thought that redistribution should aim at the reduction of poverty; once this had been achieved, it was no business of the state to close the gap between the best and worst-off in society.

Blair also differed from social democrats in his marked preference for private industry, even in the provision of state services like health and education. Before he became Prime Minister, Blair made it clear that he would not reverse any of the privatisations of the Conservative years. In fact, although the government was forced to take over the functions of Railtrack, the privatised company which maintained Britain's railways, New Labour was keen to explore the possibility of further sales of state assets, and to involve private sector companies in publicly-financed enterprises through the Private Finance Initiative (PFI).

After the 2005 general election, when Blair was faced with constant backbench rebellions as he fought to secure a tangible legacy in domestic policy, he tried to reconnect himself with the social democratic tradition. But by that time it was clear to most observers that this was a rhetorical device, which could not be reconciled with his policy priorities in the public services. Overall, Blair's ideas can best be understood in the context of the continental European tradition of Christian democracy, which has been particularly influential in Italy, Germany and Norway. In turn, Christian Democratic ideas are very closely related to new liberalism, which

Controversy:	15.2

Blair and 'the forces of conservatism'

In his speech to the Labour Party conference in September 1999, Tony Blair launched a savage attack on what he called 'the forces of conservatism'. Part of this was aimed directly at the opposition. Among other things, Blair accused the Conservatives of having fought against giving the vote to women (in fact, their rejection of female suffrage had been shared by many supposedly progressive Liberal MPs), and he even tried to connect British conservatives with the murderers of Dr Martin Luther King. However, he had a wider target in mind. In his mind, the 'forces of conservatism' included anyone who opposed New Labour, including union members who were currently resisting reform of the public services.

As so often when politicians attack the ideology of their opponents, Blair's speech told us far more about himself. His use of the blanket term 'forces of conservatism' was obviously intended to make his 'Old' Labour critics think carefully before opposing him, in case they inadvertently assisted people who wanted to turn the clock back to the days of unchecked racism and sexism. The example shows how important it is for serious students of politics to subject political rhetoric to careful analysis, rather than accepting statements at face value. As we have seen, there are no significant 'forces of conservatism' left in the UK, in an ideological sense. It certainly makes no sense at all to accuse socialists, who continue to hope for radical change and an egalitarian society, of secretive conservative leanings.

also emerged at the end of the nineteenth century. The only significant difference is that Christian democracy – like Blair – has a stronger emphasis on the community (as opposed to the state), stressing individual duties as well as rights. On the continent of Europe – particularly in Italy and Germany – Christian democracy has provided the basis for powerful and consistent opposition to socialist parties since the Second World War. It is a remarkable irony that (for various reasons, not all related to ideology) Labour chose an overtly *anti*-socialist leader at a time when the perceived threat from Communist states had disappeared. Blair made no secret of his desire to overturn many of his party's most cherished traditions, but even he was prudent enough to be evasive about the true character of his thinking.

Despite Blair's election-winning charisma, he did not succeed in converting the bulk of his party. His ideological opponents, given the collective (and insulting) name of 'Old Labour', are mostly adherents of social democracy. Some party members would still like to see themselves as socialists, but almost all of them have accepted that the days of great nationalised industries are over. Their main goal is defensive – to obstruct the intrusion of free market principles into the public services, particularly in the fields of health and education. Although they can agree with Blair's stated aspiration of extending opportunity, they doubt whether his words can mean very much when economic inequalities are continuing to grow. From the perspective of Labour loyalists, it may appear that Blair's main achievement was not to make his party 'electable' – it would have won in 1997 under any other competent leader – but his ability to make people who disagreed with him so fundamentally follow him for so long.

It is commonly assumed that Blair's rivalry with his Chancellor of the Exchequer, Gordon Brown, was based at least in part on ideological differences. In fact, the uneasy relationship between the two provides some fascinating insights into the respective roles of ideology and personality in internal party politics. Many of the Labour MPs and activists who disagreed with Blair's principles looked to Brown as an alternative leader. This meant that the 'Brownites' tended to sympathise with Old Labour ideas, while the 'Blairites' were determined to stick to the New Labour course. Brown himself seemed happy to encourage his supporters to think that there would be a significant shift in government policy if he succeeded Blair as Prime Minister. However, the evidence suggests that Brown was only a 'Brownite' to the extent that, like his supporters, he wanted to remove Blair from Number 10. He insisted on full control of economic policy, but it is doubtful that Blair would have changed any of his important decisions. Certainly Blair agreed with Brown's drive to reduce the number of children in poverty; but, as we have seen, this did not involve a serious attempt to reduce economic inequality by imposing heavy taxation on the rich. Brown was also a passionate advocate of involving the private sector in state activities like health and education. Thus if Brown does succeed Blair there is no reason to expect any reduction of the drive to 'modernise' the public services.

The Liberal party and liberalism

Blair often expressed regret that the close relationship between the Liberals and Labour in the early years of the twentieth century had proved short-lived. He argued that their separation had allowed the Conservatives to dominate the century, and set back the cause of 'progressive' politics. Blair's view says more about his approach to politics than it does about the true relationship between Labour and the Liberals. The main obstacles to a merger – considerations of social class, and the emotional, almost tribal loyalty that parties generate – are political factors which Blair has consistently downplayed. But if the two parties had been able to overlook these points and strike a deal before Labour was fully established, they would have imported significant ideological differences within the ranks of the merged organisation.

As we have seen, the ideological history of the two main parties is extremely complicated. By contrast, the Liberals (now the Liberal Democrats) have been much more straightforward. For more than a century the party has been dominated by new liberals. The Asquith government (1908–16) introduced several important social reforms, which are often cited as laying the foundations of the welfare state. True to this legacy, during the 2001 general election campaign the party argued for tax increases to fund better public services. In 2004 several prominent Liberal Democrats contributed to a book which reminded the party that liberalism has always been suspicious of the state (its title, *The Orange Book*, was a mischievous echo of *The Yellow Book* (1928), which had promoted more active state intervention). However, in the 2005 general election the Liberal Democrats again argued for higher taxes and a modest increase in public spending. But the subsequent deposition of Charles Kennedy as Liberal Democrat leader reflected the growing influence of the *Orange Book* faction, some of whom had become MPs. Ironically, while the contributors to the *Orange Book* imagined that they were being radical, they were actually working to bring their party closer to the new 'consensus' in British politics (see below), and thus making the Liberal Democrats *less* distinctive in ideological terms. Kennedy's replacement as leader, Sir Menzies Campbell, was seen as the most likely candidate to unite the party membership. This meant that Campbell would have to come to terms with the *Orange Book* faction, and within a few days of becoming leader he had persuaded his party to drop its objections to privatisation of the Royal Mail. Later the party also abandoned its pledge to increase taxes on the better-off.

While social democracy and new liberalism have several common characteristics, the *Orange Book* emphasised a crucial difference. It reminded its readers that all liberals take the individual as their primary focus, whereas social democrats concentrate on collective interests. So although from Blair's perspective it seems tragic that the Liberal Party and Labour did not unite, a merger between the Liberals and the Conservatives (while they remained under new liberal leadership, until 1979) would have been no less congenial. But we have also seen that after the Liberal Party split during the First World War the Conservatives were regarded as providing the best chance of preventing Labour from winning elections. As a result, members of the Liberal Party who feared the possibility of a truly socialist Labour government tended to defect to the Conservatives, while those who accepted the need for state intervention and recognised that Labour was never a full-blooded socialist party moved in the other direction. Thus, while Churchill rejoined the Conservatives when the Liberals faltered, Richard Haldane, who had been a senior minister under Asquith, ended up as a Labour Lord Chancellor.

As Prime Minister (1940–45, 1951–55), Churchill continued to hope that the remaining Liberals would follow his example and join the main anti-socialist party. But the Liberals struggled on, and seemed set to benefit from their perseverance at the beginning of the 1980s, when Labour adopted a more socialist outlook and the Conservatives plumped for Thatcherism. If ideology had been the main political factor, a significant number of Conservative and Labour MPs would have defected to the Liberals. They might even have emerged as the largest parliamentary grouping, reflecting the fact that a majority of the electorate continued to sympathise with new liberal ideas about the role of the state throughout the Thatcher period. But institutional ties proved so strong that no more than a handful of Labour MPs, and only a single Conservative, left their parties – and even then they joined the newly-founded SDP rather than going straight to the Liberals. Even the founder-members of the SDP were divided in their attitudes towards the Liberals, and this made the eventual merger between the parties (in 1988) a very messy affair, with senior figures like David Owen of the SDP remaining aloof.

In view of the consistent ideological approach of the Liberals and their successors over the last century, it is ironic that the party has often been accused of electoral opportunism. Like its more powerful rivals, it has adopted policies for tactical reasons from time to time. But in ideological terms it has been much more consistent than the Conservatives and Labour. One can imagine Asquith as an enthusiastic Liberal Democrat today; but Asquith's contemporaries, like Arthur Balfour (Conservative) and Keir Hardie (Labour), would find it almost impossible to recognise the parties they once led.

A new 'consensus'?

In June 2004 Labour and the Conservatives began to introduce their main campaign themes for the following year's general election. Both Blair and Michael Howard emphasised the importance of choice in public service provision. During the campaign itself, this appeal was directed towards 'hard-working families'. There was a clear assumption shared by the two leading parties that members of such families would have very similar ideas. The Conservatives reinforced this point with the main slogan for their advertising campaign: 'Are you thinking what we're thinking?'.

If there had been a significant ideological difference between the two party leaders, we would expect them to mean different things even though they use the same words, due to contrasting views of human nature. In this case Blair and Howard certainly found scope to attack each other's ideas. Howard was far more explicit than Blair in urging the direct involvement of private enterprise in the delivery of public services. But the practical impact of each programme would be greatly to expand the role of the private sector.

Both Blair and Howard argued that their policies would ensure that everyone enjoyed the range of choice in services which is currently available only to the well-off. The concept of choice is rightly associated with liberalism, which focuses on the rational individual. One of the intellectual 'gurus' of Thatcherism, Milton Friedman, published an influential book entitled *Free to Choose* in 1980. For all the bickering over policy details, Blair and Howard clearly shared Friedman's core assumptions about human nature, seeing the average Briton as a 'consumer–citizen' (see Chapter 2). Before the 2005 general election, this theme was made explicit in speeches by the Health Secretary, John Reid, and Labour's campaign coordinator Alan Milburn. It was left to Charles Kennedy of the Liberal Democrats to argue that the emphasis in public services should be on quality rather than choice.

The debate over choice added weight to the claim that there is a new consensus in British politics. Despite two landslide victories, Labour has done very little to change the broad framework of policy that it inherited from the Conservatives. In some respects it has gone further, for example in the government's use of the PFI, which guarantees a high rate of return for private companies which invest in public sector projects such as new hospitals and schools.

The emergence of this new consensus is best understood against a background of socio-economic change, combined with the influence of democratic institutions. The old terminology of class no longer makes much sense in Britain (see Chapter 3). At the same time, much greater geographic mobility and insecurity in the job market have combined to generate a more individualistic ethos in Britain as in other Western countries. The advertising industry works on the assumption that individuals are preoccupied with the material status of themselves and their immediate families. When parties call in the advertisers to enhance their appeal to the public, it is no surprise that their broadcasts and slogans echo similar assumptions about human nature.

These developments complement institutions which reflect liberal ideas. The principle of one person, one vote is, of course, in itself distinctively liberal, and the main theoretical support for universal franchise has come from liberals like John Stuart Mill. As a pluralist, Mill wanted elections to be free and equal contests between people of divergent views. He argued that principled disagreement is healthy, since even the truth becomes stale when everyone thinks the same way.

Of course, liberal democratic institutions do not ensure the success of parties which profess liberal principles. The example of Hitler's National Socialists between the wars shows that even parties which detest democracy can win significant support under the system. Even so, the necessity of playing for power by liberal rules does have a tendency to make the most serious competitors think along liberal lines. For example, political campaigning nowadays is geared towards attracting floating voters in key constituencies (see Chapter 16). These voters are assumed to exercise 'rational choice' in elections, opting for the party offering policies which will benefit themselves and their families. If the crucial voters in general elections are assumed to be distinctively liberal in their preferences, it is hardly surprising that all the parties with any chance of securing a parliamentary majority tend to adopt policies (and use rhetoric) of a liberal flavour.

Within the broad framework of liberal ideas, *laissez-faire* is the one which focuses on individual self-interest. Thus, even if the leaders of the two main parties were not already sympathetic to *laissez-faire*, they would have plenty of good reasons for devising policies which conform to that tradition. Tellingly, the most radical 2005 manifesto commitments from both main parties were those which would have found most favour with *laissez-faire* liberals (by contrast, the tax increases proposed by the Liberal Democrats were extremely modest compared to the corresponding rates in the 1970s). But it would be wrong to suggest that British politics is now dominated by a straight-forward *laissez-faire* consensus; after all, even under Thatcher, the Conservatives continued to accept the welfare state, which is highly suspect to any *laissez-faire* liberal, and since 1997 the Conservatives have become increasingly convincing when they argue that the state should help the poorest in society. Despite their desire to 'think the unthinkable' in order to achieve practical results, ambitious British politicians are still partly constrained by the legacy of the consensus which prevailed between 1945 and the mid-1970s. Senior policy-makers – whether Labour or Conservative – all want to reduce the role of the state and to boost the private sector, in contrast to the situation in the mid-1970s when the tendency was to increase the role of the state. But above all, politicians want to be elected; and that means that for all the rhetoric about extending 'choice' for rational individuals, certain aspects of public service provision will continue to be provided free for all, funded by taxpayers' money.

Alternative voices

While the decline of conservatism and socialism means that liberalism is the dominant ideology in Britain, it does not enjoy an unchallenged monopoly of political thinking. Three 'alternative' perspectives – environmentalism, nationalism and feminism – are discussed below.

Environmentalism

We have already seen how the industrial revolution affected the three main ideological traditions. Environmentalism, by contrast, can be seen as the ideology of post-industrialism. As evidence mounts of the damage done by more than two centuries of intensive exploitation of the earth's natural resources, the environmental (or 'green') movement has grown from a small fringe grouping to an important force in many Western countries.

The most committed environmentalists (often described as 'dark greens' or 'deep ecologists') believe that human beings are an integral part of nature and not superior to the rest of creation. From this perspective, they argue for a radical change in Western lifestyles. The throwaway, affluent consumer society is utterly short-sighted, they insist. It has made human beings into an endangered species. In order to save themselves from environmental catastrophe, people should start treating the world and all of its inhabitants with proper respect.

While deep ecology is clearly a distinctive ideological position, many people who think of themselves as greens flinch from its full implications. Concern for the environment is compatible with traditional conservatism in several respects; in particular, conservatives who deny that human beings can be fully 'rational' must always suspect the claims of science and technology. Meanwhile, socialists can argue for environmental protection from the same viewpoint which inspires their opposition to the exploitation of human beings. But the ideology which has most difficulty in accommodating green thought is liberalism. Typically, the environmentally-conscious liberal will buy lead-free petrol, recycle empty wine bottles, and think seriously about investing in roof insulation to reduce energy consumption at home. To the deep ecologist, this response to environmental damage is wholly inadequate; but it is only to be predicted given the liberal view of human nature. New liberals can accept limited state intervention, either through regulation or the tax system, to tackle the problem at the margin. But *laissez-faire* liberals oppose even this, and usually give their backing to any scientist who disputes the evidence for climate changes. Perhaps one day this evidence will become too glaring even for *laissez-faire* liberals to ignore; but if they ever take it seriously enough to change their lifestyles, they will have undergone an ideological conversion and ceased to be *laissez-faire* liberals. David Cameron's pronouncements on this subject, and Liberal Democrat proposals on the taxation of the aviation industry, suggest some movement in this direction. But all of the major UK parties would have to go much further to be classified as 'true' greens.

Nationalism

Green parties have been reasonably successful throughout Europe in recent elections. Their performance, though, has been more than matched by new nationalistic parties. Their rise has been greeted with considerable dismay by the more established parties, as if their ideas represented a real challenge to the dominant liberal tradition.

But does modern nationalism constitute a distinct ideology, on our definition of the term? The problem is that nationalists agree on only one thing: the need for a nation to govern itself. They have different ideas about nationhood. Culture, language, religion and geographical boundaries can all be used by nationalists to define 'their' community. Some deny that newly-arrived immigrants can form part of the nation, while others (like Zionists in Israel) welcome all newcomers who share their views. Politicians who assert the right of self-government for their own nation often deny the same right to others abroad.

We have seen that all ideologies are affected by circumstances. But it would hardly be an exaggeration to say that everyone can become a nationalist under the right circumstances. Nationalism is characteristically found whenever a community (however defined) feels that its identity is under threat. Thus it can arise when a community is denied the right to self-government, or when members of an established nation perceive that they are in danger of losing that right. In modern Britain the first kind of nationalism is represented by Scottish and Welsh supporters of devolved power within the UK (or complete independence), and by opponents of the Union in Northern Ireland. The second variety has been increasing over the last few decades, among people throughout the UK who oppose European integration, and others (not always, but very often the same people) who are troubled by the consequences of mass immigration. Nationalist views are variously represented by the Scottish National Party (SNP), by Plaid Cymru in Wales, Sinn Fein and the Social and Democratic Labour Party (SDLP) in Northern Ireland, and in England by the British National Party (BNP) and the United Kingdom Independence Party (UKIP).

These parties illustrate the wide range of tactics and demands characteristic of nationalist movements. At one end of the scale, Plaid Cymru has traditionally been concerned with the preservation of Welsh language and culture. This partly explains why the Blair government did not feel the need to offer tax-raising powers to the Welsh Assembly. At the other extreme, Sinn Fein has intimate links with the Irish Republican Army (IRA), and until the Good Friday agreement of 1998 it refused to disavow the use of violence to secure its objectives.

In Britain nationalism is normally associated with relatively small Westminster parties (although, of course, they are much more strongly represented in their devolved institutions). These groups can play a crucial role on occasion, as when the 1974–79 Labour government depended upon nationalist votes to keep it in office. But it would be a mistake to underestimate the influence of nationalism within the main parties. Labour and the Liberals/Liberal Democrats were consistent supporters of devolution, and even the Conservatives adopted the policy (for Scotland) in the early 1970s. The Conservatives, in particular, have been sensitive to possible challenges from parties like the National Front (NF), whose anti-immigration stance has now been inherited by the BNP. In the 1979 general election NF support dropped considerably, largely due to the hard line on immigration pursued by the Conservatives under Thatcher.

Labour and the Conservatives are currently appealing to nationalist sentiment in their attitude to asylum seekers, and are engaged in a long-running battle for 'ownership' of national symbols like the Union flag. On the European Union, all three main parties can be said to be nationalistic; they might disagree profoundly on where the national interest lies, but all of them regularly assert that they would stand up for it in any European negotiations. The most dramatic example of nationalism cutting across ideological lines came in the 1975 referendum on membership of the European Economic Community, when the leading figures in the 'no' campaign were Enoch Powell, an apostle of *laissez-faire* in domestic matters, and Tony Benn, who was a figurehead for socialists within the Labour Party.

Feminism

Feminism was probably the most successful political movement in Britain during the twentieth century. Indeed, it can be argued that any loss of impetus by feminism today is a direct result of considerable improvements in women's rights, in the home and at work. The significant advances over the last century are symbolised by the election of 102 women Labour MPs in 1997, the introduction of all-women shortlists in winnable constituencies, and a record seven female Cabinet ministers appointed in 2001. Some commentators believe that women already enjoy equal status to men in all important respects, and that we are now in a world of 'post-feminism'. This view is open to serious objections (see Chapter 2); but it is not confined to men who dislike the results of this social revolution.

However, rather than regarding feminism as a separate ideology, it can be argued that the victories of the feminist movement have almost all accompanied the rise of liberalism. That is, reforms such as votes for women (1918 and 1928), and the Equal Pay Act 1970 could not have been resisted by any consistent male liberal. Liberals oppose discrimination on any grounds apart from the merits of the individual, so those Liberal MPs who set their faces against female suffrage in the early twentieth century were untrue to the creed they purported to follow. By contrast, socialist feminists have very little to celebrate today. For them, meaningful women's liberation could only come with an end to the economic exploitation of both sexes. The proportion of women who have entered the workforce on a part-time basis since the 1970s is celebrated by many liberals, on the grounds that it undermines the traditional idea of dependency on a male bread-winner. But consistent socialists can only interpret this development as a backward step for humanity as a whole, since it has provided capitalism with a new pool of labour, often willing to take on low-paid, semi-skilled work.

On this view, feminism is rather like environmentalism and nationalism. In its mainstream forms, it is not an ideology at all, but rather an integral part of other belief systems which give rise to ideas about the best way of living for human beings as a whole. But one variety of feminism does conform to our interpretation of ideology. This is 'radical' feminism, which focuses on the oppression of women by men. On this view, male aggression causes wars, and creates antagonism in the workplace. Far from being a separate, 'private' domain, radical feminists argue that the family is a 'patriarchal' institution which reflects the unequal power relations found in all walks of life. For some radical feminists the only solution is strict segregation of the sexes. Indeed, technological developments hold out the prospect that the male of the species will soon be redundant even for reproductive purposes.

Radical feminism has brought several important practical gains for women, particularly by drawing attention to the under-reported crime of rape within marriage. Its insistence that 'the personal is the political' has also enhanced understanding of the political sphere. But like 'deep ecology', it gains limited (and usually hostile) coverage in the media, precisely because it cannot be assimilated by the dominant ideology, liberalism. The extent to which the popular image of feminism has been infiltrated by liberal assumptions is symbolised by the long-running debate about women 'having it all' – i.e. raising a family as well as enjoying material success in a competitive capitalist environment. Ultimately this debate is concerned with equal rights to free competition in the marketplace – a characteristic liberal argument, like almost every other topic in contemporary British politics which is taken seriously in parliament or the media.

Conclusion and summary

This chapter has shown that ideology does play an important role in British politics, but that it needs to be assessed in the context of other influences, notably institutional factors and socio-economic developments. Politicians are well aware of the importance of ideological traditions, and tend to use labels to boost their own credibility with party members, or to discredit their opponents. As a result, their statements need to be appraised very carefully rather than being taken at face value.

Ideology is best understood as a set of beliefs ultimately arising from a particular view of human nature. The introduction of democratic institutions in Britain, starting with the Great Reform Act of 1832, has encouraged politicians to address the perceived interests of the 'rational' individual voter. This tendency, combined with significant social change since the nineteenth century, has helped to produce a distinctively liberal 'consensus'. Today, the dominant assumptions underlying the policy proposals of all three main parties can only be understood as falling within the liberal tradition, despite the survival of alternative labels (which are often used as insults). This consensus should not be confused with 'the end of ideology'; the fact that one ideology is dominant does not make ideas any less important. However, political apathy in Britain can partly be attributed to the coincidence between the ideas of all three main parties. In such circumstances, it is natural for people to look around for alternatives. Almost certainly, the current party system will be able to absorb any rise in nationalism. A more serious challenge would arise if the electorate became alarmed by evidence of environmental damage, because this would demand a radical change in lifestyles and bring key liberal assumptions about rational individualism into question.

Further reading

The literature on ideology is voluminous, but not all of it is relevant to an understanding of British politics. On ideology in general, there are accessible and balanced accounts such as A. Heywood, *Political Ideologies: An Introduction* (London: Palgrave, 3rd edition, 2003) and A. Vincent, *Modern Political ideologies* (Oxford: Blackwell, 2nd edition, 1995). Far less has been written about the relationship between ideas and practice in Britain. The two best recent books are I. Adams, *Ideology and Politics in Britain Today* (Manchester: Manchester University Press, 1998) and R. Leach, *Political Ideology in Britain* (London: Palgrave, 2002). There is a concise discussion of recent developments in M. Garnett, 'Lack of Substance', *Politics Review*, Vol. 13, No. 4 (2004), pp. 10–12.

The advent of New Labour has provoked a great deal of discussion about 'Blairism'. There is a thoughtful account by S. Driver and L. Martell, *Blair's Britain* (Cambridge: Polity, 2002). Anthony Giddens, a key participant in the debate, has defended Blair in a series of books. See in particular his *The Third Way. The Renewal of Social Democracy* (Cambridge: Polity, 1998) for a contrast to the view presented in this chapter. An alternative interpretation is presented by T. Bale and N. Huntington in 'New Labour: New Christian Democracy?', *Political Quarterly*, Vol. 73, No. 1 (2002), pp. 44–50. Another strongly-argued account from a different perspective is R. Heffernan, *New Labour and Thatcherism* (London: Palgrave, 2001). For brief surveys see P. Kelly, 'Ideas and Policy Agendas in Contemporary Politics', in P. Dunleavy, A. Gamble, R. Heffernan and G. Peele (eds), *Developments in British Politics 7* (London: Palgrave, 2003), and R. Plant, 'Blair and Ideology' in A. Seldon (ed.), *The Blair Effect* (London: Little, Brown, 2001).

Most writers on conservatism – whether hostile or favourable – tend to equate it with the current beliefs of Conservative Party leaders. With this caution in mind, readers should consult D. Willetts, *Modern Conservatism* (London: Penguin, 1992). A hostile account of Thatcherism, I. Gilmour, *Inside Right: Conservatism, Policies and the People* (London: Quartet, 1978) is still relevant today. A. Gamble, *The Free Economy and the Strong State* (London: Macmillan, 2nd edition, 1994) explores the internal contradictions of Thatcherism. Some interesting ideas for the party's future direction are contained in E. Vaizey, N. Boles and M. Gove (eds), *A Blue Tomorrow: New Visions for Modern Conservatives* (London: Politico's, 2001). M. Garnett, 'The Free Economy and the Schizophrenic State: Ideology and the Conservatives', *Political Quarterly*, Vol. 75, No. 4 (2004), pp. 367–72 assesses the character of contemporary Conservatism.

The Liberal Party has been virtually ignored by academic writers, partly because of the unfounded assumption that it is they, rather than their main rivals, who adopt policies out of opportunism more than conviction. The most comprehensive study is A. Russell and E. Fieldhouse, *Neither Left nor Right? The Liberal Democrats and the Electorate* (Manchester: Manchester University Press, 2004). A useful but brief account (still relevant after more than a decade) is R. Behrens, 'The Centre: Social Democracy and Liberalism', in L. Tivey and A. Wright (eds), *Party Ideology in Britain* (London: Routledge, 1989). For more recent debates within the party, the best source is D. Laws and P. Marshall (eds), *The Orange Book: Reclaiming Liberalism* (London: Profile Books, 2004). There is an insightful discussion of the ideology in J. Gray, *Liberalism* (Buckingham: Open University Press, 1986).

On the other ideas discussed in the chapter, see A. Dobson, *Green Political Thought* (London: Routledge, 2nd edition, 1996), J. Lovenduski and V. Randall, *Contemporary*

Feminist Politics (Oxford: Oxford University Press, 1993) and, for two contrasting views of nationalism in Britain, T. Nairn, *After Britain* (London: Granta, 2000) and S. Heffer, *Nor Shall My Sword: The Reinvention of England* (London: Weidenfeld & Nicolson, 1999).

Websites

Probably the most useful sources on the internet for this chapter are the sites of the parties themselves, where students will find statements of general aims as well as links to speeches and press releases. See, in particular, www.bnp.org.uk (British National Party), www.conservative-party.org.uk, www.labour.org.uk, www.libdems. org.uk, www.sinnfein.ie/, www.snp.org.uk (Scottish National Party), www.plaid-cymru.wales.com, and www.independenceuk.org.uk (UK Independence Party).

By completing an online questionnaire, the Political Compass www.politicalcompass. org/ will place respondents on a left–right axis and an authoritarian–libertarian axis. The site also locates political parties and politicians and includes some interesting commentary on the problems of the left–right dichotomy.

Part 5
Participation

Chapter 16

Elections and electoral systems

Learning outcomes

After reading this chapter, you will:

- Understand the main features of the electoral process and electoral systems used in the UK.
- Be able to evaluate the strengths and weaknesses of the simple plurality system.
- Be able to assess the various systems used to elect supranational, subnational and local bodies.

Introduction

Elections are central to democratic politics, providing a direct link between government and citizens. At a general election, voters reach a verdict on the record of the party in office and the relative merits of the policies offered by rival political parties, express a political preference by voting for their favoured candidate and thereby choose a representative to act on their behalf in the decision-making process. In combination, the votes of individual citizens in geographical constituencies determine both the make-up of the legislature and the political colour of the government. Voting remains the primary political activity undertaken by many citizens, but election turnout has declined prompting concerns about the health of democracy in the UK.

Elections in the UK

Elections in a liberal democracy should be competitive, free and fair. A competitive election is one contested by a number of parties, presenting voters with a meaningful choice. For an election to be free, citizens must enjoy basic civil liberties such as freedom of speech and association, the right to vote in secret, and the right to join a political party and stand as a candidate. In a fair election, the votes of individual citizens should be of equal worth: 'one person, one vote, one value'. High standards are required in the administration of the electoral process: citizens should have easy access to polling places, the counting of votes should be transparent and, if disputes arise, there should be recourse to the courts. Governments should not be able arbitrarily to change electoral law to their own benefit. More exacting criteria include equitable treatment of candidates and parties in terms of resources (e.g. campaign funding) and balanced reporting by the media. The electoral system should also accurately translate votes cast into seats won.

General elections are the most important electoral contests held in the UK: all 646 members of the House of Commons are elected in single member constituencies using the simple plurality system. The timing of general elections is not fixed, though an election must be called once a parliament has run its full five-year term. The Prime Minister can call a general election at a time of his or her choosing and can determine the length of the campaign. This gives the governing party a distinct advantage. The Prime Minister can call an election when circumstances are favourable or when policies (e.g. tax cuts) have maximum impact. If a government is defeated on a motion of censure in the Commons, it is expected to resign and call an election. This last occurred in 1979 when James Callaghan's Labour government lost a vote of confidence – and the ensuing general election.

Supranational, regional and local bodies are also elected, using a variety of electoral systems. Elections to the European Parliament take place at fixed five-year intervals; devolved assemblies in Scotland, Wales and Northern Ireland are elected at four-year intervals. Councillors serve four-year terms of office but local authorities have different electoral cycles. In some, all councillors face the electorate at the same time; in others, a third or a half of members are elected at a time. Some local authorities have directly-elected mayors whose term of office varies from two-and-a-half to five-and-a-half years.

Constituency: a geographical territory in which electors choose one or more representatives to serve in the legislature.

Should a vacancy arise in a contest in which the simple plurality system is used, a by-election is called to choose a new representative. (In proportional representation list systems, the next candidate of the same party from the original party list fills the vacancy.) This is a one-off contest held in the **constituency** where the vacancy has arisen. By-elections to the House of Commons attract considerable publicity and often produce shock results as electors protest against the main parties. The Conservatives failed to win any of the 18 by-elections contested in the 1992–97 parliament, losing eight seats in the process. Labour bucked the trend by not losing a single seat in by-elections held between 1997 and 2001. But it suffered heavy defeats in Brent East (2003), Leicester South (2004) and Dunfermline and West Fife (2006). The poor showing by the Tories in the September 2003 Brent East by-election persuaded many Conservative MPs to back the vote of no confidence that ended Iain Duncan Smith's tenure as party leader the following month.

As we have seen in earlier chapters, significant parts of the UK polity are not elected. These include the head of state (the hereditary monarch), the second chamber of the legislature (the House of Lords) and quangos that distribute public funds. In common with many liberal democracies, judges and civil servants are appointed on merit rather than elected.

The electoral process

The Department for Constitutional Affairs is responsible for the conduct of general and European Parliament elections, and coordinates electoral issues concerning the devolved assemblies with territorial ministries. The Department for Communities and Local Government is responsible for local and mayoral elections. Electoral law is not subject to special constitutional procedures and can be changed through normal parliamentary procedures. The Blair government has introduced new electoral systems for elections to the European Parliament, devolved assemblies and executive mayors; extended the franchise to groups such as the homeless; imposed limits on national campaign spending, and created an independent Electoral Commission to oversee the conduct of elections and run pilot schemes on alternative methods of voting.

The Electoral Commission also maintains a register of political parties and scrutinises their funding. The two main parties spend large amounts on general election campaigns. In 1997, the Conservatives spent £28.3 million, Labour £25.7 million and the Liberal Democrats just £3.5 million. Following recommendations made by the Neill Committee on Standards in Public Life, the Political Parties, Elections and Referendum Act 2000 set a ceiling on national campaign expenditure. The maximum spending limit for parties contesting every constituency in Great Britain was £18.84 million in 2005. Labour and the Conservatives each spent close to £18 million in 2005 compared to the £4 million spent by the Liberal Democrats (see Table 16.1). Limits on constituency spending by local parties were already in place. The maximum limits on spending by candidates in 2005 were £7150 plus 7 pence per elector in county constituencies and £7150 plus 5 pence per elector in borough constituencies.

Table 16.1 Spending (£) during the 2005 general election campaign

	Conservative	Labour	Lib Dem
Party political broadcasts	293446	470218	124871
Advertising	8175166	5286997	1583058
Unsolicited material to electors	4493021	2698114	1235295
Manifesto and party documents	98956	356640	134611
Market research and canvassing	1291847	1577017	165185
Media	448277	375410	105793
Transport	934224	2188153	663513
Rallies and events	1148218	2916969	68994
Overheads and general administration	969094	2070100	243254
TOTAL	17852240	17939617	4324574

Note: Total includes miscellaneous expenditure not included in the table.

Source: Electoral Commission, 'Register of Campaign Expenditure', www.electoralcommission.org.uk/

Challenges to the validity of an election are heard in the High Court, though proven cases of fraud in general elections are rare. In 1997 the High Court ruled that the contest in Winchester should be re-run because of procedural irregularities (rather than fraud) at the count. At the subsequent by-election, the Liberal Democrats turned their initial majority of two votes into one of almost 22,000.

Four independent Boundary Commissions, one for each nation of the UK, determine the boundaries of Westminster constituencies. They review the size of the electorate in each constituency every eight to twelve years and recommend changes based on population movements. Constituencies should be as equal 'as is practicable' in terms of the size of their electorate, but more than fifty constituencies had a population 20 per cent higher or lower than the aggregate electoral quota. The Isle of Wight has an electorate of 108,000 while, at the other extreme, Na h-Eileanan an Iar (the Western Isles) has fewer than 22,000 voters. The number of Scottish seats fell from 72 to 59 in 2005; before then Scottish constituencies had averaged 55,000 voters but English constituencies 69,000.

Voting

Elections are traditionally held on a Thursday with voting taking place from 7am to 10pm. Schools and village halls are transformed into polling stations. On entering, the voter identifies themselves to officials and is given a ballot paper bearing an official stamp. This lists all candidates standing in the constituency in alphabetical order and includes party names and logos. The act of voting is secret to prevent electors being induced or pressurised into voting in a particular way. On general election ballot papers, a cross (✗) is placed in the box next to the name of one's chosen candidate. Where **proportional representation** (PR) is used, voters enter one or more numbers on the ballot paper to indicate their preferences. Failure to indicate one's choice clearly may result in the ballot paper being spoiled, rendering it invalid.

An unusal polling station – or an attempt to increase turnout? (© Reuters/Corbis)

Citizens who are unable to vote in person can apply for a proxy vote – where another person undertakes the act of voting on their behalf – or a postal vote. Those eligible for a proxy vote include people working away from home (e.g. in the armed forces). Postal votes were available on demand for all citizens at the 2001 and 2005 general elections. Prior to this, people requesting a postal vote had to state a reason and have their application approved by Electoral Registration Officers. In 2005, 6.5 million people requested postal ballots (15 per cent of the electorate) compared to 1.7 million in 2001 and 0.7 million in 1997.

Concerns about falling turnout prompted the government to authorise the Electoral Commission to carry out pilot schemes on alternative methods of voting at local elections. They tested the practicality and impact on turnout of:

- All-postal ballots.

Case study: 16.1

All-postal ballots

In an all-postal ballot voting by post is the standard method of voting: only in exceptional circumstances will electors be able to go to a polling station. To complete a postal ballot, a voter must (i) complete the ballot paper and place it in a sealed envelope, (ii) complete a declaration of identity, have their signature witnessed and place this declaration in a separate envelope; (iii) place both in a pre-paid envelope and send it by post to the Local Returning Officer before the specified deadline.

All-postal ballots have been the most successful of the pilot schemes conducted by the Electoral Commission. Of the 53 pilots held at local elections between 2000 and 2003, all but three saw an increase in turnout. The average increase was 15 per cent. The largest trial took place at the 2004 European Parliament election when four regions with a combined electorate of 14 million voters – the East Midlands, the North-East, the North-West, and Yorkshire and Humberside – held all-postal ballots. Turnout increased by more than 20 percentage points in the four regions, although increases of between 6 per cent and 14 per cent occurred in the seven other regions of Great Britain.

But the 2004 European Parliament pilots were undermined by a series of mishaps and, more worryingly, by electoral fraud. The Electoral Commission had recommended that all-postal ballots be held in only two regions but the government insisted they be held in four, despite suffering a number of defeats on this in the House of Lords. Critics alleged that Labour was motivated by a desire to increase turnout among its own supporters and had paid insufficient attention to practical concerns. Local authorities were left with little time to arrange for the printing and distribution of ballot papers.

Among the fraudulent practices reported in 2004 were multiple voting, intimidation and vote stealing. Agents of political parties were permitted to handle postal ballot papers. A High Court judge presiding over a case of vote rigging in Birmingham described the all-postal ballot system as 'an open invitation to fraud'. Concerns about the security of postal ballots also surfaced at the 2005 general election. The government responded by proposing a tightening of regulations. But these did not go as far as the Electoral Commission's recommendations that all-postal ballots should not be held again and that a system of individual registration similar to that used in Northern Ireland be used in Great Britain.

- Touch-screen electronic voting in polling stations.
- Remote electronic voting via text message and internet.
- Weekend voting and extended voting hours.
- Voting in supermarkets.

Trials of all-postal voting have produced the biggest increase in turnout. More than 50 all-postal voting pilots were held at local elections between 2000 and 2004. There were significant increases in turnout in many cases: the 32 areas using all-postal ballots in 2003 had an average turnout of 49 per cent compared to an average elsewhere of 35 per cent. Turnout rose by 22 per cent in the four regions that used all postal-ballots in the 2004 European Parliament elections. However, there was also evidence of fraudulent practice in the latter (see Case Study 16.1). The Electoral Commission recommended that all-postal ballots should not be held again. Doubts about the security of postal voting in the 2005 general election prompted the government to tighten the regulations.

Remote electronic voting allows an individual to transmit an encrypted vote using the internet, telephone, mobile phone text message or digital television. E-voting has the potential to increase participation as more people have access to the requisite technology, but the local pilot schemes produced only a small increase in turnout. Ministers had talked of an 'e-enabled' general election in the near future but concerns about the security and secrecy of e-voting saw the Electoral Commission warn against its usage. More than 20 schemes have tested extended hours, weekend voting and mobile polling at local elections but the impact on turnout was limited.

Opinion polls suggest that most electors welcomed the availability of alternative forms of voting. Concerns about security and secrecy are likely to delay any nationwide rolling out of alternative methods. Although many of the pilot schemes saw an increase, politicians should not regard them as a panacea: new methods of voting are no substitute for engaging electors in politics.

Functions of elections

Elections serve a number of functions, the relative importance of which is disputed. Standard democratic theories focus on 'bottom-up' functions, concentrating on the opportunity that elections provide for voters to participate in politics, hold decision-makers accountable and get issues on the political agenda (see Analysis 16.1). Democratic elitists play down the role of ordinary citizens: general elections occur only once every four or five years, voters have a limited choice and political participation for most citizens is limited to the act of voting. This perspective stresses the 'top-down' functions: elections are a means of bolstering the legitimacy of the political system and providing consent for the government.

British elections fall between these two poles as they provide resources for both voters (e.g. the chance to hold politicians accountable and choose between competing parties) and the government (e.g. a **mandate** to govern). Three key functions of elections – representation, participation and popular control – are now considered in relation to the UK.

Mandate: an authoritative instruction.

Direct democracy

Direct democracy involves citizens in the decision-making process in their own right: they vote directly on issues rather than electing representatives to act on their behalf. Examples found in Switzerland and the United States include referendums in which electors vote on government proposals, popular initiatives in which a group of citizens get a policy proposal placed on the ballot paper, and the recall of elected officials.

Supporters of direct democracy argue that representation requires the individual to give up their autonomy (i.e. their capacity to be self-governing). Furthermore, no person can fully appreciate the breadth and depth of another individual's experiences, interests and values. Nor can an MP represent the variety of views held by their constituents; aggregating interests leaves minority voices unheard. Direct democracy would, its supporters claim, boost participation and improve political education. They also argue that new communications would enable citizens to watch a televised political debate before voting on the issue by telephone, text message, internet or through digital television.

Representative democracy, however, should also mean more than voting in a general election every five years. Citizens can make representative democracy work more effectively by expressing their views through other forms of participation, for example by contacting their local councillor or MP, organising a petition or joining a pressure group.

Representation

Delegate: an individual who is authorised to act on behalf of others but who is bound by their instructions.

Representative: (noun) an individual who acts on behalf of a larger group but is permitted to exercise his or her judgement in doing so; (adjective) exhibiting a likeness or being a typical example.

In a representative democracy, voters elect a small number of people to act on their behalf in the decision-making process. But there are competing views on who or what a Member of Parliament should represent. It is generally accepted that an MP is a representative rather than a **delegate**. A delegate is chosen to act on behalf of others on the basis of clear instructions: they must faithfully relay the views of those they represent. A **representative**, by contrast, is free to decide how to vote based on their independent judgement. This model of representation originally drew upon the elitist notion that MPs are better informed and more skilled in affairs of state than their constituents, but it also recognises the problems an MP would face in ascertaining the views of constituents and translating their opinions into a single parliamentary vote.

While MPs are theoretically free to reach their own decisions, they are likely to come under pressure to act in the interests of their constituency and their party. An MP is a representative of *all* citizens within their constituency, not just those who voted for them. They act on behalf of both individual constituents and the collective interests of their constituency. All MPs receive numerous requests for help and may take up those grievances with public bodies. An official request from an MP can open doors that remain frustratingly closed to the average citizen. An MP defends the interests of their constituency as a whole by, for example, lobbying for public goods and protesting against decisions that would adversely affect the locality. Some MPs have particular difficulty in balancing the interests of constituency and party. Jack Cunningham was long-time Labour MP for Copeland, the Cumbrian

Analysis: 16.2

Positive action

Positive action (also known as 'positive discrimination') refers to schemes that apply special arrangements for social groups that are historically under-represented or politically disadvantaged. These schemes might include all-women shortlists or quota systems under which a percentage of seats is reserved for individuals from a particular section of society. In the United States, positive action has been used to boost the representation of ethnic minority groups in educational institutions. Positive action has also proved effective in bringing about greater gender equality in assemblies in other EU member states.

Proponents argue that only positive action will overcome structural inequalities in the representation of women. Existing selection methods perpetuate under-representation. The Conservatives, with just 17 female MPs out of 197 in the 2005 Parliament, oppose positive action preferring to persuade autonomous local associations to adopt women candidates rather than impose them. A 2002 study of Conservative selection procedures by the Fawcett Society – *Experiences of Conservative Party Women in Parliamentary Selections* (London: Fawcett Society, 2002) – found that 'overt discrimination and sexual harassment' were significant factors in the failure of women to get selected in winnable seats. But career choice, wealth and political connections also prevented women from seeking political office in the first place. David Cameron has included a significant number of women on an 'A list' of favoured Conservative candidates.

Female politicians often see themselves as having a 'feminised' style of politics that is more consensual than the confrontational culture of the House of Commons. The presence of women MPs has also had a positive impact on female participation. A 2004 Electoral Commission study – *Gender and Political Participation* (London: Electoral Commission, 2004) – reported that turnout amongst women in 2001 was 4 per cent higher than amongst men in seats that had a woman MP. Women were more likely to agree that 'government benefits people like me' in seats with a female MP (49 per cent compared to 38 per cent).

Supporters of positive action believe that women MPs best understand issues such as motherhood, abortion and sexual discrimination. In *New Labour's MPs: Women Representing Women* (London: Routledge, 2004) Sarah Childs examines the parliamentary activities of the 102 women Labour MPs elected in 1997. She found that they are more likely to take up women's issues but that the House of Commons, as a gendered environment, has limited their impact. Opponents of positive action argue that an individual need not have suffered discrimination themselves to regard it as wrong. It would be wrong to assume that the values and interests of all women are identical simply because of their shared gender. Finally, critics also argue that positive action runs counter to the principles of equality of opportunity and selection on the basis of merit.

constituency that includes the Sellafield nuclear reprocessing plant. Labour opposed nuclear power in the 1980s but Cunningham was a strong supporter with Sellafield the major employer in his constituency.

Almost all MPs represent a political party. They owe their position, to some extent at least, to the party that selected them and resourced their campaign. In return, party whips demand loyalty at parliamentary votes. Elections provide parties with a means of elite recruitment. Activists are mobilised, candidates are recruited and successful ones join the party ranks in the House of Commons and possibly the government. A handful of independent MPs have been elected in recent years. Former BBC reporter Martin Bell beat Neil Hamilton, tainted by 'cash for questions' allegations, in Tatton in 1997 helped by the absence of Labour and Liberal Democrat candidates. Dr Richard Taylor campaigned against the closure of a local hospital to win Wyre Forest in 2001 and retain the seat in 2005. Peter Law resigned from the Labour Party after a dispute over the use of an all-women shortlist for his Welsh Assembly seat and won Blaenau Gwent in the 2005 general election.

To stand for parliament, an individual must be at least 21 years old. Certain groups are disqualified from sitting in the House of Commons, including non-UK citizens, prisoners serving their sentence, bankrupts, members of the House of Lords, ordained members of the clergy, judges, police officers and civil servants. Candidates must pay a deposit of £500 which is forfeited if they secure less than 5 per cent of the vote.

An alternative perspective on representation suggests that parliament should be a microcosm of society. Major social groups should be represented in numbers proportional to their presence in society. The House of Commons scores poorly: most MPs are white, male and middle class (see Chapter 7). Only 15 MPs elected in 2005 were members of minority ethnic groups. A record 128 women MPs were elected in 2005, a major improvement on the 23 women MPs in 1983, but still only 20 per cent of the House of Commons. This put the UK 41st in a league table of women's representation in assemblies across the world. The record is better in the devolved assemblies where women constituted 50 per cent of the National Assembly for Wales and almost 40 per cent of the Scottish Parliament in 2003. The Sex Discrimination (Election Candidates) Act 2002 permits parties to use positive measures to reduce inequality in the numbers of women and men elected in Britain. This is permissive rather than obligatory: parties are not compelled to adopt positive action (see Analysis 16.2).

Participation

Elections give citizens an opportunity to participate in the political process by voting for the candidate of their favoured party. Competitive elections were a feature of British politics long before the democratic era. But the UK has only been a mass democracy since 1928 when full adult suffrage was achieved (see Timeline 16.1). The minimum voting age was reduced to 18 in 1969 and there is some support for a further reduction to 16 (see Controversy 16.1).

To be eligible to vote, an individual must be included on the electoral register. Registration forms are sent to each household by local authorities every autumn. Rolling registration also allows people who move house, for example, to register throughout the year. Some individuals (e.g. students) may be registered in two different constituencies but can only vote in one of them. People without a permanent address can register using a declaration of local connection. Rules on registration were tightened in Northern Ireland in 2002. Here individuals must provide more information when registering and show photographic identification at the polling station. A full version of the electoral register is available for public

TIMELINE 16.1

The development of the electoral system

1832   Great Reform Act. Extends the franchise to middle-class property owners in urban and rural areas, reforms electoral law and redistributes seats. The electorate totals 700,000 people, 5 per cent of the adult population

1867   Parliamentary Reform Act. Extends the franchise to urban householders and redistributes seats. The electorate reaches 2.2 million, 13 per cent of the adult population

1872   Ballot Act. Introduces the secret ballot

1884   Franchise Act. Extends the franchise to rural labourers and redistributes seats. Electorate tops 5 million, 25 per cent of the adult population

1918   Representation of the People Act. Abolishes the property qualification and extends the franchise to men aged 21 and over, bringing about full male suffrage. Extends the franchise to women aged 30 and over. Reform of electoral law. Electorate makes up 75 per cent of the adult population

1928   Representation of the People Act. Extends the franchise to all women aged 21 and over. Universal adult suffrage is achieved

1948   Representation of the People Act. Ends plural voting, achieving principle of 'one person, one vote'

1969   Representation of the People Act. Reduces the minimum voting age to 18

1985   Representation of the People Act. Extends the franchise to British citizens living abroad and extends absent voting to people on holiday

2000   Representation of the People Act. Allows those without a permanent residence to join the electoral register. Paves the way for pilot schemes to test alternative methods of voting

2000   Political Parties, Elections and Referendums Act. Establishes an Electoral Commission to oversee the conduct of elections and referendums. Sets a ceiling on spending by political parties during general election campaigns

scrutiny but since 2002 individuals have been able to choose not to have their names and addresses included in an edited version that marketing companies may purchase.

The 2001 register included more than 44 million people. Only a small number of people are denied the right to vote in general elections. These include children, members of the House of Lords, people convicted of electoral fraud within the last five years and those judged incapable of reasoned judgement because of mental illness. Prisoners detained at the time of a general election have long been denied the vote. The European Court of Human Rights ruled against this restriction in 2004 but the government has been reluctant to change the law. Citizens of Commonwealth countries and of the Irish Republic who are resident in the UK are permitted to vote in general elections. The Maastricht Treaty gave citizens of EU member states resident in the UK the right to vote in local elections and European Parliament elections, but not general elections. Residents of Gibraltar were included in the South-West region for the 2004 European Parliament elections. Some 10,000 UK citizens living abroad can vote in general elections by post.

Controversy: **16.1**

Votes at sixteen

A campaign to reduce the voting age from 18 to 16 gathered momentum in 2003 when the Electoral Commission launched a study of the issue and the main political parties debated it at their annual conferences. The 'Votes at 16 Campaign', which included a range of youth organisations within its ranks, pressed for change. Some government ministers expressed support (though Tony Blair was 'undecided') as did the Liberal Democrats. But in 'Votes at 16?', *Talking Politics*, Vol. 16, No. 2, 2004, pp. 62–4, David Denver and Philip Cowley present a compelling argument against a reduction in the voting age.

The Votes at 16 Campaign noted that 16-year-olds have some rights and duties, but not the right to vote. But the rights it highlighted are limited in practice. Sixteen is the school leaving age but only 5 per cent of 16-year-olds were in full-time employment in 2001. People can legally engage in sexual activity at 16 but require parental consent to marry in England and Wales until they reach 18. It is illogical to suggest that the right to have sex or leave school at 16 means that this should be the minimum voting age. Nor can the 'no taxation without representation' argument be reasonably extended to children who pay VAT on goods such as mobile phones and CDs. Eighteen is the minimum voting age in most liberal democracies.

Supporters of a reduction in the voting age claim that 16-year-olds are better equipped to engage in political activity than previous generations because of citizenship education in secondary schools in England. We might expect this to improve the political literacy of young people, but there is little concrete evidence because citizenship teaching has only been compulsory since 2002. Giving the vote to 16- and 17-year-olds would increase the electorate but turnout would probably fall because people under 25 are less likely to vote than other age groups. A lowering of the voting age is not a panacea: politicians would be better advised to focus their efforts on engaging young people in political issues and addressing their cynicism about party politics. Finally, a survey conducted by ICM found that 78 per cent of voters believed that the minimum voting age should remain at 18, with insufficient life experience and immaturity the main reasons cited. Only 33 per cent of people aged under 25 backed votes at 16.

The Electoral Commission's 2004 report *Age of Electoral Majority* (London: Electoral Commission, 2004) ultimately recommended that the minimum voting age should remain 18 although it did say that people should be able to stand for parliament at 18 rather than 21. The 2006 report *Power to the People* (London: the Power Commission, 2006) supported the vote at 16 and was backed by Gordon Brown.

Declining turnout

Turnout: the proportion of eligible members of the electorate who vote in an election.

Recent elections have been notable for a sharp decline in **turnout**. At the 2001 general election turnout fell to just 59.4 per cent, the lowest ever under the full franchise. Five million fewer people voted than in 1997, which itself had seen turnout hit a then low mark of 71.4 per cent. In 2005 turnout rose slightly to 61.3 per cent but this was still well below the then post-war average of 78 per cent (see Table 16.2). 'Second-order elections' tend to see a lower turnout than general elections, but the downward trend is evident here too (see Analysis 16.3, page 417). Only 24 per cent voted in the 1999 European Parliament election and 29.6 per cent

Table 16.2 Turnout at the 2005 general election

Category	Turnout (%)	Change since 2001 (%)
Gender		
Men	62	+1
Women	61	+3
Age		
18–24	37	−2
25–34	49	+3
35–44	61	+2
45–54	65	+0
55–64	71	+2
65+	75	+5
Social class		
AB	71	+3
C1	62	+2
C2	58	+2
DE	54	+1
All voters (GB)	61	+2

Source: Ipsos MORI, www.ipsos-mori.com

at the 2000 local elections but subsequent contests saw an increase, in part because of all-postal ballots. This is not an exclusively British phenomenon for turnout has fallen in many liberal democracies.

A number of explanations have been offered for the decline:

• Rational choice theories.
• The changing relationship between voters and parties.
• Sociological accounts focusing on differential turnout among different social groups.

Rational choice theory suggests that voters will abstain if the costs of voting outweigh the potential benefits. When asked why they abstained in the 2001 election, many non-voters cited practical matters such as inconvenience or absence. Trials of all-postal ballots in local and European Parliament elections have produced increases in turnout. Studies confirm that people are more likely to vote when the contest in their constituency is close and their vote is more likely to matter. Turnout was lower in safe seats than in marginal seats in 2001 and 2005. Labour's big opinion poll lead was also a factor in the low turnout in 2001.

A second group of explanations focuses on the relationship between parties and voters. Dissatisfaction with Westminster politics and the main political parties also contributed to the low turnouts of 2001 and 2005. Trust in politicians has waned and the number of voters feeling a strong attachment to a party has declined (to just 5 per cent of the electorate in 2001). Only around one in six voters feels a very strong attachment to a political party; those without a strong attachment are less likely to vote. Non-voters were also more likely to believe that there was little difference between Labour and the Conservatives in 2001 and 2005. Former Labour supporters who abstained were often disillusioned by the position the party had adopted in government and by Tony Blair's leadership. Turnout among working class voters in Labour heartlands, many of them disillusioned by New Labour's

Young people and voting

People aged under 25 are some of the least likely to vote at a general election. Only 35 per cent of young people voted in 2001 compared to 76 per cent of those aged over 65 – and this may be an overestimate because relatively high numbers of young people are not registered to vote. We would expect turnout to be lower in 'second-order elections', but the 15 per cent turnout among people under 35 at the 2003 Welsh Assembly elections is particularly poor.

A MORI survey carried out for the Electoral Commission after the 2001 general election suggested that young people were the most likely to say that 'no one party stands for me' and that they felt 'powerless' in the electoral process. Young people were more likely than other non-voters to claim that voting was 'unimportant'. Negative attitudes about Westminster politics and the established political parties were prevalent, with politicians viewed as unrepresentative of the wider population. Much was made of the fact that viewers cast over 15 million votes during Big Brother 2 in 2001, more than any of the main parties managed at the general election.

The Electoral Commission reports *Voter Engagement and Young People* (London: Electoral Commission, 2002 and 2004) found that young people had relatively low levels of interest in politics at Westminster and the election campaign. However, when politics is recognised as meaning far more than the activities of the Westminster village, then young people clearly show an interest in political issues such as the war in Iraq, the state of the environment and university tuition fees. Young people were reportedly the most likely group to talk with family and friends about political issues during the 2001 campaign.

The MORI survey found that young people who did feel that voting mattered cited participation ('having a say') as more significant than civic duty. This suggests that the onus is on politicians and the media to mobilise young people rather than expecting them to vote as a matter of course. To overcome apathy, political issues must be explained effectively and made relevant to the lives and interests of young people. Greater availability of e-voting may also persuade those who complain about the inconvenience of going to the polling station to vote.

record on public spending, was notably low in 2001 and 2005. The 2001 campaign failed to mobilise voters (only 27 per cent were 'very interested') and those with little interest in it were less likely to vote.

These may turn out to be short-term factors but if disengagement persists, the legitimacy of election outcomes and the political system as a whole will be endangered. However, the low turnout in 2001 and 2005 should not be taken automatically as symptomatic of a general disinterest in politics. Rather, surveys show that most people are interested in politics, broadly-defined, and see voting as both important and a civic duty (see Chapter 18).

Sociological accounts concentrate on differential turnout among social groups. Turnout was highest in constituencies with high proportions of elderly, university-educated and middle-class voters in the 2001 and 2005 elections. Groups least likely to vote were the working class and young people. The 18 to 24 age group was the only major social group in which turnout fell in 2005. People aged over 65 were almost twice as likely to vote as those aged 18 to 24 (see Case study 16.2). Low

Controversy: **16.2**

Compulsory voting

A radical suggestion for improving election turnout is to make voting compulsory. Voting would be mandatory for all eligible electors; non-compliance would result in a fine. A number of states operate compulsory voting, including Australia and Belgium, and turnout is indeed significantly higher than in the UK. Advocates argue that voting is not just a right but a civic duty. Nor is it a burden as the costs of voting are low compared to other social activities. Compulsory voting would improve the representation of social groups among whom turnout is currently low. It would also encourage electors to take an interest in politics and political parties to provide better quality campaigns.

Opponents claim that compulsory voting infringes the individual liberties that are the bedrock of liberal democracy. Apathetic electors would be forced to take part in a process about which they know little and have no real interest. Those who choose to abstain because they do not want to give a positive endorsement to any of the mainstream parties in a contest with a limited field would have to spoil their ballot paper. Alternatively, the ballot paper might give electors the chance to vote for 'none of the above'. Were 'none of the above' to garner more votes than the other candidates, a new field would then be required. Finally, as has been noted about other proposals for boosting turnout, compulsory voting disguises rather than addresses the root cause of the problem, namely disengagement from contemporary party politics.

turnout is particularly problematic. Young people and other minority social classes do not participate and are thus under-represented in the political process.

These interpretations of declining turnout offer different perspectives on how participation might be improved. The rational choice view implies that making the act of voting easier, for example through postal voting, or making it compulsory will improve turnout (see Controversy 16.2). Interpretations focusing on the relationship between parties and voters suggest that politicians must engage people in the political process more effectively. The final interpretation suggests that efforts must be targeted at certain groups, particularly young people.

Popular control

At a general election, voters can hold the government accountable for its record in office. If it has performed poorly, it will lose support. MPs can be held accountable individually for their record as constituency representative, though this is a minor consideration for electors.

Elections offer the prospect of a two-way exchange between parties and voters. Parties inform voters of their policies and seek to persuade them of their merits. Voters may get the chance to make candidates aware of their policy preferences during a campaign, for example at public meetings or on the doorstep. But the exchange is an unequal one and the scope for voters to influence policy at election time is limited. Instances of direct popular control over the political agenda via the electoral process are infrequent. Defeats may persuade a party to ditch unpopular

An Electoral Commission poster encouraging voting in the 2004 European Parliament elections (Courtesy of The Electoral Commission)

policies and pitch its appeal at a different group of target voters, as with the emergence of the New Labour project after 1992. Parties gauge public opinion through private polls and focus groups prior to an election, adapting their message before the formal campaign begins.

The mandate

Manifesto: a document in which a political party sets out its policy programme.

The doctrine of the mandate holds that the winning party at a general election receives an authoritative instruction from the electorate to implement the programme it put forward during the campaign. Parties issue **manifestos** setting out their main policies should they win office. This amounts to a promise of legislative action, though the governing party determines their relative priority. But the doctrine is problematic. Relatively few voters are aware of the details of party manifestos. Non-party members have no say over a manifesto, nor can they use the ballot box to veto some proposals. The doctrine of the mandate does imply that governments should not introduce a major policy change that was not put before voters at a general election.

In recent elections parties have issued headline pledges which simplify the idea of a mandate and, in theory, made it easier for voters to judge whether they have fulfilled their promises. Labour's pledges have included specific commitments, for example to cut class sizes to 30 for 5–7-year-olds (1997) and to recruit 10,000 extra secondary school teachers (2001). Labour and the Conservatives both issued six key pledges in 2005 and the Liberal Democrats ten. Post-war governments have a reasonable record in implementing their manifesto commitments. Labour claimed in 2001 and 2005 to have achieved its headline pledges and the majority of its commitments, though the methodology behind these claims has been questioned. Exceptions to the doctrine of the mandate arise regularly. Labour's 2001 manifesto stated that 'we will not introduce "top-up" fees and have legislated against them' but two years later the government brought forward legislation on differential university tuition fees. Days after the 1997 election, the Blair government gave the Bank of England the authority to set interest rates but no mention had been made of this in Labour's manifesto.

Choice

In 2005, 3555 candidates stood for election, an average of 5.5 candidates per seat. This suggests that voters had a meaningful choice, but in practice it was limited. Many constituencies are 'safe seats' in which one party has a substantial lead over its nearest rival that almost guarantees it victory. Here, supporters of other parties have little prospect of influencing the outcome. In ideological terms, choice is limited if there is little difference between the positions of the main parties. Radical positions tend to be confined to the fringes and barely feature in media coverage.

Finally, it is worth noting that in the British parliamentary system, general elections determine the composition of the House of Commons. Control of the executive is decided indirectly as the party with a majority of seats forms the government and its leader becomes Prime Minister. But when making their choice, most electors think in terms of choosing the government and Prime Minister rather than their local MP.

Election campaigns

Election campaigns should ideally educate citizens about key issues and the policies of the main parties, enabling electors to reach an informed decision about how to vote. In practice, the information provided by parties and the media is imperfect and many citizens show limited interest. Parties have two main aims in a campaign: to persuade voters of the merits of their policies and personnel, and to ensure that their supporters make the effort to vote. The national campaign is the key vehicle for the former, whereas the latter is undertaken by activists at constituency level. Parties run carefully planned campaigns that use new technology and techniques imported from the United States. They employ spin-doctors and advertising organisations to put their message across, and use private polls and focus groups to track its impact. Parties must adhere to national and local campaign spending limits, but their communications efforts are not confined to formal campaigns.

Party strategists try to set the campaign agenda by promoting issues they believe are vote-winners. Candidates are expected to follow instructions and avoid going 'off-message'. Recent contests have also seen an increase in negative campaigning in which the policies and integrity of rival parties are challenged ruthlessly. Careful planning cannot guarantee a successful campaign, nor will a good campaign necessarily bring electoral success. Observers judged Labour to have run the best campaigns in 1987 and 1992, but the Conservatives won both elections. John Major made a public appeal for unity on Europe to rebel Conservative MPs during the 1997 campaign, further exposing the divisions in his party. The dull 2001 campaign sprang to life on 16 May when Labour's manifesto launch was overshadowed by the barracking of Jack Straw at a police conference, the haranguing of Tony Blair by the partner of a patient at a Birmingham hospital, and the punch John Prescott landed on an egg-throwing protestor in North Wales. The press response to the day's events was relatively restrained and the incidents had little impact on the polls.

Television is the crucial medium for political communications. Most voters get their political news from television, so parties expend much energy on efforts to get favourable coverage. This has lessened the direct contact between politicians and voters, with voters treated as spectators rather than participants in the electoral process. Television news tends to simplify difficult issues by relaying soundbites and concentrating on party leaders rather than providing incisive analysis. The age of 24-hour news has brought overexposure: viewing figures for television news fell during the 2001 campaign. Unlike terrestrial TV broadcasters, the print media do not have to adhere to guidelines on equitable coverage of the main parties. Most newspapers endorse a party during a campaign and this support frequently colours reporting by the tabloids. The impact of the media and the relationship between politicians and journalists was explored in more detail in Chapter 4.

Parties have traditionally used billboard posters and newspaper advertisements to relay their message. These have produced some memorable slogans and images – for example, the 1979 Conservative poster showing a long dole queue under the caption 'Labour isn't working' – but their impact on voting behaviour is limited. Television election broadcasts are allocated to parties according to the number of candidates standing in the election. They have the reputation of being dull, though some have employed innovative techniques (e.g. *Chariots of Fire* director Hugh Hudson's 1987 biopic of Labour leader Neil Kinnock) or have courted controversy (e.g. those by the British National Party).

Parties have also embraced new technologies to get their message across. Labour and the Conservatives use sophisticated computer programs to identify target voters, particularly those in marginal seats. They then contact them by telephone, email or text message and may even send a campaign DVD. Labour sent a text message implying that opening hours for pubs would be extended to 100,000 young people at 10.45pm on the final Friday of the 2001 election campaign. Direct contact can be crucial in converting voters, but people's dislike of cold calls and spam email means that it can also be counter-productive. The internet is used by parties to relay information to activists, journalists and voters. The significance of the internet in 2001 was minimal as only a third of homes had internet access. It figured more prominently in 2005 but its impact on the election outcome was again limited.

Parties focus their resources on a relatively small number of marginal and target seats, the results in which may be crucial in deciding the election outcome. The

Conservatives and Labour directed much of their campaign efforts at 800,000 voters in crucial marginal seats in 2005. Voter mobilisation was traditionally the responsibility of constituency parties, but national party headquarters now use computerised records and telephone canvassing to target key voters. Nonetheless, activists still engage in doorstep canvassing to get the vote out. Most voters received campaign literature in 2001 while a quarter were canvassed by a party representative. Studies show that strong local campaigns produce an increase in support that can be decisive in close contests.

The significance of the national campaign is less clear. A majority of voters decide how to vote before the campaign gets underway, but opinion polls often register some movement as undecided voters make up their minds and waverers switch sides (see Case study 16.3). This 'churning' will not be decisive unless most of those who change allegiance move in the same direction. Labour's lead slipped during the 1997, 2001 and 2005 campaigns and support for the Liberal Democrats increased, perhaps because of their greater than normal exposure.

Case study: 16.3

Opinion polls

Opinion polls are surveys of the views and political behaviour of a sample group of the population at a particular moment in time. They are conducted by professional organisations (e.g. MORI or Gallup) on behalf of the media and political parties. Polls tend to be based on a sample of between 1000 and 2000 people who form a representative sample of the electorate. Traditionally, polls were conducted through face-to-face interviews but some organisations now undertake questioning by telephone or via the internet. Opinion polls usually have a margin of error of plus or minus three per cent. This means that the actual support for a party on 30 per cent in the polls is between 27 per cent and 33 per cent.

During a general election campaign, opinion polls appear frequently and are pored over by politicians and commentators looking for signs of change in the mood of the electorate. Critics are concerned that the media often focus on opinion polls rather than the policies of the main parties. Some would like opinion polls to be banned during the final stages of an election campaign, as happens in France.

The 1992 general election exposed concerns about the reliability of opinion polls. Virtually all the polls conducted during the campaign failed to predict a Conservative victory: they had systematically underestimated Conservative support. A post-election review conducted by the polling organisations put their inaccuracy down to the reluctance of some Conservative voters to reveal their true intentions. The pollsters have subsequently adjusted their calculations to take account of these 'shy Conservatives'. All polling organisations correctly predicted comfortable Labour victories in 1997 and 2001 but still exaggerated their support.

Labour's lead in the final opinion polls conducted in the 2005 election campaign was marginally higher than the actual result. But the MORI/NOP 'exit poll', based on a survey of 20,000 actual voters, correctly predicted a 66-seat Labour majority. More sophisticated techniques had been employed to measure turnout and support among different social groups.

Electoral systems in the UK

Electoral systems translate votes cast by citizens into seats for candidates. There are three main types:

Majoritarian system: an electoral system in which the candidate with the most votes is elected.

Proportional representation: an electoral system using multi-member constituencies in which a mathematical formula is used to match the share of the vote to the allocation of seats.

Mixed system: an electoral system in which a proportion of representatives are elected by a majoritarian system in a single-member constituency and the others are elected by proportional representation in multi-member seats and allocated to parties on a corrective basis.

1. **Majoritarian systems,** in which the winning candidate is the one who secures the most votes. These are non-proportional systems and produce significant disparities between votes won and seats allotted. Candidates are normally elected in single-member constituencies.
2. **Proportional systems,** which produce a closer fit between votes cast and seats allocated. Electors rank candidates in order of preference in multi-member constituencies.
3. **Mixed systems,** in which some representatives are elected using a majoritarian system in single member constituencies and the remainder elected by proportional representation in multi-member constituencies. These 'list seats' are allocated to parties on a corrective basis.

Proponents of majoritarian systems believe that the chief function of an electoral system is to produce a decisive outcome, strong government and a clear relationship between an MP and his or her constituents. Those who favour proportional systems hold that an electoral system should accurately translate votes into seats, ensure that votes are of equal value and provide a real choice for voters.

The simple plurality system

The simple plurality system – commonly known as first-past-the-post – is used at general elections in the UK and for local elections in England, Wales and (until 2007) Scotland. The victorious candidate does not need to obtain a majority of the votes cast (50 per cent + 1 vote) but only a plurality, that is one more vote than the second-placed candidate. In contests involving three or more candidates, the winner may fall well short of an overall majority. Simple plurality is used in single-member constituencies for general elections and in local elections in Wales and for many local elections in England. Some English local elections are, though, conducted under a system sometimes referred to as the 'block vote'. Multi-member constituencies are used and electors have as many votes as there are seats to fill. Votes are not ranked or transferred.

For much of the post-war era, the simple plurality system has offered the main parties the prospect of winning power with comfortable parliamentary majorities. It favours parties with strong nationwide support but disadvantages smaller parties whose support is spread thinly. Simple plurality often gives the party that scores most votes a 'winner's bonus' in terms of seats. A small swing can produce a landslide victory. The Conservatives won majorities of over a hundred seats on just over 42 per cent of the popular vote in 1983 and 1987. Labour's 43.4 per cent of the vote in 1997 and 40.7 per cent in 2001 produced parliamentary majorities of 179 and 167 respectively.

The electoral system is now biased in favour of Labour. In 1992 the Conservatives 41.9 per cent of the popular vote translated into a 51.6 per cent share of seats in the

Commons and a 21-seat parliamentary majority. Labour won a 167-seat majority in 2001 on 40.7 per cent of the vote and in 2005 won 55.1 per cent of seats on 35.2 per cent of the vote. The bias towards Labour results from a number of factors:

- Differences in constituency size. The average electorate in Labour-held seats in 2005 was 67,000 but was 73,000 in Conservative-held seats. The difference is explained mainly by population movements from urban to suburban and rural constituencies since the pre-1997 revision of boundaries.
- Turnout is lower in Labour-held seats. Turnout in Labour-held seats was 58 per cent in 2005 compared to 65.5 per cent in seats won by the Conservatives.
- Labour secured its largest vote swings in constituencies where it mattered most in 1997, winning a series of seats from the Conservatives. It held on to many of these in 2001 when the swing to the Tories in these seats was less than the national average.
- Anti-Conservative tactical voting helped Labour win additional seats in 1997 and 2001 but declined significantly in 2005.
- Labour benefited from the over-representation of Scotland at Westminster in the 1997 and 2001 elections. But the number of Scottish constituencies was reduced in 2005.

In short, Labour's vote is more efficiently distributed: it requires fewer votes to win seats. Labour won one MP for every 26,900 votes it secured in 2005, the Conservatives one MP per 44,500 votes and the Liberal Democrats one MP for every 96,400 votes. If Labour and the Conservatives had polled the same share of the vote in 2005, Labour would still have enjoyed a comfortable parliamentary majority. The Conservatives' share of the vote (32.3 per cent) was only 0.6 per cent higher than in 2001, but they made a net gain of 33 seats thanks to a higher than average swing in Greater London, the fragmentation of the Labour vote in some constituencies and a concentration of Tory campaign resources in marginal seats. A redrawing of constituencies by the Boundary Commissions will reduce, but not eliminate, the pro-Labour bias at the next general election. Labour will also be defending 41 ultra-marginal seats (those with majorities of less than 5 per cent of the vote).

The simple plurality system disadvantages those third and minor parties whose support is spread thinly across the country rather than concentrated in particular regions. There are no rewards for coming second. The Liberal Democrats have been consistent losers under simple plurality. In 1983 the Liberal/SDP Alliance won 25 per cent of the popular vote, 2 per cent less than Labour, but secured only 23 seats compared to Labour's 186. The Liberal Democrats won fewer seats than their vote merited in 1997, 2001 and 2005 but managed to add to their tally of seats on each occasion (despite their share of the vote falling in 1997). The 62 seats they won in 2005 was the highest third-party total since 1923. The Scottish Nationalist Party (SNP) and Plaid Cymru, who have regional strongholds, fare relatively better.

Parliaments between 1945 and 1970 contained an average of 10 MPs from third or minor parties. For the period 1974–2005 the figure is 53 MPs, with the 93 MPs from outside the two main parties making up almost one-fifth of the House of Commons in 2005. Their success owes much to a concentration of resources on target seats, tactical voting and disillusionment with the main parties.

Advantages and disadvantages

Supporters of the simple plurality system believe that it has a number of advantages over other systems. First, it is easy to understand and operate. Voters are familiar with the system; most view it as legitimate and do not feel that electoral reform is a major issue. Single-member constituencies create a clear relationship between an MP and electors. General elections usually produce a clear outcome: the party securing the largest number of votes tends to get a majority of seats in the House of Commons. Simple plurality is thus said to produce strong and responsible government. Governing parties normally have working majorities that allow them to exercise significant control over the legislative process and implement their manifesto commitments. Voters are presented with a clear choice between two main parties and can hold the governing party accountable for its record in office. Proponents of the simple plurality system depict coalition governments, common in PR systems, as less effective and less accountable – although coalitions in states such as Germany have been stable and successful. The negotiations that precede coalition formation weaken the relationship between electors and the government as they are

Table 16.3 Deviation from proportionality (DV) in general elections, 1945–2005

Year	Con Vote (%)	Con Seats (%)	Con Difference (%)	Lab Vote (%)	Lab Seats (%)	Lab Difference (%)	Lib Vote (%)	Lib Seats (%)	Lib Difference (%)	Others Vote (%)	Others Seats (%)	Others Difference (%)	DV (%)
1945	39.6	31.1	−8.5	48.0	61.4	+13.4	9.0	1.9	−7.1	3.4	3.9	+0.5	14.8
1950	43.4	47.7	+4.3	46.1	50.4	+4.3	9.1	1.4	−7.7	1.4	0.5	−0.9	8.6
1951	48.0	51.4	+3.4	48.8	47.2	−1.6	2.6	1.0	−1.6	0.6	0.5	−0.1	3.4
1955	49.7	54.8	+5.1	46.4	44.0	−2.4	2.7	1.0	−1.7	1.2	0.3	−0.9	4.8
1959	49.4	57.9	+8.5	43.8	41.0	−2.8	5.9	1.0	−4.9	0.9	0.2	−0.7	8.5
1964	43.4	48.3	+4.9	44.1	50.3	+6.2	11.2	1.4	−9.8	1.3	0.0	−1.3	11.1
1966	41.9	40.2	−1.7	48.0	57.8	+9.8	8.5	1.9	−6.6	1.5	0.2	−1.3	9.7
1970	46.4	52.4	+6.0	43.1	45.7	+2.6	7.5	1.0	−6.5	3.0	0.9	−2.1	8.6
1974 Feb	37.9	46.8	+8.9	37.2	47.4	+10.2	19.3	2.2	−17.1	5.6	3.6	−2.0	19.1
1974 Oct	35.8	43.6	+7.8	39.2	50.2	+11.0	18.3	2.0	−16.3	6.7	4.1	−2.6	18.9
1979	43.9	53.4	+9.5	36.9	42.4	+5.5	13.8	1.7	−12.1	5.4	2.5	−2.9	15.0
1983	42.4	61.1	+18.7	27.6	32.2	+4.6	25.4	3.5	−21.9	4.6	3.2	−1.4	23.3
1987	42.3	57.8	+15.5	30.8	35.2	+4.4	22.5	3.4	−19.1	4.4	3.5	−0.9	20.0
1992	41.8	51.6	+9.8	34.4	41.6	+7.2	17.9	3.1	−14.8	5.9	3.7	−2.2	17.0
1997	30.7	25.0	−5.7	43.4	63.4	+20.0	16.8	7.0	−9.8	9.3	4.5	−4.8	20.2
2001	31.7	25.2	−6.5	40.7	62.7	+22.0	18.3	7.9	−10.4	9.3	4.2	−5.1	22.0
2005	32.3	30.5	−1.8	35.2	55.1	+19.9	22.1	9.6	−12.4	10.4	4.8	−5.6	19.9

Notes: DV = deviation from proportionality. It is calculated by: calculating the difference between each party's percentage vote-share and seat-share; summing all deviations (ignoring minus signs) and halving the total. 'Others' includes Northern Ireland MPs from February 1974 onwards. Liberal includes the Liberal/SDP Alliance (1983 and 1987) and the Liberal Democrats (1992–2001).

secretive and may see a party dropping some of its policies. A minority party in a coalition might exercise more influence than its limited popular support merits.

In summary, the main advantages of simple plurality are:

- It is easy for electors to understand and use.
- Single-member constituencies mean that MPs are representatives of clearly-defined geographical areas.
- By giving the party with a plurality of votes a majority of parliamentary seats, it produces strong and stable government.
- It fosters a two-party system in which electors have a clear choice between alternative governments.

A major counter-argument made by critics of the simple plurality system is that it does not allocate seats equitably. It is disproportionate: the number of seats won by parties does not accurately reflect their share of the nationwide vote. Parliament is not a microcosm of political opinion in the country. As noted above, simple plurality gives an unfair advantage to the two main parties, an additional bonus to the election 'winner', has become biased towards Labour and often discriminates against small parties. 'Deviation from proportionality' (DV) is a simple way of assessing the proportionality of electoral systems. Table 16.3 shows that results under simple plurality have been least proportional since the post-1970 emergence of a multi-party system. The landslide results of 1983, 1997 and 2001 are the most disproportional.

The party winning most votes in a general election has twice since 1945 received fewer seats than its nearest rival. The last time a UK political party won a majority of the vote at a general election was in 1935 when a National Coalition scored 54.5 per cent. No single party has won a majority of the popular vote since 1900. The highest post-war share of the vote is the 48.8 per cent won by Labour in 1951 but the Conservatives (48 per cent) actually won 26 more seats. In February 1974 the Conservatives scored more votes (37.9 per cent) than Labour (37.2 per cent) who won 4 more seats. Labour's 35.2 per cent of the vote in 2005 was the lowest ever recorded by a winning party. Only 21.6 per cent of the electorate (9.6 million people) voted for them.

As winning candidates only need to secure a plurality of votes, many MPs are elected on a minority of the popular vote in their constituency. Two-thirds of MPs elected in 2005 (426 MPs) did not secure an absolute majority of the vote in their constituency, the highest proportion in UK electoral history. Fifty-five MPs were elected on less than 40 per cent of the vote. Gordon Banks MP won Ochill and South Perthshire on just 31.4 per cent. The low turnout also meant that a substantial majority of MPs were supported by less than one in three of the eligible electorate.

The simple plurality system does not meet squarely the requirement for 'one person, one vote, one value'. As we have seen, Labour was able to secure seats with an average vote size that was significantly less than that of their rivals. Disparities in constituency size mean that votes are of different value. A vote cast by a resident of a relatively small constituency is more likely to influence the outcome of that contest than a voter in a larger constituency. A substantial number of votes are 'wasted' because they do not help to elect an MP. Wasted votes include those for a losing candidate – 52 per cent of votes cast in the UK in 2005 – and those cast for the victor over and above their one vote lead over their nearest rival. The latter accounted for a further 18 per cent of votes cast in the UK in 2005.

Many voters have a constituency MP who is not a member of their chosen political party, raising questions about the quality of representation. Parties can be grossly over-represented: in 2005 the Liberal Democrats won all five seats in Cornwall on 44.4 per cent of the vote across the country and Labour all 13 seats in Tyne and Wear with 55.8 per cent. The other side of the coin is that parties can also be under-represented. Large parts of urban Britain are 'electoral deserts' for the Tories at parliamentary level. They won 24 per cent of the vote in the six English metropolitan counties outside London in 2005 but only 5 out of 124 seats.

Critics of simple plurality also claim that many voters are denied an effective choice. A single official candidate, selected by local party members from a shortlist of names approved by the national party, stands on behalf of each political party. Voters are denied a choice between different candidates from the same party – though the same applies under the 'closed list' system of PR. The poor prospects for small parties persuade some electors to vote tactically. Here an elector whose first choice party has little chance of victory votes instead for the candidate best placed to prevent their least-favoured party from winning. This is a tactical decision rather than a positive endorsement.

Finally, the simple plurality system is said to foster division rather than political cooperation. Critics blamed the electoral system for the 'adversary politics' of the 1970s when small shifts in voting behaviour brought frequent changes of government, dramatic reversals of policy and political instability. Since the 1980s, the simple plurality system has been cited as a key factor in periods of one-party rule in which the Conservatives won four successive general elections and Labour two landslide victories without securing more than 44 per cent of the vote.

In summary, the main disadvantages of simple plurality are:

- It does not translate votes cast into seats won effectively, producing dispro-portional outcomes that reward the largest party and disadvantage some small parties.
- Parties and MPs need only secure a plurality of the vote to win.
- Votes are not of equal worth and a substantial number are 'wasted'.
- Electors have a limited choice of candidates.

Other electoral systems

Alternative vote (AV): an electoral system in which the winning candidate must secure an absolute majority in a single-member constituency. Voters rank their preferences and votes are redistributed until one candidate secures an absolute majority.

Aside from simple plurality there are two other main types of majoritarian electoral system, the Alternative Vote and the Supplementary Vote. In the **Alternative vote** (**AV**) system, the victorious candidate in a single-member constituency has to achieve an overall majority of votes cast. Electors number all candidates in order of preference. If no candidate secures an absolute majority of first preferences, the lowest placed candidate is eliminated and their second preferences are transferred to the remaining candidates. This process continues until one candidate secures an absolute majority. AV is not used in the UK, but it was suggested as part of a mixed system by the 1999 Jenkins Report on electoral reform (see below).

Table 16.4 Election of Mayor of London, 2004

Candidate	Party	First preference (%)	Second preference (%)	Final vote tally (%)
Ken Livingstone	Labour	35.7	13.0	55.4
Steven Norris	Conservative	28.2	11.6	44.6
Simon Hughes	Liberal Democrat	14.8	24.3	
Lindsey German	Respect	6.2	3.3	
Frank Maloney	UKIP	6.0	10.0	
Julian Leppert	BNP	3.0	3.7	
Darren Johnson	Green	2.9	10.9	
Others (3)		3.1	6.1	

The main advantages of AV are:

- Winning candidates have secured an absolute majority of votes cast.
- The close link between MPs and their constituencies is retained.

The major disadvantage is:

- AV is not a proportional system. If used in recent general elections, it would have produced even greater discrepancies between votes won and seats allocated than simple plurality by increasing Labour's tally of seats. It is possible for a candidate to win 49 per cent of first preference votes but still lose the election.

Supplementary vote (SV): an electoral system in which voters indicate their first and second preferences only. If no candidate wins an absolute majority, all but the top two candidates are eliminated. Second preference votes are added to their tally and the candidate with most votes is elected.

The **supplementary vote (SV)** is a variant of AV. Here the elector records only their first and second preferences by putting a cross in the first preference column and another in the second preference column on the ballot paper. If no candidate in the single-member constituency wins more than half of the first preference votes, all but the top two candidates are eliminated. The second preference votes from eliminated candidates are examined and any for the remaining two candidates are redistributed. The candidate with the highest total is then declared elected. SV is used to elect mayors in a number of British towns and cities, including London (see Table 16.4).

The main advantages of SV are:

- The winning candidate is likely to have secured wide-ranging support.
- Second preferences of voters who supported minor parties are not counted (unlike in AV).

The main disadvantages of SV are:

- Winning candidates need not secure an absolute majority of votes cast.
- It is not a proportional system.

Proportional representation systems

The term 'proportional representation' (PR) is a general one for hundreds of different voting systems. These systems tend to produce a closer fit between votes and seats but the level of proportionality depends on district magnitude, i.e. the size of the multi-member constituencies. Minor parties will get more seats in a contest in which the entire country is a treated as a single multi-member constituency than in one in which regions return only four candidates.

The list system and the single transferable vote (STV) are examples of proportional representation systems used in the UK. In the **list system**, political parties submit a list of candidates in multi-member constituencies (often known as 'regions'), the size of the list reflecting the number of available seats. Seats are allocated according to the proportion of votes won by each party in the constituency. Electors cast a single vote. In an 'open list' system, electors can vote for a particular candidate from within a party list or for or a non-aligned candidate. In a 'closed list' system, electors can only vote for a party slate or for an independent candidate; party managers determine the rank ordering of their candidates within the party list. A closed list system is used for elections to the European Parliament in Great Britain where 75 of the UK's 78 members are elected in multi-member regions in England, Scotland and Wales. These regions elect between three and eleven members.

In the UK, the d'Hondt system is used to calculate the allocation of seats on a proportional basis (see Case study 16.4). This employs a 'highest average formula': the total votes of each party are divided by the number of seats it already has, plus the next seat to be allocated. Thus, the party totals are divided first by 1 (0 seats plus 1), then by 2 (1 seat plus 1), then by 3 (2 seats plus 1) and so on. The first seat goes to the party with the largest number, the next seat to the next highest number and so on, until all seats are allocated.

List system: a system of proportional representation in which electors vote for a party list. Seats are allocated proportionally according to the share of votes secured by each party.

Case study: 16.4

The d'Hondt formula

The d'Hondt formula is a 'highest average' system that uses a divisor method rather than a quota to allocate seats. It was devised by Belgian lawyer and mathematician Victor d'Hondt in 1878. Under d'Hondt, the total votes of each party are divided by the number of seats it already has, plus the next seat to be allocated. The first seat goes to the party with the largest number, the next seat to the next highest number and so on.

The following example is taken from a hypothetical election to the Scottish Parliament in which the d'Hondt formula is used to allocate list seats. The Conservatives, who did not win any constituency seats, win the first two list seats to be allocated. The SNP wins the third and Labour the fourth; the Liberal Democrats are not allocated a list seat.

	Con	Lab	Lib Dem	SNP	Winner
Constituency seats won	0	4	2	2	
List votes	35000	80000	30000	50000	
First divisor	1	5	3	3	
First seat	**35000**	16000	10000	16666	*Con*
Second divisor	2	5	3	3	
Second seat	**17500**	16000	10000	16666	Con
Third divisor	3	5	3	3	
Third seat	11666	16000	10000	**16666**	*SNP*
Fourth divisor	3	5	3	4	
Fourth seat	11666	**16000**	10000	12500	Lab

The main advantages of the list system are:

- The high degree of proportionality between votes cast and seats won.
- Each vote has the same value.
- It is easy for electors to understand as they cast just one vote.

The main disadvantages of the list system are:

- The d'Hondt formula can favour large parties over smaller ones, albeit to a limited extent.
- Electors have a restricted choice of candidates in closed list systems where party officials determine the order of candidates and can stifle dissent by placing non-conformists at the bottom of the list.
- Multi-member regions can weaken the bond between elected representatives and their constituents.

Single transferable vote (STV): a system of proportional representation in which voters rank candidates in multi-member constituencies in order of preference. Votes are transferred from lowest placed candidates until the required number of candidates reach a quota.

Droop quota: an electoral quota used in proportional representation systems that was originally devised by Henry Richmond Droop in 1868.

In the **single transferable vote (STV)** system, electors number their preferences and can vote for as many or few candidates as they like in multi-member constituencies. To be elected a candidate must achieve a quota. In the UK, the '**Droop quota**' is used and is calculated as follows: [votes/(seats + 1)] + 1. Any votes in excess of this quota are redistributed on the basis of second preferences. If a candidate reaches the quota on the first count, they are elected and their surplus second preferences redistributed. If this does not occur, the lowest placed candidate is eliminated and their second preferences are transferred. This process continues until the required number of seats is filled by candidates meeting the quota.

STV is used to elect the Northern Ireland Assembly where 108 members are elected from 17 multi-member constituencies which each return six members. Using the Droop quota, a candidate must secure 14.3 per cent of the vote to be elected. In Northern Ireland STV is also used for elections to the European Parliament and in local elections. It will be used in local elections in Scotland from 2007.

The main advantages of STV are:

- It is broadly proportional and ensures that votes are largely of equal value.
- Only a party or coalition of parties that win an absolute majority of the popular vote can form a government.
- Electors have a wide choice of candidates, including a choice between candidates of the same party.

The main disadvantages of STV are:

- It is less accurate in translating votes into seats than list systems or some versions of AMS (see below), particularly if multi-member constituencies contain few seats.
- It is possible to win an election without gaining an absolute majority of votes.
- Large multi-member regions weaken the relationship between representatives and their constituencies.
- It is likely to produce coalition government, which may give disproportional power to minor parties that hold the 'balance of power'.

Mixed systems

Additional member system (AMS): a mixed electoral system in which a proportion of representatives are elected by a majoritarian system in single-member constituencies; the remainder are elected by the list system in multi-member constituencies and these list seats allocated to parties to produce a more proportional outcome.

The **additional member system (AMS)** is the leading example of a mixed electoral system. The elector has two votes, one for a constituency representative and the other for a party list. Constituency MPs make up at least half of the legislative assembly and are elected by the single-member plurality system (or possibly the alternative vote). The remaining members are elected through a party list in multi-member regional constituencies (or from one national list). The list seats are allocated to political parties on a corrective basis, often by the d'Hondt formula, producing a more proportional outcome. Members elected for list seats are known as 'additional members'; list seats are also referred to as 'top-up seats'.

AMS is used in the UK for elections to the Scottish Parliament, the Welsh Assembly and the Greater London Assembly. The Scottish Parliament has 129 members, 73 of whom (or 57 per cent) are elected in single-member constituencies with the remaining 56 being 'list members' (43 per cent) elected in eight multi-member regions (see Table 16.6, page 418). The Welsh Assembly has 60 members, 40 of whom are elected in single-member constituencies (67 per cent) while 20 are 'list members' (33 per cent) chosen from five multi-member regions. Full analysis is provided in Chapter 11. There are 25 members of the Greater London Assembly, 14 of them elected in single-member constituencies (57 per cent) and 11 list members (43 per cent) chosen from a single multi-member area encompassing all of Greater London. The closed list system and d'Hondt formula are used in all three cases. The variant of AMS used for the London Assembly is distinctive as parties must reach a threshold of 5 per cent of the vote to be eligible for seats.

The main advantages of AMS are:

- The results are broadly proportional and votes are less likely to be 'wasted'.
- A proportion of MPs represent single-member constituencies, fostering a link between representatives and their constituents.
- Electors have two votes: the first can be used to support a candidate and the second a political party.

The main disadvantages of AMS are:

- It creates two categories of representative in the legislative assembly, one with constituency duties and one without a distinct base.
- The closed list system restricts voter choice and may give party bosses significant influence over the order of candidates.
- Small parties may be under-represented.

Electoral reform

Campaigners have been pressing for change to the electoral system for over a century. The Proportional Representation Society, a forerunner of the Electoral Reform Society, was formed in the 1880s. In 1918 a Speaker's Conference recommended that a mixed electoral system should be used for general elections. A Bill introducing the alternative vote system was passed by the House of Commons but rejected by the House of Lords in 1931.

Labour's belief that it must take office in its own right to achieve its objectives has historically led the party to support the simple plurality system. But support for electoral reform gained ground in the Labour movement during its long spell in opposition between 1979 and 1997. Neil Kinnock established a committee chaired by Professor Raymond Plant to examine alternatives to simple plurality. It backed the additional member system for elections for a Scottish Parliament and a regional list system for European parliamentary elections, which the Labour leadership accepted. But Plant's recommendation that the supplementary vote be used for Westminster elections was more contentious. Party leader John Smith did not support it but committed Labour to holding a referendum on electoral reform.

Tony Blair was unconvinced about electoral reform for Westminster, but maintained the referendum pledge. Labour agreed a joint agenda for constitutional reform with the Liberal Democrats that supported proportional representation for other contests. As Prime Minister, Blair established an Independent Commission on the Voting System chaired by Lord Jenkins. It proposed the hybrid system 'AV+' (also known as 'AV top up') for general elections. Most MPs would be elected in single-member constituencies using the alternative vote system which requires the victorious candidate to secure an absolute majority. Some 15–20 per cent of MPs would be list members elected from open lists in 80 multi-member constituencies and allocated to parties on a corrective basis. This would have produced a hung parliament in 1992 and a comfortable Labour majority in 1997.

The government has not acted upon the Jenkins Report and the impetus for reform has dissipated. In its 2001 and 2005 manifestos, Labour promised a review of the operation of the new electoral systems; but a referendum on 'AV+' appeared a distant prospect. The review got underway in 2005 but two key players, Secretary of State for Constitutional Affairs, Lord Falconer and John Prescott, the chair of a Cabinet sub-committee on electoral issues, are known opponents of PR. Blair's position has also hardened: he has described PR as unfair because it delivers undue influence to small parties holding the balance of power. AMS had denied Labour the prospect of governing in its own right in Scotland (and in Wales for a period) forcing the party to make concessions to the Liberal Democrats.

At Westminster political self-interest dictated that electoral reform was attractive to Labour MPs when they were in Opposition but was now unattractive as the simple plurality system had delivered big election wins. Nonetheless some Labour MPs declared their support for electoral reform after the 2005 election. The Liberal Democrats preferred system is STV which the Labour–Liberal Democrat coalition has put in place for local elections in Scotland from 2007. They did, though, back the Jenkins Report recommendations in 1999. The Conservatives oppose electoral reform even though they have benefited from it in Scotland and Wales. They fear that proportional representation would see Labour–Liberal Democrat coalitions returned at Westminster and the Tories excluded from power for the foreseeable future.

Impact of the new electoral systems

Despite its relative inaction on electoral reform for Westminster, the Blair government has introduced multiple electoral systems into the UK polity. The simple plurality system is only used for general elections and local elections in Great Britain. The devolved assemblies in Scotland and Wales are elected by the additional member system, as is the Greater London Assembly. Great Britain's representatives in the European Parliament are elected by the regional list system of proportional representation. The single transferable vote is used for elections to the Northern Ireland Assembly and for the Province's three MEPs. Elected mayors in eleven English towns and cities are chosen by the supplementary vote.

A more complex pattern of voting behaviour has developed under the new electoral systems. The multi-level UK polity clearly has a number of party systems rather than a standardised two-party system. Minor parties and independent candidates have performed better in the above contests than in Westminster elections. This is to be expected in 'second-order elections' that do not determine the government of the UK (see Analysis 16.3), but PR has been a factor in the improved showing of smaller parties. It has produced more proportional results, awarding minor parties seats they would not have won if the simple plurality system were used. The Liberal Democrats were under-represented in the European Parliament until the change to PR in 1999. The UK Independence Party and the Greens have also won seats in the European Parliament and on the London Assembly. The Conservatives failed to win any constituency seats in the 1999 Scottish Parliament election despite scoring 15.5 per cent of the constituency vote, but were allocated 18 list seats.

No electoral system can translate votes into seats with complete accuracy. PR systems are more effective than majoritarian ones, as the 'deviation from proportionality' figures in Table 16.5 show, but anomalies still occur (see Table 16.5). The number of seats in a constituency (the 'district magnitude') is a factor. Minor

Analysis: **16.3**

Second-order elections

Political scientists classify national parliamentary and presidential elections as 'first-order elections' whereas subnational, local, European Parliament and by-elections are 'second-order elections'. The introduction of proportional representation for many second-order elections in the UK has increased the likelihood that small parties will fare better than in general elections.

The main characteristics of second-order elections can be summarised as:

- Turnout is lower than for first-order elections.
- Support for the governing party is likely to decline as electors take the chance to register a protest vote against its record in office.
- Smaller parties perform better.
- Electors vote on the basis of national issues rather than issues specific to the institution that is being elected.

Table 16.5 Deviation from proportionality (DV) under different electoral systems

Institution	Electoral system	Year of election	Deviation from proportionality (%)
House of Commons	Simple plurality	2001	22
House of Commons	Simple plurality	2005	20
European Parliament (GB only)	List PR	1999	14
European Parliament (GB only)	List PR	2004	15
Scottish Parliament	AMS (57:43)	1999	11
Scottish Parliament	AMS (57:43)	2003	12
National Assembly for Wales	AMS (66:33)	1999	11
National Assembly for Wales	AMS (66:33)	2003	14
Northern Ireland Assembly	STV	1998	6
Northern Ireland Assembly	STV	2003	6

Note: DV is calculated by: calculating the difference between each party's percentage vote-share and seat-share; summing all deviations (ignoring minus signs) and halving the total.

Source: Adapted from 'Table 5.1: Disproportionality under different electoral systems', in *Changed Voting Changed Politics: Lessons of Britain's Experience of PR since 1997*, p. 34 (London, Final Report of the Independent Commission to Review Britain's Experience of PR Voting Systems, 2004)

parties are often under-represented when the d'Hondt formula or STV are used in small multi-member constituencies. Small parties were thus under-represented in the European Parliament after the 1999 and 2004 elections. Labour and the Liberal Democrats won marginally more seats in the 2003 Scottish Parliament election than they would have done under a strictly proportional system, though Labour would have won a parliamentary majority under simple plurality. The SNP, Scottish Socialists and Greens won fewer seats than their share of the vote merited. Small parties fared less well in the 2003 Welsh Assembly elections where a party needed to win 8 per cent of the vote (compared to about 6 per cent in Scotland) to be sure of a list seat. To be entitled to a seat in the London Assembly, a party must reach an electoral threshold of 5 per cent of the vote. The British National Party and Respect (a coalition of groups opposed to the war in Iraq) fell just short in 2004.

Electors have realised that their vote is less likely to be wasted under PR. Significant numbers have engaged in 'split ticket' voting at the Scottish Parliament and Welsh Assembly elections, supporting a major party in the constituency vote but giving their list vote to a minor party. The four main parties in Scotland all polled fewer list votes than constituency votes in 2003 (see Table 16.6). Minor parties and

Table 16.6 Elections to the Scottish Parliament, 2003

	Share of constituency vote (%)	Constituency seats won	Share of regional list vote (%)	List seats won	Total seats
Conservative	16.6	3	15.5	15	18
Labour	34.6	46	29.3	4	50
Lib Dem	15.4	13	11.8	4	17
SNP	23.8	9	20.9	18	27
Green	0.0	0	6.9	7	7
Scottish Socialist	6.2	0	6.7	6	6
Others	3.4	2	8.9	2	4

independents won 17 seats in the Scottish Parliament in 2003, all but two of them list seats. The Greens did not field candidates in the constituency section but scored 6.9 per cent of the list vote. Even when having a single vote under the list system, 35.8 per cent of voters in the 2004 European Parliament election supported a minor party or independent. In the 1998 Northern Ireland Assembly elections, the nationalist SDLP won the most first preference votes but the Ulster Unionist Party took the most seats as its vote was more effectively distributed and it benefited from vote transfers. The transfer of votes had a significant impact on the composition of the Assembly, turning an 'anti-Agreement' majority of first preference votes within the unionist bloc into a 'pro-Agreement' majority amongst unionists in the Assembly.

The two rounds of elections to the devolved assemblies have yet to produce a decisive winner. No party scored a majority of the popular vote or won a majority of seats, though Labour came close when winning 30 of the 60 seats in the Welsh Assembly in 2003. Peace-time coalitions are rare at Westminster but the Scottish Executive (since 1997) and Welsh Assembly government (2000–2003) have seen coalition rule. The Good Friday Agreement effectively requires that the Northern Ireland Executive include members of the main unionist and nationalist parties.

Electors are becoming more familiar with the new electoral systems and are generally supportive, though a minority find them confusing. Electors in London took part in five contests in June 2004, each using a different electoral system. In the mayoral election, 329,000 second preference votes were ruled out (17.1 per cent), many of them because voters had erroneously placed their first and second choices in the same column on the ballot paper rather than adjacent columns. In total, more than half-a-million votes in the 2004 London mayoral and Assembly elections were ruled invalid. This was actually lower than in 2000, but lessons about guidance to voters or the design of the ballot papers had not been fully learned. The new electoral systems have not brought about an increase in turnout, but surveys suggest their complexity has not been a factor in the low turnouts.

The 2005 *Better Governance for Wales* White Paper signalled that changes will be made to the way AMS operates in elections to the Welsh Assembly. But it rejected the recommendation of the independent Richard Commission that AMS be replaced by STV. The Blair government has set up a Commission on Boundary Differences and Voting Systems (the Arbuthnott Commission) to assess the impact of using four different electoral systems in Scotland after 2007: simple plurality for Westminster, AMS for the Scottish Parliament, the regional list for the European Parliament and STV for local elections. The Commission will examine the use of different boundaries for Westminster and Scottish Parliament elections, plus the representation of electors by constituency and list members. The Scottish Affairs Select Committee has already backed a reduction in the number of list MSPs to eleven having heard concerns about the imbalance in constituency work undertaken by constituency and list MSPs.

Experience of different electoral systems has not had a significant impact on popular support for electoral reform at Westminster. But, as we have seen, it has hardened opposition to PR in the top echelons of the Blair government thus lessening the likelihood of a change from the simple plurality system to a form of proportional representation for general elections.

Conclusion and summary

Elections in the UK generally meet the 'competitive, free and fair' criteria outlined at the start of this chapter, but some elements of the electoral process are problematic. Electoral law is not enshrined within a written constitution, leaving the government free to change the electoral system or enfranchise new voters by following normal legislative procedures. Some of the changes introduced by the Blair governments have been criticised by opposition parties and independent commentators, including the use of the closed list system for European parliamentary elections and the decision to hold all-postal ballots in four regions at the 2004 European parliamentary elections. Spending limits have been introduced for national election campaigns, but Labour and the Conservatives continue to far outspend other parties. Terrestrial television broadcasters must follow strict guidelines in their coverage of election campaigns, but the press are free to present issues in a partisan way. The quality of media coverage of major issues is also questionable.

The simple plurality system produces disproportional results and as such discriminates against small parties and many votes are wasted. But it has contributed to long periods of stable government by parties that have a good record in putting their manifesto commitments into practice. Low turnout is perhaps the most pressing concern, particularly if some social groups or shades of opinion are under-represented. Yet efforts to improve turnout by introducing postal or e-voting themselves raise questions about electoral fraud and the secret ballot. Greater political engagement is the key to improving the health of electoral democracy in Britain and this depends on a positive two-way relationship between political parties and electors.

Further reading

Every general election since 1945 has been the subject of a detailed study in the 'Nuffield series'. The most recent is D. Kavanagh and D. Butler (eds), *The British General Election of 2005* (London: Palgrave, 2005). P. Norris and C. Wlezien (eds) *Britain Votes 2005* (Oxford: Oxford University Press, 2005) is the latest in an excellent series that also appear as special editions of *Parliamentary Affairs*. A. Geddes and J. Tonge (eds), *Britain Decides. The 2005 General Election* (London: Palgrave, 2005) is also recommended.

Campaigning is explored in J. Bartle, R. Mortimore and S. Atkinson (eds), *Political Communications: The General Election Campaign of 2001* (London: Frank Cass, 2002). D. Kavanagh, *Election Campaigning: The New Marketing of Politics* (Oxford: Blackwell, 1995) is a useful but rather dated introduction. More detailed pieces include D. Denver, G. Hands and I. McAllister, 'The Electoral Impact of Constituency Campaigning in Britain, 1992–2001', *Political Studies*, 52:2 (2004), pp. 289–306; I. Crewe, 'The Opinion Polls: still Biased to Labour' in P. Norris (ed.), *Britain Votes 2001* (Oxford: Oxford University Press, 2001), pp. 86–101 and J. Fisher, 'Campaign Finance: Elections under new Rules', in the same volume (pp. 125–36).

The decline in turnout is examined in P. Whiteley, H. Clarke, D. Sanders and M. Stewart, 'Turnout', in P. Norris (ed.), *Britain Votes 2001* (Oxford: Oxford University Press, 2001), pp. 211–24 and J. Curtice, 'Turnout: Electors Stay Home – Again', in P. Norris and C. Wlezien (eds) *Britain Votes 2005* (Oxford: Oxford University Press, 2005), pp. 120–9 and *Voter*

Engagement and Young People (London: Electoral Commission, 2004). Possible solutions are assessed in *May 2003 Pilot Schemes* (London: Electoral Commission, 2003), *Age of Electoral Majority* (Electoral Commission, 2004) and K. Faulks, 'Should Voting be Compulsory?', *Politics Review*, Vol. 10, No. 3, (2001) pp. 24–5. On the representation of women, see *Gender and Political Participation* (London: Electoral Commission, 2004) and R. Campbell and J. Lovenduski, 'Winning Women's Votes? The Incremental Track to Equality', in P. Norris and C. Wlezien (eds) *Britain Votes 2005* (Oxford: Oxford University Press, 2005), pp. 181–97.

The best text on electoral systems is D. Farrell, *Electoral Systems: A Comparative Introduction* (London: Palgrave, 2001). J. Curtice, 'The electoral system: Biased to Blair?' in P. Norris (ed.), *Britain Votes 2001* (Oxford: Oxford University Press, 2001), pp. 239–50 exposes the bias in Britain's single member plurality system. *5 May 2005. Worst. Election. Ever* (London: Electoral Reform Society, 2005) provides a wealth of detail on the inequities of the simple plurality system. P. Dunleavy and H. Margetts, 'Comparing UK Electoral Systems', in P. Norris and C. Wlezien (eds) *Britain Votes 2005* (Oxford: Oxford University Press, 2005), pp. 198–213 examines the systems used in the UK.

Two detailed reports on electoral reform are *Changed Voting Changed Politics: Lessons of Britain's Experience of PR since 1997* (Independent Commission on PR, 2004) and the *Report of the Independent Commission on the Voting System*, Cmnd 4090 (the 'Jenkins Report') (HMSO, 1998). Britain's new electoral systems are assessed in P. Dunleavy and H. Margetts, 'Mixed electoral systems in Britain and the Jenkins Commission in electoral reform', *British Journal of Politics and International Relations*, 1:1 (1999).

Websites

The Electoral Commission's website www.electoralcommission.org.uk/ provides a wealth of information including official results from recent elections and reports on turnout and alternative methods of voting. Background material and assessments of recent developments can be found on the sites for the Constitution Unit www. ucl.ac.uk/constitution-unit/, the Electoral Reform Society www.electoral-reform. org.uk/ and Charter 88 www.charter88.org.uk/. All include copies of their excellent newsletters.

Richard Kimber's Political Science Resources page www.psr.keele.ac.uk/election. htm has links to a multitude of sites on elections and electoral systems, as does the Gateway at the Political Studies Association site www.psa.ac.uk. UK election results can be found at www.election.demon.co.uk/. The opinion poll organisations ICM www.icmresearch.co.uk/, MORI www.impsos-mori.co.uk/, Populus www.populus-limited.com/ and You Gov www.yougov.com/ provide data from past and present polls. The Fawcett Society www.fawcettsociety.org.uk/ campaigns for increased representation of women, and the Votes at 16 Campaign www.votesat16.org.uk for a reduction in the minimum voting age.

Chapter 17

Voting behaviour

Learning outcomes

After reading this chapter you will:

- Be able to evaluate the importance of social class in voting behaviour.
- Be able to assess the importance of issues, party leaders, personal economic prospects and voter perceptions of parties.
- Be able to evaluate which theories of voting behaviour provide the most convincing accounts of the outcomes of recent general elections.

Introduction

Two major approaches have dominated the study of voting behaviour in the UK since the end of the Second World War. The first focuses on the social characteristics of voters, particularly occupational class, and their long-term attachments to the Labour and Conservative parties. This perspective was the dominant one from 1945 to 1970, a period in which most electors voted for the party that represented the interests of their social class. Since 1970, social class has become less effective in predicting how people will vote. Political scientists now concentrate on a series of short-term factors, such as issues, party leaders and voter perceptions of the main parties which influence an individual's decision how to vote. This chapter focuses on these approaches and assesses voting behaviour in recent general elections. However, it should be remembered that the simple plurality electoral system does not translate votes into seats in the House of Commons accurately and that one in four electors did not vote in the 2001 and 2005 general elections (see Chapter 16).

Class voting and partisanship

Social class: a social group defined by economic and social status.

The period 1945–1970 was one of relative stability in voting behaviour in Britain. Studies of voting behaviour at this time concentrated on the social attributes of voters, particularly class alignment and partisan alignment. Election analysts identified a strong relationship between **social class** and voting. Peter Pulzer proclaimed in *Political Representation and Elections in Britain* (George Allen & Unwin, 1967) that 'class is the basis of British party politics; all else is embellishment and detail'. Social class was determined by occupation: the working class consisted of people in manual occupations, the middle class those in non-manual jobs. A majority of people voted for their 'natural class party', that is the party representing the interests of their social class. Some two-thirds of the working class voted for the Labour Party; three-quarters of the middle class voted Conservative.

Table 17.1 UK general election results, 1945–2005

Year	Con vote (%)	Con seats	Lab vote (%)	Lab seats	Lib Dem vote (%)	Lib Dem seats	Others, votes (%)	Others, seats	Turnout (%)
1945	39.6	210	48.0	393	9.0	12	3.4	25	72.8
1950	43.4	298	46.1	315	9.1	9	1.4	3	83.9
1951	48.0	321	48.8	295	2.6	6	0.6	3	82.6
1955	49.7	345	46.4	277	2.7	6	1.2	2	76.8
1959	49.4	365	43.8	258	5.9	6	0.9	1	78.7
1964	43.4	304	44.1	317	11.2	9	1.3	0	77.1
1966	41.9	253	48.0	364	8.6	12	1.5	1	75.8
1970	46.4	330	43.1	288	7.5	6	3.0	6	72.0
1974 Feb.	37.9	297	37.2	301	19.3	14	5.6	23	78.8
1974 Oct.	35.8	277	39.2	319	18.3	13	6.7	26	72.8
1979	43.9	339	36.9	269	13.8	11	5.4	16	76.0
1983	42.4	397	27.6	209	25.4	23	4.6	21	72.7
1987	42.3	376	30.8	229	22.5	22	4.4	23	75.3
1992	41.8	336	34.2	271	17.9	20	6.1	24	77.7
1997	30.7	165	43.4	419	16.8	46	9.3	29	71.5
2001	31.7	166	40.7	413	18.3	52	9.3	28	59.4
2005	32.3	197	35.2	355	22.1	62	10.4	31	61.3
Mean 1945–70	45.1		46.5		7.0		1.5		78.2
Mean 1974–2005	37.6		36.1		19.4		6.9		71.7

Note: Liberal Democrats includes Liberals (1945–79) and SDP/Liberal Alliance (1983–87). Northern Ireland MPs are included as 'Others' from 1974.

Social class formed the main political cleavage in the UK at this time. Labour self-consciously represented the interests of the working class and the Conservatives the interests of middle-class property owners. Within British society, class consciousness was more pronounced and class boundaries less porous than is the case today. Economic and political elites were largely made up of upper-class and middle-class men, many of them educated at public school and Oxbridge. Social mobility was limited: few working-class men (and fewer women) went to university or entered the company boardroom.

Partisanship was another key feature of UK politics in the early post-war period. More than three-quarters of voters had a positive attachment to a major party, identifying themselves as either a Labour supporter or a Conservative supporter. Of these, 43 per cent 'very strongly identified' with a party at the time of the 1964 and 1966 general elections. The two main parties thus had a large pool of loyal supporters, their 'core vote', which voted for them habitually.

Socialisation: the process by which individuals acquire values and beliefs in their formative years.

Class identity and partisanship were fostered during the process of **socialisation** which began in childhood. Political views developed through social learning in the home, at school and university, in the neighbourhood and workplace. An individual brought up in a council-owned property in a northern city who left school at 16 to work in a manual occupation where they joined a trade union, would be likely to identify themselves as working class and vote Labour.

Other factors also contributed to the stability of voting behaviour between 1945 and 1970. Britain had a stable two-party system in which the Conservatives and Labour averaged more than 91 per cent of the vote in the eight general elections in this period (see Table 17.1). At 78 per cent, election turnout was relatively high. Between them, the two main parties held almost 98 per cent of seats in the House of Commons. The two parties were well matched: the Conservatives spent 13 years in office and Labour 12, while the gap between their shares of the vote exceeded 4 per cent in only three elections.

Finally, this was an age of consensus politics in which neither Labour nor the Conservatives strayed far from the median voter – that is, the hypothetical voter who occupies the electoral centre ground with equivalent numbers of voters to their left and right. The electoral centre ground is not necessarily the same as the ideological centre ground. In this period, the median voter was positioned on the centre-left of the political spectrum and the main parties shared similar commitments to Keynesianism and the welfare state.

Limits of class voting

Although most electors voted along class lines in the period 1945–70, not all did. There were two main deviant groups, working-class Conservatives and middle-class socialists. If they had not captured the votes of up to one-third of the vote from the then numerically-dominant working class, the Conservative Party would not have achieved its three general election victories in the 1950s. Some explanations of working-class Conservatism focused on the values held by working-class Tories, including feelings of deference towards the Conservative Party given the social status of its leaders, its authoritarian values and support for the Union. Others looked at the location of Conservative supporters within the working class, suggesting that the increased affluence of skilled workers might account for their allegiance. Studies of support for Labour among middle-class voters also examined their values (e.g. egalitarianism) and status (e.g. employment in the public sector, particularly education and local government).

A further problem with the class voting model is its inference that the actions of governments and political parties are of limited importance for election outcomes because most voters have stable allegiances. Political parties in the 1950s and 1960s recognised that they had to both mobilise their core vote and try to win support from 'floating voters' (i.e. undecided voters who might switch support). The government's record in office, party policy on key issues and the image of the main parties and their leaders might not have been as significant in the period 1945–70 as they have been subsequently, but they nonetheless helped shape people's perceptions of party politics.

Dealignment

Class dealignment: the decline in the correlation between social class and voting behaviour.

Class and partisan dealignment have brought about a significant decline in the incidence of both class voting and partisanship since 1970. **Class dealignment** refers to the weakening of the relationship between social class and voting. Since 1970, fewer people vote for their 'natural class party'. Working-class support for Labour has waned as has middle-class support for the Conservatives. The Alford Index of relative class voting is one way of measuring the incidence of class voting. It is calculated by subtracting Labour's percentage share of the middle-class vote from its share of the working-class vote. The more supportive the working class is of Labour relative to the middle class, the higher the Alford Index score. In 1964 it stood at 42 but fell as low as 20 in 1997 before recovering slightly.

Partisan dealignment: the decline in the strength of attachments that voters have to a political party.

Partisan dealignment refers to the decline in voter identification with the main political parties. Fewer voters have a strong attachment to either Labour or the Conservatives. In 2001 only 13 per cent of people described themselves as 'very strong' supporters of one of the main parties compared to 43 per cent in 1964. This means that their core vote has shrunk. Party membership has also declined: the Conservatives had 2.5 million members in the mid-1950s but fewer than 300,000 in 2005, while Labour Party membership fell from 750,000 to 215,000 in the same period. Dealignment has produced greater electoral volatility, with more people switching support from election to election. One million voters switched directly from the Conservatives to Labour between 1992 and 1997.

The era of two-party politics also gave way to a more complex picture in which the foundations of bipolar party politics have been undermined but not overhauled. The post-1970 era has been one of dealignment rather than fundamental realignment. The share of the vote won by Labour and the Conservatives in the nine general elections held since 1970 has fallen from the 1945–70 average of 91 per cent to less than 75 per cent (see Table 17.1). At the 2005 general election, the two main parties together polled only 67.5 per cent of the UK vote. Support for the third party has more than doubled. In the 1945–70 period the Liberals averaged 7 per cent whereas after 1974 the average share of the vote won by the Liberals and their successors was 17 per cent. Nationalist parties in Scotland and Wales made electoral breakthroughs at

Westminster in the 1970s. Minor parties such as the United Kingdom Independence Party (UKIP) and the British National Party (BNP) have improved their share of the vote in recent years but have not won seats at Westminster. One in ten electors in the UK voted for minor parties in 2005 (if Northern Ireland is excluded, minor parties in Great Britain won 7.9 per cent of the vote).

Explaining dealignment

Social and economic change over the last 40 years have eroded traditional class identities and weakened the relationship between class and voting. The proportion of people working in manual occupations has declined since the 1960s, with notable falls in industries such as shipbuilding, mining and car production. Employment has risen in service industries (e.g. in catering, advertising and computing) and parts of the public sector (e.g. in social services). From being the largest social class in the early post-war period, the working class is now smaller than the middle class. The character of the labour market has also undergone profound change. Notions of 'nine-to-five' jobs and 'jobs-for-life' have receded as more people (especially women) work on a part-time basis, are employed on flexible contracts or are self-employed. The proportion of women in the workforce has increased dramatically, reaching 70 per cent in 2001.

The most popular typology of social class used by social scientists and opinion pollsters uses the following categories:

- A – higher managerial, administrative or professional.
- B – intermediate managerial, administrative or professional.
- C1 – supervisory, clerical and junior white-collar workers.
- C2 – skilled manual workers.
- D – semi-skilled and unskilled manual workers.
- E – casual workers, people reliant on state benefits (e.g. pensioners and the long-term unemployed).

The highest two categories are often merged (as AB) as are the lowest two (DE).

The working class has decreased in size since the 1960s. According to MORI, the AB group made up 24 per cent of the electorate in 2005, C1 29 per cent, C2 21 per cent and DE 25 per cent. Greater social mobility and increased affluence have also blurred the boundaries between the middle class and working class. More people from working-class backgrounds enter further or higher education, have non-manual occupations and own their homes than was the case in the 1950s. Standards of living have increased and the ownership of consumer goods widened. Social change led some academics to challenge the traditional typology of social class. The psephologists Anthony Heath, Roger Jowell and John Curtice devised an alternative typology in the 1980s (see Analysis 17.1). They also disputed claims that there had been a decline in *absolute* class voting, instead arguing that there had only been a fall in *relative* class voting. A decline in working-class support for Labour would produce a fall in the level of absolute class voting, but for relative class voting to decline, there would also have to be an increase in the number of working-class voters supporting parties other than Labour. This debate exercised psephologists

Analysis:	17.1

Social class

In studies of voting behaviour, social class is defined in terms of occupation. This approach is considerably narrower than concepts of class used by Marxist theories of conflict between the owners of the means of production (the bourgeoisie or capitalist class) and those forced to sell their own labour (the proletariat or working class). Social scientists engaged in empirical work have constructed various typologies of social class to distinguish between occupations and income levels. The most important has been the ABC1 classification which has been used by opinion pollsters and most social scientists.

Election analysts Anthony Heath, Roger Jowell and John Curtice argued in *How Britain Votes* (London: Pergamon, 1985) that the ABC1 typology failed to take account of social and economic change. They devised their own categories in which the working class formed a smaller proportion of the electorate:

- I   Salariat (managers, administrators, professionals, semi-professionals).
- II   Routine non-manual (clerks, secretaries, sales workers).
- III   Petty bourgeoisie (small proprietors, self-employed manual workers, farmers).
- IV   Foremen and technicians (blue-collar workers with supervisory functions).
- V   Working class (rank-and-file manual workers in industry and agriculture).

The limitations of the ABC1 typology have also been recognised by government statisticians who now use a new typology:

- 1. Higher managerial and professional occupations (e.g. company directors, doctors and lawyers).
- 2. Lower managerial and professional occupations (e.g. nurses, journalists and junior police officers).
- 3. Intermediate occupations (e.g. secretaries).
- 4. Small employers (e.g. farmers).
- 5. Lower supervisory occupations (e.g. train drivers).
- 6. Semi-routine occupations (e.g. shop assistants).
- 7. Routine occupations (e.g. waiters, refuse collectors).
- 8. Long-term unemployed.

Political parties identify small groups of voters whose support is believed to be crucial to their prospects of electoral success. Some of the categories they use have entered political folklore. In the 1980s the Conservatives targeted aspiring skilled and semi-skilled working-class voters in southern England – a group labelled as 'Essex man'. A decade later, Conservative attention had shifted to 'Worcester woman', middle-class women in provincial cities. These groups were identified on the basis of electoral geography; others have been labelled according to lifestyle. Tony Blair coined the term 'Mondeo man' for the thirty-something middle-class homeowner whose support New Labour needed if it was to win the 1997 election. In the 2005 general election, Labour and the Conservatives employed databases (e.g. 'Voter Vault') similar to those used by supermarkets to profile customers according to their lifestyle preferences. These used 61 demographic sub-categories with obscure labels such as 'Dinky Developments' and 'White Van Culture'.

(i.e. experts on voting behaviour) into the 1990s but the academic consensus now holds that class voting has declined in both absolute and relative terms over the last 30 years.

Assumptions that the working class and middle class were homogenous groups had always been simplistic given the differences in income between skilled and unskilled manual workers. But social change made the traditional typology more problematic. Many people now occupy 'cross-class' positions, having some working-class attributes (e.g. a manual occupation) but others associated with the middle class (e.g. home ownership). Patrick Dunleavy argued that a new public sector–private sector cleavage had emerged by the 1980s. This division had two dimensions: first between people employed in the public sector and those working in the private sector and second between people who relied on the public provision of goods (e.g. housing and transport) and those using private suppliers.

Class dealignment had a knock-on effect on party identification. People without strong class identities were less likely to feel a strong attachment to their 'natural class party'. Better education and a less deferential style of political reporting in the media were also cited as factors in partisan dealignment. But political parties themselves bore some responsibility for the weakening of party identification. In the 1970s Conservative and Labour governments failed to deliver on policy commitments or arrest the UK's economic decline. Opinion polls registered declining levels of satisfaction with the performance of the main parties and their leaders. Furthermore, gaps emerged between the ideological positions of the main parties and their supporters. Labour moved to the left in the late 1970s, while the Conservatives shifted to the right after Margaret Thatcher became party leader in 1975. Many voters committed to the post-war consensus defected to the Liberals or the Social Democratic Party (SDP) which was formed in 1981 by disillusioned members of Labour's right wing. The Liberal/SDP Alliance won 25 per cent of the vote in 1983 but was denied a breakthrough at Westminster by the simple plurality electoral system (see Chapter 16).

Consequences of dealignment

Class and partisan dealignment posed particular problems for the Labour Party. The decline in the size of the working class meant that Labour's core vote was shrinking. Ivor Crewe distinguished between the 'old working class', which was decreasing in numbers, and the emerging 'new working class'. The former consisted of manual workers who belonged to trade unions, were employed in heavy industry, were council tenants and lived in Scotland, Wales or urban areas of northern England. Members of the new working class worked in the private sector, lived in southern England, owned their own home and had more qualifications. Much of the old working class remained loyal to Labour, but the Conservatives attracted significant support from the new working class. Crewe predicted a 'glacial shift to the right' which would make it difficult for Labour to win power. Between 1979 and 1992 Labour lost four general elections, averaging just 32 per cent of the vote. Its share of the skilled working class (C2) vote fell from the 49 per cent it achieved when winning the October 1974 election to 32 per cent in 1983 (see Table 17.2).

Table 17.2 Class voting since 1974

Party	Middle class (ABC1)	Skilled working class (C2)	Unskilled working class (DE)
Conservative			
1974 (October)	56	26	22
1979	59	41	34
1983	55	40	33
1987	54	40	30
1992	54	39	31
1997	39	27	21
2001	38	29	24
2005	37	33	25
Labour			
1974 (October)	19	49	57
1979	24	41	49
1983	16	32	41
1987	18	36	48
1992	22	40	49
1997	34	50	59
2001	34	49	55
2005	31	40	48

Source: Ipsos MORI, www.ipsos-mori.com

The Conservatives and Labour (belatedly) reacted to dealignment by adapting their ideology and targeting groups of voters beyond their core support. From the late 1970s, Thatcher's popular capitalism attracted support from the new working class with policies such as lower taxes and the sale of council houses which matched their aspirations. Support for the Conservatives among skilled working-class voters rose from 25 per cent in October 1974 to an average of 40 per cent between 1979 and 1992. In the 1990s, New Labour strategists recognised that the party had to extend its appeal to skilled workers and middle-class voters in southern England. Middle-class (ABC1) support for Labour increased from just 16 per cent in 1983 to 34 per cent in 1997. In the early 1990s Labour won support from middle-class voters who worked in the public sector and regarded Thatcherism as hostile to the NHS, local government and state education. Under Tony Blair, it then added support from middle-class voters who worked in the private sector and felt that New Labour could be trusted to manage the economy.

Recent elections have provided further confirmation of class and partisan dealignment. Support for Labour increased across all social groups in 1997 but its most significant gains were among middle-class voters where it enjoyed a 12 per cent increase in support. Labour maintained its cross-class appeal in 2001 and 2005, though its working-class vote declined by 10 per cent. The Conservatives made gains among working-class voters (C2 support was up 7 per cent between 1997 and 2005) but continued to lose ground among professional and managerial voters (down a further 3 per cent between 1997 and 2005). The 2001 and 2005 elections thus produced a pattern that ran counter to the post-war norm: the Conservatives made gains among working-class voters but lost further middle-class support; Labour experienced sharper falls in its working-class vote than its middle-class vote.

The national two-party system has become more unstable since 1970. The share of the vote won by Labour and the Conservatives in general elections has declined to under 75 per cent and other parties feature more prominently in the legislature. Multi-party systems operate at subnational level and in some local authorities, with three or more parties in close competition in these elections but frequently sharing power in devolved assemblies and 'hung councils'. Turnout at general elections has also fallen from an average of 78 per cent in the period 1945–70 to 72 per cent since then and a nadir of 59 per cent in 1997 (see Chapter 16).

Social class is, then, a less important predictor of voting behaviour than it was in the early post-war period. But Labour remains the most popular party among working-class voters and the Conservatives perform best among middle-class voters. People in manual occupations are also still more likely to vote for Labour than are non-manual workers.

Other social factors

Other social factors are also relevant to voting behaviour. There are, for example, important regional variations in voting in Britain. A 'north–south' divide in electoral geography has become more pronounced in the last thirty years. Conservative support has become concentrated in the south of England, the suburbs and rural areas. Only in the south-east and east of England have the Conservatives averaged over 40 per cent of the vote since 1997. The Conservative share of the vote in northern England and the Midlands fell by more than 10 per cent at the 1997 general election and has barely recovered since. The Conservatives improved their position in Greater London in 2005, but won just five seats in the six English metropolitan areas outside London. They won only one seat in Scotland and three in Wales. Labour's traditional electoral strongholds have been in Scotland, Wales and northern England, in large urban areas and on council estates. Labour gained ground in London and the suburban south of England in 1997 (with an average increase of 10 per cent), but continues to perform best in the north and in urban areas. Full coverage of elections in Northern Ireland, which has a distinctive party system, Scotland and Wales is provided in Chapter 11.

Regional patterns of support reflect in large part the geographical distribution of social classes and differences in regional economies. Manual workers tend to be concentrated in urban areas, for example, and employment in the financial sector is concentrated in the south-east. Local politics may also be important as in south-west England where Liberal Democrat campaigning has been effective in local and parliamentary elections, the party winning all five seats in Cornwall in the 2005 general election. But differences within regions are often greater than those between them. Greater London contains some of the richest as well as some of the poorest parts of the UK. An example of different electoral outcomes in the same region was provided by neighbouring Enfield Southgate and Enfield North in 2005. The Conservatives overturned a 5500 Labour majority to win the former but not a 2300 Labour majority in the latter.

For much of the period since female suffrage, the Conservatives outperformed Labour among women voters. In the mid-twentieth century this gender gap was said to reflect social attitudes of the time (e.g. support for the family unit) and the low numbers of women in the workforce. The Conservative lead among women voters disappeared in the 1990s (see Table 17.3). Labour has enjoyed a healthy lead over the Conservatives among women voters in the last three elections (e.g. of 12 per cent in 1997). As Table 17.3 also shows, there was little difference between the voting behaviour of men and women in 1997 and 2001. Support for Labour has been particularly strong among young women: in the last three elections the pro-Labour gender gap has been much higher among women aged under-35 than among older women. This group strongly preferred Labour's policies on traditional issues (e.g. health and education) and on so-called 'women's issues' (e.g. childcare). Labour's efforts to target women voters and their success in increasing the number of female candidates in winnable seats are also significant.

Older voters have historically been more likely to support the Conservatives, while younger voters are more likely to vote Labour. This may be a result of life-cycle changes: people become more conservative as they grow older, losing their youthful idealism and taking on more responsibilities at home and at work. The political climate of an individual's formative years may also colour their long-term political attitudes. Young voters in 1997 would have recalled the problems endured by the Conservatives under John Major but not those experienced by Labour governments in the 1970s. The difference in the voting behaviour of old and young voters has survived New Labour's broad appeal. Conservative support is ageing: they led Labour only among voters aged over 55 in 2001 and 2005. Political parties are increasingly targeting older voters. The UK population is ageing as improvements in healthcare mean that people are living longer. Older people are also more likely to vote than young people. Those aged over 55 constituted 35 per cent of the electorate but 42 per cent of voters in 2005. Labour has been the most popular party with young voters in recent general elections, although the Liberal Democrats gained some ground (up 8 per cent in the 24–35 age group) in 2005.

Table 17.3 Gender and voting since 1974

	Men	Women
Conservative		
1974 (Oct.)	32	39
1979	43	47
1983	42	46
1987	43	43
1992	41	44
1997	31	32
2001	32	33
2005	34	32
Labour		
1974 (Oct.)	43	38
1979	40	35
1983	30	26
1987	32	32
1992	37	44
1997	45	44
2001	42	42
2005	34	38

Source: Ipsos MORI, www.ipsos-mori.com

Religion formed an important political and societal cleavage in the UK until the mid-twentieth century. Anglicans were more likely to support the Conservative Party, in part because of its opposition to Irish Home Rule, whereas the Liberals were favoured by Non-Conformists. The Conservatives were able to win industrial seats in the west of Scotland into the 1960s thanks to the support of working-class Protestants. Roman Catholics in Great Britain are more likely to support Labour but the decline of religion in public life has weakened the relationship between religious denomination and voting. As we saw in Chapter 11, it remains important in Northern Ireland, where most Protestants vote for unionist parties and most Roman Catholics for nationalist parties.

Ethnic minorities make up 7.8 per cent of the UK population. 'Operation Black Vote' identified 70 constituencies in 2005 in which the size of the ethnic minority population exceeded that of the winning party's margin of victory. Turnout among black voters has, though, been consistently lower than among the white population. Political parties have stepped up their efforts to attract ethnic minority voters in recent years. But the effectiveness of campaigns targeted at ethnic minorities is open to question. In *Race and British Electoral Politics* (London: Routledge, 1997), Shamit Saggar notes that ethnic minority electors tend to vote on class lines (many are in low-paid occupations) rather than on the basis of 'race' issues. Nor should ethnic minority voters be viewed as a homogeneous group. Those from South Asian backgrounds are more likely to vote Conservative than African-Caribbeans but Labour enjoys comfortable leads in both groups, winning over 80 per cent support from the latter. The war in Iraq contributed to a significant drop in support for Labour in 2005 in constituencies with large Muslim populations (see Case study 17.2, page 445).

Rational choice approaches

Models of voting behaviour that focus on the social characteristics of voters downplay the significance of short-term political factors. Voters have stable partisan loyalties and tend to vote for the same party throughout their lifetime. This approach is also deterministic: voting behaviour is determined by the individual's position within society and upbringing. But sociological approaches to voting behaviour have been rendered far less effective by class and partisan dealignment.

Rational choice theory: a theory that interprets political behaviour on the basis that individuals act rationally and explore the costs and benefits of their actions before reaching a decision.

Alternative approaches to voting behaviour, drawing upon **rational choice theory**, put the individual voter at the heart of their analysis. They focus on the processes by which electors decide how to cast their vote. Individuals make informed political choices by examining the relative merits of the main parties and/or judging which party will make them better off. There is no single rational choice model of voting behaviour, but a number of variants which identify different factors as being significant notably:

- Issues.
- Party leaders.
- The economy.
- Governing competence.

The most convincing explanations of recent election outcomes focus on voter perceptions of the competence of the main parties and their leaders. This is a diluted variant of the rational choice approach which contends that voters use these perceptions as short-cuts when making judgements about issues and election campaigns.

Issues

The issue voting model claims that people decide how to vote by comparing the policies put forward by political parties on key issues. To have a significant impact on the outcome of an election, issue voting must be disproportional: that is, a significant number of electors must identify a particular issue as being important, recognise differences in the policies put forward by the main parties on the issue, identify the same party as having the best policy and vote for it accordingly. In the 1983 election, Labour proposed unilateral nuclear disarmament whereas the Conservatives advocated a strong nuclear deterrent. Most voters opposed unilateral disarmament and thus favoured the Conservatives.

New Labour enjoyed healthy opinion poll leads over the Conservatives on most of the issues rated by voters as important in determining how they would vote in the 1997, 2001 and 2005 general elections. In the last three general elections, Labour maintained big leads on issues on which Labour had been traditionally strong such as health and education. These were the top two issues identified as important by voters in 1997 and 2001; the Labour lead over the Conservatives as the party seen as best on these issues was more than 25 per cent. New Labour also established leads on issues where the Conservatives had previously scored well, notably on law and order which was ranked the third most important issue by voters and on which Labour enjoyed a slender 2 per cent lead in 2001. Labour still led on health and education in 2005 but its lead had fallen and it trailed the Conservatives badly on

Table 17.4 Party strengths on key issues, 2005

Issues	Per cent saying issue was important in helping them decide which party to vote for	Per cent Labour lead over Conservatives on issue
Healthcare	67	+14
Education	61	+15
Law and order	56	−12
Pensions	49	+2
Taxation	42	−6
Asylum	37	−41
Economy	35	+30
Environment	28	+6
Housing	27	+20
Public transport	26	+21
Unemployment	25	+31
Defence	19	−14
Europe	19	−11
Iraq	18	−9

Source: Ipsos MORI, www.ipsos-mori.com

immigration and asylum (see Table 17.4). Significantly, Labour was also the party considered best able to manage the economy at each of these general elections (see below).

There are, however, a number of problems with the issue voting model. First, general elections are rarely decided on the basis of a single issue. It is also likely that voters will favour some of a party's policies, but dislike others. Many voters will not be aware of detailed policy commitments. The limitations of the issue voting model were illustrated by the Conservatives' four election victories between 1979 and 1992. Thatcherite values were never widely accepted by the electorate. A Gallup poll conducted on the tenth anniversary of Thatcher's arrival in Downing Street found when asked if it was more important to cut taxes or extend public services even if this required tax increases, 73 per cent chose the latter. Labour was the preferred party on issues such as health and unemployment which voters placed near the top of the list of key issues facing the country. But voters' perceptions that they would be better off under the Conservatives proved more significant in determining how people voted.

Not all issues provoke clear differences between the parties. Labour and the Conservatives put forward similar policies on the economy and public service reform at the 2001 and 2005 elections, for example. In such cases, a variant of the rational choice approach known as the 'valence model' is useful (see Analysis 17.2). It focuses on voter perceptions of party competence. Issues on which there is widespread agreement on a desirable outcome, such as low inflation or quality healthcare, are referred to as **valence issues**. It is not ideological differences that are crucial on these issues as these tend to be narrow, but voter perceptions about which

Valence issues: policy outcomes that most parties view as desirable and on which voters make judgements about the ability of parties to deliver them.

Analysis: | **17.2**

Valence issues

The valence model of voting, originally developed by Donald Stokes – see for example, D. Stokes, 'Spatial Models of Party Competition', *American Political Science Review*, Vol. 57, No. 2 (1963), pp. 368–77 – recognises that most voters and political parties agree on the desirability of issues such as a healthy economy. It thus differs from the issue voting model (or the spatial model) which focuses on issues on which the main political parties offer rival programmes. Party competition on valence issues is not structured around different perspectives on policy ends but in terms of the competence of parties to deliver the desired goal. Voters form judgements about the likelihood of political parties delivering low inflation, low levels of crime, quality healthcare and education, and national security. To enhance their prospects of election success, political parties concentrate on valence issues on which they are viewed by the public as being the party most likely to achieve policy success.

The valence model has been employed convincingly in studies of recent British general elections, notably by the British Election Study team, H. Clarke, D. Sanders, M. Stewart and P. Whiteley in *Political Choice in Britain* (Oxford: Oxford University Press, 2004). In 2001 and 2005, Labour and the Conservatives put forward similar policies on the economy and public services but a plurality of voters judged Labour to be the party most likely to deliver a sound economy and better public services.

party is most likely to deliver the desired policy outcomes. Perceptions of trust and governing competence are also significant. By focusing on voter judgements about the overall competence of the main parties, the valence model avoids some of the problems associated with pure rational choice theories (e.g. low levels of voter knowledge about party policies). The significance of governing competence will be discussed further below.

A rational choice model of party strategy first developed by Anthony Downs in *An Economic Theory of Democracy* (Harper and Row, 1957) has also been influential. It suggests that to maximise their vote, parties should position themselves close to the median voter. Electors vote for the party that has the policies closest to their own on a left–right continuum: someone with right of centre views, for example, would be likely to support the Conservatives. The median voter need not be positioned at dead centre of a left–right continuum: if a plurality of voters has centre-right views then the median voter will be positioned to the right of centre. The Downsian model suggests that if parties stray too far from the ideological territory where the median voter is situated, their prospects of election victory will be severely hampered. It is too simplistic to assume that the ideological positions adopted by political parties are simply a response to voter preferences because parties attempt to shape the values and perceptions of voters. Nonetheless, parties are punished for being out-of-touch with the mood of the electorate. Labour's move to the left in the early 1980s reflected the preferences of its activists but not the electorate, who rejected them decisively in 1983. From the late 1990s the Conservatives drifted to the right of the median voter, thereby limiting their appeal, while New Labour broadened its appeal by moving towards the electoral centre ground. As a **catch-all party** with a broad appeal, it enjoyed the support of working-class Labour loyalists, skilled workers who had voted for Thatcher in the 1980s and middle-class voters in former Conservative strongholds in southern England.

Catch-all party: a non-ideological party with a broad rather than sectional appeal.

New issue cleavages?

As the class cleavage that underpinned the post-war party system faded because of class and partisan dealignment, new issue cleavages structured around identity politics have emerged. Identity politics is crucial to an understanding of the rise of the Scottish Nationalist Party and Plaid Cymru. It also helps explain the decline of the Scottish Conservative Party which, unlike Labour, was not able to persuade voters that it was representing Scottish interests and identity. Identity issues are also critical to the party system in Northern Ireland (see Chapter 11).

Immigration and asylum, and European integration have featured prominently in recent general elections but have had the greatest impact in local and European Parliament elections. Immigration has risen up the political agenda periodically, notably in the 1970s and since the late 1990s. The Conservatives have exploited popular concerns by adopting authoritarian positions on illegal immigration and asylum, while New Labour has responded with tough measures and populist rhetoric. Extreme right-wing parties such as the BNP have taken council seats in parts of London, Lancashire and West Yorkshire but have failed to make a break-through in other contests (see Controversy 17.1). Immigration and asylum has become an important election issue in recent years. It barely featured in elections in the 1980s and 1990s, was rated by voters as the ninth most important issue in

Who votes for the BNP?

Between 2002 and 2005, the British National Party (BNP) achieved the highest levels of support for a far-right party in Britain since the 1970s. It held seventeen council seats in 2004, having polled more than a quarter of the vote in wards it contested in northern industrial towns such as Burnley and Oldham. The BNP narrowly failed to win seats in the European Parliament and London Assembly in 2004 having polled just under 5 per cent of the vote. It accrued 193,000 votes in the 2005 general election, averaging 4.3 per cent of the vote in the 119 constituencies it contested. The party won more than 10 per cent of the vote in Barking, Dewsbury and Burnley. Support for the BNP is concentrated among working-class and less-educated voters in constituencies with high levels of social deprivation.

Research undertaken by Peter John, Helen Margetts and Stuart Weir and reported in 'One in Five Britons Could Vote Far Right', *The New Statesman*, 24 January 2005, found that up to 20 per cent of the electorate would consider voting for the BNP. Unsurprisingly, three-quarters of BNP voters identified immigration as the 'most important issue facing Britain today' as did more than half of United Kingdom Independence Party (UKIP) supporters. One of the reasons immigration featured so prominently in the Conservatives' 2005 election campaign was the party's desire to shore up its right-wing support and minimise defections to UKIP and the BNP.

2001, but increased in saliency to become the second most important issue in 2005. Immigration was the issue on which the Conservatives enjoyed their biggest lead (41 per cent) over Labour in 2005 and was the most prominent issue in their election campaign. But it did not persuade significant numbers of middle-class voters to switch directly from Labour to the Conservatives.

The issue of Britain's relationship with the European Union appeared a potential vote winner for the Conservatives at the 1997 and 2001 elections. Conservative policy on membership of the European single currency was more popular than Labour's. But the Conservatives did not reap significant electoral rewards. Conservative divisions on the issue damaged the party in 1997. A 'save the Pound' message featured prominently in the 2001 Tory election campaign, but Europe was ranked only tenth among voter concerns. The Conservatives did gain some ground among elderly and working-class voters, but the Eurosceptic position also reinforced perceptions that the Conservatives were extreme and 'out of touch'. Europe barely figured in the 2005 general election campaign, in part because Labour had promised a referendum on the EU Constitution.

Though colouring party competition, identity politics has not opened up a political cleavage equivalent to the class cleavage of the early post-war period, nor brought about a fundamental realignment in the party system.

Party leaders

Party leaders have been an important factor in recent election outcomes. In an era when fewer people have strong party loyalties, perceptions of the relative strengths and weaknesses of the main party leaders are more likely to sway voters. Modern

William Hague did not convince voters that he had prime ministerial qualities (© Mirrorpix)

television and press coverage of politics is heavily skewed towards party leaders. They are the public face of their party and carry much of the responsibility for 'selling' party policy to the electorate. Voters use judgements about the character and leadership qualities of party leaders as short-cuts to help them reach verdicts on political parties. But there are limits to the impact of party leaders. Supporters of a party tend to have the most favourable opinions of its leader, making it difficult to establish the importance of a leader to their party's electoral fortunes. But a popular leader will not bring victory for their party if the message and policies that party espouses are unpopular. James Callaghan was preferred to Margaret Thatcher in 1979 but Labour lost the election.

Public perceptions of party leaders will be most significant for voting behaviour if a sizeable gap exists in popular views of the leaders of the two main parties. In 1983, MORI reported that 46 per cent of voters thought Margaret Thatcher would be the most capable Prime Minister whereas only 15 per cent thought Labour leader Michael Foot would. John Major was viewed as a more capable Prime Minister than Neil Kinnock in 1992 (38 per cent to 27 per cent) and, in a close contest, this may

Table 17.5 Most capable Prime Minister, 1992–2005 (%)

1992	
John Major	38
Neil Kinnock	27
Paddy Ashdown	20
1997	
John Major	23
Tony Blair	40
Paddy Ashdown	15
2001	
William Hague	14
Tony Blair	51
Charles Kennedy	14
2005	
Michael Howard	21
Tony Blair	40
Charles Kennedy	16

Source: Ipsos MORI, www.ipsos-mori.com

have been significant. Tony Blair outscored Major in 1997 (40 per cent to 23 per cent), William Hague in 2001 (51 per cent to 14 per cent) and Michael Howard in 2005 (40 per cent to 21 per cent) on the same question (see Table 17.5). Blair was undoubtedly an electoral asset to his party when Leader of the Opposition and in his early years in Downing Street. In his first term as Prime Minister, an average of 56 per cent of those surveyed by MORI said they were 'satisfied' with Blair's performance (see Table 17.6). Only 23 per cent were satisfied with Hague. The Conservatives did not lose the 2001 election because Hague was unpopular, but he did become an obstacle to Tory recovery rather than a catalyst for it.

Blair's popularity declined during his second term as the conduct of the war in Iraq raised questions about his integrity. Dissatisfaction with Blair was the key factor in the desertion or abstention of former Labour voters at the 2005 election. Blair's unpopularity cost Labour seats: Labour won in 2005 despite Blair rather than because of him. One opinion poll suggested that if Gordon Brown had been leader instead Labour's support would have increased by a third. Although his popularity had declined dramatically, voters still preferred Blair to the alternatives. Hague and Howard were notably unpopular among non-Conservative supporters in 2001 and 2005, undermining the party's prospects of winning new support.

Table 17.6 Satisfaction with the government, Prime Minister and Leader of the Opposition, 1992–2005 (%)

Year	Satisfied with the government	Satisfied with the Prime Minister	Satisfied with the Leader of the Opposition
1992	25 (Conservative)	43 (Major)	34 (Kinnock)
1993	13	23	36 (Smith)
1994	11	21	37
1995	12	24	49 (Blair)
1996	16	29	48
1997	21	32	50
1998	52 (Labour)	63 (Blair)	24 (Hague)
1999	45	57	23
2000	33	44	25
2001	44	54	25
2002	36	43	24 (Duncan Smith)
2003	28	34	21
2004	27	31	21 (Howard)
2005	34	37	26

Note: Figures are the average for the year or part year.

Source: Ipsos MORI, www.ipsos-mori.com

Economic factors

Economic voting models point to a correlation between the performance of the economy and voting behaviour. If the economy is performing well, voters are more likely to support the governing party at a general election. But it is not just objective factors such as the levels of inflation, interest rates and employment that are important. Personal economic expectations – will you be better or worse off under the governing party in the next year – are significant. An economic voting model developed by David Sanders used economic data (e.g. interest rates, inflation and unemployment) and perceptions to predict election outcomes. His economic voting model predicted accurately the outcome of the 1992 general election when, despite a recession, the Conservatives convinced enough people that they were the party most likely to provide future economic prosperity.

The economy was in better shape in 1997 but the Conservatives were defeated heavily. Crucially, economic recovery had not been accompanied by a widespread 'feel-good factor'. Though inflation and interest rates were low, many voters were worried about their personal economic prospects given job insecurity and problems in the housing market. Nor did the Conservatives get the credit for the economic upturn. Instead, the Major government was associated with tax rises, high interest rates and, most importantly, sterling's exit from the Exchange Rate Mechanism (ERM) in 1992. This collapse of their economic policy on Black Wednesday was a defining moment in the demise of the Conservative Party: their opinion poll ratings dropped dramatically shortly after and never recovered. More than half of voters identified the Conservatives as the best party to manage the economy at the 1992 election; by 1997 Labour was narrowly ahead.

Having persuaded voters that it could be trusted to run the economy, the Blair governments then benefited from its economic record in office. Inflation, interest rates and unemployment levels were all lower in 2001 and 2005 than they had been in 1992 and 1997. On the issue of economic management, Labour enjoyed a 34 per cent lead over the Conservatives in 2001 and a 20 per cent lead in 2005. More voters felt that the economy would improve or stay the same than thought it would get worse. During these campaigns, Labour also ensured that memories of economic problems under the Conservatives remained fresh in the minds of voters.

Governing competence

A persuasive perspective on voting behaviour claims that voters make a judgement about the overall performance of the government when deciding how to vote. In *Elections and Voters in Britain* (Palgrave, 2002), David Denver refers to this as 'judgemental voting'. If the governing party is widely perceived to have performed well in office, it will be well placed to win a general election. Voter judgements on governing competence are based on many factors, including policy success, the state of the economy, the performance of the Prime Minister and party unity. Voters without strong partisan loyalties will respond positively to a governing party that has implemented popular policies, presided over a healthy economy, has an effective leader and offers a coherent vision.

Conversely, governments that are judged to have failed to achieve a modicum of governing competence can expect to be punished at the polls. Policy failures, weak leadership, a lack of direction and obvious disunity will undermine a governing party's chances of securing another term in office. In a general election, voters are presented with a choice between possible alternative governments. As well as considering the government's record, voters also judge whether the main opposition party would be likely to perform better if it were in power. They compare the relative merits of the parties, including their ideology, policies, leaders and general fitness to run the country.

The judgemental voting perspective offers a convincing account of the outcome of recent general elections. The Conservatives won in 1992 despite the weakness of the economy because many voters still felt that they would be better off under the Tories than a Labour Party still associated with high taxes and economic instability. But in 1997 voters reached a negative verdict on the Conservatives' performance in government and believed New Labour would prove more effective. The image of the Conservative Party had been damaged by 'sleaze', party disunity, weak leadership and perceptions that they were out-of-touch with the concerns of ordinary voters. After Black Wednesday, only one in five voters expressed satisfaction with the way the Major government was running the country. In a MORI poll taken during the 1997 campaign, half of voters viewed the Conservatives as 'out of touch' whereas only 7 per cent thought New Labour was. New Labour was widely viewed as moderate, united and able to manage the economy. Blair was a more popular leader than Major and New Labour secured the backing of much of the press.

Voter dissatisfaction with the Blair government had reached 52 per cent by 2001 and climbed further to a peak of 67 per cent in 2003 as controversy over the invasion of Iraq intensified. The Iraq war was deeply unpopular by the 2005 election and contributed to a lack of trust in Blair. A MORI poll during the 2005 campaign found that 62 per cent of voters believed that Blair had lied on Iraq. However, public perceptions of the Conservatives had not improved sufficiently for them to take advantage. MORI found that the number of voters viewing the Conservatives as out of touch had fallen from 50 per cent in 1997 to 32 per cent in 2005, but only 17 per cent believed they had sensible policies and just 15 per cent felt they had a professional approach. They led Labour on issues such as immigration and law and order, but still trailed Labour on health, education and the economy. Michael Howard was not popular with non-Conservatives.

The 1997, 2001 and 2005 general elections

The 1997 general election produced a stunning landslide victory for the Labour Party. Labour won its highest ever total of seats and largest parliamentary majority. It increased its support across all classes and all regions, achieving a record post-war swing of 10.5 per cent from the Conservatives (see Table 17.7). Labour's strongest support came from the working class and it won 50 per cent of the vote among the C2 social group (skilled workers). Crucially, Labour also made significant gains in

Table 17.7 The 1997 general election

	Conservative	Labour	Liberal Democrat
Share of the GB vote (%)	31 (−12)	44 (+9)	17 (−1)
Social class			
AB	41 (−15)	31 (+12)	22 (0)
C1	37 (−15)	37 (+12)	18 (−2)
C2	27 (−12)	50 (+10)	16 (1)
DE	21 (−10)	59 (+10)	13 (−3)
Gender			
Men	31 (−10)	45 (+8)	17 (−1)
Women	32 (−12)	44 (+10)	18 (0)
Age			
18–24	27 (−8)	49 (+11)	16 (−3)
25–34	28 (−12)	49 (+12)	16 (−2)
35–44	28 (−12)	48 (+12)	17 (−3)
45–54	31 (−16)	41 (+10)	20 (+2)
55–64	36 (−8)	39 (+4)	17 (−2)
65+	36 (−12)	41 (+7)	17 (0)
Region			
Northern	22 (−11)	61 (+11)	13 (0)
Yorkshire and Humber	28 (−10)	52 (+8)	16 (−1)
North West	27 (−11)	54 (+9)	14 (−2)
West Midlands	34 (−11)	48 (+9)	14 (−1)
East Midlands	35 (−12)	48 (+10)	13 (−2)
East Anglia	39 (−12)	38 (+10)	18 (−2)
Greater London	31 (−14)	49 (+12)	15 (−1)
South East	41 (−13)	32 (+11)	21 (−2)
South West	37 (−11)	26 (+7)	31 (0)
Scotland	18 (−8)	45 (+7)	13 (0)
Wales	20 (−9)	55 (+5)	12 (0)

Note: Figures in brackets refer to change since 1992.

Source: 'How Britain Voted 1997', Ipsos MORI, www.ipsos-mori.com

Tactical voting

Tactical voting occurs when a voter decides to transfer his or her support from their favoured party to the party that is best placed to defeat the political party they like least. This was evident in the 1997 general election when some Labour supporters in Conservative-held constituencies where Labour came third in 1992 switched their support to the second-placed Liberal Democrats as they had the best chance of defeating the incumbent Conservative MP. Pippa Norris estimated that tactical voting cost the Conservatives 48 seats in 1997. Anti-Conservative tactical voting in 2001 helped Labour and the Liberal Democrats hold on to many of the seats they won four years earlier. About one-in-eight electors voted tactically in 2001.

The ideological proximity of Labour and the Liberal Democrats meant that their supporters were more willing to vote for their second-choice party to defeat the Conservatives. Effective local campaigning and media publicity also made voters more knowledgeable about the likely impact of tactical voting.

Anti-Conservative tactical voting appeared to be in decline at the 2005 general election. First, the Liberal Democrats did not make significant inroads in Conservative-held constituencies in southern England because few Labour voters switched support to them. Second, the Conservative vote increased in seats they held suggesting that anti-Tory tactical voting was declining. The Liberal Democrats may, however, have benefited from small-scale anti-Labour tactical voting in constituencies where they were Labour's closest challenger.

the lower-middle-class C1 social group (up 12 per cent). The regional voting pattern also illustrated the breadth of New Labour's appeal: it strengthened its grip in its geographical heartlands and made spectacular gains in once solid Conservative suburban areas. One million voters switched directly from the Conservatives to Labour, illustrating the willingness of electors to discard their old perceptions about the parties and form new ones in an era of partisan dealignment.

The Conservatives' polled their lowest share of the vote (30.7 per cent) since 1832 and lowest number of seats (165) since 1906. The party was pushed back into its heartlands in rural and southern England, failing to win a single seat in Scotland, Wales and most large English cities. The total Conservative vote fell from the record 14 million achieved in 1992 to 9.6 million as former voters switched to Labour, to minor Eurosceptic parties or abstained. Anti-Conservative tactical voting by Labour and Liberal Democrat supporters is estimated to have cost the Tories 48 seats (see Case study 17.1). The Liberal Democrats made a net gain of seats although their share of the popular vote declined.

The 2001 general election saw a near repeat of the 1997 result. It was generally regarded as a dull contest, enlivened only by John Prescott punching an egg-throwing demonstrator during the campaign. But the election was significant because it confirmed that Labour's 1997 landslide was not a one-off but a contest that had reshaped the electoral landscape. The electoral coalition of traditional working-class Labour voters and middle-class voters who switched to New Labour in 1997 had become frayed at the edges but held together. Opinion polls recorded disappointment at the limited progress in health, education and transport, but

Making an impact? John Prescott's punch was not the blow to Labour's 2001 election campaign that some predicted (© Rex 50 years)

voters still preferred Labour on these issues. Public perceptions of the Conservatives had not changed greatly; few saw them as a credible alternative government. They made a net gain of just one seat and one percentage point of the popular vote, but Conservative support among the middle-class fell further. In pursuing a right-wing agenda of tax cuts and Euroscepticism when voters were most concerned about failing public services, the Conservatives misread the public mood. Discontent with the two main parties was a factor in the record low turnout of 59.4 per cent, but so was the expectation that Labour would secure a comfortable victory (see Chapter 16).

The 2005 general election

Labour, the Conservatives and the Liberal Democrats all found reasons to be cheerful at the outcome of the 2005 general election, but there was also cause for concern for each of them (see Table 17.8). Labour won a 66-seat majority but its share of the vote fell to 35.2 per cent, an all-time low for a winning party. The Conservatives made a net gain of 33 seats and polled 32.3 per cent of the vote, but their increased share of the vote (just 0.6 per cent) was smaller than that posted in 2001. The Liberal Democrats won 62 seats on 22.1 per cent of the vote, their highest vote share since 1987. They took twelve seats from Labour but suffered a net loss of two seats to the Conservatives.

Support for Labour dropped in all regions and among all major social groups. Its share of the vote dropped by 9 per cent among C2 voters (skilled workers)

Table 17.8 The 2005 general election

	Conservative	Labour	Liberal Democrat
Share of the GB vote (%)	33 (0)	36 (−6)	23 (+4)
Social class			
AB	37 (−2)	28 (−2)	29 (+4)
C1	37 (+1)	32 (−6)	23 (+3)
C2	33 (+4)	40 (−9)	19 (+4)
DE	25 (+1)	48 (−7)	18 (+5)
Gender			
Men	34 (+2)	34 (−8)	22 (+4)
Women	32 (−1)	38 (−4)	23 (+4)
Age			
18–24	28 (+1)	38 (−3)	26 (+2)
25–34	25 (+1)	38 (−13)	27 (+8)
35–44	27 (−1)	41 (−4)	23 (+4)
45–54	31 (−1)	35 (−6)	25 (+5)
55–64	39 (0)	31 (−6)	22 (+5)
65+	41 (+1)	35 (−4)	18 (+1)
Region			
North-east	20 (−1)	53 (−6)	23 (+6)
Yorkshire and Humber	29 (−1)	44 (−5)	21 (+4)
North-west	29 (0)	45 (−6)	21 (+4)
West Midlands	35 (0)	39 (−6)	19 (+4)
East Midlands	37 (0)	39 (−6)	19 (+3)
Eastern	43 (+1)	30 (−7)	22 (+5)
London	32 (+2)	39 (−8)	22 (+5)
South-east	45 (+2)	24 (−5)	25 (+1)
South-west	39 (0)	23 (−3)	33 (+2)
Scotland	16 (0)	39 (−4)	23 (+7)
Wales	21 (0)	43 (−6)	18 (+4)

Note: Figures in brackets refer to change since 2001.

Source: Ipsos MORI, final aggregate analysis, www.ipsos-mori.com

and lost its lead among C1 (lower middle class) voters. Looking at constituency results, Labour's vote fell most sharply in its own seats as its core support waned. The biggest falls came in constituencies with sizeable Muslim populations and in university constituencies containing large numbers of students and academics. Higher than average swings from Labour to the Liberal Democrats in these seats reflected the unpopularity of the Blair government's policies on Iraq and tuition fees (see Case study 17.2).

The Conservative share of the vote remained static in six regions, declined in two and rose in three: Eastern (up 1 per cent), Greater London (2 per cent) and the South-east (2 per cent). The net gain of 31 seats was higher than the miserly 0.6 per cent increase in the national share of the vote suggested because of effective campaigning and the fragmentation of the Labour vote in target seats. But their total of 197 seats was still lower than the 209 seats Labour won at its 1983 nadir. Once again the Tories had not benefited greatly from popular discontent with the government. They once more lost ground among middle-class and women voters and performed poorly in middle-class suburban constituencies in the provinces.

Case study: **17.2**

The Iraq effect

The decision to join American forces in an invasion of Iraq in March 2003 was the most contentious of the second term of the Blair government. Saddam Hussein was rapidly removed from power, but American and British troops found no evidence that Iraq possessed weapons of mass destruction. Public opinion turned against the war as it became apparent that the decision to commit British troops had been based upon unreliable evidence on Iraq's weapons capability.

The impact of the war in Iraq on the 2005 general election took a number of forms. In April 2005 MORI reported that Iraq ranked only fourteenth in a list of issues identified by voters as very important in helping them decide how to vote. Only 18 per cent of voters viewed Iraq as a crucial issue, but this rose to 27 per cent among people who voted Labour in 2001 but were unlikely to do so in 2005. Controversy over the manner in which the government decided to commit to war was also a critical factor in the decline of voter satisfaction with the Prime Minister and the government. The number of voters approving of Blair's record and viewing him as trustworthy declined from late 2003.

The direct impact of the war was felt in constituencies with large numbers of Muslim voters. The table below shows that the drop in Labour's share of the vote in the ten constituencies with the highest proportion of Muslim voters was much greater than the national average. Support for the Conservatives, who supported the war, also fell in most cases. The Liberal Democrats, consistent critics of the war, were the main beneficiaries in all but Bethnal Green and Bow. This seat was won by George Galloway, leader of the anti-war party 'Respect – the Unity Coalition'. Clare Short, MP for Birmingham Ladywood, resigned from the Cabinet as she disagreed with government policy on Iraq but still suffered a 17 per cent fall in support at the election. Finally, the war in Iraq and tuition fees contributed to larger than average swings against the government in constituencies with large student populations.

Change in share of the vote (%) in constituencies with large Muslim populations

Constituency	Muslim (%)	Con	Lab	Lib Dem
Birmingham Sparkbrook and Small Heath	48.8	−1.7	−21.4	+7.0
Bethnal Green and Bow	39.2	−10.1	−16.4	−4.3
Bradford West	37.6	−5.4	−7.9	+11.9
East Ham	29.7	−3.5	−19.2	+3.9
Birmingham, Ladywood	29.5	−0.7	−17.0	+23.3
Blackburn	25.7	−8.3	−12.1	+12.5
Poplar and Canning Town	25.4	+2.0	−21.1	+2.8
West Ham	23.6	−4.7	−18.7	+3.5
Bradford North	20.6	−7.9	−7.2	+12.5
Ilford South	19.6	+1.5	−10.8	+9.3

Source: A. Mellows-Facer, R. Young and R. Cracknell, *General Election 2005*, House of Commons Research Paper 05/33, p. 62

For the second election in a row, the Conservatives had shored up their own core support but had failed to convert many floating voters. In Labour-held constituencies, the Conservative share of the vote actually showed a slight decline.

The 2005 election illustrated the dilemma facing the Liberal Democrats. Much of their campaign efforts were focused on winning seats from the Conservatives, but the party's centre-left position (e.g. its opposition to the war in Iraq and pledge to introduce a local income tax) was unlikely to appeal to disillusioned Conservative voters. In the election itself, the Liberal Democrats did not gain much ground in middle-class constituencies in southern England. Instead they benefited from disenchantment with the Blair government, taking 12 seats from Labour and becoming its main challenger in a further 100 constituencies. But the Liberal Democrats have found it difficult to convert protest voters or tactical voters into committed supporters. The inequities of the simple plurality electoral system represent a major hurdle for the third party. Elections held under proportional representation (PR) in the UK since 1999 suggest that the share of the vote won by the Liberal Democrats and minor parties would increase if a PR system was used for Westminster elections.

Realignment or dealignment?

The last three general elections have been of historic significance. For the first time in its history, Labour won three successive victories and on each occasion secured sizeable parliamentary majorities. The 1997 general election was the Conservatives' worst performance in a century and was followed by their second and fourth worst performances. The Liberal Democrats have made steady progress, securing the highest number of third-party MPs for more than 70 years in 2005.

The significance of New Labour's 1997 landslide victory can be assessed by applying a typology of general elections used by electoral analysts such as Pippa Norris. It identifies three categories of election outcomes:

1. *Maintaining elections*: traditional left–right issues dominate the campaign and existing patterns of support remain largely intact.
2. *Deviating elections*: there is a temporary downturn in the normal share of the vote for the majority party, caused primarily by short-term issues or personalities.
3. *Critical elections*: significant and durable realignments in the electorate which have major consequences for the party system occur. Realignment is evident in three areas: the social basis of party support, the partisan loyalty of voters, and the ideological basis of party competition.

Critical elections are unusual occurrences, Labour's 1945 victory being the only clear post-war case in the UK. It produced Labour's first majority government, marked the rebirth of a two-party system and paved the way for 30 years of ideological consensus. The 1997 contest brought important changes, but questions remain about their significance and durability:

1. The social basis of party support has been markedly different since the mid-1990s. New Labour is a catch-all party with a broad appeal rather than a narrow,

class-based one. It made significant gains from middle-class voters in 1997 and maintained much of this middle-class support in 2001 and 2005. Middle-class support for the Conservatives fell in each of the three contests, but they made small gains among working class voters in 2001 and 2005.

2. The partisan loyalties of voters have declined. An unusually large number of voters (around one million) switched directly from the Conservatives to Labour in 1997. Declining loyalties are also apparent in the low turnouts in the 2001 and 2005 elections, and in the willingness of voters to support different parties at different elections. This has been evident in elections to the European Parliament (where UKIP polled 16 per cent in 2004) and to the Scottish Parliament (where minor parties polled 8.9 per cent of the regional list vote in 2003).

3. The ideological basis of party competition was transformed by the emergence of New Labour. It achieved this by positioning itself in the electoral centre ground, the position of the median voter, and persuading voters that it could be trusted to manage the economy. By accepting the market economy, abandoning its 'tax and spend' outlook and promising not to raise income tax, New Labour won over voters who were dissatisfied with the Conservatives' performance in office in the 1990s. The ideological gap between the two main parties has narrowed. Only one in five voters detected a great deal of difference between Labour and the Conservatives in 2001 and 2005. As differences on socio-economic policy waned, so issues such as Europe and asylum became more significant in party competition. In the 1997, 2001 and 2005 elections, New Labour was positioned in the electoral centre ground with the Liberal Democrats to their left and the Conservatives placed on the right of centre.

It is doubtful whether these developments represent the significant and durable realignment necessary for the 1997 contest to be labelled a 'critical election'. The trends outlined above are better viewed as further evidence of electoral dealignment rather than realignment. Class voting has fallen to new lows, but recent elections mark a continuation of a trend, not its beginning or end. New Labour's cross-class appeal and the big fall in the Conservative vote mark a sharp change from the 1979 to 1992 period in which the Tories won four successive general elections. The Conservatives' standing in the opinion polls has barely moved since 1997, hovering around the 30–33 per cent mark for much of this time. The narrowing of the gap between the two main parties since 2001 resulted mainly from a fall in support for Labour, rather than an increase in Tory support. But relatively few New Labour voters feel a strong sense of attachment to the party, as low turnout and the decline in working class support for Labour confirm. The number of people voting for the two main parties has also fallen in each of the last three elections, reaching 67 per cent in 2005.

Conclusion and summary

There are clear limits to Labour's electoral hegemony. The electoral coalition of middle-class and working-class voters held together in 2001 and, to a lesser extent, 2005. But this was a result of a combination of short-term factors – a healthy economy, Labour leads on key issues and the unpopularity of the Conservatives

– rather than an enduring shift in allegiance. As we saw above, voter perceptions about the competence of the governing party have been crucial to the outcome of recent general elections. The belief that Labour is the party best able to manage the economy has been a significant factor. The economy remained relatively strong during New Labour's first two terms in office. But trust in the government and satisfaction with Blair's performance declined in the second term, fuelled by the war in Iraq. These difficulties were not as severe as those that brought the period of Conservative predominance to an end in the 1990s, but show that New Labour's reputation for competence cannot last indefinitely.

Voting behaviour in the UK is less predictable than was the case some forty years ago. Then Labour and the Conservatives had large core votes made up of people with strong class and party loyalties. Since the 1970s, class and partisan dealignment have brought about greater electoral volatility. Voters often decide how to vote on the basis of their perceptions of governing competence. Judgements about which political party would provide a sound economy and effective public services, and which has the most able leader have been critical factors in recent general elections. The three general election victories won by New Labour with its cross-class appeal may suggest a sea-change in voting behaviour. However, detailed analysis confirms that the UK has a dealigned electorate with few strong ties to the main political parties.

Further reading

The best introductions to voting behaviour in post-war Britain are D. Denver, *Elections and Voters in Britain* (London: Palgrave, 2002) and P. Norris, *Electoral Change since 1945* (London: Blackwell, 1997). H. Clarke, D. Sanders, M. Stewart and P. Whiteley, *Political Choice in Britain* (Oxford: Oxford University Press, 2004) is the definitive study of voting behaviour since the 1960s, but the statistical analysis is accessible only to specialists in the field. D. Denver and G. Hands (eds), *Issues and Controversies in Voting Behaviour* (London: Prentice Hall, 1992) is a collection of important articles.

Each general election since 1945 has been the subject of a detailed study in the 'Nuffield series'. The most recent is D. Kavanagh and D. Butler (eds), *The British General Election of 2005* (London: Palgrave, 2005). P. Norris and C. Wlezien (eds), *Britain Votes 2005* (Oxford: Oxford University Press, 2005) is the latest in an excellent series of essays analysing voting behaviour in general elections. A. Geddes and J. Tonge (eds), *Britain Decides. The 2005 General Election* (London: Palgrave, 2005) is also recommended. G. Evans and P. Norris (eds), *Critical Elections* (London: Sage, 1999) examines whether the 1997 election should be viewed as a 'critical election'.

For debates on class dealignment, see A. Heath, R. Jowell and J. Curtice, *How Britain Votes* (London: Pergamon, 1985) and the review in I. Crewe, 'On the Death and Resurrection of Class Voting', *Political Studies*, Vol. 35 (1986), pp. 620–38. The impact of social change is explored in P. Dunleavy, 'The Political Implications of Sectoral Cleavages and the Growth of State Employment', *Political Studies*, Vol. 28 (1980), pp. 364–83 and pp. 527–49. Partisan dealignment is examined in I. Crewe and K. Thomson, 'Party Loyalties: Dealignment or Realignment', in G. Evans and P. Norris (eds), *Critical Elections* (London: Sage, 1999), pp. 64–86.

The economic model of voting is set out in D. Sanders *et al.*, 'The Economy and Voting', in P. Norris (ed.), *Britain Votes 2001* (Oxford: Oxford University Press, 2001), pp. 225–38.

On party leaders, see G. Evans and R. Andersen, 'The Impact of Party Leaders: How Blair Cost Labour Votes', in P. Norris and C. Wlezien (eds) *Britain Votes 2005* (Oxford: Oxford University Press, 2005), pp. 162–80 and on issues P. Whiteley *et al.*, 'The Issue Agenda and Voting in 2005' in the same volume (pp. 146–61).

S. Saggar, *Race and British Electoral Politics* (London: Routledge, 1997) is a detailed study of ethnicity and voting behaviour. On women and voting, see R. Campbell and J. Lovenduski, 'Winning Women's Votes. The Incremental Track to Equality', in P. Norris and C. Wlezien (eds) *Britain Votes 2005* (Oxford: Oxford University Press, 2005), pp. 181–97.

Websites

General election results are available on a number of sites. The Electoral Commission www.electoralcommission.org.uk publishes detailed breakdowns of the results, while the BBC general election site has results and news at http://news.bbc.co.uk/nol/ukfs_news/hi/uk_politics/vote_2005/default.stm. Richard Kimber's 2005 general election site www.psr.keele.ac.uk/area/uk/ge05.htm provides links to hundreds of election-related sites. The website of Harvard academic Pippa Norris www.pippanorris.com/ includes both commentary and data.

Extensive data and analysis of the 2005 general election can be found on the British Election Study 2005 website www.essex.ac.uk/bes/. Data on past elections are at www.data-archive.ac.uk/findingData/besTitles.asp. Most opinion poll organisations post their poll findings online. The best site is that of MORI, www.ipsos-mori.com, as it includes detailed information from the last twenty years and expert commentary. You Gov's site www.yougov.com/, includes commentary from political analyst Peter Kellner. Other polling organisations include Populus www.populus-limited.com and ICM www.icmresearch.co.uk. The Electoral Calculus site www.electoralcalculus.co.uk/ predicts the results of UK general elections.

Campaign organisations include Operation Black Vote www.obv.org.uk/, and the Fawcett Society www.fawcettsociety.org.uk/, which promote participation by ethnic minorities and women respectively.

Chapter 18

Referendums and pressure groups

Learning outcomes

After reading this chapter, you will:

- Be able to outline the major forms of non-electoral participation in the UK.
- Appreciate the chequered history of referendums in UK politics.
- Understand the complex relationship between pressure groups and liberal democracy.

Introduction

The French philosopher Jean-Jacques Rousseau (1712–78) once jeered that the English people are only 'free' during elections. He meant that these were the only occasions when members of the public could behave like true citizens, and take a meaningful part in making the laws by which they were governed. Even at election time, during the eighteenth century this citizenship was a privilege enjoyed by a few rather than a right extended to the many. Women were not allowed to vote, and most men were ruled out by the wide range of qualifications applied in different constituencies.

Despite the different context of today, Rousseau's remark is a convenient summary of a major dilemma for all representative democracies. Elections give citizens a regular opportunity to dismiss unsatisfactory representatives. But normally that judgement can only be delivered at the end of a term of office, by which time many unpopular or damaging decisions could have been made. In the UK, instead of submitting themselves to the electorate as soon as they lose public confidence, governments usually hang on in the hope that their prospects will improve. There are, though, ways in which citizens can register their feelings between elections. In this chapter we will look at referendums, pressure groups and other forms of participation in the UK, in order to assess whether or not they overcome Rousseau's challenge.

Referendums

Referendum: a mechanism allowing voters to choose between different courses of action in a particular policy area.

Referendums are ballots in which citizens are asked to give their views on specific policies. As such, they can be seen as a return to the kind of direct democracy which was practised in Athens and elsewhere in the ancient world, and which inspired Rousseau (see Chapter 1).

| Case study: | 18.1 |

Referendums in the UK

1973. The 'Border poll' in Northern Ireland

Voters in Northern Ireland were asked if they wanted to remain within the UK. There was an overwhelming 'yes' vote, but this proved very little since opponents of the Union organised an effective boycott. Critics claimed that the referendum was nothing more than a way of confirming what everyone knew already – that the majority in Northern Ireland was Protestant and favoured the link with the rest of Britain. In their eyes the real problem was the status of the Catholic minority.

1975. Continued UK membership of the European Economic Community

The first UK-wide referendum was held on 5 June 1975, over Britain's membership of what was then the European Economic Community (EEC). The Labour Prime Minister, Harold Wilson, resorted to the vote because his party was seriously divided. A 'yes' vote, he hoped, would give him the authority to override the objections of colleagues who wanted the UK to withdraw. On a high turnout (nearly two-thirds) the 'yes' campaign secured what could be presented as a conclusive result. Almost every region of the UK voted in favour of membership. In England, there was a 69 per cent 'yes' vote. But critics could argue that the poll had been held too late. On a question of such importance, voters should have been asked whether they wanted to join in the first place. By 1975 the 'no' camp was fighting an uphill battle, asking people to overturn a decision which had already been taken. Furthermore, the 'yes' campaign was much better funded.

1979. Devolution for Scotland and Wales

Voters in Scotland and Wales were asked if they wanted devolved assemblies, with limited powers. In Scotland, the 'yes' campaign secured a very narrow victory – by less than 100,000 votes – on a turnout of less than two-thirds. In practice, this meant that the case for a Scottish assembly had been rejected, because the required level of support had been set at 40 per cent of qualified voters. The eventual figure was less than 33 per cent. The Welsh had been offered an assembly without independent law-making powers. The measure was opposed even by some government MPs, like the future Labour leader Neil Kinnock. Only about 20 per cent of those who voted endorsed the proposal, on a turnout of less than 60 per cent. In neither of these abortive attempts to secure popular approval for devolution were English voters asked for their opinions. The failure of the project led directly to the downfall of the Labour government, which was deserted by members of the nationalist parties and defeated on a House of Commons vote of confidence in March 1979 – less than a month after the ill-fated referendums.

1997. Devolution for Scotland and Wales

Eighteen years after the 1979 polls a new Labour government made another attempt to secure approval for devolution. In Scotland and Wales the turnout was lower than it had been first time round. This was somewhat surprising since opinion was still sharply divided. In Scotland the 'yes' campaign fared better, winning 63.5 per cent of the votes on 11 September 1997. But the Welsh poll, held a week later, was a cliff-hanger; only 50.3 per cent of those who voted said 'yes'. This partly reflected the fact that the powers conferred on the Welsh assembly would be strictly limited, whereas the Scottish people were given a parliament with the authority to make laws and raise additional taxes (see Chapter 11).

1998. Devolution for Northern Ireland

Northern Ireland held its second referendum on 22 May 1998, after the Belfast Agreement of the previous month. The deal was accepted by more than 70 per cent of those voting (turnout was exceptionally high, at almost 90 per cent). A poll was also conducted in the Irish Republic, which also registered a resounding 'yes'. The vote paved the way for a new devolved assembly, which embarked on a somewhat chequered history (see Chapter 11).

2004. Regional assembly for the north-east

New Labour hoped to extend its devolution project to the English regions, proposing that assemblies should be established with strictly limited powers and budgets. Initially there was strong support for the idea; in five regions (the north-east, north-west, the west and east midlands, and Yorkshire and Humberside) a 2002 BBC poll found that almost three-quarters of respondents were in favour. However, by 2004 government confidence in positive outcomes had been sapped. Only one poll was held, in the north-east in November 2004. On an all-postal ballot almost 50 per cent cast a vote. The result was almost a mirror-image of the 2002 BBC poll; 78 per cent of voters were against the plan. It was felt that a north-east assembly on the proposed lines would be a 'white elephant' – a talking-shop which increased local taxes without taking any useful action.

Since 1998. Elected mayors

On 7 May 1998 London voters agreed in a referendum to hold elections for a directly-elected mayor and a Greater London Authority. Although the 'yes' campaign secured more than two-thirds of the votes, turnout was miserable at 34 per cent. Other towns and cities have held referendums on the subject of an elected mayor. By the beginning of 2005 there had been 31 polls. In only 11 of these was the proposition accepted, and the turnout has usually been low (in 2002 Ealing managed just 10 per cent). Even the Prime Minister's constituents in Sedgefield turned down the idea.

Local referendums

Councils sometimes hold local referendums on issues like the level of spending or development projects. For example, in February 2005 Edinburgh voted against its council's proposed congestion charging scheme to control city traffic. But under the terms of the Local Government Act 1972, voters working through their parish councils are allowed to call local referendums on their own initiative. Only a small number of supporters are necessary. These 'do-it-yourself' referendums are not binding, but councillors would be unwise to ignore clear results on sizeable turnouts. Local polls generated in this way are likely to become more popular, as people become aware of their frequent use in other countries (notably the US). They can be used as ways of generating publicity for national issues – for example, anti-euro campaigners have forced referendums to stop their councils preparing for UK adoption of the single currency.

On the face of it, the history in Case study 18.1 suggests that after a slow start the British have become very keen on the referendum, following the long-established practice of many other European countries and the United States. But this impression should be qualified. Three decades after the EEC poll, this remains the only time that the population of the UK as a whole has been asked to vote on an issue. The main general principles concerning the suitability of referendums are:

- They can be appropriate ways of deciding constitutional issues of over-riding importance.
- Although in principle their verdicts can be overturned, they have more 'entrenched' status than Acts of Parliament.
- They can be called when an important proposal affects a specific constituency within the UK. In these instances the vote should be restricted to the people who are directly affected.

Referendums: for and against

The increasing use of the referendum in the UK gives rise to interesting possibilities at a time of technological change. The internet and the text-message have been exploited by the media to facilitate instant polls on a wide range of issues. Could these innovations be used by governments – or even make traditional understandings of government redundant? The old ideas of direct democracy envisaged 'face-to-face' societies where citizens could discuss topical issues in person, without having to appoint an elected intermediary. Might we be able to achieve the same effect in virtual reality?

The subject of e-voting is discussed elsewhere (see Chapter 16). At present, there is no likelihood of routine government decision-making being entrusted to voters. More likely, innovations like all-postal ballots, which encourage voter participation, might foster the use of a referendum whenever a reasonable case can be made for one, rather than reserving it for situations which clearly fall into the categories listed above. However, such ballots have already come under suspicion because of allegations of fraud, and in a contentious referendum the dangers of abuse are obvious. Internet voting would be liable to the same objections.

There is much to be said in favour of more frequent referendums. Some issues are clearly too important to be decided exclusively by politicians who may no longer reflect the views of their constituents, and it can be argued that local residents are the best people to judge proposals which crucially affect their interests. More generally, participation in referendums can enhance the level of public interest in political issues.

However, referendums are still viewed with suspicion in some quarters. Professional politicians tend to regard them as a danger to parliamentary sovereignty. However, this is a difficult case to argue in a democracy, where the legislature is supposed to reflect the views of the public. A more serious point was advanced by Margaret Thatcher (then Leader of the Opposition), when she spoke against the Bill which paved the way for the 1975 referendum on EEC membership. She associated the use of the referendum with dictatorships. There is plenty of evidence to support that view: the referendum (or '**plebiscite**') was a favoured instrument of Nazi rule in Europe, and in October 2002 Saddam Hussein of Iraq was rewarded with almost unanimous support in a poll on his leadership, despite the fact that his rule was detested in many parts of the country. However, in the context of intimidation, violence and vote-rigging, any supposedly democratic device can be manipulated by an unscrupulous regime; the referendum is not really any more susceptible to these abuses than elections.

In a liberal democracy like the UK some of the obvious sources of manipulation can be avoided. For example, the independent Electoral Commission must inspect the wording of the questions put to voters, to ensure that the referendum options are presented as objectively as possible. The Blair government also accepted many of the recommendations put forward by the 1998 Neill committee, to restrict the official funding which can be provided in referendum campaigns. However, the referendum is still open to abuse even by elected governments which are generally benign. There is an old saying in business that no-one should call a meeting unless the outcome is already known, and the same could be said of the referendum. Critics argued that the 1975 referendum on continued membership of the European Economic Community (EEC) was a cynical exercise on the part of Harold Wilson, who claimed that the UK terms had been significantly improved although in truth they had barely changed. He called the referendum to satisfy 'anti-marketeers' within his own party, and suspended the usual conventions of 'collective responsibility' so that Cabinet colleagues could campaign for a 'no' vote; but given the balance of forces on either side he could always be confident that his own preferred 'yes' option would prevail.

Equally cynical, though, have been more recent decisions *not* to hold referendums. The first two Blair governments resisted polls on the two European issues of a single

Plebiscite: a referendum; sometimes used derogatively to refer to referendums held to boost the authority of the government or leader.

Case study: 18.2

Focus groups and citizens' panels

An alternative to the formal referendum is a system of regular consultation with relatively large groups of voters who can be held to be 'representative' of the population as a whole. The Blair Government has made considerable use of focus groups which allows it to monitor public opinion. At Labour's National Policy Forum in November 2003 Blair launched an even more ambitious project: a 'Big Conversation' with British voters, inviting anyone to express their views on the policy choices facing the country. It was hoped that this process would provide ideas for the party's next election manifesto, but the response was disappointing.

Since the late 1990s local councils have also been consulting 'Citizens' Panels', with membership in some cases running to thousands. The panellists offer their views on subjects like the quality of local services. The obvious difficulty with these bodies is that they are liable to present a distorted view of public opinion. In itself, being selected as 'representative' figures can make people unrepresentative. They might become more inclined to voice opinions which they think will be pleasing to the organisers, or to agree with the most vocal panel members. In a public setting, faced with determined advocates for widely held views, participants may decide to keep dissenting opinions to themselves. Thus while these consultative bodies can provide political organisations with valuable information, it would be prudent for them to evaluate the findings in conjunction with information unearthed by independent polling companies.

currency and a constitution at least in part because of a fear that the public would defy its wishes. Also, having planned to hold referendums on devolution in four English regions, it ended up calling only one – in the north-east, where the opinion polls had indicated that there was the best chance of securing a 'yes' vote (in fact, the government ending up losing even that decision, persuading it to scrap plans to hold the other three). At the same time, the government was facing passionate opposition to its plans to outlaw hunting with hounds, but there was never a possibility that this would be subject to a referendum even though it clearly affected the way of life of many citizens.

Another difficulty with referendums is the question of turnout. Should there be a minimum level, which has to be exceeded before the results are binding? Against the wishes of the then Labour government, in 1978 provisions of this kind were included in the legislation for referendums on devolution for Scotland and Wales. In the case of Scotland, the 'yes' campaign won narrowly when the vote was held in 1979, but it did not secure the necessary level of support in the electorate as a whole. It could also be argued that on issues of far-reaching constitutional significance something more than a simple majority of votes would have to be registered; for example, the proposal might require the support of two-thirds of voters. A more mundane consideration is that referendums are expensive, whatever the method of voting.

Pressure groups

Referendums and party-run focus groups do allow members of the public to have some say in policy decisions between elections. But in these instances the decision to consult the public rests with the politicians. In that sense, for advocates of direct democracy they merely underline the limitations of public control over the policy process.

By contrast, pressure groups often communicate their opinions when politicians would prefer to be left in peace. There is a wide variety of such groups in the UK, and in recent decades their popularity has been growing (see Table 18.1). Increasing activity of this kind need not be a source of unease; on the contrary, it could be taken as a sign that **civil society** in Britain is healthy, with a highly-motivated citizen body, ready to exploit any opportunity to participate in public debate. However, when party membership and voting turnout is declining, the simultaneous rise of pressure groups suggests that people are increasingly dissatisfied with the orthodox political process, and are searching for alternative avenues to influence.

Civil society: the sphere of voluntary activity, where associations can be formed independently of the state. Such organisations (sometimes referred to as 'intermediate institutions') include clubs, pressure groups, political parties and religious organisations. A strong civil society is regarded as an essential element in any liberal democracy.

The nature of pressure groups

Pressure groups are voluntary organisations which resemble political parties in some important respects. Their growth need not be at the expense of the parties; people can be members of both kinds of organisation. The key differences between parties and pressure groups are:

- One of the main functions of political parties is to contest elections. Pressure groups do not normally put up candidates; if they do so, they are usually aiming to win publicity rather than form a government (or even to win a single seat).
- The goal of pressure groups is to exert influence over office-holders. Political parties seek to hold office themselves.

Table 18.1 Pressure group activity in the UK, 2000–2001

A recent survey of political participation in the UK found that 62 per cent of respondents claimed to have 'Donated money to an organisation'. Other activities were undertaken by the following proportions:

Signed a petition	42 per cent
Boycotted certain products	31 per cent
Raised funds for an organisation	30 per cent
Worn or displayed a campaign badge or sticker	22 per cent
Contacted a politician	13 per cent
Attended a political meeting or rally	5 per cent
Taken part in a public demonstration	5 per cent
Participated in illegal protest activities	2 per cent

The same survey found that 22 per cent of the population (or around 9 million if the finding was representative of the UK population as a whole) spent 11 or more hours per week involved in a variety of organisations. Some 41 per cent of the population was involved in one or more groups. However, the findings do not necessarily reflect a widespread desire for political participation; a large number of respondents (29 per cent) were members of motoring organisations, which can be involved in serious political issues but which are usually joined by people who want a breakdown service for their cars.

Source: Citizen Audit, Economic and Social Research Council

- Parties develop policies over a wide range of issues. Pressure groups tend to focus on one specific area of policy (although subjects like the environment generate proposals which affect many policy areas).

An interesting illustration of these distinctions was the emergence of the Referendum Party which contested 547 seats at the 1997 general election, securing around 2.5 per cent of the UK vote. The party's sole aim was to bring about a referendum on Britain's membership of the European Union (EU), in the hope that this would result in a vote for UK withdrawal. Realistically, its best chance was to force the Conservative Party to adopt this policy. Its members could have attempted to do so by the familiar pressure group tactic of lobbying Conservative candidates, and threatening to vote for their opponents unless they adopted a more Eurosceptic stance. But Sir James Goldsmith, who founded the party, was a multi-millionaire who could afford the more dramatic gesture of underwriting a nationwide election campaign. He never had the remotest chance of forming a government – or indeed much realistic hope of winning a single seat under the simple plurality electoral system.

In other words, the Referendum Party is best understood as a pressure group which was able to indulge in a dramatic strategy to advertise its goals. Even though it fared poorly, it outperformed the UK Independence Party (UKIP, founded 1993), which has remained in existence and become more like the older parties by developing policies on a wider range of issues. In the absence of the Referendum Party, UKIP polled well in the 2004 European Parliament elections but lapsed back into insignificance in the 2005 general election, when Europe was barely mentioned as an issue.

The Green Party is another interesting example. Founded in 1973 as the People Party (then renamed the Ecology Party), it fielded only 53 candidates in the 1979 general election and received just 0.1 per cent of the UK vote. However, in the 1989 Euro-elections the Greens secured 15 per cent of the vote. The response of the main parties was to register the popularity of green arguments for the first time, and adopt a more environmentally-friendly stance (at least on paper). Partly as a result (and because of internal disagreements about the political future of the ecology movement) the Greens failed to sustain their momentum in the short term. But the party continued in existence, because it was far more than a single-issue group like the Referendum Party. It developed distinctive policies across a wide range of issues, and under proportional representation has now won seats in the European Parliament, the Scottish Parliament, Greater London Assembly and many local councils.

Policy networks: made up of ministers, officials and pressure groups which share an interest in a specific policy area. Non-governmental members of a policy network can expect to be consulted on a fairly regular basis, and such groups have 'insider' status.

Policy communities: *some groups (e.g.* some financial institutions in the City of London) are *always* consulted by governments when their interests are affected. Their relationship with government is so close that they are said to participate in a policy *community*, making it difficult for any other groups to have a meaningful influence.

Insiders and outsiders

Political scientists also try to distinguish between different kinds of pressure group. For example, an important distinction has been drawn between *insider* and *outsider* groups (see Analysis 18.1). Insider groups work in close cooperation with their target audience (politicians and officials at the most appropriate level). They are accepted as members of **policy networks** (or **policy communities**), and are usually consulted during the preparation of any legislation which might affect them. The outsiders, by contrast, are only consulted by governments if and when this has become unavoidable. While they are excluded from the corridors of power they tend to favour tactics which will win them widespread media coverage.

A long series of discussions between outsider groups and their target organisations can result in a change in their status and behaviour. Over time, they may be recognised as new insider groups, and begin to place less emphasis on public campaigning since they now enjoy private access. The same development is likely to push some former insider groups into the cold. In turn, they can be expected to adopt more vigorous tactics in order to attract publicity and win back their former influence over policy (see Case study 18.3).

The debate on hunting with dogs is a good example of this process at work. Under the Conservative governments of Margaret Thatcher and John Major (1979–97) opposition to hunting was a guarantee of outsider status. Parts of the 1994 Criminal Justice Act were seen as attempts to criminalise even peaceful demonstrations in rural areas. In general, media coverage was unsympathetic to hunt saboteurs. But with the election of the Blair government in 1997 the tables were turned. The previously complacent hunting lobby felt threatened, and formed the Countryside Alliance to uphold what it saw as a human right. Mass demonstrations in favour of hunting were held in London in 1999, 2002 and 2004. On the latter occasion a group of activists managed to get inside the chamber of the House of Commons before being apprehended. After the government invoked the Parliament Act 1949 to push the ban on hunting with dogs through the House of Lords in November 2004, the Home Secretary David Blunkett announced that the police would not be given extra resources to keep track of illegal hunting, because they could now use the money previously allocated to a crackdown on hunt saboteurs!

Analysis:	18.1

Insider and outsider groups

Professor Wyn Grant, a leading academic commentator on pressure groups, has identified sub-groups within the broad categories of insiders and outsiders (in his *Pressure Groups, Politics and Democracy and Britain* (Deddington: Philip Allan, 1989)).

Among the insiders, Grant lists the following:

- High profile groups, which enjoy close contacts with the government but are also willing and able to reinforce their position by using the media.
- Low profile groups, which work behind the scenes and try not to advertise their influence.
- 'Prisoner' groups, which can sometimes be taken for granted by governments because they are dependent upon it.

Grant's outsider sub-categories are:

- Potential insiders, dedicated to winning close contact with the government.
- Outsiders by necessity, excluded from the corridors of power because they lack the necessary importance or skills.
- Ideological outsiders, whose principles cannot be accommodated within the existing political system.

Case study: **18.3**

Pressure group tactics

The tactics adopted by a pressure group depend heavily on circumstances. An 'insider' group, which is recognised as a member of a policy network, can operate quietly behind the scenes, attending meetings with officials and ministers. It will be kept informed of all relevant departmental decisions, and will be given the chance to influence legislation before it is introduced in parliament (or even before the proposal has taken shape).

'Outsider' groups, by contrast, must try to bring pressure to bear on ministers through activities such as demonstrations and boycotts, or by organising petitions. The recent tendency of groups to perform attention-grabbing stunts shows the perceived power of the media to influence public opinion and thus, indirectly, politicians. But it will also tend to alienate important decision-makers even further. Thus although groups can still move from 'outsider' to 'insider' status, there is a tendency for their initial position to be self-reinforcing. Outsiders will often feel compelled to behave in ways which make it difficult for politicians to speak to them even if they wanted to, while insiders will get to know the key people, thus consolidating their place in the policy network with social ties.

Ironically, although evidence had been produced which indicated that hunted animals suffer acute stress, the dramatic reversal of roles in this dispute owed little to new arguments or scientific findings. A party with a long history of opposition to hunting – some of it undoubtedly inspired by class considerations as well as real concern for animal welfare – had won a landslide electoral victory and felt that hunting was one issue on which it could take action. Not every supporter of the ban was a Labour MP, and the party included some passionate opponents of the measure; but there was always an overwhelming majority in the Commons as a whole. In all, it passed Bills outlawing hunting with dogs on ten separate occasions (every time the Lords rejected the measure; see Chapter 7). Nearly three hundred hours of parliamentary time were absorbed in these debates; but most of those hours were occupied by arguments which had been heard many times before. The outcome reflected a changed parliamentary situation which itself owed little or nothing to the issue of hunting. Thus the changing fortunes of pressure groups can often be influenced by circumstances outside their control.

'Sectional' and 'cause' groups

Another helpful distinction can be made between groups which coalesce around some economic interest, and those that campaign for a principle which has no relevance to their material situation. The first of these are usually designated 'sectional' groups, although this label gives the misleading impression that such bodies invariably have a divisive effect on society. Although most 'cause' groups consist of well-meaning activists who just want to make the world a better place, some are quite capable of polarising opinion. The difference is that unlike the sectional groups they are not

Lovers of democracy, enemies of the fox. The Countryside Alliance
speaks out in defence of rural life (© Dan Ching/Reuters/Corbis)

Analysis:	18.2

Pressure groups and the New Right

According to representatives of the New Right, who were prominent among the supporters of Margaret Thatcher, all human activity is self-interested. Thus there can be no distinction between 'sectional' and 'cause' groups. Even if they are not conscious of their real motivation, people who campaign for a moral cause are doing so because they derive some benefit from their activity, even if it is the psychological benefit of being recognised as a 'do-gooder'.

The New Right also deplores the practical effect of pressure groups. They argue that campaigning activity distracts government from the pursuit of the general interest, leading to misguided policy decisions and, all too often, the misuse of taxpayers' money.

normally motivated by selfish considerations (although this view is contested by the New Right; see Analysis 18.2 and Chapter 15).

Since sectional groups are generally perceived to fight for their own material interests, wherever possible they try to convince the public that some principle is involved in their struggle. This makes the task of analysis more complicated in practice than the two categories might suggest on paper. It is difficult to categorise an organisation like the Countryside Alliance, whose members support the freedom to hunt in principle, as well as upholding the economic interests of people who are employed by hunting. But the Alliance has many unusual features; it is one group which can actually expect more public support from its 'sectional' case of avoiding rural unemployment than its 'cause' of upholding the freedom to do whatever one likes so long as no-one else suffers physical harm. On the other hand, critics often point out that many successful 'cause' groups, like charities, have developed 'sectional' interests, with their top personnel demanding high salaries and seeking to extend their activities for the purposes of self-promotion. This view has been fostered by the tendency of pressure groups – even 'outsiders' like the Countryside Alliance – to employ people with grandiose business-style titles, like Chief Executive. Equally, while many activists have opposed the construction of new roads as a matter of principle, others have betrayed the so-called 'NIMBY' (Not In My Back Yard) syndrome, feeling far less strongly about road-building in other parts of the UK. These qualifications mean that students of pressure group politics need to treat the distinction between cause and sectional groups with some caution, and make informed judgements on the primary purpose of the organisations under review.

One important difference between sectional and cause groups is that the former usually have a specific catchment area from which they can hope to draw support. In other words, they will be able to target their recruitment efforts at people who share the same economic interest (e.g. trade unions can appeal to workers who do

---

Case study: 18.4

Pressure groups, the EU and devolution

The establishment of devolved institutions in Scotland and Wales has provided pressure groups with important new opportunities. Despite the limitations on their powers, they still have the scope to satisfy many pressure group demands within those territories. In themselves, victories in these forums are heartening for pressure groups; but they can also set precedents for action elsewhere. Thus, for example, the Scottish Parliament took action against hunting and smoking before the UK parliament had done so; almost certainly the moves influenced the decision-making process at Westminster and Whitehall.

One advantage of the devolved institutions is that, since they are relatively new, they provide opportunities for groups which have been crowded out in London by longer-established 'insider' groups. Hiring lobbyists at Edinburgh and Cardiff is therefore a shrewd investment for new groups. UK pressure groups have also been active at Brussels and Strasbourg for many years. This is not just because of the importance of EU law. The EU also actively encourages pressure groups, currently providing support for about a thousand organisations.

similar jobs). The membership of cause groups, by contrast, is usually subject to no such limits. This means that such groups will have to devote more energy to the task of tracking down potential sympathisers.

Some cause groups, of course, are spectacularly successful in these efforts; the Royal Society for the Prevention of Cruelty to Animals (RSPCA), for example, has around 550,000 active members organised in almost 200 local branches, and can afford to employ 1500 staff. And the difficulty of mobilisation does affect larger sectional groups, like pensioners. Campaigners trying to energise such groups face the problem of the 'free rider' – someone who expects to derive material advantage from a policy change, but abstains from any activity on the assumption that others will make the necessary effort. The difficulty of mobilising large sectional groups sometimes lures a complacent government into disastrous decisions. Thus, for example, ministers were taken by surprise by the furious response to the poll tax after its implementation in 1990, and in 2000 had to scrap plans for an increase in fuel taxes in the face of mass protests.

Other distinctions can be drawn in the increasingly crowded cast of pressure groups. Some, like the environmental groups Greenpeace and Friends of the Earth, are trans-national in the scope of their activities. Others are strictly local, like the groups that spring up to protest against the construction of a new road or the closure of a hospital. However, new forms of communication make it easy for such small organisations to liaise with larger, more experienced campaigning groups. The internet is an obvious channel of communication, but cheap air travel makes it possible even for groups with limited resources to share information face-to-face. For example, in September 1998 environmental campaigners from Sweden, Poland, France and Germany attended a training camp in Staffordshire to learn such skills as tunnelling and tree-house building. The UK animal rights movement is respected by similar groups across the world, and is very happy to give advice to advance the worldwide cause.

'Peak' organisations and neo-corporatism

Sectional groups in the UK were most prominent in the two decades after 1960. During that period, both Conservative and Labour governments consulted closely with representatives from both sides of industry – the employers, organised in the Confederation of British Industry (CBI, formerly known as the Federation of British Industry) and employees whose trade unions are affiliated to the Trade Union Congress (TUC). Such bodies are described as 'peak' (or 'umbrella') organisations, because they represent a number of groups linked by a similar interest.

Corporatism: a system in which representatives of employers and trade unions are formally incorporated within the policy-making process.

Neo-corporatism: a system in which the government seeks to facilitate agreements between trade unions and employers.

This close government cooperation with key peak organisations is a variety of **corporatism** (see Chapter 2). In its pure form, corporatism is a method of decision-making which overrides democratic institutions, and is associated with the Italian fascist regime of Benito Mussolini. In the UK, the system never came close to that totalitarian state, and is probably best described as 'liberal corporatism' or **neo-corporatism**. Under this arrangement the elected government's role was to act as an 'honest broker' in the national interest, facilitating agreements between trade unions and employers. The key assumption was that decisions were most likely to be accepted by both sides of industry if they were taken in consultation with senior representatives of the most prominent 'peak' organisations.

The key landmark in the history of British corporatism was the formation of the National Economic Development Council (NEDC, or 'NEDDY') by the Conservative government of Harold Macmillan in July 1961. The NEDC provided a forum for regular discussions between the government, the FBI (later the CBI) and the TUC. However, the arrangement never lived up to original hopes, and broke down in the early 1970s. The usual explanation for the failure of neo-corporatism in the UK is that the trade unions became too powerful. Instead of trying to reduce their power, successive governments felt compelled to appease the unions, with the result that the British economy came close to collapse. Another explanation is that the 'peak' organisations on both sides were unable to deliver, despite good intentions, because they were unable to command the obedience of their members. Thus, while the TUC was usually ready to compromise, individual trade unions continued to prioritise the economic interests of their members rather than national goals. Equally, while larger companies within the CBI usually avoided confrontation with the unions for the sake of an easy life, smaller businesses were more willing to break off negotiations and take the risk of provoking strike action.

The end of corporatism

By the mid-1970s many commentators were worried that the UK was becoming 'ungovernable' (see Chapter 2), largely because of the demands of various sectional groups who were powerful or persuasive enough to win concessions from the government. When Margaret Thatcher came to office in 1979 she was determined to avoid this predicament. She did not abolish the NEDC – that decision was left for her successor John Major – but in opposition she showed no inclination to talk with the TUC, and before the end of her first term in Downing Street she had provoked a public clash with the CBI.

Although she had no love for employers' organisations, Thatcher was on close terms with many influential business figures, and was determined above all to curb the power of the trade unions. Almost every year of her premiership featured a new piece of restrictive legislation. But a more potent weapon was the government's economic policy, which accelerated the decline of the manufacturing industries that were most heavily unionised. In 1979 there were more than 12 million workers affiliated to the TUC; by the time of Thatcher's departure the figure was down to about 8.5 million. However, while it was losing members the trade union movement actually won back much of its old popularity with the general public. But there was no prospect that trade unionists would recover the influence they had enjoyed in their heyday, when their leaders seemed to be at least as powerful as elected politicians.

While Thatcher's critics claim that her attitude towards the trade unions was vindictive and driven by partisan considerations, she proved more than willing to pick squabbles with 'establishment' bodies like the British Medical Association (BMA) and the Bar Council (which managed to fight off most of her proposed reforms of the legal profession). Even the Police Federation was occasionally restive, despite the allegation by left-wing activists that the police had become no more than 'Maggie Thatcher's boot-boys'.

New social movements

Whatever the fate of the neo-corporatist bodies which formerly wielded so much influence, a reasonable case can be made for depicting Thatcher as the inadvertent friend of the pressure group. Many existing bodies were re-activated by the perceived need to oppose her reforms; and others owed their foundation to the impetus of Thatcherite policies. For example, Stonewall was set up to campaign for homosexual rights in the wake of the controversial Clause 28 of the Local Government Act 1988, and the Anti-Poll Tax Federation was created by the Community Charge which became law in the same year. But even before Thatcher's attack on long-established organisations, it was possible to identify a change in the nature of pressure groups and the style of campaigning. Commentators now refer to 'new social movements', which can be distinguished from traditional pressure groups because:

- Their membership tends to be diverse, cutting across old class boundaries.
- They have broad ideological objectives rather than focusing on specific issues.
- Their immediate aim is to win publicity and to bring pressure to bear on decision-makers through the media, rather than engaging in discreet lobbying of decision-makers.
- They build coalitions of different groups with broadly similar objectives, often coming together for single campaigns then diverging without establishing a settled hierarchical structure, or even a formal system of membership.

The first new social movement in the UK is usually taken to be the Campaign for Nuclear Disarmament (CND, founded in 1958). CND tended to attract young, middle-class supporters, who marched every year from the nuclear weapons research facility at Aldermaston, Berkshire, to a rally in London's Trafalgar Square. At that time, CND was widely regarded as a 'subversive' organisation whose activities threatened to leave the West defenceless against the Soviet Union. But in 1960 the Labour Party conference passed a motion endorsing CND's aims, against the fierce opposition of the party leadership. A similar motion was passed in 1981 and Labour fought the next two elections on an anti-nuclear defence policy.

CND's concern for the future of the planet and its varied inhabitants was shared by members of environmental groups which sprang up in the 1970s, such as Friends of the Earth (1970), Greenpeace (1973), and the Animal Liberation Front (1976). These organisations were far more radical than older groups concerned with the environment, such as the National Trust (1895), the Campaign for the Protection of Rural England (1926), and the League Against Cruel Sports (1926). However, over time the older bodies were themselves influenced by the new climate of activism; the National Trust, for example, had a long-running and bitter debate in the 1990s about allowing hunting on its land.

Other new groups which arose at this time were inspired by the American civil rights movement of the 1960s. In the second half of that decade the Labour government implemented a series of measures designed to help women, homosexuals and ethnic minorities. The success of these campaigns owed much to the sympathetic stance of Roy Jenkins (Home Secretary from 1965–67). The 1970s saw further legislation, like the Equal Pay Act 1970 and Sex Discrimination Act 1975, which improved working conditions for women, and the Race Relations Act 1976 which

SHAC and Huntingdon Life Sciences

On 11 September 2004 around 300 people held an anniversary march in Stamford, Lincolnshire. However, they were not remembering the terrorist attack in New York three years earlier. Rather, they were celebrating the fifth anniversary of a successful mission to release several hundred guinea-pigs which had been bred for animal testing.

The demonstrators supported a long-running campaign to close down Huntingdon Life Sciences (HLS), branded by its critics as 'Europe's leading vivisectionist'. The campaign, which began after a Channel 4 documentary in 1997, has made national headlines and inspired the creation of a new police group, the National Extremist Tactical Co-ordination Unit. Workers at HLS have suffered intimidation, and the SHAC campaign has also affected HLS's financial backers and customers in the pharmaceutical industry. Special measures have now been taken to protect the anonymity of investors, and the government has stepped in with promises of financial support. In 2003 HLS took out an injunction against nine named individuals, together with SHAC, London Animal Action and the Animal Liberation Front. It was claimed that less than 50 agitators were endangering the whole of Britain's pharmaceutical industry, worth billions of pounds.

In October 2004 protestors against animal testing dug up the grave of a woman whose relatives bred animals for research. Despite the resulting media outcry, and new legislation designed specifically to curtail its activities, SHAC remains committed to the closure of HLS, and the government clearly regards the case as a trial of strength from which it cannot back down. Sections of the media have given outspoken support to HLS, and it can be argued that far from advancing the cause of animal welfare SHAC's shock tactics have prevented it from winning a fair hearing.

tightened previous legislation on racial discrimination. Other groups were founded to campaign on behalf of the poor and the disabled.

In recent years pressure groups have continued to proliferate and to form alliances of varying duration. In 1991, 250 groups opposing the government's road-building programme were brought together under a loose umbrella organisation, Alarm UK. UK groups participated in anti-globalisation demonstrations, notably at Quebec and Seattle in 1999, and before the G8 meeting at Gleneagles, Scotland, in 2005. In another relatively new development, although these campaigners do target politicians they believe that governments are increasingly powerless to restrain vast multinational firms. Thus they also direct their activities against companies like McDonald's, Esso and Coca-Cola. As well as demonstrating, they try to mobilise the power of the consumer through boycotts.

Until quite recently it was possible to advance persuasive general explanations for the emergence of new social movements. Increasing affluence is usually identified as a factor. The prominence of middle-class activists in the ranks of environmental campaigners, for example, suggests the rise of a 'post-materialist' consciousness among people who enjoy the necessary leisure-time for activism. Such campaigners are likely to be well-educated, and to note with indignation the persistence of anomalous discrimination against women, ethnic minorities and others. The drive to extend rights from humans to animals can partly be explained from the same perspective, since technological change means that animals are no longer essential suppliers of transport and labour-power in industry. Meanwhile, people who give up eating meat on principle can now choose from a wide range of meat-flavoured vegetable products.

On this view, prosperity has generated many of its own critics, who are well-motivated and resourceful enough to use the mass media (which is, of course, another product of the modernity they reject). These activists are difficult to equate with any of the traditional ideologies, and their prominence in pressure groups suggests a degree of disillusionment with the main UK political parties.

There is usually an assumption that the members of such movements are 'progressive' or left-wing in the old ideological terminology. However, since the election of the Labour government in 1997 the best-publicised pressure groups have come from a different mould. Hunters, motorists and fathers separated from their children have all used tactics typical of the new social movements, trying to win media publicity with spectacular campaigns which are often planned and coordinated by means of new technology like the internet and mobile telephones (see also Case study 18.3). Yet all three causes can be said to be reactions against the success of new social movements. The pro-hunting lobby has been mobilised by the prospect that animal welfare groups would finally get their way. In 2000 motorists took direct action to oppose fuel taxes which had been advocated by environmentalists. And the pressure group Fathers 4 Justice, which demonstrated inside the House of Commons, at Buckingham Palace and at other famous public buildings, could be seen as an indirect product of the feminist movement, since its members protested against the alleged tendency of the courts to give the benefit of any doubt to female parents in disputed custody cases.

Clearly the era of new social movements is far from over; people will continue to join together in campaigns for enhanced rights, a safer environment, and

Batman makes a point on behalf of Fathers 4 Justice (© Rex 50 years)

global justice. But while these movements tend to demand positive action from governments, another trend has emerged of campaigning *against* actions which governments have already taken (or are threatening to take). These activists can take heart from the success of the Anti-Poll Tax Federation, which managed not only to secure the abolition of the poll tax but also contributed to the departure of Prime Minister Margaret Thatcher (see also Case study 18.5). While this example gives heart to protestors, governments seem more capable of provoking them, by taking legislative action in areas which have traditionally been seen as essentially private matters such as hunting. And this is not the only source of provocation. The million-strong march in protest against the prospect of war on Iraq in 2003 represented only a small proportion of the widespread opposition to Tony Blair's foreign policy.

Pressure groups and democracy

Positive assessments of pressure group activity usually arise from a pluralist perspective (see Chapter 1). That is, it is assumed that a multitude of such groups, covering a wide variety of subjects, is a sign of a healthy liberal democracy with an active citizen body. Free competition amongst such groups is likely to promote good government, because campaigners on all sides of a question can be expected to present evidence in support of their favourite cause. With guaranteed access to a free press, they have reason to hope that the most rational case will win the argument and be reflected in government decisions.

From the pluralist viewpoint, the recent decline of the old sectional pressure groups is a welcome development. While pluralists acknowledge that unions and businesses are important interests in British society, they monopolised government attention, and the voice of the consumer was often neglected in the 1960s and 1970s. The relative decline of these powerful organisations leaves an opening for other groups to be heard.

But a more pessimistic view of recent developments is also possible. From the perspective of the New Right (see Analysis 18.2), any increase in pressure group activity is deplorable in itself. Even those who reject this ideological perspective can have similar grounds for questioning the benefits of pressure group competition. In its most familiar form the pluralist case assumes that there will be something like a level playing field for the competing groups, which ensures that rational decision-makers will tend to accept the most persuasive argument. However, during the 1990s a series of scandals revealed the extent to which privileged access to politicians could be bought, regardless of the quality of the case they were hired to present, or the extent to which it enjoyed public support. Apart from rare cases of direct bribery, well-financed organisations could hire the most skilful and eloquent lobbyists, some of whom obviously gave a higher priority to money-making than to the cause of good government. This approach would come naturally to 'sectional' groups, which are themselves primarily concerned with the material interests of their members. However, the lasting legacy of lobbying activity in this period was greater public disillusionment with the political system, despite the conclusions of the Nolan Committee (see Chapter 7) which promised tighter regulation of the links between decision-makers and extra-parliamentary organisations.

Case study:	18.5

Recent pressure group successes

Nowadays there are so many pressure groups, many of which oppose each other, that it is rarely possible to say whether their arguments have proved decisive. One should also keep in mind pressure group failures. For example, the Keep Sunday Special campaign could not prevent legislation to allow the extension of Sunday shopping; and despite the activities of CND, American Cruise Missiles were sited in British bases in the early 1980s. The Stop the War coalition, which claimed that over a million supporters had marched through London in February 2003, failed to change Tony Blair's policy towards Iraq.

However, there are some instances where the work of one or more pressure group has undoubtedly made a difference:

- 1989. The South African government releases Nelson Mandela and lifts restrictions on parties opposed to the apartheid system, at least in part because of worldwide boycotts of firms which traded with South Africa.
- 1995. Greenpeace protested against Shell's decision to dispose of an oil platform, the Brent Spar, at sea. Despite strong backing from the UK government Shell capitulated in the face of a Europe-wide boycott.
- 1996. The 'Snowdrop' campaign was formed to press for a ban on privately-owned handguns after the massacre of children and teachers at Dunblane, Scotland, in March 1996. Despite furious protests from the shooting lobby, a total ban on private ownership of handguns was introduced in 1997. Ironically, in the next two years the use of handguns in criminal activities actually increased by more than a third.
- 2000. The government withdrew proposed increases in fuel tax in the wake of mass countrywide protests.
- 2005. The celebrity chef, Jamie Oliver, forced the government to rethink its policy on school meals. While this could be regarded as a success for a one-man pressure group, other bodies had been campaigning for some time on this issue.
- In recent years, environmental groups like Greenpeace have also disrupted and delayed the Labour government's plans to permit commercial exploitation of genetically modified (GM) crops.

For pluralists, it can only be an additional cause for concern that the recent growth of pressure group activity has coincided with a fall in more orthodox forms of democratic participation. In their view, government has a crucial part to play in mediating between the different groups; and, ideally, the government at any time should represent a large proportion (if not an overall majority) of the public. However, with electoral turnout falling, political parties can win decisive parliamentary majorities with the support of a relatively modest proportion of the UK electorate. It would be highly dangerous to assume that the low turnout in recent general elections reflects widespread contentment among the public as a whole. The continued popularity of new social movements suggests an increasing number of people who hold beliefs which cannot be accommodated by the main political parties. The marked tendency for movements to spring up in determined opposition to government policies is an indication that discontent is spreading far beyond habitual malcontents who refuse to see anything good in the modern world.

Given the new prominence of pressure groups, it is pertinent to ask whether their own internal procedures satisfy democratic criteria. In the 1980s Conservative governments criticised trade unions because their leaders were not truly accountable to members; for example, officials like Arthur Scargill, the controversial President of the National Union of Mineworkers (NUM), were elected for life. Legislation was introduced to rectify this situation, and also to force unions to ballot their members before they made financial contributions to the Labour Party. However, the Conservatives seemed less troubled by the extent to which quite secretive business organisations, like Aims of Industry, channelled funds into their own party.

Questions about the democratic credentials of pressure groups extend beyond the most familiar sectional groups. Some organisations, like CND, have actively encouraged the autonomy of local groups rather than trying to coordinate their campaigning from the centre. However, the 'iron law of oligarchy' (see Chapter 14) suggests that there is a tendency for all organisations to fall under the direction of small groups as they grow larger. This problem is accentuated in the contemporary context, as media outlets try to identify specific individuals who are capable of speaking on behalf of organised groups. Equally, the need to avoid bad publicity provides an incentive to impose discipline on the membership, to the extent of expelling activists who do not toe the 'official' line.

The new dilemmas facing pressure groups in the media age were neatly illustrated in January 2006, when Fathers 4 Justice revealed that they had expelled several members who wanted to take the group's headline-grabbing stunts even further. It was reported that some members had even considered kidnapping Tony Blair's-five year-old son. Such activities are hardly compatible with the healthy democratic activities favoured by pluralists. Fathers 4 Justice recognised this by announcing that it would disband in the wake of the controversy. This example is further evidence that the relationship between pressure groups and democracy is more complex than many pluralists assume.

Conclusion and summary

The rise in pressure group activity, and the increasing demand for referendums on a variety of subjects, constitute a serious challenge to representative democracy in the UK. Recent developments draw attention to the fact that the current system of representation is a means to an end, not an end in itself. No political system can provide satisfactory outcomes for everyone; but unless representative democracy satisfies a significant majority of the people most of the time, its legitimacy will be called into question.

However, those looking for alternative methods in the referendum and the pressure group are confronted with obvious difficulties. Despite recent technological advances, the referendum is still at best a very cumbersome device. It is also possible to envisage circumstances in which, far from providing authoritative decisions on emotive issues, closely-fought referendums could actually reinforce and inflame existing divisions within society.

Pluralists argue that government can act as an impartial arbiter between competing pressure groups. This idea is more persuasive as a theory than as a guide to actual practice; no government can be wholly impartial. But this does not mean that things would be any better if the existing system of representative democracy was replaced by a grand parliament of pressure groups. The ideas of such groups often conflict in a way which leaves no room for compromise. Furthermore, pressure groups themselves are not invariably democratic organisations which allow their members a realistic chance of meaningful participation.

Further reading

A useful brief introduction to referendums is E. Magee and D. Outhwaite, 'Referendums and Initiatives', *Politics Review*, Vol. 10, No. 3 (2001), pp. 26–8. I. Horrocks and D. Wring raise questions about technology and participation in 'The Myth of E-thenian Democracy', *Politics Review*, Vol. 10, No. 4 (2001), pp. 31–2. It is still worth consulting D. Butler and U. Kitzinger, *The 1975 Referendum* (London: Macmillan, 1976), which provides a comprehensive and incisive account of the issues involved in the first (and so far, only) UK-wide referendum.

On pressure groups, see W. Grant, *Pressure Groups and British Politics* (Palgrave, 2000), and the same author's 'Pressure Politics; The Challenges for Democracy' in *Parliamentary Affairs*, Vol. 56, No. 2 (2003), pp. 297–308. B. Coxall's *Pressure Groups in British Politics* (Harlow: Pearson, 2001) is concise and accessible. Although its findings are slightly dated, R. Baggott's *Pressure Groups Today* (Manchester: Manchester University Press, 1995) is still well worth reading. On new social movements, see P. Byrne, *Social Movements in Britain* (London: Routledge, 1997) and, on environmentalism, R. Garner, *Environmental Politics* (London: Palgrave, 2nd edition, 2000). Two special issues of the journal *Parliamentary Affairs* are highly recommended: Vol. 56, No. 4 (2003) focuses on participation and includes articles on pressure groups and protest politics; Vol. 51, No. 3 (1998) looks at new social movements. The Electoral Commission has issued a number of detailed reports on political participation in Britain. The most useful are the regular surveys, *An Audit of Political Engagement* (London: Electoral Commission, 2004, 2005 and 2006).

Websites

On referendums, see the Electoral Commission website www.electoralcommission.org.uk.

There is a wealth of pressure group material on the internet. This is only a sample list:

British Medical Association www.bma.org.uk

Campaign for Nuclear Disarmament www.cnduk.org

Child Poverty Action Group www.cpag.org.uk/

Confederation of British Industry www.cbi.org.uk

Countryside Alliance www.countryside-alliance.org

Direct Democracy Campaign www.homeusers.prestel.co.uk/rodmell/index.htm

Fathers4Justice www.fathers-4-justice.org

Friends of the Earth www.foe.co.uk

Greenpeace www.greenpeace.org

League Against Cruel Sports www.league.uk.com

National Trust www.nationaltrust.org.uk

Royal Society for the Prevention of Cruelty to Animals www.rspca.org.uk

Royal Society for the Protection of Birds www.rspb.org.uk

Stop Huntingdon Animal Cruelty www.shac.net

Part 6
Conclusions

Chapter 19

Governance and democracy in the UK

Learning outcomes

After reading this chapter, you will:
- Be aware of key areas of continuity and change in British politics.
- Be able to evaluate the 'health of democracy' in Britain.

Introduction

This concluding chapter reviews the two main themes of the book, the transition from government to governance and the changing nature of British democracy. It examines the major changes that these developments have brought in British politics but also points to significant areas of continuity.

The old order changes

The standard view of British politics in the twentieth century depicted the United Kingdom as a highly centralised state in which decision-making authority was concentrated at the centre. The British constitution encouraged this centralisation of power. The doctrine of parliamentary sovereignty, the cornerstone of the traditional constitution, established the legislative supremacy of Parliament – it could legislate on any matter of its choosing and no other body had the authority to overturn Acts of Parliament. Unlike most other liberal democracies, Britain had an uncodified constitution which did not establish a clear separation of powers between the legislative, executive and judicial branches of the state. The legislature and executive were in practice fused. The majority party in the House of Commons formed the government and could use its parliamentary majority to enact its legislative programme largely unchecked. The simple plurality electoral system and two-party system added to the executive's institutional advantages by translating a plurality of votes garnered in general elections into working parliamentary majorities. Beyond Westminster, local government was weak and there was no other tier of elected subnational government in Great Britain.

As we have seen in this book, many of these defining features of the Westminster Model of British politics have come under strain in recent years. The shift from government to governance and the constitutional reforms introduced since 1997 have been important drivers of change in British government and politics.

Government to governance

Government involves decision-making through formal institutions and rules; it is hierarchical with clear lines of control and accountability. Governance refers to the role of multiple non-state actors and networks in decision-making. It is characterised by fragmentation rather than centralisation, interdependence rather than hierarchy, regulation rather than command. Governance requires bargaining and cooperation between actors working within the same or linked policy fields whereas government involves clear lines of command and control.

Adherents of the Westminster Model held that decision-making power in the executive resided with either the Cabinet or, as was increasingly the case in the twentieth century, the Prime Minister. The latter thus sat at the apex of a hierarchical system of government. A more sophisticated approach is offered by the core executive model which views the core executive as fragmented and the relationships between its key actors as characterised by dependence rather than command.

Organisational change within the civil service has added to the complexity of central government. The post-1988 'Next Steps' reforms separated the policy-making and policy implementation roles of government departments, the latter being transferred to executive agencies which have significant autonomy. The private sector's role in delivering public goods has been extended through market-testing and the Private Finance Initiative (PFI). This dispersal of functions away from the core executive makes it more difficult for the centre to control the policy process. The Blair governments have tried to address this by embracing the concept of 'joined-up government' and strengthening Downing Street's capacity to coordinate policy implementation.

The state's socio-economic role has diminished since the early years of the post-war period when it controlled nationalised industries (e.g. coal and electricity), used economic policy instruments to maximise employment and expanded the welfare state (e.g. creating the National Health Service). The Conservative governments of Margaret Thatcher and John Major (1979–97) reduced the state's role in economic management and the provision of public goods by privatising nationalised industries and extending the role of market forces in the welfare state. These trends continued under the Blair governments. The post-war interventionist state has been replaced by an enabling or regulatory state which sets the framework through which public goods are provided by the private sector or specialised agencies.

The shift from government to governance has also been evident at local level where service provision functions have been transferred from elected local authorities to quangos, private companies and voluntary bodies. Local authorities used to be the predominant actors in the delivery of services such as education and housing but, under pressure from the centre, have had to reinvent themselves as policy facilitators within their communities.

Multi-level governance

The UK is now a multi-level polity. Central government does not monopolise decision-making authority having transferred legislative competence to supranational and subnational tiers of government. The European Union (EU) has sole authority in some policy areas (e.g. trade and agriculture) and shares competences with its member states in others (e.g. the single market) where national governments do not have veto powers. European Union law has direct application in the UK and overrides domestic law should conflict arise. Membership of the EU has had significant implications for British government, requiring Whitehall departments, local authorities and the courts to adapt their practices to conform to those of the EU. British government and politics has, to some extent, been 'Europeanised'.

Westminster has delegated legislative authority in a range of policy areas to devolved bodies in Scotland, Wales and Northern Ireland. It remains sovereign but does not have full supremacy over policy across the UK, accepting a position of non-intervention in devolved matters. Devolution has had significant implications not only for politics in these parts of the UK, but for the UK political system as a whole. In health and education, devolved bodies have pursued policies different from those implemented in England by the UK government. New machinery for managing intergovernmental relations has also been put in place.

Constitutional reform

Devolution is one of the most significant elements of the programme of constitutional reform put in place by New Labour since 1997. Few major institutions have been untouched. The House of Lords now consists primarily of appointed members and Conservative dominance has ended. Radical changes to the judiciary such as the creation of a Supreme Court are intended to create a clearer demarcation between the executive, legislature and judiciary. The Human Rights Act 1998 provides a clear framework for the courts on cases concerning the relationship between the individual and the state. Government departments have changed their procedures in response to the Act and to devolution.

These reforms have challenged some of the key principles and practices that underpinned the traditional constitution, prompting talk of a 'new constitutional settlement'. Legislation such as the Human Rights Act 1998 and the Scotland Act 1998 introduced an element of codification into the constitution by setting out in statute law the relationship between institutions and between the state and its citizens. This legislation can be viewed as *de facto* fundamental law – although a future parliament could overturn these acts, the problems this would provoke suggest that they will instead become an entrenched feature of the constitution.

The post-devolution UK no longer satisfies the typology of a unitary state – one in which all component parts of the state are governed in the same way from a strong centre – which was a key feature of the Westminster Model. Rather, the UK state is quasi-federal in character with a formal division of legislative authority between different tiers of government and institutional arrangements to handle intergovernmental relations.

The more things change ...

Constitutional reform and the trend towards governance have brought about significant change in British politics. But the story of the development of the UK polity in recent years must also emphasise continuity. Although often radical, the changes to the constitution identified above have not brought about a wholesale transformation of the UK polity. Key features of the Westminster Model persist. Change has often been incremental rather than fundamental: evolutionary not revolutionary. Political actors have also responded in a pragmatic fashion to the challenges they face, adapting existing practices rather than ditching them completely.

Labour's reforms have not provided the UK with a codified constitution. The sovereignty of Westminster has, in constitutional theory at least, been preserved. The Scotland Act 1998 states that the Westminster parliament remains sovereign and retains the power to make laws for Scotland. The Human Rights Act 1998 also seeks to preserve the sovereignty of parliament. If the courts find legislation incompatible with the ECHR, that legislation is not automatically struck down: it is for

Ancient rituals have survived the modernisation of the constitution (© AP/EMPICS)

parliament to decide on amendments. Nor will the new Supreme Court be able to overturn legislation. The rule of law is still susceptible to the authoritarian whims of central government.

Liberal and radical critics have questioned the coherence and comprehensiveness of the New Labour's reforms. They argue that the Blair governments opted for limited change to the House of Lords, territorial politics, electoral reform and citizens' rights. A more radical approach would have seen an elected upper house, greater powers for the devolved assemblies, proportional representation for Westminster elections and a UK Bill of Rights.

A strong centre

The core executive model notes that many actors within the core executive have resources and that no one individual monopolises decision-making. But the Prime Minister has significant advantages as he or she has access to resources that are not available to other actors. He or she has the power of patronage, can set the strategic direction of the government and intervene in specific policy areas of their choosing. Margaret Thatcher was not the first Prime Minister to delegate crucial decisions to Cabinet committees or rely on personal advisers, but she took full advantage of these devices in order to avoid protracted arguments in the full Cabinet. The decision-making role of Cabinet has continued to decline as Tony Blair has developed a 'sofa government' in which decisions are taken in informal meetings with ministers and advisers. A concentration of resources at the centre has further increased the potential for prime ministerial predominance. The Prime Minister's Office has been bolstered and strategic units created to coordinate policy making and set targets for policy delivery. The reach of the Treasury has also been extended through the Comprehensive Spending Review process and the development of Public Service Agreements.

The centre remains strong. Actors in the core executive have much greater access to important resources compared to other tiers of government. Government departments are the most powerful actors in policy networks because they have the greatest resources. The core executive remains the heart of UK politics. The most important decision-making bodies in the EU are the European Council and the Council of Ministers – intergovernmental institutions in which decisions emerge from negotiations between national governments. Member states have retained substantial decision-making authority over major policy areas such as Treaty change, taxation and foreign policy. Under the devolution settlement the UK government is responsible for economic, constitutional and foreign policy. The UK government is the dominant actor in intergovernmental institutions such as the Joint Ministerial Council. The centre has also been able to restructure English local government and curtail its powers.

Central government has responded pragmatically to the challenges posed by European integration and devolution, adapting existing procedures rather than creating new institutional frameworks. A 'Whitehall ethos' that values centralised decision-making and policy coordination remains largely intact. Downing Street and the Foreign Office ensure that governmental departments and devolved administrations stick rigidly to a policy line developed at the centre while the Treasury keeps EU-related expenditure in the UK on a tight rein.

The enabling state is less active in the economy and society than was the case during the post-war Keynesian welfare state consensus. But government maintains a critical macroeconomic policy role and under New Labour has intervened to promote competitiveness, training and social justice. The state may have been 'rolled back' in the economic sphere where market forces are more prominent, but it maintains authoritarian tendencies in other spheres. Libertarians bemoan the development of a 'nanny state' which has regulated people's lifestyles by criminalising smoking in public places and fox hunting. The 9/11 terrorist attacks in the United States have led to a greater emphasis on national security in most liberal democracies. In the UK funding for the security services has increased, the surveillance of people has been extended and terrorist suspects have been detained without trial.

The condition of British democracy

The UK remains an unusual example of a liberal democratic state (but see Case study 19.1). It is one of only a small number not to have a codified constitution. Other features which have marked the UK out as different from other liberal democracies in Western Europe include the concentration of power at the centre, the weakness

Case study: 19.1

The Westminster Model abroad

The Westminster parliament is often described as the 'mother of parliaments'. This is a reference to the longevity of the English parliament, although Iceland and the Isle of Man vie for the honour of having the oldest parliamentary system. It also reflects the export of the Westminster system of parliamentary democracy in a constitutional monarchy to many countries in the Commonwealth. These include Australia, Canada, Jamaica and New Zealand. Here the British monarch is the head of state while the head of government is usually the leader of the largest party in parliament. The executive branch is made up of members of the legislature and operates a Cabinet system in which the Prime Minister is the key actor. Bicameral legislatures are the norm (except in New Zealand) and parliamentary ceremony often replicates that found in England. Two-party systems and simple plurality electoral systems are found in many Commonwealth states. Another similarity is that civil law is based on English common law.

But there are significant differences in the way a Westminster-style system operates in Commonwealth states that adopted the British model of government. Almost all have written constitutions and codified Bill of Rights (New Zealand does not have a single codified constitutional document) but conventions remain important. Australia and Canada are federal states. The suitability of the Westminster Model has also been a subject of political controversy in some Commonwealth states. New Zealand moved to a mixed electoral system in 1996 while the British monarch's position as head of state is a thorny issue in Australia.

The Westminster Model was not exported to continental Europe where codified constitutions, elected second chambers, strong regional government, proportional representation and multiparty systems are common.

of local and regional government, an unelected second chamber of parliament, a relatively weak rights culture, the simple plurality electoral system and a two-party system. Claims from liberal and radical critics that the UK was insufficiently democratic were influential in the Labour Party during the 1990s. New Labour's programme of constitutional reform has improved the health of British democracy in some respects but has also created new problems and left others untouched. The following section offers a brief examination of the condition of British democracy by assessing shortcomings in four areas central to New Labour's reforms: modernisation of the constitution, improved accountability, stronger rights for citizens and higher levels of political participation.

Modernisation

The Scottish Parliament and Welsh Assembly buildings represent the new face of UK politics. But the most familiar images of the UK state are still the Westminster Parliament, 10 Downing Street and Whitehall. Ancient parliamentary traditions have also survived constitutional modernisation unscathed. Many are of little consequence. Some of the hangovers from a pre-democratic *ancien regime* are, however, of political significance. The post of Lord Chancellor, for example, survived the Blair government's plan to abolish it as to do so would have required a redrafting of centuries-old legislation. Most hereditary peers have been removed from the House of Lords but it remains an unelected body despite Labour's 1997 manifesto commitment to democratisation. Proposals for a chamber in which a significant proportion of members are directly elected were shelved (perhaps temporarily) by a government which feared that an upper house with a significant elected element could challenge the supremacy of the House of Commons.

Gordon Brown and David Cameron have both suggested that the prerogative powers of the Crown may be the subject of a new wave of constitutional reform. Most prerogative powers are exercised by ministers on behalf of the Crown rather than by the monarch in person but remain anomalous (see Table 19.1). They cover some of the most important functions of the state including the deployment of the armed forces and declarations of war. The monarch also retains powers such

Table 19.1 The Royal prerogative

The main prerogative powers are:

- The summoning, prorogation and dissolution of parliament
- The granting of Royal Assent to Bills
- The appointment of ministers, judges, diplomats and many other holders of public office
- The granting of honours
- The issue and withdrawal of passports
- The pardoning of convicted offenders or reduction in their sentences
- The control and disposition of the armed forces
- The declaration of war
- The making of treaties and recognition of foreign states
- The personal immunity of the monarch from prosecution in the courts
- Miscellaneous prerogatives (e.g. the creation of corporations by charter, the issue of coinage, etc.).

as appointment of the Prime Minister, assent to legislation and dissolution of parliament which in certain circumstances may be contentious.

The devolution project remains unfinished. The Welsh Assembly is to be given greater powers, the electoral system used for the Scottish Parliament is likely to be modified and the future character of devolution in Northern Ireland remains uncertain. With the demise of plans for elected assemblies in the English regions and controversy over the voting rights of Scottish MPs at Westminster, the 'English Question' has also emerged as an important political issue.

Accountability

The countervailing trends of centralisation and fragmentation in the core executive have both prompted concerns about the accountability of central government. Tony Blair's preference has been for a 'sofa government' in which decisions are made in informal meetings of advisers and ministers. A greater reliance on special advisers has undermined the policy advice function of the civil service. The neglect of formal mechanisms of collective decision-making which results from 'sofa government' was criticised in the Butler Report which pointed to the absence of checks and balances in the Cabinet system in the run up to the war in Iraq. The increased incidence of policy disasters such as the poll tax, the Millennium Dome and the Child Support Agency also indicate that for many years policy proposals have not been scrutinised sufficiently within the core executive or in Parliament.

But claims of 'elective dictatorship' are not a new feature of British politics. The fusion of the executive and legislative branches allows the government to force legislation through parliament without effective scrutiny. It controls the parliamentary timetable and utilises the whip system to make it difficult for backbench MPs to amend government Bills. But parliament's cause is not lost. MPs are now more willing to assert their independence, extracting concessions from the Blair governments by rebelling or threatening to rebel. The House of Lords has also inflicted defeats on the government, notably on civil liberties issues. Parliament has greater opportunity for pre-legislative scrutiny and Select Committees carry out important investigations into the work of government departments and agencies. But parliament continues to produce badly-framed primary legislation and is ill-equipped to scrutinise secondary legislation.

The publication of the *Ministerial Code* clarified ministerial accountability to parliament. Even so, the circumstances in which ministers should resign remain unclear. Political pressure exerted by the Prime Minister and media appears more significant than the constitutional convention that ministers should resign when they or their department are found to be guilty of serious political errors. Reform of the civil service has blurred the lines of accountability still further. The distinction between policy strategy (for which ministers are responsible) and operational decisions (made by agency chief executives) sheds only limited light on the issue.

Local government is, in some respects, in a healthier position than it was a decade ago. The Blair government has given greater discretionary powers to local authorities which are deemed to be delivering high quality services and has encouraged them to play a more active community leadership role. But local authorities have only limited discretionary powers, must meet centrally-determined targets and have little financial autonomy. The local quango state has also expanded with the creation of bodies such as Regional Development Agencies and registered social landlords. Hundreds of unelected bodies take decisions on public money with little scrutiny of their work by elected bodies at either local or national level.

Ministers enjoy considerable patronage powers and the process of appointments to quangos is opaque. Special advisers often have greater policy influence than senior civil servants. But independent panels are now responsible for some appointments to the House of Lords and judiciary. Despite some serious scandals in recent years, British politics is happily free of the systemic corruption found in some liberal democracies.

Concerns about the accountability of policy-makers extend beyond the nation state given the significance of decisions taken in the European Union, global institutions and international non-governmental organisations for politics in the UK. The democratic deficit in the EU has arisen because policy competences have been transferred from national governments, which are accountable to their legislatures and electorates, to the EU where the main executive body (the European Commission) is not directly elected and there is limited scrutiny of decisions made by the Council of Ministers. The European Parliament has been given greater legislative and scrutiny powers in an attempt to close the democratic deficit but it does not enjoy the levels of legitimacy of national parliaments.

Rights

The Human Rights Act 1998 strengthened the rule of law by entrenching basic civil liberties in statute law. The Freedom of Information Act 2000 gave citizens a statutory right to access much information held on them by public bodies. However,

The state has taken on new powers to tackle terrorism (© Nicholas Bailey/Rex Features)

the government ensured that there were significant exemptions. Meanwhile civil liberties have been curtailed by the anti-terrorism legislation introduced after the 9/11 attacks in the United States and the July 2005 London bombings. The House of Lords and judiciary have asserted their independence fiercely on these and other rights issues. The legality of the 2003 invasion of Iraq under international law has also been questioned.

The record of the Blair governments on non-terrorism-related domestic matters has also been criticised by civil liberties campaigners. Legislation introduced under Blair allows complex fraud cases, and cases where jury-nobbling is suspected to be heard by judges alone, thereby restricting the right to trial by jury. The double jeopardy rule – namely, that individuals acquitted of a serious crime should not be tried again for the same offence – was overturned by the Criminal Justice Act 2003. This also enabled judges to allow juries to hear details of defendants' previous offences. Controversial proposals for the introduction of identity cards were reintroduced at the start of Labour's third term.

Participation

Low turnout has been a depressing feature of recent elections in the UK. Fewer than six out of ten registered electors voted at the 2001 general election, a figure that improved only marginally in 2005. Turnout is even lower in local and European Parliament elections. Such dismal levels of voter participation undermine the legitimacy of the political system and bring into question the representative function of elected bodies. Parties which win elections invariably claim a mandate to govern even though they have failed to win support from a majority of those eligible to vote. The views of social groups that exhibit low levels of turnout (e.g. those aged under 35) are under-represented in the political process. Women and ethnic minorities are also under-represented in the House of Commons.

The low levels of turnout also pose questions about the efficacy of political parties, election campaigns and the electoral system. Partisan dealignment has seen a loosening of the bonds between parties and voters so that only around one in six people now feel a 'very strong' attachment to a party. Those without a strong attachment are less likely to vote. Party membership has also declined: the mass parties of the 1950s have been replaced by 'electoral professional' parties that target a relatively small number of voters. Election campaigns and a partisan press that focuses on spin rather than substance have alienated large numbers of electors.

Non-voters are more likely to feel that the two main parties offer the same sort of policies. Broad agreement between New Labour and the Conservatives on the primacy of the free market has brought greater political stability than was the case in the adversarial politics of the 1970s when parties in power sought to unravel the policies introduced by their rival. But it means that electors are presented with a limited choice and radical perspectives are rarely aired. In the absence of strong class or party loyalties and ideological differences between the parties, judgements about which party would provide a sound economy and effective public services and which has the most media-friendly leaders have become critical factors in determining election outcomes.

A classic two-party system was a central feature of the Westminster Model. The period since 1970 has, however, seen the development of multi-party systems in local, subnational, national and European electoral arenas. There is genuine multi-party competition in elections to the devolved assemblies and European Parliament. At Westminster the two-party system has been eroded but not overturned completely: Labour and the Conservatives hold a majority of seats despite a sharp decline in support. Competition between three or more parties is the norm in general elections but the simple plurality electoral system means that this is not translated accurately into multi-party politics in the House of Commons. The electoral system is also biased to Labour, rewarding it with large parliamentary majorities despite a fall in share of the vote. The Conservatives (1979–97) and Labour (since 1997) have held office alone for considerable periods giving the UK some of the features of a dominant party system.

Evidence from other liberal democracies suggests that proportional representation has a positive effect on turnout as electors are less likely to feel that these votes are wasted. The Blair government introduced proportional representation for elections to the devolved assemblies, European Parliament and executive mayors, contests in which turnout tends to be lower than for general elections. But it has maintained the simple plurality system for Westminster. Meanwhile, trials of new voting methods such as all-postal ballots and e-voting produced higher turnout but also raised concerns about the security of the ballot.

Low turnout is often said to be a symptom of a wider malaise of British democracy. Opinion poll evidence has revealed significant levels of dissatisfaction with traditional party politics and a lack of trust in politicians. But disillusionment with politics at Westminster does not, however, equate automatically to a lack of interest in politics. Democracy in Britain is, in some areas at least, as healthy as it has ever been (see Table 19.2). Surveys suggest that most people are interested in politics (broadly-defined) and participation in political activities such as demonstrations and consumer boycotts has increased. New interest groups and single issue movements have emerged, many of which focus on civil liberties and lifestyle issues. Despite concern from politicians and the media about a decline of respect and community, Britain has also retained its strong tradition of civic activism. This is evidenced in the large number of people who belong to a voluntary organisation or serve on community bodies such as school boards. New technologies are also being utilised by political activists, a notable example being the boom in internet 'blog' sites devoted to British politics.

Table 19.2 Rating the system of governing Britain

Question: Which of these statements best describe your opinion on the present system of governing Britain?

	1973	1995	2003
Works extremely well and could not be improved	5	3	3
Could be improved in small ways but mainly works well	43	19	42
Could be improved quite a lot	35	40	38
Needs a great deal of improvement	14	35	13

Source: Ipsos MORI, www.ipsos-mori.com

Election turnout is lowest among young people. In 2005, for example, only 37 per cent of 18–24-year-olds voted. This is a particular cause for concern as it suggests that political parties are failing to engage young adults in the political process and that their interests are not represented fully. Again, though, non-voting is not the whole story: young people may be reluctant voters but many have been mobilised by issues such as university tuition fees and the war in Iraq. The number of students studying politics at school, college and university has also been on an upward curve.

Conclusion and summary

Political scientists have been more effective at explaining the recent past than predicting the near future. But it seems likely that the next few years will be interesting times for students of British politics. Many of the issues reviewed in this concluding chapter will remain on the agenda. The process of constitutional reform is set to continue with further changes to the House of Lords, the Welsh Assembly and the judiciary taking effect. A new round of reform of the structure of local government is likely. The trend from government to governance may also get a higher political profile as problems with PFI and bodies such as the Child Support Agency become more apparent.

Tony Blair's resignation will be a key moment. Gordon Brown, his likely successor, is expected to maintain much of his Blairite policy inheritance while his time at the Treasury suggests that he will also favour a centralised style of decision-making. Each of the three main political parties will fight the next general election with a different leader from the one who fought the 2005 contest – the first time this will have happened since 1979. The Conservatives and the Liberal Democrats will also have undergone an ideological repositioning. Experts on voting behaviour are already predicting a close contest with a hung parliament a greater possibility than in the recent past. This combination of factors may even bring about a significant increase in turnout.

Further reading

The academic journals *Parliamentary Affairs*, *Political Quarterly*, *British Journal of Politics and International Relations* and *British Politics* include articles on developments in British politics and in British political science. P. Dunleavy, R. Heffernan, P. Cowley and C. Hay (eds), *Developments in British Politics 8* (London: Palgrave, 2006) is a good supplement to the main textbooks – see in particular, P. Dunleavy, 'The "Westminster Model" and the Distinctiveness of British Politics'. The Democratic Audit has produced a number of important studies of British democracy including S. Weir and D. Beetham, *Political Power and Democratic Control in Britain: The Democratic Audit of the United Kingdom* (London: Routledge, 2002) and D. Beetham et al, *Democracy under Blair* (London: Politico's, 2003).

Websites

The Democratic Audit site www.democraticaudit.com includes briefings on the health of British democracy and the Constitution Unit www.ucl.ac.uk/constitution-unit/ regular updates on constitutional reform. The report of the independent Power Commission www.powerinquiry.org/home.php offers a critical perspective on democracy in Britain. The BBC News website http://news.bbc.co.uk/ is an excellent source of information on developments in British politics; Epolitix www.epolitix.com/EN/ is also recommended. New 'blogs' on British politics are emerging on a weekly basis, although the quality varies greatly. Among the most informative and entertaining are http://politicalbetting.com/, http://ukpollingreport.co.uk/blog/index.php, http://5thnovember.blogspot.com/ and http://conservativehome.blogs.com/.

Index

HOW PARLIAMENT WORKS

6th edition

ROBERT ROGERS & RHODRI WALTERS

July 2006
Pbk 504pp £19.99
ISBN 1405 83255X

"When the British constitution is in such flux, describing today's Parliament might seem like drawing on water. But in this account Robert Rogers and Rhodri Walters have achieved the near-impossible; it is clear, elegant, invaluable, bang up-to-date and full of dry wit."

Andrew Marr, BBC Political Editor, 2000–2005

"Acute observation and analysis of the tensions and potential of Parliament. This book is required reading for anyone interested in the evolution of democracy."

**Tam Dalyell, MP from 1962–2005
and Father of the House, 2001-2005**

"A must for everyone who needs to know about Parliament. Comprehensive and authoritative, this really is how Parliament works."

**Betty Boothroyd (Baroness Boothroyd, OM),
Speaker of the House of Commons, 1992–2000**

"Much more than a clear and concise introduction to Parliament. Despite my years as a political scientist, I gained a lot of new insights."

Professor Gerry Stoker, Manchester University

Complete the form below and save 20% when you buy How Parliament Works 6e

✂

YOUR DETAILS (please write in BLOCK CAPITALS)

Name:

Address:

Postcode:

Tel: Email:

Your reference code is LAO1OA

YES! Please send me the following title

Title	ISBN
How Parliament Works 6e	140583255X
Price	Qty
£19.99 £15.99	

METHOD OF PAYMENT

Please debit my:

☐ Mastercard ☐ Visa ☐ Amex ☐ Switch ☐ I enclose a cheque made payable to Pearson Education for £

Card No:

Expiry Date: /   Issue No: (Switch only)   Start Date: /   Security No. (4 digits for Amex):

Signature: Date:

Send your form to us:
Elton Daddow, Pearson Education, Edinburgh Gate, Harlow, Essex CM20 2JE   Call us on: +44 (0) 870 607 3777   Online at: www.pearson-books.co.uk/LA010